SQL Server MVP Deep Dives
Volume 2

SQL Server MVP
Deep Dives
Volume 2

Edited by Kalen Delaney ▪ Louis Davidson ▪ Greg Low
Brad McGehee ▪ Paul Nielsen ▪ Paul Randal ▪ Kimberly Tripp

MANNING

SHELTER ISLAND

For online information and ordering of this and other Manning books, please visit www.manning.com. The publisher offers discounts on this book when ordered in quantity. For more information, please contact

Special Sales Department
Manning Publications Co.
20 Baldwin Road
PO Box 261
Shelter Island, NY 11964
Email: orders@manning.com

♾ Recognizing the importance of preserving what has been written, it is Manning's policy to have the books we publish printed on acid-free paper, and we exert our best efforts to that end. Recognizing also our responsibility to conserve the resources of our planet, Manning books are printed on paper that is at least 15 percent recycled and processed without the use of elemental chlorine.

Manning Publications Co.	Development editor: Cynthia Kane
20 Baldwin Road	Copyeditor: Liz Welch, Linda Recktenwald
PO Box 261	Project editor: Barbara Mirecki
Shelter Island, NY 11964	Typesetter: Marija Tudor
	Cover designer: Marija Tudor

ISBN 9781617290473
Printed in the United States of America

1 2 3 4 5 6 7 8 9 10 – MAL – 16 15 14 13 12 11

To all the children of Operation Smile

MVP authors and their chapters

Johan Åhlén   53
Gogula Aryalingam   57
Glenn Berry   31
Aaron Bertrand   19
Kevin G. Boles   20
Robert Cain   45
Tim Chapman   38
Denny Cherry   5
Michael Coles   46
Rod Collcdge   14
John Paul Cook   21
Louis Davidson   4
Rob Farley   2
Grant Fritchey   32
Darren Gosbell   54
Sergio Govoni   22
Allan Hirt   7
Satya Jayanty   16
Tibor Karaszi   17
Jungsun Kim   39
Tobiasz Koprowski   18
Hugo Kornelis   23
Ted Krueger   50
Matija Lah   24
Rodney Landrum   15
Greg Larsen   9
Peter Larsson   25
Andy Leonard   47
Ami Levin   1
Greg Low   41
John Magnabosco   11

Jennifer McCown   37
Brad McGehee   36
Siddharth Mehta   60
Ben Miller   26
Allan Mitchell   59
Tim Mitchell   51
Luciano Moreira   27
Jessica M. Moss   40
Paul Nielsen   6
Shahriar Nikkhah   48
Robert Pearl   34
Boyan Penev   55
Pedro Perfeito   58
Pawel Potasinski   12
Mladen Prajdić   28
Abolfazl Radgoudarzi   48
Denis Reznik   29
Rafael Salas   52
Edwin Sarmiento   44
Chris Shaw   3
Gail Shaw   8
Linchi Shea   35
Jason Strate   33
Paul Turley   43
William Vaughn   42
Peter Ward   13
Joe Webb   10
John Welch   49
Allen White   30
Thiago Zavaschi   56

brief contents

PART 1 ARCHITECTURE **1**

    1 ▪ Where are my keys? 3

    2 ▪ "Yes, we are all individuals"
       A look at uniqueness in the world of SQL 16

    3 ▪ Architectural growth pains 26

    4 ▪ Characteristics of a great relational database 37

    5 ▪ Storage design considerations 49

    6 ▪ Generalization: the key to a well-designed schema 60

PART 2 DATABASE ADMINISTRATION **65**

    7 ▪ Increasing availability through testing 67

    8 ▪ Page restores 79

    9 ▪ Capacity planning 87

    10 ▪ Discovering your servers with PowerShell and SMO 95

    11 ▪ Will the real Mr. Smith please stand up? 105

    12 ▪ Build your own SQL Server 2008 performance dashboard 111

    13 ▪ SQL Server cost recovery 121

    14 ▪ Best practice compliance with Policy-Based Management 128

    15 ▪ Using SQL Server Management Studio to the fullest 138

    16 ▪ Multiserver management and Utility Explorer—best tools for
       the DBA 146

17 ▪ Top 10 SQL Server admin student misconceptions   157

18 ▪ High availability of SQL Server in the context of Service
     Level Agreements   167

PART 3   DATABASE DEVELOPMENT............................. 175

19 ▪ T-SQL: bad habits to kick   177

20 ▪ Death by UDF   185

21 ▪ Using regular expressions in SSMS   195

22 ▪ SQL Server Denali: what's coming next in T-SQL   200

23 ▪ Creating your own data type   211

24 ▪ Extracting data with regular expressions   223

25 ▪ Relational division   234

26 ▪ SQL FILESTREAM: to BLOB or not to BLOB   245

27 ▪ Writing unit tests for Transact-SQL   255

28 ▪ Getting asynchronous with Service Broker   267

29 ▪ Effective use of HierarchyId   278

30 ▪ Let Service Broker help you scale your application   287

PART 4   PERFORMANCE TUNING AND OPTIMIZATION 297

31 ▪ Hardware 201: selecting and sizing database server
     hardware   299

32 ▪ Parameter sniffing: your best friend…except when it isn't   309

33 ▪ Investigating the plan cache   320

34 ▪ What are you waiting for? An introduction to waits and
     queues   331

35 ▪ You see sets, and I see loops   343

36 ▪ Performance-tuning the transaction log
     for OLTP workloads   353

37 ▪ Strategies for unraveling tangled code   362

38 ▪ Using PAL to analyze SQL Server performance   374

39 ▪ Tuning JDBC for SQL Server   384

PART 5   BUSINESS INTELLIGENCE 395

40 ▪ Creating a formal Reporting Services report part library   397

41 ▪ Improving report layout and visualization 405

42 ▪ Developing sharable managed code expressions in SSRS 411

43 ▪ Designing reports with custom MDX queries 424

44 ▪ Building a scale-out Reporting Services farm 436

45 ▪ Creating SSRS reports from SSAS 448

46 ▪ Optimizing SSIS for dimensional data loads 457

47 ▪ SSIS configurations management 469

48 ▪ Exploring different types of enumerators in the SSIS Foreach Loop container 480

49 ▪ Late-arriving dimensions in SSIS 494

50 ▪ Why automate tasks with SSIS? 503

51 ▪ Extending SSIS using the Script component 515

52 ▪ ETL design checklist 526

53 ▪ Autogenerating SSAS cubes 538

54 ▪ Scripting SSAS databases – AMO and PowerShell, Better Together 548

55 ▪ Managing context in MDX 557

56 ▪ Using time intelligence functions in PowerPivot 569

57 ▪ Easy BI with Silverlight PivotViewer 577

58 ▪ Excel as a BI frontend tool 585

59 ▪ Real-time BI with StreamInsight 597

60 ▪ BI solution development design considerations 608

contents

preface xxxv
acknowledgments xxxix
about Operation Smile xli
about this book xliii
about the editors xlv
about SQL Server MVPs xlvi

PART 1 ARCHITECTURE **1**

EDITED BY LOUIS DAVIDSON

1 ***Where are my keys? 3***

AMI LEVIN

Keys in the relational model 4

The debate 5

The arguments 6

Pro artificial keys 6 ▪ Pro natural keys 8

Additional considerations 10

Natural keys assist the optimizer 11 ▪ Artificial keys are the de facto standard 12 ▪ Modularity, portability, and foreseeing the future 12 IDENTITY columns may result in value gaps and "run out" of values 13

Recommendations 13

Simplicity and aesthetics 14

Summary 14

2 *"Yes, we are all individuals"*
A look at uniqueness in the world of SQL **16**
ROB FARLEY

Introducing uniqueness 16

Constrained to uniqueness 16

Primary keys 17 ▪ Unique constraints 18 ▪ Unique indexes 19

Unique constraint or unique index? 19

Advantages of the unique index 19 ▪ Advantages of the unique constraint 20

Uniqueness in results 20

The good and the bad of DISTINCT 20 ▪ DISTINCT or GROUP BY 21 ▪ Are they needed at all? 22 ▪ Unnecessary grouping 23 Being guided by "that" error 24

Summary 25

3 *Architectural growth pains* **26**
CHRIS SHAW

Manage your data types 27

IDENTITY case in point 27 ▪ Database design and scalability 28

Naming conventions 28

Inconsistent design 29

Normalization 30

Overnormalized 30 ▪ Undernormalized 30

Primary keys and foreign keys 31

GUIDs as primary keys 31 ▪ System-generated integers as primary keys 32 ▪ Generating your own ID values 32

Indexes 33

Underindexing 33 ▪ Overindexing 35 ▪ Maintenance 35 Fill factor 36

Summary 36

4 *Characteristics of a great relational database* **37**
LOUIS DAVIDSON

Coherent 38

Standards based 38 ▪ Reasonable names and data types 39 Cohesive 40 ▪ Needs little documentation 40

Normal   40

Fundamentally sound   41

Documented   42

Secure   43

Encapsulated   44

Well performing   46

Summary   47

5 *Storage design considerations   49*
DENNY CHERRY

Selecting the correct RAID type   49

*RAID 0   49 ▪ RAID 1   50 ▪ RAID 5   51 ▪ RAID 6   51
RAID 10   52 ▪ RAID 50   52 ▪ When to use RAID 5   52
When to use RAID 6   53 ▪ When to use RAID 10   53*

File placement   53

Index files   54 ▪ Transaction log files   54 ▪ tempdb database   54

Disk alignment   54

*Correcting disk alignment on Windows 2003 and earlier   55
Correcting disk alignment in Windows 2008 and later   56
Correcting after the partition has been created   56 ▪ Aligning
on the array   56*

Snapshots   56

*Snapshots with a VSS-enabled storage array   57 ▪ Snapshots
with a non-VSS-enabled storage array   57 ▪ Snapshots as a backup
process   58 ▪ Using snapshots to present storage to downstream
environments   58*

Clones   59

Summary   59

6 *Generalization: the key to a well-designed schema   60*
PAUL NIELSEN

A place for normalization   60

Lessons from the UIX discipline   61

Generalization defined   62

Benefits of generalization   63

Summary   64

PART 2 DATABASE ADMINISTRATION 65

EDITED BY PAUL RANDAL AND KIMBERLY TRIPP

7 *Increasing availability through testing 67*
ALLAN HIRT

Testing—it's not just for application functionality 68

The missing link 69

Knowledge is power 71

Test early, test often 72

Automated versus manual testing 73

What needs to be tested? 73

First things first 75

Remember the big picture, too 77

Summary 78

8 *Page restores 79*
GAIL SHAW

Restore granularities 79

Requirements and limitations 80

*Recovery model and availability of log backups 80 ▪ SQL Server
Edition 80 ▪ Page type of the damaged page 80*

Performing a page restore 81

What's coming? 84

Summary 85

9 *Capacity planning 87*
GREG LARSEN

What is capacity planning? 87

Gathering current database disk space usage 88

Performance metrics 90

Summary 94

10 *Discovering your servers with PowerShell and SMO 95*
JOE WEBB

Using PowerShell and Excel 95

Using SMO with PowerShell 96

Collecting instance and machine information 97
Collecting SQL Agent job information 98
Collecting database information 100
Summary 103

11 Will the real Mr. Smith please stand up? 105
JOHN MAGNABOSCO

Personally identifiable data 106
Today's superhero: the DBA 106

Our superpowers 106 ▪ *Tools of the trade 107*

Summary 109

12 Build your own SQL Server 2008 performance dashboard 111
PAWEL POTASINSKI

DMVs as the source of performance-related information 111
Using SQLCLR to get the performance counter values 112
Sample solution for performance monitoring 115
Use Reporting Services for performance monitoring 118
Some ideas to improve the solution 119
Summary 119

13 SQL Server cost recovery 121
PETER WARD

The context for SQL Server as a Service 121
What's SQL Server as a Service? 122
An introduction to chargebacks 123
Implementing a chargeback model 125
Summary 127

14 Best practice compliance with Policy-Based Management 128
ROD COLLEDGE

The context for contemporary database administration 128
The importance of best practice compliance 129

Central Management Servers   130

Policy-Based Management   131

Surface area configuration   132 ▪ *Sysadmin membership   134*

Policy-Based Management with Central Management
Servers   135

Summary   137

15 *Using SQL Server Management Studio to the fullest   138*
RODNEY LANDRUM

Querying many servers at once   138

Creating and using a scripting solution with templates   141

Scripting multiple objects and now data, too   143

Summary   145

16 *Multiserver management and
Utility Explorer—best tools for the DBA   146*
SATYA SHYAM K JAYANTY

SQL Server 2008 R2 tools for the DBA   146

Tools of the trade   147

Managing multiple instances using Utility Control Point   148

Multiserver management and administration   152

Best practices   155

Summary   156

17 *Top 10 SQL Server admin student misconceptions   157*
TIBOR KARASZI

Simple recovery model   157

Default collation   158

Table-level backups   159

Using replication for high availability   160

Timing query performance   162

Shrinking databases   163

Auditing login access   163

Tail-log backups   165

Database defaults   165

Difficulty   166

Summary   166

18   *High availability of SQL Server in the context of Service Level Agreements*   167

TOBIASZ JANUSZ KOPROWSKI

High availability—a definition   167

Types of unavailability   169

Unavailability indicators   169

High availability options in SQL Server   170

Service Level Agreement   171

Measurement indicators   171

The structure of a Service Level Agreement   172

Service Level Agreements: the context for high availability   173

Summary   174

Useful links   174

PART 3   DATABASE DEVELOPMENT 175

EDITED BY PAUL NIELSEN

19   *T-SQL: bad habits to kick*   177

AARON BERTRAND

SELECT *   177

Declaring VARCHAR without length   179

Not choosing the right data type   181

Mishandling date range queries   182

Making assumptions about ORDER BY   183

Summary   184

20   *Death by UDF*   185

KEVIN BOLES

Poor estimates   185

Row-by-row processing   188

What can you do about it?   190

  Inline table valued function solution   190 ▪ *Set-based solution*   191

What about code reuse?   192

One last example of how bad scalar UDFs can be   193

Summary   194

21   *Using regular expressions in SSMS   195*
         JOHN PAUL COOK

Eliminating blank lines   195

Removing extra newline characters   196

Collapsing multiple lines into a single line   197

Using the beginning-of-line metacharacter   197

Using the end-of-line metacharacter   198

Summary   198

22   *SQL Server Denali: what's coming next in T-SQL   200*
         SERGIO GOVONI

OFFSET and FETCH   200

  SQL Server 2005 and 2008 solution   201 ▪ *SQL Server Denali
  solution*   201 ▪ *Comparing execution plan results*   202

SEQUENCE   202

  Tips for using SEQUENCE   203 ▪ *Restrictions*   203

EXECUTE...WITH RESULT SETS   205

THROW   208

Summary   209

23   *Creating your own data type   211*
         HUGO KORNELIS

Anatomy of a CLR user-defined type   212

  ...But do you need it at all?   212 ▪ *Representations and
  conversions*   213 ▪ *How about NULL?*   214

Building the data type: the bare basics   214

  Starting the project   214 ▪ *Adding the fields for the native
  representation*   215 ▪ *Editing the signature*   215 ▪ *Converting between*

.NET and text   216 ▪ *Converting between .NET and serialized   219*
Handling NULLs   220 ▪ *Using the data type   222*

Summary   222

24 *Extracting data with regular expressions   223*
MATIJA LAH

Understanding before coding   223

Background   224 ▪ *An incredibly brief introduction to regular
expressions, matches, and groups   225* ▪ *Regular expressions and SQL
Server   226* ▪ *Regular expressions and the .NET Framework   226*

The solution   227

The core   227 ▪ *The SQL CLR user-defined function   229* ▪ *The SSIS
script component   230*

Homework   232
Summary   232

25 *Relational division   234*
PETER LARSSON

Why use relational division?   234
Defining relational division   234
Background   235
Sample data for two simple cases   236
Comparison charts   238
Let's go on with the real stuff   240
Set-based solution to common relational division   240
Does one query exist for all types of relational division?   242
Summary   243

26 *SQL FILESTREAM: to BLOB or not to BLOB   245*
BEN MILLER

To FILESTREAM or not to FILESTREAM   245
Configuring FILESTREAM in SQL Server   247

Operating system configuration   247 ▪ *SQL Server configuration   248*

Database configuration   249

Creating a table that uses FILESTREAM   250
Things to consider   251
How do I use FILESTREAM?   252
Summary   254

27   Writing unit tests for Transact-SQL   255
LUCIANO MOREIRA

Unit test basics   255
   Unit test for databases   256 ▪ *T-SQL unit test walkthrough   257*

Automating unit test execution   265
Summary   265

28   Getting asynchronous with Service Broker   267
MLADEN PRAJDIĆ

The Service Broker usage template   267
Creating Service Broker objects   270
Summary   277

29   Effective use of HierarchyId   278
DENIS REZNIK

Hierarchies in a database   278
Introduction to the HierarchyId data type   279
   Using the HierarchyId data type   279 ▪ *Physical HierarchyId data
   organization   280*

Effective indexing   282
   Depth-first indexes   283 ▪ *Breadth-first indexes   284*

More information about HierarchyId   285
Summary   286

30   Let Service Broker help you scale your application   287
ALLEN WHITE

Scalable solutions   287
Service Broker objects   288
   Security   288 ▪ *Message types   289* ▪ *Contracts   289*
   Queues   289 ▪ *Services   289* ▪ *Conversations   290*
   Endpoints   290 ▪ *Routes   290* ▪ *Remote service binding   291*

ETL trigger demonstration 292

Summary 295

PART 4 PERFORMANCE TUNING AND OPTIMIZATION...... 297
EDITED BY BRAD M. MCGEHEE

31 Hardware 201: selecting and sizing database server hardware 299
GLENN BERRY 299

Why database server hardware is important 300

Scaling up or scaling out 300

SQL Server and hardware selection 301

Database server–specific hardware factors 302

Intel vs. AMD processors 304

Memory recommendations 304

Traditional storage subsystems 305

New developments in storage subsystems 306

Benchmarking and sizing tools 307

Summary 308

32 Parameter sniffing: your best friend...except when it isn't 309
GRANT FRITCHEY

Understanding parameter sniffing 309

Parameter sniffing gone wrong 312

Dealing with bad parameter sniffing 313
OPTIMIZE FOR 313 ▪ WITH RECOMPILE 315 ▪ Local
variables 316 ▪ Plan guides 316 ▪ Turn off parameter sniffing 318

Summary 318

33 Investigating the plan cache 320
JASON STRATE

Plan cache dynamic management objects 320
sys.dm_exec_cached_plans 321 ▪ sys.dm_exec_query_plan 321

Investigating missing indexes 322

Investigating index usage   324

Investigating operations   325

Investigating index scans   327

Investigating parameters   328

Plan cache considerations   329

Summary   330

34 *What are you waiting for?* *An introduction to waits and queues*   331

ROBERT PEARL

Introduction to total response time   331

What are wait stats?   332

Why use wait stats?   332 ▪ Wait type categories   332

The execution model   333

Viewing and reporting on wait statistics   335

Calculating wait time: signal waits vs. resource waits   337

Correlating performance data: putting it together   339

General I/O issues   339 ▪ Buffer I/O latch issues   339 ▪ Blocking and locking   340 ▪ CPU pressure   340 ▪ Parallelism   340 ▪ Memory pressure   341

Summary   341

35 *You see sets, and I see loops*   343

LINCHI SHEA

What loops?   343

The loop perspective   344

Loops in a query execution plan   346

Loops in complex queries   348

User-defined scalar functions in implicit loops   349

Merging multiple loops into one   350

Parallelizing loops   350

Linked server calls in a loop   351

Squeezing the fat out of loops with a slim table   352

Summary   352

36 *Performance-tuning the transaction log for OLTP workloads 353*
BRAD M. MCGEHEE

How can the transaction log be a bottleneck? 353

Factors that contribute to transaction log bottlenecks 354

Determining whether the transaction log is a bottleneck 356

Strategies for dealing with transaction log I/O bottlenecks 357

Start with standard performance-tuning techniques 357 ▪ *Take advantage of minimally logged operations if appropriate 358 Select a fast I/O subsystem 358* ▪ *Align disk partitions 358 Remove physical file fragmentation 358* ▪ *Preallocate transaction log file size 359* ▪ *Separating data and log files 359* ▪ *Managing virtual log files 360* ▪ *Perform transaction log backups often 360* ▪ *Schedule database maintenance during slow times 361*

Summary 361

37 *Strategies for unraveling tangled code 362*
JENNIFER MCCOWN

Organize: make it readable 362

Formatting 362 ▪ *Comments 364*

Break down: what does it do? 364

SELECT columns 364 ▪ *Data 364* ▪ *Sketch 365 Pseudocode 366*

Streamline: resolve obvious issues 366

Too much data 367 ▪ *Functions 367* ▪ *Non-SARGable WHERE Clauses 368*

Streamline: optimize joins 369

Streamline: similar subqueries and queries 370

Streamline: dynamic SQL 371

Summary 373

38 *Using PAL to analyze SQL Server performance 374*
TIM CHAPMAN

Performance Analysis of Logs (PAL) 374

Using PAL with SQL Server 375

Capturing performance counter data   375
   Data collector sets using PAL template files   375 ▪ *Logman   376*
   SQLDiag   376

Performing PAL analysis   377
   Counter Log   377 ▪ *Threshold File   378* ▪ *Questions   380*
   Output Options   380 ▪ *File Output   381* ▪ *Queue   381*
   Execute   381

The PAL report   382
Summary   382

39   *Tuning JDBC for SQL Server*   384
JUNGSUN KIM

JDBC performance tuning can be effective   384
Recommendations for tuning jTDS configuration   386
Unicode character issues   386
API cursor issues   388
ResultSet Type issue   389
Prepared statement mechanism issue   391
Controlling global configuration   393
Summary   394

PART 5   BUSINESS INTELLIGENCE 395
EDITED BY GREG LOW

40   *Creating a formal Reporting Services report part library*   397
JESSICA M. MOSS

Report parts defined   397
Deciding to create a report part library   398
Selecting report parts   399
   Level 1   400 ▪ *Level 2   400* ▪ *Level 3   401* ▪ *Level 4   401*

Using a report part library   401
   Creating the initial report part   402 ▪ *Using report parts
   and change requests   403* ▪ *Existing report part changes and
   publication   403*

Summary   404

41 *Improving report layout and visualization* **405**
GREG LOW

Target-based rendering 405

Control over pagination 406

Joining across datasets 407

Aggregates of aggregates 407

Writing mode 407

Domain scope 408

Databars 408

Sparklines 409

Summary 410

42 *Developing sharable managed code expressions in SSRS* **411**
WILLIAM (BILL) VAUGHN

Coding report expressions 411

Adding a report element property expression 412 ▪ *Coding a report Code property expression 414*

Creating sharable managed code expressions 419

Referencing DLLs from your report 421

Summary 422

43 *Designing reports with custom MDX queries* **424**
PAUL TURLEY

Using the Adventure Works sample data 425

MDX query builder 425

Building a report 425

Adding a calculated member 426

Handling parameters 429

Passing parameters 430 ▪ *Parameterizing measures 432*

Summary 434

44 *Building a scale-out Reporting Services farm* **436**
EDWIN SARMIENTO

What is network load balancing? 436

Preparing your network 436

*Create a DNS entry for the NLB cluster application   437 ▪ Configure the
server network cards   437*

Adding the network load balancing feature   437

Creating the NLB cluster   438

Adding hosts to the NLB cluster   440

Installing Reporting Services on the NLB cluster   440

Configuring the first Reporting Services instance   441

Configuring the second Reporting Services instance   442

Joining the second Reporting Services instance   443

Configuring view state validation   444

Configuring the hostname and UrlRoot   445

Workarounds for the HTTP 401 error message   446

Summary   447

45   *Creating SSRS reports from SSAS   448*
ROBERT CAIN

Creating the report project   449

Adding a shared data source   449

Creating shared datasets   449

*Creating the main dataset   450 ▪ Creating the parameter list shared
dataset   451*

The report   452

*Datasets   453 ▪ The matrix   453 ▪ Adding hierarchy drill-down
capabilities   453 ▪ Parameters   453 ▪ Charts   455*

Summary   456

46   *Optimizing SSIS for dimensional data loads   457*
MICHAEL COLES

Optimization quick wins   457

Type 0 dimensions   459

Type 1 SCDs   460

Type 2 SCDs   465

Summary   468

47 *SSIS configurations management* *469*
ANDY LEONARD

Building the demo database 470

Starting in the middle 470

Changing the connection 472

Externalizing the connection 473

Taking a step back 473

Abstracting a bit 474

Let's take a peek *478* ▪ *Runtime overrides* *478*

Summary 478

48 *Exploring different types of enumerators in the SSIS Foreach Loop container* *480*
ABOLFAZL RADGOUDARZI AND SHAHRIAR NIKKHAH

Make it dynamic 480

Foreach Loop enumerators *480*

Summary 492

49 *Late-arriving dimensions in SSIS* *494*
JOHN WELCH

A late-arriving dimension scenario 494

Natural keys and surrogate keys 495

The example data structure 495

Working around late-arriving dimensions 496

File it *496* ▪ *Ignore it* *496* ▪ *Update the fact later* *497*

Handling late-arriving dimension members in fact processing 497

Processing the dimension update 500

Summary 501

50 *Why automate tasks with SSIS?* *503*
TED KRUEGER

Automation by example 504

SSIS key tasks and components 505

Creating reusable and mobile SSIS packages   509

Precedence and manipulating control flow   511

Monitoring the results   513

Summary   514

51 *Extending SSIS using the Script component*   *515*
TIM MITCHELL

The Swiss Army knife of SSIS   515

Before we get started...a word of caution   516 ▪ *Sources, destinations, and transformations...oh my!   516* ▪ *Synchronous and asynchronous behavior   518* ▪ *Script component inputs and outputs   519* ▪ *Into the code   520*

Summary   525

52 *ETL design checklist*   *526*
RAFAEL SALAS

Discovering data realities   526

Extract phase   527

Detecting changed data   527 ▪ *Data staging   528*

Transform phase   529

Load phase   531

Surrogate key generation   531 ▪ *Data update strategy   532*

ETL system instrumentation and management   533

Alerting   533 ▪ *Recovery and restart ability   533* ▪ *Audit, balance, and control support   535* ▪ *Runtime event logging   535* ▪ *ETL metadata and reporting   536*

Summary   537

53 *Autogenerating SSAS cubes*   *538*
JOHAN ÅHLÉN

Background   538

Sample usage scenarios   539 ▪ *Technology overview   539*

Developing InstantCube, a simple cube generator   539

Creating the Visual Studio project   539 ▪ *Creating the relational database emitter   540* ▪ *Creating the Analysis Services emitter   540*

Creating the SSAS database   540 ▪ *Creating the data sources   541*
Creating the Data Source View   542 ▪ *Creating the dimensions   543*
Creating the cubes   545

Summary   546

References   547

54 Scripting SSAS databases – AMO and PowerShell, Better Together   548

DARREN GOSBELL

Advantages of PowerShell   548

Advantages of compiled code   549

Automating processing   549

Repetitive design changes   551

Scripting databases   554 ▪ *Modules and snap-ins   555*

Summary   556

55 Managing context in MDX   557

BOYAN PENEV

Named sets   559

Calculated members   560

Scope assignments   565

Summary   568

56 Using time intelligence functions in PowerPivot   569

THIAGO ZAVASCHI

Introducing Data Analysis Expressions   569

DAX data types   569 ▪ *Sample database   570*

Time intelligence functions   570

Golden rules   571 ▪ *Functions that return a single date   571*
Functions that return a table of dates   572 ▪ *Functions that evaluate*
expressions over a time period   573

Samples   573

Summary   576

57 *Easy BI with Silverlight PivotViewer* **577**

GOGULA ARYALINGAM

Presenting Silverlight PivotViewer 577

What makes up your pivot 578

Cards (or images) 578 ▪ *Slicing and dicing options* 579 ▪ *Filtering and sorting options* 579

The way to go 579

Which seat should I take? 579 ▪ *The source* 580 ▪ *Preparation* 580
Implementation 582

Summary 584

58 *Excel as a BI frontend tool* **585**

PEDRO PERFEITO

Key points to consider when choosing a BI frontend tool 585

Why Excel? 586

Assumptions 586

Why use OLAP as a source? 587

Dashboard implementation 587

The business perspective 587 ▪ *The technology perspective* 588

Summary 596

59 *Real-time BI with StreamInsight* **597**

ALLAN MITCHELL

What is StreamInsight? 597

What are events and event streams? 598

Event shapes 598

Deployment 599

Architecture 599

How does querying streams differ from querying an RDBMS? 600

Where is StreamInsight useful? 602

Time 602

Querying the streams 603

Summary 606

60 *BI solution development design considerations   608*
SIDDHARTH MEHTA

Architecture design   608

Other aspects influencing architecture design   610

Solution development   611

Conceptual design   611 ▪ ETL layer   611 ▪ Dimensional modeling and cube design   612 ▪ Reporting platform   613 ▪ Dashboard development   614

Summary   615

index   617

This is the second volume of a book that many people thought would never see the light of day. In early 2007, the editor of the first volume, Paul Nielsen, had an extraordinary idea. I'll let him tell you about how this idea came into being, by including a section from the preface to Volume 1:

> Each year Microsoft invites all the MVPs from every technology and country to Redmond for an MVP Summit—all top secret—"don't tweet what you see!" During the MVP Summit, each product team holds a series of presentations where they explain their technologies, share their vision, and listen to some honest feedback. At the 2007 MVP Summit in Seattle, Bill Gates presented his vision of the future of computing to the MVPs and then took questions for about an hour. I really enjoy these dialogues. I get the sense that if BillG wasn't the founder of Microsoft, he'd make a great MVP. You can tell he likes us as fellow Geeks, and he's rather candid in the MVP Q&A time. It's one of my favorite parts of the MVP Summit.
>
> During the Q&A, the lines at the microphones are far too long to bother to join, so I daydream a few questions I'd ask BillG:
>
> - As the world's wealthiest Geek, what can you tell me about your PC?
> - Even with all your accomplishments, do you still find the most happiness and satisfaction with your family?
> - Do you play Age of Empires 2, and if so, want to join me in a game?
> - Kirk or Picard?
> - Can I buy you lunch?
>
> And then I thought of a good, deep, Charlie Rose-type of question: "Centuries from now, would you rather be remembered as the guy who put a computer on every desk, or as the guy who ended malaria and fought the good fight against poverty?" As I try to guess what BillG might say, the answer is obvious. I'm glad that BillG's intellect and resources are being directed at improving the human condition, and as an original Windows fan I'm proud of BillG. But the answer to

my question is both—Windows has already done as much to fight poverty as will the Bill and Melinda Gates Foundation.

Toward the end of the Q&A time, which was mostly taken up with technical questions, I was thrilled to hear one of the MVPs ask for his advice as a philanthropist. BillG said that we should all be involved in our communities and give of ourselves in creative ways: at the library, at schools, and with charities. "Do philanthropy where you are." This idea of giving of ourselves is central to the MVP community.

Paul then went on to describe how he decided he could make a difference "where he was" by writing about his passion, SQL Server, and using it to create a charity book to help children. He enticed me into the project, and after communicating with the rest of the SQL Server MVPs to determine if there was enough interest to make a project of this type viable, together we started approaching publishers.

It didn't take long to find that Manning Publications was extremely interested in producing this kind of project. Michael Stephens liked both the community aspect of the project and the charity goals. Manning also offered us a higher-than-usual author royalty, because we were giving it all to charity. We recruited four other prominent MVPs to help with the editing, and the project was underway.

A project such as this had never been done before. We had 53 independent authors from all around the world trying to collaborate. Figuring out how to manage the technical editing and rewrites, and dealing with writers who were technically extraordinary but lacking in some writing skills, and deciding what to do with a chapter that came in at 40 pages when all the rest were 10–15 pages, made the project much more time-consuming than we expected. Many of the MVPs who had written chapters early in the process despaired of ever seeing their work in print.

But then it all seemed to come together, just in time for the 2009 PASS Conference, which is the largest conference in the world for SQL Server professionals. The book had been available for preorder, and by the time the conference started, the preorders alone had earned the chosen charity more than $10,000! Manning made an all-out effort to get 200 copies of the book available in print to sell at the conference. Almost three dozen of the MVP authors were speaking at the conference, and they told their audiences about this remarkable work we had done. On the Thursday of the conference, right after lunch, we launched Volume 1 in a special event in the vendor area and followed this with the most popular book-signing in PASS history. Most of the attending authors stood behind a long table, and eager readers flowed by in front of us, getting autographs from all the authors present. All 200 copies of the book were sold, which was another PASS record, and many people who wanted a copy weren't able to get one and participate in the signing. Although my hand was numb from signing my name so many times, it was the most exciting event of my professional life. Volume 1 was so well received that there was immediate talk of another one. We all needed a rest, however, and we needed to give the community time to absorb the first terrific volume. But in late 2010, Paul and I decided it was time to start thinking about Volume 2.

Paul and I switched roles: he stepped down from the overall editor role to become a section editor, and I became the overall editor. Kimberly Tripp, Paul Randal, and Greg Low stayed on as section editors for the new volume, and we brought in Louis Davidson and Brad McGehee as new section editors. Manning was more than happy to continue to support us with its publishing team.

Like the first volume, this one is divided into five sections aligned with the five job roles dealing with SQL Server: database architecture and design, database development, database administration, performance tuning and optimization, and business intelligence. There was no rigid organization to the outline—MVPs were simply asked to submit abstracts for chapters that they wanted to write, and those abstracts were directed to the appropriate section editors. As in the first volume, the contents are driven by the MVPs' individual passions, not by a comprehensive feature list. The section editors selected the best abstracts, but we committed to the idea that every MVP who wanted to contribute to the book could contribute. We had a much tighter deadline for this volume and also a much stricter page count limit, and we limited each author to a single chapter. But we didn't restrict what the authors could write, and only insisted that it be never-published material in a topic area that wasn't specifically addressed in Volume 1. So this volume is completely new material!

To select the charity, we collected nominations from the participating MVPs with the restriction that the charity had to be a secular group that benefited children around the world. And we wanted to give to a smaller charity—we didn't want our contribution to be added to a billion-dollar fund. The vote this time was overwhelming in favor of Operation Smile, which you can read about on page xli.

I'd like to include another paragraph from the preface to the first volume, because there is no way I can say this better than Paul did:

> If you are reading this book, then you are "rich." Considering your place in human history, you're wealthier than most kings of centuries past—you are well educated, your grocery store shelves are full, you have a family doctor. For too many in the world, that is not the case. There are communities without clean water, children hurting from war, and AIDS orphans who have no family or place to sleep. When one ponders the immense need and poverty in the world, it's easy to become overwhelmed with hopelessness. How can a single drop of ink change the color of an ocean? But we have no other option than to do what we can. My philosophy is that of Confucius: "It is better to light one small candle than to curse the darkness." Even BillG can't heal the world, but we can each make a difference.

By buying this book, you've supported Operation Smile. We want to reiterate BillG's suggestion that we can all find ways to do philanthropy where we are, and this book is one way to start doing that, both for the authors and for the readers.

Welcome to *SQL Server MVP Deep Dives, Volume 2*—a collaborative work by 64 passionate SQL Server MVPs.

KALEN DELANEY

acknowledgments

The first thank-you has to go to the 63 MVPs who wrote and edited this book, and to their families, and in some cases their employers, for supporting them in the effort.

To my fellow editors, Louis Davidson, Greg Low, Brad McGehee, Paul Nielsen, Paul S. Randal, and Kimberly L. Tripp, who went above and beyond the call to make sure their sections contained quality content: thank you.

To Marjan Bace, our publisher, thank you for helping us refine the original concept, supporting the project from the very first day of Volume 1, and partnering with us.

To Michael Stephens, Cynthia Kane, Liz Welch, Linda Recktenwald, Mary Piergies, Barbara Mirecki, Candace Gillhoolley, Ozren Harlovic, Marija Tudor, and the rest of the team at Manning Publications—thanks for believing in this project and sticking with it to the end.

A big thanks to Victor Isakov, Dave Dustin, Aaron Nelson, Denis Gobo, and Mike Walsh for contributing their time as technical editors. Your help was invaluable! And a huge showering of gratitude to Stacia Misner, Jen Stirrup, Rob Farley, and Robert Pearl who stepped up at the last minute to help us deal with an unexpected crunch!

To the reviewers who read early versions of the manuscript and provided helpful feedback: Amos Bannister, Nikander Bruggeman, Margriet Bruggeman, Dave Corun, Sanchet Dighe, Richard Handloff, Peter Lee, Massimo Perga, Richard Siddaway, Ian Stirk, and Deepak Vohra.

Many thanks to Ed Lehman and Ed Hickey, our SQL Server product team MVP Liaisons, for their support and the many good times.

To our MVP leads through the years—Shawn Aebi, Paul Wehland, Stephen Dybing, Ben Miller, Alison Brooks, Suzanna Moran, Ryan Bolz, and others internationally—thank you for supporting our community efforts.

To everyone in the Microsoft SQL Server product team, our enthusiastic thanks for developing a product worthy of our passion.

A heartfelt thank-you to Operation Smile for all you do for the children.

And finally, thank you, readers, for supporting our project and helping us support Operation Smile.

about Operation Smile

Operation Smile, headquartered in Norfolk, Virginia, is an international children's medical charity with programs and foundations in more than 60 countries, whose network of more than 5,000 medical volunteers from 76 countries is dedicated to helping improve the health and lives of children and young adults. Since its founding in 1982, Operation Smile has provided more than 2 million patient evaluations and has conducted over 200,000 free surgeries for children and young adults born with cleft lips, cleft palates, and other facial deformities. To lay the groundwork for long-term self-sufficiency in developing countries, Operation Smile donates medical equipment and trains local medical professionals in its partner countries so they are empowered to treat their own local communities. Visit www.operationsmile.org for more information.

A letter from Operation Smile follows on the next page.

Operation ⊕ Smile

August 15, 2011

To Kalen, Kimberly, Paul, Paul, Greg, Louis, Brad, and all the other
SQL Server MVPs who participated in producing this book:

On behalf of Operation Smile, we want to thank all of you for selecting Operation Smile as the beneficiary for Volume 2 in the *SQL Server Deep Dives* series. We are indeed privileged and humbled knowing you have joined us in helping children around the world who just want a chance to smile and play like every other child.

Approximately one in 500–700 children, or 200,000 globally, are born each year with a cleft lip or cleft palate deformity. These children face numerous challenges to their everyday survival and are often ostracized due to difficulty in speaking and eating.

Because of our dedicated medical volunteers and generous financial supporters, we are able to continue our mission to heal children's smiles and transform lives across the globe.

Thanks again to everyone who contributed to this book and for making the decision to make a difference in the lives of children who may never know your name, but will never forget your kindness.

Lisa Jardanhazy

Lisa Jardanhazy
Vice President, Strategic Partnerships & Cause Marketing

about this book

In this book, the world's leading practitioners of SQL Server present a collection of articles on techniques and best practices for SQL Server development and administration based on their many years of combined experience. The 64 MVPs who contributed to the book each picked an area of special interest to them and shared their insights and practical know-how with you. The topics covered will appeal to a broad range of readers with varied levels of SQL Server experience, from beginner to advanced.

How the book is organized

This book has 60 chapters divided into five parts that correspond to the 5 job roles involving SQL Server:

- Part 1   Database architecture and design
- Part 2   Database development
- Part 3   Database administration
- Part 4   Performance tuning and optimization
- Part 5   Business intelligence

There is no rigid construction to the book, no list of SQL Server features or versions that needed to be covered. The contributors to the book submitted abstracts on their topics of expertise, and these were added to the appropriate sections. The section editors reviewed the abstracts and chose the ones that best fit into their grouping of chapters.

Source code

All source code in listings or in text is in a `fixed-width font like this` to separate it from ordinary text. The source code for the examples in this book is available online from the publisher's website at www.manning.com/SQLServerMVPDeep DivesVol2. The source code is organized by chapter, but please note that not all chapters have code listings in them.

Author Online

The purchase of *SQL Server MVP Deep Dives, Volume 2* includes free access to a private web forum run by Manning Publications, where you can make comments about the book, ask technical questions, and receive help from the authors and from other users. To access the forum and subscribe to it, point your web browser to www.manning.com/ SQLServerMVPDeepDivesVol2.

This page provides information about how to get on the forum once you're registered, what kind of help is available, and the rules of conduct on the forum. Manning's commitment to our readers is to provide a venue where a meaningful dialogue between individual readers and between readers and the authors can take place. It's not a commitment to any specific amount of participation on the part of the authors, whose contributions to the book's forum (as well as all authors' contributions to the book itself) remain voluntary (and unpaid).

The Author Online forum and the archives of previous discussions will be accessible from the publisher's website as long as the book is in print.

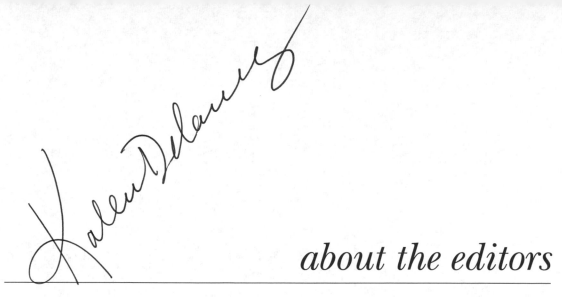

about the editors

Kalen Delaney is the lead editor of *SQL Server MVP Deep Dives, Volume 2*. The bios and photographs of the section editors can be found at the end of the introductions to each part, as follows:

- Part 1   Database architecture and design, edited by Louis Davidson
- Part 2   Database development, edited by Paul Randal and Kimberly Tripp
- Part 3   Database administration, edited by Paul Nielsen
- Part 4   Performance tuning and optimization, edited by Brad McGehee
- Part 5   Business intelligence, edited by Greg Low

KALEN DELANEY

Kalen Delaney has worked with SQL Server for nearly 24 years and has written about it for more than 20. In addition to writing deeply technical books such as *Inside SQL Server* and *SQL Server 2008 Internals*, she writes courseware and delivers advanced SQL Server training around the world. Find out more about Kalen's writing and training on her website at www.SQLServerInternals.com

Kalen has been invited by Microsoft to present special internal training on many occasions. She has spoken at Microsoft TechEd and presented at every PASS (Professional Association for SQL Server) Summit since the organization's inception. She is delighted that her love for SQL Server can once again be put to such good use in the publication of this second volume of *SQL Server MVP Deep Dives*.

about SQL Server MVPs

The Microsoft Most Valuable Professional (MVP) award is given in recognition of contributions to the community and can be renewed on a yearly basis. Only MVPs who have been actively contributing to the community during the previous year are renewed, so MVPs can't rest on their laurels and expect to continue to be members of this generous, vibrant group of professionals. Contributions can take many forms, and those forms are constantly evolving. MVPs are the top influencers in many different kinds of communities. They all give their time to the community in one or more significant ways. They may be forum or newsgroup moderators, authors, bloggers, trainers, speakers, and user group or SQL PASS leaders, to name just a few.

MVPs are also usually the most highly skilled individuals on Microsoft's technology outside of Microsoft. In recognition of their place as the best aggregators of customer feedback and the broadest channel of communications out to customers, MVPs are given more access to product-development teams than any group of customers in order to maximize both inbound and outbound communications with the community. MVPs are awarded in many other technologies in addition to SQL Server, but it is the SQL Server MVPs who have put together the book you're reading. Even within SQL Server, there are a wide variety of focus areas, and many SQL Server MVPs work across a number of SQL Server areas. Having a single broad category allows MVPs more access to the breadth of the product. In addition, if you browse through the table of contents for this volume, you'll see that having a single broad category for SQL Server MVPs gives you a wide variety of SQL Server topics to read about.

You can find out more about MVPs on Microsoft's site at http://mvp.support .microsoft.com/. You can see the full list of SQL Server MVPs here: https://mvp .support.microsoft.com/communities/mvp.aspx?product=1&competency=SQL+Server.

PART 1

Architecture

Edited by Louis Davidson

Database design and architecture are subjects that can be quite polarizing. You're either super excited by them, or they tend to make you bored to tears and ready to hurl cartoon birds at cartoon pigs. At the SQL PASS conference last year, a keynote was given by Dr. David DeWitte, a Technical Fellow in Microsoft's Data and Storage Platform Division. For a great number of people, it was amazing stuff that made us sad when he finished talking. For quite a few more, it was painfully uninteresting, because, quoting a person I overheard, "I'm not going to use this." As a speaker, I've given a number of sessions on normalization that get an average speaker score for usefulness that was just above 3 out of 5, because half of the people loved it and the other half wanted me to speak about something else entirely but were kind enough to give me a 2 instead of the dreaded 1.

There in a nutshell loomed the $64,000 question. Is knowing about the architecture of SQL Server internals useful? Is understanding the proper way to do database design of any real value, even if you're never going to directly design a query optimizer or even a database? Architectural understanding is like understanding why certain foods are good for you. A little understanding will help guide your eating habits, just like a bit of architectural knowledge will give you some insight into how to design and program to meet the needs of SQL Server's architecture.

One of the underlying goals of SQL is to be a completely declarative language where you tell the computer what you want to do and it does so almost magically.

In reality, though, it's not quite that simple unless you have very big hardware and very small needs. SQL Server doesn't run like an Xbox game on a console, where all programs are built to work on one set of hardware parameters. It's architected to run on lowly computers like my little laptop and on computers with more CPUs than you can count on your fingers and toes. Understanding the architecture of the SQL Server engine and how it works with the hardware will help you optimize your code and the servers where it operates. And understanding how the optimizer works will help you see why normalization and constraints are usually good for performance rather than bad.

Architecture is a wide topic, so with six chapters we have an interesting range of subjects. We have two chapters that largely center on different aspects of keys and uniqueness, two that are general database architecture overviews, one on generalizing your designs, and even one that's about physical storage architecture. A bit of a hodge-podge to be sure, but as you read the rest of this book, you'll notice that the coding, reporting, and operational types of chapters are far more plentiful because, as a whole, MVPs aren't theorists or deep internal architecture implementers but expert users of the technology with a solid knowledge of how the architecture affects them and a desire to share their knowledge with you.

The focus on data architecture in the lion's share of the sections shouldn't surprise you. Database design is something that everyone has to do, and it's quite difficult to do correctly, not so much due to the fact that the task is difficult from a technical or theoretical side (in fact it turns out to be easy to apply), but because it's rare to start a completely new database with completely new code to access it. In this section you'll get some guidance on how to implement a solid, working, and well-formed database prepared for today's business as well as tomorrow's.

About the editor

 Louis Davidson has been in the IT industry for 17 years as a corporate database developer and architect. He's been a Microsoft MVP for 7 years and has written 4 books on database design. Currently, Louis serves as the Data Architect for the Christian Broadcasting Network, supporting offices in Virginia Beach, Virginia, and Nashville, Tennessee. Louis has a bachelor's degree in computer science from the University of Tennessee at Chattanooga, with a minor in mathematics. For more information, please visit his website at http://drsql.org.

1 Where are my keys?

Ami Levin

If you walk into a room full of DBAs or DB developers and you feel like having the same kind of fun as setting fire to a dry hayfield, just drop this question: "What's a better design, using natural keys or artificial keys?" Satisfaction guaranteed. When I started to study database design, this was one of the first hot controversies I encountered. If you Google the phrase "natural vs. artificial keys," you'll come up with more than 150 million results, including endless debates, numerous articles, blog posts with passionate replies, long theoretical and practical arguments, and even the occasional profanity. In this chapter, I would like to take you on a tour, very much the same way I have traveled with this dispute, and I hope that together we can reach some useful insights into the essence of both positions. Who can tell? Perhaps things won't look as stark afterward.

The seeds of the dispute, curiously, were planted by the inventors of the relational model. The basis for all major databases today was first introduced by Edgar F. Codd of IBM in 1969 and later extended in collaboration with Chris Date and others. Although they were in accord on the main tenets of the model, the relational database forefathers held slightly different views on certain aspects of the model, and this early difference of opinions led to current-day repercussions, as you'll see later. Date seemed to be a keen supporter of using artificial keys, but Codd had quite a few reservations on the matter.

What caused this difference of opinion to grow into a controversy, and what has kept the battle alive for so long? Its growth to the rank of controversy stems from the fact that database design has a crucial impact on performance, modularity, consistency, and scalability. This makes the issue of correct database design ever so important. Moreover, once in production the basic design of a database is probably the hardest aspect to revise.

I hope that when you approach your next design project, this chapter will prompt you to take the few extra hours, days, or weeks to consider your key selection with the seriousness that it truly deserves. If this chapter will help you save even one hour of work or one dollar of unnecessary expense in the future, it was worth all the work I've invested in it.

The unforeseen consequences of database design flaws

I've seen numerous cases where the DBAs and developers admit that there are serious flaws in the database design ("I inherited it this way"), but they'll probably have to live with those flaws for many years to come. Their very valid reason is that the original design was created many years ago when the design characteristics, now recognized as flaws, had little or no negative impact. Since then, the natural evolution and expansion of the database have magnified the impact of those flaws. If the original designers had known the true extent of the resources that would be spent as a direct result of their design flaws, I'm sure they would have taken the time to think things over once more.

Keys in the relational model

The importance of keys is apparent in seminal works, and in particular the works regarding data normalization. The concept of normalization was first introduced by Codd in his ground-breaking paper "A Relational Model of Data for Large Shared Data Banks." This paper, which set the foundations for all relational databases as we know them today, is freely available on the internet, and I highly recommend it to anyone who deals with database design. A few years later, Codd and Date elaborated this concept into the normal forms as we know them today.

It's obvious from the normalization rules that keys are a fundamental entity that plays a critical role in the design of a relational database. The schema design is tested and validated for correctness based on the keys and how they relate to all the nonkey columns that make up your database tables. Choosing the correct model to represent the reality the database will serve is fully key dependent. How much thought have you given your keys until now?

Databases are a mirror of reality

I'd like to emphasize the fact that a relational model database is (surprise, surprise)... a *model*. That may sound obvious, but it does carry a lot of meaning and corresponding responsibility. Dictionary.com defines *model* as "a simplified represen-tation of a system or phenomenon, as in the sciences or economics, with any hypotheses required to describe the system or explain the phenomenon, often mathematically." A database models, in relational form or some other form, some physical or logical universe, entity, or phenomenon (or a part of one of those). It's designed to be a mirror, in relational language and terms, of its real characteristics and functions.

A *key* was originally defined by Codd as follows: "Normally, one domain [column] (or combination of domains) of a given relation [table] has values which uniquely identify each element [row] (n-tuple) of that relation. Such a domain is called a primary key." Codd realized that there may be multiple columns within a table that may be candidates to identify the row. Therefore he offers, "Whenever a relation has two or more non-redundant primary keys, one of them is arbitrarily selected and called the primary key of that relation."

So the primary key is an arbitrary selection! Or is it? Although logically any of the candidate keys can be used to identify the row, a primary key must shoulder several other responsibilities besides unique identification. These include most often serving as the parent node in foreign key relationships, being used by default as the clustering key for the table's physical index structure, and not allowing NULL values. In this chapter, I'll use the following highly simplified definitions of the various types of keys:

- A *simple key* is a key that consists of a single column.
- A *composite key* is a key that consists of more than one column.
- A *candidate key* is a key (simple or composite) that could be used to uniquely identify the row.
- A *primary key* is the key selected from among the candidate keys to serve as the authoritative row identifier.
- An *artificial* (or *surrogate*) *key* is a key that doesn't contain any information about the entity that the table represents—for example, a GUID.
- A *natural key* is a key that consists of columns that contain information natural to the entity that the table represents. An example is the vehicle identification number (VIN) of a car.

The deeper theoretical aspects of key definitions and all the various subtypes of keys are useful in other discussions but don't contribute to the purpose of this chapter. This chapter's purpose is to present the practical aspects and ramifications of the choices you make for your keys when designing your database. Therefore, I'll focus on what I've found to be the most common choices for key selection that SQL Server database designers face: should you use a column or a set of columns that are already a part of your row and contain information about the entity (broadly called the *natural key*), or should you add an IDENTITY or similar column (broadly called here the *artificial key*) to generate values that will identify the row and serve as the primary key?

The debate

The overwhelming majority of database designs that I've encountered use artificial sequential enumerator keys such as IDENTITY for just about every table in the database. College classes about databases, books about database development, web articles, and most other materials include examples that use artificial keys almost exclusively. I believe that this practice is so widespread that new students, learning to become database developers, take it as a fact of life that this is how it should be done. Moreover, many database developers have come from a background of procedural programming, where the concept of object handles, pointers, and physical addresses fits perfectly with the notion of a "row handle," which an artificial key seems to offer. Joe Celko, a well-known relational database expert and author, often claims that the origins of this practice are rooted all the way back in the 1950s when magnetic tapes were used to store sequential chunks of data and physical pointers were the only available means for the programming languages of those days to access the data. Celko is among the very few who wholeheartedly (some claim overly so) preaches for using natural keys. So who is right?

The arguments

For this chapter, I've researched many books, articles, blogs, and forum posts. I've tried to narrow this topic down to the most commonly found arguments for each camp. Although it seems that the pro–artificial keys camp represents the vast majority of the relevant population, I'll try to give similar weight to the arguments and at the same time serve as devil's advocate for both camps. Without further ado, let's looks at the claims of the supporters of each type of key.

Pro artificial keys

Let's begin with the claims of the pro–artificial keys camp.

ARTIFICIAL KEY VALUES NEVER CHANGE

The reason key value permanence is so meaningful is that it's hard to propagate changes in key values throughout all referencing tables without disrupting the database. Although cascading referential constraints can be used in most cases to handle this task, it can incur significant data modification overhead. It's a potential cost that never needs to be estimated when using an artificial identifier whose value never needs to change, regardless of what other property values change.

Yet how frequently does a key property of an entity change in the real world? A true natural key such as a human retina scan will never change. A well-established industry standard identifier such as an ISBN might change. The 9-digit SBN code was established in 1966, to be replaced in 1970 by the ISO 10-digit ISBN, and 27 years later changed again to its current 13-digit format. Databases that used ISBNs as primary keys needed to accommodate these changes. Databases that didn't implement cascading referential constraints might have required significant work to accommodate these changes and could have experienced potential disruptions to the database.

I'd like to add that the claim that an artificial key will never change should be qualified. When two or more databases need to be merged, some of the artificial key values will probably need to change to avoid logically duplicate rows.

ARTIFICIAL KEYS ARE SHORT AND SIMPLE

Natural keys can be long. Sometimes, the natural key will consist of quite a few columns. Even if the top parent table has a relatively simple one-column natural key, each child table will require adding its own attributes to the key. The deeper you dive in this hierarchy, the longer and more complex the natural key will become. Because primary keys must be indexed in SQL Server to enable efficient enforcement of uniqueness, you might hit the 900-byte maximum index key size limit, which will prevent you from using the natural key altogether.

Using multicolumn keys for joins results in long and complex join conditions, requiring long queries and potentially more complex plans that may lead to performance degradation. These multicolumn join conditions are used for enforcing foreign keys as well. This in turn may lead to degraded performance in data modifications.

Artificial keys, on the other hand—especially the most common integer type IDEN-TITY columns—are short and simple. If you use them for every table, they will remain short and simple regardless of the hierarchy level. They're meaningless, so they can be whatever form and size you want them to be.

ARTIFICIAL KEYS CAN IMPROVE PERFORMANCE

There are several aspects to this claim. First is the fact that the SQL optimizer has an easier time estimating join-predicate selectivity when it only needs to deal with simpler joins based on a single column, resulting in more efficient execution plans. Second, the clustering effect of using an ever-increasing primary key such as IDENTITY, which by default is also used as the clustered index key, will ensure that the rows are inserted sequentially into the last page of the index. The result is better cache use as the most recent page will remain in cache for reuse when the next insert arrives. This may reduce I/O costs for sequential inserts.

> ### Artificial keys and index sizes
>
> Another claim I hear often is that using short keys will result in smaller indexes and hence better overall performance. This would be true only if the artificial key was the only unique key required on a table. However, the natural key attributes are also unique, and this means additional unique constraints (and their corresponding indexes) must be maintained for data-consistency enforcement. So in many cases, the presence of an artificial key may result in larger index requirements.

IN SOME CASES, AN ARTIFICIAL KEY IS THE ONLY OPTION

When I ask database designers for an example of tables that have no natural keys, the most frequent reply I receive is that of an event log table. A Profiler trace is an excellent example of an event log. Even if you consider all the properties of a trace event, they might not be enough to uniquely identify it.

But one could also claim that a simple event log is a flat, nonrelational bulk storage structure to begin with. If these log events are the main business entity that your database deals with, you should probably design it quite differently, splitting this flat structure into a truly normalized relational form.

While we can certainly find some great examples of real-world objects that are best identified by an artificial key, it would seem that they would be in the minority. After all, a well-designed relational model that truly mirrors the reality it serves must have a natural way of uniquely identifying each individual entity. If not, it means that these entities can't be distinguished in the real world. Celko once claimed that not having a natural key is a violation of Aristotle's law of identity: "To be is to be something in particular."

USING ARTIFICIAL KEYS REDUCES FRAGMENTATION OF CLUSTERED INDEXES

The clustered index of an ever-increasing value that never changes will never get fragmented by INSERTs or UPDATEs (except UPDATEs that increase row size), thus reducing the need for index maintenance. A clustered index requires an exclusive, table-level lock in order to be rebuilt. Consequently, during a clustered index rebuild, table data is unavailable to the application except for transactions that are using the read-uncommitted isolation level. Therefore, using IDENTITY keys as clustered primary keys can reduce potential downtime.

DELETEs are quite a different story and hide a very risky aspect. Because the primary key value is ever increasing, the space left by a row that was deleted will never be reclaimed until the index is rebuilt or until the page is empty. This is not the case when using natural keys, which tend to have more or less even distribution patterns. Even if you choose to use artificial clustered keys, you'll need to deal with the fragmentation effect of the natural keys anyway. As previously mentioned, their unique (nonclustered by default) indexes will be required to enforce data consistency and will suffer from the same fragmentation. It's true that rebuilding a nonclustered index is cheaper in terms of locking and potential downtime. This brings me to the question of whether or not it's a good idea to have the clustered index of the table on the primary key. Because in my opinion this issue deserves a full chapter by itself, I won't address it here.

ARTIFICIAL KEYS HAVE MEANING BY VIRTUE OF BEING USED

Once generated and communicated back into the real world, artificial keys can move from a starting position of *meaningless* to a position of *meaningful* by virtue of being used and hence become semi-natural. For example, it's easier for the warehouse manager to communicate specific products to employees using a short integer number than to use a barcode or a combination of five different properties that constitute the natural key. These arbitrary numbers eventually make sense to this cloistered group of people, regardless of whether they have any meaning to the people in the warehouse next door. And on their lunch breaks, they canrelax with no confusion at all over a nice hot cup of 593482.

Pro natural keys

Next I'll address the claims of the pro–natural keys camp.

NATURAL KEYS HAVE BUSINESS MEANING

Natural keys, as their name suggests, are natural to the entity that the table represents. These are attributes that must be stored anyway and have a real role to play for the database application. Adding additional (meaningless) data in the form of an artificial key is redundant and inflates the database. Moreover, because the value of the artificial key isn't visible or even known to the application's end users, they will never query for it. For example, no user would ever ask, "Which customers live in the country that happens to be represented in this particular database by the number 5?" They would query the database with a question like, "Show me all Canadian customers."

Codd said something very interesting about using artificial (surrogate) keys: "Database users may cause the system to generate or delete a surrogate, but they have no control over its value, nor is its value ever displayed to them."

QUERIES ON TABLES USING NATURAL KEYS REQUIRE FEWER JOINS

Naturally, when your keys contain the data you're after, the need for joins is drastically reduced. For example, a query on an [Order Details] row that already has the natural [Product] identifier in it may be enough for some queries and eliminate the need to join the [Products] table, as would be required when an artificial [ProductID] is used, because it holds no information about the product. The product key may be the product name, the manufacturer's proprietary product number, barcode, and so on. When the most natural identifier is used—meaning the one that the particular business requires most often—the number of required joins will be reduced to a minimum.

Having fewer joins makes your queries more elegant, shorter, simpler, and in most cases, better performing. Here's an example of a simple query from AdventureWorks, Microsoft's sample database that was designed using artificial keys exclusively:

```
SELECT    SOH.SalesOrderID, C.AccountNumber, ST.Name AS Territory
FROM      Sales.SalesOrderHeader AS SOH
          INNER JOIN    Sales.Customer AS C
              ON        C.CustomerID = SOH.CustomerID
          INNER JOIN    Sales.SalesTerritory AS ST
              ON        ST.TerritoryID = SOH.TerritoryID
```

Note that two joins are necessary to access the desired information. Let's see how this same query would eliminate joins if no artificial keys were used. Assuming that the columns in the select list are the natural keys for these entities, and assuming that the designer used them as the primary keys, the same query would've been written as

```
SELECT    SalesOrderID, CustomerAccountNumber, Territory
FROM      Sales.SalesOrderHeader
```

NATURAL KEYS MAINTAIN DATA CONSISTENCY

This extremely important aspect of using natural keys has several levels to it. The most obvious one is the fact that uniqueness must be enforced on the table by relying on the unique properties that identify the entities rather than on a meaningless IDENTITY column. For example, consider a [Countries] table that has only an IDENTITY primary key named [CountryID]. For such a table, nothing prevents you from inserting multiple rows for the same country, each using a different ID. When an artificial key is used, an additional unique constraint *must* be placed on the country's name to keep data consistent. Unfortunately, it's often not the case, and more unfortunately, this situation often leads to data inconsistencies.

Data consistency concerns

It's true that even with a unique constraint in place on the natural key, improperly designed applications can still allow duplication by way of spelling variations (for example "USA," "U.S.A."). I've taken active part in purifying the data of several such databases. This relates to another bad practice of database design: failing to enforce standardized sets of values for global entities such as countries. In my database designs, you'll often find a [Countries] table that consists of a single primary key column, [Country]. Only the application administrator has the required privileges to change it. Simple foreign keys reference it from all tables that require a [Country] attribute. The countries list is populated using standardized names, and when "Ceylon" changes its name to "Sri Lanka," it's easily dealt with using cascading referential integrity constraints.

NATURAL KEYS ELIMINATE LOCK CONTENTIONS DUE TO PHYSICAL CLUSTERING

This issue is the counter aspect of the ever-increasing insert performance improvement mentioned in the pro–artificial keys section. Although benchmarks have proven that using an ever-increasing clustering key may improve performance for sequential inserts, the issue becomes more complex when at the same time the table data is also queried by SELECT statements. Remember that these selects aren't necessarily user initiated but may be initiated by the database engine enforcing foreign keys when referencing tables' data is modified. When the same physical data pages are being modified and selected at the same time, serious locking contentions may occur. Natural keys, which usually have a naturally random distribution, suffer much less from this issue.

Solving clustered page locking contentions

I've encountered several cases in the past where the database designers were called on to solve this issue, and they simply redesigned the keys to use randomly distributed GUIDs instead of IDENTITY to eliminate this locking contention. Of course, this strategy also eliminated the benefits of insert performance page caching and reduced fragmentation, in some cases introducing an even more severe performance problem due to the high levels of fragmentation and page splits. Interestingly enough, I didn't witness a single case where the designers even considered the solution of using a natural key. When I mentioned the option, usually a few eyebrows were raised in response to my "weird" ideas.

Additional considerations

The following points are less frequently mentioned in the natural versus artificial key debate. Nevertheless, I do believe they're no less important than the commonly mentioned ones.

Natural keys assist the optimizer

I discovered this issue while preparing a demonstration for a class back in 2006. I was surprised that I never saw it mentioned elsewhere as I have found it to be a serious issue that designers need to be aware of. SQL Server maintains statistical histograms of data distribution to optimize execution plans. The query optimizer uses this information to select the best plan, based on the actual parameter values used in the query. Here's a simple query that lists all US customers from a table that uses a natural country key, its name:

```
SELECT   *
FROM     Customers
WHERE    Country = 'USA'
```

For this query, the optimizer will "sniff" the predicate literal value USA and consult the statistics on the [Country] column. It will decide, based on the estimated number of US customers, whether it's best to scan the [Customers] table (the most efficient approach when the number of US customers is high) or to use a noncovering, nonclustered index with a key lookup (the most efficient approach when this number is low).

An important point: the optimizer can only take advantage of statistics if it can sniff the value of the predicate. In the previous query, the natural key of the country—its name—was used and therefore the optimizer was able to use the statistics to make the best choice.

But what would happen if the designer of the database chose to use an artificial key for countries? In that case, the query would need to be written as follows:

```
SELECT   Customers.*
FROM     Customers INNER JOIN Countries
         ON Customers.CountryId = Countries.CountryID
WHERE    Countries.CountryName = 'USA'
```

Now the optimizer is in trouble. At optimization time, it doesn't know what [CountryID] value is used for USA and therefore can't use the distribution statistics to estimate how many US customers are there. Crippled in its ability to sniff the value, it now can only make a best effort guess based on the average selectivity of the column—a less precise piece of information. As a result, the execution plan it selects won't be as certain.

The optimizer's execution plan options when it can't consult statistics

Extending the previous example, if the optimizer uses the average selectivity of the column instead of sniffing the actual value, here are the possible outcomes.

In case you have only US and Canadian customers, it will see a low average selectivity (exactly 2), indicating that the number of customers with a country value of USA is probably high, and will likely perform a table scan. This might prove to be a good choice if you have a lot of US customers, and a worse choice if you happen to have only a few.

(continued)

The penalty becomes much more expensive in the more common scenario of uneven distribution. In this scenario, you have customers from all over the world, but (being a US-based company) a large portion of them are from the US. For example, you may have 100,000 customers from 100 different countries, but 30,000 of them are from the US. The overall selectivity of the [CountryID] column is pretty high—on average, you have 1,000 customers from each country. This would lead the optimizer to perform an index seek, because it expects just 1,000 key lookups. But this would prove to be a poor decision for this particular country, because 30 times more lookups are required. The penalty becomes much worse when the pages are accessed in a nonsequential order, potentially causing excessive I/O and when subsequent operations (in more complex queries) rely on this far-off estimation to make additional plan choices.

One way of working around this issue is to split the query into two queries. First, query for the [CountryID] of USA, and then use this value in a second query to retrieve the relevant customers. Issuing two queries instead of one will also carry a price tag, but this seems to me an unnecessary and awkward way to solve a problem that could have been avoided in the first place by using the natural key.

Artificial keys are the de facto standard

As I mentioned earlier, the use of artificial keys is extremely widespread and is considered by the vast majority of designers to be the only option for primary keys. This fact has led third-party software products, mainly object-relational mapping (ORM) data access layer products, not to even consider the alternatives. Older versions of common ORMs such as Hibernate generated an artificial key for each entity created through it and only allowed the use of existing single column keys. Only EJB 3.0 allowed the use of composite keys. Even modern ORM frameworks such as LINQ, although allowing composite keys, impose serious barriers to their usage. For example, LINQ won't cache rows that have composite keys. I found that one out the hard way...

Although it makes perfect sense for a generic ORM not to try to guess what your natural keys are when you use it to generate the schema, it doesn't make sense that ORMs should pay relatively less attention to supporting natural and composite keys. Doing so seriously limits the schema design options of those few people who have use for natural and composite keys, and who like the advantages of designing with such third-party products.

Modularity, portability, and foreseeing the future

Although when you initially design your database you tend to look at it as an individual entity, your single beloved baby, you should consider how parts of this baby could change over time, requiring you to readdress its care in the unseen future. Businesses change and therefore the databases that support them will change as well. The design patterns used will determine how easy it will be to accommodate these changes in the future, although it won't necessarily be you who needs to deal with it. Adding additional functionality support to the database usually means adding new tables and new references to existing ones. I don't think there's a rule of thumb stating whether it will be easier to accommodate all possible changes with either natural or artificial keys, but it definitely will be easier to accommodate with whatever pattern you've chosen to begin with. You might, for example, conclude that natural keys are your best friend in a particular design today, but the future will bring additional multiple levels of hierarchy that will make keys huge. On the other hand, you might use an artificial key for a particular table because it seems to be of minor importance and contains only a handful of rows, only to find later that it has become a major entity and you have to deal with the implications of your initial decision.

IDENTITY columns may result in value gaps and "run out" of values

Remember that IDENTITY doesn't guarantee sequential monotonically spaced values. When an IDENTITY value is assigned to a transaction performing an INSERT, that value is lost if the transaction rolls back and a value gap is created in the table. If regulations require no-gap, sequential values (such as tax invoices), IDENTITY is not your friend.

Also remember that the data type you choose for your artificial primary key will determine the maximal number of rows the table can accommodate. Using an INT data type and starting the numbering from 0, with an increment of 1, means that the table can hold approximately 2 billion rows. It may seem to you today that this is a far-fetched, imaginary limit, but keep in mind that this is what the designers of TCP/IP thought when they decided to use a 32-bit address space. I've witnessed cases where this limit was reached. In most cases it came as a surprise when transactions started to fail in production. Trust me on this; you really don't want to find yourself in that position...

Recommendations

Before you finalize the design you're working on now, or whenever you're called upon to design a relational model, stop for a minute, review this chapter, and ask yourself these questions for each table design you are about to submit:

- *Is there a natural key that I can use as primary key?* If the answer is "no," make sure it's not due to a specification or design flaw. Reevaluate your design. If you think it's good, don't be shy: talk to the person who wrote the specifications. Ask if it was their intention to include entities that can't be distinguished from each other.
- *If there are a few natural candidates, is one of them familiar and simple?* When more than one natural candidate key exists, identify the one that's most familiar to the users, simple to use, and small enough to allow a unique index.

- *Is the key stable?* How often will this property change? How complex will it be to accommodate these changes? Will cascading referential constraints be enough to deal with changes, or will you need to disrupt the database somewhat when they change?
- *How will it be used logically?* Will most queries require just this property, and might using it save you a lot of joins? Is it the parent of a deep hierarchy, and might it get to be long and complex down the line?
- *How will it affect the physical usage considerations for this table?* Will this table require ultrafast sequential insert performance, or should it accommodate concurrent inserts and deletes? What are the maintenance windows available for this table? How much fragmentation do you expect it to get over time?

You probably won't be able to fully answer all these questions for every table, but it's not about the answers—it's about the questions!

Simplicity and aesthetics

I've designed quite a few databases during my 15-year career with SQL Server. Although initially I used nothing but artificial keys, once I started experimenting with natural keys I discovered a hidden beauty in the relational model that was unrevealed to me before. Using natural keys makes the schema look like a true reflection of the reality it represents. The queries become shorter, simpler, and much more similar to the plain human language that stands behind them. Eventually, every SQL query is a result of a human requiring some information from the database. When the schema is nothing but natural data, everything seems to fall in place elegantly. Moreover, I've found that using natural keys forced me to improve my design in many other aspects as well. The importance of a high level of normalization becomes much more evident with natural keys. Table hierarchies that seem to vanish in importance when using artificial keys, suddenly become crystal clear. At first, using natural keys seemed weird, but after the revelation of their beauty, I could no longer go back to the old way of blindly defaulting to artificial keys.

Summary

A few years ago, I had a passionate debate with several fellow MVPs on the issue of natural keys. I recall that of a dozen or so participants, only one was even partly open-minded about using natural keys. That's exactly why I have biased this chapter in favor of "the road less traveled." I don't need to convince anyone to use IDENTITY for keys; 99 percent of people do it anyway. On the other hand, I don't want to convince anyone to do the opposite. I just want to make you stop for a brief moment and think again before blindly adding an IDENTITY column to every table and using it as the primary key. If I managed to achieve this goal with the words of this chapter, my mission is accomplished (for now).

> **A final word of advice**
>
> Become familiar and practice with designing simple databases using only natural keys. Doing so will help you to quickly evaluate these guidelines for the more complex tasks of your job. Even if you decide never to use a single natural key for your databases, at least you'll know you made an intelligent choice—your choice—and you'll know you aren't just blindly following the masses.

About the author

 Ami Levin, CTO and co-founder of DBSophic, has been a Microsoft SQL Server MVP since 2006, and has over 20 years of experience in the IT industry. For the past 14 years Ami has been consulting, teaching, and speaking on SQL Server worldwide. Ami leads the Israeli SQL Server user group, moderates the local Microsoft support forum, and is a regular speaker at SQL Server conferences worldwide. His latest articles can be found at www.dbsophic.com.

2 "Yes, we are all individuals" A look at uniqueness in the world of SQL

Rob Farley

This chapter looks at the idea of uniqueness, in both database design and query design. I explain the ways in which uniqueness can be enforced and compare the features of each. I then examine the idea of uniqueness within datasets, and challenge some basic methods that people use to create GROUP BY clauses. I hope you gain a new appreciation for uniqueness so that you can echo the Monty Python team in shouting "Yes, we are all individuals!"

NOTE For all my examples, I'll use the AdventureWorks sample database, running on a SQL Server 2005 instance, connecting with SQL Server 2008 R2 Management Studio. I prefer the way that the later versions of SSMS display execution plans, but want to demonstrate functionality that applies in earlier versions as well as the newer ones. You can download AdventureWorks by searching for it at codeplex.com.

Introducing uniqueness

Uniqueness is often taken for granted—we learned about it in our earliest days of database development. But I plan to show you that uniqueness is something that shouldn't be taken lightly at all. It's a powerful feature that you should consider carefully—not only when designing databases, but also when writing queries.

Constrained to uniqueness

With unconstrained data, anything goes. This isn't the way you like it—right from the word "Go," you define your tables as having a list of columns and constrain those columns to use particular types. You freely implement columns that are automatically populated with the next number in a list, or that use default constraints to

16

provide an initial value. You even use computed columns for those times when you want a column to be forced into a particular value. As much as the idea of constraining your systems sounds restricting, it's a design feature on which we all thrive.

Without uniqueness, you might not be able to tell the difference between two rows. Even though you might want to record the same data twice, you'd still like to be able to tell the difference between two rows, so having a way of making sure each row is uniquely identifiable is an incredibly useful feature—one that you often take for granted.

You have a few choices for constraining your tables to unique values.

Primary keys

Probably the most common cry of database architects is that every table must have a *primary key*—that is, a column (or collection of columns) whose values uniquely identify each row (and that don't allow NULL values). Many argue that without a primary key, that thing you've created isn't actually a table, despite what SQL Server calls it. I'm not going to try to argue one way or the other—I think everyone agrees that having primary keys on tables is a good idea.

In SQL Server Management Studio's Object Explorer pane, you see primary keys reflected using a gold key icon in the list of Columns, and listed again in the Keys section of the table properties (see figure 1).

By default, the primary key columns of a table are used as the keys of a unique clustered index on the table. You can see one listed in figure 1, called

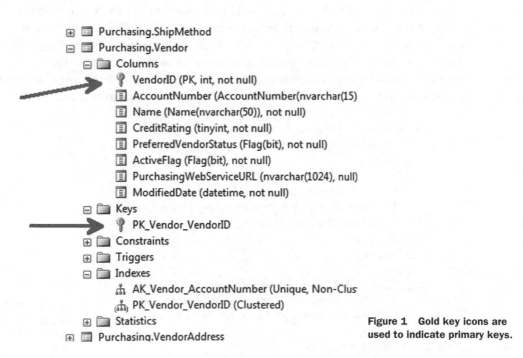

Figure 1   Gold key icons are used to indicate primary keys.

PK_Vendor_VendorID. If I try to drop this index, using the command DROP INDEX Purchasing.Vendor.PK_Vendor_VendorID;, I get an error, as shown here:

```
Msg 3723, Level 16, State 4, Line 3
An explicit DROP INDEX is not allowed on index 'Purchasing.Vendor.
PK_Vendor_VendorID'. It is being used for PRIMARY KEY constraint enforcement.
```

A primary key doesn't need to be enforced by the clustered index; it can be done with a nonclustered index instead. Attempting to remove a nonclustered index that enforces a primary key causes the same error to occur.

In your databases, you use the values stored in tables' primary key columns to identify the items represented in the table. In this example, the vendor is represented by their VendorID, and you'd refer to them as Vendors 1, 2, and 3, despite calling them by Name or Account Number in the nontechnical world.

Unique constraints

Another option for enforcing uniqueness is to use a unique constraint. This isn't designed to replace the primary key, but rather to provide an alternative to the primary key. This kind of constraint is often used for natural keys—a column (or set of columns) that you recognize as uniquely identifying each row in the real world but that hasn't been used as the primary key for practical or technical reasons (such as its ability to allow a NULL value—a unique constraint can have a single NULL value, whereas a primary key can't—or its size, particularly if they're referenced in many other tables). A set of columns that could potentially be used as a primary key is known as a candidate key.

Good examples of these can be found in the names of things. You can usually identify things by their names. Despite there being many Rob Farleys in the world, in many contexts my name is unique. On Twitter I'm @rob_farley, a handle that (hopefully quite obviously) no one else has. My profile also identifies me as user 14146019. In Adventure-Works, if I constrain the names of Product subcategories using a unique constraint, this is represented by a blue key icon in Object Explorer, as you can see in figure 2.

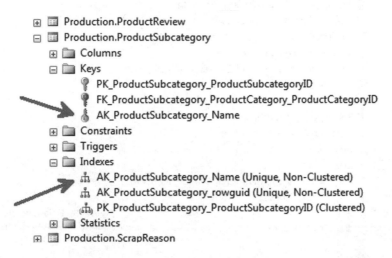

Figure 2   Blue key icons are used to indicate unique constraints.

Notice that the unique constraint is enforced by a unique index. The experience of attempting to drop this index is different from that of trying to drop one used by a primary key. This time the DROP command is successful, but the unique constraint is also dropped. Similarly, if the unique constraint is dropped, the unique index is also (and perhaps predictably) dropped.

Unique indexes

You've already seen that unique indexes are created to maintain both primary keys and unique constraints. But what if a unique index is created without an accompanying constraint? Is the effect the same, or is something lost?

Even without a primary key or unique constraint, a unique index will provide the same functionality as far as the ability to restrict the data. No entry in the Keys section of Object Explorer is seen, but a unique index can be seen in the Indexes section, as expected.

Unique constraint or unique index?

Having suggested that uniqueness can be maintained by either a unique constraint or a unique index, let's consider the differences between them, and I'll point out a couple of misconceptions about them, as well.

Advantages of the unique index

A unique index is created in the same way that any index is created, with the exception that it involves the word UNIQUE:

```
CREATE UNIQUE INDEX uix_Product_Name ON Production.Product(Name);
```

A number of additional options are available that are specific to indexes, as well as many that are also available when creating a unique constraint. The most common example I can think of is FILLFACTOR, but there are a couple of other options that aren't available to unique constraints—ones that I consider important and a significant factor in the decision about whether to use a unique constraint or a unique index:

- Included columns
- Filters

I'm sure all readers of this chapter will appreciate the significance of included columns as a performance-tuning tool. If an index INCLUDEs additional columns, then a copy of that data is stored at the leaf level of the index, potentially avoiding the need for an expensive lookup to find that data in the underlying table storage (clustered index or heap). Any time an index is used, whether it be a scan or a seek, there's a benefit to be seen from included columns. Included columns do add to the size of the index, and this data must be kept up-to-date whenever data in an included column is altered. But these downsides are often considered minor in comparison to the benefits of avoiding lookups.

Filtered indexes, new in SQL 2008, provide another significant tool in the performance tuner's utility belt. When I think of indexes, I often consider the analogy of the phonebook, and consider the Yellow Pages to be like a filtered index, listing phone numbers ordered by business type, but with a filter such as `WHERE IsBusiness = 'Y'` (or more strictly `WHERE HasPaidToAdvertiseInTheYellowPages = 'Y'`). We all use the Yellow Pages and realize its significance in helping us find the information we need, so I expect I don't need to describe the benefits of filtered indexes.

In the context of uniqueness, a filtered index presents an interesting situation. It means you can constrain your data so that Products that are colored Red must have different names from each other, but there can be duplicate names among other colors. A filtered index doesn't constrain all your data—just the data that satisfies the filter. Although this scenario is useful, you end up with a unique index that's only applicable to certain parts of the data.

Advantages of the unique constraint

In my experience, the benefits of using unique constraints are more about people than technology. Unique constraints are a logical feature used in database design, whereas indexes (of any kind) are a physical feature often seen primarily as a performance tool. Performance-tuning consultants may recommend that indexes be created, but database architects may recommend that constraints be created. I play both roles and find myself seeing things somewhere in between.

It's completely correct to have the database architect (designer, if you prefer) indicate when a field should be constrained to uniqueness. They're the ones who need to understand the business and the impact of such a decision. The performance-tuning expert should seek to understand the business, but ultimately is more concerned about the execution plans that are being created by queries and deciding whether a carefully constructed index would help. I'd like to suggest that the database architect consider the queries that will be needed and take a more active part in designing the indexes to be used, and that the performance-tuning expert consider the significance of unique constraints and appreciate the part that uniqueness (and all aspects of database design) have on performance.

Uniqueness in results

It's one thing to be able to constrain a table so that it's only populated with unique data, but to have unique data in a result set is a slightly different matter. The keyword `DISTINCT` is one of the first that you learn when beginning T-SQL, but it's also the first one to earn the stigma of "keyword to be avoided where possible."

The good and the bad of DISTINCT

`DISTINCT` has obvious uses. If there are duplicates in a dataset, then slipping the keyword `DISTINCT` in after `SELECT` will manage to de-duplicate the result set data. This is the good. But as most database professionals know, simply using `DISTINCT` in a `SELECT` query to filter out duplicates from the entire dataset can often hide bigger problems.

A better way of removing duplicate rows from a result set is to ask why they're there in the first place. Duplicates are often present because of mistakes (by query writers) in join predicates, or for a variety of other reasons. DISTINCT should never be used to "fix" a query, but only when you know ahead of time it'll be required, such as when you're querying to find the list of different Product colors sold:

```
SELECT DISTINCT p.Color
FROM Production.Product AS p
WHERE EXISTS (      SELECT *
                    FROM Sales.SalesOrderDetail AS s
                    WHERE s.ProductID = p.ProductID);
```

DISTINCT or GROUP BY

As anyone who's ever written a query like this knows, the next question that the client asks is "How many are there of each color?" At this point, you rewrite the query to use GROUP BY instead, which allows aggregate functions to be applied over the rows that share the same color:

```
SELECT p.Color, COUNT(*) AS NumProducts
FROM Production.Product AS p
WHERE EXISTS (      SELECT *
                    FROM Sales.SalesOrderDetail AS s
                    WHERE s.ProductID = p.ProductID)
GROUP BY p.Color;
```

The functionality provided here is similar to using the DISTINCT keyword, with the difference being slightly beyond the accessibility of aggregates. The most significant difference between the two is regarding the treatment of nonaggregate functions and subqueries. Figure 3 shows two queries (and their plans) that might seem similar in functionality but that are subtly and significantly different.

Notice the order of operations and widths of arrows. Using DISTINCT, the de-duplication happens on the dataset including the computed data. It applies the concatenation on every row before looking for duplicates. With GROUP BY, the query optimizer

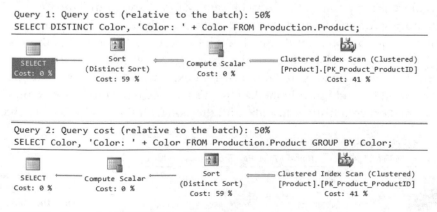

Figure 3 Comparing DISTINCT and GROUP BY

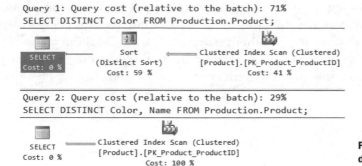

```
Query 1: Query cost (relative to the batch): 71%
SELECT DISTINCT Color FROM Production.Product;
```

```
Query 2: Query cost (relative to the batch): 29%
SELECT DISTINCT Color, Name FROM Production.Product;
```

Figure 4 The sort operation disappears with an extra column.

does a little more work, realizing that the computation can be applied on the distinct values. In this scenario, it uses slightly less effort in comparing the values for making them unique, and then only needs to apply the computation 10 times, rather than more than 500 times.

I can't think of a single situation where DISTINCT is a better option than GROUP BY, except for readability and conciseness. The fact that GROUP BY requires that things be listed in the GROUP BY to allow their use in the SELECT clause—thereby forcing query writers to type more—encourages the lazy use of DISTINCT and frequently queries that perform more poorly. More on that soon.

Are they needed at all?

I ran a simple query, selecting the different colors in the Production.Product table, and I accomplished this using a sort (Distinct Sort) operator. If I add an extra column (the Name column), though, you see that the sort disappears, as shown in figure 4.

Of course, there's trickery going on here. I'm adding a column that's already known to be unique. Because the query optimizer knows that the Name column is already unique, it realizes that the combination of Name and Color must also be unique. Applying an operation couldn't make it anymore unique—there aren't degrees of uniqueness. Notice that the unique index isn't even being used here, but if you remove it temporarily, the impact is significant, as shown in figure 5.

Removing the constraint doesn't suddenly cause the data to be nonunique; it's simply that the query optimizer doesn't know it for certain. This is one of those scenarios that I described in Chapter 40 of the first *SQL Server MVP Deep Dives* book, titled "When is an unused index not an unused index?" If you don't have that book, I recommend you go and buy it immediately—it's an excellent resource, and none of the authors make a cent from it. Just like with this book, all the proceeds go to charity.

```
Query 1: Query cost (relative to the batch): 100%
SELECT DISTINCT Color, Name FROM Production.Product;
```

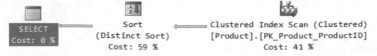

Figure 5 The Sort operation reappears when the uniqueness isn't already known.

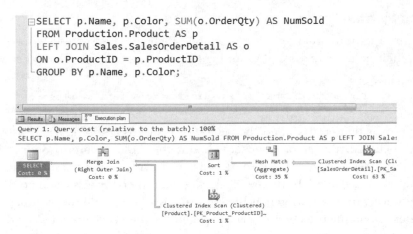

Figure 6 Counting the number of products sold by product name and color, using a unique constraint

Unnecessary grouping

The same effect as in figures 4 and 5 can be seen using the GROUP BY clause as well as DISTINCT, but you have more options available to you. Consider a GROUP BY clause in which you're grouping by the product name and color. Perhaps you're counting how much of a product has been sold. A query and plan can be seen in figure 6.

In this situation, you see that the aggregation is performed using only data from the table of order details. The product details are added to the mix later. You're grouping by the product itself, displaying the name and color. Because the product name is unique, there's no difference whether you group by the name or any other unique feature of the product.

If the product name weren't unique, you'd be in a situation similar to counting the population of towns by their name. You might not want the population of Boston to be listed as more than 4 million if you're thinking of Boston in Lincolnshire, UK (population approximately 60,000). Differentiating by name simply doesn't always cut it. Let's remove the unique constraint and look at the query again (see figure 7). The cost of this plan is significantly more, as you'd expect.

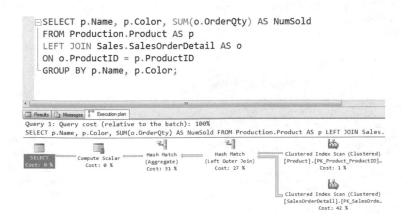

Figure 7 Counting the number of products sold by product name and color, without using a unique constraint

Being guided by "that" error

At this point, I want to break you of a common practice. When people write a GROUP BY clause, their behavior is driven by wanting to avoid that error we all know so well:

```
Msg 8120, Level 16, State 1, Line 1
Column 'Production.Product.Name' is invalid in the select list because
it is not contained in either an aggregate function or the GROUP BY clause.
```

This is the error that occurs when the GROUP BY clause is ignored. When GROUP BY p.Name is included, the error complains about the Color column. Soon, all the required fields are added and the error disappears, leaving you with a valid query that probably works but that might not be ideal. Naturally, query writers don't go through this process every time, knowing how the construct works, but still the vast majority of query writers create their GROUP BY clause using only the nonaggregated fields from their SELECT clause.

But if you ignore the SELECT clause (and the HAVING clause and ORDER BY clause, which can also produce that error) and acknowledge that you want to group by the product itself, rather than just its name and color, then you can introduce a unique set of columns to the GROUP BY clause and see the old plan return. This unique set of columns would be the product's primary key. Grouping by the product's primary key means that every other column from p in the GROUP BY clause can be completely ignored—you can't make it any more unique (see figure 8). The extra columns are now only present in the GROUP BY clause to satisfy that error, giving you a far more ideal query. (Please don't use this as an excuse to remove other unique constraints and indexes—they're still important for data consistency.)

This change would mean that two products with the same name and color would appear with a corresponding row each. But in many situations, this would make sense. It could be fine to list both Bostons with their corresponding populations, rather than

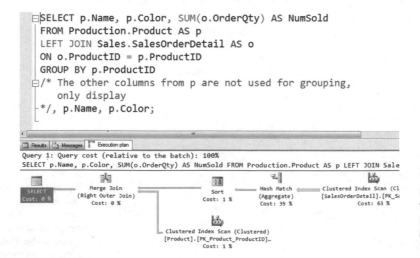

Figure 8 Counting the number of products sold, grouping by the primary key

combining them into a single row (even if only to highlight the need for further distinguishing information).

Summary

Uniqueness can be applied to data in a number of ways, to tables using primary keys, unique constraints and unique indexes, and to datasets using DISTINCT and GROUP BY. However it's done, it's important to consider the impact on data and the advantages to having data constrained like this. You should also consider the idea of grouping by the primary key on a table, even if that field doesn't appear in the HAVING, SELECT, or ORDER BY clauses.

About the author

 Rob Farley is the owner and principal consultant of LobsterPot Solutions Pty Ltd., an Australian-based company specializing in SQL Server and business intelligence and the first Australian company to be a Gold Competency Partner in the Microsoft Partner Network. He's a Microsoft Certified Trainer and a regular conference presenter both around Australia and overseas. He heads up the Adelaide SQL Server User Group and has received the Microsoft MVP Award for SQL Server every year since 2006. Rob is a past branch executive committee member of the Australian Computer Society, and he's recently been appointed to the PASS Board of Directors. He's a dedicated husband and father, the author of two chapters in the first volume of *SQL Server MVP Deep Dives,* and is proud to be able to contribute again to this volume.

3 Architectural growth pains

Chris Shaw

When I was 19 years old, I took a big step onto what United States Marines know as the yellow footprints. The yellow footprints are symbolic of the steps a recruit needs to take to become a Marine. The first and longest-lasting impression is how this marks the starting point of your Marine Corps career. To the drill instructors looking at recruits standing on the yellow footprints, it symbolizes the beginning of molding young men and women into Marines. During this molding process, recruits are exposed to a number of experiences that are designed to teach them all the skills needed to reach the end goal. Some of these experiences are going to hurt; some of these experiences may appear redundant, such as learning to brush your teeth. But all of these experiences are specifically put in place because someone understands that each of these young people will need to know these skills in order to become a successful Marine.

As part of the process, a recruit must pass specific tests, including a three-mile run as well as a certain number of sit-ups and pull-ups. In addition to my sports participation the year before, I made sure I could run the required distance before leaving for boot camp. Without being proactive in my conditioning beforehand, my Marine training would have been that much more difficult and painful. As time passed and my body grew stronger, the pain of working out hard started to subside.

Today when I look back on some of my personal growing pains, I recall graduating from boot camp, as well as the accomplishment I felt during the precise moment I was called a Marine for the first time. I also recall my discussion with one of the drill instructors as he reminded me that all the pain we pushed through and all the training we'd endured was designed for us to become better Marines. This training ensured we'd have a better chance of surviving events that could happen in the future.

When I work on databases today, I apply the same principles I gained from my Marine training. I look at the future aspects of the database requirements. I reflect back on other database designs with similar requirements that either worked well or didn't work as well. I then apply the lessons learned from those experiences.

Just as with my Marine training, in which decisions made early in my training impacted the outcome, long-term performance and ease of use is affected by architectural decisions made early in the database design process—decisions such as what data types, keys, and indexes to use, in addition to how records will be uniquely identified. What makes your databases any different? Databases need change, technology changes, and most of all, changes related to your understanding of how SQL Server works affect your database. Likewise, in the many SQL Server career paths, many decisions made early in a career change as time goes on. This chapter illustrates the decisions that are made when databases are first architected and how these initial decisions can have a lasting impact.

Manage your data types

Identity values are easy to use. Often new designers are eager to use identities after they've learned how each table should have a primary key, allowing each record to be uniquely identified. There are many places where using an identity as a table's primary key works well. In some situations using an identity may require special attention. One issue I see often is using the identity value and forecasting the next value without validating the identity value. Events that occur on the table could impact the identity value, causing gaps in the numbering or even starting the numbering again from the original seed.

I've witnessed two different occasions when the data type selected for an identity didn't allow enough values to be inserted, causing data loss in the tables. In some cases identities are used without a complete understanding of their behavior—for example, when data is truncated from a table rather than deleted from a table. Consider these two statements, which remove data from the UserTable:

```
CREATE TABLE UserTable
(
 UniqueId INT IDENTITY(1,1) NOT NULL,
 Data VARCHAR(30) NOT NULL,
);
```

Statement 1:

```
Delete from UserTable;
```

Statement 2:

```
Truncate Table UserTable;
```

The delete statement won't reseed an identity value in the table, but a truncate table will. If the UserTable in this example had tables that referenced it without foreign keys, the data integrity would be lost.

IDENTITY case in point

In 2010, a company whose business is public safety ran into an issue on a table where they stored mass amounts of collected data. The company monitored locations of individuals by taking readings from a device that the individuals wear. Readings were taken repeatedly, tracking items such as whether the wearer had interfered with the device, where the wearer was located, and whether the device was operating correctly. The specifics on the table structure and exactly what data was stored were never released. But we could gather pieces of information based on press releases that show the design included an identity column. We could also discern that multiple rows were being inserted into this table for each individual that wore the aforementioned device. The information tends to point to a table design that looks like this:

```
Create Table CollectedData(
CollectedDataID int IDENTITY not null PRIMARY KEY,
--collected data columns
)
```

After reviewing the requirements, you can see there's an issue with the table's design. The limit for the numbers of rows that can be inserted in the table is 2,147,483,647. This restriction creates a table that has an upper limit and additional data will trigger an arithmetic overflow error. The same remains true with the use of tiny int as well; I recommend that you go one size larger than you think you'll need, unless storage is the primary concern.

Database design and scalability

Let's return to our example. When the table reached the upper limit on the number of records that could be inserted, the database started to refuse information coming from the monitoring devices. (This meant that individuals who should be monitored were no longer being monitored.) The solution was to grow the size of the data allowed. The data type of the identity column was changed from an integer to a big integer by increasing the number of records that could be stored to 9,223,372,036,854,775,807. In addition, development time was devoted to making sure all the applications that reported, processed, or inserted this data also had to be prepared for the new data type.

The complete outage lasted close to 12 hours. During these 12 hours the data collection stopped, revenue stopped, and well...the safety of everyone involved was in jeopardy. When you start to look at database designs and the architecture, always validate that the database is scalable and meets current requirements. The issue with the design occurred with the choice of data types and not with the use of the identities.

Naming conventions

When you create stored procedures, views, and triggers, the code is going to refer back to a table or another object a large percentage of the time. Code can be completed much quicker and have a much better flow if all the referenced objects are named using the same consistent pattern. I've found that when I suggest a naming convention, many times it comes under attack because different people have different preferences. For example, rather than spaces in my object names, I prefer an underscore (_). To my eye, it's very clean and easy to read, and at the same time keeps my object names as one continuous, space-free string. In any case, benefits to using a naming convention include the promotion of code reuse, simplified troubleshooting, and enhanced object search.

Often in their first attempts at a naming convention, developers will model naming conventions after what they're seeing in the database. A good example of this are the stored procedures that are installed with SQL Server. These stored procedures begin with `sp_` so many novice developers use this as their standard and will prefix their own stored procedures with `sp_`. But `sp_` is a prefix that's allocated to system stored procedures in SQL Server and means the stored procedure exists in the system databases (the master and the hidden resource database). Using the `sp_` prefix could impact the performance of your stored procedures.

A simple stored procedure that gathers client information from a table could be named so many ways. When working on an application, how do developers know what stored procedure to call unless all the stored procedures are formatted the same, or unless they go back and search for the stored procedure in the database? For example, consider these names:

- `Get Customer Info`
- `Get_Customer_Info`
- `GetCustomerInfo`

All three of these stored procedures may return the same information, but because of the naming convention they'll be three different objects. Many naming conventions have been adopted, and searching the internet will provide you with many options to choose from for establishing your own implementation standards. A consistently applied poor naming convention is better than multiple good ones inconsistently applied to the same database.

Inconsistent design

Designing databases to make them functional isn't a difficult process, but designing a database where the tables are designed consistently and normalized correctly and that meet all of the aspects of either spoken or documented requirements can be a daunting task. I believe that the most important part of a database design is the requirements. Some first-generation or initial database designs can resemble an organized spreadsheet collection. Other first-generation database designs resemble a lab assignment straight out of a database normalization class and contain such a large degree of normalization in them that retrieving even the most basic information is difficult or requires more than a basic understanding of T-SQL.

As the lifecycle of a database progresses beyond the first generation and requirements change often, new individuals will work on the design of the database. The issue of inconsistent design becomes serious when the technology debt doesn't allow for a proper redesign of the database. It's at this point that a single database may be both *over*normalized and *under*normalized. The key to success as a designer of the database is being able to balance the time and cost of a redesign with the changing requirements of the database.

Normalization

The topic of normalization is a big one, with its roots coming from E.F. Codd in the 1980s. The importance of the topic can be seen in other chapters found in this book that discuss normalization. If you're new to normalization, I recommend looking at these chapters in depth, because understanding normalization is a key component of database design. Even with a complete understanding of normalization and all the degrees that it can be applied, there are time when a database can be overnormalized to the point where using the database can be difficult. The complete opposite of overnormalization is the lack of normalization, making data referential integrity difficult to maintain.

Overnormalized

Properly identifying an overnormalized database isn't easy, because the design of a database is driven by the requirements that were available at the time of the design, in addition to the skill of the designer at that time. The definition of overnormalization alone is something that's debated in the database community at length. I'd declare a database overnormalized when the data has been broken down to the point where there's little or no benefit of the additional tables. Overnormalization of data can cause queries to be overly complex and perform poorly.

Outside of the design theory, it could be argued that database designs need to be efficient. Efficiency can be defined in many ways; one is the amount of effort that it takes for a report designer to access the core information in the database. Another way is the amount of time that it takes for a query to return data to the end user on the other side of a web page. No matter how efficiency is defined in your database, consider watching for sections of the database that appear overengineered.

Undernormalized

A database that's undernormalized may have issues with data integrity, storage, and flexibility in working with new requirements. Consider a database that requires storing customer information. A table that stores a customer's information with a single address attribute may look something like this:

```
Create Table Customer(
Name varchar(50) not null,
CustomerID int identity(1,1) not null,
Address varchar(50) not null,
City varchar(50) not null,
State char(2) not null,
…
)
```

In the case of an undernormalized database, there are a couple of key issues with this table that will likely arise, depending on the requirements. The address is a classic example; for a company that may have multiple locations, a table designed like this would require multiple entries, in turn generating multiple CustomerID values that may be related to one parent company. This would also mean that the name is duplicated along with all the other information in the table. An application that applies business logic may violate that entry and not allow it, or a unique constraint may reject it, as well. (A unique constraint on company name could be a valid rule based on the original requirement.)

The flexibility issues become even more apparent when new addresses, such as a billing address or a headquarters address, need to be stored in the database. With the undernormalized example, each of those columns would have to be added to the table. The City attribute and the State attribute would have to be duplicated as well.

A normalized design would add a location table, with a location ID. The Customer table would no longer store the Address, City, and State attributes but would store the LocationID values, with a foreign key from the location table to the customer table based on LocationID. This flexibility allows for multiple locations to be added to a customer without having to add columns to the Customer table.

Primary keys and foreign keys

Primary keys are designated on a column in a table to define the rows unique to the table. A primary key can consist of multiple columns or a single column. The power of data referential integrity lies in the ability to show a relation between tables by using foreign keys based on the primary key values. For example, an address table may contain addresses and may have a primary key on it to distinguish unique addresses, but the referential integrity lies in the relationship of a foreign key to a customer table. The relationship can require the database to mandate that a customer have at least one address. The biggest mistake made when looking at primary keys and foreign keys in a database is not using them.

GUIDs as primary keys

Deciding how to define the unique values can often lead to mistakes. Some designs use a natural key or a column that will naturally be unique on the table. An example of a natural key could be a phone number for a business table or a Social Security number for tables that hold information about people.

When a table doesn't have a natural key or it isn't used, the most common options for a primary key are either a globally unique ID (GUID) or an identity column. GUIDs are guaranteed unique values globally, making them a good option if data from tables on many systems is going to be combined into a single table. Identities are values that are issued in sequential order as the record appears in the table. A key difference between the two values is the sequential order.

A good practice is to define your primary keys as the clustered index. When the primary key is defined as such, the bookmark lookups operate more efficiently and the difference in the database's performance is noticeable. Because GUIDS aren't issued in sequential order, page splits and excessive disk I/O will occur when the primary key is used as a clustered index. For those situations when a GUID is required as a primary key, you can use the function NEWSEQUENTIALID in place of the NEWID function. The main drawback to NEWSEQUENTIALID is the potential ability to predict the next value. Although using this function can dramatically reduce fragmentation by ensuring each GUID will be sequential, it is not always guaranteed. Fragmentation can still occur, decreasing overall performance. You can't limit the use of the NEWSEQUENTIALID function to stored procedures—table rules and constraints will be enforced. You must also ensure that proper primary keys are issued with ad hoc statements as well a default value of NEWSEQUENTIALID.

System-generated integers as primary keys

A common practice when assigning a primary key to a table is to use the identity value. An identity value will automatically insert a new value into the column based on the maximum value and the increment value of the last row inserted into the table. A common scenario is to have the identity start at a value of 1 and then increment by 1 each time a new row is inserted into the table.

Identities are easy for the human eye to read as well as being easy to type. If a person is viewing a record set, it's easy to determine what makes each of the rows a unique row. In addition to the readability, identity values have a natural order to them, unlike the unique values of GUIDs discussed earlier. Another compelling reason to use an identity value for a primary key is the improved speed in searching and joining; SQL Server will be able to search on the integer value much more quickly.

Generating your own ID values

An option that can work for smaller databases that have fewer numbers of transactions is a system where a table internal to the database stores a value that can be used to determine the next ID. A function is created or statements in stored procedures are used to get the next primary key value. The benefits to a process like this are few in comparison to some of the impacts.

A self-maintained key table can experience a number of locks as the number of database users starts to grow. The contention between issuing new IDs, saving the most recently used, and waiting for inserts to complete can mean the beginning of extended lock waits. Complexity can become unnecessary when trying to grab a group of IDs when batch operations are needed.

For each best practice there are exceptions. One of the databases I helped design and manage had to do with global customers. The customers would access the service by entering a unique number in the phone, so the keys had to be easy for the customers to memorize and enter in their phones. Each client could have many records in the customer table for different staff members, and because of security reasons we didn't want the issued IDs to be sequential.

It was completely plausible that a new customer could sign up for the service on Monday morning in the United States, but by that afternoon they could be in a different zone wanting to use that service. The solution that worked best for the database was to generate our own IDs.

Indexes

When a table in a database grows over time and new records are inserted, the data in the table can become a bit jumbled, or in database-speak, fragmented. The more data is inserted, the faster a table becomes fragmented. Index fragmentation occurs when index contents are no longer stored continuously on the storage. This fragmentation causes SQL Server to look at and address each row in the search criteria, an action otherwise referred to as a table scan. Table scans, where ideally table seeks should occur, can be the cause of your phone ringing off the hook when the performance of the database starts to decline.

Underindexing

The biggest indicator of a table having an insufficient number of indexes is the performance. Queries that retrieve data will take a long time to run, and as data is added to the table, the performance worsens. If you review a common query's execution plan, you'll find a number of table scans throughout the plan. (You can view execution plans in SQL Server Management Studio by choosing Query > Include Actual Execution Plan or by pressing Ctrl+M.) The execution plans will appear on a tab called Execution Plan in SQL Server Management Studio.

Performance Monitor counters can be drastically affected by queries being run on tables that have insufficient indexes. The counters that provide information on the disk drive can show a large impact. The counters that I often see affected are Physical Disk counters.

To learn about potential missing indexes, you can query the dynamic management views (DMVs), such as `sys.dm_db_index_usage_stats`. Author Glenn Berry (http:// sqlserverperformance.wordpress.com/), who wrote the chapter "Hardware 201: Selecting and Sizing Database Server Hardware" for this book, has done great work with these DMVs. Glenn wrote the following query, which you can run in your database to highlight the indexes your database may be missing:

```
SELECT user_seeks * avg_total_user_cost * (avg_user_impact * 0.01) AS
[index_advantage],
migs.last_user_seek, mid.[statement] AS [Database.Schema.Table],
mid.equality_columns, mid.inequality_columns, mid.included_columns,
migs.unique_compiles, migs.user_seeks, migs.avg_total_user_cost,
migs.avg_user_impact
FROM sys.dm_db_missing_index_group_stats AS migs WITH (NOLOCK)
INNER JOIN sys.dm_db_missing_index_groups AS mig WITH (NOLOCK)
ON migs.group_handle = mig.index_group_handle
INNER JOIN sys.dm_db_missing_index_details AS mid WITH (NOLOCK)
ON mig.index_handle = mid.index_handle
WHERE mid.database_id = DB_ID() -- Remove this to see for entire instance
ORDER BY index_advantage DESC OPTION (RECOMPILE);
```

The results are easy to read and will give you a lot of useful information, including the following:

- *Index Advantage*—A formula that takes into account the number of seeks and the average cost of performing those seeks on the table

- *Last User Seek*—Indicates the last time that seek was performed
- *Database.Schema.Table*—The table that would see the benefits from the index
- *Equality columns*—Columns where the data is a positive match on its value, such as an equal to
- *Inequality columns*—Columns where the data isn't a positive match on its value, such as a not equal to
- *Include columns*—Columns in the missing index that should be included to make the index a covering index
- *Unique Compiles*—The number of compiled and recompiled SQL Statements that would benefit from the index
- *User Seeks*—The number of seeks that would benefit from the index
- *Average Total User Cost*—The average savings to the user queries
- *Average User Impact*—The percentage of performance increase that would be seen by adding the index

When building the indexes that would be added by running this result set, be sure to list the columns in the tables in the order of equality columns and then inequality columns, with the included columns last. The included columns can also be added to the include portion of the index. As with anything done in production, it's a good idea to completely review these indexes and not blindly add them into a production environment.

Another useful query shows which objects in the plan cache have missing indexes:

```
SELECT TOP(25) OBJECT_NAME(objectid) AS [ObjectName],
               query_plan, cp.objtype, cp.usecounts
FROM sys.dm_exec_cached_plans AS cp
CROSS APPLY sys.dm_exec_query_plan(cp.plan_handle) AS qp
WHERE CAST(query_plan AS NVARCHAR(MAX)) LIKE N'%MissingIndex%'
AND dbid = DB_ID()
ORDER BY cp.usecounts DESC;
```

The results of this query will display the following information:

- *Object Name*—Specifies the name of the object that could benefit from adding indexes
- *Query Plan*—Specifies the query plan for the object that could benefit from adding indexes
- *Object Type*—Defines the source of the SQL Statement, such as stored procedure, triggers, and views
- *Use Counts*—Provides the number of times that object had been used

The data in this query is sorted on the number of times the plan has been called where the plan has identified that additional indexes would be beneficial. Now you have a good place to start looking for possible queries to tune to improve performance, possibly drastically, with minimal effort.

Overindexing

A problem that I see occurring more and more is overindexing. When an index is added to a table, that index needs to be maintained. As new data is inserted into a table, it could require that one or more indexes need to be adjusted so the new data is indexed correctly. This new data could mean a page splits so that data can be inserted in the correct location. Poorly performing inserts can be an indicator of a table that has too many indexes.

A quick way to see all the indexes on a table is by using the system stored procedure sp_help. This stored procedure will return a lot of valuable information about a table, such as columns, defaults, keys, indexes, and the properties of the table. After executing sp_help, review the results; in the index section of the results, index_keys will return a list of the columns in the individual index you're looking at. Repeating columns in different indexes could be an indication of overindexing.

Just as the DMV returns information about indexes that are missing, the same can be found for indexes that aren't being used:

```
SELECT OBJECT_NAME(s.[object_id]) AS [Table Name], i.name AS [Index Name],
i.index_id,
user_updates AS [Total Writes], user_seeks + user_scans + user_lookups AS
[Total Reads],
user_updates - (user_seeks + user_scans + user_lookups) AS [Difference]
FROM sys.dm_db_index_usage_stats AS s WITH (NOLOCK)
INNER JOIN sys.indexes AS i WITH (NOLOCK)
ON s.[object_id] = i.[object_id]
AND i.index_id = s.index_id
WHERE OBJECTPROPERTY(s.[object_id],'IsUserTable') = 1
AND s.database_id = DB_ID()
AND user_updates > (user_seeks + user_scans + user_lookups)
AND i.index_id > 1
ORDER BY [Difference] DESC, [Total Writes] DESC, [Total Reads] ASC OPTION
    (RECOMPILE);
```

When it comes to dropping an index, it's important to understand the complete impact of the action before doing so. Always review all indexes before dropping them. To determine whether an index has been used, this query compares the number of times the index has been used to the number of times the index has to be maintained. If an index is being maintained more often than it has been used, give strong consideration to removing that index.

Maintenance

Indexes need to be maintained long term. As data is inserted into a table, existing indexes can become fragmented. As the fragmentation on a table increases, query plans may see the index isn't being useful and determine that it's more beneficial to scan the index for that query. Creating the index to meet search requirements is just the beginning of battling poor performance; keeping the indexes free of fragmentation and optimal for performance on high-transaction tables is a necessary task to keep poor performance at bay.

Fill factor

A common issue or design consideration that's often overlooked is the fill factor on the indexes. The default as assigned by SQL Server is 0, or to fill the pages 100 percent on leaf-level pages before moving the data to an additional page. If the fill factor on a page is 60 percent, then only 60 percent of the space on that page will be filled, and 40 percent will remain free upon creation or maintenance of that index. If your indexes have to be adjusted often to keep up with new data in the tables, you can avoid page splits by inserting data into the free space left by the fill factor configuration. On the flip side, adjusting the fill factor for indexes to allow free space on each page will also increase the amount of disk space that's required by the table to store those indexes.

Summary

Designing a database that performs well, scales well with new requirements, and is easy to use isn't a simple task. The difference between a senior-level and a mid-level designer is often defined by the experiences that each designer possesses. A senior-level database architect has made mistakes and found solutions to those mistakes. The true wisdom comes from these experiences and knowing what key elements of a set of requirements will work best for each design.

After boot camp is over and a Marine enters what's called the FMF (Fleet Marine Force), decisions are made to help further each Marine's career. Each Marine needs to determine what area of his or her career he or she needs to dedicate more time to so he or she can improve as an individual. In the same fashion, commanders review the troops to determine what the group needs to improve on to enhance it as a whole. Although some choose to focus on physical fitness and others choose areas such as education, all of them choose to continue to learn from past experiences to improve the future.

Over the last 15 years of my career, I've learned a number of things. The thing that I've learned the most about—and continue to learn the most about—is how *not* to do things. As an instructor, I strive to continually add information that can only be drawn from experience.

About the author

Chris Shaw started his database career while in the Marine Corps working with Lotus Ami Pro databases in 1993. From there he went on to companies such as Wells Fargo, Pulte Mortgage, and Yellow Pages Inc., and later consulted with insurance companies, including Anthem Blue Cross and Blue Shield. Chris has enjoyed writing and speaking about SQL Server over the last 10 years at events such as SQL Connections, PASS (Professional Association for SQL Server), and SQL Server Worldwide User Group (SSWUG) ultimate conferences (where Chris was the Conference Chair). He's the founding member of the Colorado Springs SQL Server User Group and is currently writing on chrisshaw.wordpress.com and www.sswug.org.

4 Characteristics of a great relational database

Louis Davidson

Relational theory isn't a religion no matter how it may appear—although it has about the same argument-to-agreement ratio. Relational theory is a fairly strict set of principles that have been set up and reasonably well adhered to, not just by intolerant, unbendable, and downright ornery data architects, but by the people who create relational engines to process data. Why are data architect types so interested in doing things in a manner that's uncomfortable for programmers? Because our goal is to satisfy the relational engine's need and we don't worry too much about the fact that a C# coder has to write a bit more code on occasion. Heck, if lines of code and ease of programming were our primary motivators, our job as data architects would be easy; we'd just create one big, generic table to store all data. No, the reason is that we must match the data structures to the needs of the engine and satisfy programmer needs as a secondary (albeit extremely important) need.

The more I write and teach, the more I've noticed that on a large scale, people struggle with how to know what makes a database "good." Throughout this book you have in your hands, you'll notice that a lot of the material is devoted to making an existing database go faster. Although these are great skills to have, getting the design right is the most important goal. Too many people try to toss hardware at the problem and achieve only linear gains in performance, whereas a slight redesign of the database could give you immense gains with less hardware.

There may be an art to concocting a beautiful, elegant solution to a problem, but there should be no ambiguity in interpretation of the solution once it's complete. As a guide to writing and evaluating databases, I've identified seven characteristics that can be helpful to cover the entire process of database design. These characteristics will refer to what makes a database "great," but I'll assume it meets the most fundamental characteristic: it works. For example, if you've just implemented a payroll system, everyone is getting paid the right amount and proper accounting for these payments is being done. Almost every system out there meets the "it works" criterion, even if the database is in reality a horrible tangle of poorly conceived structures and code.

Here are the characteristics we'll cover:

- **Coherent**
- **Normal**
- **Fundamentally sound**
- **Documented**
- **Secure**
- **Encapsulated**
- **Well performing**

Coherent

I like a puzzle as much as the next person. Sudoku, mazes, adventure videogames, and so forth are all somewhat fun or at least a good mental workout. If there weren't a definite solution to them, though, it'd be hard to tell the difference between a well-designed puzzle and the chicken scratch of, well, a chicken. The same is true of database design. You follow a common pattern of design and naming to make sure your database makes sense to you and the developers now, as well as those poor unlucky people who will follow you in a few years (sometimes it'll be you who suffers!)

The crux of coherency is that whenever you query for some data, modify some data, alter the database structure, or implement some manner of data validation, you shouldn't have to think too hard about how to accomplish it. One of the best books I read when I was working for an internet startup was *Don't Make Me Think* by Steve Krug (New Riders Press 2005). It highlighted a bunch of mostly horrible websites and discussed why they were horrible (many sucked like a battalion of Roombas). In most cases it was because when you wanted to perform a typical task, you had to think hard about how to accomplish it, requiring you to go to nonstandard places to do common tasks.

The same concepts apply to database designs. The easier it is to look at a table as an individual object, as well as part of a holistic solution, the better. One of the definitions on wiktionary.org for coherence is "a logical arrangement." I defined "coherent" for database designs as having these traits (which I'll expand upon):

- They are standards based.
- They have reasonable names and data types.
- They are cohesive.
- They need little documentation. (Probably the most important criterion of all.)

Standards based

In any computer programming, any standard is better than *no* standard (and no, the standard to have no standard is cheating and will make Genie angry). Adherence to standards ensures that when you start to look for something, you can determine the meaning in a common manner. Obviously the best standards are the ones that make it easy to understand the system without going to the documentation to decode the meaning of a name; you should have to use documentation only for clarification purposes.

Of course, the most important word in the previous paragraph is "adherence." Take the practice of naming stored procedures usp_ followed by a name. Okay, so this is a user stored procedure. But if someone names one without the usp_, then what happens? Is this not a stored procedure? What about data type usage? Say one user uses char(9) for the account number, and another varchar(12) with a check constraint to limit data to 9 characters only to make data easier to see in SSMS. What does this say to the users, other than they need to do a better job of interviewing? So as much as I abhor some standards, not following those standards you've set up or not having standards is a major issue that will cause people to have to think about what the structure means rather than what the data means.

Reasonable names and data types

Many designers are far too careless with the names of objects. Names are the first line of documentation that you present to users, developers, and even the future-you who gets called at 1:00 a.m. because the SniggleStr column value was considered invalid. What's the SniggleStr? If it were obvious you probably wouldn't be called at 1:00 a.m. to help figure it out. And you hope it makes sense to someone in the organization or not only will you be up all night trying to figure it out, but you'll also have a meeting with the CIO to discuss your failures as a database designer.

Data types are the other big piece of the "making sense" picture. Too many databases have just two distinct types in the database: something like varchar(200) and varchar(max). Sure, you can store everything from numbers, values, names, and so forth in these two data types, but you'll encounter two problems with this approach:

- *It isn't very efficient for the engine*—You can store the number 15,000,000 as a string, but it will take 8 bytes instead of 4 for an integer. And if you want to add that number to another number, you'll have to convert it to an integer anyway or you'll get the two values concatenated.
- *No help for data integrity*—If a column is supposed to hold only numbers but it will allow storing 'Fred', errors are going to occur—for example, if some code tries to use a text value that's supposed to be a number and outputs NaN and stores it!

The fact is, name plus data type should give the user a solid clue of what can go in the column. When a column is typed int, it's obvious that the data in the column will be an integer. If the type is varchar(200), you assume that any ASCII character string of 0–200 characters will be acceptable. The better job you do with your naming of columns, tables, and so forth, the more focused you can be when creating types. You'll have happier users and programmers, and even performance will improve, because adding integer typed data is faster than having to typecast the values for each row.

Cohesive

By *cohesive*, I mean that all of the pieces and parts come together to provide the expected functionality. You'd rarely have one database that serves 20 fundamentally different things, such as having your customer base and your CD collection documented in the same database. A database is a container, generally used to facilitate managing like sets of data in a container that can be managed as a single unit.

A rule of thumb is that you want to have the objects that work together in one place, but only ones that will come in contact with one another. Coordination of backup and recovery is a big reason for having one database. Similar to when you're organizing your tool chest or utility closet in your house, like items go together and dissimilar items go in separate containers that make locating and utilizing resources easier.

Needs little documentation

Documentation is probably your least favorite part of any project, but you can tell the quality of a software package by how often you need to go to the documentation. If you're a nerd, you've probably been picked on for not reading documentation, and there's a reason for this. Good electronics work basically the same way. You can drive most cars because they have the same basic controls. Toasters toast the same way; even my Hamilton Beach combination toaster/toaster oven didn't take more than 15 seconds to figure out. Only features that are complex require documentation (my car stereo's voice control contains quite a few nonobvious but cool features whose operation required me to read the manual).

You should design your databases the same way. Follow common patterns and include documentation, in standard locations, that people can access to find out the few things that don't work in a straightforward manner. Give me too much information and I'll ignore it. Why don't I read the toaster instructions? Because it's 20 pages that mostly tell me stuff that a 4-year-old Siamese cat could figure out. Sure, there's probably a feature that I'm not immediately taking advantage of because I don't read the docs, but I'll risk that to avoid being told one more time not to use the toaster while taking a shower.

Write documentation like a technical writer edits their work. Use the software; anything you had to think about, document that first. Remember that users aren't programmers and won't know everything you do immediately. In the end, though, the more you can do to avoid the need to document by making the object coherent, the better off you and your users will be.

Normal

Normalization is the central topic when discussing database design in that it describes a set of standards that tables ought to conform to in order to work with the relational engine. It's specified as a list of "forms," each more restrictive than the next, and each attempting to eliminate some form of problem by storing less structured data.

I generally define normal as follows: "The design should be normalized as far as is reasonable." Reasonable is in the eye of the beholder, but the problem is that there's a lack of understanding as to what normalized means, and to be honest, why you'd want to do it in the first place. If you don't know the answers, well, reasonable is just translated to what you know well enough to think it's useful.

Briefly, the basic gist of normalization is that you don't duplicate data. Every single piece of data in a relational database has a specific job and it's the *only* point of data that does that job. It's not the source of another piece of data, nor is it sourced from some other piece (or pieces) of data. Sounds easy enough, but we'd need an entire chapter of this book to illustrate the concept fully. In this brief introduction I just want to establish that it's a good thing to make sure that every value has a single purpose.

The concept of a single purpose extends not only to multiple columns but to the single column as well. If you regularly need to break down a value in a SQL statement to use it (like using substring), then you probably don't have it right. There are plenty of reasonable anti-examples where this concept breaks down, such as searching in a large string object on occasion, but even that can depend on the purpose of the large string. Having data at this "atomic" (can't be reasonably broken down further) level means less need for code to manage duplicate data whether copied or summarized for performance. (It'll also be important to you when you want to index data to make a search go faster.)

The reason that this is so important is that normalized data follows the same pattern of usage that the relational engine was built to handle. Most of us would never use a hammer to screw in a nail, and we'd be even less likely to drive a nail with a screwdriver. Why do people expect SQL Server to do a good job as a data manipulation tool when they won't learn how it's supposed to be used? Frequently, you see a messy data solution to a problem that could easily be formulated with a proper relational solution that works in a much easier fashion and still have the ability to produce a friendly, usable interface.

On the programming side, the less normalized the system, the more likely you are to need iterative, one row = one object instance solutions, leading to lots of singleton retrieves from the database to do data manipulation. But to relational programmers, taking the normalized structures and letting the SQL engine take their set-based queries and do all the ugly work for them almost always provides a solution that works and works fast.

It all starts with shaping the data architecture in the correct manner.

Fundamentally sound

The basic goal of a relational database system is to store data in a correct manner that allows the user to avoid spending lots of time validating what's been saved. When a database can be considered fundamentally sound, it means that the users can be certain that a minimum set of rules are enforced. Unfortunately for the DBA, there are a large number of non–database programmer types who'd prefer it if the database was treated as nothing more than a lightly formatted hard drive device with some search capabilities built in. SQL Server is happy to serve in this capacity, but what a waste of resources; it can be harder to query, and data has to be validated to be used. ETL type processes are all too often processes where instead of Extract, Transform, and Load, there's a bunch of Clean, Clean, and More Clean processes tossed in, as well. The problem is that no matter how good you are, without using at least uniqueness and foreign key constraints and transactions, you'll end up with less than pleasant data once users and the reality of concurrent data access get hold of your data.

Some forms of validation are difficult to do outside of the data layer, starting with foreign key constraints, and this list is larger than you might imagine. An example is any validation where another table or multiple rows is involved, like a check constraint that checks the cardinality of a relationship. Uniqueness enforcement should always be done in a UNIQUE constraint. In the worst case, you're going to end up with a unique index that's very helpful to the query processor.

Loading data then becomes far safer. If you rely completely on a layer of disparate code to manage the integrity of the data, what happens when the ETL layer is pointed directly at your data? Can you afford to load large amounts of data with a complex object layer or do you have to recode all the rules in every ETL process? Do you just hope that the rules are all followed, or do you test with every usage? Unfortunately, hope springs eternal in a lot of situations where it wasn't such a dandy idea, and the UI starts failing because of unknown data rules.

In the early days of client-server programming, we tried using the data layer as the be-all and end-all layer of data programming, and it stank. T-SQL is not the greatest language for doing everything. And note that this topic is also *not* about stored procedures. Stored procedures are part of the data access layer, not the data layer. They should be used to replace queries from the application, not as a place to put complex validation code. (They're just as ineffectual when dealing with ETL types of data validation.) In either case (procedures or ad hoc), the goal of a well-designed database is the fundamental data integrity that can be done in the table layer and that all users can honor.

Documented

This topic probably won't stir up a hornet's nest or anything, but I'd also expect that it would be the least popular in practice. The person who feels they can disagree with the need for a reasonable amount of documentation is probably a bit off their rocker to start with. Initially, I defined the need for documentation as follows: "Anything that can't be inferred from just looking at the built-in metadata should be documented in writing." And yes, I know documentation is more boring than a whole oilfield of derricks. So let me give you a life lesson. Documentation is a lot more fun when it's done *before* you build.

Yes, you heard me. If you've chosen names for things that seem right, the definitions you make may just fall out of the name. So it isn't that much work. The payoff is probably a lot better than you might imagine. Be careful, though; too much documentation can easily be worse than no documentation. Sometimes systems have so much documentation that it's impossible to know how to find information, or there are conflicting bits of documentation. Keep it sparse, with just enough information that you communicate what was on your mind when you were designing your objects.

Names can only be so descriptive; you get just 128 characters for a name, and if you come close to that your users are going to beat you with whatever they can find handy. Names should be succinct versions of the definitions. Names shouldn't typically include purpose—purpose can be tricky. Who wanted this, why they wanted it, and how it's to be used should only be gleaned from documentation.

The beauty of having documentation written down is that your analysts and users have a way to check out the design to make sure they "approve." They see a lot of names, fine. They see some diagrams, decent. They read your definitions and...wait. What do you mean by "This attribute is here for X"? Did we agree to that? Well, yeah, I thought you did, you'll indignantly think, but sometimes, no matter how sure you are that you're right (and no matter how right you are that this was in fact the design you'd agreed on) a communication gap was opened and things went sideways.

For you Agile readers, I don't mean documenting things to death or even spending all that much time on it. If you're creating 30 tables with 10 columns on average and 20 relationships, you only need to document 320 independent items. Add a bit more to the documentation for constraints, and then for processes, and you might have a few hours of work. And if you find this taking too long, either you have messed up the Coherent bit or your team has communication problems that can't easily be solved. And the more Agile you are, the more important coherent designs and concise documentation is. What happens if you get it wrong and can't ship because you didn't get clear direction and your team didn't realize it until they started seeing the "results"? Pretty sure that can't be good for the manifesto.

So, yeah, all I'm trying to say is that documentation is communication—not just to you, not just to other programmers, but to future programmers, users, and even a future version of yourself whom you'd treat better if you could see the pain in his or her eyes.

Secure

The secure characteristic deals with the common need of most systems of keeping eyes out of the places where eyes shouldn't be. In basic terms, everything is hunky-dory until the janitor clicks on the wrong place in the time entry app and finds out that the CEO is making $2.5 million a month, or until a "devious" employee starts digging around and gives himself a raise... and it's impossible to track who did it.

In the introduction to this chapter I defined *secure* simply as users being able to see only data to which they're privy. Sounds easy enough, but when you start to consider what it means, it's more complicated than you might imagine. There are multiple layers of security to be concerned with, as well as multiple enemies, from hackers on the internet to a clerk who could accidentally stumble on data they shouldn't see.

There are many forms of security that people tend to implement, and often you leave it up to the application to enforce security. But even when taking that path, you're still going to need to lock down the database from application mistakes, and you'll most likely need extra tables, columns, and coordination in the application to make it work. For example, a time entry system is an easy thing to implement—until you hit security. Everyone has someone they report to. So rights to see everyone who works for you seems like a given, but this starts to be a hierarchy. Then people have dotted-line bosses, and people who enter time for them (such as an assistant or time-keeper). And if you do any cost analysis, all of these people probably have some entry defining how much they're costing to work there, particularly if they get any overtime. These relationships require a lot of tricky code to get things right.

Security needs to be considered in terms of access from both external and internal sources. I don't just mean a novice hacker who works for you who whines about his salary in comparison to a coworker, but what about Harry the Hacker out there? If he gets access to the data, what then? Could your company fall apart because someone gets your customer list? It doesn't matter whether you're a top-secret company, if Harry the Hacker sends your entire customer list in an email stating "I have your name because I stole _____'s database," how many more times will customers give their name to that company?

To get the entire security picture correct, you have to build an impenetrable fortress around your data, making completely certain that while friends can use the data from inside the fortress and outside, too, baddies can't get in from any layer. How you do that could consume an entire book. The process usually includes people from multiple departments in an organization, including programmers, DBAs, system administrators, network folks, and such to make sure that you're protected, that all activity is logged, and so on. The greater your need for security, the greater emphasis you should place on checking background and implementing checks and balances.

Does this make you feel less secure? It should! If the security of your data doesn't scare the crud out of you, you're not thinking hard enough. But if you take the time to make sure your implementation design considers the needs of the users and their rights to access data while keeping others out, you'll be fine…probably.

Encapsulated

The next to last of the characteristics in this chapter is probably the most contestable part of the design and implementation process: encapsulation. The concept of encapsulation isn't contested (or even contestable by sane programmers in any field of the art of system creation). Every time you use a Windows API call you're participating in encapsulation. Every language that you don't have to program using a series of ones and zeros is using some level of encapsulation to make life easier. The problem isn't encapsulation; it's how you perform the encapsulation.

It's at this point in the process that I have to make something clear. As a writer in a nonreligious instructional topic, I need to be reasonably open to other people's ideas and concepts. Nowhere in database design does this get as contentious as when talking about encapsulation. I'll define *encapsulated* in the following terms: "Changes to the structures should cause minimal impact to the user of the data structures."

The obvious answer to any long-term DBA is that establishing a solid layer of stored procedures to allow others to access the data is the easiest way to achieve these goals. This is analogous to the Windows API that you call to get a message box on a 64-bit server. The data programmer can adjust the API if desired, but he or she can also remove the entire database and replace all the tables with new tables. Rarely does this occur, but it's not uncommon to have multiple apps using the same database structures, and sometimes the needs differ (perhaps one app only needs one address for a person; the other can use all of them).

So at this point, the common question is "Why go through all of this when I can let my ORM [object relational mapping, generally highly automated] deal with the database?" And it's a fair question. As a bona fide lazy person, I hate to do more work than necessary. The problem is the future. I learned a long time ago to honor future-me in as many ways as I can (well, eating right and exercising notwithstanding) and future-me wants to hang out and admire all the work current-me did and either relax or build something new for even later-in-the-future-me. I hate doing rework. The motto of my website (drsql.org)—"An ounce of design is worth a pound of rework"—is a direct reflection of that. Design now...enjoy later. Some of my favorite production moves were done on stored procedure access systems. I'd built and tested the heck out of the database and was ready for nearly anything; the other layers, not so much. The database team was there in case of trouble, but mostly we played chess and taunted the programmers, whose hair always seemed a bit thinner at the end of the night.

To be honest, I said that the argument for ORMs was valid, and with some reservations, I find it all too frequent that I have to give in to the argument for ORM-based programming. The only concern I have is that the database is becoming less of a platform that we code to and more of a storage-only platform. Initially this sounds as if I'm trying to protect my job, but it really isn't that at all. My problem is that there are a few consumers of the data that ORMs won't do an adequate job for unless the database is built for the database server, and not for the ORM:

- *Report writers*—Best case, you have a business intelligence solution so that users don't have to access the OLTP database. But someone has to write queries to get the data out.
- *Future ORMs*—No one likes to get nailed down to one programming methodology other than SQL programmers. Most of the products that were around when I was doing SQL Server 4.21 programming (read: a long time ago) are gone now or morphed into something bizarrely different (like VB). What's good for ORM A might not be good for ORM B.
- *Importers/outside sources*—Poorly normalized databases make it harder to import data from outside sources without using the API, and most shops are going to do bulk loading of data at some point.

Note that in the last bullet I said *poorly* normalized databases. Is this guaranteed to be the case? No, but any database I've seen designed primarily for the needs of the screen or object mapping always looks vastly "different" than a database designed for the needs of the data to work with a relational engine.

Unlike the other characteristics, this one seems to veer toward being opinion rather than straight facts. It's just that sort of problem, but any solution that meets the criterion "Changes to the structures cause only changes to usage where a table/column directly accessed it"—or even one that *recognizes* the problem—is a major step in the right direction. If you're attending a session on database design, you probably care about doing database design right. It's the same with the concept of encapsulation. If you're paying attention to the future and not just racing against an arbitrary deadline, at the very least you probably won't leave future-you in a bind, even if future-you is a totally different person.

Well performing

Well performing is last in the list for a reason. It's the least important characteristic of any data-oriented system—just don't let the user know. Just as when a person buys a sports car, performance is the second thing that a user will notice about the system. The first will be the UI (just like the pretty shell on the outside of the car). But a pretty, fast sports car is useless if it only works occasionally. If the car runs 100 miles an hour in first gear, it doesn't matter if the seats aren't bolted in and the steering wheel works backward. I initially defined *well performing* as "Gives you answers fast," and solely in the context of performance, that's true. But in reality, that's a simplistic attitude. Maybe a better criterion would be "Do all operations required in a minimal amount of time hold up in consideration of the realities of physics?" When considering performance, you have to deal with many facets to the problem:

- *Initial database design*—Designing the database with the concept of normalization close at hand is the first step in getting things to work fast. The relational engine of SQL Server is named *relational* because it likes data to be formed in a relational manner. As you make more and more tables, it often seems counter-intuitive, but the right normalized design almost always outperforms the alternative.

- *Concurrency*—If all you ever had to work on were single-user systems, life would be easy. But the fact is, on every database system I've worked with, there are always far more than one user. And lots of "users" aren't humans (no, not zombies) but rather machines, reading in data from mail, internet, and phone calls and processing the data. To make sure that the data isn't worked on by multiple users, you have to use locks, and locks slow things down but ensure that multiple users don't make conflicting updates.

- *Indexing*—This is the first thing most people think of when they're adjusting performance—and for a good reason. An index can turn a full table scan operation into a single-row operation simply by giving the query processor a place to look first for data. Indexes aren't free, and you need to avoid using useless and irrelevant indexes on "just in case."

- *Hardware*—SQL Server can be run on simple cheap hardware, and for most situations you wouldn't notice if it was run on a server that was configured like a file server. Unfortunately, the problem is that as you start to need "real" power, the hardware configuration can't be so simplistic. Adding CPU power and RAM is simple, but the usual weak link in the process is disks. Until solid state drives hit it big, disk drive speed and redundancy are critical in making your server run fast.
- *Good code that accesses your data*—No matter how well your database is designed, if you code in an incorrect manner—such as using loops where set-based queries would work better, lots of unnecessary temp tables, or poorly formatted search arguments like `WHERE datediff(day, columnName, getdate()) > 1`—you're still going to be hosed.

I'm not numb to the fact that performance is an issue. It's really a major pain point, because it changes so much with all of the aforementioned factors, but also because it's negotiable. The fact is, though, data integrity is *not* a negotiable factor. You can't say "Bah!" to users because they complain that their numbers aren't adding up, but "The server seems kind of slow" can easily be written off as whining (mostly because it usually is). Time is money, and if a user has to do a task 200 times a day and performance issues make it take 10 seconds instead of 4 seconds, it doesn't seem like much. But 1,200 seconds isn't a small amount of time in the least. And if there are a hundred people doing these same repetitive tasks, that's a lot of time (and not uncommon in, say, a call center).

Summary

In this chapter, I presented seven characteristics that make up a great database design and implementation. None of these factors can be considered outside of the primary design consideration: that the database works. I didn't make that a characteristic because it's the overall goal.

Once you have that working database, that's not the end of your work. Here's where achieving a great relational database implementation will come in handy. Using the techniques I showed in this chapter will give you a great foundation.

Because you have normalized, queries will be easier to write and understand. Your design is coherent, so you don't have to spend hours blankly staring at the tables thinking, "What the heck does this mean?" The documentation you created helps clarify what you were thinking in complex cases. You've covered the fundamentals of data integrity, so queries and reports all make sense. Because you've implemented solid security, your temp worker hasn't emailed off a list of your customers to his friend Mugsy for 20 bucks. And you have tuned the system so it runs faster. So not only does it work, but it works well and is easy to change when the need arises.

About the author

Louis Davidson has been in the IT industry for 17 years as a corporate database developer and architect. He has been a Microsoft MVP for seven years and has written four books on database design. Currently he serves as the data architect for the Christian Broadcasting Network, supporting offices in Virginia Beach, Virginia and Nashville, Tennessee. Louis has a bachelor's degree from the University of Tennessee at Chattanooga in computer science with a minor in mathematics. For more information, visit his website at http://drsql.org.

5 Storage design considerations

Denny Cherry

As a DBA, you need to have at least a basic understanding of the hardware underneath the databases. If you don't know what's going on under the covers, you can't make intelligent decisions about your database servers' configuration. Many storage array vendors tout their arrays as a black box that can fix all problems. But in reality that isn't the case, and you need to be careful when making storage design decisions.

Selecting the correct RAID type

There are several types of RAID (redundant array of independent disks, or redundant array of inexpensive disks) configurations you can choose from, and each has specific pros and cons.

RAID 0

RAID 0 is a stripe set with no parity and therefore no redundancy. This is a fast RAID type to use—and inexpensive as well, because no space is wasted when building the RAID array. For every gigabyte of data that's written to the array, one gigabyte of space must be purchased. Because there's no redundancy in a RAID 0 array, there's no protection from disk failure. If a single disk in a RAID 0 array fails, all data on the RAID array is lost. Because of this lack of redundancy, RAID 0 arrays aren't good for use with a SQL Server. Some people consider RAID 0 a good level to be used for the tempdb database. But this isn't the case; if you were to use RAID 0 for the tempdb database and the RAID 0 array were to fail, the tempdb database would become unavailable. The SQL Server engine would thus fail and the applications that use the database would become unavailable until you rebuilt the RAID array, as well as the folders that hold the tempdb database. RAID 0 arrays require at least 2 disks and support up to the number of disks the storage vendor supports, typically 15 disks.

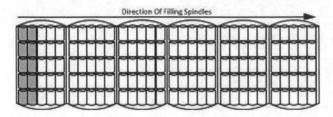

Figure 1
RAID 0 array using concatenation

You can build RAID 0 arrays using striping or concatenation. RAID 0 arrays that are built using concatenation will fill the first disk in the RAID array, then the second, then the third, and so on, as shown in figure 1. RAID arrays that are built using concatenation are designed for maximum space, without providing any performance benefit. Eventually performance will improve, because the data has been spread across all the disks in the RAID array.

RAID 0 arrays that are built using striping will have the blocks striped across the disks, as shown in figure 2. This arrangement allows for maximum performance starting with the first block of data that is written to the RAID 0 array. As each new block is written to the array, the next block is written to the next spindle in the array, starting with the first disk. The second block is written to the second disk, then the third block is written to the next disk, and so on. When the last disk is used—disk 6 in figure 2—the next block (block 7 in this case) would be written to disk 1, block 2, with the next disk (block 8 in this example) written to disk 2, block 2, and so on.

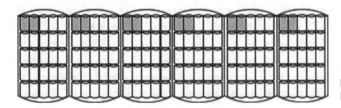

Figure 2
RAID 0 array using striping

RAID 1

RAID 1 arrays are a straight mirror between two spindles. All writes that are made to the primary disk are synchronously written to the slave disk of the pair. This offers no speed improvement but provides full redundancy of the data on disk. Some vendors allow for reads from the slave disk, but most don't, because doing so could cause latency while waiting for the slave drive to spin to the correct position to handle write requests. As blocks are written to the master disk of the pair, the block is also written to the slave disk in the pair, as shown in figure 3.

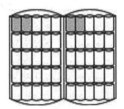

Figure 3
RAID 1 array

The block must be written to both disks before the storage array will send an acknowledgment back to the host computer saying that the write has been accepted. Because RAID 1 arrays are a direct mirror, they support only two disks in the RAID array.

RAID 5

RAID 5 arrays are a stripe set with parity for redundancy. No matter the size of the RAID group, the parity information will require approximately a single disk's worth of space. If a five-disk RAID 5 array is used (typically called a 4+1 RAID 5 set), then four disks are used for data storage and a single disk is used for storing the parity information. When reads are being performed against a RAID 5 array, the performance will be approximately that of a similar RAID 0 array. When writes are being performed against a RAID 5 array, they'll be much slower than a similar-sized RAID 0 array.

The slowdown for writes is due to the parity calculation that's performed against the block of data being written. Because of this parity slowdown, RAID 5 arrays should be used for disks that are mostly read, with no to low writes happening to the volume. RAID 5 disks are popular because they're fairly inexpensive, while still providing a decent amount of protection for spindle failure. When a five-disk RAID 5 array is used, there's roughly a 20 percent cost penalty when storing data—which means that for every gigabyte of information that's stored, 1.2 GB of data is written to disk; the 1 GB of information as well as approximately 200 MB of parity information. The easiest way to figure out the lost space is to assume that n–1 spindles are usable for a RAID 5 array.

In all modern arrays, the parity information will be striped across all the disks in the RAID 5 array. Older arrays may store all the parity information on a single spindle within the RAID array, which can result in a hotspot on the disks, causing the disk that holds the parity information to fail more often than the other disks. In either case, in the event of a disk failure when the disk is replaced, the missing information is rebuilt from a combination of the surviving information and the parity information.

A RAID 5 array requires at least three spindles, two for data and one for parity. A RAID 5 array can survive a single spindle failure without data loss. If the failed disk isn't replaced and a second disk fails, then all data on the RAID 5 array will be lost.

RAID 6

RAID 6 arrays are similar to RAID 5 arrays in that a RAID 6 array is a stripe set with dual parity. The RAID 6 array has a performance impact similar to that of the RAID 5 array: the performance impact will be against the writes to the RAID 6 array whereas the reads against the RAID 6 array aren't affected. A minimal performance difference exists between RAID 5 and RAID 6 arrays—RAID 6 arrays are typically one to two percent slower than RAID 5 arrays.

Like the newer RAID 5 arrays, the parity information for the RAID 6 array will be written across all the spindles in the RAID 6 array to distribute the parity information across the spindles and to prevent a hotspot. RAID 6 is becoming more popular with storage administrators thanks to its good read performance, good redundancy, and low cost per gigabyte. With a five-disk RAID 6 array, the parity cost is high—approximately 40 percent. But when the RAID 6 array is increased to 10 disks, the parity cost is reduced to approximately 20 percent, while still allowing for up to two disks to fail with no data loss. The easiest way to figure out the lost space is to assume that n–2 spindles are usable for a RAID 6 array.

NOTE   RAID 6 is a newer standard and isn't supported on older storage arrays, so it may not be available on your storage array.

A RAID 6 array requires at least four spindles: two for data and two for parity. A RAID 6 array can survive two spindle failures without data loss. If the failed disks aren't replaced and a third disk fails, all data on the RAID 6 array will be lost.

RAID 10

RAID 10 arrays are a combination of RAID 1 and RAID 0 arrays. With RAID 10 arrays, the disks are paired up and mirrored using traditional RAID 1. These RAID 1 arrays are then striped using RAID 0, which allows for multiple spindles to fail, depending on which spindles fail. The RAID 10 array supports between 1 and $n/2$ disks failing (where n is the number of disks in the RAID 10 array). If the array were to lose two disks from a single RAID 1 array pair of the RAID 10 array, all data on the RAID 10 array would be lost and the RAID 0 stripe would be broken. If a single disk from each RAID 1 pair is lost, the RAID 0 stripe wouldn't be broken, leaving the data intact on the array.

For all the potential redundancy that RAID 10 provides, some high costs accompany it. Because all the data is mirrored, there's a 100 percent capacity penalty: each gigabyte of data that's stored requires 2 GB of space.

RAID 50

RAID 50, also called a meta-LUN, is a combination of RAID 5 and RAID 0. Two or more RAID 5 arrays are built with a logical unit number (LUN) created on each one. These two RAID 5 LUNs are then combined using either striping (to increase speed) or concatenation (to increase space). These RAID 50 arrays aren't actually using a RAID type called RAID 50 but are instead using RAID 5 and RAID 0 separately. When using a meta-LUN, you aren't limited to RAID 5 and RAID 0; you can also use RAID 6, RAID 1, or even RAID 10 as the base LUNs and then stripe over those.

When to use RAID 5

RAID 5 should be used for the majority of database servers. Most database servers don't have the write workload required to make a RAID 10 storage solution for the data files a requirement. If your data change rate is 10 percent or less per week, you should seriously consider RAID 5 as a viable storage configuration for your database servers. When the data change rate is greater than 10 percent per week, RAID 5 is too slow to accept the writes and you should use RAID 10.

This 10 percent data change rate per week isn't a hard-and-fast number and can be adjusted up or down based on the amount of data within the database. The larger the database is, the smaller the data change rate should be before the storage configuration should be changed from RAID 5 to RAID 10. For example, on a 100 GB database, a

10 percent weekly change rate should be a good limit because this is 10 GB of data change. But for a 1 TB database, this 10 percent weekly change rate is much too high, because this would be 100 GB of data change. In this case, if the weekly data change rate were somewhere in the neighborhood of two to three percent, RAID 5 may still provide you with an acceptable level of performance.

When to use RAID 6

RAID 6 should be used at times when RAID 5 is giving you an acceptable level of performance but the disk failure rate has become unacceptable and the system is left exposed to data loss too frequently. In this case, consider using RAID 6 because it offers a performance metric similar to RAID 5 while allowing for additional disk failures without leaving the data within the database in an exposed state.

When to use RAID 10

Use RAID 10 when RAID 5 and RAID 6 can't provide enough write I/O capacity to support the write I/O of the database application as measured by Windows Performance Monitor's physical disk activity counters. Additionally, if the workload that's on the storage solution is high write, such as the transaction log or tempdb database, then RAID 10 is the preferred option. In these cases, you want to default to RAID 10 not only to increase the performance of the writes, but also to reduce the storage platform's CPU workload.

All storage arrays have CPUs just like traditional servers do. Switching from RAID 5 or RAID 6 to RAID 10 will reduce the CPU load on the storage array, allowing more overall workload to be placed on the array. Because transaction logs and the tempdb database (specifically the transaction logs) are basically all writes, this places a lot of CPU pressure on the storage arrays' CPU. To reduce this CPU load, you must sacrifice hard drive space. Although expensive within a storage array, disk space is much cheaper than putting additional CPUs within the array. Much like when you add indexes to a database, you have to make intelligent design decisions to consume additional hard drive space to save CPU power. You could put everything on RAID 10, but that's not an intelligent use of your resources.

File placement

Placing SQL Server files is half art and half science. The science half comes from understanding the I/O capabilities of the storage solution that you're using. The art half comes from being able to see how the database server will, in the abstract, push I/O down to the storage array. As you move files around the server from disk to disk, RAID array to RAID array, you have to be able to visualize how the I/O for each RAID array will change on both sets of disks, and how these changes will impact the overall storage array, such as the cache workload, frontend loops, and backend loops.

As databases grow, data file placement becomes increasingly important. Planning correctly before the system grows will make your life much easier in the long run. The larger the system gets, the harder it will be to change the disk configuration. Data files should be placed on RAID 5, RAID 6, or RAID 10, depending on their requirements. Systems with lower write I/O requirements should be placed on RAID 5 or RAID 6, whereas systems that have higher write I/O requirements should be placed on RAID 10.

Proper data file placement when used in combination with table-level partitioning can allow current important data to reside on high-speed expensive RAID 10 arrays. You can then move older data that doesn't need to be accessed as frequently to less expensive, slower RAID 5 or RAID 6 storage.

NOTE   Sadly, there are no hard-and-fast rules for when to use RAID 5, RAID 6, or RAID 10. Every database is different and requires a different configuration to ensure that it's performing at its peak.

Index files

Index files or the index partitions that are updated should be kept on storage of a design similar to the base tables of these indexes. Indexes for tables or partitions that are read-only should use RAID 5 or RAID 6 so as to maximize the number of spindles used for reading data.

Transaction log files

The transaction log files should be stored on RAID 1 or RAID 10 storage depending on the size of the transaction logs and the required write throughput. Unless a database is read-only, there's no good reason to store the transaction log on a RAID 5 or RAID 6 array. The write I/O for writable databases would typically be too high for a RAID 5 or RAID 6 array, unless the database is small and has a minimal workload.

tempdb database

Typically, the tempdb database should reside on RAID 1 or RAID 10 arrays because the workload for the tempdb database will typically be at least 50 percent write, if not higher. In a perfect world, each of the data files for the tempdb database should be on its own RAID 1 or RAID 10 array.

If you've put the tempdb database's data files on their own volumes, you should also put the transaction log file on its own volume. If the tempdb database's data files are all on a single hard drive, place the transaction log on its own hard drive. If this isn't possible, place the transaction log on the same disk as the tempdb database. Most operations on the tempdb database are logged to the tempdb database's transaction log just as normal operations to the user databases. Therefore, the correct amount of I/O must be made available to the tempdb database's transaction log.

Disk alignment

The issue of disk alignment is extremely important from a performance standpoint. The issue comes down to the way that the master boot record (MBR) was defined when the first partition was created. The first 32k of space on the physical hard drive was

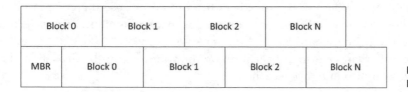

Figure 4
Poor disk alignment

originally used for the MBR, when storage was expensive. Today, disk space is fairly inexpensive.

Modern hard drives perform I/O in 64k blocks; having a 32k MBR means that the first block of data is written starting at the 33rd 1k block in 64k blocks, as shown in figure 4. Because the logical partition isn't aligned with the physical boundaries of the storage array, the number of physical operations the storage array needs to complete all operations is doubled.

When the disk is correctly aligned, blocks of the partition are properly aligned with the physical blocks, as shown in figure 5. When the physical blocks are aligned with the blocks within the partitions, the extra physical I/O operations are no longer needed.

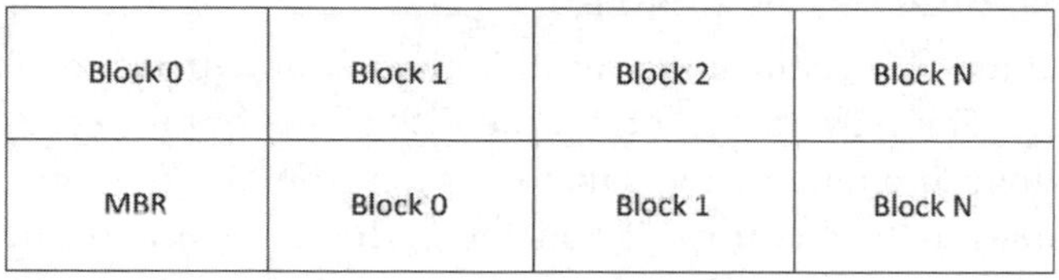

Block 0	Block 1	Block 2	Block N
MBR	Block 0	Block 1	Block N

Figure 5
Correct disk alignment

Correction of misaligned disks is critical in ensuring that the disk subsystem of the server is running at its peak efficiency. The more volumes that share spindles with each other, the greater the impact on system performance because the storage array is doing work that doesn't need to be done.

Correcting disk alignment on Windows 2003 and earlier

You must correct the disk alignment before putting data onto the volume. On Windows Server 2003, you accomplish this task by using the diskpart.exe command-line application (included with the OS); on Windows Server 2000, you use diskpar.exe (included with the Windows 2000 Server Resource Kit, a separate download and install).

The diskpart.exe and diskpar.exe applications are similar in their function, but the switches are slightly different. Because of the minimal number of installations of SQL Server on Windows 2000 operating systems, I won't discuss the specifics of diskpar.exe.

You run diskpart.exe from a command-line window or by choosing Start > Run and typing `diskpart.exe` in the Run box. After launching diskpart.exe, you'll see the prompt DISKPART>. From this prompt you can run `list disk` to view a list of the available disks. This list will match the disks that are shown in the Computer Management MMC snap-in.

After identifying the disk that needs to be configured, use the command `select disk N` where *N* is the number shown by the `list disk` statement. After selecting the disk, create the primary partition by typing `CREATE PARTITION PRIMARY ALIGN=64`. This command creates a primary partition on the volume with the disk aligned at the 64k marker, as shown in figure 5 earlier.

Correcting disk alignment in Windows 2008 and later

Correcting disk alignment in Windows Server 2008 and later is much easier than using the diskpart.exe or diskpar.exe command-line applications. When new partitions are created in Windows Server 2008, they're aligned automatically, but Windows aligns the volumes at the 1024k boundary instead of the 64k boundary. Microsoft made the decision for this 1 MB alignment instead of a 64k alignment to be compliant with all possible storage solution architectures. When using a storage array with a 64k block size, this 1M alignment won't affect performance. You may notice that slightly less than 1 MB of space is missing from the volume, instead of the 64k of space missing that you might otherwise see.

Correcting after the partition has been created

The most important thing to remember about disk alignment is that it can't be corrected for after the fact. The only way to correct the disk alignment is to create a new partition on a new volume and migrate the data to this new volume. You can't use storage array-side techniques to correct for this issue after the fact, because the storage array sees the MBR simply as data stored on the partition and not as an actual offset.

Aligning on the array

Many storage array vendors allow you to handle disk alignment on the storage array itself. Although this may appear to be a good idea, in the long run it's not. If you move the array to another location on the storage array, you have to manually re-create the array-side offset on the destination. If you don't, the offset will be lost and performance will suffer.

Snapshots

Most storage arrays support snapshots, which are much like the snapshot technology introduced in Microsoft SQL Server 2005. Snapshots allow you to create a point-in-time view of a LUN, which can then be presented to another server for a variety of purposes (such as backups or QA testing). Although the technique used by storage arrays is similar to the one used by SQL Server, the snapshots aren't compatible with SQL Server. These array-level snapshots won't show up in the database snapshot menu tree of SQL Server Management Studio, nor can they be queried for using the SQL Server dynamic management views.

A similar method is called *copy on first write*. With this technique, after a snapshot is taken the first time a write is made to the disk, the block is copied to the snapshot space (which was predefined on the storage array). A pointer within the snapshot's configuration is updated to show that the snapshot should look at the block within this space instead of the original block (which the source volume continues to use).

Snapshots with a VSS-enabled storage array

Many storage arrays use a native SQL Server process called VSS (Volume Snapshot Service), which integrates with the Windows VSS process. When you take array-level snapshots using a storage array integrated with VSS, the databases are considered to be *crash recoverable*. This means that the database files will be in the same state they'd be in if the database server had crashed or if the database server had blue-screened and restarted. In 99.9 percent or more of cases, a database in which a snapshot has been taken using VSS will come on line and run through the normal recovery process.

The VSS process is pretty basic. When the storage array is ready to take a snapshot, the array communicates with the Windows OS and requests from VSS a list of the writers on the server. These writers include all the available disks, the databases, and database instances (among other potential items such as Exchange Server databases). The array will then determine, based on the information received from VSS, which volumes need to be snapped, as well as which databases and instances those objects are a part of. Once this is done, the storage array creates a "snap-set" of the needed LUNs so the databases will be snapped in a consistent set. At this point, the array requests that the snapshot be created.

VSS then tells all the various writers that are within the snapshot to prepare for the process. Within the context of SQL Server, this means that a checkpoint is issued for the databases in question. When all the VSS writers report that they're ready (which means that all the checkpoints have been completed), VSS instructs the writers to freeze all write I/O in order to prevent new writes from being sent to the disk. This doesn't mean that the SQL Server will stop accepting writes but that the writes will be captured into the write buffer. But the write buffer won't be flushed to disk, nor will the writes be written to the physical transaction log. When all the writers report back to VSS that the writes have been halted, VSS instructs the storage array to complete the snapshot. Once that process is finished, the array informs VSS of the completion, and VSS then instructs the writers to begin allowing writes to the disk again.

All this must take place within a timeout period. By default, this timeout period is 10 seconds. If the process isn't completed within the 10-second window, VSS tells the array to cancel the snapshot, and the writers are told to begin writing to disk.

Snapshots with a non-VSS-enabled storage array

Storage arrays that aren't VSS enabled don't create crash-recoverable databases; they create what are called *crash-consistent* databases. Because the write buffer wasn't flushed before the snapshot, the database and files may not be in a recoverable state.

Just because the storage array doesn't integrate with VSS natively, data isn't necessarily lost. If the storage array supports taking the snapshots via a command-line application, you can control everything from a single script. This approach requires building an application to integrate with the Windows VSS API to trigger the VSS process, waiting for the response to trigger the snapshot on the array, and then informing VSS that the process has been completed.

Snapshots as a backup process

Some people advocate using snapshots as a backup process instead of doing traditional SQL Server backups. This strategy isn't the best idea, because when you take a snapshot, only the changed blocks are copied into the snapshot space. If the RAID array that holds the production volumes fails, all the blocks that make up the base of the snapshot will also be lost. The same is true if a block on the base LUN of the snapshot becomes corrupted—that block will be corrupted for all the snapshots that point to that block, as well.

Snapshots can be used as part of a larger backup process by taking snapshots, presenting those snapshots to another server, and having that server then back up the snapshot version of the volume to tape for long-term protection. But keep in mind that using array-based snapshots as the sole backup process isn't a viable backup solution.

Using snapshots to present storage to downstream environments

When you need to present storage to your downstream database instances (development, QA, testing, user acceptance testing, etc.), you can use snapshots to do so. In this case you can take a series of snapshots from the production environment, which you can then present to these other environments. Snapshots can be presented to servers in either read-only or read-write mode. By presenting the LUN to the server in read-write mode, the SQL Server can mount the databases in read-write mode, updating the few records that need to be updated via the development and QA testing phase, without any changes made to the production LUN.

This approach can save a massive amount of space, especially on large databases. If your production database environment is a 1 TB database, maintaining all five environments with a full copy of the database will take approximately 5 TB of space. But by using database snapshots, you'll use approximately 1.5–2 TB of space (depending on your production growth rate, how often you refresh your downstream environments, and how much data change occurs within your downstream environments).

If you need to obfuscate the data before it can be used in your downstream environments, you can do this, as well. You can take a snapshot of the production environment and obfuscate the data within this snapshot, and then take snapshots of the snapshot and present these snapshots to the other down-level environments. You can then refresh your downstream environments quickly. You simply shut down the SQL Server in the downstream environment, delete the old snapshot, take a new snapshot of the production system, and present the snapshots to the downstream environment. If you powered off the downstream environment, simply power back up the server; it'll pick up the LUNs on boot-up as new disks and SQL Server should start up as expected.

Clones

Clones are a synchronous duplicate copy of the production LUN within the array. Any time a write is made to the production LUN, that write is duplicated to the secondary LUN. This helps protect against disk failures on the production LUN by keeping a duplicate copy of the data available on another set of spindles. Clones are different from the various "instant clones" or "zero copy clones" that some vendors present as options.

A traditional clone will take time to complete and will end up with a fully synchronous copy of the LUN. The instant clones or zero copy clones start the clone process, and when they report that the process is done, you can mount the clone to another machine. In the background, the clone is backfilled with the missing blocks. If the instant clone or zero copy clone isn't configured to maintain a synchronous copy after completion, it effectively takes a snapshot of the LUN and then backfills the snapshot with the unchanged blocks.

When you make a synchronous clone of a LUN, you can separate this LUN so that it's no longer being written to when the production LUN is written to. This puts the LUN into a fractured state (your vendor may use a different term). At this point, the clone is its own LUN. You can mount it to a server or take snapshots of it. The clone is now ready for use.

Summary

Several storage options are available to you when you're designing your storage environment for your SQL Server. Knowing all the available options will help you get the right level of performance at the best possible cost. When selecting your storage solution, getting the right storage and the right cost is critical to not only getting optimal performance but also doing so in a fiscally responsible way.

About the author

Denny Cherry is an independent consultant with more than a decade of experience working with platforms such as Microsoft SQL Server, Hyper-V, vSphere, and Enterprise Storage solutions. Denny's areas of technical expertise include system architecture, performance tuning, replication, and troubleshooting. Denny currently holds several of the Microsoft Certifications related to SQL Server for versions 2000 through 2008, including the Microsoft Certified Master, as well as being a Microsoft MVP for several years. Denny has written several books and dozens of technical articles on SQL Server management and how SQL Server integrates with various other technologies..

6 Generalization: the key to a well-designed schema

Paul Nielsen

The year: 2002. The project: approximately a year late and $1.5 million greater than budget. The team had grown from a small handful of developers to 19, but the work was getting further behind by the day. The project was mission critical to the organization, but because the organization's culture valued friendship over performance, the delays were accepted. The situation had degraded to the point where management wanted a second opinion. I was told there were "no sacred cows—challenge everything." (In hindsight, they should've known that was a challenge I'd relish).

The project collected data for monthly reporting—not a complicated project. Once I understood the requirements, I modeled the data using 17 tables. Yet the project's database had 87 tables and would be easily characterized by most DBAs as "highly overnormalized."

You're reading this book, so I have no doubt that you, too, have run across databases that are proclaimed to be perfectly normalized yet are difficult to understand and query. Too many data modelers generate designs that are overly complex and painful to understand, query, or maintain. Why?

There's a popular phrase: "Normalize until it hurts, then denormalize until it works." Must normalization mean unwieldy? I don't think so. I believe the problem is that normalization is only half of the design equation. The missing half is generalization.

A place for normalization

For the record, for online transaction processing (OLTP) projects, I believe in normalization and I don't denormalize for performance. Normalization buys data integrity, and without data integrity, the database might just as well be null and void.

Normalization also buys performance. Denormalized data requires additional code to normalize the data for clean retrieval, check duplicate data, and write duplicate data. Denormalization can cause more performance issues than its misguided application can seem to solve. I once developed a large, heavy-load database and compared a normalized to a denormalized schema. The normalized was about 15 percent faster. So "denormalize until it works" isn't true for OLTP performance.

Denormalization is the norm, and a good idea, for reporting tables. And it's true that most OLTP databases include some portion of reporting tables. But for OLTP tables—those that regularly see inserts and updates in business transactions—I never denormalize.

As useful as normalization is, it's a means to an end and not the goal of the schema. I like to think of normalization as the grammar of the data. For English, the grammar rules determine how words should be placed in a sentence, but merely following good grammar won't guarantee that the sentence is worth reading. It's assumed that a well-written story will have good grammar (for the most part), but I don't recall thinking to myself after I read the last Tom Clancy novel, "Wow, that Tom sure writes with good grammar." Nope. I thought, "I sure enjoyed how Tom tells a story, and I like his characters." Grammar is there for the integrity of the sentence structure, but it takes style and substance to tell a good yarn.

English departments go beyond basic grammar and teach story, plot, character development, and creative writing. What are the corresponding skills for database design? And why don't we codify and teach the skill of designing a well-crafted database schema—one that's both normalized and elegant, has excellent data integrity, and is easy to query?

Lessons from the UIX discipline

Recently, I've been working in the area of user interface design and user experience (UIX). Two UIX principles might apply to database design. First, there's no such thing as intuitive—there's only familiar. This means that when you see a new UI, it's not that you can magically figure it out, but that it builds on what you already know. It's intuitive because it's familiar. It might appear slick and amazing, but if it was completely foreign then you wouldn't have a clue where to begin.

The same can be said of database design; understanding a database design requires a certain level of understanding of both databases and the knowledge domain that the design represents. To take this one step further, understanding and designing databases requires a certain repertoire of both database design patterns and data typically seen in databases.

The second UIX principle that might apply to database design is regular usability testing. In his book *Rocket Surgery Made Easy: The Do-It-Yourself Guide to Finding and Fixing Usability Problems* (New Riders Press, 2009), Steve Krug makes the case for a simple form of usability testing. With no instruction, the test subject sits before the UI and attempts to complete simple tasks while telling the tester every thought that goes through her brain. Within two to three rounds of this simple form of usability testing, the major issues are sure to bubble to the top and the developers will have a fresh insight as to how users will see their UI.

What would happen if database modelers brought report writers and developers into a room and asked them to write queries from the schema without any instruction or help from the data modeler? Without a doubt, the difficult area of the schema would be quickly revealed.

Designing a UI and modeling a database are both a bit like designing a puzzle. The puzzle doesn't hold any secrets from its designer. But for the rest of the world, it's often a different story. For both disciplines, one of the primary goals is to create a design that meets the requirements and is readily usable.

Now, I understand that I've made a logical leap or assumption that usability is a goal of the database schema. Some of you will strongly disagree with my assumption. I know, I've seen you cross your arms and say that the only job of the data modeler is to preserve the integrity of the data through normalization, and if that means it's hard to query, then you've done your job well. As someone who's had to write queries against your database, I respectfully disagree. If the database isn't readily understandable and easy to consume by those with reasonable professional skills, then the design is less than it could be. I'll put it plainly: your baby is ugly.

So the question is, how can you create a well-designed database that's both normalized and has great data integrity, and is highly usable as well?

Generalization defined

Whether or not you realize it, one of the first steps of normalizing is deciding on the scope of the entities (tables) being modeled. First normal form includes the concept of a single entity storing data about a single grouping of similar or related items. The definition of what constitutes a grouping of similar things can be broad or narrow, as similar types of things in reality are modeled in the database. The modeler has the option of creating specific entities or more generalized entities. The art of modeling often comes down to choosing the sweet spot on the generalization-specialization continuum.

Generalization therefore is defined as the entity's scope—broad versus narrow and specific (see figure 1). On the generalization extreme of the continuum, there's one mega-table holding every instance of things being tracked in the database. At the other end of the continuum is a design that has a different table for every grouping that differs ever so slightly from another grouping.

An example helps illustrate the question. Consider your current environment wherever you might happen to be. If you're in a room, it might include furniture, computers, other people, electrical outlets, books, flooring, lighting, musical devices…the list goes on. How would you design a schema to inventory everything in your current environment?

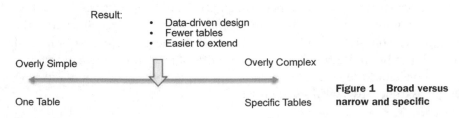

Figure 1   Broad versus narrow and specific

An overly generalized schema would use a single entity to hold a list of items. It may use a column to indicate the type of object. Attributes that differ between types of items might be stored in nullable columns. These are the kind of nullable columns that risk domain integrity and cause data modeling purists to reject nullable columns completely. Clearly, the extremely generalized design is a problem.

At the other end of the continuum, an overly specific schema might use a separate entity for each type of item—an entity for furniture, humans, computers, monitors, flooring, projectors, food, drink, and so on. A common justification for this level of detail is that different types of items have different attributes. But this kind of overly specific design is difficult to query, tends to include lots of unions in the abstraction layer, hurts performance, and causes project bloat. In the end, it's these designs that cause developers to complain about overnormalization and conclude that normalization hurts.

To be clear, an overly complicated database, often called overnormalized and what I'm referring to as overly specific, isn't the fault of normalization. And some might say that an overly specific database could be considered a poorly normalized database.

The sweet spot is someplace in the continuum between these two extremes. A design that respects data integrity and leverages generalization might include a single entity for the attributes common to all item types and super-type subtype entities to hold the attributes specific to each item type.

In figure 2, the common Object table is organized by the ObjectType table. Humans and computers can have attributes specific to them stored in the subtype tables. If a new type of object enters the environment, the type could be added to the data in the ObjectType table and the new object could be tracked immediately without any code change. If the new type becomes important, a new subtype table could be added to the model, but this means less code change than adding a completely new table and modifying all the queries to union data from the new specific table.

Benefits of generalization

Normalization is good for every goal of the database. It increases the performance, data integrity, usability, and extensibility of the database. But an overly specific design,

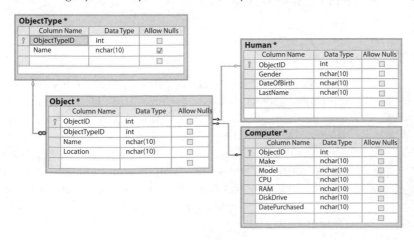

Figure 2   Common Object table organized by the ObjectType table

often called overnormalized, will severely limit performance, data integrity, usability, and extensibility.

When normalization is applied with generalization, the result can be a data-driven design that performs well, has excellent data integrity, and is easy to understand.

A database that's difficult to extend is perhaps the greatest risk to an organization. The most common workaround is to store the new data in a new database. These silos are strategically dangerous to the organization. A generalized database will be data-driven and far easier to extend than an overly specific database.

Data schemas that employ generalization are sometimes referred to as data-driven, and it's true that generalization and data-driven are compatible, almost symbiotic, concepts. But think of *generalization* as the decision to scope the group of like items into entities and *data-driven* as the technique that allows a common entity to store similar but different entities.

One benefit of data-driven is that when taken to an extreme, many business rules can be driven lower than a UI code-behind button, lower than the business layer, lower than procs, lower even than the schema. The ultimate place to store business rules is in the data—metadata specifically. A completely data-driven design can achieve this goal, which yields a highly flexible application.

Summary

Not only does generalization make the data model more nimble, but it can also help make the abstraction layer and the code above the database easier to develop and extend.

Generalizing common objects may seem like common sense to you. If this is the case, I congratulate you for applying the principle of generalization perhaps without knowing that term. And continue modeling data because you have a mind for data patterns.

As you design data schemas, I encourage you to consciously consider how you can apply the principle of generalization to some of the entities. Think carefully about the scope of the entities and choose the scope that best fits the situation. As you mature in your data modeling, my hope is that you begin to think of normalization as the basic grammar and generalization as the style of the story.

About the author

Paul Nielsen is the founder of Ministry Weaver, a software startup offering an object database for ministries. He focuses on extreme data modeling, database development, and the occasional XMAL and C#, and he was the author of the SQL Server Bible series and the editor of the first volume of the SQL Server MVP Deep Dives. Paul offers consulting and seminars on data modeling and schema optimization. He lives in Colorado with his family, and he's passionate about marriage, adoption, theology, music, writing, and their next family trip to Maui.

PART 2

Database administration

Edited by Paul Randal and Kimberly Tripp

In the two years since the first collectively authored *SQL Server MVP Deep Dives* book, it seems as if many more people labor under the title of DBA. There has been an explosion in the use of products that utilize SQL Server as the data store (e.g., Microsoft's SharePoint, Team Foundation Server, and Dynamics) and so many more people have been thrust into the DBA role. It also seems as if more companies are building on SQL Server as they grow their businesses.

Altogether this means a lot more people are seeking education on SQL Server use and practices. During those same two years there has been a commensurate explosion in the number of people blogging about SQL Server and the number of community events (such as SQL Saturdays) where DBAs can find information about SQL Server. Does this mean that print is dead for technical books such as this?

Absolutely not!

Whether in a "real" book or the electronic version, this section of the book contains the impassioned writing of MVPs who are either full-time DBAs or work as consultants with full-time DBAs. They've considered what would make the most impact to easing the burden of being a DBA and chosen to donate their time writing about it to make this section useful to all.

From using the tools—with chapters focused on multiserver management, SMO, PowerShell, and Central Management Servers—to chapters focused on capacity planning and increased availability through testing, these active MVPs and DBAs have put together some of their best practices and tips and tricks that help them do their jobs better (and help you do yours!). We enjoyed reading these chapters and hearing what items ail our colleagues and friends, as well as hearing a few additional myths.

We'd like to thank those authors from this section for their time and dedication. With the pressures of work these days, we can understand how hard it is to carve out time for a project such as this, but their passion for SQL Server and giving back something to the community drives them on. And that's the same reason we're involved with the book again—because we still love using SQL Server, learning about SQL Server, and teaching about SQL Server. We hope you enjoy this section!

About the editors

Paul Randal and Kimberly Tripp are a husband-and-wife team who own and run SQLskills.com, a world-renowned SQL Server consulting and training company. They're both SQL Server MVPs and Microsoft Regional Directors, with more than 30 years of combined SQL Server experience.

7 Increasing availability through testing

Allan Hirt

As a DBA, your sphere of influence is often limited to instances of SQL Server and their databases. Influence may or may not extend to the underlying servers hosting those instances and databases because those components are often managed by other groups within your organization. For DBAs, this can be a potential problem. Why? Consider this example: on Friday night, the SAN administrator decides to update the firmware on the storage unit that has all of your mission-critical databases. The SAN administrator doesn't tell you this is going to happen, because it should be no big deal and happens at a layer that's not exposed to the databases.

It's the weekend, and you're looking forward to catching up with friends and family before going back to the office on Monday morning. Unfortunately, your mobile phone wakes you at 3:30 a.m. on Saturday. The on-call DBA (who's new to the organization) is on the other end frantically asking you what she should do—all the important databases are offline. This means that all the processing done in the early hours of the morning that must be completed before other time-sensitive work can be done may be impacted if the databases can't come online quickly. Because it only appears to be a database problem at the moment, the spotlight is on the DBAs. Because the on-call DBA wasn't equipped to deal with this scenario, you get up and remotely log into the environment to do some initial troubleshooting. After doing a bit of investigation, you notice errors in the logs that are indicative of a storage problem. All systems with local storage are fine, but any server configured with SQL Server and connected to that particular SAN has been affected.

When you call the SAN administrator, he flatly denies anything is wrong and claims there were no issues with the SAN after the update. After a few more hours of trying to determine what went wrong so that you can bring the databases on line, the situation escalates. More applications that are *not* SQL Server based but also use the SAN are offline as users try to access their files to get an important report finished for

Monday morning. The more the various administrators for the systems with problems troubleshoot their respective issues, the more it appears to be a storage issue. The SAN administrator is finally called in and as it turns out, the update package rolled out to the SAN had a bug in it that affected the configuration of the SAN and corrupted the storage. Although the spotlight is temporarily off the DBAs as the SAN is being repaired, it will return when the storage is up and you need to ensure the databases are available.

Consider another example: the in-house developers decide to roll out an update to your company's most visible application on a Friday night. The update involves not only updating the application servers, but also rolling out new objects in the databases with corresponding schema updates to support them. The developers email the update script to the DBAs before they leave the office for the weekend.

When the time comes for the DBA to execute the script, everything seems fine. But on Monday morning the users are inundating the help desk with calls that the application isn't returning the data expected and the DBA team is now involved. As it turns out, the script not only added objects, but also updated the biggest and most used table's data with an unqualified WHERE clause that modified every row. Because you're the DBA, you're automatically in the hot seat: it's up to you to get the data back. Although you have backups, the database is 1 TB and it'll take some time to get the file from the centralized backup solution and restore it.

Could either of these situations have been prevented? The answer is yes, and the how is simple: by testing prior to their production rollouts.

Testing—it's not just for application functionality

When most people think of testing (sometimes known as quality assurance), they equate it with the testing of things like application functionality. Testing is an offshoot of development, right? Wrong. Testing doesn't stop with the application. Just as application functionality must be tested in development, it's up to IT to ensure that the planned implementation or deployment—be it rolling out a new patch to a server or updating a schema—works properly *before* it's completed in production. Administrators are on the front line, and a big part of their responsibility is to ensure that the respective service level agreements (SLAs), recovery time objectives (RTOs), and recovery point objectives (RPOs) can be met. Consider these facts:

- *Change is the only thing that's constant*—Do you implement a production server and never patch it, meaning it's the same today as it was from day one in production? For anyone reading this book, the answer should be no. For example, the SQL Server development team releases various updates over the course of a SQL Server version's lifetime. As of this writing, SQL Server 2008 has had two service packs (SPs), all of the cumulative updates (CUs) released every other month for each currently supported version, as well as several individual hotfixes that aren't specifically included in the core CU package. Whether or not you plan to apply or have already installed any of those updates doesn't matter;

the point is that SQL Server is a moving target. A DBA needs to manage and account for this moving target. It's a matter of when, not if, at least one of those updates will need to be installed.

- *Change may introduce risk*—Change means there's a difference. Difference introduces the unknown. The unknown equates to some level of risk. Sometimes that risk is extremely small, and other times it's astronomical. Which part of the spectrum you'll fall under depends on many factors, including what aspect the update is affecting and how crucial that component being updated is as it relates to the overall workings of your solution. Whether you're working in a 9-to-5 environment or one that is 24/7, anything that introduces risk poses a threat to your uptime if it causes a problem that requires downtime to fix. A big part of preventing downtime and increasing availability is mitigating the risk (small or large) to minimize potential threats to the environment.

- *The only way to understand the risk of a change is to test it*—A committee can sit in a room and debate whether a change should be applied, but talking doesn't substitute for understanding what happens if it's installed. The change may fix the problem for which it's intended but also introduce an undesirable side effect, such as decreasing performance, which in turn decreases productivity and ultimately impacts the business. That's not something you want to discover for the first time in production because it'll most likely require a separate outage to fix. The more you know up front, the better.

The missing link

Features like failover clustering, database mirroring, availability groups, and log shipping increase availability, but they don't prevent all failures. They protect against certain scenarios and not others. For example, if you apply the wrong patch to your SQL Server instance on all cluster nodes, that's not something that a failover will cure. All the nodes have that update installed. Although you may be able to remove the patch, doing so may impact the availability of the instance to finish the task. So now your highly available cluster will be down to fix a problem. That's not good. The reason that a cluster is used in this example is that in many environments, a cluster is purchased only for production. No cluster exists anywhere else. That's clearly a problem because the process for updating a SQL Server failover cluster is vastly different than applying the update to a standalone server. You don't want the first place the update is installed to be production. The solution is to have another cluster in a different environment to use for testing purposes (if not for other reasons).

In a perfect world, there would be at least four distinct environments for all systems (including mission-critical ones): development, testing, staging, and production. Most environments are lucky to have two or maybe three of those different environments. It's important to note that all environments should mirror, or be as close as possible to, the configuration of the target production environment in terms of configuration (and size, if possible). This includes matching right down to patch levels, versions, and editions of all software. The following list highlights why each of the four environments is unique:

- Having a dedicated development environment allows developers to have their own sandbox in which to design and prototype without affecting anyone else. Development environments are highly volatile because developers are changing and updating code constantly.

- Testers have different needs than developers. Testers are usually working against specific builds of code that require specific (and more stable) configurations that change only in a more controlled manner. Sharing an environment with developers may not meet those needs. If developers and testers share one environment, what happens when one or the other makes a change or reboots a server? Everyone is potentially affected. This is why having a dedicated test environment for testers is important.

- Staging (sometimes referred to as preproduction) could be an important element to increase availability. If you can afford only one environment to be a copy of production (even if in configuration, not size), it should be staging. It's the final place where you could test the rollout of an update or patch, and assuming it has the same configuration as production, you can see how things will work and behave when you finally roll it out. Without a staging environment, you may be faced with the situation described at the beginning of this section: production is truly the first time you're performing an action based on that configuration.

- Production is the day-to-day environment that applications and end users access. Combining it with any other one would definitely add risk. Production should be considered a "hands-off" environment for anyone but production administrators, and even they should use standard best practices such as remote administration where possible to minimize the risk of doing something such as accidentally powering off the box. Developers and testers shouldn't have access to production unless they're assisting in a troubleshooting effort. This approach minimizes the risk of someone accidentally updating or bringing down a production server, instance, or database by connecting to production instead of another environment where the task should be executed. Other issues, such as who has access to sensitive data, is also a concern in production environments. Don't put yourself in a position where that could be a problem.

One environment not mentioned earlier would be an additional one for the administrators (DBAs, Windows, and so on) to do their own testing. This would be different from the environments already used for development, testing, and staging. Like developers and testers, all administrators need their own sandbox to allow them to further test before implementing changes in production. It may not be specific application testing, but proving that a PowerShell script written to perform a specific task does exactly that, or understanding the steps and dependencies of an update package, is crucial. You don't want any doubt in production that it's going to work. The environment should reflect the current state of production and would be somewhat like a hybrid testing and staging environment in terms of its configuration.

Cost is obviously a factor in how many and which specific environments are deployed where you work. Having four environments, some of which may be copies of each other down to the hardware, can get expensive. This is where using virtualization for some environments can come into play. The bottom line is that the more diverse environments you have to test and prove things over time, the smaller the overall risk when it comes time to do things in production.

Knowledge is power

With each update, Microsoft usually publishes a list of the fixes included with relevant links for additional information. You should know that in some cases, not all the fixes contained in an update will be listed, which is another reason you have to test. Your vendors or internal developers should know their applications well enough to be able to use the list as a starting point to identify potential code paths that the fixes may touch in the application. For example, if an application uses transactional replication and there's a replication fix included in the update you're considering applying, that update (or specific hotfix if being installed outside of a CU or SP) would be one that's a strong candidate for testing because of the potential for adversely affecting the application.

This means that every release has to be properly evaluated and vetted by multiple groups—maybe even external ones (such as a vendor if there's integration with their application). Some third-party vendors will publish a list of SQL Server patches they support. For example, if a new SQL Server SP is released, a vendor may not support it until they've done their testing. If your company policy is to apply the SP as soon as possible, that policy may be at odds with the application vendor. You have three options:

- Push the vendor to support the SP to meet your implementation timeframe.
- Have an exception and only apply the SP when it's supported, putting it at odds with your internal policies but maintaining supportability with the vendor.
- Assume the risk of not being supported by the vendor and apply the SP after doing your own testing.

Which option you choose depends on your environment. A vendor who's more proactive than reactive would test and certify as soon as possible after a CU or SP is released to help their customers. The reality is often different, because vendors can be slow in certifying the new SQL Server update. This can be an even bigger problem after a major version of SQL Server is released (such as SQL Server 2008 or SQL Server 2008 R2) and the vendor hasn't yet done any work to support it, whether it's one month or one year after the ship date. This situation hurts customers who may want to use the new version, and over a longer period of time, ultimately affects supportability of the entire solution if the vendor continues to require older versions of SQL Server and/or Windows.

If at all possible, never blindly apply an update "just because." *Just because* it's released doesn't mean you need it, or at least need it immediately. SQL Server updates such as CUs and SPs are cumulative, which means everything that was in the update prior to it is included in a later update. An SP may also have a few more fixes than a CU, but what's in a CU is always in an SP. Some later CUs and its fixes may not be in an SP depending on what cutoff point was made for the SP. A hotfix fixes a specific problem; it may or may not make it into a CU or SP because it could've been devised as a one-off for a customer and may not be public. Only install hotfixes if you have the specific problem the hotfix addresses.

A good example of "not everything makes it into a release" is SQL Server 2008 R2. When the code was branched for SQL Server 2008 R2 and subsequently released, it didn't contain any of the fixes that shipped as part of SQL Server 2008 CU5, CU6, and CU7. All of those fixes were then rolled up and shipped as part of SQL Server 2008 R2 CU1 so that those fixes were rolled forward into the new version. This example is a case where ignoring a CU for your product version could be harmful if you need a fix contained in any one of those listed CUs that also applied to the previous version.

Test early, test often

Assume for a moment your company has a policy of applying SPs and not the CUs that ship every other month. There's nothing wrong with this policy, but there's a way you can minimize the testing needed to be done for an SP as well as minimize your risk overall when the SP ships from Microsoft. Achieving these two goals is simple: test along the way before you reach the SP.

If your policy is to apply only an SP and not the CUs, realize that SPs happen less frequently than a CU. There may be an SP released once a year or possibly longer from one SP to another. Because CUs are released every other month, the longer the delta of time between SPs, the more change (and more risk) there is. Even though you wouldn't be applying them in production, you could be installing the CUs all along in development and/or test environments to see if the fixes impact your applications and address any issues as they arise. That way, by the time the SP is released the amount of work everyone (including the DBAs) would need to do should be fairly trivial. If you don't do this testing all along, it could mean a lot of work when it comes time to apply the SP. This is especially true if it's found that there are quite a few fixes you'd need to address. If you'd been taking care of this testing all along, you wouldn't be in the predicament. You may not have to test every CU, but do so at reasonable intervals (such as every other one).

Microsoft often releases advance versions of the service packs (such as betas or release candidates). Even if you haven't been testing using the CUs, those early pre-RTM releases are also opportunities to do a lot of the same work you'd do with CUs, a bit later in the cycle. You choose to tackle this challenge, there are plenty of chances to make life easier for yourself instead of being under the gun at the last minute.

Automated versus manual testing

There seems to be a movement these days to automate everything. From starting your car's ignition via a mobile phone to turning on the lights in your house at a certain time with a specific luminosity, technology has come a long way. In the dark days of the development and IT world not so long ago, testers didn't have automated tools. They relied on specifications from developers (or elsewhere) to write test plans. The plans were then executed and the results documented. If problems were found, either bugs were filed for an application or other things were fixed or altered as a result of the findings. These days, the trend is to use software specifically designed to be a testing harness and generate a file that claims success or failure. The reality? Both approaches are still valid because each has pros and cons.

When does it make sense to automate? If certain tests are repeated often or have predictable outcomes, automation is a good thing. It allows you to do things like "smokescreen" tests after installing the update in production to see if the most important parts of functionality are working. There are quite a few tools today to automate tests, and your company may even be using one already. Sometimes you can automate things easily in scripts such as Windows Management Instrumentation (WMI) or Power-Shell, but for applications you generally need something more specialized to drive the interface. If doing automated testing, make sure that it generates a report that can either be processed or is easily readable to see whether it was a success. Testing for testing's sake is worthless.

Realize that some tests may be too complex or have elements that can't be automated using existing tools or processes. These would be manual tests. Manual testing can potentially be time consuming, but there are times where the time and effort invested in automating may not be worth the trouble even if the task isn't complex. For example, executing a query to verify one of the SQL Server properties using `SERVERPROPERTY` may be faster through a `sqlcmd` session or SQL Server Management Studio than it'd be to create a script, execute it, and then analyze the output.

What needs to be tested?

Until now, this chapter has focused mainly on the patch management aspect of testing. But patch management isn't the only thing that needs to be tested when it comes to your SQL Server environment. These other things, in the following list, will provide you with increased reliability and lower risks, and give you predictability. The list represents the most common testing situations that must be addressed; there may be others not listed that would be specific to your environment that you'd need to account for.

- *Restore your backups*—Every DBA should know that the only way to completely verify a backup is to restore it. Generating backups is only part of what you need to do to ensure that you can recover from a disaster. The verification tests that are an optional component of SQL Server's backup functionality provide reassurance that the backup should be fine, but make no mistake: that is *not* the same as performing the restore. Unfortunately, most organizations still don't restore any database for a variety of reasons (not enough hardware, not enough time, etc.). It may be impractical to restore every backup, but picking random ones at various times is better than doing nothing at all. This will not only instill confidence that the backups themselves are good, it will also give you an estimated time of how long the restoration process will take should the restore need to take place. As an important bonus, in the event you should find yourself having to restore from a backup and management wants to know how long it will take, you can provide an answer based on your tests.

- *Test disaster recovery plans*—As any natural disaster that has occurred in recent memory should demonstrate, being prepared (on many levels, not only technological) for a disaster is crucial. Some problems that may be accounted for in your disaster recovery plans could be man-made, whereas others are designed to protect against natural disasters like floods, earthquakes, and tornadoes. The reason this is so important is that despite the human catastrophe that may have happened after the disaster, at some point when things calm down, life will need to go on. People will need to go to work and businesses will need to get back on track. The only way that happens is to ensure business continuity.

  It's not enough to have plans—they have to be tested. How do you know if they work or are adequate otherwise? Testing a disaster scenario could potentially be disruptive. That's the point. You need to know what works, what doesn't work, and if something doesn't work, how to fix it. You'll never account for every "what if," but you can certainly cover the major ones.

  Disaster recovery testing is usually not just doing things like ensuring you can perform a log shipping role change. It involves simulating an entire site failure and what you would do to get systems up from bare metal. This includes flying people to your data center, accounting for the time it takes to get there, and so on. This testing could be a significant expense, but is it worth losing the business if you don't know? Every second in a server- or site-down scenario matters.

- *Test relevant processes*—Two core components of availability success are people and process. Process is something no one likes because it means structure. Two examples that come to mind are retrieving backup files and testing handoff points. For the first, not everyone will have their backups stored locally. That means integrating with another group to get them from some centralized system before the restore process can begin. If that process is broken (for example, you can't get in touch with the backup operator immediately because they don't work 24/7), it needs to be corrected. As a DBA, you're responsible for getting the database back up and running. No one cares if you're dependent on others for making part of that happen. If you have tight RTOs and RPOs, a blunder by someone else could, at the worst, cost you your job because a mission-critical system is down too long.

- *Test application functionality after updates are applied*—The DBA's job may be finished after installing the update for SQL Server, but before allowing production use of the entire system, someone from the application side (developers or testers) should verify the application. A DBA is usually not the expert on the application itself. Even if the DBA can run queries to verify that data is fine, that doesn't necessarily correspond to the functionality within the application. It's usually not possible to do a full regression test when your maintenance window is short, so you should devise a list of the top tasks performed by end users and execute those. Doing so should provide sufficient coverage to demonstrate that the update was successful and didn't adversely impact the application. Extensive testing should've already been done in nonproduction environments; this is an extension of that process that should support the findings from the completed application testing against the update. This step is important because the last thing you want to do is have users notify you of problems; you want to catch them before they're even seen.

- *Test specific hardware configurations before you install SQL Server or after (depending on the particular item and where it's installed or configured in relation to SQL Server)*—Whether you're clustering your servers or installing instances on a standalone box, there are some specific "advanced" configurations that you must fully test. Four good examples are multisite (also known as geographically dispersed) clusters, storage-based backups, multipath I/O, and storage mirroring (which is sometimes a component of multisite clusters depending on the configuration). Storage-based backups often require a specific disk configuration and dictate how SQL Server data and log files can be placed. Once SQL Server is installed, test that it's working as expected (both with backups and restores). If you're using storage such as a SAN, chances are you're configured to use multiple network paths for redundancy as well as performance. You want to ensure that in the event of one path failing, the redundant path works. The only real way to do this effectively is to pull the cables and check the behavior. This is an effective test on a cluster to see that the failover mechanism works. Finally, if you're going to be mirroring the storage for something like a multisite cluster, each hardware vendor has their own way of implementing such a solution. Not only would you have to follow their guidelines, but the configuration should be thoroughly verified prior to installing SQL Server. Whether or not you have mirrored storage, if your configuration is to allow a clustered instance to move between two sites, test its failover as well.

First things first

Testing itself isn't enough. To truly be successful, you must also implement change control, because it goes hand in hand with testing. Change control isn't technology (although technology may be part of the solution). Change control is a series of formal processes that govern how changes can be rolled out and executed, whether it's a non-production or production environment. It not only adds accountability, but documents things like the reason for applying the update, the exact steps of what will be done, the plan and steps to roll the update back, the teams (or stakeholders) that approved the update to be applied, who did the work, and finally, when the work was done. These things may sound trivial but are important to track.

Change control should increase communication and knowledge between everyone. For example, one of the most disruptive things causing downtime in nearly every environment is the patching of the underlying operating system. DBAs should be notified when the systems running SQL Server will be affected so they can take the appropriate measures (such as doing a full backup of all databases prior to the update) in the unlikely event that a problem occurs during the update process. If the DBA isn't notified and the update needs something like a reboot, their pager or mobile phone may go off notifying them that SQL Server is down. No maintenance on a system for which a DBA is responsible should be a surprise. This speaks to that first example with the SAN earlier in the chapter: administrators, DBAs or otherwise, can't work as if what they do has no impact on anyone else.

Heed this warning: change control should be a transparent process that's simple and easy to follow. For all of its benefits, change control can also hamper a company and have the opposite effects of the benefits it should provide. There are times, such as in a server down situation, where utilizing the change control process would hamper relief efforts to get back up and running. If you need a committee decision for everything in a crisis, it'll add to the outage time. Stakeholders should agree on emergency procedures and approve provisions to ensure that whatever is done during the downtime to fix the problem is accounted for and properly dealt with *after* the event is over. For example, any work done would be documented and subsequently submitted to change control where it would be approved as ex post facto.

Besides change control, all your systems (or at least the most mission-critical ones) should have baselines. A *baseline* is a snapshot of what the system looks like under normal usage. The baseline may have different aspects (at rest, under load, and so on). The reason this is important is that you can easily identify when the system in question doesn't appear to be behaving normal (increased I/O, using more CPU, and so on). Information like this is invaluable after an update because you'll most likely be monitoring it a bit more closely for a few days. How to baseline is out of scope for this chapter, but it involves measuring items like disk I/O, memory, and processor usage for the systems themselves as well as at a database level.

Your company may want to consider leveraging existing frameworks for the standardization of processes such as the Microsoft Operations Framework (MOF; http://technet.microsoft.com/en-us/solutionaccelerators/dd320379) and Information Technology Infrastructure Library (ITIL; www.itil-officialsite.com/). MOF and ITIL are proven methodologies and solid foundations to build on.

Remember the big picture, too

Testing updates and patches slated for production deployment or disaster plans are tactical efforts; they're a means to a specific end. Your company also needs to develop a supportability and platform roadmap for everything from hardware and operating systems to applications and relational database systems, including SQL Server.

For example, you may have a mix of SQL Server 2000, SQL Server 2005, and SQL Server 2008 deployments. What's the long-term strategy to migrate and retire everything on SQL Server 2000? The longer they remain in production, the more risk it presents to your environment. Forget the fact that SQL Server 2000 is long out of support. You may not have used Microsoft's support much (if at all) when that version was supported, but as time goes on the systems are older, running on less efficient and larger hardware that drives up costs and consumes rack space; internal components such as network cards are more prone to failure over time; and most important, the expertise of those who still know how to use older versions dwindles. Keeping older systems (and their associated applications) up and running becomes a burden. You can probably think of at least one system in your current or former workplace that has an old configuration (such as SQL Server 7.0 on Windows NT 4.0) but that is still up and running because one application that can't be retired or upgraded still uses it. That system is one where no one who's currently an administrator knows much about it and everyone is too scared to do anything for fear of bringing the server down. This is a scenario that should be avoided; there needs to be a way forward to upgrade that solution to later versions you're familiar with.

This strategy wouldn't apply only to retiring old systems. Everything in your environment from the SAN to SQL Server releases updates and changes. Some of them are even predictable. As noted earlier, SQL Server releases CUs every other month. You may not need a specific CU if it doesn't contain any fixes you need, but that fix in the CU will ultimately end up in an SP you *will* apply at some point because it's cumulative. What happens if your company has a policy that an SP must be installed within three months after its release, with no exceptions? You install it and hopefully test beforehand, but if a problem was found in an application that needs to be fixed too late in the cycle, it may mean long hours for everyone. If you'd been testing the CUs all along—even if it wasn't in production—you may have identified and fixed the problem well before the mandate to install the service pack would even be in effect. Risk would've been mitigated and your support costs dramatically reduced because you were proactive and not reactive.

A good reference for developing a long-term strategy is the whitepaper "Testing Hot Fixes, Cumulative Updates and Service Packs," which can be found at http://blogs .technet.com/b/sql_server_isv/archive/2010/10/20/hot-fixes-and-cus-and-service-packs -oh-my.aspx. The information is invaluable to all SQL Server professionals with information on concepts like general distribution release (GDR) branching that should be understood so that you make truly informed choices for updates.

Summary

Testing is arguably a crucial, but often ignored, link to minimizing or eliminating downtime. Not being prepared is a preventable cause of downtime. Not knowing how things like an update work or what other things you may need to do in addition to the installation will come back and haunt you. Having untested processes that in theory should work as they're documented is a big risk. When you have tight maintenance windows, there's little—if any—room for error. Add to that your SLAs, RTOs, and RPOs, and the need to test before production becomes even more important. The one time you expect things will be fine and fail to test is the one time you'll have problems. Depending on the impact to the business, the downtime incurred may even impact your job to the point you could be fired. Don't put yourself in that position. Testing is an easy way to minimize risk, increase availability, and instill peace of mind.

About the author

Cluster MVP Allan Hirt is a consultant, published author, speaker, and trainer who has been using Microsoft SQL Server in various guises since 1992. He's based in the Boston area and for the past 10 years has traveled all over the world to work with and train clients. His most recent book is *Pro SQL Server 2008 Failover Clustering* (Apress 2009), and he is currently working on a mission-critical book for SQL Server Denali.

8 Page restores

Gail Shaw

It's said that taking and verifying backups is a DBA's first responsibility, but I believe that the most important thing is the ability to restore data when necessary, in as short a time as possible. That ability requires real knowledge and practical experience of effectively using the restore command, as well as the less commonly used page restore feature.

Restore granularities

There are several possible granularities at which a database can be fully or partially restored. I suspect that everyone is familiar with the full restore, a replacement of the entire database with whatever was in the backup, but that's far from the only option you have.

The database can also be restored at a filegroup level if filegroups other than the primary one exist. It can also be restored at a file level, if there are multiple data files in the database. Such a restore can be used either to replace the database and bring it up piece by piece, or to replace a damaged file or filegroup while leaving the rest of the database intact. Additionally, it can be used to perform partial restores of the database to an alternate location. Complete coverage of these operations, known as piecemeal and partial restores, is beyond the scope of this chapter.

One additional granularity that was added in SQL 2005 is the ability to restore individual pages within the data files. Instead of restoring entire files or the entire database, specific pages within the database can be restored from a backup. So why would you want to do this? The primary use would be in the case of minor database corruption in a large database.

Imagine a multiterabyte database that has five pages corrupted in its largest filegroup. The affected table is critical, and data loss can't be tolerated. If the entire database was restored to fix the corruption, or even if only a single file was restored, substantial downtime could result due to the time required to restore the large volume of data. If only the five corrupted pages could be restored from the backup, the downtime would be substantially reduced.

One thing that page restores are *not* is a way to restore a table or part of a table to an earlier point in time. The reason for that will become clear later in this chapter.

Requirements and limitations

Like many nice features, this one comes with a laundry list of limitations and restrictions. Fortunately it's a small enough list that the feature is still usable.

Recovery model and availability of log backups

Here's one of the most important points to note: the database *must* be in full or bulk-logged recovery model for page restore to be possible. You can't do a page restore on a database using the simple recovery model.

Furthermore, there must be an unbroken chain of log backups from the full backup used (or the differential backup if one is used in addition to the full backup) up to the time that the page restore started. That means the following:

- The transaction log must not have been explicitly truncated (BACKUP LOG … TRUNCATE_ONLY or NO_LOG).
- There must not have been a change to the simple recovery model during the period that the log backups are required.
- No log backup in the chain can be missing or damaged.

Although page restores in bulk-logged recovery do theoretically work, problems can occur if there have been minimally logged operations affecting the (assumedly damaged) pages that are going to be restored.

Books Online (http://msdn.microsoft.com/en-us/library/ms175168.aspx) recommends that if you're attempting a page restore on a database in bulk-logged recovery, you should switch the database to full recovery first and take a log backup. If the log backup succeeds, it means that none of the minimally logged operations affected damaged pages; hence the page restore will succeed.

SQL Server Edition

The SQL Server Edition, interestingly enough, isn't a limitation, though many would likely guess that page restores would only work in Enterprise Edition or above. In reality, page restores can be done in any edition of SQL Server, right down to SQL Express.

In the Enterprise and DataCenter editions, the restore is an online restore in most cases and the database remains available for the duration, but in other editions the restore is offline with the database unavailable during the restore. That said, even if the restore is offline, the downtime will be minimized by restoring the smallest portion of the database possible (which is a huge benefit of page restores).

Page type of the damaged page

Not all pages can be restored. Data, index, and text pages can all be restored at the page level, and in Enterprise Edition, they can be restored online (with the database available).

Pages belonging to the critical system tables can be single-page restored, but the database must be offline for the restore, regardless of the edition.

Allocation pages can't be restored using page restores. This includes the GAM, SGAM, PFS, ML, and DIFF pages. The IAM pages, despite being a form of allocation page, can be restored using single page restore in the same way as for data, index, and text pages. This is because the IAM pages are specific to individual tables and indexes, whereas the other allocation pages are database-wide.

The database boot page (page 9 in file 1) and file header pages (page 0 in each file) can't be restored using single-page restore.

Performing a page restore

Let's walk through how to do a page restore. Assume for the purposes of this demo that the database in question is a rather important production database.

Some queries that are executed against the database result in an invalid page checksum error (error 824). Analysis reveals that five pages in the database are corrupted: 1:56610, 1:56611, 1:56612, 1:56613, and 1:56614 (pages are identified using the notation *file id:page number*, so 1:56610 is the page numbered 56610 in file 1).

> ### Identifying corrupted pages
>
> Damaged pages can be identified in multiple ways. In some cases the error message that SQL Server returns when it encounters the corruption includes the page number.
>
> The most common method of identifying damaged pages is to run DBCC CHECKDB and analyze the errors returned. Such an analysis is far beyond the scope of this chapter.
>
> Additionally the suspect_pages table in msdb contains a list of damaged pages that SQL Server has encountered recently, although some aren't listed in that table.
>
> Finally, a read through the SQL Error Log will show high-severity errors, including damaged pages, and may list the page numbers within the logged error message.

Looking at the msdb backup history, the backup files shown in figure 1 exist.

	database_name	backup_finish_date	physical_device_name	Backup Type
1	WebForums_Prod	2011-03-26 13:47:28.000	D:\Backups\WebForums_Prod.bak	Full backup
2	WebForums_Prod	2011-03-26 14:15:11.000	D:\Backups\WebForums_Prod\WebForums_Prod_backup_2011_03_26_141511_4394531.trn	Log Backup
3	WebForums_Prod	2011-03-26 14:30:08.000	D:\Backups\WebForums_Prod\WebForums_Prod_backup_2011_03_26_143008_5771484.trn	Log Backup
4	WebForums_Prod	2011-03-26 14:45:15.000	D:\Backups\WebForums_Prod\WebForums_Prod_backup_2011_03_26_144515_7509765.trn	Log Backup
5	WebForums_Prod	2011-03-26 15:00:15.000	D:\Backups\WebForums_Prod\WebForums_Prod_backup_2011_03_26_150015_1005859.trn	Log Backup
6	WebForums_Prod	2011-03-26 15:30:08.000	D:\Backups\WebForums_Prod\WebForums_Prod_backup_2011_03_26_153008_0693359.trn	Log Backup
7	WebForums_Prod	2011-03-26 15:47:10.000	D:\Backups\WebForums_Prod\WebForums_Prod_backup_2011_03_26_154656_2109375.trn	Log Backup
8	WebForums_Prod	2011-03-26 16:00:16.000	D:\Backups\WebForums_Prod\WebForums_Prod_backup_2011_03_26_160015_7773437.trn	Log Backup
9	WebForums_Prod	2011-03-26 16:15:06.000	D:\Backups\WebForums_Prod\WebForums_Prod_backup_2011_03_26_161505_9892578.trn	Log Backup
10	WebForums_Prod	2011-03-26 16:30:05.000	D:\Backups\WebForums_Prod\WebForums_Prod_backup_2011_03_26_163005_0781250.trn	Log Backup
11	WebForums_Prod	2011-03-26 16:45:01.000	D:\Backups\WebForums_Prod\WebForums_Prod_backup_2011_03_26_164501_4775390.trn	Log Backup
12	WebForums_Prod	2011-03-26 17:00:01.000	D:\Backups\WebForums_Prod\WebForums_Prod_backup_2011_03_26_170001_4794921.trn	Log Backup
13	WebForums_Prod	2011-03-26 17:15:01.000	D:\Backups\WebForums_Prod\WebForums_Prod_backup_2011_03_26_171501_4423828.trn	Log Backup
14	WebForums_Prod	2011-03-26 17:30:02.000	D:\Backups\WebForums_Prod\WebForums_Prod_backup_2011_03_26_173002_0498046.trn	Log Backup
15	WebForums_Prod	2011-03-26 17:45:03.000	D:\Backups\WebForums_Prod\WebForums_Prod_backup_2011_03_26_174503_2470703.trn	Log Backup
16	WebForums_Prod	2011-03-26 18:00:02.000	D:\Backups\WebForums_Prod\WebForums_Prod_backup_2011_03_26_180002_3300781.trn	Log Backup

Figure 1   Backup history

Previously performed database integrity checks confirm that the database was undamaged at the time that the full backup was taken. Therefore, it's safe to use for the restore. If the corruption was present in that full backup, it'd be necessary to go back and find a previous full backup that didn't have the corruption present in it and use that backup (assuming that an unbroken log chain existed from that backup).

To start the restore, you need a full backup. This can be a full database backup, a full filegroup backup, or a full file backup, as long as the backup used contains all the pages that need restoring. Because we have a full database backup here, use that.

It's interesting to note that in general a differential backup can't be used as the starting backup for a page restore, even if all the pages listed for restore are part of that differential backup. An attempt to do so throws error 3195:

```
Msg 3195, Level 16, State 1, Line 1
Page (1:56610) cannot be restored from this backup set. RESTORE PAGE can
only be used from full backup sets or from the first log or differential
backup taken since the file was added to the database.
```

The syntax is much the same as a normal database restore, with only the additional specification of the pages to be restored. Up to a maximum of a thousand pages can be specified in a single restore statement:

```
RESTORE DATABASE WebForums_Prod
    PAGE = '1:56610, 1:56611, 1:56612, 1:56613, 1:56614'
    FROM DISK = 'D:\Backups\WebForums_Prod.bak'
    WITH NORECOVERY;
```

It's quick to run (21 seconds on my test database, which is 1.6 GB in size), far quicker than a full database restore would be. The messages returned indicate 5 pages were processed, as you'd expect.

NOTE If the restore is to be an offline restore (Standard Edition or below, or damaged critical system tables), the tail of the log needs to be backed up before starting the restore, and the norecovery option must be specified on the log backup. This changes the database state to "recovering."

We're not done yet, though. If you query the table that contains the pages that you've restored, the query runs fine—until it hits the first of the restored pages and returns an error:

```
Msg 829, Level 21, State 1, Line 1
Database ID 22, Page (1:56610) is marked RestorePending, which may indicate
disk corruption. To recover from this state, perform a restore.
```

For the page restore to be complete, the restored pages must be brought up-to-date with the rest of the online portion of the database by restoring log backups. This is why page restores can't be used to restore a table or part of a table to an earlier point in time and why page restores can't be done on a database that's in simple recovery model (as log backups aren't possible in the simple recovery mode).

If you had a differential backup, or several of them, now would be the time to restore the latest of the differential backups (because a differential backup means you can skip all the log backups between the time the full backup was taken and the time the differential backup was taken). The syntax is the same as for the full backup. In this particular scenario there are no differential backups, so you'll move straight on to the log backups.

What you need to do now is to restore all of the log backups, right up to the latest one, all using WITH NORECOVERY. To simplify the process, use the msdb backup tables to generate the restore statements. There's no point in more typing than necessary.

```
DECLARE @DatabaseName VARCHAR(50) = 'WebForums_Prod'

SELECT database_name, backup_start_date,
        CASE Type
                WHEN 'D' THEN 'Full backup'
                WHEN 'I' then 'Differential backup'
        END AS BackupType
    FROM msdb..backupset bs
        INNER JOIN msdb..backupmediafamily bmf
                ON bs.media_set_id = bmf.media_set_id
        WHERE database_name = @DatabaseName
                AND type IN ('D','I')

-- pick the start date of the appropriate full or diff backup from that list
-- and replace the constant below with that value.
DECLARE @BackupStartDate DATETIME = '2011-03-26 13:46:34.000'

SELECT 'RESTORE LOG [' + @DatabaseName + ']
    FROM DISK = ''' + bmf.physical_device_name + '''
    WITH NORECOVERY'
FROM msdb..backupset bs
    INNER JOIN msdb..backupmediafamily bmf
            ON bs.media_set_id = bmf.media_set_id
    WHERE database_name = @DatabaseName
            AND backup_start_date >= @BackupStartDate
            AND type = 'L'
    ORDER BY backup_start_date
```

That generates a nice list of RESTORE LOG commands that can be run. Note that all of them are run using WITH NORECOVERY because there's still one step more to go.

If you query the table again, you get the same error as previously; the pages are still marked RestorePending.

The last thing that you need to do is to take another log backup. This one must be taken after the page restore started. It must have a starting log sequence number (LSN) that's higher than the LSN for any transaction that could've affected those pages.

Note that with an offline restore, the tail-log backup would've been taken prior to the restore starting, and as such no additional log backup would be taken at this point.

If there are scheduled log backups running, then, assuming that you're doing an online restore, you could wait for the next one to run, or you could take an ad hoc log backup immediately. This is not a tail-log backup (though it's referred to as that in some places); it's not taken with the NO_TRUNCATE or NORECOVERY options. It's also worth noting that this log backup can (and probably should) be taken with the COPY_ONLY option so as not to affect the existing log backup chain or any log shipping that may be present.

Once that log backup has been taken, it can then be restored, and this time the restore log can to be run WITH RECOVERY:

```
RESTORE LOG [WebForums_Prod] from DISK =
'D:\Backups\WebForums_Prod\WebForums_Prod_backup_final.trn' WITH RECOVERY
```

That log backup can also run WITH NORECOVERY; often even the last log restore is done with that option to ensure that the database isn't accidentally recovered too soon. If the last log restore is run WITH NORECOVERY, one additional step is needed to recover the database:

```
RESTORE DATABASE [WebForums_Prod] WITH RECOVERY
```

And now that table can be queried without error and the corruption has been repaired. The restored pages are fully available, and (assuming Enterprise Edition) the rest of the database and even the rest of the table were online and available the whole time.

What's coming?

In the current versions of SQL Server (2005, 2008, and 2008 R2) no GUI interface is available for doing page restores. In SQL Server Denali, a GUI wizard has been added to perform page restores. The wizard is fairly straightforward.

First, you need to specify that you want to perform a page-level restore (see figure 2). Then you have to specify the pages you want to restore and verify that backup set (see figure 3).

Once you've done that, click OK to restore the pages from the backup, restore all log backups, take the final log backup and restore that, leaving the pages online and available.

The Check Database Pages button allows you to ensure that the pages entered you entered are valid database pages.

For the paranoid DBA, the Script button produces a T-SQL script detailing what the wizard would do and performs a double-check before running (or perhaps scheduling) the restore.

Figure 2   You'll perform a page-level restore.

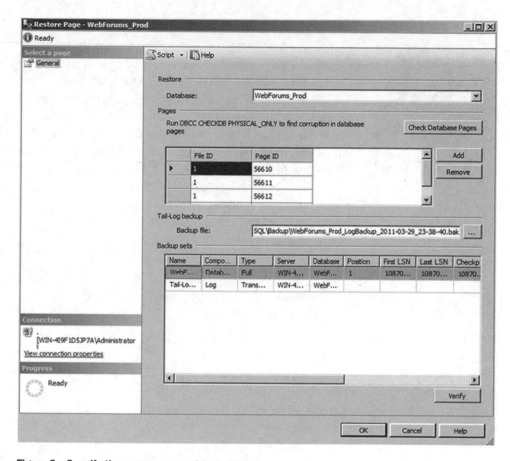

Figure 3 Specify the pages you want to restore.

There's no way to manually add a backup set. The backup sets are read from the backup history tables in msdb. Therefore, if the page restore is being done on a server other than the one where the backups were taken, either you'll have to copy over the backup history or you'll have to perform a page restore using T-SQL scripts.

Summary

The ability to restore individual pages of a database lends a great deal of flexibility when it comes to recovering a critical database in the case of corruption. Restoring only the damaged pages can result in much lower downtime than any other level of restores, an important consideration if you're dealing with a mission-critical database with high availability requirements.

Although performing page restores isn't likely to be something that has to be done on a regular basis, anyone working with large databases should at least be familiar with the technique and requirements in case page restores should become necessary.

About the author

Gail Shaw is a database consultant from Johannesburg, South Africa, specializing in performance tuning and database optimization. Before moving to consulting, she worked at a large South African investment bank and was responsible for the performance of the major systems there. Gail is a frequent poster on the SQLServerCentral forums and writes for the same site. She has presented multiple times at both TechEd Africa and the PASS Community Summit. She was awarded MVP for SQL Server in July 2008.

9 Capacity planning

Greg Larsen

[handwritten: THANK FOR THE WORK ON BOARD]

As a DBA, you have lots of different tasks to take on to manage and maintain your SQL Server environment. You need to install and configure SQL Server, make database schema changes, and perform a slew of other tasks like implementing backups and managing user access security. The list goes on and on. One of the tasks that is occasionally overlooked is capacity planning.

Capacity planning isn't just one task but a number of different tasks. Some people think capacity planning is just disk space management. It's partly that, but it's also more than that. In this chapter I'll discuss managing the space and performance capacity of your SQL Server environment.

There's no single formula for capacity planning. The goal of this chapter is to help you capture capacity planning information and to help you understand why capturing this information is important. It's up to you to decide what capacity planning information is appropriate for your environment and determine how to use that information to better manage your environment. Ultimately, you'll define the rules to adopt for your environment and then modify them over time.

In addition to exploring the concepts of capacity planning, I'll provide some snippets of code. These code snippets will allow you to collect snapshots of capacity information. You can then use these code snippets as the basis for developing an automated collection process for your environment. Keep in mind that most of the code snippets use dynamic management views (DMVs) so they can only be run in SQL Server 2005 or later.

What is capacity planning?

How do we define *capacity planning*? Is it the amount of data SQL Server is currently storing? Is it the amount of disk space being used on each one of your SQL Server drives? Is it the process you use to determine how much data a new system is going to consume when it's implemented on your server? Is it the amount of CPU, memory, and I/O the existing workload is using? Is it the amount of offsite tape storage space being used? Is it the process you use to capture disk space and performance metrics?

Capacity planning is not just one task but is a series of tasks that are performed proactively by DBAs over time to ensure adequate capacity is available before it's too late.

The series of tasks that DBAs take on to do capacity planning covers a broad spectrum of monitoring and managing of SQL Server resources. They measure the physical aspects of hardware, such as disk space, CPU, and memory. But they also take a series of separate hardware measurements over time to produce trend reports of resource usage. By periodically reviewing trend reports, DBAs are able to make sure enough capacity exists to handle todays SQL Server loads, as well as plan appropriately to acquire additional capacity for handling future resource needs.

Gathering current database disk space usage

To show how much disk space each database is using over time, you need to capture the amount of disk space each database is using periodically. How often you capture your disk space usage information depends on how granular you want this information. Keep in mind that the more often you capture this information, the more disk space you'll need to store these metrics. Ironically, you may need to do capacity planning for your metrics database.

What kind of disk space information is important to capture? A database consists of a data and log file, or a series of data and log files if you have multiple files and filegroups. Also, data and log files have both allocated space information and used space information. You need to determine what make sense for you to capture.

I like to capture disk space information weekly. I find it's nice to have disk allocation amount by database as well as the amount used. Having the used space enables me to show more accurately the growth rate of a database.

By having disk space usage information for all databases over time, I can answer the following questions:

- Which database is consuming the most disk space monthly?
- What are the top five database disk space consumers?
- What how much disk space is being consumed monthly by all databases?
- Based on current growth rate, when will I run out of disk space?

There are many more questions that can be asked and answered with disk space usage information. The point is, unless you capture disk space information and do trend analysis you won't have metrics that you can use to predict your future disk space needs.

Enough theory about why capturing disk space information is an important item for capacity management. It's time to move on and talk about methods for capturing this information.

There are two aspects of capturing disk space information you need to think about. The first is how to get the disk space information, and the second is how to store that information. In this chapter I'm not going to discuss where or how to store disk space information, but instead I'll show you how to capture disk space information. Listing 1 shows sample code that you can use to gather the current disk space usage information.

Listing 1   Code that returns disk space usage information

```
-- create temporary table that will store data space used information
CREATE TABLE ##tmp_sfs (
fileid int,
filegroup int,
totalextents int,
usedextents int,
name varchar(1024),
filename varchar(1024) ,
DBName  varchar(128)
);

-- Declare variables
DECLARE @CMD varchar(2000);

-- Command to gather space for each database
SET @CMD = 'DECLARE @DBName varchar(128);
            SET @DBName = ''?'';
            INSERT INTO ##tmp_sfs (fileid,filegroup,totalextents,
                                   usedextents,name,filenamc)
            EXEC (''USE ['' + @DBName + '']
                DBCC SHOWFILESTATS WITH NO_INFOMSGS'');
            UPDATE ##tmp_sfs SET DBName = @DBName WHERE DBName is NULL';

-- Run command against each database
EXEC master.sys.sp_MSforeachdb @CMD ;

SELECT DBName,
       [LOG File(s) Size (KB)] / 1024.0 AS [LogAllocMB],
       [DataAllocMB],
       [DataUsedMB]
FROM
(
   SELECT instance_name as DBName, cntr_value, counter_name
   FROM sys.dm_os_performance_counters
   WHERE counter_name IN
   (
       'Log File(s) Size (KB)'
   )
     AND instance_name not in ('_Total','mssqlsystemresource')
   UNION ALL
   SELECT DBname
     ,totalextents * 8 / 128.0 AS cntr_value
     , 'DataAllocMB' AS counter_name
   FROM ##tmp_sfs
   UNION ALL
   SELECT DBname
     ,usedextents * 8 / 128.0 AS cntr_value
     , 'DataUsedMB' AS counter_name
   FROM ##tmp_sfs
) AS PerfCounters
PIVOT
(
   SUM(cntr_value)
   FOR counter_name IN
   (
       [LOG File(s) Size (KB)],
```

```
        [DataAllocMB],
        [DataUsedMB]
    )
) AS pvt;

-- drop temporary table
DROP TABLE ##tmp_sfs;
```

First, a comment about this code: it uses an undocumented and sometimes unreliable stored procedure, `master.sys.sp_MSforeachdd`. An alternative solution would be to deploy Aaron Bertrand's rewrite of this stored procedure, which you can find at http://mssqltips.com/tip.asp?tip=2201.

This code uses `DBCC SHOWFILESTATS` to collect space information for the data files. This DBCC command is executed against each database and stores space information in a temporary table. The log information is obtained by using the `sys.dm_os_performance_counters` DMV. The data from both these methods is then joined together to output a single record by database showing the disk space usage information, as shown here:

```
DBName              LogAllocMB    DataAllocMB    DataUsedMB
------------------- -----------   -------------  -----------
AdventureWorks      1.992187      176.750000     129.062500
AdventureWorks2008R2 1.992187     284.687500     183.812500
master              8.179687      6.562500       4.375000
model               0.492187      1.250000       1.250000
msdb                0.492187      12.125000      11.500000
tempdb              1.992187      3.125000       1.562500
```

Remember, this chapter is about capacity planning. To perform capacity planning, you need to collect database space usage information over time. I suggest you build a process that uses the code in listing 1 or similar code to periodically save space usage metric information in a SQL Server database table for later analysis.

Performance metrics

Another aspect of managing capacity is managing the performance growth of your server. By *performance growth*, I mean understanding the performance characteristics of your server and how they change. If you're able to track how your SQL Server performance is changing, you'll be able to better understand how new databases and database changes affect your SQL Server performance.

Tracking performance metrics will allow you to produce performance trend graphs that will show how your SQL Server instances performance capacity changes. You won't believe how quickly management will authorize the purchasing of a new machine when you produce a nice colorful graph showing how the various performance metrics are getting close to reaching your machine's theoretical hardware limits. But before you ask for a more powerful machine, you should do everything you can to tune up the machine and applications you have. By taking on the performance improvement effort, you might not even need to purchase a new machine (or you can at least put off the purchase for a while longer).

By regularly capturing various performance metrics, you can answer the following questions:

- How much CPU capacity is being used this month? Compare that to last month, last year, and so on.
- Is the page life expectancy better now that we implemented those coding changes?
- Is the number of concurrent users on our system growing?

There are several ways to capture performance metrics. But because this discussion focuses on DBAs capturing performance metrics, I'm going to focus on how you can capture performance metrics using T-SQL. SQL Server 2005 added DMVs that you can use to capture various performance metrics.

Understanding the CPU load on your system is important. Knowing when you have extended periods of high CPU will provide you with greater insight into when intensive CPU workloads are being run. That way, you can better understand which workloads are using your CPU bandwidth. Also, knowing your CPU trend will let you discover things like whether or not that new application you implemented last month drastically increased the CPU load on your system.

You can use the `sys.dm_os_ring_buffer` DMV to extract CPU utilization. The code snippet in the following listing shows how to use the system health record from the `sys.dm_os_ring_buffer` to retrieve the current processor utilization.

Listing 2   Extract CPU utilization with T-SQL

```
SELECT TOP(1) SQLProcessUtilization AS [SQLServerProcessCPUUtilization]
 FROM (
    SELECT record.value('(./Record/@id)[1]', 'int') AS record_id,
     record.value('(./Record/SchedulerMonitorEvent/SystemHealth
/ProcessUtilization)[1]',
    'int') AS [SQLProcessUtilization], [timestamp]
    FROM (
       SELECT [timestamp], CONVERT(xml, record) AS [record]
       FROM sys.dm_os_ring_buffers
       WHERE ring_buffer_type = N'RING_BUFFER_SCHEDULER_MONITOR'
         AND record LIKE '%<SystemHealth>%') AS x
     ) AS y
 ORDER BY record_id DESC;
```

How you use the CPU utilization number returned from this query will need to be factored into how you've configured your SQL Server machine. Today there are many configurations that use non-uniform memory access (NUMA) or virtual machine technology that may skew the CPU utilization of your physical machine.

You might already be familiar with System Monitor counters like page life expectancy, buffer cache hit ratio, and batch requests per second. These counters are also available by using the `sys.dm_os_performance_counters` DMV. But in order to extract these counters from the DMV, you need to understand how the data is exposed via the DVM.

The sys.dm_os_performance_counters DMV contains a number of counter types and values. Some of these counter values can be used directly to obtain a performance metric, whereas some metrics require you to perform processing logic to obtain a counter value. I'll go through three examples that will show you how to extract performance metrics using this DMV.

First, let me show you how to extract page life expectancy from the sys.dm_os _performance DMV. This DMV returns several counters. Each counter is associated with a cntr_type column; the different cntr_types appear in the following list. For each counter type, I've noted the types of counters that are associated with that type:

- 65792—A counter value that doesn't require calculations to get metrics
- 272696576—Per-second counters; takes two samples to get metrics
- 537003264 and 1073939712—Ratio and ratio base counters; use both counters to calculate metrics

The page life expectancy is associated with cntr_type = 65792. All the counters associated with this counter type can be used directly from this DMV. The following SELECT statement extracts the page life expectancy from this DMV:

```
SELECT cntr_value as PageLifeExpectancy FROM sys.dm_os_performance_counters
    WHERE counter_name = 'Page life expectancy'
      AND object_name = CASE WHEN @@SERVICENAME = 'MSSQLSERVER'
                        THEN    'SQLServer:Buffer Manager'
                        ELSE 'MSSQL$' + rtrim(@@SERVICENAME) +
                            ':Buffer Manager' END;
```

All you'd need to do is change the counter_name and object_name information appropriately to use this coding method to extract those other performance metrics from the DMV provided they're of cntr_type 65792.

The next type of performance counters you can collect from the sys.dm_os _performance_counters DMV are per-second counters. There are a number of per-second counters, such as Page lookups/sec and Page reads/sec. To use these per-second counters, you need to capture two samples of the counter value and then perform some calculations to obtain the per-second counter value. The next listing shows an example of capturing the number of page reads per second.

Listing 3   Capturing the number of page reads per second with T-SQL

```
-- Collect first sample
DECLARE @old_cntr_value INT;
DECLARE @first_sample_date DATETIME;
SELECT @old_cntr_value = cntr_value,
       @first_sample_date = getdate()
FROM sys.dm_os_performance_counters
WHERE counter_name = 'Page reads/sec';

-- Time frame to wait before collecting second sample
WAITFOR DELAY '00:00:10';
```

```
-- Collect second sample and calculate per-second counter
SELECT (cntr_value - @old_cntr_value) /
       DATEDIFF(ss,@first_sample_date, GETDATE()) as PageReadPerSec
FROM sys.dm_os_performance_counters
WHERE counter_name = 'Page reads/sec'
  AND object_name = CASE WHEN @@SERVICENAME = 'MSSQLSERVER'
                         THEN  'SQLServer:Buffer Manager'
                         ELSE 'MSSQL$' + rtrim(@@SERVICENAME)
                              + ':Buffer Manager' END;
```

By looking at this code you can see I captured the first sample of the Page reads/sec counter and placed the value in a local variable, and then waited 10 seconds before capturing the second sample. While capturing the second sample, I subtracted the first sample value from the second sample counter value and then divided that by the number of seconds between the first and second sample. This provided me with the per-second value for the Page reads/sec counter. The reason I have to do this is because the actual cntr_value for per-second counters is the total number for counter items, in this case page reads, since SQL Server started up. You can use this technique to capture any one of the various per-second counter metrics (those counters that have a cntr_type of 272696576).

The last type of counters you can collect from the sys.dm_os_performance _counters DMV are ratio counters. To obtain these counter values, you need to use the counter values from two different related records: the ratio and the base. You can identify these ratio counters by looking at either the object_name or the cntr_type column. If the object name has the word "ratio" in it, then it's a ratio counter. Another way to identify a ratio counter is to see if the cntr_type column entry is either 537003264 or 1073939712. The next listing calculates the buffer cache hit ratio.

Listing 4 Calculating the BufferCacheHitRatio with T-SQL

```
SELECT (a.cntr_value * 1.0 / b.cntr_value) * 100.0 [BufferCacheHitRatio]
FROM (SELECT * FROM sys.dm_os_performance_counters
          WHERE counter_name = 'Buffer cache hit ratio'
            AND object_name = CASE WHEN @@SERVICENAME = 'MSSQLSERVER'
                                   THEN  'SQLServer:Buffer Manager'
                                   ELSE 'MSSQL$' + rtrim(@@SERVICENAME) +
                                        ':Buffer Manager' END ) a
      CROSS JOIN
      (SELECT * from sys.dm_os_performance_counters
          WHERE counter_name = 'Buffer cache hit ratio base'
            and object_name = CASE WHEN @@SERVICENAME = 'MSSQLSERVER'
                                   THEN  'SQLServer:Buffer Manager'
                                   ELSE 'MSSQL$' + rtrim(@@SERVICENAME) +
                                        ':Buffer Manager' END ) b;
```

By looking at this code, you can see that I selected two different sys.dm_os _performance_counter records; one had a counter_name of 'Buffer cache hit ratio' and the other had a counter_name of 'Buffer cache hit ratio base'. I then calculated the buffer cache hit ratio by dividing the cntr_value for the 'Buffer cache hit ratio' record by the cntr_value of the 'Buffer cache hit ratio base' record. You can calculate a ratio metric for any of the ratio/base counters in the sys.dm_os_performance_counter DMV by dividing the cntr_value of the ratio record by the cntr_value of the base record.

To jump-start your effort of collection performance statistics, I have a code sample I'd like to share. This sample code uses the techniques identified earlier to output a single record with multiple performance counters. You can find this sample in listing 5, located at www.manning.com/SQLServerMVPDeepDivesVol2. Use this code as a starting point for helping you develop code to capture performance samples.

Once you have some code to capture performance statistics, you should build a process to periodically collect these statistics. When considering how often to track the statistics, settle on a happy medium where you capture enough information to track performance at the desired granularity but not too much that the performance metric capture process causes a performance impact itself and is hard to maintain.

Summary

In this chapter I discussed a number of aspects of capacity planning. I didn't much discuss the importance of collecting the metrics in a repository, which allows better trend analysis and reporting based on different metrics. These trend reports will provide you with powerful graphical representations of your capacity and performance footprint and are important tools that can be used to identify system performance changes.

As a DBA you owe it to yourself, your customers, and your management to take on some form of capacity planning. By doing so, you can show how fast your databases are growing and how many performance resources are being used over time. This information can be extremely valuable when you're trying to make your point that a new application has adversely impacted performance or when you're trying to justify the purchase of new hardware to management. If you aren't capturing space and performance information for your SQL Server environment today, then I hope this chapter has convinced you to do so and provided ideas on how to capture capacity planning information.

About the author

Greg Larsen has been working with SQL Server since version 6.5. He works for the state of Washington and does part-time consulting for DesignMind, a San Francisco–based consulting company. Greg has written over 150 articles on topics related to SQL Server. He runs a website that contains numerous SQL Server example scripts at www.sqlserverexamples.com. Greg is also an adjunct professor at South Puget Sound Community College. He has been an MVP since 2009. In his spare time, he races and cruises on his sailboat in and around the Pacific Northwest.

10 Discovering your servers with PowerShell and SMO

Joe Webb

You've inherited a SQL Server and you need to collect the relevant information about it. How many databases does it have? When were the backup jobs last run, and were they successful? Are triggers being used in any of the databases? There's a lot to capture and analyze. Fortunately, you don't have to point and click to gather this information. You can use PowerShell and SQL Server Management Objects (SMO) to automatically collect the data and display it in a Microsoft Excel spreadsheet. You can even compare the values to industry-recognized best practices and highlight any differences that need your immediate attention.

In this chapter we'll examine how PowerShell and SMO can be used to automate the analysis and documentation of your SQL Servers.

Using PowerShell and Excel

One of the great things about PowerShell is that it's inherently aware of the Windows platform and many of the software applications installed on it. Accessing email or working with the Windows Management Interface (WMI) can be accomplished easily using PowerShell. That's also the case with Excel.

Excel provides a rich environment for reporting and storing information about your servers. You can use this spreadsheet (sometimes called a *runbook*) to quickly reference a server's configuration information and dependencies.

Fortunately, you can use PowerShell to collect information about your servers and document the findings in an Excel spreadsheet. Listing 1 shows how to instantiate a new Excel worksheet from within PowerShell.

Listing 1   Creating an Excel worksheet using PowerShell

```
#Create a new Excel object using COM
$Excel = New-Object -ComObject Excel.Application;
$Excel.visible = $True;
$Excel = $Excel.Workbooks.Add();
$Sheet = $Excel.Worksheets.Item(1);
```

Notice that a new workbook and worksheet is being added to an instance of the Excel application. Throughout the rest of this chapter, you'll reference the $Sheet variable as you populate it with configuration properties and other relevant information collected from the SQL Server instance.

Using SMO with PowerShell

SQL Server Management Objects (SMO) is a class library that allows you to programmatically administer SQL Server 2000, SQL Server 2005, SQL Server 2008, and SQL Server 2008 R2 instances. You can easily access SMO through a variety of programming languages, including PowerShell.

NOTE   The SMO class library assemblies are installed automatically during the installation of SQL Server client tools such as Management Studio. If you don't have the client tools on your computer, you can download and install the SMO assemblies from the Microsoft website.

To use SMO in PowerShell, you must first load the assembly in your PowerShell script. This may be done using the LoadWithPartialName static method of the assembly class, as demonstrated in the following listing. The command is piped to the out-null cmdlet to suppress output to the console window.

Listing 2   Loading the SMO reference library

```
#Load the assembly and read the list of servers from a file
[System.Reflection.Assembly]::LoadWithPartialName
('Microsoft.SqlServer.SMO') | out-null;
```

Once the assembly has been loaded, you can use it to instantiate objects from its class library. For the examples in this chapter, you'll create a Server object, as illustrated in the next listing. The $instance variable contains the name of the SQL Server instance to which you wish to connect in the form of servername\instancename. For this example, you'll connect to the default instance of the local machine.

Listing 3   Creating a `Server` object from the SMO class library

```
#Create an SMO connection to the instance
$instance = "(local)";
$server = New-Object ('Microsoft.SqlServer.Management.Smo.Server')
 $instance;
```

Collecting instance and machine information

To prepare the Excel spreadsheet to receive the instance and machine information, you'll first add some column header information to the spreadsheet. You'll start in the first column of the third row and add column header information, and then work your way across the spreadsheet. The following listing provides the PowerShell script used to add the headers.

> **Listing 4   Creating the column headers in Excel**

```
#Define the start row
$row = 3;

#Create column headers for the instance
$Sheet.Cells.Item($row,1) = "INSTANCE NAME:";
$Sheet.Cells.Item($row,2) = $instance;
$Sheet.Cells.Item($row,1).Font.Bold = $True;
$Sheet.Cells.Item($row,2).Font.Bold = $True;

$row++;

#Create server column headers
$Sheet.Cells.Item($row,1) = "Edition";
$Sheet.Cells.Item($row,2) = "OS Version";
$Sheet.Cells.Item($row,3) = "Physical Memory";
$Sheet.Cells.Item($row,4) = "Product";
$Sheet.Cells.Item($row,5) = "Platform";
$Sheet.Cells.Item($row,6) = "Processors";
$Sheet.Cells.Item($row,7) = "Version";
$Sheet.Cells.Item($row,8) = "Product Level";
$Sheet.Cells.Item($row,9) = "Login Mode";
$Sheet.Cells.Item($row,10) = "Linked Servers";
$Sheet.Cells.Item($row,11) = "Databases";
$Sheet.Cells.Item($row,12) = "Min. Memory";
$Sheet.Cells.Item($row,13) = "Max. Memory";
$Sheet.Cells.Item($row,14) = "CLR Enabled";
$Sheet.Cells.Item($row,15) = "Collation";
$Sheet.Cells.Item($row,16) = "Num Of Log Files";
$Sheet.Cells.Item($row,17) = "Total Jobs";


#Format the server column headers
for ($col = 1; $col -le 17; $col++){
    $Sheet.Cells.Item($row,$col).Font.Bold = $True;
    $Sheet.Cells.Item($row,$col).Interior.ColorIndex = 48;
    $Sheet.Cells.Item($row,$col).Font.ColorIndex = 34;
    }
```

The first portion of the script places the instance name just above the column headers. This can be helpful if you're looping through a collection of servers rather than only one.

The next section of the script creates 17 column headers for properties such as the edition of SQL Server, the amount of memory available in the computer, and the total number of SQL Agent jobs defined. The final section of the script formats the column headers.

Once the column headers have been created, you can collect the values for the properties described by the headers. You'll use the Information property to gather much of the required information, such as the edition, the OS version, and the amount of physical memory in the machine. The next listing demonstrates how the server object may be examined programmatically with PowerShell.

Listing 5   Collecting the SQL Server instance and machine information

```
#Collect the SQL Server and machine information
$Sheet.Cells.Item($row, 1) = $server.Information.Edition;
$Sheet.Cells.Item($row, 2) = $server.Information.OSVersion;
$Sheet.Cells.Item($row, 3) = $server.Information.PhysicalMemory;
$Sheet.Cells.Item($row, 4) = $server.Information.Product;
$Sheet.Cells.Item($row, 5) = $server.Information.Platform;
$Sheet.Cells.Item($row, 6) = $server.Information.Processors;
$Sheet.Cells.Item($row, 7) = $server.Information.Version;
$Sheet.Cells.Item($row, 8) = $server.Information.ProductLevel;
$Sheet.Cells.Item($row, 9) = $server.Settings.LoginMode.ToString();
$Sheet.Cells.Item($row, 10) = $server.LinkedServers.Count;
$Sheet.Cells.Item($row, 11) = $server.Databases.Count;
$Sheet.Cells.Item($row, 12) =
    $server.Configuration.MinServerMemory.ConfigValue;
$Sheet.Cells.Item($row, 13) =
    $server.Configuration.MaxServerMemory.ConfigValue;
$Sheet.Cells.Item($row, 14) = $server.Configuration.IsSqlClrEnabled.RunValue;
$Sheet.Cells.Item($row, 15) = $server.Information.Collation;
$Sheet.Cells.Item($row, 16) = $server.numberOfLogFiles;
$Sheet.Cells.Item($row, 17) = $server.JobServer.Jobs.Count;
```

Notice that the Server.Information.Edition property reveals the SQL Server edition of the instance. This information is being saved to the column of the current row in the Excel spreadsheet. The OSVersion is being saved to the second column, and so on. The Server.Settings.LoginMode property is used to determine the authentication mode set for the instance.

The Count property of the LinkedServers, Databases, and JobServer.Jobs properties are used to determine the number of linked servers, databases, and SQL Agent jobs for this server.

Collecting SQL Agent job information

After collecting information, you'll interrogate the job server for scheduled jobs and their statuses. Once again, you'll create some column headers in the Excel spreadsheet.

The following listing documents the column information to be collected and formats the headers.

Listing 6   Creating row headers for job information

```
#Increment the row counter
$row++;
$row++;

#Create the column headers for the jobs in this instance
$Sheet.Cells.Item($row,1) = "JOB NAME";
$Sheet.Cells.Item($row,2) = "ENABLED";
$Sheet.Cells.Item($row,3) = "LAST RUN DATE";
$Sheet.Cells.Item($row,4) = "LAST RUN OUTCOME";

#Format the job column headers
for ($col = 1; $col -le 4; $col++){
    $Sheet.Cells.Item($row,$col).Font.Bold = $True;
    $Sheet.Cells.Item($row,$col).Interior.ColorIndex = 48;
    $Sheet.Cells.Item($row,$col).Font.ColorIndex = 34;
        }
```

The `server.JobServer.Jobs` property contains much of the information you'll want to examine as part of your SQL Server audit. For each job, you'll report its name, whether or not it's enabled, the last time it ran, and whether or not it completed successfully during its last run. This next listing shows the PowerShell script used to collect and format this information.

Listing 7   Collecting SQL Server Agent job information

```
#Collect information for each job on this instance
foreach($job in $server.JobServer.Jobs){
    $Sheet.Cells.Item($row, 1) = $job.Name;
    $Sheet.Cells.Item($row, 2) = $job.IsEnabled;
    $Sheet.Cells.Item($row, 3) = $job.LastRunDate;
    $Sheet.Cells.Item($row, 4) = $job.LastRunOutcome.ToString();
    switch ($job.LastRunOutcome.ToString()){
        "Failed" {$Sheet.Cells.item($row, 4).Interior.ColorIndex = 3}
        "Succeeded" {$Sheet.Cells.item($row, 4).Interior.ColorIndex = 0}
        }

    $row++;
}
```

Notice that a value of 0 for the `LastRunOutcome` property indicates that the job didn't complete successfully during its last run. Also notice that the script uses the `switch` flow control statement to highlight any job failures by turning the color of the cell bright red.

Collecting database information

Now that the job information has been recorded in the spreadsheet, let's examine each database attached to the SQL Server instance. The following listing creates the column header for the database information.

Listing 8   Creating the row headers for database information

```
$row++
$row++;

#Create column headers for the databases in this instance
$Sheet.Cells.Item($row,1) = "DATABASE NAME";
$Sheet.Cells.Item($row,2) = "COLLATION";
$Sheet.Cells.Item($row,3) = "COMPATIBILITY LEVEL";
$Sheet.Cells.Item($row,4) = "AUTOSHRINK";
$Sheet.Cells.Item($row,5) = "RECOVERY MODEL";
$Sheet.Cells.Item($row,6) = "SIZE (MB)";
$Sheet.Cells.Item($row,7) = "SPACE AVAILABLE (MB)";
$Sheet.Cells.Item($row,8) = "AUTOCLOSE";
$Sheet.Cells.Item($row,9) = "CREATEDATE";
$Sheet.Cells.Item($row,10) = "AUTOCREATESTATISTICSENABLED";
$Sheet.Cells.Item($row,11) = "AUTOUPDATESTATISTICSENABLED";
$Sheet.Cells.Item($row,12) = "DATASPACEUSAGE (MB)";
$Sheet.Cells.Item($row,13) = "INDEXSPACEUSAGE (MB)";
$Sheet.Cells.Item($row,14) = "LASTBACKUPDATE";
$Sheet.Cells.Item($row,15) = "LASTDIFFERENTIALBACKUPDATE";
$Sheet.Cells.Item($row,16) = "LASTLOGBACKUPDATE";
$Sheet.Cells.Item($row,17) = "LOGFILES";
$Sheet.Cells.Item($row,18) = "LOGSIZE";
$Sheet.Cells.Item($row,19) = "LOGLOCATION";
$Sheet.Cells.Item($row,20) = "OWNER";
$Sheet.Cells.Item($row,21) = "PRIMARYFILEPATH";
$Sheet.Cells.Item($row,22) = "TABLES";
$Sheet.Cells.Item($row,23) = "VIEWS";
$Sheet.Cells.Item($row,24) = "PROCEDURES";
$Sheet.Cells.Item($row,25) = "FUNCTIONS";
$Sheet.Cells.Item($row,26) = "TRIGGERS";
$Sheet.Cells.Item($row,27) = "STATUS";
$Sheet.Cells.Item($row,28) = "PAGEVERIFYCHECKSUM";

#Format the database column headers
for ($col = 1; $col -le 28; $col++){
    $Sheet.Cells.Item($row,$col).Font.Bold = $True;
    $Sheet.Cells.Item($row,$col).Interior.ColorIndex = 48;
    $Sheet.Cells.Item($row,$col).Font.ColorIndex = 34;
    }

$row++;
```

To gather database information from the SQL Server instance, you'll employ the Databases collection of the Server object. You'll iterate through each database attached to the instance using a `foreach` flow control construct and examine its properties. This next listing demonstrates this technique.

Listing 9 Collecting database information

```
$dbs = $server.Databases;

#Examine each database in the collection
foreach ($db in $dbs) {
    #Perform some calculations and format the results
    $dbSpaceAvailable = $db.SpaceAvailable/1KB;
    $dbDataSpaceUsage = $db.DataSpaceUsage/1KB;
        $dbIndexSpaceUsage= $db.IndexSpaceUsage/1KB;
    $dbSpaceAvailable = "{0:N3}" -f $dbSpaceAvailable;


    $Sheet.Cells.Item($row, 1) = $db.Name;
    $Sheet.Cells.Item($row, 2) = $db.Collation;
    $Sheet.Cells.Item($row, 3) = $db.CompatibilityLevel;
    $Sheet.Cells.Item($row, 4) = $db.AutoShrink;
    switch ($db.AutoShrink){
        "False" {$Sheet.Cells.item($row, 4).Interior.ColorIndex = 0}
        "True" {$Sheet.Cells.item($row, 4).Interior.ColorIndex = 3}
        }
    $Sheet.Cells.Item($row, 5) = $db.RecoveryModel.ToString();
    $Sheet.Cells.Item($row, 6) = "{0:N3}" -f $db.Size;
    if ($dbSpaceAvailable -lt 1.00){
        $fgColor = 3;
        }
    else{
        $fgColor = 0;
        }
    $Sheet.Cells.Item($row, 7) = $dbSpaceAvailable ;
    $Sheet.Cells.item($intRow, 7).Interior.ColorIndex = $fgColor;

    $Sheet.Cells.Item($row, 8) =  $db.AUTOCLOSE ;
    switch ($db.AutoClose){
        "False" {$Sheet.Cells.item($row, 8).Interior.ColorIndex = 0}
        "True" {$Sheet.Cells.item($row, 8).Interior.ColorIndex = 3}
        }
    $Sheet.Cells.Item($row, 9) =  $db.CREATEDATE;
    $Sheet.Cells.Item($row, 10) = $db.AUTOCREATESTATISTICSENABLED;
    switch ($db.AUTOCREATESTATISTICSENABLED){
        "True" {$Sheet.Cells.item($row, 10).Interior.ColorIndex = 0}
        "False" {$Sheet.Cells.item($row, 10).Interior.ColorIndex = 3}
        }
    $Sheet.Cells.Item($row, 11) = $db.AUTOUPDATESTATISTICSENABLED;
    switch ($db.AUTOUPDATESTATISTICSENABLED){
        "True" {$Sheet.Cells.item($row, 11).Interior.ColorIndex = 0}
        "False" {$Sheet.Cells.item($row, 11).Interior.ColorIndex = 3}
        }
    $Sheet.Cells.Item($row,12) = $dbDataSpaceUsage;
    $Sheet.Cells.Item($row,13) = $dbIndexSpaceUsage;
```

```
$Sheet.Cells.Item($row,14) = $db.LastBackupDate;

if (((get-date) - $db.LastBackupDate).days -gt 1) {
    $fgColor = 3;
    }
else {
    $fgColor = 0;
    }
$Sheet.Cells.Item($intRow,14) = $db.LastBackupDate;
$Sheet.Cells.item($intRow,14).Interior.ColorIndex = $fgColor;


$Sheet.Cells.Item($row,15) = $db.LASTDIFFERENTIALBACKUPDATE;

if (($db.RecoveryModel -ne 3) -and ($db.LASTLOGBACKUPDATE -eq
"12:00:00 AM")) {
    $fgColor = 3;
    }
else{
    $fgColor = 0;
    }
$Sheet.Cells.Item($row,16) = $db.LASTLOGBACKUPDATE;
$Sheet.Cells.item($row,16).Interior.ColorIndex = $fgColor;

$i = 0;
$logFileSize = 0;
$logFileName = "";

$logs = $db.LogFiles;
foreach ($log in $logs) {
    $i++;
    $logName = $log.Name;
    $logFileName = $log.FileName;
    $logFileSize += $log.Size;
    }

$Sheet.Cells.Item($row,17) = $i;
$Sheet.Cells.Item($row,18) = $logFileSize;

if($i -eq 1) {
    $Sheet.Cells.Item($row,19) = $logFileName;
    }
else {
    $Sheet.Cells.Item($row,19) = "(multiple)";
    }


$Sheet.Cells.Item($row,20) = $db.OWNER;
switch ($db.Owner){
    "sa" {$Sheet.Cells.item($row, 20).Interior.ColorIndex = 0}
    default {$Sheet.Cells.item($row, 20).Interior.ColorIndex = 3}
    }
```

```
$dbpath = $db.PRIMARYFILEPATH;
if($logFileName.SubString(0, 3) -eq $dbpath.SubString(0,3)) {
    $fgColor = 3;
    }
else {
    $fgColor = 0;
    }

$Sheet.Cells.Item($row,21) = $dbpath;
$Sheet.Cells.item($row,21).Interior.ColorIndex = $fgColor;


$Sheet.Cells.Item($row,22) = $db.Tables.Count;
$Sheet.Cells.Item($row,23) = $db.Views.Count;
$Sheet.Cells.Item($row,24) = $db.StoredProcedures.Count;
$Sheet.Cells.Item($row,25) = $db.UserDefinedFunctions.Count;
$Sheet.Cells.Item($row,26) = $db.Triggers.Count;
$Sheet.Cells.Item($row,27) = $db.Status;

$Sheet.Cells.Item($row,28) = $db.pageVerify;
switch ($db.Owner){
    "Checksum" {$Sheet.Cells.item($row, 28).Interior.ColorIndex = 0}
    default {$Sheet.Cells.item($row, 28).Interior.ColorIndex = 3}
    }

    $row++;
}
```

Notice that the script loops through each database in the Databases collection and retrieves its name, collation, and compatibility level, among other things. As with prior scripts, some settings are interpreted as they're being reported.

The script compares some values against commonly accepted best practices and highlights any departures from those best practices in red. The AutoClose setting is an example of this analysis during the collection.

NOTE A highlighted cell in the spreadsheet doesn't necessarily indicate that the setting is wrong or inherently bad. It may make sense in this instance to have that setting. A highlighted cell only indicates that further investigation into the setting is warranted.

Summary

When combined with SMO and Microsoft Excel, PowerShell can make for an incredibly robust and rich automation environment, allowing administrators to collect, analyze, and document SQL Server settings with a minimal amount of effort. With a little additional effort, the scripts provided in this chapter may be extended to collect settings and information from a collection of SQL Servers from across the corporate network.

About the author

Joe Webb has served as Chief Operating Manager for WebbTech Solutions, a Nashville-based consulting company, since its inception. He has more than 15 years of industry experience and has consulted extensively with companies in the areas of business process analysis and improvements, database design and architecture, software development, and technical training.

In addition to helping his consulting clients, Joe enjoys writing and speaking at technical conferences. He has spoken at conferences in Europe and North America and has authored or coauthored three books: *SQL Server MVP Deep Dives* (Manning, 2009), *The Rational Guide to SQL Server Notification Services* (Rational Press, 2004), and *The Rational Guide to IT Consulting* (Rational Press, 2004).

Joe is a seven-time recipient of the prestigious Microsoft MVP Award for demonstrating a willingness to share his expertise with the SQL Server Community.

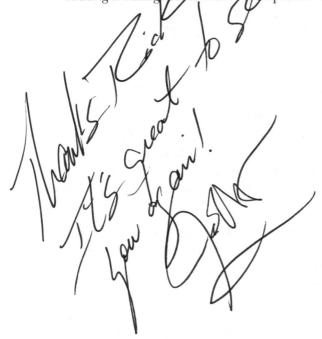

11 Will the real Mr. Smith please stand up?

John Magnabosco

A glittery wall of yellow, adorned with the images of three blue figures of questionable candor, slides quickly to the left to reveal three mysteriously silhouetted individuals. As the television camera spans the stage and the lights illuminate each one, the host begins to paint an individual's life story, describing how that person has beaten the odds and found his own slice of success. With the final question from the host, "What is your name, please?" each person confidently responds "I am Mr. Smith!"

This puzzling scenario comes straight from the classic television archives of a game show titled "To Tell the Truth." The premise is that through a series of questions and answers, the true holder of the claimed identity is revealed. This scenario staged on a Burbank, California television set offers a great deal of entertainment—but when presented with the nightmare of having to prove your identity amid a host of disingenuous characters claiming it for their own, it's not anyone's idea of a good time.

The databases that you architect and maintain often contain data that's utilized for identification purposes. This type of information in the right hands can be powerful in various aspects, such as diagnosing and treating illnesses, performing financial transactions, and analyzing statistics. In the wrong hands, the impact of accessing this information can be devastating. It can result in identity theft, discrimination, and in some cases violent harassment. Data security and integrity has been a long-standing pillar of our profession. In this day and age, where personally identifiable data is shoveled into your databases like coal into a locomotive, you're challenged to expand the vista of security and embrace your role as a guardian who advocates for those who have entrusted us with their most valuable asset: their data.

Personally identifiable data

What is this thing called *personally identifiable data*? In a nutshell, personally identifiable data is information that uniquely describes an individual. It's the data captured in the database that designates you as a purchaser of an order. It's the data that can be used to contact you or identify your location. It's the information that you provide to the bank teller who grants you access to funds in an account. It's the information that provides the means to obtain a license to drive.

An extensive, all-inclusive list of the data elements that are categorized as personally identifiable data can be challenging to obtain. It can vary from country to country depending on the privacy laws that have been established by governing bodies and industry regulators. There are, though, some data elements that are generally recognized. Here are a few examples:

- Federal identification number
- Driver's license number
- Date of birth
- Individual's full name, especially if unique, rare, or well known
- Financial account numbers, such as credit card or banking account numbers
- Fingerprints (and other biometric information)
- DNA molecule information

To the person whose identity this data validates, it's their passport to maneuver through society. To the person fraudulently claiming the personally identifiable data as their own, it can grant them access to another person's funds or the ability to commit crimes under a stolen identity, presenting legal issues for the valid and innocent holder of the identity.

The responsibility for a database that contains personally identifiable data is one that exceeds the typical concerns of the latest backup or tuning the latest resource-gorging query. A DBA must take on the roles of a guardian, defender, and superhero.

Today's superhero: the DBA

As a child I thoroughly enjoyed waking early on a Saturday morning, grabbing my bowl of brightly colored rings floating in a sea of milk, and watching "The Justice League." This was a cartoon series that presented a dream team of superheroes collaborating to fight the forces of evil in the world. If the Justice League was assembled today, I believe that it'd have a slightly different lineup. It would be one that would include a superhero who represents the protection of the innocent from the diabolical activities of those who misuse personally identifiable data. This superhero would be none other than the DBA.

Our superpowers

Every superhero possesses superpowers. Some may be able bend steel with their bare hands whereas others can run fast as a lightning bolt. The DBA is no exception. As a

DBA, you truly do have superpowers that you must develop and maintain to protect personally identifiable data. These superpowers are *data conservation* and *ambassadorship*.

DATA CONSERVATION

The first superpower that you possess is a deep understanding of the power and value of data. Although other roles in a business may value data as something that's consumed for the benefit of a project or periodic task, as a DBA you value data as a living entity. It's something to be conserved, nurtured, and protected. You're in a natural position to be concerned about your customer's personally identifiable data and are quick to question why it needs to be stored and how it's going to be used. You're literally the last line of defense when it comes to consumer data advocacy.

AMBASSADORSHIP

The second superpower that you possess is the magic combination of regulatory compliance and technical acumen. When you're knowledgeable about governmental laws in regard to data, industry requirements with which your business must comply, and general information security best practices, you are indeed an asset. In a business that has a department that focuses on compliance issues, you're a partner in determining the most effective and efficient solutions to protect the business from noncompliance. For the IT department, you can interpret the compliance requirements into actionable tasks so that they can be successfully implemented.

Tools of the trade

Superpowers are nice, but there are times when a simple tool will suffice. Our favorite superhero would never use his laser beam eyes to cook a can of pork and beans when a microwave will do the job. The following are a handful of tools that are available to you as a DBA.

RETENTION POLICIES

It's easy for a business to claim the need for data to be perpetually available online. The "You never know when you need it" anthem can be heard in boardrooms around the world and that hypnotic rhythm of convenient on-demand access to data is hard to resist. But this level of availability does come with a price. The cost of hardware and personnel to support the volume of data increases over time. In addition, you must take into account legal requirements, such as the Sarbanes–Oxley Act of 2002, that define archival and destruction requirements for personally identifiable data in an effort to protect customers and businesses.

   If your business doesn't have a retention policy in place, lead a collaborative effort to develop a policy. Once the policy is in place, become familiar with it and participate in its enforcement.

ROLE-BASED PERMISSIONS

Shakespeare once wrote, "All the world's a stage, and all the men and women merely players." There are times when I wonder if he had databases in mind. Considering that he lived before the word *data* was even a part of the common lexicon, I guess that's unlikely. Nonetheless, this statement certainly applies to anyone who desires access to data. You have players that write and read data and you have players that simply read data. There are data elements you wish to disclose to all and data elements you wish to disclose to a select few. Applying these levels of access individually can be challenging.

Role-based permissions provide the ability to define data access levels to a given collection of users, known as a *role*, in a simplified, consistent, and reliable manner. To learn more about implementing security for SQL Server databases, refer to http://msdn.microsoft.com/en-us/library/bb510418.aspx.

DATA SEPARATION

Ask the question "Why does my refrigerator have a separate compartment for a freezer?" and you'll likely receive a glare of disdain followed by the obvious answer: "To keep the items in the fridge from freezing." When it comes to sensitive data and nonsensitive data in your database, the same is true: through the separation of these types of data you can more easily manage their access and integrity.

SQL Server offers database object schemas as a security and organizational feature to database architecture. When you use this feature, you can efficiently manage role-based permissions to all database objects contained within a database object schema. For example, say a database object schema called Customer contains a collection of tables, views, and stored procedures. Another database object schema called Product also contains a collection of tables, views, and stored procedures. Access to all the items in the Customer database object schema can be granted or denied by managing the permissions to the database object schema itself rather than all the individual objects.

Consider building a schema for personally identifiable data elements that's distinct from the ones used for standard data elements. To learn more about database object schemas, visit http://msdn.microsoft.com/en-us/library/dd283095.aspx.

OBFUSCATION

There have been times, when asked for my federal identification number, that I've been tempted to respond with the hexadecimal conversion of its value. It would successfully transmit the requested data, but it wouldn't be useful to anyone unless the recipient held the key to its conversion to a recognizable format. This temptation is muted by the great chance that the federal tax authorities may not appreciate my sense of humor.

Several forms of obfuscation are available to you to help protect personally identifiable data. Here are a few examples:

- *Encryption*—This approach requires a hierarchy of symmetric keys, asymmetric keys, or passwords to encrypt plain text to an unrecognizable format and decrypt the encrypted value to its original plain-text value. To learn more about encryption and how it's implemented, refer to my book *Protecting SQL Server Data*, available through Simple-Talk Publishing (http://www.simple-talk.com/books/sql-books/).
- *Hashing*—This approach is similar to encryption with the exception that once the plain text has been encrypted it can't be decrypted. A comparison between the stored hash and a requested hash implicitly reveals the underlying value.

This approach is commonly used for storage of passwords in a database. You can use the `HASHBYTES` method to hash a plain-text value. Here's a sample of how the method is used to obfuscate plain text:

```
SELECT HASHBYTES('SHA1','Plain Text Value');
```

- *Repeating character masking*—This approach replaces a predefined number of characters with a single repeating character. Credit card receipts commonly use this method to hide the account number by replacing all the numbers, except the last four digits, with an asterisk. Character masking is accomplished through the use of the `REPLICATE` method. The following is a sample of how the `REPLICATE` method is used to obfuscate plain text:

```
SELECT REPLICATE('*',6) + RIGHT('0123456789',4);
```

- *Encoding*—This approach use a code to represent a plain-text value. This code would be understood by a finite group of individuals. This technique is often used to identify classification of diseases in health-care systems. For example, the coding used to identify a benign colon polyp is 211.3.

EDUCATION AND EVANGELISM

Among all the tools we've discussed there is one that's a matter of passion and awareness. It's a tool that doesn't require a computer, a policy, or a single digit of code. It's the education and evangelism of data conservation.

Each of us has a digital footprint that grows on a daily basis. With each transaction, purchase, or install of a cell phone application, your personally identifiable data is being transmitted and stored. You can participate in educating the general public in how to protect themselves. You can raise awareness among other data professionals whether they're DBAs, analysts, or data-hungry executives. You can help your employer by creating and participating in training for employees who handle personally identifiable data on a daily basis. As a result, your influence is expanded in a way that raises the confidence of your customers and creates an increasingly data-sensitive environment.

Summary

There are many dimensions to your responsibilities as a DBA: optimizing the performance of a database, constructing a properly normalized data structure, or efficiently and reliably moving data from one system to another. But in your daily tasks, don't lose sight of the fact that you're a superhero in the world of information security.

The superpowers that you possess must be exercised to prevent atrophy. As you gaze upon your collection of SQL Server manuals, consider expanding the bookshelf to include books on the subject of data privacy and security. Through your study on this subject, you'll build and maintain an intuitive awareness and sensitivity about personally identifiable data.

The tools available to you are more effective when you've invested time in their mastery. Exercise data retention best practices, permit access to personally identifiable data on a need-to-know basis, and isolate sensitive data from standard data. In times of storage and transmission, always use a method of obfuscation to ensure that data isn't intercepted and used by unintended parties. Most important of all, step away from the computer and passionately educate.

About the author

John Magnabosco, Data Coach at Defender Direct in Indianapolis, is passionate about the security of sensitive data that we all store in our databases. He's the author of *Protecting SQL Server Data*, published by Simple Talk Publishing. Additionally, he co-founded IndyPASS and IndyTechFest, and blogs regularly at Simple-Talk.com. In 2009 and 2010, John was honored to receive the SQL Server MVP designation. When his attention is drawn to recreation, he enjoys writing, listening to music, and tending to his chile garden.

12 Build your own SQL Server 2008 performance dashboard

Pawel Potasinski

Have you ever seen any of the fantastic applications for monitoring performance of database systems? How wonderful your life as a DBA would be if you could sit in your chair, looking at a big screen full of information showing how your server and databases are performing and, what's even more important, how to react when an issue occurs. This is why powerful tools for monitoring SQL Server databases are popular and worth their price.

But what if the budget doesn't allow you to buy any additional software and you have to rely only on the information that SQL Server itself gives you? The purpose of this chapter is to give you some ideas on how to use SQL Server features, like Common Language Runtime (CLR), dynamic management views (DMVs), and SQL Server Reporting Services (SSRS), to create your own performance dashboard that will prove helpful in your everyday DBA work.

The approach proposed in this chapter can be implemented in SQL Server 2005 and later (where CLR, DMVs, and SSRS are available).

DMVs as the source of performance-related information

I think that Books Online, the official SQL Server documentation, contains the best definition of the DMVs: "Dynamic management views and functions return server state information that can be used to monitor the health of a server instance, diagnose problems, and tune performance." DMVs are a great source of performance-related information.

I won't cover the DMVs in this chapter; instead, I encourage you to become familiar with all of them on your own. To do so, you can run the query from listing 1 to view all the dynamic objects available in your SQL Server instance, check the

SQL Server documentation for more details, and play with them to see the information they provide. For a good reference on DMVs I recommend a series of articles titled "A DMV a Day" by Glenn Berry (SQL Server MVP and author of chapter 31) available on Glenn's blog: http://sqlserverperformance.wordpress.com/2010/05/02/recap-of-april-2010-dmv-a-day-series/.

Listing 1   Query to list dynamic views and functions

```
SELECT N'sys.' + name AS [name],
    type_desc
FROM sys.system_objects
WHERE name like N'dm[_]%'
ORDER BY name
```

Later in this chapter, I use a DMV to present a sample solution for creating a performance dashboard, but you can use more of them in your own custom dashboards if you desire.

Using SQLCLR to get the performance counter values

As a DBA, you've probably used Performance Monitor (perfmon.exe) to measure hardware and operating system performance. The problem with using PerfMon is that only a subset of its counters is available for a SQL Server 2008 instance using the sys.dm_os_performance_counters DMV. But using the SQLCLR lets you create a Microsoft .NET–based user-defined scalar function in every version from SQL Server 2005 on to get the value of every counter registered in the OS of the server. Let me show you how.

First you have to enable CLR integration in SQL Server. You can do so by setting the 'clr enabled' server configuration option, as shown in the next listing.

Listing 2   T-SQL code for enabling CLR integration in SQL Server 2008

```
EXEC sp_configure 'clr enabled', 1;
RECONFIGURE;
```

NOTE Make sure your company or organization policies allow you to enable CLR integration. In some environments the security policy is rigorous and .NET-based user-defined objects can't be used in SQL Server databases.

Then you can start to develop the .NET code of the function. The easiest way to create a CLR object is to use one of the "big" Visual Studio 2008 or later editions (for example, Professional Edition) and create a new project from the SQL Server Project template (see figure 1).

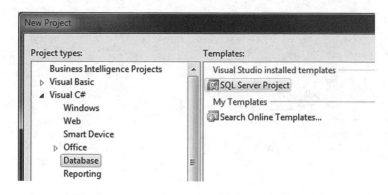

Figure 1 Creating a new project based on the SQL Server Project template in Visual Studio 2008 Professional

NOTE   If you use a version of Visual Studio that doesn't contain the SQL Server Project template, you can use the Class Library template instead. If you do so, you have to add a project reference to the Microsoft.SqlServer .Server library to be able to use the Microsoft.SqlServer.Server name-space in the code and to compile the project into a DLL file that can be imported to the SQL Server database as a new assembly. You'll find an article on how to create a SQLCLR assembly and related objects without using SQL Server Project template here: http://msdn.microsoft.com/en -us/library/ms131052.aspx.

In the project, create a user-defined function item (or a class if you're using the Class Library template). Use the `System.Diagnostics` namespace and classes from it to get the performance counter values. Example code for the function may look like that shown in the next listing.

Listing 3   C# code of user-defined function that returns value of a performance counter

```csharp
using System;
using System.Data;
using System.Data.SqlClient;
using System.Data.SqlTypes;
using Microsoft.SqlServer.Server;
using System.Diagnostics;

public partial class UserDefinedFunctions
{
    [Microsoft.SqlServer.Server.SqlFunction]
    public static SqlDouble ufn_clr_GetPerfCounterValue(
      SqlString CategoryName,
      SqlString CounterName,
      SqlString InstanceName,
      SqlString MachineName
    )
```

```
    {
        MachineName = MachineName.IsNull ? "." : MachineName.Value;
        PerformanceCounter p = new PerformanceCounter(
          CategoryName.Value,
          CounterName.Value,
          InstanceName.Value,
          MachineName.Value);
        float value = p.NextValue();
        System.Threading.Thread.Sleep(100);
        value = p.NextValue();
        return new SqlDouble(value);
    }
};
```

In listing 3 the `ufn_clr_GetPerfCounterValue` method of the `UserDefinedFunctions` class is defined with the `SqlFunction` attribute, which describes the type of an object. The `PerformanceCounter` class and its `NextValue` method are used to get the value of a particular counter.

NOTE   Notice that in this example the `NextValue` method is called twice. This is because the first call initiates the counter and the second one gets the value. You may perform the following test: remove one call of the `Next-Value` method, deploy the project to the database, use the function, and verify that the value returned by the function doesn't represent the value of the counter.

The assembly containing the code in listing 3 has to be given the `UNSAFE` permission set in SQL Server database. According to security best practices, you should do the following:

- Sign the assembly with a strong name (this can be done in Visual Studio in the project properties window or by using the sn.exe command-line utility).
- In SQL Server, create a certificate based on the strong name contained in the assembly's DLL file.
- Create a login for the created certificate and grant the UNSAFE permission to the login.

See the next listing for sample code that implements these steps.

> **Listing 4   T-SQL code for granting UNSAFE permission to the assembly**

```
USE master;
GO
CREATE ASYMMETRIC KEY SQLCLRKey
FROM EXECUTABLE FILE = 'D:\SQLPerformance.dll';
CREATE LOGIN SQLCLRLogin FROM ASYMMETRIC KEY SQLCLRKey;
GRANT UNSAFE ASSEMBLY TO SQLCLRLogin;
GO
```

Many DBAs prefer the approach of a separate administrator's database where they can store their tools and T-SQL code for common use. Let's assume you've created such a database called DBAToolbox. Put the assembly containing the `dbo.ufn_clr_GetPerf CounterValue` function in this database using the code from the following listing (assuming the DLL file is located on drive D).

Listing 5   T-SQL code for adding the assembly and the function

```
USE DBAToolbox;
GO
CREATE ASSEMBLY [SQLPerformance]
    AUTHORIZATION [dbo]
    FROM FILE = 'D:\SQLPerformance.dll'
    WITH PERMISSION_SET = UNSAFE;
GO
CREATE FUNCTION [dbo].[ufn_clr_GetPerfCounterValue](
  @CategoryName [nvarchar](4000),
  @CounterName [nvarchar](4000),
  @InstanceName [nvarchar](4000),
  @MachineName [nvarchar](4000)
)
RETURNS [float]
AS
EXTERNAL NAME
    [SQLPerformance].[UserDefinedFunctions].[ufn_clr_GetPerfCounterValue]
GO
```

NOTE   If you use Visual Studio and the SQL Server Project template, the code from listing 5 will be executed by Visual Studio during project deployment. If that's the case, you won't have to run it yourself.

Sample solution for performance monitoring

For many counters there are some well-known best practices that tell you about the acceptable values of the counter. Every time the counter goes beyond its "valid" range, pay attention to the counter because it may be a symptom of a performance problem.

One of the possible ways to evaluate performance counter values against their acceptable limits is to store the limits for each counter in a table and compare them against the values of the counters. To store the counter limits in the administrator's database, create a table and fill it with your baseline data (see the next listing).

Listing 6   T-SQL code for creating table and generating baseline

```
USE DBAToolbox;
GO
IF OBJECT_ID('dbo.PerfCounters', 'U') IS NOT NULL
  DROP TABLE dbo.PerfCounters;
GO
CREATE TABLE dbo.PerfCounters (
  PerfCounterID int NOT NULL IDENTITY(1,1) PRIMARY KEY,
  Category nvarchar(4000) NOT NULL,
  Counter nvarchar(4000) NOT NULL,
  Instance nvarchar(4000) NOT NULL DEFAULT '',
  IsSQLCounter bit NOT NULL,
```

```
    FriendlyName nvarchar(256) NOT NULL,
    IsRatioBased bit NOT NULL,
    IsActive bit NOT NULL,
    BestPractice nvarchar(4000) NULL,
    UpperLimit float NULL,
    LowerLimit float NULL
);
GO
INSERT INTO dbo.PerfCounters (
    Category, Counter, Instance,
    IsSQLCounter, FriendlyName, IsRatioBased, IsActive,
    BestPractice, UpperLimit, LowerLimit
)
VALUES
(
    'Processor', '% Processor Time', '_Total',
    0, 'CPU', 0, 1,
    'Should be less than 80%', 80, NULL
),
(
    'PhysicalDisk', 'Avg. Disk Queue Length', '_Total',
    0, 'Avg. Disk Queue', 0, 1,
    'Should not be permanently greater than 0', 1, NULL
),
(
    'MSSQL$SQL2008R2:Buffer Manager', 'Page life expectancy', '',
    1, 'Page Life Expectancy', 0, 1,
    'Should not drop below 1000', NULL, 1000
),
(
    'MSSQL$SQL2008R2:Databases', 'Percent Log Used', 'AdventureWorks',
    1, 'AdventureWorks database - % log used', 1, 1,
    'Should not reach 90%', 90, NULL
), (
    'MSSQL$SQL2008R2:Plan Cache', 'Cache hit ratio', '_Total',
    1, 'Cache hit ratio', 1, 1,
    'Should not fall below 90%', NULL, 90
);
```

Each counter instance is stored in a single row and is described by its category, name, and optionally by an instance (columns Category, Counter, and Instance). For each counter there's a flag, IsSQLCounter, indicating whether the counter comes from the sys.dm_os_performance_counters DMV (value of 1) or from the PerfMon counters set (value of 0). Each counter has its friendly name (the FriendlyName column) to display in the report so you can quickly read the report by the names of the criteria that are being measured. Moreover, there's an explanation of the acceptable range for the counter stored in the BestPractice column. This sentence can show up in the report every time a warning is raised for a particular counter. The columns Upper-Limit and LowerLimit store the upper and lower limits for the acceptable range of values for the particular counter. You can set the limits according to some best practices or reflecting the baseline that has been established for the system. The IsActive column works as the enable/disable flag for each counter. The IsRatioBased column states whether the counter should be calculated by division of two values from the sys.dm_os_performance_counters DMV.

The sys.dm_os_performance_counters view returns the data of all performance counters for the particular instance of SQL Server. Counters are grouped into objects (or categories), such as Buffer Manager. Each counter can have multiple instances measured separately. For example, there are many counters measured per database. In such a situation, a database name is usually the name of a counter instance. Counters are divided into several types. The type describes if you can read the value of a counter directly or need to perform some additional calculation, such as for ratio counters.

To present the performance data in your dashboard, you need a query that evaluates the values of the counters stored in the dbo.PerfCounters table. The next listing shows a sample query you can use in case the only monitored performance counters are those returned by the sys.dm_os_performance_counters view.

Listing 7   T-SQL for evaluating the values of monitored performance counters

```
;WITH PerfCTE AS (
  SELECT
    pc.FriendlyName,
    pc.BestPractice,
    CASE
      WHEN pc.IsRatioBased = 1 AND r.cntr_value = 0 THEN 0
      WHEN pc.IsRatioBased = 1 AND r.cntr_value <> 0 THEN 100. * c.cntr_value
      / r.cntr_value
      WHEN c.cntr_value IS NULL THEN
      dbo.ufn_clr_GetPerfCounterValue(pc.Category,
      ➥ pc.Counter, pc.Instance, '.')
      ELSE c.cntr_value
    END AS Value,
    pc.UpperLimit,
    pc.LowerLimit
  FROM dbo.PerfCounters AS pc
  LEFT JOIN sys.dm_os_performance_counters AS c
  ON pc.IsSQLCounter = 1
  AND pc.Category = c.[object_name]
  AND pc.Counter = c.counter_name
  AND pc.Instance = c.instance_name
  LEFT JOIN sys.dm_os_performance_counters AS r
  ON c.object_name = r.object_name
  AND r.counter_name LIKE RTRIM(c.counter_name) + '%'
  AND c.instance_name = r.instance_name
  AND r.cntr_type = 1073939712
  WHERE pc.IsActive = 1
)
SELECT
  FriendlyName,
  BestPractice,
  CONVERT(numeric(19,2), Value) AS Value,
  CASE
    WHEN Value BETWEEN ISNULL(LowerLimit, Value)
      AND ISNULL(UpperLimit, Value) THEN 1
```

```
    ELSE 0
  END AS KPIValue
FROM PerfCTE;
```

The idea is not only to return the value of each counter, but also to show whether the value falls into the acceptable range. If it doesn't, the KPIValue column in the result set should be of value 0 for that counter.

Use Reporting Services for performance monitoring

SSRS is a platform for designing, deploying, and managing reports. You can use this out-of-the-box reporting platform to create your custom performance dashboard.

Use Business Intelligence Development Studio (BIDS) to create a new project based on the Report Server Project template. Within the project create a report with a single dataset based on the connection to the central database DBAToolbox and the query shown in listing 7. Ignore any parsing errors and warnings in the Query Designer window, because the parsing mechanism of this window doesn't support common table expressions (CTEs) used in that query.

Some features of the SSRS report that you can use in the dashboard are as follows:

- Expressions for calculating the values; for example, you can set the following expression for the `BackgroundColor` property of a table row in the report:

  `=IIF(Fields!KPIValue.Value=1,"White","Yellow")`

- The `AutoRefresh` property of the report, which causes the report to refresh automatically on a regular basis (see figure 2).
- Graphical indicators to show the status of each counter.
- Tooltips to display descriptions for performance warnings.

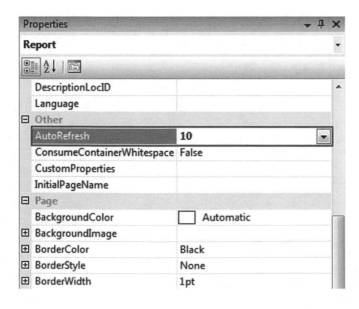

Figure 2   The Properties
window with the
`AutoRefresh` property
of the report set to
10 seconds

NOTE Try to make the report "lightweight." Don't put too many graphics into it, and try not to overload it with any unnecessary calculations and expressions, especially if you're going to use the `AutoRefresh` property to automatically refresh the report.

Figure 3 shows a preview of a sample implementation of the dashboard. In this simple report, every counter is represented by a single row in a table. Any performance warning is marked with a yellow background for the table row as well as an appropriate graphical indicator. In addition, a tooltip with the best practice description appears when you move the mouse cursor over the indicator.

Performance Dashboard

Last refresh: 7/14/2011 11:28:57 AM

Friendly Name	Value	
CPU	8.24	✓
Avg. Disk Queue	0.00	✓
Page Life Expectancy	30847.00	✓
AdventureWorks database - % log used	1.00	✓
Cache hit ratio	53.93	✗

Should not fall below 90%

Figure 3 Preview of sample custom dashboard with a performance warning raised

Some ideas to improve the solution

Here are some other tips that you might find useful:

- Add more warning levels for each counter.
- Capture performance data from other DMVs.
- Put the code for report's dataset into the stored procedure.
- Provide the ability to drill down for more details on some of the counters.
- Attach the report as a Custom Report in SQL Server Management Studio.

Keep in mind that all these changes would result in schema changes for the dbo.PerfCounters table and modifications to the query for the report.

Remember that you aren't limited to performance counters and DMVs in terms of building your own performance dashboard. You can combine these features with other mechanisms and platforms, such as Extended Events or SQL Trace, to get more reliable and in-depth monitoring results.

Summary

SQL Server provides you with a powerful set of features that when combined allow you to create your own utility for database monitoring. You can use your experience and performance baselines to define and store the appropriate set of alerting rules that can be applied against performance data and shown graphically in a Reporting Services report. Finally, the automatic refresh feature of Reporting Services reports allows these custom dashboards to be regularly refreshed to provide the most up-to-date performance data and to inform you when something looks suspicious on the server.

About the author

 Pawel Potasinski is a SQL Server Most Valuable Professional (MVP) working as a senior consultant for ABC Data IT Consulting. He's been working with SQL Server since 2000. His current focuses are data warehousing, ETL processes, performance troubleshooting, and dynamic code generation. He's held Microsoft Certified Trainer (MCT) certification since 2004. In 2007, he founded the Polish SQL Server User Group (PLSSUG). Pawel blogs at www .sqlgeek.pl.

13 SQL Server cost recovery

Peter Ward

One of the challenges facing the IT departments of many organizations today is determining who pays for the operational support of the SQL Server databases that are used by the business. Organizations are continually introducing new applications that assist in improving and streamlining business processes. It wasn't that long ago that an office looked similar to a classroom, with long rows of desks and on each desk an in tray and an out tray. Documents would move along the row of desks from one person's out tray to another person's in tray. These manual business processes and workflows have now been replaced with line-of-business applications such as CRM, ERP, and HR systems. With each new application that's adopted, there's a corresponding database that also needs to be managed. Hence, IT departments continually have to increase the number of databases that they support without having an easy way to recover the costs associated with this additional management. IT departments are being asked to do more with less as a result of their inability to recover the costs associated with database management.

The context for SQL Server as a Service

The IT industry is much like the fashion industry in that both industries are based on trends that always change with the seasons. What was considered to be best practice or fashionable last year is often no longer the case this year. One trend that's not going away any time soon is the concept of virtualization. Virtualization is typically an initiative by IT departments to assist in reducing the costs associated with providing infrastructure to the business. But the problem with many virtualization projects is that although they reduce the hardware footprint and help to reduce other infrastructure costs such as rack space, power, and cooling, they often fail to deliver on consolidating the number of SQL Server instances in the environment.

In data centers today, there's a phenomenon known as *SQL Server sprawl*. SQL Server sprawl is the uncontrolled and uncoordinated deployment of SQL Server instances. The root causes of this sprawl are often 1) attempts to ensure application performance, and 2) the fact that a business procures infrastructure and software on a project-by-project basis.

As mentioned, one of the reasons for SQL Server sprawl—and also one of the reasons that consolidation isn't performed—is that application sociability is difficult to achieve. Application sociability is the concept of applications coexisting in an environment. One of the best ways to think about the challenge of application sociability is the analogy of two children playing in a sandbox with a toy truck. Both kids want to play with the toy truck, but the truck is a finite resource that can be used by only one child at a time. Therefore, it's the bigger kid who muscles in and "steals" the toy truck so that the smaller child is only able to play with it once the bigger kid has finished with it. Applications often behave the same way in that there will be one application that wants to use all the resources on a server to the detriment of any other applications on the server. That explains the emergence of SQL Server sprawl as new instances of SQL Server are deployed so that application A doesn't affect the performance of application B.

The second reason for SQL Server sprawl is that the introduction of a new application is typically funded as a project by a particular business unit. For example, if a new Payroll application is implemented, then the Human Resources business unit will fund the project. If new hardware is required, the project funds this purchase along with the software, including the database platform. Therefore, the business unit sees the hardware as theirs; after all, they paid for it. As a result, they're unwilling to share the infrastructure because they want to ensure that the Payroll application isn't affected by sharing the infrastructure with anyone else.

If you look a little closer at this pattern of procurement, what you'll often find is that once the project has been implemented there's no longer any funding to provide ongoing support for the SQL Server instance and hardware, let alone someone to pay for upgrades. As a result, SQL Server instances aren't upgraded and they're run on legacy platforms that nobody wants to pay to upgrade.

SQL Server as a Service is designed to address these issues by providing a framework that allows the number of SQL Server instances to be reduced while increasing the elasticity in the SQL Server topology. It also provides a mechanism to recover the costs associated with the ongoing management and maintenance of the SQL Server topology.

What's SQL Server as a Service?

SQL Server as a Service is a relatively new concept. Shashank Pawar, a Microsoft Data Platform Technology Solutions Professional, provides one of the best definitions of SQL Server as a Service: "SQL Server as a service/private cloud helps in optimizing your existing SQL Server environment by reducing total costs of ownership and improves the agility for business solutions that require database platforms."

One factor that makes the discussions of SQL Server as a Service confusing is that it's also referred to as SQL Server Private Cloud. When you think of the cloud typically you're thinking about Software as a Service (SaaS) models. SaaS is a software delivery model in which software and its associated data are hosted centrally in the internet (cloud); SaaS uses the cloud as a delivery mechanism. But the term *cloud computing* only refers to the provision of computational resources on demand via a computer network.

Cloud computing has no dependency on the internet, so it's something that can be delivered using a LAN—hence the term *Private*. Private Cloud is based on on-premises infrastructure. The key, though, is that the delivery of the infrastructure creates an agile, cost-effective factory that can quickly provision and expand or collapse capacity (elasticity) based on end-user demand. Given that, what SQL Server as a Service means is that a SQL Server topology satisfies the following characteristics:

- Provides self-service functionality to allow end-users to request new, expand, or shrink the resources they've been allocated
- Proactively monitors server and database utilization and reallocates resources as required
- Provides expand or collapse capacity, with no downtime
- Provides self-service provisioning of new resources
- Meters resource utilization for chargeback

One of the key tenets of SQL Server as a Service is the metering of resource utilization and the chargeback associated with it. This is because cost is often one of the main reasons that IT departments look to implement SQL Server as a Service or any SaaS solution. The reason cost is such a big factor is that by using the service model, capital expenditure is converted to operational expenditure. It also means that IT departments don't need to provide infrastructure for one-time or infrequent intensive computing tasks that otherwise remain idle.

An introduction to chargebacks

Just as in fashion, what's old is also new again. The same way that flares and platform shoes came back into fashion, chargeback models for computing resources are also making a return.

Charging for resource utilization isn't something that's a new concept. If you cast your mind back to about the same time that flares were originally fashionable, most computing was performed on mainframe computers. These computers were expensive to purchase and maintain, and as a result there was a need to try to recover the associated costs. This cost recovery was achieved by charging for the computational units that were used. The process to perform this cost recovery was relatively easy, because the mainframe operating systems natively provided logging mechanisms that 1) identified who was using the resources, 2) identified which applications they used, and 3) showed the amount of CPU, memory, and storage they consumed by the application. You could then use this information to recover the cost of the mainframe by charging the amount of resources consumed back to an individual business unit or costs center.

A lot has changed since then (apart from the fashion). The biggest change to IT departments is the introduction of commodity computing and the ability to purchase a computer that has hundreds of times the processing power at one-hundredth the price of a mainframe. As a result of the reduction in the cost of delivering computational processing, there's no longer a need to recover the costs associated with procuring IT resources. This is also coupled with the fact that today's operating systems don't provide an easy mechanism to track resource usage by individual users. But despite the reduction in the cost of modern server infrastructure, it's not free. There's a cost associated with purchasing a server as well as a cost associated with the ongoing operation and maintenance of the server, which is often many times more than the original cost, let alone the cost of the software to run on the server.

The issue that most IT departments face today is how to introduce a paradigm shift in the business for how they charge for computing resources. Often you'll hear an end-user ask, "Why does it cost the business unit $4,000 for a laptop? I can purchase the same one for less than $1,000." Yet the end-user doesn't normally think about recovering the total cost of ownership, such as hardware and software maintenance, as well as data consumption.

The issue with this model is that it's the same as taxes that governments force individuals to pay. These taxes pay for providing public facilities such as schools, roads, and health facilities, but they aren't a "user pays" model. So someone who doesn't get sick or have any children going to school and walks everywhere is being taxed even though they don't use the resources they're paying for.

Nobody likes paying taxes for things they don't use! A chargeback model is designed to provide transparency and control to end-users regarding the resources they use. SQL Server as a Service introduces the concept of metering resource utilization. The implementation of this metering provides a mechanism to create a chargeback model that only taxes end-users for what they consume.

The concept of chargeback based on metering is designed so that a business unit is only charged based on what they use. This model is similar to bridge tolls. Someone makes an investment in the infrastructure to build the bridge along with capacity for future traffic needs. The cost of the bridge as well as the ongoing maintenance is then paid for by the people who use the bridge. If you don't use the bridge, you don't pay. Users are empowered because they know what the cost to use the bridge is and they can decide when it's appropriate to use the bridge. They know what the cost is to use the bridge when they're in a rush, or they can drive the long way to their destination.

A side effect of the toll model is that if end-users are aware of what something is costing them, they can look for ways to drive efficiencies and costs savings. For example, if they're aware that the poor code in one of their reports is costing them money due to the additional computations required, they can choose to invest to have the poor code resolved and reduce the ongoing costs associated with running the report.

This level of reporting to provide a cost breakdown by process isn't something that has been easily attainable in the past. But a number of changes have been introduced in SQL Server 2008 R2 to support chargeback mechanisms and the provision of SQL

Server as a Service. Some of these features, such as the Utility Explorer, Management Data Warehouse, and dynamic management views, are addressed in this book.

Implementing a chargeback model

The key thing to remember with a chargeback model, as in any solution, is that there's no one size that fits all. Each organization will have a slightly different way of identifying which resources to charge for as well as how much to charge for them. There's another important thing to keep in mind when implementing a chargeback model; let's return to the bridge analogy. When building a bridge, you know there's already a road in place that drivers can use and you need to entice them to use the new toll road in place of the existing road (which they see as free because they don't associate taxes paid with the use of the road).

The strategy for metering and charging based on consumption is to provide a cost-effective alternative to self-hosting SQL Server databases and attempt to entice business groups to migrate their current databases to a centrally managed service. It's critical that costs can be calculated and charged back to the business. There are four basic models of chargeback, as you can see in table 1.

Table 1 The four basic models of chargeback

Approach	Description
Overhead	All costs are absorbed by the entire business.
Allocation of expense	Component tracking is used to create a percentage of cost for each business unit.
Standard resource rates	Users are charged using a fixed rate schedule for a particular service, such as a search result or a report run.
Fixed rate	Users are charged by time on the system alone, regardless of other components.

A typical chargeback model is a combination of the allocation of expense and standard resource rates approaches. The challenge of the allocation of expense approach is to understand the expense of the service and its dependencies. To accurately recover costs, you have to know the expense of offering the service. The following items are examples of costs that should be defined for each organization:

- Capital expense, such as hardware
- Ongoing expenses, such as Software Assurance
- Support costs, including both environmental and human resources
- Operational costs, such as data centers, racking, and power
- Cost of the solution over time; what's the lifespan of the service?

When defining the standard resource rates, you must establish a measurable unit of resources known as a computational unit (CU). For the sake of simplicity, often this is defined as one processing unit and 1 GB of memory. A processing unit represents what the operating system would see as a CPU; this could be a CPU core or a hyper-threaded CPU core. In addition to the CU costs, the service is typically charged based on storage usage.

Consider the following example, where the CU is calculated at $1,000 per CU per month and the SQL Server instance for the client has two CUs assigned to it (two CPUs and 2 GB of memory).

Each month $2,000 will need to be recovered (excluding storage). Because the business group consists of multiple business teams with individual cost centers, the approach will be to measure proportional utilization of the CU assigned to the SQL Server instance. The following is an example of this scenario.

The instance, listed in table 2, has four databases; two are from cost center A, one belongs to cost center B, and another belongs to cost center C:

- Database 1 and 2 are owned by cost center A.
- Database 3 is owned by cost center B.
- Database 4 is owned by cost center C.

Table 2   Example of computational unit utilisation

Database	Cost Center	CU utilization %	Storage (GB)
Database 1	A	34	10
Database 2	A	5	100
Database 3	B	15	1
Database 4	C	25	50
Internal	N/A	21	75

Internal resources include unused CU utilization during the billing cycle and the storage required to maintain the service but that's not directly utilized by an end-user. These costs will be allocated equally to all service users because they're required to maintain the service.

In our example, the chargeback, listed in table 3, would be:

- CU cost $1,000, 2 CUs total
- Storage cost $2 per GB

Cost Center 1 will be charged 39 percent of the CU + (the internal CU cost / 3) + 110 GB of storage + (75 GB / 3).

Table 3   Sample chargeback calculation

Cost Center	CU cost	Storage cost	Total
Cost Center A	46% = $920	135 GB x $2 = $270	$1,190
Cost Center B	22% = $440	26 GB x $2 = $52	$492

Table 3 Sample chargeback calculation *(continued)*

Cost Center	CU cost	Storage cost	Total
Cost Center C	32% = $640	75 GB x $2 = $150	$790

This example is a simplified version of a chargeback model for SQL Server as a Service. There are a number of factors for the chargeback model that need to be considered, valued, and then defined in order for the chargeback model to be effective:

- Does a CU cost include DR servers?
- Does a CU cost include supporting environments such as user acceptance training (UAT), development, sandbox, and management environments, or are they a separate service?
- Does storage include backups and data recovery copies of a database?
- Does storage include supporting environments such as UAT and development?

Summary

The success of the chargeback model depends on the accuracy of the utilization data. You must develop a complete and accurate understanding of the costs in order to offer and maintain SQL Server as a Service.

About the author

Peter Ward is the Chief Technical Architect of WARDY IT Solutions, a company he founded in 2005. WARDY IT Solutions has been awarded the APAC Microsoft Data Management Solutions Partner of the year since 2009 and was a member of the 2010 Deloitte Technology Fast 500. Peter is a highly regarded speaker at SQL Server events, a sought-after SQL Server consultant, and a trainer who provides solutions for some of the largest SQL Server sites in Australia. Peter has been recognized as a Microsoft Most Valuable Professional for his technical excellence and commitment to the SQL Server community.

14 Best practice compliance with Policy-Based Management

Rod Colledge

With each new release of SQL Server introducing more features and basic administration tasks becoming either redundant or automated, the term *database administrator* is becoming ambiguous and, in some cases, misleading. In my blog post from August 2009 titled "The Great DBA Schism," available at http://bit.ly/ltajQf, I discussed the need for SQL Server professionals to develop their skills in a particular product area, describing four different groups of DBAs indicating their mastery of the product. This chapter focuses on a number of SQL Server features used by one of those groups, enterprise DBAs, for proactive administration of a large number of servers.

The context for contemporary database administration

Back in the early to mid-1990s, with hardware prices at a premium and SQL Server yet to possess the enterprise features we now take for granted, the best DBAs were those who knew how to wring every last drop of performance from the available hardware, could easily spot and tune locking problems, and could recover crucial data from corrupted hard disks. Since those days, there have been two simultaneous developments: hardware has become significantly more powerful and less expensive, and the SQL Server feature set has advanced considerably beyond the departmental level that characterized the earlier versions. As a result, the numbers specializing in the dark arts of database administration have slowly dwindled.

That's not to say that those people are no longer required; on the contrary, when something goes wrong, those with a deep understanding of the inner workings of the product are worth their weight in gold. But the frequency with which such events occur is much lower than it used to be, owing to the masking effect of powerful hardware as well as the automation and intelligence now baked into modern versions of SQL Server. As a direct consequence, "classic" DBA functions such as backups and database consistency checks are now being increasingly performed by non-DBAs such as network administrators, leading to a dilution of the traditional DBA role.

In my blog post, I argue that those remaining in the traditional DBA role will need to refine their skills in order to effectively administer large numbers of database servers. With a shift toward cloud or hosted computing, the days of having a specialist DBA on staff to administer a small number of on-premise servers are changing, with companies increasingly outsourcing these tasks or cross-training other staff in basic database administration.

In this chapter, you'll learn about two features introduced in SQL Server 2008 that assist DBAs remaining in the pure administration space to effectively and proactively manage large numbers of servers and databases according to industry best practice. Before looking at those features, let's set the scene with a quick look at the importance of best practice compliance.

The importance of best practice compliance

In a chapter from his book, *How to Become an Exceptional DBA* (Red-Gate 2008), SQL Server MVP Brad McGehee writes about the absence of an internationally recognized DBA "code of conduct" covering issues such as misconduct, ethics, and illegal activities. He points out the presence of codes for other professionals such as physicians, accountants, and realtors, and then highlights the fact that DBAs are both the protectors of an organization's data and privy to its confidential information. It seems an alarming oversight that such a code doesn't exist, and I fully support Brad in his efforts to draw attention to this.

In the absence of a formal code of conduct, as a DBA you can ensure that you're aware of, and *enforce*, best practice compliance in your day-to-day administration tasks. In the foreword to my book, *SQL Server 2008 Administration in Action* (Manning 2009), SQL Server MVP Kevin Kline described institutional knowledge as "the accumulated wisdom of many individual practitioners across many years"; the SQL Server community is fortunate to have many highly skilled practitioners willing to share their accumulated wisdom, encapsulated as widely accepted best practices. For junior database administrators, following best practices enables avoidance of common mistakes and subsequent pain experienced by others. More broadly, best practice compliance becomes important in large environments; as the number of servers under our administration grows, the harder it is to execute poorly thought-out administration routines.

Although some best practices may not be appropriate in every situation, understanding them, in a general sense, is important in determining if and when they apply. As SQL Server MVP Paul Randal is famous for saying, "It depends." Yes, it most certainly does. As SQL Server administrators, we should strive to understand not only what best practices exist, but why they're considered best practice, therefore enabling an objective assessment of their applicability in a variety of situations.

Over the years, both Microsoft and third-party vendors have released a number of tools for checking the status of a SQL Server instance for best practice compliance. The most widely used of these tools is Microsoft's SQL Server Best Practices Analyzer.

Available since SQL Server 2000, the Best Practices Analyzer tool is a free download from the Microsoft website and is used for checking a SQL Server instance for compliance with a set of common best practices. As good as the tool is, it has a number of limitations that prevent it from being truly useful in identifying and enforcing best practices. Knowing best practices is useful, implementing them is even better, but in large enterprise environments, how can you be sure that your servers *remain* in accordance with the best practices, particularly when several DBAs are involved who have a range of skills, experiences, and configuration preferences? Short of constantly running and checking the results of the Best Practices Analyzer tool (or a similar product), enterprise DBAs are faced with a significant challenge to come up with an effective administration routine.

In response to this challenge, Microsoft introduced *Policy-Based Management* in SQL Server 2008. In combination with another feature introduced in that version, *Central Management Servers*, Policy-Based Management provides enterprise DBAs with an effective platform for the ongoing best practice administration of a large number of servers.

Before we look at Policy-Based Management, let's take a quick look at the other new feature in focus for this chapter, Central Management Servers.

Central Management Servers

Like Enterprise Manager before it, SQL Server Management Studio is the tool of choice for most administration tasks. For the enterprise DBA, administering large numbers of servers means registering several of them, and the visual clutter this brings is something Microsoft addressed with the Registered Servers feature.

Using the Registered Servers feature, you can create groups in which individual servers are registered. You may create a Production Servers group, a Test Servers group, and a Development Servers group, each of which contains one or more server registrations. In addition to addressing visual clutter, such groups enable you to perform additional actions. For example, you can export the server group definition and permit other DBAs—for example, a new hire—to import the definitions, allowing them to quickly come up to speed with the enterprise environment and avoiding the manual registration of each individual server.

In SQL Server 2008, a new feature called Central Management Servers was introduced. Similar to Registered Servers, Central Management Servers allow groupings of servers, but with one important difference. In Registered Servers, the group and security definitions are stored within each DBA's PC; in Central Management Servers, as the name suggests, the group information is stored centrally within another server. DBAs register the Central Management Servers, which in turn provide access to the grouping information and servers, as long as a DBA has permissions to view the servers contained within the group.

That last point is crucial. With Registered Servers, the only way to provide access to grouping information is to export the definition to a file, provide the file to other DBAs, and ask them to import the definition. Optionally, the security details for the

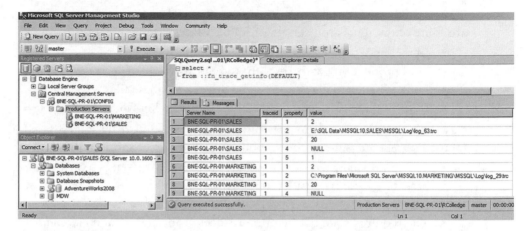

Figure 1   Using the Central Management Servers feature to execute a query against multiple servers simultaneously

registration (username and password) can be included in the export file. With Central Management Servers, this security risk doesn't exist; all connections are made using Windows Authentication, so if DBAs don't have access to the server through Windows Authentication, they won't be able to access the server. Not only is this more secure, it's also more convenient; you no longer have to export or import files to maintain consistent groupings across the DBA team.

In both cases, Registered Servers and Central Management Servers allow you to perform actions against the group of servers rather than individual servers. For example, you can execute a query against all servers in the group simultaneously. Figure 1 shows an example. Note at the top left I've registered a Central Management Server called BNE-SQL-PR-01\CONFIG, which contains a server group called Production Servers, with two servers registered: BNE-SQL-PR-01\MARKETING and BNE-SQL-PR-01\SALES. With the Production Servers group selected, I clicked New Query and executed the query shown. Notice the shaded status part at the bottom; in SSMS this defaults to pink, which indicates this is a multiserver query. Also note the additional column in the result set, showing which server each row applies to.

The ability to group servers together and then take actions against the whole group, is a powerful tool for an enterprise DBA. As you've seen, Central Management Servers provide the grouping function, and Policy-Based Management, discussed next, provides best practice management techniques. Together, they make a beautiful couple. Before I show them together, let's take a look at Policy-Based Management.

Policy-Based Management

Policy-Based Management, introduced in SQL Server 2008, can be considered a "living and active" version of the Best Practice Analyzer tool, which has been around for many years. It's "living" in the sense that it's built into SQL Server, rather than installed as a separate product, and it's "active" in the sense that its checks can prevent (or more accurately roll back) certain changes that violate best practice conditions. Here are some of the things you can do with Policy-Based Management:

- Detect unexpected system failures
- Find production databases with AutoShrink enabled
- Look for backup files on the same drive as database files
- Detecting the existence of sysadmins outside a known base of users

Now let's cover some of the new terminology introduced by Policy-Based Management. A *policy* is considered the combined state of one or more of these items:

- The entity managed by the policy; for example, a SQL Server instance, a database, or a table is considered the *target*.
- A group of properties appropriate for a particular target is called a *facet*.
- The required state of one or more facet properties is called a *condition*.

How the policy is enforced is called the *evaluation mode*. It's important to understand the differences between the various evaluation modes and in which cases they can be used. Depending on the facet, some evaluation modes aren't available. Here's a brief description of each, beginning with the least restrictive mode:

- *On Demand*—All policies support the On Demand mode. Policies using this evaluation mode run when an administrator chooses to run them, typically for ad hoc checks, checks against a version of SQL Server earlier than 2008, or when a facet, such as the Surface Area Configuration for Analysis Services, doesn't support any other evaluation mode. Administrators running policies in the On Demand mode can interact with the results, optionally choosing to reconfigure the system for policy adherence.
- *On Schedule*—This mode uses SQL Server Agent to schedule the execution of policies. Failures are sent to the SQL Server log for later analysis and, like any other error, can be the subject of an alert.
- *On Change – Log Only*—This evaluation mode, like the next in this list, is restricted to changes brought through Data Definition Language (DDL) events, such as the creation of a table. Policies using this evaluation mode actively monitor the system for changes as they occur; failures are sent to the SQL Server log.
- *On Change – Prevent*—Like the previous mode, this mode is restricted to DDL changes, but in this case, changes that violate the policy are actively prevented by rolling back the transaction. One example of how this mode can be used is a policy that enforces tables to be named in a certain manner, such as with a tbl_ prefix. Attempts to create a table without the prefix will fail and a policy error message will be issued.

To illustrate how policies work, let's walk through two examples.

Surface area configuration

SQL Server 2008 and later comes preinstalled with a range of policies that you can take advantage of straight away. The policy files are installed in the C:\Program Files\

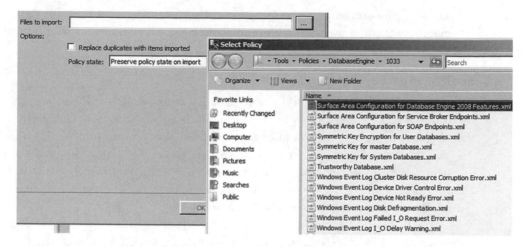

Figure 2   A range of predefined policy files are available for importing.

Microsoft SQL Server\100\Tools\Policies directory. In SQL Server Management Studio, you can import them by choosing Management > Policy Management and right-clicking Policies. As shown in figure 2, you have several policies to choose from, but for this example, choose Surface Area Configuration for Database Engine 2008 Features.

After you select the file and click OK, a new policy is created (imported) in your SQL Server instance. You can then change the evaluation mode—for example, to schedule it for nightly execution—or right-click on the policy and choose Evaluate to immediately check the SQL Server instance for policy compliance. In the example shown in figure 3, my server failed the policy check because it has Database Mail enabled and the policy stipulates that it should be disabled.

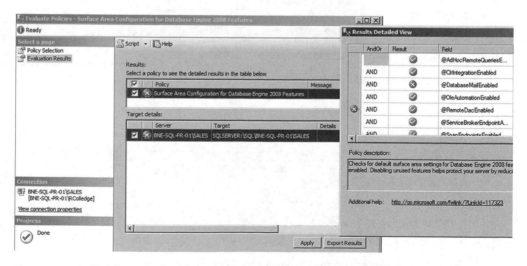

Figure 3   A failed policy execution for Surface Area Configuration

Next, as a demonstration of another type of check you can perform with Policy-Based Management, you'll use it to determine if there are any users with sysadmin privileges outside of a known base.

Sysadmin membership

For this policy example, you'll create a policy from scratch rather than import an existing one. The first step is to create a condition, so choose Management > Policy Management, right-click Conditions, and choose New Condition. As shown in figure 4, you'll create a condition named Sysadmin Check Condition against the Server Installation Settings facet using the @WindowsUsersAndGroupsInSysadminRole field. For Value, use the `Array` function to enumerate the known groups outside of which there should be no sysadmin-privileged accounts.

With this condition in place, you can now create a policy that uses it. Right-click Policies and choose New Policy; then type `Sysadmin Check Policy` in the Name field and choose the condition you created, Sysadmin Check Condition, from the Check Condition drop-down field. Figure 5 shows the definition of this policy, which you're creating using the On Schedule evaluation mode to run once a day.

In addition to the scheduled execution, you can manually execute this policy by right-clicking it and choosing Evaluate. As shown in figure 6, the policy failed evaluation, because I have sysadmin accounts defined outside the allowed set.

Policy-Based Management has a vast amount of functionality beyond what we've discussed here. One of my favorite functions is to configure a server to exactly how I

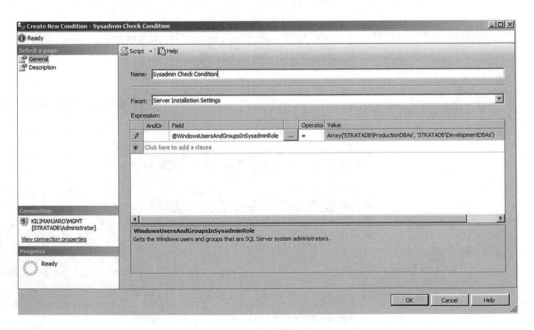

Figure 4   A condition using the WindowsUsersAndGroupsInSysadminRole field

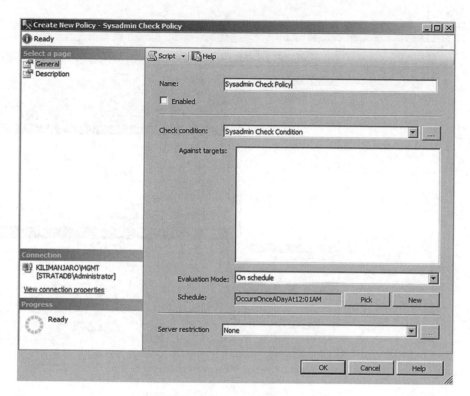

Figure 5 **A policy using the Sysadmin Check Condition**

want a group of other servers configured, and then create policies from that server's facets. I'll explain this in the next section.

Earlier I promised to illustrate the power of combining Policy-Based Management with Central Management Servers. To close the chapter, let's bring both features together and illustrate their combined power.

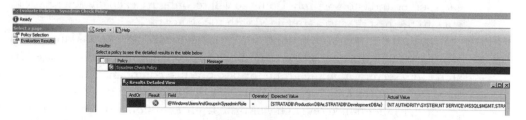

Figure 6 **A failed policy execution for sysadmin checks**

Policy-Based Management with Central Management Servers

You know how to run a query against multiple servers simultaneously by selecting a Central Management Server group and selecting the New Query option. You can also evaluate policies against a Central Management Server group, which evaluates the

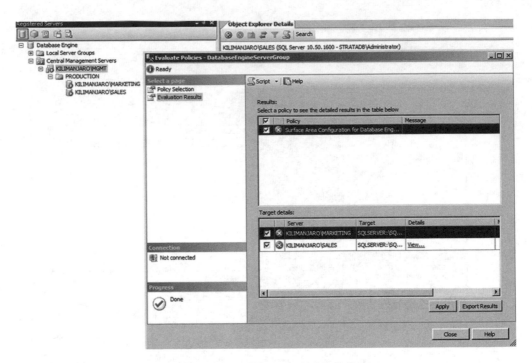

Figure 7 Evaluating policies against a Central Management Server Group

policy against each server in the group, in the one action. For example, as shown in figure 7, I right-clicked the Production Central Management Server group and chose Evaluate Policies before selecting from the predefined Surface Area Configuration for Database Engine 2008 Features policy file. I then clicked Evaluate, and as you can see both servers in the group failed evaluation.

Clicking the View link next to each server reveals the reason for each failure. What's important to point out here is that you're able to select the check box next to each server and choose Apply. Doing so will reconfigure each chosen server for adherence to the best practices contained with the policy file.

Think about what you've done here; you've created a Central Management Server group called Production, placed a number of servers within the group, and then evaluated every server within the group for best practice compliance in a single action. You then reconfigured failed servers at the click of a button!

Earlier I mentioned one of my favorite features of Policy-Based Management is the ability to configure a server to the precise state that you want a group of other servers to be configured, and then create policies from that server. You can do that by right-clicking a server instance, choosing Facets, and then clicking Export Current State as Policy after selecting the desired facet. With the resulting policy file(s), you can then evaluate a group of servers for adherence to your custom policy files, and optionally reconfigure them if any servers deviate from the policy settings.

Summary

The ultimate goal of Policy-Based Management and Central Management Servers working together is the ability to move closer toward an *intent*-based management regime, whereby you can effectively say "Make all those production servers exactly the same as this one" or "Make those test servers like this one." There are a few limitations I'd like changed, but I'm excited about the direction Microsoft is taking with these features. In an enterprise environment with hundreds or even thousands of servers, it's the only way to play.

About the author

Rod Colledge is a director and principal consultant of StrataDB, a leading Australian-based provider of SQL Server solutions and a Microsoft Certified Partner. With over 15 years of SQL Server experience, Rod's depth of knowledge and commitment to the SQL Server community was rewarded in January 2010 when he received the MVP award for SQL Server. Rod is the author of *SQL Server 2008 Administration in Action* (Manning 2009). He's a regular and sought-out speaker at local and international user groups and conferences, including the Professional Association for SQL Server (PASS) and TechEd, and blogs at http://www.RodColledge.com.

15 Using SQL Server Management Studio to the fullest

Rodney Landrum

As a DBA or SQL Developer, how often do you use SQL Server Management Studio (SSMS) in your path? That's what I thought: every day, except for the days you're on vacation (and even then you're probably *thinking* about using it). SSMS is generally our tool of choice for all manner of DBA-related activities and tasks, from backups to writing T-SQL queries. We all become accustomed to using an application the same way, over and over again through the years. In this chapter, I'll introduce you to some features that are available in SSMS 2008 and 2008 R2 that I've found raises an "Ahhh, cool" from people who were unaware of the existence of these features.

There are specifically three features in SSMS 2008 and 2008 R2 that I'd like to demonstrate; although not "undocumented," they are also not obvious. These three features are:

- Querying many servers at once
- Using script templates
- Scripting multiple objects and data

In this chapter, the goal is to show you something that you may not have seen before. But even if you have, my hope is to introduce a level of functionality that you may not have thought of that will ultimately make your life as a DBA or developer a little easier. If it doesn't make your life easier, at least you'll have something cool to show off to your DBA friends.

Querying many servers at once

In this chapter I'm going to assume that as a DBA or SQL developer you work in a SQL farm of three or more SQL Servers across several environments like development, QA/test, and production. I manage 140 servers in my SQL Server infrastructure, and although that's probably more than some, it's certainly less than others. Regardless, these tips will help you with environments of almost any size.

Let's say that you're tasked with reporting which servers in your environment are 64-bit and which are 32-bit architecture. The assumption is that you didn't install all the servers yourself and you don't have a photographic memory of each and every server in your environment. The first piece of knowledge you'd require is how to derive that information via T-SQL because you don't want to remote desktop connect (RDP) into each server to run the command-line tool Winver.exe or msinfo32.exe to find out.

Fortunately there are several ways for you to get the architecture information in T-SQL. First, by running SELECT SERVERPROPERTY('Edition') connected to the SQL instance you can easily see if a server is 64-bit (X64) or 32-bit (Intel X86). The result for Standard Edition of SQL Server will either be Standard Edition or Standard Edition (64-bit). Using SERVERPROPERTY is the best choice if you need granular information and wish to incorporate this into programmatic logic like in an IF statement. Two other ways to derive the edition information are by executing the extended stored procedure xp_msver or using @@VERSION, each of which provides much more information. You can see the output of xp_msver in figure 1. For our use in this example, because we want to see more information in a single row per server, we'll use @@VERSION.

	Index	Name	Internal_Value	Character_Value
1	1	ProductName	NULL	Microsoft SQL Server
2	2	ProductVersion	589824	9.00.4035.00
3	3	Language	1033	English (United States)
4	4	Platform	NULL	NT INTEL X86
5	5	Comments	NULL	NT INTEL X86
6	6	CompanyName	NULL	Microsoft Corporation
7	7	FileDescription	NULL	SQL Server Windows NT
8	8	FileVersion	NULL	2005.090.4035.00
9	9	InternalName	NULL	SQLSERVR
10	10	LegalCopyright	NULL	© Microsoft Corp. All rights reserved.
11	11	LegalTrademarks	NULL	Microsoft® is a registered trademark of Micros...
12	12	OriginalFilename	NULL	SQLSERVR.EXE
13	13	PrivateBuild	NULL	NULL
14	14	SpecialBuild	264437760	NULL
15	15	WindowsVersion	248381957	5.2 (3790)
16	16	ProcessorCount	1	1
17	17	ProcessorActiveMask	1	00000001
18	18	ProcessorType	586	PROCESSOR_INTEL_PENTIUM
19	19	PhysicalMemory	2047	2047 (2146926592)
20	20	Product ID	NULL	NULL

Figure 1   Output of xp_msver

Either query, SELECT @@VERSION or xp_msver, is a simple way to get the architecture from a single SQL Server instance. What if the request you receive for this information is to show all of the test server instances that are 64-bit? You could go through your documentation and find all of the test or QA SQL Servers in your environment and connect to each one via SSMS one by one, and then run the SQL to get the architecture. This approach is time consuming and I know you value your time.

In SSMS 2008 and later, you have the power of multiserver query support. This feature is one of the few I've found (besides another one I'll show you later in this chapter) that's backward compatible with SQL Server 2000, 2005, and 2008. (If you've tried using SSMS IntelliSense for a SQL Server 2005 instance you know what I mean…it doesn't work.) To prepare to run a query and receive a result set from multiple servers in one execution, you start by registering servers in the Registered Servers tab.

In figure 2 you can see that I have four servers registered under the QA group. These four servers are test/QA servers. There can be many more servers and many more groups to organize your environment, and the same server can exist in one or more groups. I wanted to choose a simple example for this demonstration.

To get the consolidated architecture information from all four servers using our SELECT

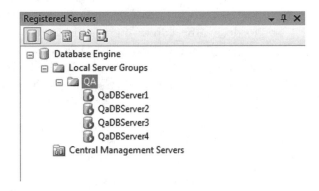

Figure 2   Four registered servers in the QA group

@@VERSION query, right-click on the group QA and select New Query from the context menu. If you're familiar with running single queries for one server, then you may recall the color at the bottom of the connected query for a single server is yellow and the text in the connection bar reads "Connected (1/1)." In a multiple-server query, it's a bit more colorful, showing a lively pink with the number of servers able to connect from the registered server group. As you can see in figure 3, all four servers are connected and you can now execute the query to return the desired results for the servers. You have the ability in SSMS to move the status bar to a more conspicuous location, like the top of your query window, so there's no doubt when your query is connected to multiple servers.

Figure 3   Showing all four test/QA servers connected

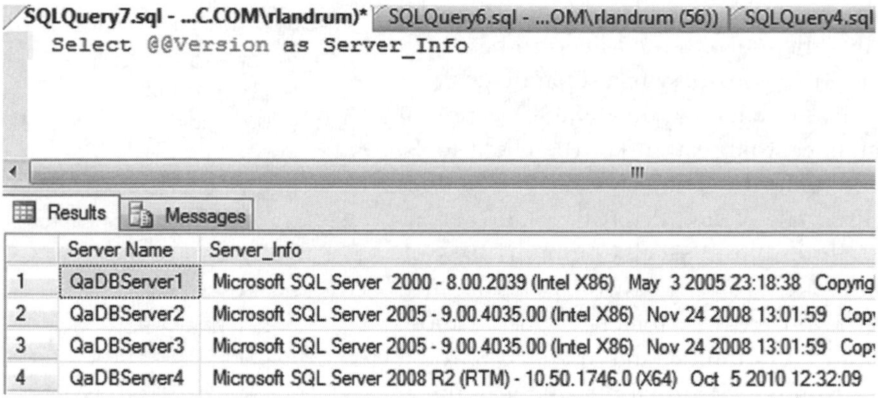

Figure 4   Consolidated results showing one 64-bit server

It's easy to see from the mix of results (figure 4) that all versions of SQL Server are supported from 2000 to 2008 R2. Of the four connected servers, only one is 64-bit, QaDBServer4. Note that the server name that's returned within the results is the description of the server you have assigned and not the server name itself. The default description when you register a server in the Registered Servers tab is also the server's name.

Finally, the standard output formats exist for your queries as well, such as sending the results to text, grid, or file. The latter is useful if you'll use the output to pull into a report or Microsoft Excel spreadsheet, because the person who requested this information from you, the trusted DBA, will be more at home in that world than in SSMS, where you live.

Creating and using a scripting solution with templates

Like other integrated development environments, such as Business Intelligence Development Studio (BIDS), SSMS supports creating a scripting solution and that solution can be shared and saved within a source control application like Team Foundation Server (TFS). I've created and "sourced" my own scripting solutions over the years in this manner. But I noticed while creating and saving scripts into a scripting solution I was limited as to the structure of how I could save and search for scripts that I needed. For example, you only have the ability to create a single folder to save your scripts.

One option that's available to explore and extend the flexibility of working with commonly used scripts is Template Explorer (which is built into SSMS). Template Explorer is a special location where common script tasks such as creating databases or tables are only a click away. These scripts typically contain template parameters, which aid in inputting values quickly. And further, anyone can add their own templates or commonly used scripts with the same technique to enter parameter values at the time of execution, which I'll show shortly. A drawback to using Template Explorer is that you'll need to manually add scripts to each installation of the client tools from a source location as opposed to a script solution. Also, the scripts themselves would need to be added to a source control system separately.

First, let's look at the default location of templates when you install the client tools. By default the templates are created in C:\Program Files\Microsoft SQL Server\ 100 \Tools\Binn\VSShell\Common7\IDE\Sql-WorkbenchProjectItems\Sql for SSMS 2008 R2. If you create a folder in this location, call it DBA Common, and open SSMS, you'll see (as in figure 5) that the folder is immediately available as a template folder. Further, if you add common scripts, as I've done with usp_Restore_Database.sql in the DBA Common folder, they'll show up for any user who opens SSMS on the workstation where SSMS is installed. You may even make it part of your company's standard

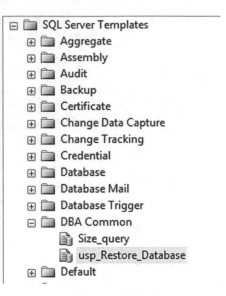

Figure 5   Custom folder and script added to Template Explorer.

SQL Client Tools install to move a DBA Common folder into this location after each installation so all the DBAs have the same template scripts.

Now, the fun begins when you open the template query, presuming it was created to accept template parameters, as the usp_Restore_Database.sql script was. You'll notice that this query is a fairly simple stored procedure that takes two parameters: @restore_file and @database_name, as shown in figure 6. Also notice that the parameter value options are enclosed by < and > and separated by two commas. This is a standard syntax for telling SSMS that you'd like to enter the values of the query by specifying template values.

Before you execute the stored procedure, you can either press Ctrl-Shift-M or click the Specify Values for Template Parameters icon on the toolbar. With the example stored procedure, usp_Restore_Database, you can see that the three-part syntax for parameter, type, and value equates to instructions of what to type, the data type expected, and the value itself. In this case, I chose to add Enter Backup File path in single quotes for the @restore_file parameter with a type of String and a value of Location. Similarly for the @Database_name parameter, there are instructions on what to enter, the data type, and the value name. With these template parameters in place,

```
SQLQuery1.sql - not connected*
  Exec [DBAMaint].[dbo].[usp_Restore_Database]
      @restore_file = <Enter Backup File path in single quotes,String 100,Location>
      @database_name = <Enter Target Database Name in single quotes,String 50, Name>
```

Figure 6   Setting up template parameters

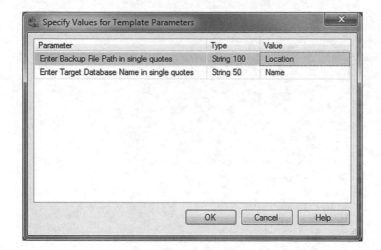

Figure 7   Entering template parameters

pressing Ctrl-Shift-M reveals an input window (see figure 7) that takes all the parameter values at once, which is much easier than having to navigate through the code to enter values yourself. You can also add special instructions as I did here to put the values in single quotes because this will be a string that's passed in to the stored procedure.

After you enter the values and click OK, the stored procedure is ready to execute to begin the process of restoring the specified file to the specified database. The code you'd execute after entering the values appears in the following listing.

Listing 1   Output query after adding template parameter values

```
Exec [DBAMaint].[dbo].[usp_Restore_Database]
     @restore_file = 'c:\Backups\MyDB.BAK'
     @database_name = 'MyDatabase'
```

You can use this technique anywhere inside a query, such as in a WHERE clause or as part of a declaration of variables. This technique comes in handy if you're writing a quick ad hoc query for someone else and you don't know exactly what values they'll use.

Scripting multiple objects and now data, too

The final new feature in SSMS 2008 and 2008 R2 that I'd like to show is one that I've found isn't familiar to many people. I ran across it by chance in SSMS 2008 when I was creating drop and create scripts for database objects. Since SSMS 2008, in addition to using the Generate Scripts wizard to script schema objects, you can now generate INSERT statements for data, as well.

To launch the Generate Scripts wizard, right-click on any database in Object Explorer inside SSMS and select Tasks\Generate Scripts. If you're using SSMS 2008 R2, it'll open the Generate and Publish Scripts page. Click the Next button to move to the Choose Objects page. You'll have the option to script the entire database or to select specific database objects. For this exercise, choose to select specific objects. At this point you're able to select tables, views, stored procedures, UDFs, users, SQL assemblies,

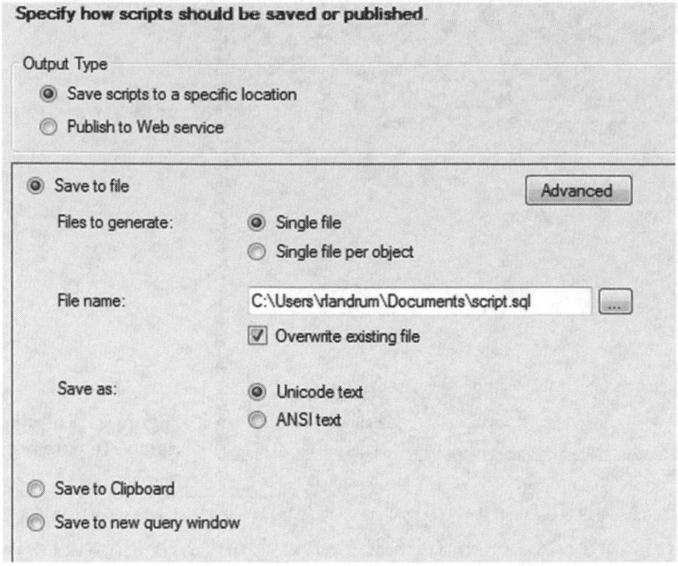

Figure 8   **Specifying how the scripts will be generated**

DDL triggers, and schemas to script. Expand the Tables list and choose a table that contains data you want to script. In my example I'm choosing a commonly used Numbers table, which has a single column to store sequential integer values 1 to N. Clicking Next brings you to the Scripting Options page, where you'll find (though not easily) the option to script the data, as shown in figure 8.

The unobtrusive Advanced button will have all the options you need, but as in SSMS 2008, finding the ability to script data isn't obvious at first. As you scroll down the list of options, like Script USE DATABASE and Script Logins, you'll see the Types of Data to Script option, as shown in figure 9. The three choices you have for this last

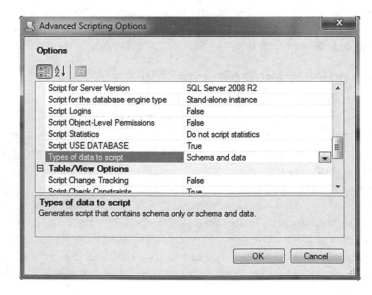

Figure 9   **Scripting schema and data**

option are Schema Only, Schema and Data, or Data Only. I've chosen Schema and Data. After clicking OK, I also chose to save to a new query window, overriding the default output to a file.

After the Summary tab, you can click Next again and the output script will be displayed in a new window, as in listing 2. There are various options that you can choose, such as to drop and create the objects or just create. You may want to play around with these options to match the script to your specification.

Listing 2   Output script from Generate Scripts

```
SET ANSI_NULLS ON
GO
SET QUOTED_IDENTIFIER ON
GO
CREATE TABLE [dbo].[Numbers](
     [Num] [int]

) ON [PRIMARY]
GO
INSERT [dbo].[Numbers] ([Num]) VALUES (1)
INSERT [dbo].[Numbers] ([Num]) VALUES (2)
INSERT [dbo].[Numbers] ([Num]) VALUES (3)
INSERT [dbo].[Numbers] ([Num]) VALUES (4)
INSERT [dbo].[Numbers] ([Num]) VALUES (5)
```

Summary

There are obviously many more hidden treasures remaining to be found in SSMS, and in this chapter I touched on three that I think you'll find useful. I certainly find myself using them more and more now that I know they're available, and I hope that you'll give them a try. I'll be willing to bet you stumble across other options you weren't aware of.

About the author

Rodney Landrum has been working with SQL Server technologies for more than a decade. He writes regularly about many SQL Server technologies, including Integration Services, Analysis Services, and Reporting Services. He's the author of *SQL Server Tacklebox* (Red Gate Books, 2009) and co-author of three books on Reporting Services. He's a regular contributor to *SQL Server Magazine*, SQLServerCentral, and Simple-Talk. He currently lives in Orlando, Florida.

16 Multiserver management and Utility Explorer—best tools for the DBA

Satya Shyam K Jayanty

As a DBA, you need to be proactive to be able to multitask database maintenance, security, availability, manageability, and performance-tuning chores. SQL Server 2008 and SQL Server 2008 R2 tools will help you accomplish the required level of responsibilities.

In this chapter, we'll go through the SQL Server tools that can help you manage and administer multiple SQL Server instances and data-tier applications. We'll also spotlight the Utility Control Point (UCP) feature, which can help DBAs to accomplish the multiserver management and administration of their data platform. This chapter highlights the importance of SQL Server 2008 R2 tools that will enable DBAs and developers to design, implement, and administer the multiserver management concept. In addition, we'll offer best practice tips.

SQL Server 2008 R2 tools for the DBA

As a DBA and data platform architect, I like to classify the SQL Server Management Studio (SSMS) as the most important of all the SQL Server tools and utilities.

SSMS started its journey with the SQL Server 2005 version and has continued with enhanced features in SQL Server 2008 onward, combining components (tools and utilities) into a single GUI interface. I'm not going into minute details of SSMS here, but this chapter uses the SSMS tools as a single focal point for multiserver management, which is essential for every SQL Server user to manage their data platform tasks effectively.

For a DBA, it's essential to understand the data flow, application usage, and, most importantly, data platform administration and management, which can extend the lifespan of an application. To administer the data platform, regardless of whether it's for a middle-tier, client/server, or web-based application, it's essential as a DBA to maintain data availability and seamless management of vital administrative tasks on multiple instances and multiple databases.

The challenging part for a DBA occurs whenever a performance or data availability problem arises. Then all fingers usually point to the database by default, irrespective of the root cause of the problem. SQL Server 2008 is equipped with a wide variety of features internally; the tools and utilities are available to monitor and troubleshoot the issues. Likewise, these tools will enable the core aspects of management, administration, and development. In this chapter we'll explore the SQL Server 2008 R2 tools and utilities to achieve multiserver management functionalities.

Tools of the trade

SQL Server Management Studio is equipped with a variety of tools and utilities that are essential to the job of a DBA. These are as follows:

- *Activity Monitor (AM)*—Activity Monitor is a tool that can be helpful for monitoring and troubleshooting an issue within the SQL Server instance. A dashboard view enables users to obtain a quick snapshot of server, database, and network activity for an instance. To invoke this tool, right-click the server name in Object Explorer and choose Activity Monitor.

- *Dynamic Management Views (DMV)* and *SSMS Reports*—The practical use of SSMS Reports is to obtain a snapshot of server-wide and database-scope information. The graphical representation of DMVs uses dashboard reports that are built in and SSRS generated, without needing to install the SQL Server Reporting Services service.

- *Management Data Warehouse (MDW) (Data Collector)*—The Data Collector is a powerful feature used to acquire in-depth information about processor, disk, and query statistics from the monitored instances. The Data Collector offers predefined collector types that provide the mechanism for collecting data and uploading it to the MDW database. The four collector types are Generic T-SQL Query, Generic SQL Trace, Performance Counters, and Query Activity.

- *Policy Based Management (PBM)*—This utility implements the standards and is ideal for configuration management of multiple instances in an automated way. Having different evaluation modes, PBM can help a DBA to check for policy compliance, log policy violations, or raise alerts on policy violations, with operation rollbacks on policy violations to ensure the instance remains in compliance with the enterprise standards.

- *Resource Governor (RG)*—This tool maintains a consistent level of service by limiting required resources (CPU and memory) and guaranteeing the resources for mission-critical processes. The resource allocation can be configured in real time, but the reconfiguration changes may take some time depending on the currently executing workloads.

- *SQLCMD*—This command-line interface allows users to execute ad hoc scripts, stored procedures, and script files at the command prompt. This utility is ideal for users who are comfortable with command syntax; by default, the utility uses OLE DB to execute TSQL batches. SQLCMD is also accessible from the Query Editor, which offers the ease of executing SQLCMD files within SSMS.
- *Utility Control Point (UCP)*—This new feature in SQL Server 2008 R2 provides several ways to view summary and detailed data for an instance. The UCP is the focus of this chapter: to construct a methodology to acquire health state data of managed instances and data-tier applications (DAC). The real-time reports and dashboard view from UCP resemble the mixed features of MDW and PBM in SQL Server 2008.

Managing multiple instances using Utility Control Point

SQL Server 2008 R2 introduced Utility Control Point, which provides multiserver management with a dashboard view. UCP provides a generic view of SQL Server–related resource usage including overutilized and underutilized resources for managed instances and data-tier applications. CPU utilization, storage utilization, and policy details for all managed instances are included with UCP.

When the resource utilization is volatile, or drastic changes in performance are noticed, UCP allows the administrator to step up the multiserver management feature to enroll the instances, which set the default resource utilization and capacity policies. All the policies and collected data are stored in the Utility Management Data Warehouse (UMDW) database called sysutility_MDW.

The minimum requirements to set up UCP are as follows:

- The SQL Server version must be 10.0.4000 (SQL Server 2008 Service Pack 2) or 10.50.1600 (SQL Server 2008 R2 RTM) or higher.
- The SQL Server edition that's hosting the UCP database must be Datacenter (SQL Server 2008 R2) or Enterprise in the production environment.
- For development and testing purposes only, you can use the Developer edition or Enterprise Evaluation edition, which is set to expire in 180 days.
- The SQL Server instance must be a database engine type.
- TCP/IP must be enabled on the instance that will host the UMDW database.
- The SQL Server Agent service must be set to autostart; during the UCP setup, this service must be up and running.
- The SQL Server service account must be a Windows domain account.
- In case the SQL Server instance is hosted on Windows Server 2003, then the SQL Server Agent account must be a member of the Performance Monitor user group. Also, the SQL Server service account must have read permission to Users in Windows Active Directory.
- For data-tier applications, there are no specific hardware or software requirements. But to enroll and manage DAC through UCP, users must consider the limitations and thresholds imposed by the data-tier application framework.

When these prerequisite steps are satisfied, then you're ready to set up the UCP feature using the SQL Server Management Studio components. Similar to the Management Data Warehouse (Data Collector) feature, UCP will collect and upload the resource data to the UMDW. Using the SQL Server 2008 R2 Management Studio Object Explorer screen, a new tab called Utility Explorer is accessible that will show the information about Utility Explorer.

To create a UCP on an instance of SQL Server, you use the UCP Wizard to specify the SQL Server instance where the UCP database is created and managed and to enable the utility collection sets as per the SQL Server Agent job schedules. The following steps are required to create a UCP on an instance of SQL Server:

1 In Management Studio, in Object Explorer, click Utility Explorer to create the Utility Control Point. The introductory screen of the UCP Wizard appears, as shown in figure 1.

   Within the Create Utility Control Point screen, specify the instance of SQL Server where the new UCP will be created and configured.

2 You must specify two values: the SQL Server instance name and the UCP name.

   On the next screen, the UCP Wizard requires that you enter the Windows domain account that will be used to run the utility collection set.

NOTE As a best practice, ensure that you use a Windows domain account (create a new account if required) to manage UCP and don't use the SQL

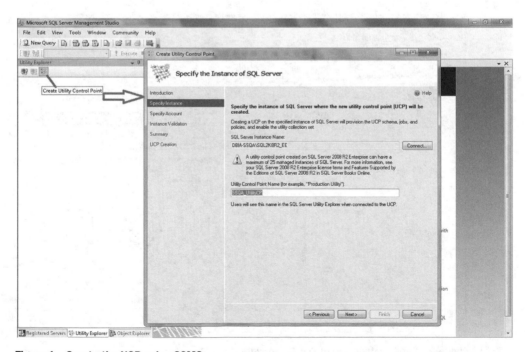

Figure 1   Create the UCP using SSMS.

Server Agent service account. If a cross-domain account is used, then ensure the domains with two-way trust relationships.

3 Click Next to continue to validate the SQL Server instance for UCP.

4 If any errors and warnings appear, click the hyperlink under the Result column, which will show the reason for failure. The Next button will be disabled and the Rerun Validation button enabled.

5 Fix the specified errors against the action, and click the Rerun Validation button to proceed. You can also choose to save the report by clicking the Save Report button, which will save the information in HTML format.

   When the validation process is completed, a screen is displayed to close the UCP Wizard.

6 You should now have a new database created called sysutility_MDW on the instance that was chosen at the beginning of UCP setup.

7 Once the UCP is created and configured, in the Utility Explorer screen in SSMS click Managed Instances > Enroll Instance, as shown in figure 2.

The next set of steps is self-explanatory (wizard driven) and requires a SQL Server instance to enroll:

8 Specify the user account to run the UCP; all the information that's provided here is reviewed as prerequisite validation results, which completes the enrollment of the specified instance.

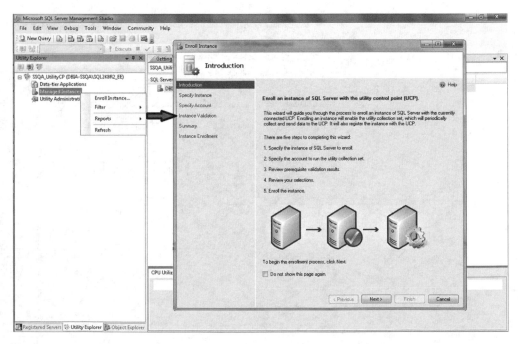

Figure 2   Enroll an instance of SQL Server with the UCP.

To enroll additional instances, repeat these steps to enable the instances to be managed by the UCP.

NOTE Remember: the instances that are managed must be SQL Server version 10.0.4000 (SQL Server 2008 Service Pack 2) or 10.50.1600 (SQL Server 2008 R2 RTM) or higher.

I've enrolled three instances to be managed by UCP. Initially, the Utility Explorer Content tab may not have the required information to show the unified view (such as resource usage spikes).

In order to generate a CPU load, I executed the following TSQL script on the three instances that are enrolled within the SSQA_Utility UCP shown in figure 2:

```
Declare     @DT DateTime,
@FB Bigint;
Set         @DT=GetDate();
While       DATEADD(Second,180,@DT)>GETDATE()
Set         @FB=POWER(2,45);
```

9 Choose Managed Instances under Utility Explorer to see the dashboard view of resource utilization for the CPU and storage for the SQL2K8 instance.

Figure 3 shows example CPU utilization for an enrolled SQL Server 2008 instance. In addition to checking the CPU utilization, you can review the storage consumption for a specific database by using the Storage Utilization tab.

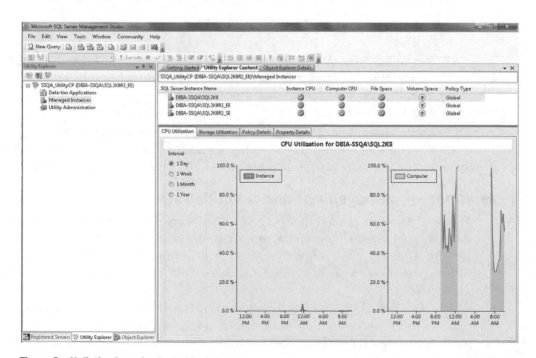

Figure 3   Holistic view of selected instance

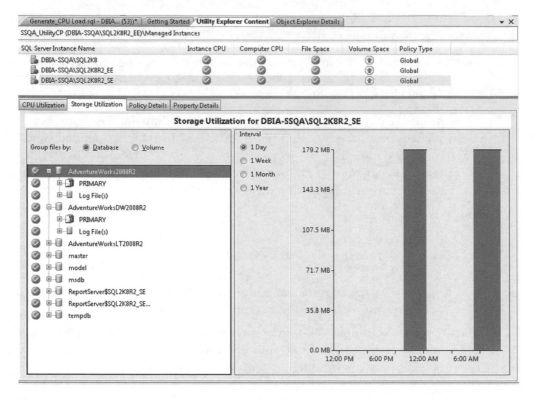

Figure 4   Storage Utilization view for the SQL2K8R2_SE instance

10   Click the Storage Utilization tab to display the information shown in figure 4.

The Managed Instances item will present data for the enrolled instances. Likewise, the data-tier applications, which are classified as an entity of database, and instance objects used by an application are enrolled automatically by the UCP.

The sample database called FoodMart2008 can be downloaded from http://www .codeplex.com and registered as a data-tier application. Refer to http://msdn.microsoft .com/en-us/library/ee240739.aspx for more information on data-tier applications.

Multiserver management and administration

Now that we've completed the setup of UCP to store data for managed instances and data-tier applications, it's essential to manage the policies and administer UCP.

The application and multiserver management functionality of UCP provides DBAs with the necessary tools to gain centralized insight of server and database resource utilization.

The UCP data collection sets are installed and started immediately on each instance that's enrolled. By default, the Managed Instances and Data-tier Application's default maximum values for CPU and Storage Utilization are at 70 percent and default minimum values are at 0 percent.

The Utility Administration node in Utility Explorer allows you to manage the system default values as follows:

- The Manage Policy tab lets you set global policies for the Managed Instances and data-tier applications; this tab also shows how frequently the CPU resource utilization violation is reported.
- The Security tab lets you remove privileges for the logins on UCP. The logins that have sysadmin privileges are administrators on the UCP. You can grant administrator privilege for the logins or add the logins to the list using the Security node in Object Explorer.
- Finally, the Data Warehouse tab enables the administrator to set the data-retention period for the Utility Management Data Warehouse. For this release of SQL Server, you can't change the default values for UMDW database name (sysutility_MDW) and collection set upload frequency (every 15 minutes).

Likewise, to help you troubleshoot the resource health issues identified by the UCP, the Utility Administration node will help identify a CPU that's overutilized by SQL Server instances or data-tier applications. It can also help identify overutilized file space for database files or allocated disk space on a storage volume.

The following options are used to perform multiserver management and administration using the UCP feature:

- Within the Utility Explorer screen, you can use the Utility Administration node to manage policies or set security for a SQL Server utility. You can use this tab to set thresholds across the Data-tier Applications or Managed Instances entities on the UCP.
- The Policy Details tab lets you set global policies for data-tier applications and managed instances. For example, you can define policies to determine when the CPU is over- or underutilized by showing when the usage is greater or less than the set value. Similarly, the space utilization policy covers data and log files when they're over- or underutilized.
- Finally, you can set the policy violation frequency on the Volatile Resource Policy Evaluation vertical tab. You can evaluate SQL Server Utility over this moving time window for six hours of reporting.
- You can set the percentage of SQL Server Utility policies in violation during the time window before the CPU is reported as overutilized to 40 percent.

These settings will report the violations over six hours; they calculate 24 policy evaluations, and 9 of them must be in violation before the CPU is marked as overutilized.

How frequently should CPU utilization policies be in violation before being reported as underutilized?

- Evaluate SQL Server Utility over this moving time window for reporting every two weeks.
- Set the percentage of SQL Server Utility policies in violation during the time window before the CPU is reported as underutilized to 90 percent.

When the system default values are changed, these settings will report the violations over two weeks; that calculates 1344 policy evaluations, and 1209 of them must be in violation before the CPU is marked as underutilized.

All the global policies and performance data (collected) that will help the UCP to identify the resource bottlenecks are stored in the UMDW and will be used to report policy violations.

The upload process is managed by the SQL Server Agent service account. UCP creation will create eight jobs on the instance that hosts UMDW. The scheduled jobs are as follows:

- collection_set_4_noncached_collect_and_upload
- mdw_purge_data_[sysutility_mdw]
- syspolicy_purge_history
- sysutility_get_cache_tables_data_into_aggregate_tables_daily
- sysutility_get_cache_tables_data_into_aggregate_tables_hourly
- sysutility_get_views_data_into_cache_tables
- sysutility_mi_collect_and_upload
- sysutility_mi_collect_performance

The Windows domain account specified will be the owner of all the jobs that are specified for UCP.

NOTE   Except for the scheduled job collection_set_4_noncached_collect_and _upload, all jobs are enabled by default.

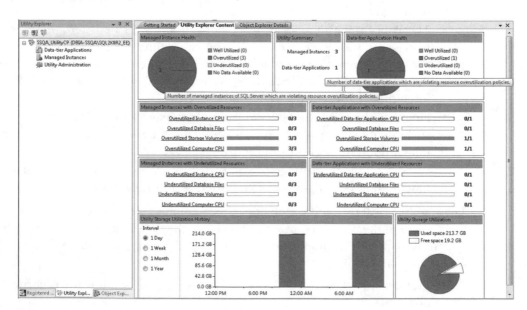

Figure 5   Dashboard view of Utility Control Point for SSQA_UtilityCP

The default directory for the UMDW database (data and log file) is *<System drive>*:\Program Files\Microsoft SQL Server\MSSQL10_50.*<UCP_Name>*\MSSQL\Data\. The *<System drive>* might be C:\ and is based on your Enterprise SQL Server operations policies. You can choose to modify the UMDW (sysutility_mdw) database files' location by using the ALTER DATABASE method.

Finally, using Utility Explorer, you can see the dashboard view of UCP by clicking the UCP name. See figure 5.

During the UCP creation, there are some issues that might restrict the enrollment of managed instances or data-tier applications. In such cases, troubleshooting SQL Server Utility issues might include resolving a failed operation to enroll an instance of SQL Server. The list of known issues is documented at http://msdn.microsoft.com/en-us/library/ee210592.aspx

Best practices

Certain recommendations presented here are categorized as best practices, and certain considerations such as capacity planning on a SQL Server instance where UCP is hosted are required:

- By default, in a typical scenario the UCP will consume 2 GB of disk space per managed instance of SQL Server per year. This estimate can vary depending on the number of databases and system objects on that managed instance.
- For the UCP administration, around 25 MB per managed instance of SQL Server are required. Likewise, the amount can vary depending on the number of managed instances and their resource utilization policies, in addition to the number of database and system objects that are collected by the managed instance.
- In addition to UMDW database, the system database msdb also plays a vital role in UCP management. All the policies (source: Policy-based framework) and job schedules are stored in the msdb database.

Therefore, the disk space usage will increase exponentially when the number of managed instances in UCP is increased to five or more. This is due to the increase in the number of policy violations and the duration of the moving window in which to report volatile resource violations. If a SQL Server instance is removed from the Managed Instances section, the UMDW database space won't reduce the disk space until the data-retention period is met on the UCP instance.

Furthermore, you must ensure that the Server Collation settings of the UCP instance and the managed instance match; for example, if the UCP instance is a case sensitive, then the managed instance of SQL Server must be, as well.

By default, the database recovery model for the sysutility_mdw database is set to SIMPLE. So it's essential to provide the required level of disaster-recovery capability for UMDW by including the database in a regular backup schedule.

Summary

The Utility Control Point feature provides multiserver management using SQL Server 2008 R2 features. The UCP viewpoints enable administrators and DBAs to manage resource health and storage capacity. For SQL Server 2008 R2 RTM and SQL Server 2008 Service Pack 1 release, you can register up to 25 instances. SSMS can help to group the managed instances as a common type for the specific set of applications, such as web applications, to manage the resources efficiently that will accomplish multiservice management and administration using a single set of tools.

About the author

Satya Shyam K Jayanty is an independent consultant working as principal architect and director for D Bi A Solutions Limited, based in Europe. In 1992, Satya started his career in the IT industry as a computer operator and assistant programmer, and then in 1996 he changed his career to Sybase DBA. He has been working with SQL Server (beginning with version 4.2) for more than 15 years and has been an accomplished Microsoft SQL Server MVP since 2006.

He's a regular speaker and SME volunteer at major technology conferences such as Microsoft Tech Ed (Europe, India, and North America), SQL PASS (Europe and North America), and SQL Bits (UK), and he manages the Scottish Area SQL Server user group based in Scotland. He's also a moderator in web-based SQL Server forums (Microsoft Technet and http://www.sql-server-performance.com), a writer and contributing editor, and a blogger at http://www.sqlserver-qa.net, http://www.sql-server-performance .com, and http://www.beyondrelational.com.

17 Top 10 SQL Server admin student misconceptions

Tibor Karaszi

Having trained SQL Server administrators for two decades now, I can anticipate many of the questions and thoughts that arise in a SQL Server admin class. Some misconceptions repeat over and over, and in this chapter I'll elaborate on some of the most common misconceptions.

Let me start by saying that it's okay to misunderstand how something works—that allows you to learn something, and learning is fun. I learn stuff all the time! Some misunderstandings are more common than others, and the reason for such common misunderstandings will vary. It might be that how the product works doesn't seem logical at first glance...or that the product doesn't work the way you want it to work...or perhaps some other product works in a different way. In the end, the reason for the misconception doesn't matter; I find it more productive to explain how things work.

Let's tackle these myths one by one.

Simple recovery model

The simple recovery model means no logging

You should be glad that this isn't the case. The transaction log is used for many things in SQL Server. One is to support transaction log backups. Because this isn't possible in the simple recovery model, you might wonder why SQL Server writes things to the transaction log in the simple recovery model. The answer is because it needs the transaction logging for *other things*. As you read the following list of reasons why logging still occurs in the simple recovery model, for some items you might think "I can do without that!" But I'm pretty certain that few of you could do without the ability to support rollbacks.

- *To support rollback*—Remember that each modification command is protected by a transaction. This also applies if you don't have BEGIN TRANSACTION and

COMMIT TRANSACTION statements. If you only have a single-statement batch (INSERT, UPDATE, DELETE, etc.), then that command is the logical unit of work (i.e., the transaction). A DELETE, for instance, while working over the rows that qualify for the WHERE clause won't only stop if something goes wrong. It will stop *and undo* the rows that were deleted. Yes, this is a rollback, and it's possible thanks to the transaction log. The same basic principle applies as well if several modification statements are grouped in the same transaction.

- *For transactional replication*—This replication type comes from the transaction log records produced as a result of your modification commands. The Log Reader Agent job reads the transaction log and reverse-engineers the modification commands from the log records, storing them in the distribution database, so that the same modification can be performed on the subscription databases.

- *For Change Data Capture (CDC)*—CDC is a new feature for SQL Server 2008, and it uses the same log reader mechanism as transactional replication. But the modification commands aren't stored in a distribution database; they're stored in the source database, ready to be read by the table functions created by the CDC configuration process.

- *Database mirroring*—This is also based on transaction logging. The log records are produced in the principal database and are then synchronously or asynchronously sent to the mirror database to be applied there.

- *Database recovery*—Every time we start SQL Server, it will use the transaction log to redo and undo operations, if necessary, to make sure the database is in a transactionally consistent state.

I'm sure that many of you can think of other things that also use the transaction log. In short, logging is an integral part of SQL Server, and although it's mainly there to support transactions (rollback, log backups, and such), it's also used for various other features. Setting the database to the simple recovery model doesn't turn off logging—it will only mean that it's no longer your responsibility to empty (also known as truncate or reuse) the transaction log; SQL Server will do that by itself. Also, you can still get large LDF files in the simple recovery model—for instance if you have old open transactions (for any reason), or large long-running transactions (like modifying many rows in the same INSERT/UPDATE/DELETE command), among other things.

Default collation

I should stick with whatever collation the setup program suggests

Yes, if you feel lucky. Do you? I'm not the type of person who wins the lottery, so I prefer to give the collation selection some thought. The setup program will pick a default collation based on the locale settings for the system account on the machine. This doesn't necessarily match what collation you want for your system databases and as the default collation for new databases.

You should pick a collation that matches how you want SQL Server to handle things like sorting of character data, case sensitivity, accent sensitivity, and code pages for non-Unicode data. If you have doubts, ask the vendor/developer of the application for which you install SQL Server:

- What collations do you support?
- What collation do you recommend?
- Do you support that I have a different collation for the system databases than what we'll have in the application database?

The answers to these questions will allow you to pick the right collation. Note that "Don't know" or "Huh?" for question three should be interpreted as "No." Also worth remembering is that when you restore or attach a database, the collation will be the same as it was on the source SQL Server. Say that the source SQL Server had collation A for the system databases, and the database you want to move to the new SQL Server also has collation A. You install the new SQL Server with collation B and restore this database. You now have a SQL Server with system database collation B and the user database has collation A. If you are lucky, the application has no problems with this, but can you assume that? The worst case is that you run in production for a while and after a week or so see errors from the application because of this.

One reason for such a problem is if the application creates a temp table, using tempdb's collation, and then compares this to some table in your application database, possibly with a "collation conflict error." You can create the temp table by specifying `database_default` as the collation for the column to get the same collation as the source database, but doing so won't help if the application doesn't specify `database_default`. The next version of SQL Server (SQL 11) will reportedly have a feature called Contained Database, a first version of that feature, which will help for these situations and also with isolating the database from its environment (the SQL Server instance) in general.

Table-level backups

Moving a table to its own filegroup allows me to do table-level backup and restore

Well, sort of, but it might not achieve your end goal. Here's the question you should ask yourself:

What do I want to achieve by doing table-level backup or table-level restore?

The answer to this question will tell you whether filegroup level backup will be helpful. The bottom line is that SQL Server won't allow you to restore a database so that different parts of the database are from different points in time. So, if the reason for you to do table-level restore is to back out of some mistake done in the database ("Oops, I just deleted the Invoice table!"), then filegroup restore won't be of much use to bring this data directly back into the database. (You *can* do partial restore into a new database—more information to follow). You might think that if the Invoice table is on its own filegroup, you could restore a backup of that filegroup from a point in time that was *before* you deleted that Invoice table. But the solution isn't quite that simple.

When you restore a part of a database (page, filc, or filegroup), you'll also have to restore all subsequent transaction log backups (unless the affected filegroup has been read-only since the backup was performed—more information to follow) so that SQL Server can apply all changes against the restored data until the current point in time. This technique wouldn't allow you to restore only a part of the database to an earlier point in time. There are exceptions to the "restore all log backups" rule, but those involve read-only databases or filegroups that don't apply to this scenario. Until you restore all your log backups up to the current point in time, you either won't be able to access the data in the filegroup you restored (if you are on Enterprise Edition or similar), or you won't be able to access *any* data in the database.

What you can do, though, is restore the filegroup in question and also the PRIMARY filegroup to a *new* database name, using the PARTIAL option of the RESTORE DATABASE command. You can do this to a desired point in time, but the possible resolution will depend on what types of backups you have. Assuming you restore the Invoice table to a point in time before you dropped that table, you can now use some means to copy the table and data to your production database. This task is doable, but it isn't as straightforward as restoring the filegroup level backup directly into the production database.

You might question the value of filegroup backup and restore in the first place, but there are definitely use cases. Say you have a large database, divided into several filegroups, and something happens with any of the file(s) that constitutes one of the filegroups. You'll now be able to restore only that filegroup, and all subsequent log backups, also known as online piecemeal restore. You can even restore a file from a filegroup (containing that file) or full backup, or restore a filegroup from a full backup. You can restore only what's broken, and the backup you restore from can contain more than what's broken (more than what you restore). Doing so can definitely be a time-saver for larger databases and possibly with partitioned tables.

Another use case is if you have some data that you only modify once a month. You can modify that data, set the filegroup to read-only, and back up the database, and for your regular backups you'll no longer need to include this seldom-modified filegroup. This approach will save space for your regular backups. If something happens with the read-only filegroup, you restore it from the earlier full backup. SQL Server won't require you to restore subsequent log backups because the filegroup hasn't been modified since the backup (this requires SQL Server 2005 or later).

So, there are use cases for filegroup-level backup and restore, but doing so isn't as simple as restoring a part of a database and getting that part to an earlier point in time.

Using replication for high availability

I'm using replication, so if something happens with my production database, I'll just switch over to the subscriber database

Let's say you want to use the SQL Server replication functionality for some type of failover or disaster recovery functionality. I'll start by saying that it's certainly possible to use replication for failover type scenarios, but don't expect to click a Next button. A subscriber database isn't a binary copy of the publisher database; it won't contain exactly the same things as the publisher. The differences will vary depending on what type of replication you're using (Transactional, Snapshot, or Merge). I won't match every aspect I mention here with every type of replication; the purpose here is to give you a general idea of why replication for failover isn't a point-and-click solution.

Merge application adds a unique identifier column to each table that doesn't have one already, which can cause problems if your application uses SELECT * or INSERT without a column list. Transactional replication requires each table you want to publish to have a primary key (PK) defined (sure, many databases have PKs defined for all tables, but that's unfortunately not always the case). There are considerations for both transactional and merge replication if you have columns using any of the old-style LOB (Large Object) data types (text, ntext, and image).

I used the Create Publication Wizard to configure replication and looked at the settings available for a table (Article Properties). There are about 40 properties you can define. Other replication types will have a different number of properties, but the basic principle applies. Here are things that *aren't* replicated by default:

- Foreign keys
- Check constraints
- Nonclustered indexes
- Defaults
- Triggers
- Filegroup associations
- Partitioning scheme
- Full-text indexes
- Permissions
- Sparse column attributes

This list isn't meant to be exhaustive but should give you an idea of factors you must consider. You can go through the configuration list, making sure that you select the options you need so you'll have as close a replica as possible. Hopefully, those who are using replication for failover have spent time on this part of the process and verified that they have what they need and also that the application will work fine if they must switch over production to the subscription database. Thinking through your configuration should be done for all solutions, but other technologies that were more directly designed for failover-type scenarios will give you a binary copy of the database if you switch over (except for the cluster support, which is the same database). The closer you come to a binary copy of the database, the fewer choices you have and the easier it will be to use such a solution for a failover scenario. I'd welcome a setting for replication such as "Configure Publication for Failover" or "Make Publication as Close a Copy to the Original as Possible," a default setting suitable for these scenarios.

Replication can have its advantages as a failover technology, but it won't be a good solution unless you spend time to ensure you have everything you need in case of a disaster.

Timing query performance

Timing that a query executes quickly is enough to guarantee good performance

The danger with this assumption is that you risk missing things that will show up when you're in production and are less likely to be able to fix them quickly and keep end users happy. I'm a fan of thinking in terms of resource usage and not only response time.

In the end, the resources you have in the machine are limited. The server can only perform so many clock cycles per second. And the server can only do so many I/O operations per second. And you're limited to a certain amount of memory, which can be used, among other things, to reduce I/O by caching data. In an environment where the resources are limited, you'll be able to co-exist more happily if you try to conserve resource usage. This rule applies to the ecosystem on Earth equally as to a computer system. You can be a better citizen by not wasting resources.

You might say now that in the computer world, you have Moore's law, or something similar to that, meaning you get more memory, clock cycles, and I/O operations for every year that goes by. That's certainly true, but people are also expecting more from you. Are your databases the same size today as they were in 1992? Probably not. Do you have more users today? You get my point. But even if that weren't the case, cheap or quick isn't the same as free or instantaneous. And the distinction is important. If something is free, you can use a lot and it's still free. Or if something is instantaneous, no matter how many times you do it, it will still be instantaneous. But because computing resources are neither free nor instantaneous, they'll add up. Execute enough queries and it will start to cost you and will take time.

The danger here is that you might not see the effect until you're in production and users are already suffering. The fix can take a long time to find and implement; meanwhile your business is hurting. As a simple example, run the following query in your Adventureworks2008 database:

```
SELECT d.ProductID, d.OrderQty, d.UnitPrice, d.ModifiedDate
FROM Sales.SalesOrderDetail
WHERE OrderQty = 30
```

Was that quick enough? By looking at only the time it took to execute the query, you'll likely say "Yes." But is it good enough? Does it conserve resources? Run SET STATIS-TICS IO ON and also enable the option Include Actual Execution Plan, and execute the query again. You'll now see that the query performs a table scan, meaning it will look at every page and every row for the order details table. This table scan can be okay when you develop the application or do your initial testing, because you probably won't yet have a production volume of data. Not only do you have a small volume of data, the data you do have is likely to fit in cache. If this query goes into production, you can probably imagine what will happen over time as you get a production volume of rows in your order details table. Not only will memory consumption start to add up, but sooner or later you won't fit the data in cache, and the table scan now starts to force physical I/Os, which are so much slower than reading from cache. Things start to get ugly pretty quickly.

There are circumstances where a table scan can be the best algorithm, and you might not be able to anticipate every query over a number of years into the future. But ignoring resource consumption and only looking at execution time can be a recipe for disaster. I've seen it countless times, as I'm sure many of you have, as well.

Shrinking databases

Shrinking the databases regularly is good housekeeping

"Are you going to beat that dead horse even more?" you might be thinking. If you are, then fine, keep moving; there's nothing more to be seen here. But as long as I see data file shrinking being performed at customer sites, recommended in forums, and reported as being included in various types of maintenance routines, I'll pound on it a bit more.

Hopefully most of you know that data file shrinking is bad, for many reasons. I won't delve into the details here—you can learn all that on the internet. I have an article on my blog that has been frequently read for some 10 years now. You can find it at http://www.karaszi.com/SQLServer/info_dont_shrink.asp.

For those of you who are curious why you don't want to do data file shrinking except in special situations, here's a short list of reasons:

- It will fragment the data in your database—badly.
- It will fragment the database files in your filesystem.
- It will cause your transaction log to grow—potentially a lot.
- It will take time.
- It can cause "out of space" errors if grow doesn't happen quickly enough.

These points are for data files; there are additional reasons to not regularly shrink transaction log files. Even if I convinced only a few of you esteemed readers to stop doing regular shrinks, I think this section is a good use of ink.

Auditing login access

I can see the Windows account name for somebody who logged in using SQL Server authentication

I wish you could. The typical background for this scenario is that you have an application that uses the same login for several, possibly all, users. This application has its own security and account handling. Now you realize that the auditing and tracking of who did what that's built into the application is no longer enough.

You want to use functionality within SQL Server to determine who did what. But the problem is how you can differentiate the users when they use the same login name (typically a SQL Server login). Whether you use Profiler and Tracing, `sp_who`, `sys.dm_exec_sessions`, Server Audit, some T-SQL function, or other means, you won't get the Windows account name when SQL Server authentication is used.

There are solutions you can try, like having a table that identifies the session ID with your login name. That would require your application to insert a row into the table when it connects to SQL Server. Or the application can use `SET CONTEXT_INFO` to set something that identifies the user. But both these solutions require the application to do something when it connects. Also, a simple `sp_who` or similar won't pick up the name of the user. You might consider using the hostname, which is designed to give you the client machine name. This can be spoofed, though (it's set by the connection string), and SQLCMD has a command-line switch to specify the value for this. Also, the machine name isn't the same thing as the account name of the user.

You'll end up requiring some changes in the application if you want to see who did what using SQL Server means. Here's one way to do it, which will also minimize the number of accounts (logins/users) you'll create in SQL Server as well as the amount of permission assignments you'll end up doing:

1 Create a Windows (Active Directory) group for this purpose.
2 Add the relevant Windows accounts to this Windows group.
3 Add the Windows group as a login to SQL Server.
4 Add a user for this login to your database.
5 If you want minimal changes made to your application, you now might make this user a member of the db_owner role. It depends on how much work you're prepared to put in to ensure that the application uses minimal privileges while working in the database. In the end, it boils down to how much work you're willing to do. If the old app did it using the same account, having high privileges, then you might be okay with the new app having the same privileges, with the added ability to see who did what.
6 Make sure the application connects using Windows authentication from now on.

    But what if the end user uses a tool like SQL Server Management Studio, connects directly to SQL Server using Windows authentication, and then wreaks havoc in your database (because the user will have the same privileges the app has)? You can handle this situation using application roles:

7 Make sure that the Windows login/user (for the Windows group) you created has as low privileges as needed in the database.
8 Create an application role in the database, and assign the relevant permissions that the application needs to the application role. An application role is password protected.
9 The application will log in using Windows authentication and then use `sp_setapprole` to change security context for the connection to the application role.

You can now see who did what assuming you look at the login name. This solution isn't for everyone, but where it fits it will allow you to see who did what, with some minor changes to the application.

Tail-log backups

SQL Server will automatically connect to the existing LDF file and use the last log records since the most recent log backup when I restore a transaction log backup

Here's the scenario. You're performing database and log backups. Something happens so you'll have to restore your database. Say that it was 10 minutes since you performed your last log backup. You have 10 minutes worth of transactions in the LDF file. If you now restore your backups into the same database name as the current database, you'd have overwritten the log records for those last 10 minutes. They're lost forever.

Microsoft added a check for this situation in SQL Server 2005. This feature will check if you're doing log backups and whether modifications have been made in the database since the last log backup was performed. If that's the case and you restore into that database name, you'll see an error message like this one:

```
Msg 3159, Level 16, State 1, Line 1
The tail of the log for the database "dbname" has not been backed
up. Use BACKUP LOG WITH NORECOVERY to backup the log if it contains
work you do not want to lose. Use the WITH REPLACE or WITH STOPAT
clause of the RESTORE statement to just overwrite the contents of
the log.
Msg 3013, Level 16, State 1, Line 1
RESTORE DATABASE is terminating abnormally.
```

I like to think of this as a friendly reminder to perform the "last" log backup (also known as the "tail-log backup") before you do the restore operation. If you don't want to perform this log backup, you can still do the restore using the REPLACE option of the RESTORE DATABASE command.

Database defaults

I should use the default specifications for file size and attributes when I create a new database

Using the defaults might be fine if you're creating a database for temporary use—something you want to play with or test things on. But for databases that will stick around for a while and will be anything but miniscule in size, reconsider.

The default number of files is two; one data file (MDF) and one log file (LDF). This might be fine, depending on your requirements. The problem is the file size and autogrow increments. The default file size is something like 2 MB for a data file and 1 MB for a log file (the exact default values depend on the size of these files for your model database).

The autogrow increment for a data file is 1 MB. Imagine a database that has grown to 25 GB, if autogrow would've grown the database file size. That would mean that you had roughly 25,000 autogrow operations for this file alone. Imagine what that does to your filesystem.

For a log file, the default is even worse: the unit is 10 percent of the current size. So although the file is small, it will grow frequently with small increments. This will cause a large number of virtual log files (VLFs)—the transaction log is internally divided in a number of VLFs—which in turn will increase things like startup time for SQL Server. And because the file is larger, 10 percent means that it will take time to grow the file. Instant File Initialization can't be used by transaction log files, so SQL Server will have to zero every bit of the transaction log file as it grows. Kimberly Tripp has written a number of great blog posts on this topic; this is a good starting point: http://www.sqlskills .com/BLOGS/KIMBERLY/post/Transaction-Log-VLFs-too-many-or-too-few.aspx.

The recommendation is as obvious as it seems: try to specify a reasonable file size and autogrow increment. And ideally, you want to monitor file space usage and manually grow the files before autogrow kicks in.

Difficulty

This is hard

No, it's fun! Working with SQL Server, implementing a production environment, and defining and implementing a backup strategy can be fun. SQL Server is a great product to work with. If you strive for doing a good job and dig in, you'll find that what could be considered difficult turns out to be challenging and intriguing. You'll also find a great community with lots of help out there in cyberspace, including Twitter, forums, and blogs. Fire up your favorite search engine and you'll soon find us!

Summary

A great thing about training is that questions, problems, and thoughts are so diverse, no two classes are alike. But some topics tend to repeat, and I've elaborated on a few of them here.

About the author

Tibor Karaszi, a SQL Server MVP since 1997, is an independent consultant and trainer focusing on the relational database engine. His experience with SQL Server goes all the way back to the late 1980s and the first version of Microsoft SQL Server. Tibor lives in Stockholm, Sweden; visit his site at http://www.karaszi.com.

18 High availability of SQL Server in the context of Service Level Agreements

Tobiasz Janusz Koprowski

For most of us, especially readers of this book, SQL Server—in any version—is the heart of the system. We take care of it, perfect it, use more and more recent versions, and spend lots of time getting to know, and, most of all, befriending it. We use many tools to employ it in a better, safer, more convenient, and more efficient way: first through procedures, scripts, and applications we create, and then through tools supplied by Microsoft and applications supplied by various vendors. This is the ideal state for us, apart from those difficult moments when a presentation is needed, or, worse still, when we have to plan a budget for the environment of which we take care.

Unfortunately, in the big picture of our database environment, we have internal and external clients. These are our supervisors, project managers, and department directors. Although they give us our tasks, our data, servers, instances, clusters, and so on take most of our time. But our clients constantly require something, demand and expect something from us. *A report for tomorrow? No, it's for this afternoon! A new set of script changes? As if I care; we have wage processing tonight! I can't enter the database; why does it take so long?* These are only a fraction of the demands I've heard this month alone.

In this chapter, you'll get to know what high availability is, how it influences your everyday work, and why Service Level Agreements are, or should be, important for you.

High availability—a definition

There are many books, courses, webcasts and workshops on high availability. We can find quite a lot of material on high availability in SQL Server as well. That's why we need to consolidate our knowledge. First, let's answer one question: what is high availability?

The definition found in various studies on the subject is clear enough: to maintain high availability is to ensure a ceaseless functioning of devices, systems, and applications, mostly for the needs of the production environment in an enterprise. Simultaneously, it's expected to prevent data loss that may result from the following:

- *Software faults*—Everyone who has carefully read the EULA (end user license agreement) must have noticed the following statement: "Microsoft shall not be held liable for any damages arising from software faults." What does it mean practically? It means that if you use an instance of SQL Server 2008 R2 Enterprise Edition in your production environment (which costs a pretty penny, as well), and suddenly, during a peak transaction load, SQL Server crashes and blue screens, Microsoft isn't liable for damages. Nevertheless, those who read EULAs may protest because the producer *is* liable to a certain extent—in the case of Microsoft Corporation, the limited amount is $5 U.S. (See http:// koprowskit.eu/licensing/2009/09/producent-oprogramowania-nie-ponosi-odpowiedzialnosci/, but this blog is in Polish. The original information is available at http://www.microsoft.com/security/scanner/en-us/Eula.aspx.)

- *Bugs*—During the development of SQL Server, there's a chance one faulty fragment of code may pass all tests undetected, and then a bug may occur at the worst moment.

- *Hardware failures*—These are the most common causes (besides human-caused failures) of environment inaccessibility. The range of inanimate objects that can fail is large: hard drives, memory cards, network cards, motherboards, fans, processors, HDD (hard disk drive) controllers (the most troublesome failures), Fibre Channel cards, SAN and NAS matrixes, power supply, air-conditioning, or network infrastructure.

- *Natural disasters*—Recently we've observed natural disasters that influence high availability; the most recent examples are the flood in Australia, the tsunami and earthquake in Japan, and the heavy snowfall in the United States. These are only a few examples of natural disasters that may cut off your server room from the rest of the world, having an effect on your availability.

- *Human-caused errors*—Often enough, you hear the saying "a human being is the weakest link" during risk analysis for your environment. This is sad, but true. It's easy enough to select the Shut Down option instead of the Log Off option to switch off a server—it happens quite often. It's not a big problem if it takes place in the vicinity of the server room because someone can power on the server again, but what if you shut down a server from a different location (overseas, for instance) and in a virtual environment, which you don't administrate?

- *Other unpredictable events*—These include other unexpected incidents that may have an adverse impact on your environment; for example, a truck that suddenly crashed into your office or an excavator bucket that snapped your fiber optic cable connecting you with the world.

Types of unavailability

There are two kinds of unavailability:

- *PSO (planned system outage)*—Planned minimal unavailability of a system to carry out necessary maintenance work, installation of updates, or replacement/upgrade of hardware, which are coordinated with the client and don't influence HA and SLA (service level agreement) resolutions until...
- *USO (unplanned system outage)*—Completely unplanned and unexpected failure partially or completely disabling performance or availability in a noticeable and measurable way, which may result in expensive repairs and/or contractual fines for failing to provide clients with agreed-on SLAs.

Let's go back to "until...." What does that mean? Well, if you need to patch your system or to upgrade your database to a newer version, it might turn out that after rebooting, your database won't work (or even worse, the system won't start). Then your planned system outage—agreed upon with the client—turns into an unplanned system outage and most often lasts too long, which results in the client's dissatisfaction and affects the binding SLA parameters.

Unavailability indicators

A closer look into various offers of outsourcing and hosting the data center or your own offer (if you provide such services) reveals the usual measure of availability of 99.99 percent or sometimes 99.95 percent. What do these three or four nines mean? Is the measure sufficient for you? Take a look at table 1.

Table 1   Table of availability—the magic nines

Availability percentage	Downtime per year	Downtime per month	Downtime per week
90	36.5 days	72 hours	16.8 hours
95	18.25 days	36 hours	8.4 hours
98	7.30 days	14.4 hours	3.36 hours
99	3.65 days	7.20 hours	1.68 hours
99.5	1.83 days	3.60 hours	50.4 min
99.8	17.52 hours	86.23 min	20.16 min
99.9 (three nines)	8.76 hours	43.2 min	10.1 min
99.95	4.38 hours	21.56 min	5.04 min
99.99 (four nines)	52.6 min	4.32 min	1.01 min
99.999 (five nines)	5.26 min	25.9 sec	6.05 sec
99.9999 (six nines)	31.5 sec	2.59 sec	0.605 sec

It turns out that "three nines" isn't such great availability. To fully understand it in the context of your production availability, you should consider the formula for calculating availability:

```
AVAILABILITY = MTBF / (MTBF + MTTR)
```

MTBF stands for "mean time between failures" and MTTR stands for "mean time to recovery/repair."

In addition, you have to exclude planned repairs, patching, and unit replacement; these don't influence availability because they're included in the planned system outage schedule.

High availability options in SQL Server

The most important options for high availability in SQL Server are listed in table 2.

Table 2   Table of high availability of SQL Server

Area	Database mirroring	Failover clustering	Transactional replication	Log shipping
Data loss	Some data loss possible; none when using synchronous mirroring	Data loss possible, unless synchronous mirroring/SAN replication used	Some data loss possible	Some data loss possible
Automatic failover	Yes (in HA mode)	Yes	No	No
Transparent to client	Yes, when configured	Yes; connect to same IP	No; NLB helps	No; NLB helps
Downtime	Variable depending on failure type and size of mirror redo queue	20 seconds or more plus time to recovery	Seconds	Seconds plus time to recovery
Standby read access	Yes, with DB snapshots	No	Yes	Yes
Data granularity	DB only	All systems and DBs	Table or view	DB only
Masking of HDD failure	Yes	No; shared disk	Yes	Yes
Special hardware	No; duplicate recommended	Cluster HCL	No; duplicate recommended	No; duplicate recommended
Complexity	Medium–high	Medium	Medium–high	Low

What's important, in addition to these four basic and most frequently allowed options, is that SQL Server introduces three more new features:

- *Live migration*—Allows you to manage resources dynamically by moving virtual devices between physical hosts, to burden hosts' systems and to improve the health management of such environments. Unavailability is practically limited to the time needed for the network to switch on (about 1/4 to 1/2 of a standard ping question).
- *Hot-add CPU and memory*—In connection with the virtualized environment mentioned previously, it enables a live addition of processing and memory resources to your database server without stopping it, much less restarting it.
- *Peer-to-peer replication*—It enables storing and sharing data on servers with diversified locations, taking into account their geographical location. It provides scale-out and high availability solutions for using data across multiple instances (often called nodes).

Service Level Agreement

Now that we've briefly defined high availability of SQL Server and its relevant features, let's look at SLAs.

SLAs were introduced in the 1980s as agreements between telecommunication operators and target clients. They are mutually negotiable service agreements (with the exception of cloud service, as practice proves) and concern primarily IT, but not always. SLAs should be seen as formal, legally binding contracts, although informal agreements are acceptable in some countries, including level and scope of service based on calculable metrics (availability level, usefulness, and efficiency). An SLA should specify the minimum and maximum scope of every service stipulated by it.

Measurement indicators

Every well-defined SLA must contain specific measurement indicators. My favorite example of a typical call center can give you an idea of specificity:

- *ABA (abandonment rate)*—Percentage of connections rejected while waiting for an answer
- *ASA (average speed to answer)*—Average time (mostly in seconds) needed to connect with the help desk
- *TSF (time service factor)*—Percentage of connections received in a precise time frame; for instance, 80 percent in 20 seconds
- *FCR (first call resolution)*—Percentage of connections during which a problem was solved without diverting the call to another expert
- *TAT (turnaround time)*—Time needed to finish specific tasks

The following extracts are from SLAs for a database environment, which are frequently used as measurement indicators of completion (or exceeding our standard SLA clauses):

- *Production time*—Time in which service/partition/table/database must be available; this may differ for different parts of the database depending on the application or other factors.

- *Percentage of service time*—Percentage of period (timc scope) when service/partition/table/database is available.
- *Hours reserved for downtime*—Defining downtime hours (maintenance breaks) in advance makes users' work easier.
- *Methods of help for users*—This means help desk response time and/or (we particularly do not like it) DBA response/reaction time.
- *Number of system users*
- *Number of transactions served in a time unit*
- *Acceptable performance levels for various operations*
- *Minimum time required for replication between physical or virtual different server*
- *Time for data recovery after a failure*—With regard to the way the data has been lost: accidental data deletion, database damage, SQL Server crash, or OS Server crash.
- *Maximum space*—Maximum space for tables/databases.
- *Number of users in specific roles*

The structure of a Service Level Agreement

Because of the great diversity of organizations with which IT agreements are made, we classify them as follows:

- *Service-oriented structure*—Agreement includes one service.
- *Client-oriented structure*—Agreement includes all services for one client.
- *Business process-oriented structure*—Agreement includes all services and their components that support a business process.
- *Multilevel structure*—Often attempted but difficult to define because it's oriented on everything (organization level, client, services).

A well-defined SLA should comprise the following components:

- *General details*—These include history of version, last update, last changes made by *xxx*, version number *x.x*.
- *Document characteristics*—These include the owner of the document and the name of document (SLA *xxx*.doc); this part comprises basic elements of every SLA.
- *Particular details*—This should be a maximum of three pages of clear, understandable text.

Most frequently, an SLA has the following structure:

- Aims of SLA
- Conditions of SLA
- Description of services offered
- Definition of service
- Scope of service
- Roles and responsibilities of parties
- Evaluation of service (service level)

- Time of service
- Service windows
- Planned improvements of service
- Long-term aims
- Periodic surveys
- Escalation procedures
- Change management

Service Level Agreements: the context for high availability

An SLA is not only a formal agreement between your boss, your company, or your representative and an external client. You're also often obliged by an unofficial agreement containing even fewer formal clauses, forcing you to comply with a certain scope of availability, and that's your daily work. You take care of SQL Server in your intranet or CRM to maintain its full functionality—at least within the working hours of internal departments and in particular during reporting or calculation of your wages. Suddenly, it seems there's an agreement, although informal, that you have to fulfill during your daily work. Let's leave these internal obligations; usually you manage to cope with them thanks to your personal charm and internal cooperation.

What we should consider now is the external agreement according to which your services must be available for the client almost constantly and almost everywhere (all exceptions must be included in the SLA definition). How can you do this if your key account manager or supervisor didn't invite you to the negotiation table when specific maintenance details were being discussed? Such a situation isn't a rare case, and as the administrator, you're expected to "work it out somehow." To perform your duties well (meaning at a normal pace, quietly, with no hurry or pressure), you need to have appropriate conditions provided.

If you're about to set up your SQL Server in a cluster, you need a minimum of two servers. But has anyone remembered to buy extra HDDs and network cards (LAN or FC) and to obtain a controller supply guarantee from their producer? Have you secured your server to such an extent that if one of the administrators quits in anger, then that administrator won't be able to purposely change or damage your databases? Human factor again. And what if the backup procedures, no matter how perfectly well described and seemingly well conceived, should fail? Try to imagine the following hypothetical example (based on my experience).

You allow 15 minutes unavailability for databases of 25 GB volume. You're able to provide a copy of the database for the user during these 15 minutes (because you have it on a second HDD), but:

- What will you do in the event of data damage?
- What will you do in the event of HDD damage?
- What will you do in the event of burnt motherboard?
- What will you do in the event of an FC cable being cut?

- How much time will it take to recover the backup?
- How much time will it take to bring a backup tape from another location 25 miles away in a big city during rush hour?

Summary

This chapter doesn't cover all aspects of the topic (it tackles only the tip of the iceberg), but it focuses on a rarely discussed yet essential particular of working with SQL Server and, in a broader perspective, any IT environment where high availability is essential.

Several conclusions are worth remembering:

- You need to know that SLAs exist.
- You should contribute to the definition of the SLAs (at least with respect to requirements, possibilities, and available technology).
- You must know the scope of your own responsibility.
- You need your plan B and plan C, fail-proof and tested.
- You need a technical capacity to fulfill your SLA agreements, meaning spare units in the storeroom where your environment is located, namely hard drives, storage devices, network cards, HDD controllers, and installation disks. You must also have serial numbers, a hard copy of emergency procedures, and a fully charged cell phone available.

Useful links

Check out the following links for more information:

Service Level Agreement and SLA Guide, http://www.service-level-agreement.net/
Business Excellence Institute, http://www.bei.org.pl/ (This site is in Polish.)
The SLA world, http://www.sla-world.com/

About the author

Linked to the ICT industry for 12 years, Tobiasz Janusz Koprowski has several years' experience in the banking sector (ICBS, AS/400). He worked in the data center of a large IT company in Wroclaw for a number of years. The leader of the community of SQL Server and SharePoint in Poland and Europe, he's frequently a speaker at meetings and conferences. He's also a member of the technical team GITCA, where he serves as vice-chair in the EMEA region. Koprowski is interested in operating procedures, SLAs, security, and communities. He's also the holder of several certificates, a consultant, auditor, freelance MCT, technical writer, blogger, photographer, journalist, and music reviewer.

PART 3

Database development

Edited by Paul Nielsen

The simple SELECT statement is still the most complex and powerful single word in computer science. I've been writing database code professionally since the mid-1980s, and I'm still amazed at SELECT's ability to draw in data from numerous sources (and types of sources) and make that data twist and shout, and present it exactly as needed.

The goal of Transact-SQL (T-SQL) is to provide the right question to SQL Server so the query optimizer can generate a query execution plan that's correct and efficient. The code is only one part of the equation. The physical schema plays a huge role in the efficiency of the code and the query execution plan, and indexing is the bridge between the data and the query. Entering the schema + the query + the indexes into the query optimizer yields the query execution plan.

I might argue that the physical schema is the foundation for database performance; nulltheless, I can't disagree that poor T-SQL code has been the source of many a database pain.

This section is where SQL Server MVPs who are passionate about their T-SQL code share their excitement for T-SQL—their passion, like mine, for making data twist and shout:

- Aaron Bertrand opens the section by sharing his ever-popular list of T-SQL best practices in the form of habits worth forgetting.
- Kevin Boles urges us to remember that the point of T-SQL is the query execution plan, not reusable code.

- John Paul Cook reveals the little-known skill of performing regular expression in Management Studio.
- Sergio Govoni explains the new T-SQL features in Denali.
- My friend and former SQL Server Bible tech editor, Hugo Kornelis shows how to create a new data type.
- Matija Lah digs deep in the CLR and comes up with how to use regular expressions in queries and SSIS packages.
- Peter Larsson returns to our Codd roots with an academic but practical chapter on relational division—a complex topic but one that must be mastered by every serious T-SQL developer.
- Ben Miller, our former MVP lead turned MVP, writes about the options for storing blobs and FILESTREAM.
- Luciano Moreira discusses a topic that's a passion of mine—running unit tests on your T-SQL code.
- Mladen Prajdić provides an excellent discussion on Service Broker.
- Denis Reznik shows how to effectively use the HierarchyID data type for coding hierarchies.
- And finally, Allen White demonstrates his ninja scalability skills with Service Broker.

Without a doubt, turning a set of SQL Server MVPs loose with the permission to write about whatever gets them excited is bound to turn up some interesting topics, and indeed it did. Happy reading.

About the editor

Paul Nielsen is the founder of Ministry Weaver, a software startup offering an object database for ministries. He focuses on extreme data modeling, database development, and the occasional XMAL and C#, and he was formerly the author of the SQL Server Bible series and the editor of the first volume of *SQL Server MVP Deep Dives*. Paul offers consulting and seminars on data modeling and schema optimization. He lives in Colorado with his family and he's passionate about marriage, adoption, theology, music, writing, and their next family trip to Maui.

19 T-SQL: bad habits to kick

Aaron Bertrand

As a longtime participant in the SQL Server community, I've seen my share of bad habits. I've even formed a few of my own, all of which I'm on the path to correcting. Whether they come from StackOverflow, the MSDN forums, or even from the #sqlhelp hash tag on Twitter, one thing is clear: bad habits can spread like poison ivy. The same is definitely true in Transact-SQL (T-SQL), where samples are borrowed, reused, and learned from on a daily basis.

Many people think SELECT * is okay because it's easy, or that following coding standards for this one stored procedure is unimportant because it needs to be deployed in a rush, or that they shouldn't have to type that ORDER BY statement because the rows "always" come back in the same order. This chapter is meant to take five of these habits and point out (a) why they're problems, and (b) what you can do to avoid them.

Please note that several of the examples in this chapter will use tables and data from the AdventureWorks2008R2 sample database, available from CodePlex at http://sqlserversamples.codeplex.com/.

SELECT *

For as long as there has been T-SQL code, there has been prevalent use of SELECT *. Although typically this is the most straightforward way to determine what a table looks like in ad hoc and troubleshooting scenarios, my characterization as a "bad habit" in this case only refers to its use in production code.

In many cases, not all the columns in the table or view are required by the application. Using SELECT * in this case can cause wasteful scans or lookups in order to return all of the columns, when the query (and application) may have been satisfied by a covering index at a much lower resource cost. Not to mention there's the additional overhead of sending all the unneeded columns over the network just to have the application ignore them in the first place—or worse, incorporate them into the code, never to be used.

Consider the following two versions of a query against the Sales.SalesOrderDetail table, and imagine that the application only cares about the columns SalesOrder-DetailID, ProductID, and SalesOrderID:

```
SELECT *
    FROM [Sales].[SalesOrderDetail]
    WHERE [ProductID] < 20;

SELECT [SalesOrderDetailID],[ProductID],[SalesOrderID]
    FROM [Sales].[SalesOrderDetail]
    WHERE [ProductID] < 20;
```

When looking at the execution plans for these two queries, you can see that the short-hand version is twice as expensive as the version that explicitly names the required columns. In this case the extra cost is caused by a key lookup, as you can see in figure 1. This figure shows SQL Sentry Plan Explorer, which you can download for free at www.sqlsentry.net/plan-explorer/.

Even when all the columns are required, there are other reasons to name your columns instead of using shorthand. One is that schema changes to the underlying

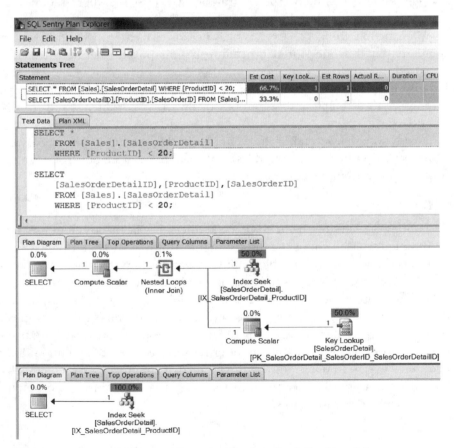

Figure 1   Comparing execution plans: SELECT * vs. explicit column list

table(s) can break code relying on ordinal position of columns or performing inserts into other tables without using an explicit column list.

NOTE Please keep in mind that the use of SELECT * within an EXISTS clause is perfectly fine. The optimizer understands that you won't be returning the columns as data and performs its work without any negative impact on the execution plan.

An example of schema changes causing problems is the case where a view is created using SELECT *. If you change the underlying schema, the view can become "confused" because it isn't automatically notified about metadata changes. This means if your view says SELECT * FROM dbo.foo and you rename the column x to y, the view will still return a column named x. This issue can get even more convoluted if you then add a different column named x with a different data type.

There's an easy workaround to fix the view in this case: a system stored procedure introduced in SQL Server 2005 named sys.sp_refreshsqlmodule. Alternatively, you can prevent SELECT * in a view by using SCHEMABINDING, which doesn't allow the syntax; this strategy also prevents underlying changes from being made to the table without the user knowingly removing the SCHEMABINDING condition from any of the views that reference it.

The excuse I hear the most from people defending the use of SELECT * is one borne out of laziness: they complain that they don't want to type out all the column names. Today's tools make this a questionable excuse at best—whether you're using Mladen Prajdic's SSMS Tools Pack, RedGate's SQLPrompt, or the native IntelliSense in SSMS, you'll rarely need to type out the columns manually, thanks to features such as keyword expansion and AutoComplete. And even if you don't use those tools and have disabled IntelliSense, you can drag the entire list of columns by expanding the table in question in Object Explorer, clicking on the Columns node, and dragging it onto the query window, as shown in figure 2.

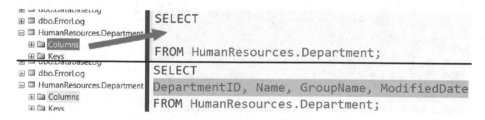

Figure 2   Dragging the Columns node onto a query window

Declaring VARCHAR without length

Another habit I see in a lot of code is declaring VARCHAR, NVARCHAR, and other string types without specifying a length. This tendency likely shows up in people with backgrounds in any number of scripting and object-oriented languages, where a string is a string, and it can be as long as you want, as long as it fits in memory. SQL

Server has some inconsistent rules about how long a string can be, depending on how the value is defined. Consider the following examples:

```
DECLARE @x CHAR = 'foo';
SELECT a = @x, b = CAST('foo' AS CHAR), c = CONVERT(CHAR, 'foo');
```

You'd expect in all three cases to see `'foo'` returned, but in fact the first column in the query returns only the letter `'f'`. This is because when a CHAR-based variable is declared without a length, the length becomes 1 (and this follows the ANSI standard). On the other hand, when you use CAST or CONVERT to specify that a string should be a CHAR-based type, the length becomes 30.

 This behavior can also come into play when you create tables. If you create a table with a column that is CHAR based and you don't specify a length, the behavior once again follows the standard, and the column is created with a maximum length of 1:

```
CREATE TABLE dbo.x(y VARCHAR);
GO
```

There are some further oddities in behavior that can make the inconsistent rules tricky to discover; for example, if you try to insert a longer string into the column, you'll get an error message about data truncation:

```
INSERT dbo.x(y) SELECT 'foo';

Msg 8152, Level 16, State 14, Line 2
String or binary data would be truncated.
The statement has been terminated.
```

But if you create a stored procedure that accepts a parameter with the exact same type (VARCHAR with no length), there's no error message, and the string is silently truncated and SQL Server quite happily puts the leading character into the column:

```
CREATE PROCEDURE dbo.x_insert
    @y VARCHAR
AS
BEGIN
    SET NOCOUNT ON;
    INSERT dbo.x(y) SELECT @y;
END
GO
EXEC dbo.x_insert @y = 'foo';
SELECT Result = y FROM dbo.x;

Results:
Result
-
f
```

This means that it can take quite a bit of manual effort, or maybe even luck, to discover that the strings you're passing into your stored procedure aren't remaining intact when they get written to the table. Hopefully this kind of thing gets discovered during testing, but having seen this issue make it into production systems, I want to be sure it becomes well known. This problem goes away if you always declare a length for your CHAR-based columns.

Not choosing the right data type

There are a lot of cases where you might be tempted to use a specific data type to store certain information, but your first instinct isn't always the best choice. Here are just a few examples I've seen:

- Using NVARCHAR(MAX) for zip codes, phone numbers, or URLs
- Using VARCHAR for proper names
- Using DATETIME when DATE or SMALLDATETIME will do
- Using TIME to store an interval or a duration
- Using VARCHAR to store DATETIME data

There are many other examples, and I could probably write an entire chapter just on this habit alone, but I want to focus here on the last example—primarily because it's one of the most common that I see out in the wild.

Many people say they want to store DATETIME using a CHAR-based data type so that they can keep their formatting. They may want to store a date as "Tuesday, April 5th, 2011" or as "04/05/2011" without having to perform any presentation formatting when they retrieve the data. Another reason I've seen for using CHAR-based data types instead of DATE/TIME types is to store a date without time, or vice versa.

The main problem with doing so is that you lose the ability to validate your data, validation that you get for free when you use a data type such as DATETIME, SMALLDATETIME, or DATE. And in most cases, you also lose the ability to sort the dates and to perform various date-related functions against the data, because SQL Server isn't going to recognize every conceivable format as DATE/TIME data—especially if the data comes from a form with free text entry, where someone is just as likely to enter "None of your business" as they are to enter a properly formatted and accurate date.

If you're concerned about formatting, please consider that presentation isn't a function of the database. You want to be able to trust your data, and every modern language has easy-to-use methods to present a DATE/TIME value coming out of SQL Server in whatever predefined or custom format you desire. The next version of SQL Server, codenamed Denali, will have a FORMAT function, which will make formatting much easier than currently possible.

If you're using SQL Server 2008 or later, and your need revolves around leaving date or time out of the equation, there's little preventing you from using the new, separate DATE and TIME types. If you must continue supporting SQL Server 2005 and older versions, you could use a DATETIME or SMALLDATETIME column with a CHECK CONSTRAINT to ensure that the time portion is always midnight, or that the date portion is always some token date (usually January 1, 1900).

If you aren't yet using SQL Server 2008 or later, there's one case that will be hard to support without using this bad habit (and I'll forgive it in this case): you need to store dates that precede 1753, the lower bound on the DATETIME data type. Because the SQL Server 2008 DATE data type supports dates from 0001-01-01 through 9999-12-31, you should be able to avoid this issue if you target that platform. (And if you're working on new development that's being targeted at SQL Server 2005, remember that this version is no longer in mainstream support, so there are likely far more concerning limitations coming your way.)

Mishandling date range queries

At my previous job, I reviewed a large number of stored procedures that ran reports against historical data, so I've seen a lot of examples of date range query abuse. The most obvious examples are making a WHERE clause "non-SARGable," which basically means that an index on the relevant column can't be used. This is easy to do by applying a function such as CONVERT() or YEAR() against the relevant column, which ties one of the optimizer's hands behind its back. Examples include stripping the date or time to get all the data for a specific day, or extracting just the year and month to pull the data for a specific month. Here are a couple of examples:

```
SELECT SalesOrderID, ProductID
    FROM Sales.SalesOrderDetail
    WHERE YEAR(ModifiedDate) = 2006;

DECLARE @date SMALLDATETIME = '20060801';

SELECT SalesOrderID, ProductID
    FROM Sales.SalesOrderDetail
    WHERE CONVERT(CHAR(8),ModifiedDate,112) = CONVERT(CHAR(8),@date,112);
```

These methodologies will yield a full scan because SQL Server doesn't know how to translate the filter into a usable seek. These queries can be rewritten as follows, and if there's an index on the ModifiedDate column, it can be used for a much more efficient plan:

```
SELECT SalesOrderID, ProductID
    FROM Sales.SalesOrderDetail
    WHERE ModifiedDate >= '20060101'
    AND ModifiedDate < '20070101';

DECLARE @date SMALLDATETIME = '20060801';

SELECT SalesOrderID, ProductID
    FROM Sales.SalesOrderDetail
    WHERE ModifiedDate >= @date
    AND ModifiedDate < DATEADD(DAY, 1, @date);
```

I also saw a lot of BETWEEN queries. The problem with using BETWEEN for DATETIME or SMALLDATETIME data is that the end of the range is quite ambiguous. Imagine you have the following data in a table called dbo.Events:

```
dt
----------------
2011-01-01 14:55
2011-01-01 23:33
2011-01-01 23:59
2011-01-02 00:00
2011-01-02 01:23
```

Now consider a query like this:

```
SELECT COUNT(dt)
    FROM dbo.Events
    WHERE dt BETWEEN '20110101' AND '20110102';
```

If you ask different people, you'll probably get different expectations about whether the count should be 3, 4, or 5. The answer, in this case, will be 4, even though the author of the query probably didn't intend to include any data that occurred on January 2…or perhaps they assumed that all the data was entered without time. So in that case, the query should have included *all* of the data on the second. These cases are much better expressed using the following queries:

```
SELECT COUNT(dt)
    FROM dbo.Events
    WHERE dt >= '20110101'
    AND dt < '20110102';

SELECT COUNT(dt)
    FROM dbo.Events
    WHERE dt >= '20110101'
    AND dt < '20110103';
```

Finally, this can get even more ambiguous if you try to determine the "end" of a day to allow you to continue using BETWEEN. This kind of code was commonplace in a former environment:

```
SELECT COUNT(dt)
    FROM dbo.Events
    WHERE dt BETWEEN '20110101' AND '20110101 23:59:59.997';
```

The problems here are numerous. One is that if the data type of the column is SMALL-DATETIME, the end of the range will round up, and the query will become (without your explicit knowledge):

```
SELECT COUNT(dt)
    FROM dbo.Events
    WHERE dt BETWEEN '20110101' AND '20110102';
```

If the data type of the column is more precise (e.g., DATETIME2), then a different problem arises: being 3 milliseconds away from midnight may leave some rows out that should've been counted.

I always use an open-ended date range like those demonstrated in these queries. This way, I know for sure that the optimizer will use an index if it can, and I don't have any doubts about whether I'll include data from the wrong time period.

Making assumptions about ORDER BY

The last bad habit I'm going to talk about here is the reliance on ordering without using an explicit ORDER BY clause. You may remember that in SQL Server 2000, you could create a view using SELECT TOP 100 PERCENT … ORDER BY, and when you ran a query against the view without an ORDER BY, it would return in the expected order.

With optimizer changes in SQL Server 2005, this behavior was no longer observed—and even though the ORDER BY was clearly documented as a filter to determine which rows to return, and not necessarily to dictate the order the rows would be returned, many people complained about the behavior change.

The fact in this case is quite simple: if you want a specific order, *always* define an explicit ORDER BY on the outer query, even if some inner component of the query or table structure makes you feel like the data should come back in a certain order. If you don't use an ORDER BY clause, you're essentially telling SQL Server "Please return this data in whatever order you deem most efficient."

It's a common misconception that a query against a table with a clustered index will always come back in the order of the clustered index. Several of my colleagues have published blog posts proving that this isn't true, so just because you see it in your environment today, don't assume that this is a given. In short, do *not* rely on unguaranteed behavior, even if you "always" observe the same thing. Tomorrow the behavior may be different, because of a statistics change, your plan being expunged from the plan cache, or optimizer behavior changes due to a service pack, hotfix, or trace flag change. These are all things that can happen that you either won't know about or won't immediately correlate with the need to now go and add ORDER BY to all of your queries where the ordering behavior has changed.

Does this mean you should add ORDER BY to every single query you have? Only if you care about order (though I've found few cases where order truly isn't important, at least when you're returning data to a user or an application). And if you're changing your queries to ensure that your order will be observed tomorrow, make sure to inspect your query plans to determine whether you're performing any unnecessary sorts, because these won't necessarily be associated with the end result. Sort operations are rarely, if ever, going to make your queries run faster.

Summary

Making exceptions to sensible rules, or making assumptions about undocumented behavior, will lead to undesirable results sooner or later. But if you strive to avoid these things, and try to turn bad habits into good habits, you'll have far fewer cases where the exceptions will cause you pain.

About the author

Aaron Bertrand is a senior consultant for SQL Sentry, makers of performance monitoring and event management software for SQL Server, Analysis Services, and Windows. He's been blogging at sqlblog.com since 2006, focusing on manageability, performance, and new features. Aaron has been an MVP since 1997, and he speaks frequently at user group meetings and SQL Saturday events.

20 Death by UDF

Kevin Boles

When Microsoft released SQL Server 2000, developers around the world rejoiced at the introduction of user-defined functions (UDFs). They were finally able to, within their Transact-SQL code, adhere to two of the main developer mantras: code encapsulation and code reuse. But unfortunately scalar UDFs weren't fully integrated into the SQL Server optimizer and relational engine. This resulted in a number of issues, some of which can lead to unbelievably horrible query performance. In this chapter I'll focus on two of these issues: bad optimizer estimates and especially row-by-row query processing. I'll use a variety of standard tuning devices, including STATISTICS IO output, query plan analysis, and Profiler tracing. You'll discover that SSMS does *not* tell the truth when it comes to UDF execution metrics. Most importantly, you'll learn two techniques for avoiding the downsides of scalar UDFs.

Poor estimates

The query optimizer in the SQL Server engine uses a wide array of numerical values, formulas, and logic to quickly and efficiently provide a "good enough" query plan to be used to perform the requested action. Among the main facets used are statistics about both row counts and value distributions in the tables and columns involved in the query.

The first problem I'll review is that when UDFs are at play, those statistics aren't necessarily directly usable anymore, and "bad" values can lead the optimizer to make (sometimes disastrously) suboptimal plan choices. Two common types of bad plans are nested loop joins for a kajillion rows, or taking perhaps tens of minutes to scan a kajillion-row table and doing a hash join when an index seek and bookmark lookup would be appropriate to bring back the few actual matching rows in a matter of milliseconds.

Listing 1 shows a straightforward scalar UDF that concatenates names into a Full-Name-style output. The index was created to allow for an efficient index seek plan where appropriate. Note that the code uses exactly the same data types found on the

Person.Contact table where those three name fields reside. All fixed strings are cast with the N prefix, and ISNULL is only used for the MiddleName value, which is the only one of the three name columns that is NULLable. The return value is exactly the largest possible size value that could exist given the definition of the Person.Contact table. The correct data types and sizes are used, and the CPU-burning ISNULL is only used where necessary. Of such small details can big wins be had in database development.

Listing 1   FullName UDF

```
CREATE NONCLUSTERED INDEX idx1 ON Person.Contact
(LastName, FirstName, EmailAddress)
GO
CREATE FUNCTION dbo.fn_FullName (@FirstName nvarchar(50), @MiddleName
 nvarchar(50), @LastName nvarchar(50))
RETURNS nvarchar(153) WITH SCHEMABINDING
AS
BEGIN
   RETURN @LastName + N', ' + @FirstName + N' ' + ISNULL(@MiddleName, N'')
END
GO
```

NOTE   All code in this chapter is coded against the AdventureWorks database, which can be freely downloaded from the CodePlex website (http://msftdbprodsamples.codeplex.com/).

The next listing shows a query that uses the user-defined function from listing 1.

Listing 2   Using the FullName UDF in a SELECT

```
SELECT dbo.fn_FullName(c.FirstName, c.MiddleName, c.LastName) as FullName,
       od.ProductID,
       SUM((UnitPrice - UnitPriceDiscount) * OrderQty) AS TotalPrice
  FROM Sales.SalesOrderHeader oh
 INNER JOIN Sales.SalesOrderDetail od ON od.SalesOrderID = oh.SalesOrderID
 INNER JOIN Sales.SalesPerson sp ON sp.SalesPersonID = oh.SalesPersonID
 INNER JOIN HumanResources.Employee e ON e.EmployeeID = sp.SalesPersonID
 INNER JOIN Person.Contact c ON c.ContactID = e.ContactID
 WHERE dbo.fn_FullName(c.FirstName, c.MiddleName, c.LastName) =
 N'Abbas, Syed E'
 GROUP BY c.LastName, c.FirstName, c.MiddleName, od.ProductID
```

Throughout this chapter, I'll be using hardcoded values instead of parameters to avoid potential plan-caching and parameter-sniffing issues and (for this section in particular) to ensure that the optimizer has exact values that will allow it to truly show the estimate differences at the heart of my first assertion.

Running the stored procedure against the AdventureWorks database on my laptop's SQL 2005 instance outputs 68 simple rows of data quickly. Code encapsulation and

TextData	CPU	Duration	Reads	Writes	RowCounts
SELECT dbo.fn_FullName(c.FirstName, c.Middle...	79	258	1311	0	153

Figure 1   Information gathered from profiler

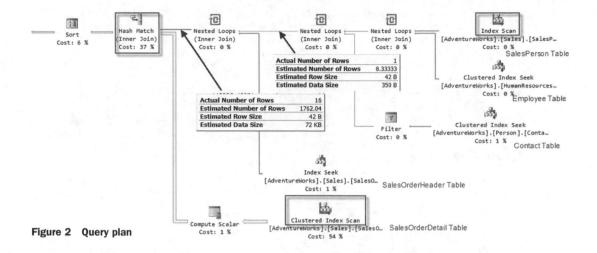

Actual Number of Rows	1
Estimated Number of Rows	8.33333
Estimated Row Size	42 B
Estimated Data Size	350 B

Actual Number of Rows	16
Estimated Number of Rows	1762.04
Estimated Row Size	42 B
Estimated Data Size	72 KB

Figure 2 Query plan

fast—this is great, right? Ummm…not if you dig just a little deeper. Profiler reveals the information shown in figure 1 when you do a Statement Completed event capture.

Let's find out what the query plan tells us about those I/Os. Take a look at figure 2. Notes:

1. There's an index scan on the SalesPerson table—not even the table you're filtering on. What if that were a million-row table? The cost could be prohibitive, and the locks taken during that scan, a serious drain on concurrency.

2. Right before you join to the SalesOrderHeader table, you're already over a factor of 8 off on your row count estimate: 8.33 rows estimated, 1 actual row.

3. Once you've completed the join to the SalesOrderHeader table, you're over *two orders of magnitude* off between the Estimated and Actual rows (1762.04 estimated, 16 actual). Believe me when I say that nothing good will be happening in your plan when that level of disparity occurs. That high estimated number crosses a tipping point, and the optimizer chooses to do a table (clustered index) scan and hash-match join to acquire the SalesOrderDetail rows. That action is the primary cause of the 258 Duration and 1311 Reads of the query.

The problem here is that the UDF prevents direct utilization of index/column statistics. Let's see what happens when you rewrite the query to allow for direct column access. The following listing shows a refactoring of the original SELECT that places the UDF code inline with the rest of the set-based statement.

Listing 3 Set-Based FullName SELECT

```
SELECT c.LastName + N', ' + c.FirstName + N' ' + ISNULL(c.MiddleName, '')
       as FullName, od.ProductID,
       SUM((UnitPrice - UnitPriceDiscount) * OrderQty) AS TotalPrice
  FROM Sales.SalesOrderHeader oh
 INNER JOIN Sales.SalesOrderDetail od ON od.SalesOrderID = oh.SalesOrderID
```

```
INNER JOIN Sales.SalesPerson sp ON sp.SalesPersonID = oh.SalesPersonID
INNER JOIN HumanResources.Employee e ON e.EmployeeID = sp.SalesPersonID
INNER JOIN Person.Contact c ON c.ContactID = e.ContactID
WHERE c.LastName = N'Abbas'
  AND c.FirstName = N'Syed'
  AND c.MiddleName = N'E'
GROUP BY c.LastName, c.FirstName, c.MiddleName, od.ProductID
```

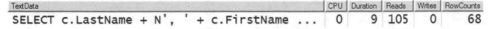

TextData	CPU	Duration	Reads	Writes	RowCounts
SELECT c.LastName + N', ' + c.FirstName ...	0	9	105	0	68

Figure 3   Profiler information

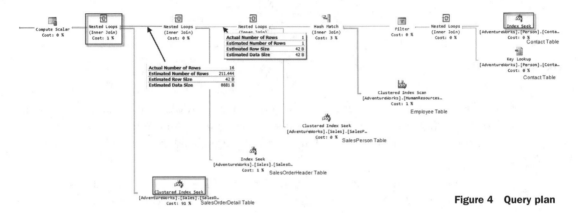

Figure 4   Query plan

Figure 3 shows the Profiler information for this statement. Figure 4 shows the query plan, which you'll compare to the UDF-based plan.

Notes:

1 You're now doing an index seek on the table (Person.Contact) you're filtering on, and the Estimated and Actual row count are both 1.

2 By the time you make it to joining to the SalesOrderHeader table, the Estimated and Actual rows are *still* both 1.

3 You see some mismatch between the Estimated and Actual row counts after rows are retrieved from SalesOrderHeader, as you often see in multijoin queries, but nowhere near the two orders of magnitude discrepancy from the UDF-based plan. Thus the optimizer correctly chooses an index seek plan to retrieve the few SalesOrderDetail rows required to fulfill the needs of your query. You can plainly see the much better performance that results.

Here you've seen how a simple scalar UDF can lead to a horribly performing query plan and that an inline refactor can eliminate the problem. On to the next class of UDF-related problem!

Row-by-row processing

The second problem I'll examine is the even more harmful "cursor under the covers" query execution that can result from using scalar UDFs. The previous example was "only" 28.7 times worse from a duration perspective and just 1.3 times worse from a reads perspective. I've come across *many* situations at clients where UDFs were five or even six orders of magnitude worse than their set-based counterparts! In listing 4 is a simple UDF that calculates a total price for a particular order and a stored procedure that uses it in the SELECT and WHERE clauses. (Again please recall that I'm using hard-coded values to avoid parameter sniffing/plan caching issues.)

Listing 4   Bad scalar UDF

```
CREATE FUNCTION dbo.fn_TotalPrice (@SalesOrderID int)
RETURNS money WITH SCHEMABINDING
AS
BEGIN
   DECLARE @result money
    SELECT @result = SUM((UnitPrice - UnitPriceDiscount) * OrderQty)
      FROM Sales.SalesOrderDetail
     WHERE SalesOrderID = @SalesOrderID
     RETURN @result
END
GO


CREATE PROC dbo.UDFsAreBad
AS
SET NOCOUNT ON
SELECT t.Name as TerritoryName, oh.OrderDate,
       dbo.fn_TotalPrice(oh.SalesOrderID) as TotalPrice
  FROM Sales.SalesOrderHeader oh
 INNER JOIN Sales.SalesTerritory t ON t.TerritoryID = oh.TerritoryID
 WHERE dbo.fn_TotalPrice(oh.SalesOrderID) > 10000
GO


EXEC dbo.UDFsAreBad
```

Again we examine the query plan (see figure 5).

Let's also look at the reads from SET STATISTICS IO ON:

```
Table 'Worktable'. Scan count 0, logical reads 0, ...
Table 'SalesOrderHeader'. Scan count 1, logical reads 703, ...
Table 'SalesTerritory'. Scan count 1, logical reads 2, ...
```

I leave it to the inquisitive reader to examine the Estimated versus Actual row counts, but they're pretty good. It's tempting to evaluate the given plan and I/O outputs and

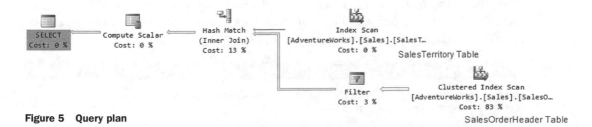

Figure 5   Query plan

TextData	CPU	Duration	Reads	Writes	RowCounts
EXEC dbo.UDFsAreBad	640	2210	102727	0	68411

Figure 6   **Profiler information**

TextData	CPU	Duration	Reads	RowCounts
SELECT @result = SUM((UnitPrice - UnitPriceDiscount) * OrderQty) FROM Sale...	0	0	3	1
SELECT @result = SUM((UnitPrice - UnitPriceDiscount) * OrderQty) FROM Sale...	0	0	3	1
SELECT @result = SUM((UnitPrice - UnitPriceDiscount) * OrderQty) FROM Sale...	0	0	3	1
SELECT @result = SUM((UnitPrice - UnitPriceDiscount) * OrderQty) FROM Sale...	0	0	3	1
SELECT @result = SUM((UnitPrice - UnitPriceDiscount) * OrderQty) FROM Sale...	0	0	3	1
SELECT @result = SUM((UnitPrice - UnitPriceDiscount) * OrderQty) FROM Sale...	0	0	3	1
SELECT @result = SUM((UnitPrice - UnitPriceDiscount) * OrderQty) FROM Sale...	0	0	3	1
SELECT t.Name as TerritoryName, oh.OrderDate, dbo.fn_TotalPrice(oh.SalesOr...	5500	21166	102729	1827
EXEC dbo.UDFsAreBad	5516	21168	102731	68411

Figure 7   **Profiler trace**

think, "I'm good to go here." As you're about to see, those outputs don't reflect the true cost of the query. Figure 6 shows what Profiler reports.

Whoa! What gives here? Over 100,000 reads? The query returned just 1,827 rows but the RowCounts column in Profiler reports 68,411! What "gives" is that this scalar UDF is evaluated individually for each row in the query. To prove this, enable the SP:StmtCompleted event in Profiler, and rerun the query.

TIP   Be wary of doing this granular profiling against production systems. The overhead can be extraordinary!

Figure 7 shows the tail end of the statement-level Profiler trace.

TIP   Be sure to disable Include Actual Execution Plan and Statistics IO in SSMS because they can skew results reported to Profiler.

And there you see it. There were 33,292 rows of the guts of that scalar UDF in the Profiler trace, just from one SELECT statement! I've shown clients millions of these for single calls to the database. Recall the query plan from SSMS and the STATISTICS IO output. They don't portray the reality of what's going on here!

What can you do about it?

Some of you might be thinking, "I've got to go fix some code right now!" You obviously need to refactor this code, and there are two main ways you can go about it.

Inline table valued function solution

The first is to create an inline table valued function (iTVF) and use CROSS APPLY against it. The inline part is critical. The following listing is an example of the original scalar fn_TotalPrice function refactored to be an iTVF.

Listing 5   **Inline table valued function**

```
CREATE FUNCTION dbo.fn_TotalPrice_TVF (@SalesOrderID int)
RETURNS TABLE WITH SCHEMABINDING
AS
```

```
        RETURN SELECT SUM((UnitPrice - UnitPriceDiscount) * OrderQty) AS
TotalPrice
            FROM Sales.SalesOrderDetail
            WHERE SalesOrderID = @SalesOrderID
GO

CREATE PROC dbo.TVFsAreBetter
AS
SET NOCOUNT ON
SELECT t.Name as TerritoryName, oh.OrderDate, fn.TotalPrice
  FROM Sales.SalesOrderHeader oh
 INNER JOIN Sales.SalesTerritory t ON t.TerritoryID = oh.TerritoryID
 CROSS APPLY dbo.fn_TotalPrice_TVF(oh.SalesOrderID) as fn
 WHERE fn.TotalPrice > 10000
GO

EXEC dbo.TVFsAreBetter
```

The fact that the body of the UDF is a single SELECT statement is the key that will allow the optimizer to integrate it into its normal set-based query plans. Figure 8 shows the iTVF execution metrics.

As you can see in the query plan in figure 9, the Compute Scalar is inlined with the set-based flow of data. The STATISTICS IO read output closely matches that reported by Profiler:

```
Table 'Worktable'. Scan count 0, logical reads 0, ...
Table 'SalesOrderHeader'. Scan count 1, logical reads 634, ...
Table 'SalesOrderDetail'. Scan count 1, logical reads 1238, ...
Table 'SalesTerritory'. Scan count 1, logical reads 2, ...
```

Most important, a statement-level Profiler capture will show that the iTVF isn't being executed per row. I'm sure you'll notice that the duration is 3 times shorter and the reads an amazing 55 times less than the Scalar UDF run.

Set-based solution

The second method of eliminating scalar UDFs from your code is to integrate the logic of the UDF into your existing statements that reference the UDF. This can be a difficult

TextData	CPU	Duration	Reads	Writes	RowCounts
EXEC dbo.TVFsAreBetter	94	712	1874	0	1827

Figure 8 iTVF execution metrics

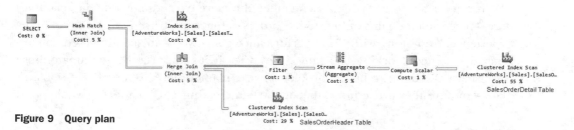

Figure 9 Query plan

undertaking, sometimes requiring using intermediate result sets or complex logic. But it's almost always worth the effort. The next listing shows a set-based version of the UDF.

Listing 6   Set-based refactor of the scalar UDF

```
SELECT t.Name as TerritoryName, oh.OrderDate, od.TotalPrice
  FROM Sales.SalesOrderHeader oh
 INNER JOIN Sales.SalesTerritory t ON t.TerritoryID = oh.TerritoryID
 INNER JOIN (SELECT od.SalesOrderID, SUM((od.UnitPrice -
                 od.UnitPriceDiscount) * od.OrderQty) AS TotalPrice
            FROM Sales.SalesOrderDetail od
            GROUP BY od.SalesOrderID) od
   ON od.SalesOrderID = oh.SalesOrderID
 WHERE od.TotalPrice > 10000
```

In listing 6, you see that the aggregation has been placed into a derived table (you could use a common table expression as well if you like that query style) and the derived table joined to the original UDF-using query code. How does it perform? Take a look at figure 10 for the Profiler output and back at figure 9 for the query plan.

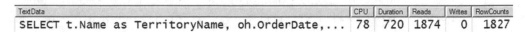

TextData	CPU	Duration	Reads	Writes	RowCounts
SELECT t.Name as TerritoryName, oh.OrderDate,...	78	720	1874	0	1827

Figure 10   Profiler output

Here's the `STATISTICS IO` output from the query in listing 6:

```
Table 'Worktable'. Scan count 0, logical reads 0, ...
Table 'SalesOrderHeader'. Scan count 1, logical reads 634, ...
Table 'SalesOrderDetail'. Scan count 1, logical reads 1238, ...
Table 'SalesTerritory'. Scan count 1, logical reads 2, ...
```

Well, how about that! In this case, the iTVF and the set-based solution are both identical in their execution metrics. Although the iTVF solution can be simpler to implement, I've come across scenarios where a set-based refactor was required to get optimal performance.

What about code reuse?

Whenever I talk on this subject at conferences or with clients, I'm invariably asked how to handle code reuse and especially impact analysis issues. "I used a UDF so if I needed to change it I'd just need to change it in one place, not all 33 places where the UDF is referenced in my T-SQL." Remember, these are exceedingly low-end examples here—performance gains of four to five orders of magnitude aren't uncommon in my experience. And along with those performance gains, you can see increased concurrency due to fewer locking/blocking issues. Clearly it's important to eliminate those bad scalar UDFs that exhibit the problems I've explained here. Remember, T-SQL isn't like C# or any other procedural language. When creating T-SQL code, the whole point is to enable the query processor to generate a good query-execution plan for a set-based operation.

To solve your impact-analysis issues, take the refactor snippet of code and place a GUID as a comment with that code. Put that in your source code control system, and have that GUID as a comment everywhere in your code where you use the refactor snippet. Now if you need to do a code change, you can simply search your source code for the associated GUID. Voilà—100 percent reliable impact analysis. Yes, you still need to touch those 33 places in the code, but it will almost certainly be a similar change at each location so it should be straightforward. As for testing, you'll have to test all 33 places, but you'd have to do that no matter whether you changed a scalar UDF, an iTVF, or the set-based refactor.

One last example of how bad scalar UDFs can be

A few years back, I came across one of the most amazingly flexible pieces of code I've ever seen. It was a scalar UDF that was used to format a date as textual output. It had 19 formatting inputs that could be used in hundreds of permutations. The client was suffering from CPU bottlenecks instead of the vastly more common I/O bottleneck. They had a large number of servers, each with just a small number of databases on it because CPU usage was so high.

My performance-tuning review quickly uncovered this UDF. It was just over 120 lines of code that included the following breakdown:

Statement	Count
CAST	9
CHARINDEX	1
DATEDIFF	3
DATENAME	2
DATEPART	6
DECLARE	24
IF	11
LEFT	3
REPLACE	42
RIGHT	9
SET	74

I found that this UDF was used throughout the database code and was responsible for upward of 75 percent of the CPU utilization on the servers! If I run the code in listing

7 on my laptop's copy of AdventureWorks (which has 113,443 rows in the referenced table), an entire CPU core is pegged at 100 percent for 25 seconds with a hot cache!

Listing 7   Format date scalar UDF

```
DECLARE @datevar char(8)
--CCYYMMDD string output
SELECT @datevar = dbo.FormatDate(TransactionDate, 'yyymmdd')
  FROM Production.TransactionHistory
```

In listing 8, the simple replacement code, which uses the built-in CONVERT function, provides the exact same output and runs essentially instantaneously. That's 25 seconds less of CPU burn and 25 seconds less of locking the object!

Listing 8   Format date equivalent refactor

```
DECLARE @datevar char(8)
SELECT @datevar = CONVERT(char(8), TransactionDate, 112)
  FROM Production.TransactionHistory
```

Summary

In this chapter, you learned just how disastrously bad scalar UDFs can be. There are a variety of ways they can harm you, with the worst probably being the per-row execution. That doesn't always happen, and the primary cause is ancillary data access from within the UDF code. But the format-date story (and countless others I've come across in the past six years) clearly shows there are other problems. If you do have scalar UDFs in your code, you should consider removing them. Look for ways to switch to inline table valued functions or preferably full set-based code. Use the GUID comment trick to help discover where the function replacement code is and thus aid any impact analysis that might need to be done. One final parting gift: scalar UDFs also void the use of parallel query plans, which is why the FormatDate UDF pegged only ONE CPU core on my laptop!

About the author

Kevin Boles is a SQL Server expert, working exclusively with the product since version 6.5. With over 15 years of database experience, he holds virtually every SQL Server–related certification, including MCT and MVP. Kevin teaches occasionally and has been a successful independent consultant for the past 10 years. He is also a mentor with SolidQ, a top-tier global SQL Server consulting firm. His passion is the relational engine, especially performance analysis and tuning.

21 Using regular expressions in SSMS

John Paul Cook

Regular expressions are known for their power and their cryptic nature. Many people avoid using them because the value isn't perceived to be worth the cost of learning an arcane syntax. But there are a few high-value regular expression edits that have simple syntax. SQL Server Management Studio (SSMS) supports the use of regular expressions when editing queries. You can reap the benefit of regular expressions without having to master the tedious subtleties of advanced regular expression syntax. This chapter shows you how to efficiently use a few simple regular expressions within SSMS.

Eliminating blank lines

When you're copying a query from an email message or web page, superfluous blank lines may appear after you paste the query into SSMS. Manually removing the blank lines by deleting them one at a time is both tedious and error prone. A simple global edit using regular expressions can safely and efficiently remove the unwanted blank lines with a minimum of effort. Here's an example of an emailed query that has unwanted blank lines in SSMS:

```
SELECT DepartmentID

    ,Name

    ,GroupName

    ,ModifiedDate

FROM AdventureWorks2008R2.HumanResources.Department
```

Saving the query to a file and examining the file in a hex editor reveals the root cause of the problem, as you can see in figure 1.

	0001	0203	0405	0607	0809	0A0B	0C0D	0E0F	0123456789ABCDEF
	0001	0203	0405	0607	0809	0A0B	0C0D	0E0F	0123456789ABCDEF
0x00	5345	4C45	4354	2044	6570	6172	746D	656E	SELECT Departmen
0x10	7449	440D	0A0D	0A20	2020	2020	202C	4E61	tID.... ,Na
0x20	6D65	0D0A	0D0A	2020	2020	2020	2C47	726F	me.... ,Gro
0x30	7570	4E61	6D65	0D0A	0D0A	2020	2020	2020	upName....
0x40	2C4D	6F64	6966	6965	6444	6174	650D	0A0D	,ModifiedDate...
0x50	0A16	524F	4D20	4164	7665	6E74	7572	6557	.FROM AdventureW
0x60	6F72	6B73	3230	3038	5232	2E48	756D	616E	orks2008R2.Human
0x70	5265	736F	7572	6365	732E	4465	7061	7274	Resources.Depart
0x80	6D65	6E74	0D0A						ment..

Figure 1   Hexadecimal view of a double-spaced SQL query with duplicate newline characters circled

Removing extra newline characters

Notice the 0D0A 0D0A pairs throughout the file. Hex 0D is a carriage return and hex 0A is the newline character. Functionally speaking, each newline character is followed by a second newline character, which is the cause of the blank lines. You can easily globally search and replace all pairs of newline characters with a single newline character. In regular expressions, the escape sequence that represents a newline is \n. By extension of this principle, two consecutive newline characters are represented by \n\n. The global change required to remove superfluous blank lines is to replace all occurrences of \n\n with \n, as shown in figure 2. Notice that you must select the Use check box and choose Regular Expressions from the drop-down list in the Find and Replace dialog box.

If the regular expression replacement doesn't remove the offending blank lines, you have a different pattern. Pasting a code sample copied from a web page may result

Figure 2   Before (top) and after (bottom) view of a query. A regular expression removed the blank lines. Notice that the Use check box is checked and that Regular Expressions is selected.

in a space character between the 0D0A pairs. When this happens, replace \n \n with \n to globally remove the superfluous blank lines.

Collapsing multiple lines into a single line

As a matter of style, a SELECT statement may have one column per line or multiple columns in the same line. Changing from one style to another is easy to do with regular expressions. In our example query, the second, third, and fourth lines of the query begin with six space characters followed by a comma. The second, third, and fourth lines are preceded by a \n. You can use this knowledge to define a pattern. As a regular expression, this pattern must begin with a \n. By replacing \n   , (\n followed by six spaces and a comma) with a single comma, newline characters and the six leading spaces are edited out, causing the first four lines to become one line (see figure 3).

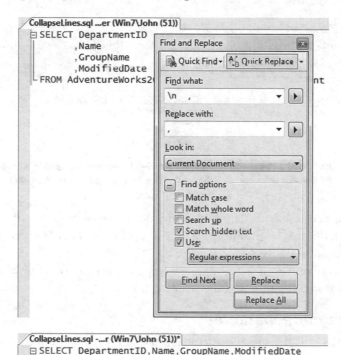

Figure 3 A regular expression collapsed the first four lines (query shown on top) into a single line (query shown on bottom).

Regular expressions are useful in turning a list of column names into a SELECT statement. You can quickly add a comma to either the beginning or the end of a selection of lines by using the appropriate metacharacter. In these examples, the changes are applied only to the selection instead of the entire file to prevent insertion of characters where they aren't wanted.

Using the beginning-of-line metacharacter

The caret symbol (^) is the metacharacter signifying the beginning of a line. Using this metacharacter can be confusing because if you want to edit the beginning of a line, you

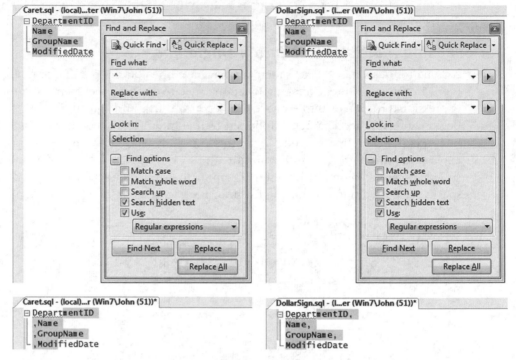

Figure 4   A regular expression added a comma to the beginning of the last three lines of the query.

Figure 5   A regular expression added a comma to the end of the first three lines of the query.

must select part of the previous line. The beginning-of-line metacharacter (the caret symbol) has no effect on the beginning of a line if none of the previous line is selected. This is illustrated in figure 4.

If you replace all occurrences of ^ in the selected region with a comma, the result is a comma appended at the beginning of the selected lines.

Using the end-of-line metacharacter

The dollar sign symbol ($) is the metacharacter signifying the end of a line. To have an edit applied to the end of a line, you must select at least part of the next line, as shown in figure 5.

If you replace all occurrences of $ in the selected region with a comma, the result is a comma appended at the end of the selected lines.

Summary

Regular expressions can provide simple and fast solutions to common editing problems in SSMS. There's no reason to fear using them. After getting comfortable using regular expressions for simple editing tasks, you may wish to graduate to more complex editing.

About the author

John Paul Cook is a database consultant based in his hometown of Houston, Texas. With more than 30 years of relational database experience, John now focuses on using information technology to improve patient outcomes. Currently a full-time nursing student, John will combine his nursing and database skills after graduation.

SQL Server Denali: what's coming next in T-SQL

Sergio Govoni

TO RICK
A BIG THANKS!

Last November when I was in Seattle for the PASS Summit 2010, Microsoft announced the first public Community Technology Preview (CTP1) of Microsoft SQL Server, code-named "Denali." In this chapter, I'll talk about some new features of the T-SQL language:

- OFFSET and FETCH
- SEQUENCE
- EXECUTE … WITH RESULT SETS
- THROW

OFFSET and FETCH

The ORDER BY clause, used to sort the query result set, has two interesting options in Denali that allow you to simplify the ad hoc paging of a query result set: OFFSET and FETCH. In the following scenario, you can see typical examples.

Here's the OFFSET option:

```
OFFSET {integer_constant | offset_row_count_expression} {ROW | ROWS}
```

This code specifies the number of rows to skip before starting to return rows from the query expression. The value can be an integer, a constant, or an expression that's greater than or equal to 0.

Here's the FETCH option:

```
FETCH {FIRST | NEXT} {integer_constant |
fetch_row_count_expression} {ROW | ROWS} ONLY
```

This code specifies the number of rows to return after the OFFSET clause has been processed. The value can be an integer, a constant, or an expression that's greater than or equal to 1.

With the OFFSET and FETCH options, you could explain in T-SQL language the following scenario: you have to extract all rows from the table Person.Contact in the AdventureWorks database, and the output must show 10 rows per page. The result of these options allows you to build up the number of rows that you want, starting from a specific row number. This is the best use of the OFFSET/FETCH clauses. Also, keep in mind that those options are ANSI SQL standard.

In previous versions of SQL Server, this scenario could be solved using two T-SQL elements—the TOP and ROW_NUMBER() functions—but neither element satisfies your request completely. The TOP expression allows you to reduce the returned number of rows, but it doesn't skip a range of rows. The ROW_NUMBER() function allows you to filter a specific range of rows, but it doesn't work in the WHERE clause.

SQL Server 2005 and 2008 solution

In earlier versions of SQL Server, the following workaround allows you to solve the issue of paging by using a common table expression (CTE):

```
-- Ad hoc paging prior SQL Server Code-Name "Denali"

-- Change database context
USE [AdventureWorks];
GO


-- First 10 rows
WITH CTE AS
(
  SELECT   ROW_NUMBER() OVER (ORDER BY LastName, FirstName) AS RowNum
           ,LastName, FirstName, Phone
  FROM     Person.Contact
)
SELECT     *
FROM       CTE
WHERE      RowNum BETWEEN 1 AND 10
ORDER BY   RowNum;
GO
```

The second group of 10 rows can be displayed by the previous CTE after changing the range on the BETWEEN operator in the outer query like this: WHERE RowNum BETWEEN 11 AND 20.

SQL Server Denali solution

The new filter options OFFSET/FETCH sound like an extension of the ORDER BY clause. The following piece of T-SQL code shows you how to extract the first 10 rows of the query result set:

```
-- First 10 rows
SELECT    LastName, FirstName, Phone
FROM      Person.Contact
ORDER BY  LastName, FirstName
OFFSET 0 ROWS FETCH NEXT 10 ROWS ONLY;
go
```

The output is shown in figure 1.

To obtain the second group of 10 rows, change the integer constant on the OFFSET option. In the next example, the result starts from the tenth row, returning 10 rows:

```
-- Next 10 rows
SELECT    LastName, FirstName, Phone
FROM      Person.Contact
ORDER BY  LastName, FirstName
OFFSET 10 ROWS FETCH NEXT 10 ROWS ONLY;
```

	LastName	FirstName	Phone
1	Abbas	Syed	926-555-0182
2	Abel	Catherine	747-555-0171
3	Abercrombie	Kim	334-555-0137
4	Abercrombie	Kim	208-555-0114
5	Abercrombie	Kim	919-555-0100
6	Abolrous	Hazem	869-555-0125
7	Abolrous	Sam	567-555-0100
8	Acevedo	Humberto	599-555-0127
9	Achong	Gustavo	398-555-0132
10	Ackerman	Pilar	1 (11) 500 555-0132

Figure 1   Ad hoc paging with SQL Server Denali (first "page")

Comparing execution plan results

By using the first 10 rows from each of the two queries, you can compare the results of the execution plan. In SQL Server Management Studio, select the Actual Execution Plan query option. The result is shown in figure 2.

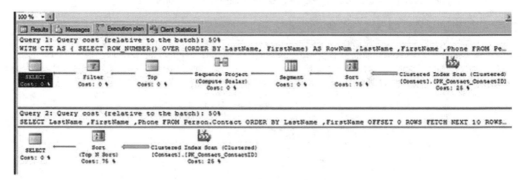

Figure 2   Query execution plan

The execution plans generated by the query optimizer are similar. In the first plan (the CTE query), there are more tasks, although the most important one is the Filter operator (the WHERE clause) and a Sequence Project Task (the ROW_NUMBER() function). Considering those tasks have an actual cost equal to 0, in this example the performance is similar; in fact, the OFFSET/FETCH options haven't been implemented in order to improve performance but to make the code easier to read and maintain.

SEQUENCE

SEQUENCE is a user-defined, schema-bound object that generates a sequence of numeric values. The values generated by the sequence can be ascending or descending, starting from any defined value. The value numbers can be cyclic, repeated until reaching the upper or lower value.

Unlike an IDENTITY column, a SEQUENCE object isn't linked to any table, so any required relationships have to be managed from the application.

Tips for using SEQUENCE

A SEQUENCE object can be used instead of the IDENTITY column in the following scenarios:

- The application requires the value before an INSERT statement is executed.
- The application requires the values to be shared between two or more tables.
- The application has to restart the sequence after a certain value has been reached.
- The application requires sequence values to be sorted by another column.

Restrictions

There are some restrictions that you have to be aware of when using a SEQUENCE:

- Unlike an IDENTITY column, the sequence values aren't protected from UPDATE, and the column that received the value can be modified.
- There aren't any unique constraints on a sequence value.
- In a table, the sequence value may have gaps, because of a rollback or a SQL Server service restart.

The new statement CREATE SEQUENCE allows you to create a SEQUENCE object, as shown here:

```
-- create new sequence object
create sequence dbo.MySequence
as
  int
  minvalue 1
  no maxvalue
  start with 1;
go
```

The SEQUENCE objects created in a database are displayed through the catalog view sys.sequences. The next statement displays how to use the NEXT VALUE FOR function for the SEQUENCE object just created. The following statement retrieves the next two values for the dbo.MySequence object:

```
select
  MySequence_Value = next value for dbo.MySequence
union all
select
  next value for dbo.MySequence;
go
```

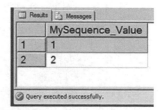

Note that the object named dbo.MySequence was created without specifying a table link; also, you didn't save any information about the SEQUENCE object on the storage engine. No tables were created, and nothing was persisted to disk. The output is shown in figure 3.

Figure 3 Output using the NEXT VALUE FOR function on the dbo.MySequence object

A typical issue for the IDENTITY column is resetting the sequence value. To reset the value for the SEQUENCE object, you could use the RESTART WITH option as shown here:

```
alter sequence dbo.MySequence
  restart with 20;
go
```

The next value that dbo.MySequence retrieves will be 20, as shown in the following statement:

```
select
  next_mysequence_value = next value for dbo.MySequence
union all
select
  next value for dbo.MySequence;
go
```

The results are the values 20 and 21 in a single result set.

It's important to specify that the sequence value won't necessarily be sequential; for example, when a transaction is rolled back, the number isn't returned back to the pool, and when several tables share numeric values from the same SEQUENCE object, there may be gaps in each table. The next example shows what happens to the sequence values when a transaction that generated them is rolled back using the ROLLBACK statement:

```
begin transaction;

select next value for dbo.MySequence;

rollback transaction;

select next value for dbo.MySequence;
go
```

The results are the values 22 and 23, each in its own result set.

The SEQUENCE object is typically used instead of an IDENTITY column. In the following example the dbo.Orders table has been created without using the IDENTITY property for the OrderID column (the primary key of the table). The unique values will be assigned to the OrderID column using the dbo.SO_OrderID SEQUENCE object. Note the use of the NEXT VALUE FOR function in the INSERT statement:

```
-- Using SEQUENCE instead of IDENTITY column

-- Create table dbo.Orders
create table dbo.Orders
(
  orderid int not null primary key
  ,ordernumber varchar(20) not null
  ,customerid int not null
  ,qty decimal(8, 3) not null
);
go
```

```
-- Create sequence dbo.SO_OrderID
create sequence dbo.SO_OrderID
as
  int
  start with 1
  increment by 1;
go

-- Insert some records
insert into dbo.Orders
(orderid, ordernumber, customerid, qty)
values
(NEXT VALUE FOR dbo.SO_OrderID, 'N0000000001', 1, 10),
(NEXT VALUE FOR dbo.SO_OrderID, 'N0000000002', 5, 80);
go
```

Now in the dbo.Orders table there are two records, and both have a unique value for the OrderID column, much like the IDENTITY property would've produced:

```
-- View the table
select * from dbo.Orders;
go
```

The output is shown in figure 4.

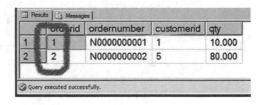

Figure 4   Data from the dbo.Orders table

EXECUTE...WITH RESULT SETS

The new WITH RESULT SETS clause is related to the EXECUTE statement. This clause will allow you to redefine the name and the data type for each column that's in the result set of the EXECUTE command.

The following piece of T-SQL code creates the dbo.SpareParts table. The INSERT statement inserts some items sold by a company in the food industry:

```
-- Setup table dbo.SpareParts
use [AdventureWorks];
go

create table dbo.SpareParts
(
  ProductID sysname not null primary key
  ,SellStartDate date not null
  ,SellEndDate date not null
  ,ProductNote varchar(40) null
  ,ListPrice decimal(8, 2) not null
  ,SafetyStockLevel integer not null
);
go

-- Insert some test data
insert into dbo.SpareParts
(ProductID, SellStartDate, SellEndDate, ProductNote, ListPrice,
➥ SafetyStockLevel)
```

```
values
('seattle crab', '20111206', '99991231', '1 kg', 16.2 , 4),
('king salmon', '20111206', '20121231', '2 kg', 11.5, 10),
('coffee', '20111208', '20120630', null, 5.0, 80),
('blueberry scone', '20111210', '20120630', '0.1 kg', 1.30, 8),
('blueberry muffin', '20111211', '20130630', '0.1 kg', 1.40, 15);
go
```

The following statement shows the data from the dbo.SpareParts table:

```
select * from dbo.SpareParts;
go
```

The output is shown in figure 5.

	ProductID	SellStartDate	SellEndDate	ProductNote	ListPrice	SafetyStockLevel
1	blueberry muffin	2011-12-11	2013-06-30	0.1 kg	1.40	15
2	blueberry scone	2011-12-10	2012-06-30	0.1 kg	1.30	8
3	coffee	2011-12-08	2012-06-30	NULL	5.00	80
4	king salmon	2011-12-06	2012-12-31	2 kg	11.50	10
5	seattle crab	2011-12-06	9999-12-31	1 kg	16.20	4

Figure 5
Data from the
dbo.SpareParts
table

The following piece of T-SQL code defines the stored procedure dbo.usp_get _product_for_sell that's used by sales agents to know the spare parts list on sale. The stored procedure accepts two input parameters. @vDate represents the date used to filter the SellStartDate and SellEndDate columns, and @vPrice represents the filter on the ListPrice column:

```
-- Setup stored procedure
use [AdventureWorks];
go

create procedure dbo.usp_get_product_for_sell
(
  @vDate as date, @vPrice as decimal (8, 2) = 0
)
as begin

  /* Name: dbo.usp_get_product_for_sell() */

  if (isnull(@vDate, '') = '')
  begin
    print ('Error: Invalid value for parameter @vDate');
    return;
  end;

  select    S.ProductID, S.ProductNote, S.SellStartDate, S.SellEndDate
  from      dbo.SpareParts as S
  where     (@vDate between S.SellStartDate and S.SellEndDate);

  if (isnull(@vPrice, 0) > 0)
  begin
    select    SL.ProductID, SL.ListPrice
```

```
    from        dbo.SpareParts as SL
    where       (SL.ListPrice <= @vPrice)
                and (@vDate between SL.SellStartDate and SL.SellEndDate)
    for xml path('root');
  end;
end;
go
```

Now you'll be executing the stored procedure `dbo.usp_get_product_for_sell` to output the spare parts list on sale on December 6, 2011. Note that the columns are renamed as specified in the `WITH RESULT SETS` clause:

```
-- Single WITH RESULT SETS
exec dbo.usp_get_product_for_sell @vDate = '20111206'
with result sets
(
  -- First result sets
  -- Column name and data type
  (
    ProductName varchar(20)
    ,Note varchar(40)
    ,SellBy date
    ,SellEnd date
  )
);
go
```

The output is shown in figure 6.

The next statement shows how to get two result sets: the first (as in the previous example) uses the `@vDate` parameter; the

Figure 6   Using the EXECUTE...WITH RESULT SETS clause

other uses the `@vPrice` parameter, which sorts out the spare parts having the price below or equal to the value. Note that the second result set is in XML format because of the `FOR XML` clause:

```
-- Multiple WITH RESULT SETS
exec dbo.usp_get_product_for_sell
  @vDate = '20111208'
  ,@vPrice = 5
with result sets
(
  -- First result sets
  -- Column name and data type
  (
    ProductName varchar(20)
    ,Note varchar(40)
    ,SellBy date
    ,SellEnd date
  ),
  -- Second result sets
  -- as XML
  as for xml
);
go
```

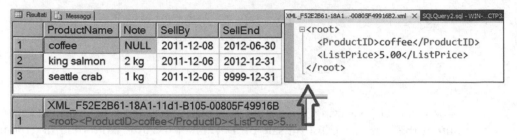

Figure 7   Output from the stored procedure using the multiple WITH RESULT SETS and AS FOR XML options

The output is shown in figure 7.

THROW

SQL Server Denali improves error handling with the new THROW (T-SQL) statement. THROW outside of a TRY...CATCH block acts similar to the RAISERROR() function, with a few notable exceptions:

- The message_id parameter doesn't need to be defined in sys.messages.
- The message_id must be INT (not BIGINT) and greater than or equal to 50000.
- THROW doesn't accept any parameter substitution for customizing the error message inline.
- The severity level is always 16.

The following T-SQL code defines the error message ID number 50001 with two bookmarks (%s) that customize the message:

```
EXEC sys.sp_addmessage
  @msgnum = 50001,
  @severity = 16,
  @msgtext = N'What''s Coming Next in %s for SQL Server Code-Named %s.';
go


-- With RAISERROR
RAISERROR(50001, 16, 1, N'T-SQL', N'"Denali"');
go
```

The output is shown in figure 8. This type of parameter substitution doesn't work with THROW.

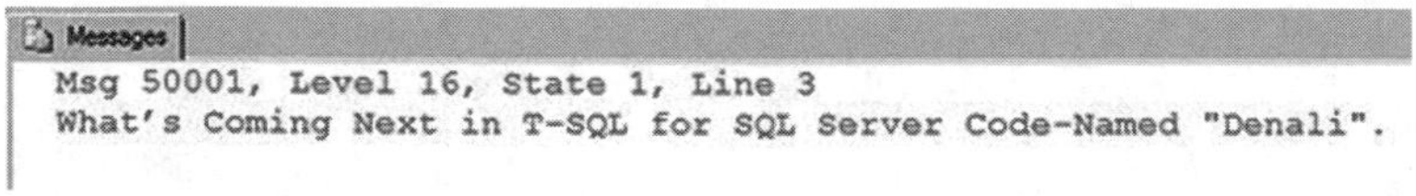

```
Messages

Msg 50001, Level 16, State 1, Line 3
What's Coming Next in T-SQL for SQL Server Code-Named "Denali".
```

Figure 8   The RAISERROR() function with substitution parameters

THROW inside a TRY...CATCH will be able to rethrow the error message that occurred in the TRY block. The next example shows a division by 0 into a TRY block. When the error occurs, the execution goes inside the CATCH block, where the error can be handled by a rollback and/or a notification. Then, the THROW command displays the error:

```
BEGIN TRY
  select 1/0
END TRY
BEGIN CATCH
  PRINT N'Message from inside CATCH.';
  -- rollback
  -- notification
  -- throwing the same errors back to the caller
  THROW;
END CATCH;
go
```

The output (error) is shown in figure 9.

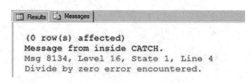

```
(0 row(s) affected)
Message from inside CATCH.
Msg 8134, Level 16, State 1, Line 4
Divide by zero error encountered.
```

Figure 9 THROW inside a TRY...CATCH block

Summary

In this chapter, you saw some of the new features of T-SQL in Denali—in particular, the new filtering option called OFFSET/FETCH, which you can think of as an extension to the ORDER BY clause. I also discussed SEQUENCE objects, which generate a sequence of numeric values that you can use instead of an IDENTITY column. I talked about the WITH RESULT SETS clause, which can change the column names and data types of the result set of an EXECUTE statement. Finally, I demonstrated the THROW statement, which improves error handling.

I've just touched the surface of the T-SQL improvements that will appear in Denali when it's released. There are many more features and language enhancements that you'll discover as you embrace the new version of SQL Server, all with the goal of increasing productivity and improving performance.

About the author

Since 1999 Sergio Govoni has been a software developer. In 2000, he received degrees in computer science from the Italy State University. He has worked for over 11 years in a software house that produces multicompany enterprise resource planning software for the Windows platform. Today, at the same company, he's a program manager and software architect and is constantly involved on several team projects, where he takes care of the architecture and the mission-critical technical details. Since version 7.0, he's been working with SQL Server and has a deep knowledge of implementation and maintenance relational databases, performance tuning, and problem-solving skills. He also trains people in SQL Server and its related technologies, writes articles, and participates actively as a speaker at conferences and workshops for UGISS (www.ugiss.org), the first and most important Italian SQL Server User Group. Sergio lives in Italy and loves to travel around the world. You can meet him at conferences or Microsoft events.

23 Creating your own data type

Thanks, Rick!

Hugo Kornelis

In SQL Server 2005, a new feature was introduced: Common Language Runtime (CLR) integration. Some people, mainly .NET developers, were enthusiastic, because they hoped they'd never need to write another line of SQL code. They were wrong. SQL code is still the best way to manipulate data. Other people, mainly DBAs, were afraid that their database would be swamped with code in all kinds of obscure .NET languages, causing them to lose all control over the data. They were wrong, too. The DBA has to enable CLR integration, and the default permission set for CLR assemblies doesn't even allow any data access.

CLR integration came in five flavors. Three of them already existed in T-SQL flavor: stored procedures, user-defined functions, and Data Definition Language (DDL) triggers. The other two are completely new and are still only available in the CLR flavor: user-defined data types (UDTs, the subject of this chapter) and user-defined aggregates (UDAs). Because these features enabled some nice, new possibilities, I expected them to have quite some uptake. And that's where *I* was wrong. Unless I'm looking in the wrong places, I see far fewer databases that use UDTs (and UDAs) than I expected. Is that because developers don't know what's possible with UDTs? Or because developers know all too well what isn't? This chapter will explore both the possibilities and the limitations of UDTs, and hopefully help some people see the exciting new functionality made possible by CLR user-defined data types.

A short (and mostly made-up) history of complex numbers

The data type I implement as an example in this chapter will be used to represent complex numbers. Because complex numbers aren't an everyday occurrence, here's a short recap.

211

(continued)

You're probably familiar with the numbers typically implemented in SQL Server's numerical data types, such as integer, money, or real. Mathematicians call this the class of "real numbers"—a fair name, because these numbers correspond to very real amounts.

You're also familiar with the square root, the inverse of the square. Because a square can never be a negative number, you've been told in high school that negative numbers have no square root.

Then, one fatal day, a somewhat wacky mathematician who completely misunderstood a popular John Lennon song asked himself, "I know negative numbers have no square root, but what if I imagine that they do?" And because mathematicians love to use letters instead of numbers, he labeled the square root of –1 i, and then defined the square root of all other negative numbers as the product of i and some real number. For instance, $3 \cdot i$ (the product of 3 and i) is the square root of –9. With this, the class of "imaginary numbers" was born—again, a very appropriate name.

As if this wasn't enough, our not-so-favorite mathematician then went on to reason about what would happen if you add a real number to an imaginary number—and voilà, yet another class of numbers was born. And for this class, "complex numbers" appeared to be the most appropriate name. Note that the class of complex numbers encompasses both the real and the imaginary numbers: a real number is a complex number where the imaginary part just happens to be $0 \cdot i$, and an imaginary number is a complex number where the real part is equal to 0.

All this would never have been more than a wasted workweek for a mathematician and maybe an obscure article in *Science Magazine*, but then it turned out that complex numbers have useful applications—for instance, in signal analysis, quantum mechanics, or algebraic number theory. So now we're stuck with these complex numbers, and for generations to come, students will be plagued with them.

I've seen two different ways to represent complex numbers. For instance, the sum of the real number 4.5 and the imaginary number $3 \cdot i$ can be represented as (4.5, 3), or as $4.5+3 \cdot i$. My personal preference is the latter method, not only because this is what I used in high school, but also because it's immediately recognizable as a complex number, whereas the first form could also represent a point in a two-dimensional space. This is the form I'll use throughout this chapter.

Anatomy of a CLR user-defined type

I'm sure you're eagerly waiting to open Visual Studio and start hammering. But we need to cover a bit of the theory first. For starters, I'll discuss in which cases a UDT is a good solution—and in which cases it isn't. You also need to have some understanding of the elements that have to be combined to successfully craft your own data type.

...But do you need it at all?

As with most features in SQL Server, it's possible to abuse UDTs in ways that should never be allowed. In my opinion, the first thing you need to do when you start creating your

UDT is to step back and reconsider whether a UDT is the best solution for your problem. Sometimes, there are far easier ways to solve the same problem.

When deciding whether a UDT is an appropriate choice, you have to consider the type within its intended context. A nice example of this is the UDT for storing points in a two-dimensional space. When SQL Server 2005 was released, this was probably the most-used example in articles about UDTs. But in many cases, the use was inappropriate. If you're only interested in the x and y coordinates as individual values, then you don't need a UDT; simply use two columns with an appropriate numerical data type, and let the representation layer handle the conversions between this format and the preferred string representation for the end users. Squeezing two individual values into a single column would violate the first normal form requirement that values need to be atomic.

But I've also seen examples where the x and y coordinates were never returned or set individually, and where instead some methods were implemented to manipulate on points as a whole—for instance, a method to calculate the distance between two points, or a method to return the point that's a given distance in a given direction removed from another point. In those examples, a point was indeed an atomic value, even if it consisted of two numbers, and no first normal form requirements were violated.

Representations and conversions

When creating a UDT, you have to consider no less than three representations of the data:

- *The native .NET representation that every VB.NET and C# developer is intimately familiar with*—Whenever any action is taken on the data represented by a UDT, it first has to be converted to this native format.
- *The so-called "serialized" representation that SQL Server needs to store values*—This is necessary because the internal structures used for native .NET data types don't match the internal format SQL Server uses for its storage. When you add data to a table that uses the UDT for one of its columns or store a value in a variable that has this UDT as its data type, the value will first be converted to this form.
- *The textual (string) representation that's used for interacting with human end users of your database application*—Because neither the native .NET format nor the serialized SQL Server format is even remotely user-friendly, you'll want to ensure that all your interactions with humans use a human-friendly representation.

All CLR code manipulates on the native format, so you won't have to write code to convert between the serialized and string formats. When such a conversion is needed, SQL Server will use two conversions, first from the given representation to native, and then from native to the target representation. That still leaves you with a total of four conversion routines to implement: `ToString()` and `Parse()` to convert between the native and string formats, and the `Read()` and `Write()` methods from the `IBinary-Serialize` interface to convert between the native and serialized formats.

How about NULL?

In a relational database, each data type must support the special value NULL to represent the absence of any real data. A CLR UDT shouldn't be an exception. Even when a specific column can forbid the NULL value by adding a `NOT NULL` constraint, the data type itself should support it.

Many native .NET data types also support a Null value. But this Null value doesn't represent the absence of any real data; it represents special things such as the end of a pointer chain or a void object. This different value also results in different behavior. In SQL, an expression that receives NULL as one of its arguments typically returns NULL; in .NET, many operations are undefined for Null and hence throw an exception.

Because a UDT shouldn't violate the fundamental rules of relational databases, you need to ensure that your UDT handles the relational NULL appropriately—which means that you should probably not represent it as the .NET Null.

Building the data type: the bare basics

This chapter focuses on the elements required for every UDT: the method's signature, its attributes (for storing the data in native format), four (or, sometimes, two) methods for converting between the different representations of the data, and two methods for handling relational NULL values. I'll describe them in logical order, which isn't the order used in the template, so you'll have to jump up and down through the code a bit.

Starting the project

The best way to get a head start on your UDT is to use the templates built into Visual Studio. To get the correct template for a UDT, start a new project; then in the list of installed templates in the New Project dialog box, click the triangle before the Database entry in the list, click the SQL Server entry, and then select either Visual Basic SQL CLR Database Project or Visual C# SQL CLR Database Project.

Visual Studio will first open a new dialog box where you can add a database reference for the project. Although not required, this step allows Visual Studio to take over much of the heavy lifting for deploying your code to the database. After confirming that you want debugging enabled for the database connection, you should be presented with an empty SQL CLR project.

The next step to add a UDT to the project is to select Project > Add User-Defined Type. Change the name in the Add New Item dialog box, and then click Add to make Visual Studio add the skeleton code for your UDT.

By default, CLR integration is disabled in SQL Server. If you want to use any form of CLR integration, including a UDT, you'll have to enable this first; use the code in listing 1. Because this is a server-wide setting, I recommend you discuss enabling this option with your DBA.

> **Listing 1   Enabling CLR integration on your server**

```
EXEC sp_configure 'clr_enabled',1;
RECONFIGURE;
```

Adding the fields for the native representation

The first thing you should do is add fields for the native representation of the data. For a complex number, the best native representation is to use two fields of data type double (one for the real part and one for the imaginary part), and a boolean to represent whether the value is a relational NULL value (in which case the values in the two double fields are irrelevant). Using a boolean to handle relational NULL values is a safe method that can always be used; in some cases, another possibility is to use an "impossible" value in one of the fields to represent NULL. For complex numbers, there are no impossible values, so you must use the boolean. But it's not a bad idea to always use the boolean—doing so increases standardization of your code.

In the skeleton, you'll find two placeholder field members (var1 and m_null) at the very end of the code. I prefer to move them to the start of the code, but they can be anywhere within the Struct. Replace the placeholder fields with the fields you actually require (as shown in the following listing).

Listing 2   Field members to represent a complex number

```
private double m_real;
private double m_imag;
private bool m_null;
```

Editing the signature

The method's signature in the skeleton code looks like the next listing.

Listing 3   The default signature

```
[Serializable]
[Microsoft.SqlServer.Server.SqlUserDefinedType(Format.Native)]
public struct Complex : INullable
```

Most of this shouldn't be changed, but here's a list of things you *can* do safely:

- You can change the Format.Native property to Format.UserDefined. If you do this, you must also add the MaxByteSize and IsFixedLength properties. This will be explained in the section "Converting between .NET and serialized" later in this chapter.
- You can add the IsByteOrdered property. This property is required if you intend to include the UDT data in an index; it tells SQL Server that the serialized representation of data can be used for meaningful comparisons of the smaller/larger than type.
- You can add the ValidationMethodName property. You should do this if you have code where SQL Server loads data from some source that uses the serialized form (for instance, when converting binary data to a UDT or when bulk-inserting data); this kind of loading bypasses the validation normally present in the methods to convert user input (in string format) to native and then serialized format, so you should write your own validation method and use this property to specify its name.

- Finally, you can add the Name property; this is only used by Visual Studio if you choose to use the automated deployment option; it has no other function.

None of these modifications are relevant for our complex type, so you don't need any changes.

Converting between .NET and text

To support human interaction, you need a method to represent a complex value in a human-friendly string format, as well as a method to parse human input to either a valid complex value or an error condition. These methods aren't exclusive to SQL CLR user-defined data types; you'd need them as well if you just implemented your own data type in a native .NET application.

PARSE()

The Parse() function (see listing 4) creates a new complex number and initializes it with the value represented by the string passed into it. If the conversion fails, it throws an exception. This function will automatically be called by SQL Server if you assign a string value (literal or variable) to a column or variable declared as complex.

Listing 4   The Parse() function

```
public static Complex Parse(SqlString s)
{
    if (s.IsNull)
        return Null;
    Complex u = new Complex();
    // Put your code here
    string tmp = s.ToString().Trim();

    // Evaluate imaginary part (if there is one) first
    if (tmp.EndsWith("i"))
    {
        // Find last - or + sign
        char[] MinusOrPlus = new char[2] { '-', '+' };
        int Last = tmp.LastIndexOfAny(MinusOrPlus);
        // No + or - is not an error; "17.3i" is a valid complex number.
        // Change -1 to 0 to prevent error in substring expression.
        if (Last < 0)
        {
            Last = 0;
        }
        string imag_str = tmp.Substring(Last, tmp.Length - Last - 1).Trim();
        switch (imag_str)
        {
            case "":
            case "+":
                u.m_imag = 1;      // Special case handling for "i" / "+i"
                break;
            case "-":
                u.m_imag = -1;     // Special case handling for "-i"
                break;
            default:
```

```
        try
        {
            u.m_imag = double.Parse(imag_str,
                    CultureInfo.InvariantCulture);
        }
        catch (Exception ex)
        {
            throw new ArgumentException(
"Error converting imaginary  part (" + imag_str + "i): " + ex.Message);
        }
        break;
    }
    // Strip off the imaginary part, to leave just the real part
    // Note special case handling for complex numbers with no real part
    tmp = (Last == 0 ? "0" : tmp.Substring(0, Last).Trim());
}

// tmp now contains only the real part; use Double.Parse()
try
{
    u.m_real = double.Parse(tmp, CultureInfo.InvariantCulture);
}
catch (Exception ex)
{
    throw new ArgumentException("Error converting real part (
        " + tmp + "): " + ex.Message);
}

return u;
}
```

The code in listing 4 is quite long, but most of it is just handling of various special cases, such as allowing the user to write -i instead of 0+-1i, or 7.3 instead of 7.3+0i.

Note that you'll have to add using System.Globalization at the start of your source code in order for the CultureInfo.InvariantCulture to be recognized.

Proper localization is impossible

The Parse() and ToString() methods use CultureInfo.InvariantCulture in an attempt to mimic how SQL server handles locale settings for the real data type. For the Parse() method, this works quite well. For instance, the Netherlands use a decimal comma instead of the decimal dot that's more common in most English-speaking countries. But even on Dutch computers, you still have to use the decimal dot when assigning a value to a real number (for example, DECLARE @Real r = 12.34; or DECLARE @Real r = '12.34';). By forcing the invariant culture, you ensure that conversions to complex numbers also consider the dot as decimal separator. Without it, the Parse() method would consider the dot to be the thousands separator, which is ignored by Double.Parse(); the effect would be that DECLARE @Cmpl dbo.Complex = '12.34-12.34i'; would assign the value 1234 - 1234i to @Cmpl.

For the String() method, even the invariant culture isn't perfect. If I output a real value to my screen, the result depends on how I do it. If I use PRINT, SQL Server

(continued)

converts the value to text using US style (decimal dot), and then sends that string to the client. But if I use SELECT, the client receives the actual value and has to do the formatting itself, using my OS locale settings. So in that case, I do get the decimal comma that's common in the Netherlands. I haven't found a way to mimic this behavior for a UDT.

TOSTRING()

The ToString() method (see listing 5) is the reverse of the Parse() function—it creates a string representation of a complex number. But unlike Parse(), ToString() won't be automatically invoked. Attempting to implicitly convert a UDT to a character data type will return an error, and when you use a UDT in a SELECT statement, SQL Server will simply send the serialized representation, because the process on the other end of the connection might be your own .NET application that uses the Complex data type, as well. If you issue a SELECT from SQL Server Management Studio, you'll see a binary dump of the internal (serialized) representation of the complex value. The ToString() method will only be invoked if you explicitly add it (for example, SELECT @Cmpl.ToString();) or if you use an explicit CAST or CONVERT to convert a complex value to a character data type.

Listing 5   The ToString() method

```
public override string ToString()
{
    StringBuilder builder = new StringBuilder();

    // Format real part
    if (m_real != 0) // Suppress real part of 0("3i" instead of "0+3i")
    {
        builder.Append(m_real.ToString(CultureInfo.InvariantCulture));
        // Add a + sign if the imaginary part is positive
        if (m_imag > 0)
        {
            builder.Append("+");
        }
    }

    // Format imaginary part
    if (m_imag == -1)
    {
        builder.Append("-i");        // Format "-1i" as "-i"
    }
    else if (m_imag == 1)
    {
        builder.Append("i");         // Format "1i" as "i"
    }
    else if (m_imag == 0)
    {
        if (m_real == 0)             // Suppress "0i"
```

```
        {
            builder.Append("0");    // Don't suppress both "0" and "0i"
        }
    }
    else
    {
        builder.Append(m_imag.ToString(CultureInfo.InvariantCulture));
        builder.Append("i");
    }

    return builder.ToString();
}
```

Because the code in listing 5 uses the `StringBuilder` type, you'll need to add `using System.Text;` to the beginning of the code.

OTHER CONVERSIONS

For complex values, converting from text is not always the best approach. You may find yourself needing to cast a floating point number to the `Complex` data type, for use in an operation that expects an argument of that type. Or maybe you have two separate arithmetic expressions to calculate the real and the imaginary part, that you then want to combine into a complex value. I haven't been able to find a way to do this, other than the awkward way of converting the numerical values to strings, concatenating them in the right order, and converting the result to a complex value.

Converting between .NET and serialized

In order for SQL Server to store your UDT data in the data pages of your table, the data has to be converted to the only format the storage engine understands: a single, consecutive series of bytes of either fixed or variable length. And the same format is also used by SQL Server for UDT variables.

Not all native .NET data types are stored as a consecutive series of bytes, so there has to be some way to convert .NET data types to the serialized format and back again. In some cases, you can use the native serialization and deserialization routines so that you don't have to do anything. When the built-in logic falls short, you'll have to supply custom methods for serialization and deserialization.

NATIVE SERIALIZATION

Native serialization is the easiest serialization method available. To implement native serialization, you only need to specify `Format.Native` in the signature of your UDT, and this property is already set this way in the skeleton code Visual Studio generates when you create a UDT. So by doing nothing, you activate native serialization, and Visual Studio and SQL Server take care of all the heavy lifting for serializing and deserializing your UDT data.

There's one catch, though: native serialization isn't always available. Two conditions have to be met:

- You have to implement your UDT as a `struct` (`structure` if you use Visual Basic.NET), not as a `class`.
- No member fields may be reference types; they have to be value types. In other words, only the C#.NET data types `bool`, `byte`, `double`, `float`, `int`, `long`, `sbyte`,

short, SqlBoolean, SqlByte, SqlDateTime, SqlDouble, SqlInt16, SqlInt32, SqlInt64, SqlMoney, SqlSingle, uint, ulong, and ushort are permitted.

The UDT for Complex satisfies both these conditions, so there's no need for custom serialization.

CUSTOM SERIALIZATION

If your UDT has to use a data type that's implemented as a reference type (which, unfortunately, includes the very custom string data type), you'll have to make changes to the signature of your UDT, and you'll have to supply the code to implement the Read() and Write() methods of the IBinarySerialize interface. An example of this can be found on the companion website.

There's no rule against using custom serialization in cases where native serialization is available, but I fail to see any good reasons to do so.

Handling NULLs

All data types in SQL Server must be able to handle NULL, so your UDT must implement two more methods. There are also two NULL-related attributes of the SqlMethod property you can add in the signature of each method in a UDT to control how it responds to NULL values.

NULL AND ISNULL

These are the last methods required for each UDT. The Null method is somewhat similar to the Parse() method in that it also creates a new Complex, but this method initializes it to the NULL value. The IsNull method is used to test if a complex value is the SQL NULL value or an actual complex number. These methods are generally very simple, as you can see in the following listing.

Listing 6   The Null and IsNull methods

```
public bool IsNull
{
    get
    {
        // Put your code here
        return m_null;
    }
}

public static Complex Null
{
    get
    {
        Complex h = new Complex();
        h.m_null = true;
        return h;
    }
}
```

If you've been following along, you'll probably notice that the code in listing 6 is exactly the same as the skeleton code that was generated when you created the UDT.

That's one of the benefits of the standard handling of SQL Server NULL values with a `bool` field m_null. If you use a different method to represent NULL, you'll probably have to modify the methods `IsNull` and `Null`.

INVOKEIFRECEIVERISNULL AND ONNULLCALL

In a relational database, most expressions are subject to NULL propagation—if any of the operands or arguments for an expression or function is NULL, the result is also NULL. There are only a few exceptions, like `COALESCE` and `ISNULL`.

This behavior is easy to replicate for the methods in your UDT. There are two attributes that you can use in the `SqlMethod` property of a method's signature to control if a NULL should propagate. Their function is similar but not the same, so you should take care not to confuse them. Also note that they have different defaults.

The first, `InvokeIfReceiverIsNull`, can be applied to any nonstatic method; this property specifies what should happen if the method is invoked on a variable or column whose current value is NULL. If this attribute is set to `false` (the default), the method won't be invoked, and the return value (if any) will be set to Null (if supported by the data type) or the default; if the returned data type is a SQL-compatible data type, this will result in the return value being NULL. When set to `true`, the method will always be executed.

In listing 7, I show how you can use this property to make sure that a NULL complex value is not displayed as NULL but as a custom text. This isn't something I recommend doing for a real UDT, though—I only did it because we don't have any methods yet where there's a real use for the `InvokeIfReceiverIsNull` property. The code in listing 7 is only given as an example, and I suggest you remove it and revert to the original code for the `ToString()` method after you've tested this.

> **Listing 7 Forcing `ToString()` to be invoked for NULL values**

```
[SqlMethod(InvokeIfReceiverIsNull=true)]
public override string ToString()
{
    if (this.IsNull)
    {
        return "No value";
    }
// rest of the code (see listing 5)
```

The second attribute, `OnNullCall`, can be used on any method that accepts one or more arguments. If set to `true` (the default), the method is always executed, even if one or more of the arguments passed in are NULL. When set to `false`, the method isn't invoked and the return value (if any) is set to NULL when at least one of the arguments is NULL.

Given the existence of this attribute, I never understood why it's not used in the skeleton code for the `Parse()` method. I always change its signature and remove the explicit code for NULL handling, as shown in listing 8.

Listing 8   Using `OnNullCall` to simplify NULL handling in `Parse()`

```
[SqlMethod(OnNullCall=false)]
public static Complex Parse(SqlString s)
{
    // The two lines of skeleton code below can be removed,
    //thanks to OnNullCall
    //if (s.IsNull)
    //    return Null;
    Complex u = new Complex();
    // Put your code here
    // rest of the code (see listing 4)
```

Using the data type

Once the five methods described so far have been created, you have a working UDT. Once the assembly has been built (using Build on the Build menu in Visual Studio), you can deploy it to your SQL Server database and start using it. On the book's web page (www.manning.com/SQLServerMVPDeepDivesVol2), you can download code that deploys and tests the new data type. This code also includes some examples of methods you could add to make the UDT more useful.

Summary

In this chapter, I demonstrated that it's not hard to build your own SQL Server data type using CLR integration. I also showed that, with the proper methods added, such a data type can bring tremendous power to your fingertips.

I also pointed out that there are several limitations. Locale-specific formatting, implicit conversions, conversion errors, arithmetic operators, and even plain selecting data are all handled differently for a CLR UDT, so it'll never be possible to create a type and use it as if it were a native data type.

If you can accept these limitations, you have a valuable instrument placed in your hands—as Microsoft has proven by implementing the hierarchy, geometry, and geography data types as CLR user-defined data types in SQL Server 2008.

About the author

Hugo Kornelis is co-founder and R&D lead of perFact BV, a Dutch company that strives to improve analysis methods and to develop computer-aided tools that will generate completely functional applications from the analysis deliverable. The chosen platform for this development is SQL Server. In his spare time, Hugo likes to share and enhance his knowledge of SQL Server by frequenting newsgroups and forums, reading and writing books and blogs, and attending and speaking at conferences.

24 Extracting data with regular expressions

Matija Lah

In most information management domains, such as resource management, sales, production, and accounting, natural language texts are only rarely used as a source of information. In contrast, there are domains, such as content and document management, where natural language texts pretty much represent the principal or sole source of information.

Before this information can be utilized, it needs to be extracted from the source texts. This task can be performed manually by a person reading the source, identifying individual pieces of data, and then copying and pasting them into a data entry application. Fortunately, the highly deterministic nature of this operation allows its automation.

In this chapter I'll discuss the use of regular expressions in extracting information from texts using SQL Server 2008 (most of this chapter also applies to SQL Server 2005) and the Microsoft .NET Framework implementation of regular expressions.

Understanding before coding

To get a better understanding of the problem at hand, let's turn to Julie "Nitpick" Eagleeyes, an imaginary analyst and editor specializing in document management. Julie not only has to deal with hundreds of thousands of documents, but also with her managers, who are interested in lowering costs, and the authors, who are interested in maintaining a steady and predictable modus operandi, performing their work in exactly the same way they have for years.

So, Julie already has her work cut out for her, but now she also has to deal with *us*, the IT professionals, who, as I guess we all can agree, are a little bit of a manager and a little bit of an author at the same time. Jean-Paul Sartre understands Julie's predicament very well: "Hell is other people."

Background

Before we focus on Julie, let's clarify your objectives: presented with a collection of texts containing various pieces of information, you'll be tasked with identifying each piece of information and then extracting and converting it appropriately before it's passed to the next component in an existing document management solution.

We meet Julie in her office after she's just come back from a meeting with the authors, where it has been decided—unanimously and contrary to Julie's objectives, but very much in line with her expectations—that the authors won't be switching from their current word processors to a brand-new application proposed by Julie's employer. Because there will be no changes to the authoring process, another process will most probably have to be modified with the following requirements, according to Julie:

- A new section of the document will be used to list the references describing the relationships between the documents, and our automated extraction process will identify and store these sections separately.
- In the end, extract all the references, identify their nature, and store them in another table in the database.

Based on Julie's explanation, you can make the following deductions:

- You'll be dealing with documents, each containing a section of text listing references to other documents. The structure of the reference is fixed and will be used consistently.
- You'll need to automate the data flow from the table holding the documents to the table holding the references, setting the reference type appropriately along the way.

Julie was also kind enough to provide two typical examples (see table 1 and table 2).

Table 1 Examples of reference lists in a document

DocumentId	Reference section
200400351	Art. 351/2004 amended by Art. 27/2006, Art. 6/2007, Art. 2/2010, Art. 31/2010.
200400451	Art. 451/2004 also found in L. 127/2001, Art. 76/2002, N. 82/2003. Art. 451/2004 amended by Art. 46/2007, Art. 213/2010.

Table 2 shows the results for document 200400351 if you were to extract the information manually.

Table 2 An example of extracted values

Part	Value
Referenced Document Identifier	Art. 351/2004
Reference Type	amended by
Referencing Document Identifiers	Art. 27/2006, Art. 6/2007, Art. 2/2010, Art. 31/2010

From these examples you can see that even though the *values* they contain are different, their *shape* is the same. What you need is a way of describing the shape of strings, and based on this the automated process can identify which strings or substrings to extract.

An incredibly brief introduction to regular expressions, matches, and groups

Regular expressions (regex, for short) can be defined as *a system of rules and operators used to describe and manipulate sets of strings.*

In Julie's examples you can identify multiple subsets of strings that would be matched by a single regex; in English you'd define their shape as follows:

> *A string beginning with "Art", "N" or "L", followed by a space, then by numbers or letters, delimited by a slash character.*

The "translation" to a corresponding regex would read

```
[ArtLN.]+\s*\d+/\d+
```

If you were to apply this regex to Julie's text samples, it'd match every document identifier in the example (shown in table 3). In other words, each occurrence of a set of strings described by the regex within the expression represents a *match*.

Table 3   Regular expressions matches

Regex	Matches (one per row)
[ArtLN.]+\s*\d+/\d+	Art. 351/2004 Art. 27/2006 Art. 6/2007 Art. 2/2010 Art. 31/2010

Based on the example in table 2, you need to extract *three* different substrings from the source string. A single reference at the beginning of the string designates the *referenced* document. It's followed by a description designating the *type of reference*, which is followed by a list of references, designating the *referencing* documents.

By enclosing each of these subsets in parentheses, you define *groups* within the matched string. The corresponding regex would read

```
([ArtLN.]+\s*\d+/\d+)(\W*)([a-zA-Z\s][^ArtLN.]+)\b(\W*)(.*)
```

If you were to apply the new regex to our example, the result would contain a single match (the entire string), with all the individual subsets corresponding to the groups defined in the regex, as shown in table 4.

NOTE   The first group returned contains the outermost group—the match itself. For brevity, the outermost group is not shown in table 4.

Table 4　Regular expressions groups

Subset of the regex	Group
`([ArtLN.]+\s*\d+/\d+)`	Art. 351/2004
`(\W*)`	
`([a-zA-Z\s][^ArtLN.]+)\b`	amended by
`(\W*)`	
`(.*)`	Art. 27/2006, Art. 6/2007, Art. 2/2010, Art. 31/2010.

Each subset of strings (enclosed in parentheses) within each occurrence of the regex inside the expression represents a *group*.

Regular expressions and SQL Server

Transact-SQL doesn't natively support regular expressions. To use regular expressions in a SQL Server 2008 database engine, you'd need to create a SQL CLR user-defined module—a CLR function or a CLR procedure.

At the heart of any SQL CLR module (regardless of whether it's vendor-supplied or user-defined) there's a .NET assembly, loaded into the database and registered with the SQL Server instance. CLR integration is a complex and comprehensive subject, and therefore very much outside the scope of this chapter, in which we'll cover only one particular assembly and its deployment.

Later in this chapter, you'll implement your own regular expressions class library in a SQL CLR user-defined function.

SQL Server Integration Services (SSIS) also provides a few ways of extending built-in functionalities. First, there are the script task and the script data flow component. Both provide a way of extending an SSIS package with custom business logic that's relatively simple to implement. In both cases, the custom code is embedded within the package definition and compiled at runtime.

Later you'll implement the same regular expressions class library mentioned earlier in a script data flow component.

Regular expressions and the .NET Framework

Both regular expression classes—`Match` and `Group`—are available in the .NET implementation of regular expressions.

There's one important thing I haven't mentioned in my incredibly brief introduction to matches and groups: grouping constructs. The following two features are ones that I use regularly:

- *Named groups*—The `(?<name>)` construct allows you to name each group, and in retrieval or replacement operations you can then refer to a group by its name, rather than by the index designating its relative position to the start of the source string.

- *Noncapturing groups*—The `(?:)` construct can be used to specify which groups won't be captured by the matching operation.

Earlier you developed a regex to be used to extract three subsets from the source string in which you're interested. In table 5 you can see that distinguishing between the results isn't quite straightforward (you'd have to rely on their order), and also groups exist there that you don't need. You can correct this with grouping constructs. Here's an improved regex:

```
(?<item>[ArtLN.]+\s*\d+/\d+)(?:\W*)(?<ref_type>[a-zA-Z\s][^ArtLN.]+)\b(?:\W*)(?<ref_items>.*)(?:\W*)
```

Table 5 Regular expressions groups utilizing grouping constructs

Subset of the regex	Group	Name
`(?<item>[ArtLN.]+\s*\d+/\d+)`	Art. 351/2004	item
`(?:\W*)`		*(not captured)*
`(?<ref_type>[a-zA-Z\s][^ArtLN.]+)\b`	amended by	ref_type
`(?:\W*)`		*(not captured)*
`(?<ref_items>.*)`	Art. 27/2006, Art. 6/2007, Art. 2/2010, Art. 31/2010.	ref_items
`(?:\W*)`		*(not captured)*

Compare the results displayed in table 5 with the results of "manual labor" displayed in table 2. Is this what Julie expects? Does the famous quote by Sartre still apply to *us*?

The solution

You're going to create a .NET Framework class library using the C# programming language, implementing the appropriate .NET Framework regular expressions classes. This class library will provide you with the core functionalities and will be used by every other assembly you create later.

The solution assumes that you're familiar with the `Regex` class of the .NET Framework, its constructors, and the most vital of its members, namely `Matches` and `Groups`. You should also be familiar with regular expressions *options*, provided by the `Regex-Options` enumeration.

The core

The first step of the main function (named `Match`) is to apply the regex to the expression and retrieve a collection of matches:

```
// Create a new Regular Expression based on pattern and options
Regex re = RegexCreate(pattern, options);
// Retrieve Matches of pattern in expression as IEnumerable
IEnumerable<Match> matchCollection = re.Matches(expression).Cast<Match>();
```

You can't know in advance whether the regex will contain group definitions, so the function should handle both situations. You'll select all matches containing only a single group (the default group) and place them in the final result set:

```
// Collect Matches containing only the "default" group.
matchItemCollection = matchCollection.Where
(match => match.Groups.Count == 1).SelectMany<Match, MatchedItem>
    ((match, matchNumber) =>
        new List<MatchedItem>
        {
        new MatchedItem
            (
            (int)(matchNumber + 1),
            (string)match.Value
            )
        }
    );
```

Next, you'll select the matches containing more than one group and add them to the result set:

```
// Collect Groups (from Matches with Groups)...
matchItemCollection = matchCollection.Where
(match => match.Groups.Count > 1).SelectMany
    ((match, matchNumber) =>
    // ...but skip the "default" Group...
    match.Groups.Cast<Group>().Skip(_groupsToSkip)
    .SelectMany<Group, MatchedItem>
        ((group, groupNumber) =>
            new List<MatchedItem>
            {
            new MatchedItem
            (
            (int)(matchNumber + 1),
            (Nullable<int>)(groupNumber + groupsToSkip),
            (string)re.GroupNameFromNumber(groupNumber + _groupsToSkip),
            (string)group.Value
            )
            }
        )
    // ...then union with the previous results.
    ).Union(matchItemCollection);
```

With the `Skip` method, you omit the outermost group from the result set (groups-ToSkip is set at 1, meaning that the first group is skipped).

To extend the usability of group names to the caller, the `Match` function also implements a special `IEnumerable` parameter, named `requestedGroups`. The caller can use this parameter to specify the groups to be placed into the final result set; if the parameter isn't set or empty, the result set will contain all groups:

```
// If Group names were specified...
if (requestedGroups != null && requestedGroups.Count() > 0)
{
```

```
// ...only return Groups with corresponding names
// (by joining the Matched Item and the Requested Groups collections)
return matchItemCollection.Join<MatchedItem, string, string, MatchedItem>
    (requestedGroups,
    group => group.GroupName,
    groupRestriction => groupRestriction,
    (group, groupRestriction) =>
        new MatchedItem
        {
        MatchNumber = group.MatchNumber,
        GroupNumber = group.GroupNumber,
        GroupName = group.GroupName,
        Item = group.Item
        }
    );
}
else
// ...otherwise return all Groups.
{
return matchItemCollection;
}
```

To simplify maintenance and deployment, I suggest you place the core function in an assembly of its own.

The SQL CLR user-defined function

Because all the functionalities already exist in the core Match function, the definition of the SQL CLR function is quite simple. All you need here is to invoke the core function:

```
[SqlFunction(
    ...
    )]
public static IEnumerable Match(string expression, string pattern,
string groups, Nullable<Int64> options)
{
    IEnumerable<string> groupList =
        groups.Tokenize(_supportedSeparators, true);

    RegexOptions regexOptions =
        (RegexOptions)(options == null ? 0 : options);

    return MVPDeepDives.Common.RegularExpressions.Match
        (expression, pattern, groupList, regexOptions);
}
```

For maintenance and deployment purposes, I suggest you place the SQL CLR function in its own assembly (with a reference to the core class library developed earlier).

To be able to use these functions in the database engine (using T-SQL), the compiled assembly containing the SQL CLR function must be deployed to the SQL Server database. To deploy the assembly, use the CREATE ASSEMBLY DDL statement. Then to create a user-defined CLR function, use the CREATE FUNCTION DDL statement, using the EXTERNAL NAME syntax. For documentation of these two DDL statements, you can refer to Microsoft SQL Server Books Online.

The scripts used to deploy the assembly and to create a user-defined function in SQL Server are available at this book's web page.

The SSIS script component

To utilize the core Match function in an SSIS package, you could use a data flow script component, either by extending an existing data flow task or creating a new one. The script component should be defined as a *transformation component*, with a single input and a single output. The input columns will be determined by the preceding data flow component (for example, a source or a transformation component), but you'll configure the output columns manually. The core Match function could return more than a single row per each input row, so you should also define the output as asynchronous.

The function returns a set containing four columns as specified in table 6; these columns should be added to the output (in addition to those representing the input columns).

Table 6   The output columns corresponding to the result set of the core Match function

Name	Data type	Purpose
MatchNumber	DT_I4	The match's ordinal number
GroupNumber	DT_I4	The group's ordinal number
GroupName	DT_WSTR(450)	The group's name
Item	DT_NTEXT	The group's value

Next, you need to take care of two arguments expected by the core Match function:

- pattern—The regular expressions pattern to be used to identify and extract data
- options—The regular expressions options (as Int64 or DT_I8) to be used to control the operation

These two arguments could be passed to the script component via SSIS variables or via input columns. In the example accompanying this chapter, SSIS variables have been used.

To make the core Match function accessible to the script component, its assembly must be referenced in the script component's definition. You'll use the core Match function in the script component by extending the overridden Input0_Process-InputRow method:

```
public override void Input0_ProcessInputRow(Input0Buffer Row)
{
```

```
string expression = Encoding.Unicode.GetString
    (Row.%expression_column%.GetBlobData
        (0, (int)Row.%expression_column%.Length)
    );
List<RegularExpressions.MatchedItem> matchedItemCollection =
    new List<RegularExpressions.MatchedItem>();
matchedItemCollection.AddRange
    ((IEnumerable<RegularExpressions.MatchedItem>)RegularExpressions
        .Match(expression, pattern, (RegexOptions)options
    ));
if (matchedItemCollection.Count > 0)
{
    this.CreateNewOutputRows(ref Row, ref matchedItemCollection);
}
}
```

In this definition, the text `%expression_column%` represents the name of the column containing the expression to be searched.

The results (if any) produced by the core `Match` function are passed to the script component's output in an overload of the `CreateNewOutputRows` method:

```
public void CreateNewOutputRows(Input0Buffer row, ref
    List<RegularExpressions.MatchedItem> matchedItemCollection)
{
    foreach (RegularExpressions.MatchedItem matchedItem in
matchedItemCollection)
    {
        Output0Buffer.AddRow();

        ...

        Output0Buffer.MatchNumber = matchedItem.MatchNumber;

        if (matchedItem.GroupNumber == null)
            Output0Buffer.GroupNumber_IsNull = true;
        else
            Output0Buffer.GroupNumber = (int)matchedItem.GroupNumber;

        if (matchedItem.GroupName == null)
            Output0Buffer.GroupName_IsNull = true;
        else
            Output0Buffer.GroupName = matchedItem.GroupName;

        Output0Buffer.Item.ResetBlobData();
        Output0Buffer.Item.AddBlobData
            (Encoding.Unicode.GetBytes(matchedItem.Item));
    }
}
```

An example SSIS package demonstrating the use of the core `Match` function in a data flow script component and an example SSIS package including the data flow task implementing the custom SSIS component is available at this book's web page.

Homework

Using the code accompanying this chapter, you'll be able to build and test a complete solution. After reviewing the code carefully and experimenting with the samples provided, you'll also understand how the solution works. But from my experience, the learning process yields the best results when you design a solution "from scratch." To help you continue exploring what else you can do with regular expressions and SQL Server, here are a couple of ideas:

1 Our core `Match` function implements the `groupRestriction` parameter, which allows a list of regular expressions group names to be used to filter the result set returned by the function. But this parameter isn't used by any of the functions in the solution accompanying the chapter.

   1a Extend the SQL CLR function and utilize the `groupRestriction` parameter.

   1b Extend the Custom Data Flow Component to also take advantage of this optional argument.

2 Explore additional pattern matching methods of the .NET Framework `Regex` class.

   2a Consider the `Regex` class's `Split` method; can you think of a common problem that you could solve by implementing it?

   2b Which `Regex` method would you implement to extend the built-in T-SQL string replacement methods?

3 Study the `IsMatch Regex` method, and then implement it in a data flow transformation, either in an SSIS script component or a custom SSIS data flow component.

   3a Can you think of a use case where the objective would be to test whether a value is matched by a specific pattern?

   3b Would a synchronous or an asynchronous output be appropriate for this kind of transformation? Why?

4 The script data flow component is not the only method available for extending SSIS functionalities.

   4a Consider using the suggestions in this chapter to design a custom SSIS data flow component.

Summary

You analyzed a real-life business problem, identified several functionalities available that could help you solve it, and then instead of focusing on just one of them, you developed both—each one in its own specific environment, but both of them implementing the same core functionality.

Additionally you learned how to extend the built-in functionalities of Microsoft SQL Server with custom ones. You saw how to utilize SQL Server CLR integration, which you used to integrate a powerful technique of data identification, extraction, and transformation into the SQL Server Database Engine, as well as SQL Server Integration Services.

Most important, you provided the customers with a way of achieving their objectives, to solve a real-life problem—which is what counts in the end.

All of the code used in this chapter is also published online and can be downloaded from www.manning.com/SQLServerMVPDeepDivesVol2.

About the author

Matija Lah graduated from the Faculty of Law at the University of Maribor, Slovenia, in 1999. As a lawyer with extensive experience in IT, in 2001 he joined IUS SOFTWARE d.o.o., the leading provider of legal information in Slovenia, where he first came in contact with Microsoft SQL Server. In 2005 he decided to pursue a career of freelance consultant in the domain of general, business, and legal information, which in 2006 led him to join AI-in-Law Future Technologies Inc., introducing artificial intelligence into the legal information domain. Based on his continuous contributions to the SQL community, he was awarded the Most Valuable Professional award for SQL Server by Microsoft in 2007.

25 Relational division

Peter Larsson

Relational division is one of the hardest-to-understand areas in relational theory because of the complexity involved. Yet relational division is one of the areas that can be most useful when programming for relational databases.

Why use relational division?

There are many situations where relational division is a good solution. A simple way to think about relational division's usefulness is to consider situations where you need data from one set that matches ALL the values in another set. For example, you may want to find all customers who have been served by both James and Gabrielle. Or you may want to find all applicants who have experience with Reporting Services, SharePoint, and Integration Services. What if you run a dating site and you want your clients to be able to search for certain criteria such as eye color, number of children, and so on? Possible dating choices will only be returned when someone matches ALL of the specified criteria.

A common mistake is to think you can use a series of INNER JOIN(s) to find the solution, but you can't do that in an efficient way. INNER JOIN will allow you to find rows in one set that match any one of the rows from another set, but in order to find those that match ALL, you'd have to build a temporary table of intermediate results, and then use a loop to check for each value of interest. A relational division algorithm deals with this special problem.

Defining relational division

Relational division is a binary operation involving two sets, R and S. The operation can be written just like a mathematical division—that is, R ÷ S. Set R should have at least two attributes, A1 and A2. The result, Q will be a set of values from A1 in set R for which there's a corresponding A2 value to match every row in set S. This definition will hopefully become clear to you when we look at an example. If you'd like an even more mathematical definition of relational division, take at look at this Wikipedia article: http://en.wikipedia.org/wiki/Relational_algebra.

The relational division operation is normally a time-consuming and complex operation, because it involves using the tuples of one set to partition a second set. The relational division operator is effectively the opposite of the Cartesian product operator. You can think of it this way. In mathematical division, when dividing R by S, R is the dividend and S is the divisor, and the result is a quotient, Q. In mathematical division, when you have R ÷ S = Q, it's also true that Q x S = R. When translating this to set operations (or relational algebra), you can treat x as the Cartesian product or cross join operator, and say that after performing relational division, the result, Q is the set that can be cross joined with the divisor, S to return the dividend, R. In numerical terms, Q would be [0, 2).

Use R ÷ S when you wish to express queries with ALL; you want the dividends (the rows in R) that match ALL divisors (rows in S). E.F. Codd didn't limit the result to an exact division; he allowed for a remainder. In fact, remainder division is the default and exact division is a special case, and you'll see what this means when we look at some specific examples.

In this chapter you'll learn about an algorithm that's very efficient for performing either exact relational division or division with a remainder. To compare the efficiency, I've searched for algorithms that are most commonly used today for implementing relational division (and also some not-so-common ones), and I've used them for a comparison baseline.

I'll also show you that you're already using relational division without even knowing it!

Background

Relational algebra received little or no attention until the publication of Codd's relational data model in 1970. Codd proposed such algebra as a basis for database query languages. Relational algebra is essentially equivalent in expressive power to relational calculus. This result is known as Codd's theorem.

Some care has to be taken with negation to avoid a mismatch. The difference operator of relational algebra always returns a finite result. To overcome these difficulties, Codd restricted the operands of relational algebra to finite relations only and also proposed restricted support for negation (NOT) and disjunction (OR).

Relational algebra is similar to normal algebra, except you use sets (relations) as values instead of numbers. Relational algebra isn't used as a query language in any actual relational database management systems (RDBMSs); instead you use the SQL language, and in Microsoft SQL Server you have the Transact-SQL dialect.

You need to know about relational algebra to understand query execution and optimization in an RDBMS. Relations are seen as sets of tuples, which means that no duplicates are allowed.

The difference in syntax and performance among various RDBMSs is due to the actual implementation of the various relational operators.

Sample data for two simple cases

Figure 1 shows the contents of a table containing stockholder names and stock names. Using this table, you've been asked to get all stockholders who own IBM stock. How do you write that query?

```
SELECT   Stockholder
FROM     dbo.Stockholders
WHERE    Stockname = 'IBM';
```

The result is Peso and White. This is something you might write and use almost every day, so now you know you're already performing relational division!

What you just did was relational division using one row and one column. The query can be extended to use multiple columns; for example, if you added a column Type to the Stockholders table, it increases the difficulty but is solved with adding an AND to the WHERE clause:

```
SELECT Stockholder
FROM   dbo.Stockholders
WHERE  Stockname = 'Enron'
       AND Type = 'A';
```

Stockholder	Stockname
Peso	IBM
Peso	Microsoft
Peso	Apple
Green	Enron
Green	BP
White	IBM
White	Enron
White	Xerox
White	Apple
Yellow	McDonalds
Yellow	Microsoft
Yellow	Siemens
Blue	McDonalds
Blue	Microsoft

Figure 1   Stockholders table

With this simple query you now have performed relational division using multiple columns for one row. So how many types of relational division are there?

I've already mentioned exact division and division with a remainder, so there are two types. I've also shown that there can be single column and multiple column division, so there are two more types. And finally, there are two more types because you can use one row or multiple rows to divide by. This adds up to eight different types, as shown in figure 2.

Rows	Columns	Remainder	You
Single	Single	Yes	★
Single	Multiple	Yes	★
Single	Single	No	
Single	Multiple	No	
Multiple	Single	Yes	
Multiple	Multiple	Yes	
Multiple	Single	No	
Multiple	Multiple	No	

Figure 2   Types of relational division

Now, let's continue and write a query that checks for multiple rows. You want a query that returns the stockholders who own both Apple and Microsoft. This is a common operation.

```
SELECT    Stockholder
FROM      dbo.Stockholders
WHERE     Stockname IN ('Apple', 'Microsoft')
GROUP BY  Stockholder
HAVING    COUNT(Stockname) = 2;
```

As expected, the query returns only Peso. Notice that Peso additionally owns IBM and that's considered the remainder in this division.

How would you write a query the returns the stockholders who own only McDonald's and Microsoft? (The *only* makes this an exact division; if you wanted stockholders who owned at least these two stocks, you'd use remainder division.) Listing 1 shows one possible solution.

NOTE The online code contains scripts to build the needed tables. You can run these scripts in any database, but I suggest you use a test database.

Listing 1   First solution

```
-- Query 1
SELECT     sh.Stockholder
FROM       dbo.Stockholders AS sh
WHERE      sh.Stockname IN ('McDonalds', 'Microsoft')
GROUP BY   sh.Stockholder
HAVING     COUNT(sh.Stockname) = 2
           -- Remove below AND for remainder division, or change "=" to "<="
           AND COUNT(sh.Stockname) = (SELECT COUNT(*)
                                      FROM   dbo.Stockholders AS x
                                      WHERE  x.Stockholder = sh.Stockholder);
```

The type of query in listing 1, made popular by Joe Celko, has a built-in performance issue. There's a correlated subquery that executes for each stockholder, so for a large dataset this query isn't recommended. The second check is necessary because the filter for Stockname only includes those stockholders who own the Stockname, and any of those stockholders could also own additional stocks. It's necessary to add the second filter to check that those stockholders passing the first filter have no other Stock-Name associated with them. If you want remainder division, you can either leave off the second check or change the equals (=) to less than or equal to (<=). For exact division, listing 1 will return only stockholder Blue, and for remainder division, it will return Blue and Yellow.

There's another approach to coding relational division that Joe Celko made popular, and that approach is to use a double negative and find all stockholders who don't have one of the desired Stocknames and exclude them. (In pseudocode this would be "Give me all the stockholders where there does *not* exist one of the desired Stock-names that the stockholder does *not* have.") This solution is shown in listing 2.

Listing 2   Second solution

```
-- Query 2
SELECT  DISTINCT sh1.Stockholder
FROM    dbo.Stockholders AS sh1
WHERE   NOT EXISTS (SELECT *
                    FROM   (SELECT 'McDonalds' AS Stockname UNION ALL
                            SELECT 'Microsoft') AS Portfolio
                    WHERE  NOT EXISTS
                           (SELECT *
                            FROM   dbo.Stockholders AS sh2
                            WHERE  sh1.Stockholder = sh2.Stockholder
                                   AND sh2.Stockname = Portfolio.Stockname
                           )
                   );
```

Unfortunately, the second query can't do exact division. (That is, it can't find those stockholders who only have the specified `Stocknames` and no others.) It can only return both Blue and Yellow. I've come up with a solution, shown in listing 3, that takes care of both exact division and remainder division with just one simple parameter value and no change in the query at all.

Listing 3   Third solution

```
-- Query 3
SELECT     Stockholder
FROM       dbo.Stockholders
GROUP BY   Stockholder
HAVING     SUM(CASE
               WHEN Stockname IN ('McDonalds', 'Microsoft')
                  THEN 1
                  ELSE 0 END)
           = 2
           AND MIN(CASE
                  WHEN Stockname IN ('McDonalds', 'Microsoft')
                     THEN 1
                     ELSE 0 END)
           >= 0; -- Change to 1 for exact division
```

For the query in listing 3, if the final value is 0, only Blue is returned, because stockholder Blue owns no other stocks besides McDonald's and Microsoft. If the final value is changed to 1, both Blue and Yellow are returned.

Comparison charts

Now let's see how the solutions scale for remainder division. Figure 3 shows the CPU time for the three solutions performing remainder division. The three vertical bars for each solution are based on different numbers of rows. As you can see, Query 1

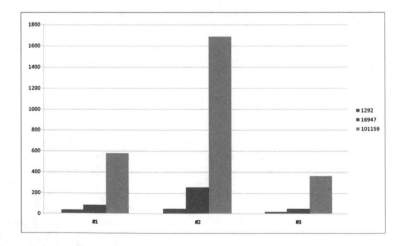

Figure 3
CPU comparison

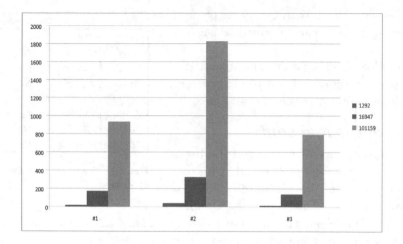

**Figure 4
Duration comparison**

doesn't scale linearly. Query 2 is the worst performing, and Query 3 scales quite well and also uses almost half the CPU as Query 1.

Figure 4 shows the duration for the three solutions, again with three bars for three different table sizes. Duration follows same pattern as CPU. Query 1 is better than Query 2, and Query 3 finishes faster than Query 1.

Figure 5 indicates the number of reads for each of the solutions. (I had to present this graph using a logarithmic scale because it wasn't possible to display the graph linearly.) The reads follow the same pattern as CPU and duration for Query 1 and Query 3, where Query 3 uses fewer reads than Query 1. Query 2 shoots through the roof!

So what makes Query 3 more efficient? The obvious reason is that it only does one pass over the Stockholder table. The performance comparisons for exact division for Query 1 and Query 3 follow the same pattern, where Query 3 less CPU, finishes in less

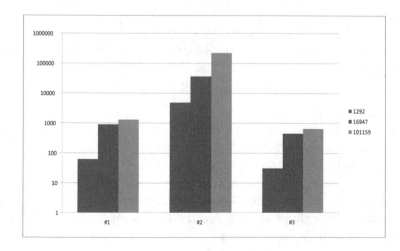

**Figure 5   Logical
reads comparison**

time, and uses fewer reads than Query 1. (Query 2 isn't included because it can't perform exact division.)

Now you've learned to master more than half of the division types. As figure 6 shows, you've now seen code to implement five of the eight possibilities.

Rows	Columns	Remainder	You
Single	Single	Yes	★
Single	Multiple	Yes	★
Single	Single	No	★
Single	Multiple	No	
Multiple	Single	Yes	★
Multiple	Multiple	Yes	
Multiple	Single	No	★
Multiple	Multiple	No	

Figure 6   We've explored five of the eight types.

Let's go on with the real stuff

In the previous section, you hardcoded the list of desired values, which forms the dividend in our relational division. Now you'll work with set-based solutions, working with both a dividend (Stockholder)

Stockname
IBM
Apple

table and a divisor (Portfolio) table. This is also a more real-life scenario. Figure 7 shows the Portfolio table that you'll use as the divisor.

Figure 7   The Portfolio table you'll use as the divisor

Set-based solution to common relational division

Listing 4 shows how you'd transform the previous query to deal with two tables.

Listing 4   Relational division with two tables

```
SELECT      sh.Stockholder
FROM        (
                SELECT      Stockholder,
                            COUNT(*) AS Stockitems
                FROM        Stockholders
                GROUP BY    Stockholder
            ) AS sh
INNER JOIN  (
                SELECT  COUNT(*) AS Stockitems
                FROM    Portfolio
            ) AS pf ON pf.Stockitems = sh.Stockitems
INNER JOIN  Stockholders AS s ON s.Stockholder = sh.Stockholder
INNER JOIN  Portfolio AS p ON p.Stockname = s.Stockname
GROUP BY    sh.Stockholder
HAVING      COUNT(*) = MIN(pf.Stockitems);
```

This is a direct transformation of Query 3. The part AS pf ON pf.Stockitems = sh.Stockitems is the same as AND MIN(CASE ... END) >= 1. If you change the pf.Stockitems = sh.Stockitems to pf.Stockitems <= sh.Stockitems, then the query will return remainder division.

By building the query in a set-based fashion, you can extend the previous query to include multiple columns as well, with a simple extension to the Portfolio join condition. Assume both the Stockholders table and the Portfolio table have an additional column Type, and in addition to matching the Stockname values between the tables,

Stockholders		
Stockholder	*Stockname*	*Type*
Peso	IBM	A
Peso	Microsoft	A
Peso	Apple	B
Green	Enron	A
Green	BP	A
White	IBM	A
White	Enron	B
White	Xerox	A
White	Apple	A
Yellow	McDonalds	A
Yellow	Microsoft	B

Portfolio	
Stockname	*Type*
IBM	A
Apple	B

Stockholders ÷ Portfolio
Stockholder
White

Figure 8   Tables used for relational division on multiple columns

you want the Type value to also match. Figure 8 shows a subset of the Stockholders table, along with the Portfolio table and the result.

Listing 5 shows how you could code this. The scripts will create a new Stockholders table called StockholdersT and a new Portfolio table called PortfolioT, both of which contain the column Type.

Listing 5   Code for relational division on multiple columns

```
SELECT      sh.Stockholder
FROM        (
                SELECT      Stockholder,
                            COUNT(*) AS Stockitems
                FROM        StockholdersT
                GROUP BY    Stockholder
            ) AS sh
INNER JOIN  (
                SELECT   COUNT(*) AS Stockitems
                FROM     PortfolioT
            ) AS pf ON pf.Stockitems <= sh.Stockitems
INNER JOIN  StockholdersT AS s ON s.Stockholder = sh.Stockholder
INNER JOIN  PortfolioT AS p ON p.Stockname = s.Stockname
                AND p.Type = s.Type
GROUP BY    sh.Stockholder
HAVING      COUNT(*) = MIN(pf.Stockitems);
```

Figure 9 shows you've now explored all types of division!

But wait! There's more to come. There's an extension to the eight types of division, and it allows dividing over multiple divisor sets, which will be described in the next section. So there are actually 16 types of division!

Rows	Columns	Remainder	You
Single	Single	Yes	★
Single	Multiple	Yes	★
Single	Single	No	★
Single	Multiple	No	★
Multiple	Single	Yes	★
Multiple	Multiple	Yes	★
Multiple	Single	No	★
Multiple	Multiple	No	★

Figure 9   You're now familiar with all eight types of relational division.

Stockholders		
Stockholder	*Stockname*	*Type*
Peso	IBM	A
Peso	Microsoft	A
Peso	Apple	B
Green	Enron	A
Green	BP	A
White	IBM	A
White	Enron	B
White	Xerox	A
White	Apple	A
Yellow	McDonalds	A
Yellow	Microsoft	B

Portfolio		
SetID	*Stockname*	*Type*
1	IBM	A
1	Apple	B
1	Microsoft	A
2	IBM	A
3	McDonalds	A
3	Microsoft	A

Stockholders ÷ Portfolio	
Stockholder	*SetID*
Peso	1
Peso	2
White	2

Figure 10   Tables you can use for relational divisor sets with multiple divisor sets

Does one query exist for all types of relational division?

Yes, there does exist one query that works for all types of relational division—and this is one reason I wanted to write this chapter. I'm hoping Microsoft will someday make the T-SQL language more complete and incorporate relational division into the language. Meanwhile, you have to use all sorts of queries to accomplish the same thing. The query you'll see in listing 6 can be extended to handle multiple divisor sets, as well.

What's a divisor set? You can think of it as providing a way to perform multiple divisions in a single query. Assume you want to search for a subset of rows matching one set of divisor values, and also search for a second subset of rows matching a different set of divisor values. Also assume that there's a priority you can assign to each subject that will indicate the order that the result rows should be returned. Figure 10 shows the same Stockholders data that appeared in figure 8, but the Portfolio divisor table now has an additional column indicating a SetID. All rows in the divisor with the same SetID are considered one divisor.

In the Portfolio table in figure 10, there are three divisor sets. The first consists of IBM with type A, Apple with type B, and Microsoft with type A. Only stockholder Peso matches all those rows. The second divisor set consists of only IBM with type A, and both Peso and White matches that row. The third divisor set contains McDonald's with type A and Microsoft with type A, and no rows in the Stockholders table match both of those, so no SetID 3 rows are returned in the result. Listing 6, using a variation of the Portfolio table with a SetID column, shows the code you can use to perform relational division with multiple divisor sets.

Listing 6   Relational division with multiple divisor sets

```
SELECT      sh.Stockholder,
            pf.SetID
FROM        (
            SELECT      Stockholder,
            COUNT(*) AS Stockitems
```

```
                 FROM         StockholdersT
                 GROUP BY     Stockholder
             ) AS sh
INNER JOIN   (
                 SELECT       SetID,
                              COUNT(*) AS Stockitems
                 FROM         PortfolioTS
                 GROUP BY     SetID
             ) AS pf ON pf.Stockitems = sh.Stockitems
INNER JOIN   StockholdersT AS s ON s.Stockholder = sh.Stockholder
INNER JOIN   PortfolioTS AS p ON p.Stockname = s.Stockname
                 AND p.Type = s.Type
WHERE        pf.SetID = p.SetID
GROUP BY     sh.Stockholder,
             pf.SetID
HAVING       COUNT(*) = MIN(pf.Stockitems);
```

Summary

When writing production code, you should keep two important things in mind to achieve professional-quality work. First, you need to pay attention to the maintainability of your code; second, you have to tune your queries for performance and speed.

I've used this new algorithm with a few of my clients. For example, rewriting a stored procedure for Sony Ericsson brought the execution time for the stored procedure from 21 minutes down to 2 seconds. For another customer, rewriting a stored procedure brought the execution time from 10 hours down to 3 minutes!

Can you make the algorithm even simpler? The short and direct answer is probably no. When I designed this algorithm, I didn't pay that much attention to theory. I was more focused on how SQL Server works. And after a few tries, I managed to get the algorithm to work. As a bonus, it works on all current versions of SQL Server and it's portable.

I've filed a Connect proposal to Microsoft to include relational division in SQL Server to move the T-SQL language closer to completion. I propose the following:

```
DIVIDE     DividendSet AS t
USING      DivisorSet AS n ON n.Col1 = t.Col1
             { AND n.Col2 = t.Col2 }
{ PARTITION BY    n.DivisorSetID }
MATCHING   { REMAINDER | EXACT }
OUTPUT     t.Stockholder
           { , n.DivisorSetID }
{
  INTO     TargetTable
           (
               Col1
               { , Col2 }
           )
}
```

The proposal isn't far from how MERGE works. You can make a difference by voting on this Connect proposal here: http://connect.microsoft.com/SQLServer/feedback/

details/670531/move-t-sql-language-closer-to-completion-with-a-divide-by-operator. As you can see, the DIVIDE BY operator can be made compact and easy to remember.

At this point, I hope you've learned what relational division is and how to recognize when you should use it.

About the author

Peter Larsson has been an international consultant and lecturer since 1993. He is a SQL Server Microsoft MVP (since 2009), leader and co-founder of the local PASS chapter Scania, and a mentor for SQLUG (the Swedish SQL Server User Group). Peter joined SolidQ in 2011.

Peter's key expertise is high-performance querying, and he's well known for his unorthodox mindset when solving complex problem statements. It's not unusual for Peter to refactor an algorithm or query and reduce the runtime from hours to just a few seconds or minutes. When not working, Peter spends his time with his wife and four kids.

26 SQL FILESTREAM: to BLOB or not to BLOB

Ben Miller

Coming from a development background, I understand streaming and I/O operations; the two concepts fall close together in my mind. So, when I think about SQL Server, I think about data in rows and columns and managed by an engine—files don't enter my mind.

`FILESTREAM` is a new SQL Server data type for SQL 2008 and later. More precisely, it's an attribute on an existing `varbinary(max)` data type in SQL 2008 and later. There are requirements to use it, as you'll see in this chapter. `FILESTREAM` gives the SQL Server engine the ability to store a reference to a file in a SQL Server column and have the actual file stored in the filesystem instead of inside the column itself. But the question is, as this chapter's title asks, do you store the file in a BLOB, inside the column (to BLOB), or is it better to store it in the filesystem (not to BLOB)?

In this chapter I'll show you the requirements and configuration steps to get this attribute to correctly apply to a column in a table so the file is stored in the filesystem instead of in the data pages. I'll also discuss when you might want to use `FILESTREAM` and when you might not.

To FILESTREAM or not to FILESTREAM

In the early days of content management systems (CMSs), there were various ways to handle files in databases. Here are the main three methods often used for storing files:

- Store the file in the filesystem, and store the absolute path to a disk file in a column.
- Store the file at a URL, and put that URL in the column as a reference.
- Store the file in the table column; retrieve the file at each call or cache it to disk.

Now you have a fourth option: using `FILESTREAM`, store the file in the filesystem and stream it.

Risks are associated with any of these options. You must specify the permissions that govern access to these files and determine how to prevent the accidental deletion of files. You must also ensure that the files are backed up with the database and kept in sync. In regard to the storage of the files in the database, two potential concerns are size and retrieval performance. Say you store the file in the column with the data type `varbinary(max)`. Then when you retrieve the file, it will be pulled through the engine and clutter up the buffer pool. You'll have to decide which method is more efficient, secure, and safe, and you'll have to weigh your decision carefully. But maybe most important today, you also have to decide which method is the most recoverable.

Answering these questions causes some degree of angst, because when you start to go down a certain road, changing paths is neither quick nor easy. So what would make you want to use one over the other? Let's look at each of the four options:

- *Store the file in the filesystem, and store the absolute path in the column*—With this option, the filesystem is still leveraged, but files are often moved, deleted, or renamed, and many system administrators don't update the table to reflect the new name or location. On the web in particular, you get broken-image symbols in the browser. This is a risk with disjointed storage: one part in SQL Server and one part in the filesystem with no links between them.

- *Store the file at a URL, and put the URL in the column*—This option is fairly similar to the first, except today many developers use content delivery systems to store their files. This strategy allows them to store the file somewhere else for storage purposes or to use their caching mechanisms to deliver the content to the web. You're still relying on another system to maintain the locations of the files. In some cases, you're not in control of the store in the content delivery system and are vulnerable to the pitfalls of the first case.

- *Store the file in the table column, and decide on the retrieval mechanism*—This approach is a little more self-contained and less vulnerable than the first two. You've put the content with the metadata and you can back it up when you back up the database. You have the ability to put permissions on that column or table so that permission vulnerabilities can be addressed. But here's the challenge: the size of the files are growing, which poses problems with scalability and storage concerns. The issue isn't just the sheer size of the database: with BLOBs getting larger, the buffer pool is taking a hit on putting those files through and out the stream to the client. How do you know where to put these bigger files?

- *Using FILESTREAM, store the file in the filesystem and stream it*—With this option, when you put the file in the table, the file gets stored outside of SQL Server in the filesystem container controlled by SQL Server. This approach doesn't eliminate all risk, because the files are in the filesystem. But even with proper controls in place, the sysadmins with potential access to the files should tread lightly. I believe that it has less risk if the sysadmins respect the containers that aren't normal stores, like a directory full of files. Other benefits of using `FILESTREAM` include improved administration and transactional consistency.

Configuring FILESTREAM in SQL Server

You must have two configuration items in place to use the SQL Server `FILESTREAM` method of storing files: the OS configuration and the SQL Server configuration. Once these are in place, you'll be ready to use the `FILESTREAM` attribute on your `varbinary(max)` columns.

Operating system configuration

First, you must configure the OS to allow the desired functionality. Each option has a different effect on the OS and SQL Server:

- Enable `FILESTREAM` for Transact-SQL Access
- Enable `FILESTREAM` for File I/O Streaming Access
- Allow Remote Clients to Have Streaming Access to `FILESTREAM` Data

The first option enables `FILESTREAM` for use in T-SQL so that you can have a file that's accessed through the filesystem and retrieved using standard T-SQL. This approach blends the BLOB and the `FILESTREAM` together. The file is stored in the filesystem, but when retrieved it's brought through the engine as part of the rowset.

The second option enables streaming of the file using Win32 streaming. This requires a share name to be created, which lets you use the Win32 Streaming APIs to retrieve the file outside the buffer pool of SQL Server's engine. The second option doesn't allow for a remote client to retrieve the file via streaming, though—that's where the third option comes into play. The third option tells SQL Server that remote clients are allowed to use Win32 streaming to get the file

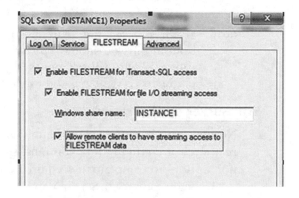

Figure 1   OS configuration options

from the filesystem. With all three options checked, as shown in figure 1, `FILESTREAM` is fully enabled for use by T-SQL and Win32 streaming, both local to the SQL Server and remotely.

There are two places that you can configure these options. The first is when you're installing SQL 2008 and later while setting up the data directories. You'll see a FILESTREAM tab that contains these options on the Data Engine Configuration page. You'll have a second opportunity to configure these options by using SQL Server Configuration Manager once SQL Server is installed. In the Configuration Manager, you'll see an identical FILESTREAM tab. When changing the options via Configuration Manager, you won't be prompted to restart the SQL Server, but in order for the settings to take effect, you must restart.

```
C:\>net share

Share name     Resource                                Remark

-----------------------------------------------------------------------------
C$             C:\                                     Default share
G$             G:\                                     Default share
IPC$                                                   Remote IPC
ADMIN$         C:\Windows                              Remote Admin
I01            \\?\GLOBALROOT\Device\RsFx0150\<localmachine>\I01
                                                       SQL Server FILESTREAM share
                                                       Caching disabled
The command completed successfully.
```

Figure 2   Enter NET SHARE at the command prompt.

To validate the configuration of the OS, choose Start > Run and type `cmd.exe`. At the command prompt, enter `NET SHARE`. The results show that a special share has been created and labeled for use by SQL Server as a `FILESTREAM` share (see figure 2). Also, you can go into SQL Server and run the query shown in the following listing to see the levels of configuration.

Listing 1   Server properties

```
SELECT
     SERVERPROPERTY ('FilestreamShareName') ShareName
     ,SERVERPROPERTY ('FilestreamConfiguredLevel') ConfiguredLevel
     ,SERVERPROPERTY ('FilestreamEffectiveLevel') EffectiveLevel
GO
```

NOTE   You'll still see the share if you've selected the second configuration option, but you should validate the configuration by using the query in listing 1. This will tell you the level of configuration that the SQL Server engine is recognizing and will honor when you go to use it.

SQL Server configuration

Now that you have the OS configured and the SQL Server engine is reporting the correct level of configuration, you must specify the SQL Server and database configuration options to complete the requirements to use SQL Server `FILESTREAM`.

To begin, open SQL Server Management Studio (SSMS) and connect to a server. In Object Explorer, press F8 or select View > Object Explorer, right-click the SQL Server instance, and choose Properties to open the dialog box shown in figure 3. In the Advanced section, the first option on the right is Filestream Access Level with a drop-down arrow beside it. This is where you allow SQL Server to use the `FILESTREAM` attribute on a `varbinary(max)` column. Click the drop-down arrow to see your options: Disabled, Transact-SQL Access Enabled, and Full Access Enabled. If you plan to use Win32 I/O streaming, you need to enable Full Access.

Figure 3   Configuring the Filestream Access Level setting

The `sp_configure` procedure can be used to change or display global configuration settings for the current server. You can also use `sp_configure` to configure SQL Server rather than use SSMS. The command is shown in listing 2. The options defined for `sp_configure` are as follows:

- 0—Disables `FILESTREAM` support for this instance
- 1—Enables `FILESTREAM` for Transact-SQL access
- 2—Enables `FILESTREAM` for Transact-SQL and Win32 streaming access

Listing 2   `sp_configure` options

```
USE master
GO
/* This will get the setting, show advanced options not required */
EXEC sp_configure 'filestream access level'
GO
/* To use this to set it, you will use 0, 1, 2 */
EXEC sp_configure 'filestream access level', 2
GO
RECONFIGURE
GO
```

A SQL Server restart isn't required for these options to take effect, but you need to issue a `RECONFIGURE` statement to complete the process.

With this configuration in place, you're now ready to enable a database to use `FILESTREAM` on a `varbinary(max)` column.

Database configuration

When creating a normal database, you define at least two files: one for the database data and one for the log. You can define any number of additional filegroups and files for a database. When working with `FILESTREAM` filegroups, you create a filegroup with the `CONTAINS FILESTREAM` attribute and then add a file that defines the path where the `FILESTREAM` store will be created. You can create multiple `FILESTREAM` filegroups in a database.

Listing 3 shows how to create a database, listing 4 shows how to create filegroups that contain `FILESTREAM` containers, and listing 5 shows how to enable `FILESTREAM` columns in tables and put them on the filegroups.

Listing 3   The Create Database script

```
CREATE DATABASE [MyProductionDB] ON  PRIMARY
(
    NAME = N'MyProductionDB_data',
    FILENAME = N'F:\SQLDATA\MyProductionDB.mdf'
)
LOG ON
(
    NAME = N'MyProductionDB_log',
    FILENAME = N'F:\SQLDATA\MyProductionDB_log.ldf'
)
GO
```

Listing 4   Adding a filegroup with FILESTREAM

```
ALTER DATABASE [MyProductionDB]
    ADD FILEGROUP FilestreamGroup1
    CONTAINS FILESTREAM
GO
```

NOTE   If you try to create a filegroup using CONTAINS FILESTREAM and the FILESTREAM feature hasn't been enabled correctly, you'll receive an error:

```
Msg 5591, Level 16, State 3, Line X
  FILESTREAM feature is disabled.
```

Listing 5   Adding a file to the FILESTREAM filegroup

```
ALTER DATABASE [MyProductionDB]
 ADD FILE
 (
    NAME = Photos,
    FILENAME = 'F:\FSDATA\Files'
 )
 TO FILEGROUP FilestreamGroup1
GO
```

In listing 5, notice the requirement for the defining of the filename for the FILESTREAM filegroup. When you define the path or filename, ensure that the directories exist *up to* the last directory you specified. In listing 5, F:\FSDATA must exist, but the directory Files must not exist, or you'll get an error telling you that the directory already exists and SQL Server won't be able to create the path for the FILESTREAM store. When you have the directory structure created correctly, SQL Server will create the folder Files and assign special permissions to that folder. By default, the SQL Server Service and the BUILTIN\Administrators accounts have permissions to this directory (or container). Keep in mind that because the files reside on the filesystem, they're vulnerable to manipulation by those with privileges.

WARNING   You can introduce corruption into the database by altering permissions and the files in the filesystem under this container.

Creating a table that uses FILESTREAM

Next, let's go over the requirements to creating a table with a FILESTREAM attribute on a varbinary(max) column:

- Each table must have a uniqueidentifier column that's a UNIQUE ROWGUIDCOL.
- You must specify the FILESTREAM attribute on the varbinary(max) column.
- You must use the FILESTREAM_ON clause to designate which filegroup to store FILESTREAM data.

The code in the following listing will create a table with one FILESTREAM column and then designate your FILESTREAM filegroup as the place for the FILESTREAM column.

Listing 6   Creating a table with a FILESTREAM column

```
CREATE TABLE dbo.[PhotoContainer] (
    [PhotoID] [int] IDENTITY(1,1) NOT NULL PRIMARY KEY,
    [PhotoFile] varbinary(max) FILESTREAM NULL,
    [PhotoGuid] UNIQUEIDENTIFIER NOT NULL ROWGUIDCOL
                    UNIQUE DEFAULT NEWID()
)
FILESTREAM_ON FilestreamGroup1
GO
```

As you'll recall, you can create multiple FILESTREAM columns in one table, but they all must be in the same FILESTREAM filegroup. So be careful if you want to separate them in different locations.

At this point you have a fully configured table that can now accept the files and store them in the FILESTREAM container on disk, using either T-SQL or Win32 streaming.

Things to consider

With the configuration of FILESTREAM complete, I'll discuss factors that you should take into account when using FILESTREAM or BLOB storage. There's always going to be overhead associated with either FILESTREAM or BLOB storage and retrieval. This overhead will be the main consideration in this section.

Files come in all sizes and types, each type with its own challenges. The following file size ranges will help you think about your situation and what fits:

- 256 KB or less
- 256 KB to 1 MB
- 1 MB and greater

For files that are 256 KB or less, there's less overhead if you store them in BLOB or varbinary(max) columns and retrieve them via T-SQL. For those 1 MB or greater, the overhead gets worse for BLOB storage but improves with FILESTREAM using Win32 streaming. Paul Randall wrote a whitepaper that shows the overhead of FILESTREAM (http://msdn.microsoft.com/en-us/library/cc949109(v=sql.100).aspx).

The number of rows wasn't part of this discussion, but that's something you'll need to be aware of in your testing and decision.

Backups are an additional consideration. When you back up a database that has FILESTREAM columns, just as a database with BLOBs in the columns, the data is all backed up. There's one advantage to the FILESTREAM configuration: if you don't wish to back up the FILESTREAM files, you can do a partial backup and omit the backup of that filegroup.

How do I use FILESTREAM?

Next, I'll show you the new keywords you can use to gain access to the FILESTREAM columns in order to use Win32 streaming. When retrieving files in FILESTREAM, you need just a SELECT statement naming the column.

There are two new elements that you need to use to access FILESTREAM columns. The first is PathName(), the extension to the FILESTREAM column, which returns the symbolic path (the actual physical path is hidden) of the file that allows you to stream the data (see listing 7). Also, you'll need to use GET_FILESTREAM_TRANSACTION _CONTEXT() to get the transaction context of the statement (see listing 8). This also implies that for streaming the file, you need to be within a transaction. If you aren't in a transaction, GET_FILESTREAM_TRANSACTION_CONTEXT() returns NULL.

Listing 7   Example of PathName()

```
DECLARE @ID UNIQUEIDENTIFIER
SET @ID = NEWID()
INSERT INTO dbo.PhotoContainer(PhotoGuid, PhotoFile)
VALUES (@ID, CAST('Photo Placeholder' AS VARBINARY(MAX)))

SELECT PhotoFile.PathName() as [PhotoFile.PathName()]
FROM dbo.PhotoContainer
WHERE PhotoGuid = @ID
```

Listing 8   Example of GET_FILESTREAM_TRANSACTION_CONTEXT()

```
BEGIN TRAN

SELECT PhotoGuid,
     GET_FILESTREAM_TRANSACTION_CONTEXT() as TransactionContext
FROM dbo.PhotoContainer
```

There are other important things to remember about Win32 streaming. When you use Win32 streaming, you can use the transaction context one time per file. When you're finished with that file, you need to commit the transaction and open another one. So unlike the BLOB query, where you can retrieve a set of files, if you stream you can only stream one file at a time.

The next example will show how to use the .NET API for streaming files from the FILESTREAM columns. There's a SqlFileStream object in the namespace System .Data.SqlDataTypes. This class allows you to stream files from SQL Server FILESTREAM columns. Listing 9 shows you how to use this class and illustrates the features of the new constructs introduced for use with the FILESTREAM data type. I'm including a snippet of .NET code that shows how to insert a row with a FILESTREAM column and how to stream the file to the filesystem.

Listing 9   Code sample for the SqlFileStream object

```
var connStr = "Data Source=SQLInstance;Initial Catalog=DBName
;Integrated Security=True";
SqlConnection con = new SqlConnection(connStr);
```

```csharp
//  Retrieve the FilePath() of the image file
SqlCommand sqlCmd = new SqlCommand(
        "INSERT INTO dbo.PhotosWithFileStream (PhotoFile) " +
          "OUTPUT inserted.PhotoID, " +
            "inserted.RowGuid, " +
            "inserted.PhotoFile.PathName() as PathName, " +
            "GET_FILESTREAM_TRANSACTION_CONTEXT() as Context " +
          "VALUES (CAST('' as varbinary(max)))", con);

con.Open();

SqlTransaction transaction = con.BeginTransaction("PhotoTran");
sqlCmd.Transaction = transaction;

SqlDataReader dr = sqlCmd.ExecuteReader(CommandBehavior.SingleRow);
if (dr.Read())
{
    // Get the PhotoFile.PathName to write the file to.
    string filePath = dr["PathName"].ToString();

    // Obtain a Transaction Context
    byte[] txContext = dr["Context"] as byte[];

    FileStream file = new FileStream(txtInsertFile.Text,
    FileMode.Open);

    // Create the SqlFileStream Class with the PathName()
    // and GET_FILESTREAM_TRANSACTION_CONTEXT()
    SqlFileStream sqlFS = new SqlFileStream(filePath, txContext,
FileAccess.Write);

    // Get the file and put it into the buffer
    byte[] buffer = new byte[file.Length];
    int bytes = file.Read(buffer, 0, buffer.Length);

    // Write buffer to the stream
    sqlFS.Write(buffer, 0, buffer.Length);

        // Cleanup
        sqlFS.Close();
    }
    // Must close the DataReader before you Commit.
    dr.Close();
    // Now Commit the Transaction
    sqlCmd.Transaction.Commit();
    con.Close();
    con.Dispose();
```

In listing 9, a `SqlFileStream` object is created, along with an open `SqlConnection`, and a transaction is opened on that connection. Open a file and use that transaction context to stream the file to SQL Server using the `SqlFileStream.Write` method. The explanation is a little beyond the subject of this chapter, but I wanted to give you the example that allows you to see the way to stream. This approach uses the .NET wrapper of the Win32 streaming method.

Summary

In this chapter you learned what FILESTREAM is and why it's better compared to the old ways of handling files. You also saw how to configure FILESTREAM and how to use it.

About the author

Ben Miller has over 14 years working with SQL Server. Currently he's the director of database administration for Nature's Sunshine Products. He has worked in IT for over 20 years in both development and IT admin functions. Ben is the president of the SQL Server User Group in Utah County, Utah and the Virtual PowerShell User Group at SQLPASS. He's a frequent speaker on SQL topics and loves to share information with the community.

@DBADuck

27 Writing unit tests for Transact-SQL

Luciano Moreira

Unit testing is a known methodology among developers around the world, be they Java, C#, VB.NET, or C++ programmers. Unit testing helps you produce code with fewer bugs and achieve a higher degree of quality. Although this has become a well-known practice, when it comes to databases, we haven't seen the same adoption rate.

The objective of this chapter is to introduce some basic concepts of unit testing that you can apply when programming with T-SQL, without using any third-party tool or external framework. I'll show you how to make the necessary adjustments and bend some rules to adapt unit tests to databases.

Unit test basics

The primary goal of unit testing is to take the smallest piece of testable code from your project and write tests to verify that the code behaves exactly as it's supposed to. This behavior is usually driven by the parameters you provide as the input for the call, expecting an output from the callable code (usually a function or method). This outcome may be a return value, an exception (yes, it can be the right output), or even some changes in the state of the object, a term in object-oriented programming that represents a change in an object property.

Here are some of the benefits of unit tests:

- *Higher application quality*—Although testing individual modules doesn't guarantee they'll work together, it's a huge step to achieve higher application quality and fewer bugs.
- *Easier to make changes*—If the business changes and you need to reflect that in your code, you can do so by changing (or writing more) unit tests and modifying the application code accordingly.

- *Easier to refactor the code*—Refactoring is a discipline for restructuring your code, usually to achieve better reusability and maintainability, without changing its external behavior.
- *Living documentation*—Instead of having to maintain all sorts of documents when some minor change occurs, the tests become a living documentation, because it clearly states all the input and expected outputs.
- *Better design*—To be able to test some code, you usually have to isolate that code, work with programming interfaces, and adhere to the project guidelines. These basic principles usually lead developers to a design with a better separation of responsibilities among classes and functions.

Here are several best practices that dictate some of the guidelines for good unit tests:

- *Automatic to execute*—There should be a way to execute it in an automated way, so you can easily invoke the tests and check the results.
- *Repeatable*—If you run the test 20 times in a row, all the tests should run smoothly and the expected outcome should be the same.
- *Detailed and extensive*—Unit tests are supposed to test everything that's likely to break, ideally testing every single line of code, but at least covering some basic scenarios of problems, like boundaries, conditions, expected exceptions, and the correct course of action.
- *Different verification path from the code*—If your code library is supposed to store some data in a data structure, let's say a hash table, the way to verify its value shouldn't be using another method from the same API but writing a direct access to the hash table values.
- *Small and independent*—Each test should test only one given scenario at a time, such as a small part of a complex method with some assertions, and tests also should be independent, so the execution order doesn't influence the tests' outcome.
- *Runs quickly and in an easy way*—The purpose of unit tests is to constantly check for the desired output during coding and when something changes. The results should come out quickly, raising developer productivity.

To become familiar with writing unit tests, you have to practice a lot. Many people think that when they're coding tests, they're wasting time that could be used to write new functionality. But in the long run, the developer will reap the benefits of a code with higher quality and fewer bugs. But you'll have to see it with your own eyes (and code!) to prove that unit tests are worth the trouble.

Unit test for databases

When developers are testing their code, tests will invariably touch the database or some kind of data store, which is usually managed by a data access layer (DAL). This interaction is perhaps more cumbersome because you have to deal with database state and more complex setup and teardown of your tests, raising questions such as "How do I set up the database?" "Because tests are independent, should I re-create the database between every test?" and "Is restoring a backup efficient?"

There are many ways to solve those problems, like using a database snapshot to quickly revert a database to its original state (my favorite) or running scripts that create and destroy the database automatically. But what you usually see is that developers end up writing mocks and stubs that simulate the behavior of a database to avoid the burden of accessing it, because the expected behavior is commonly known.

This approach works fine if all your code and business rules are written outside the database, but let's face it, we still have many, many applications that encapsulate some of the core business logic within stored procedures in your database. And even worse, those stored procedures may be called from a command-line interface, that doesn't have a pretty C# application with a DAL to test it, or it may be a central repository accessed by many different clients reusing the same procedures (will you write the "same" tests for each application?). So how do you, as the DBA who wrote the procedure, guarantee it's working as expected?

NOTE I don't want to initiate a debate of which is the right approach to access your database: using stored procedures or an object-relational mapping (ORM), like Entity Framework or Hibernate. My point is that many organizations work with code on the database side and a team is usually responsible for implementing it and passing the usage guidance to the developers, so they should care about maintenance and quality.

I firmly believe that the database (or T-SQL) developer should follow the steps of our C# or Java developers and embrace unit testing as a core skill in their team, allowing them to write better software. Let's raise our quality bar, shall we?

Based on the principle that you have to use it to understand the value of unit tests, in the next section, I'll guide you through basic steps to simulate unit-testing creation and execution, allowing you to experience it by yourself, so feel free to try out the scripts and later apply the testing methodology to your own code.

The approach described here is what I call the "poor man's T-SQL unit test solution," because it won't use any fancy tool (like Visual Studio) or any third-party framework. It's a homemade implementation that can be carried to your environment and extended, as appropriate.

Another aspect of our approach is that it will, let's say... *bend* some guidelines of unit testing, like being independent. Because the database usage characteristic is a sequence of data manipulations, I found that some minor adjustments to the way I do unit tests in C# have proven to be useful and simpler. You may follow all the best practices to the letter, but it'll require a bit more effort to do so.

T-SQL unit test walkthrough

In our scenario, let's suppose you'll have a central database that holds data common to many applications, such as customer information. To avoid data quality issues caused by bad data management, you have to guarantee that access is through stored procedures following the company guidelines.

At first, you'll have a data model and your database script with the basic schema of your objects. To organize this solution, you'll use SQL Server Management Studio (SSMS) and start with a file named Create Database.sql (in the next listing), holding the creation of a database named TSQLUnitTest and a simple table named Customer

Listing 1   Create Database.sql

```
IF NOT EXISTS (SELECT NAME FROM sys.databases WHERE name = 'TSQLUnitTest')
    CREATE DATABASE TSQLUnitTest
GO


USE TSQLUnitTest
GO


IF OBJECT_ID('dbo.Customer') IS NOT NULL
    DROP TABLE dbo.Customer
GO


CREATE TABLE dbo.Customer
(ID INT IDENTITY(1,1) NOT NULL PRIMARY KEY,
 Name VARCHAR(100) NOT NULL,
 SSN CHAR(11) NOT NULL,
 DateOfBirth DATE NULL,
 Sex CHAR(1) NULL,
 MaritalStatus VARCHAR(30) NULL,
 AnnualIncome DECIMAL(15,2) NULL
)
GO
```

The procedure usp_RegisterCustomer (listing 2) inserts a customer in the table and is straightforward: it'll accept some parameters, execute an insert, and return the identity value of the inserted row.

The usp_RegisterCustomer procedure is the application code, so you won't do test-driven development (TDD) right now. Using TDD you're supposed to write the tests first, execute those tests (they'll fail, because the code they test doesn't exist yet), and only then will you write the code that'll give the desired outcome. If the tests run successfully, the expected behavior is correct and so is the code.

Listing 2   usp_RegisterCustomer.sql

```
IF OBJECT_ID('dbo.usp_RegisterCustomer') IS NOT NULL
    DROP PROCEDURE dbo.usp_RegisterCustomer
GO


CREATE PROCEDURE dbo.usp_RegisterCustomer
    @SSN CHAR(11)
```

```
        , @Name VARCHAR(100)
        , @DateOfBirth DATE
        , @Sex CHAR(1) = NULL
        , @MaritalStatus VARCHAR(30) = NULL
        , @AnnualIncome DECIMAL(15,2) = NULL
AS
INSERT INTO dbo.Customer (SSN, Name, DateOfBirth, Sex, MaritalStatus,
AnnualIncome)
VALUES (@SSN, @Name, @DateOfBirth, @Sex, @MaritalStatus, @AnnualIncome)

        RETURN @@IDENTITY
GO
```

As a way to validate the procedure (see the next listing), many DBAs and developers would be satisfied to run the procedure with a simple EXEC, check the return value, and execute a SELECT * statement against the Customer table.

Listing 3 Not structured (wrong!) test approach

```
DECLARE @i INT
EXEC @i = usp_RegisterCustomer '999-99-9999', 'Luciano Moreira',
'1979-12-29', 'M', 'Married', '50000'
PRINT @i

SELECT * FROM dbo.Customer
```

After your manual tests are executed and with all results acceptable, the procedure is ready for production, simple as that. Am I right?

Not so fast, coder... let's start the testing methodology by adding another file to the project: Tests - usp_RegisterCustomer.sql. The idea behind this file is that it'll contain all the tests related to this procedure that can be executed to verify if it's working as expected and will help you organize your solution.

This script will contain two parts: the test setup and the unit tests. The first one is the test setup space, where you should put all the data manipulation language (DML) needed to set up your environment. That way, if you're testing a procedure that'll insert a sale record, some basic product, customer, and employee data should be inserted to support the new record.

The second part of the script will hold the unit tests you create. For this simple scenario, you should create at least two tests for the basic course of execution. The first one will be your minimal record insertion that tests only the parameters that are required (verifying procedure signature), and you'll need a second one for the complete customer record. Listing 4 shows these two unit tests.

The basic foundation of unit testing is to verify some assertion. If you're testing the add method for a calculator class, the assertion should be the sum of the provided parameters. For this procedure, your assertion will have to verify if the record is correctly inserted and that the correct value is returned.

If your conditions aren't met, you'll raise an error to alert that the test has failed so that the developer can work through the problem and correct the issue.

Listing 4   Basic tests

```
DECLARE @ReturnValue INT

/*************************************************************************
 Minimal record
 *************************************************************************/
EXEC @ReturnValue = dbo.usp_RegisterCustomer
     @SSN = '999-99-9999'
    ,@Name = 'Luciano Moreira'
    ,@DateOfBirth = '1979-12-29'
IF NOT EXISTS
(SELECT ID
  FROM dbo.Customer AS C
  WHERE @ReturnValue = 1 AND C.ID = 1
     AND C.Name = 'Luciano Moreira' AND C.SSN = '999-99-9999'
     AND C.DateOfBirth = '1979-12-29' AND C.MaritalStatus IS NULL
     AND C.Sex IS NULL AND C.AnnualIncome IS NULL)
RAISERROR (
'ERROR! Problem with the test related to usp_RegisterCustomer'
, 16, 1)


/*************************************************************************
 Complete record
 *************************************************************************/
EXEC @ReturnValue = dbo.usp_RegisterCustomer
     @SSN = '999-99-9999'
    ,@Name = 'Bernardo Moreira'
    ,@DateOfBirth = '2010-10-25'
    ,@Sex = 'M'
    ,@MaritalStatus = 'Single'
    ,@AnnualIncome = 10000
IF NOT EXISTS
(SELECT ID
  FROM dbo.Customer AS C
  WHERE @ReturnValue = 2 AND C.ID = 2
     AND C.Name = 'Bernardo Moreira' AND C.SSN = '999-99-9999'
     AND C.DateOfBirth = '2010-10-25' AND C.MaritalStatus = 'Single'
     AND C.Sex = 'M' AND C.AnnualIncome = 10000)
RAISERROR (
'ERROR! Problem with the test related to usp_RegisterCustomer'
, 16, 1)
```

When you execute all the create scripts, followed by the testing script, you'll see that no error message is shown, meaning that all your tests succeeded. This is what you expect to see, a clean output with the message "Command(s) completed successfully."

Note that you could write two IF statements (assertions) to verify the desired outcome, one for the table record and one for the return value. This probably would be more readable and maintainable than sticking it all in a WHERE clause, but for the purpose of this walkthrough, let's keep it shorter, using only one assertion.

To partially automate the testing process and avoid having the developer execute every setup script, you should add a new project item called Setup.bat. This script will reside under the Miscellaneous folder and contain all the calls needed to create your database and procedure. So for now it'll contain two lines of code, but as the project grows it can hold hundreds of setup lines:

```
SQLCMD -S lutinote -E -I -i "Create Database.sql"
SQLCMD -S lutinote -E -I -i "usp_RegisterCustomer.sql"
```

During your development and testing, you'll always have a command prompt window open, pointing to your solution directory. When a new test is written or some adjustment is made, you execute setup.bat followed by your test script, achieving a better productivity when testing your code.

You should be wondering where the real value is behind unit tests, and, I have to admit, it's not easy to realize it right away. And as you may have noticed, the simpler the procedure, the simpler the test is, but as code evolves over time, more complex assertions and business changes will bring a bigger value to your tests.

Continuing with our example, you'll add some complexity to it. One thing is noticeable: using the tests, you've stated what the basic procedure signature is and created some direction on how to use your procedure. Besides the documentation, I always point a developer to the unit tests as a way to explain how to use some module of code.

To fulfill a security request, all data manipulation should be logged in a table, which will be coded in the create database script. For the sake of simplicity, the table will have a generic structure without getting much relevant data (as in a real-world system). All the manipulation will be recorded by an insert trigger—for now let's ignore deletes and updates—that does all the work to register the action (see the following listing).

Listing 5　Log table and trigger

```
IF OBJECT_ID('dbo.ManipulationLog') IS NOT NULL
    DROP TABLE dbo.ManipulationLog
GO

CREATE TABLE dbo.ManipulationLog
(ID INT IDENTITY(1,1) NOT NULL PRIMARY KEY,
 ObjectName VARCHAR(100) NOT NULL,
 Operation VARCHAR(20) NOT NULL,
 [Description] VARCHAR(400) NOT NULL,
 RegisteredTime DATETIME2 DEFAULT SYSDATETIME()
)
GO

INSERT INTO dbo.ManipulationLog (ObjectName, Operation, [Description])
VALUES ('Database', 'CREATE', 'All tables created')
go

CREATE TRIGGER trgI_Customer ON dbo.Customer
FOR INSERT
AS
```

```
      INSERT INTO dbo.ManipulationLog (ObjectName, Operation, [Description])
      SELECT 'Customer', 'INSERT', 'ID: ' + CAST(I.ID AS VARCHAR)
      FROM inserted as I
GO
```

As you may have noticed, the procedure has a subtle problem that may lead to different return values, related to the use of @@IDENTITY. In an unstructured approach (listing 3), this may not have been noticed, but if you execute the environment setup, run your BAT file from the open command prompt, and execute the tests, you'll receive two error messages:

```
Msg 50000, Level 16, State 1, Line 28
ERROR! Problem with the test related to usp_RegisterCustomer
Msg 50000, Level 16, State 1, Line 47
ERROR! Problem with the test related to usp_RegisterCustomer
```

Because our assertion SELECT statement includes validation of the return value @ReturnValue = 1 in the WHERE clause, both tests failed, because the identity returned from the ManipulationLog table is the wrong one. Changing the return command to use SCOPE_IDENTITY() instead of @@IDENTITY will solve the problem, so if you rerun your tests all error messages will be gone.

You could write some assertions to verify whether the records have been correctly inserted in the ManipulationLog table, but because this table isn't something specific to the customer data, it's more efficient not to create those assertions. The correct approach would be to create a test file and write some tests for the ManipulationLog table to verify that inserts, updates, and deletes in every table are correctly logged.

A simple change in the underlying structure wouldn't cause the procedure to break, but would instead return different values that could cause serious side effects in the application, such as retrieving IDs that would map sales to a different (and incorrect) customer, for example. The tests failed due to a combination mismatch of IDs from both tables and eventually it could result in the same ID being returned and an error-free execution of the tests, even with the incorrect behavior. But as you evolve as a unit test developer, you'll learn that creating some disruption (like inserting a dummy record in the ManipulationLog table) will be beneficial, because it brings variation to your tests.

Continuing our coding, let's experiment with TDD methodology. A new business rule dictates that all the non-nullable fields should be tested before the insert occurs, and if some NULL value is found, an exception should be raised and the procedure aborted.

Your new test condition should cause an exception to occur when you pass a NULL value to some parameters, so coding the test for the @SSN parameter should follow the structure depicted in the following listing.

Listing 6   Expected exception with @SSN parameter

```
/*************************************************************************
 Parameter problem - @SSN
 *************************************************************************/
BEGIN TRY
    EXEC @ReturnValue = dbo.usp_RegisterCustomer
            @SSN = NULL
            ,@Name = 'Luciano Moreira'
            ,@DateOfBirth = '1979-12-29'
    RAISERROR('ERROR! This instruction should never be executed.', 16, 1)
END TRY
BEGIN CATCH
    IF ((ERROR_MESSAGE() <> 'The parameter @SSN cannot be NULL')
 OR ERROR_PROCEDURE() <> 'usp_RegisterCustomer')
    BEGIN
            RAISERROR (
'ERROR! Problem with the test related to usp_RegisterCustomer.'
, 16, 1)
            PRINT ERROR_MESSAGE()
    END
END CATCH
```

The test executes the procedure, passing it a NULL value for @SSN. The correct course of execution would be to generate an exception with the message "The parameter @SSN cannot be NULL." If the error message is different or isn't generated by the correct procedure you're testing (maybe some inner procedure is the one causing the exception), you'll raise another error, because this isn't the intended behavior.

Besides checking for an exception inside the CATCH block, it's important to add a RAISERROR statement after the EXEC. Suppose that the table structure allows nulls in the SSN column and your validation isn't working correctly. In this scenario, the row would be inserted and the CATCH block never executed, so you might believe that your code is correct because all tests run fine, when in reality the behavior is wrong. Placing a RAISERROR after the EXEC statement will guarantee that if an exception isn't raised during the procedure execution, another error with the wrong message is thrown and the CATCH block will be executed, verifying that the message is incorrect and causing the test to fail. If the procedure raises any exception inside a TRY block, the following statement won't be executed and the control flow will be correctly redirected to the CATCH block, as expected.

After the test is coded, you should run your test and see it fail. Printing the error message is optional but may help you understand why your test is failing. For this execution, because you have no parameter verification, the insert is executed and the error message is "Cannot insert the value NULL into column 'SSN', table 'TSQLUnitTest.dbo.Customer'; column does not allow nulls. INSERT fails." That goes against the business rule.

Inserting a simple parameter verification in the procedure, raising the correct error message, and returning execution to the caller (see the following code) will make all the tests run successfully. So far you coded the test, saw it fail, corrected your

code, and ran the test again, verifying that it executed successfully. So you've con-
cluded your first TDD implementation!

```
IF (@SSN IS NULL)
BEGIN
    RAISERROR ('The parameter @SSN cannot be NULL', 16, 1)
    RETURN
END
```

To complete the parameter testing, write two more tests for the @Name and @Date-
OfBirth parameters, using the same structure described earlier. Run your tests (which
will fail), alter the procedure to verify the parameters' values, and rerun all the tests.
When no error is reported, you're all set.

One important aspect of parameter testing is related to standards. If the company
or team has some standards on message format (or error numbers), the correct test
would be testing that, so you're forcing some sort of contract between test and code,
also serving as the base for future documentation.

Continuing with structure changes in the Customer table, let's create a unique
nonclustered index on the SSN column to avoid duplicates. The create database script
now has another instruction in its body:

```
CREATE UNIQUE NONCLUSTERED INDEX idxNCL_Customer_SSN
ON dbo.Customer(SSN)
GO
```

After this change, if you re-execute all the tests you'll see that the second test failed,
because both inserts use the same SSN, 999-99-9999. Changing the wrong test related
to the customer Bernardo Moreira to use SSN 999-99-9998 will make the tests pass
without errors; this isn't a correct test. To correctly test this scenario, you should have
a test (in the following listing) for the expected exception, related to the column's
unique property.

Listing 7 Expected exception with duplicate SSN

```
/*************************************************************************
 Duplicate SSN
 *************************************************************************/
BEGIN TRY
    EXEC @ReturnValue = dbo.usp_RegisterCustomer
            @SSN = '999-99-9999'
            ,@Name = 'Luciano Moreira'
            ,@DateOfBirth = '1979-12-29'
    RAISERROR('ERROR! This instruction should never be executed.', 16, 1)
END TRY
BEGIN CATCH
    IF ((ERROR_MESSAGE() <> 'Cannot insert duplicate key row in
➥ object ''dbo.Customer'' with unique index ''idxNCL_Customer_SSN''.
➥ The duplicate key value is (999-99-9999).')
OR ERROR_PROCEDURE() <> 'usp_RegisterCustomer')
    BEGIN
            RAISERROR (
```

```
'ERROR! Problem with the test related to usp_RegisterCustomer.'
, 16, 1)
              PRINT ERROR_MESSAGE()
      END
END CATCH
```

On the book's web page (www.manning.com/SQLServerMVPDeepDivesVol2), you'll find additional scripts demonstrating unit tests for updating, a complete update/delete procedure, and schema refactoring.

Automating unit test execution

So far, you have an open command prompt with a BAT file that re-creates all the structure you need to run the tests with all the related procedures to help you during test and code development. But what if you have hundreds of testing files and after some database change you want to execute all the tests at once? Doing it manually wouldn't be an option, so you can create a more complete batch file called "Run all tests.bat" (in the next listing).

Listing 8   Run all tests.bat

```
@echo off
ECHO ************** Setup *************************
CALL Setup.bat
ECHO ************** Unit Test Script *************************
ECHO Tests - usp_RegisterCustomer.sql
SQLCMD -S lutinote -E -I -i "Tests - usp_RegisterCustomer.sql"
```

The execution of the file in listing 8 will fire the setup batch and later execute all the tests contained in the script Tests - usp_RegisterCustomer.sql. If you replicate the same structure for all test files, re-creating and executing a test suite and putting all of them in the same batch file, you can run all the tests at once and register the output in a text file (for example, UnitTests_Output.txt). You can do so using the following code:

```
C:> "Run all tests.bat" > UnitTests_Output.txt
```

If you follow the testing guidelines described in this chapter, when a problem occurs the ERROR! text will be placed in the output file, so you can easily find where the problem occurred in the test script execution (file and line) and rerun it separately, starting a troubleshooting process to spot and correct the issue.

   You can improve this approach with a PowerShell script or other more elaborate mechanism, but I think you get the idea.

Summary

In this chapter, you learned how unit tests can help you leverage a better code quality and avoid bugs in your database modules. This rather simple and direct approach to unit tests can be accomplished with BAT files, Notepad, and SQLCMD. Visual Studio also has tools for database unit testing that you can explore.

   The more you write unit tests, the more successful you'll be at achieving the right balance between testing coverage and testing scenarios.

About the author

 Luciano Moreira is co-founder of Sr. Nimbus, a consulting company in Brazil, where he serves as chief data architect and provides consulting and training services in SQL Server and the .NET platform. He's worked with the Microsoft platform since 2000, always focused on development and databases. He has the following certifications: MCP, MCAD .NET, MCSD .NET, MCDBA, MCTS (SQL Server 2005/2008, .NET 3.5, .NET 4.0 Data Access), and MCITP (SQL Server 2005 and 2008), and has been an MCT since 2002.

Luciano received the SQL Server Microsoft MVP title in July 2010. He blogs at http://luticm.blogspot.com.

28 Getting asynchronous with Service Broker

Mladen Prajdić

SQL Server Service Broker is an asynchronous messaging system built into the database engine. Because it resides in the database, it fully complies with ACID (atomicity, consistency, isolation, durability) principles. Messages are stored, they can't be lost, and they're a part of the transactional system. Having a system like this in the database engine opens up a world of new possibilities in database programming. Quite a few things are implemented on the Service Broker architecture inside the database engine, such as event notifications, database mail, server-to-client notifications of changed data, and database mirroring.

Service Broker has been a part of SQL Server since its 2005 version, but it's still not widely used. This may be due to the lack of a graphical user interface in SSMS, an overly complex setup, and the need to learn XML programming in SQL Server (all messages are in XML format). This is why I'll give you a template that you can use for secure communication between two instances of SQL Server.

I've successfully used this template in a project that required gathering auditing data from multiple servers to a single central location and another project that used Service Broker for custom replication between two databases in combination with Change Data Capture in SQL Server 2008. Another use for Service Broker is having an order-receiving stored procedure switch to an asynchronous execution in peak time. This involved no change to application code at all. The possibilities are endless.

The Service Broker usage template

I'm assuming you're familiar with Service Broker terminology and objects so I won't describe them. Our template will set up a direct communication between two instances using transport security with certificates. This means that the communication channel between SQL Servers will be encrypted, but the messages themselves won't be. Look into implementing dialog security if there's a need for message encryption.

You'll have two instances: DataSender (the initiator) and DataReceiver (the target). Data will be sent from the initiator to the target. There are two parts of the Service Broker set up on each instance. The first step is to enable the Service Broker functionality at the instance level (endpoint, certificate-based security, and so forth) in the master database. The second step is to create Service Broker objects (for example, message types, contracts, queues, and routes) and functionality (such as activation stored procedures and programming) at the database level.

Let's look at what you have to do in the master database on the DataReceiver instance. All the code is run under the SA account. You use two databases: DBSender on the DataSender instance and DBReceiver on the DataReceiver instance. Note that if you have the instances on the same physical server, you need to use different ports for each instance. To make the scripts shorter, I've omitted the object existence check and cleanup if they exist. The following listing shows the code that enables Service Broker and sets up transport security on the DataReceiver instance.

Listing 1   Enabling Service Broker and setting up transport security: DataReceiver

```
USE master
-- SET UP TRANSPORT SECURITY

-- create a master key for the master database
-- DO NOT FORGET THIS PASSWORD AND STORE IT SOMEWHERE SAFE
CREATE MASTER KEY ENCRYPTION
BY PASSWORD = 'Put_Your_Custom_Password_For_DataReceiver_Master_DB_Here'

GO
-- create certificate for the service broker TCP endpoint for secure
--communication between servers
CREATE CERTIFICATE CertificateDataTransferReceiver
WITH
    -- BOL: The term subject refers to a field in the metadata of
    --      the certificate as defined in the X.509 standard
    SUBJECT = 'CertDataTransferReceiver',
    -- set the start date yyyyMMdd format
    START_DATE = '20111001',
    -- set the expiry date
    EXPIRY_DATE = '20500101'
    -- enables the certificate for service broker initiator
    ACTIVE FOR BEGIN_DIALOG = ON

GO
-- save certificate to a file and copy it to the DataSender instance
-- so we can enable secure connection
BACKUP CERTIFICATE CertificateDataTransferReceiver
    -- this path must be somewhere where we have permissions
    TO FILE = 'c:\CertificateDataTransferReceiver.cer'

GO
```

```
-- create endpoint which will be used to receive data from DataSender
-- instance
CREATE ENDPOINT ServiceBrokerEndPoint
    -- set endpoint to actively listen for connections
    STATE = STARTED
    -- set it for TCP traffic only since service broker only supports TCP
    --protocol
    -- by convention, 4022 is used but any number between 1024 and 32767
    -- is valid.
    AS TCP (LISTENER_PORT = 4022)
    FOR SERVICE_BROKER
     (
            -- authenticate connections with our certificate
            AUTHENTICATION = CERTIFICATE CertificateDataTransferReceiver,
            -- default value is REQUIRED encryption but let's just set it
            --to SUPPORTED
            -- SUPPORTED means that the data is encrypted only if the
            -- opposite endpoint specifies either SUPPORTED or REQUIRED.
            ENCRYPTION = SUPPORTED
     )

GO
-- Finally grant the connect permissions to public.
GRANT CONNECT ON ENDPOINT::ServiceBrokerEndPoint TO PUBLIC
```

As you can see, not much code is needed to enable Service Broker; comments take up most of it. The most important parts are saving the master key password somewhere safe and copying the certificate to the DataSender instance. You'll use this certificate on the DataSender instance to authorize the login that will be sending data through Service Broker. This is why the setup in the master database on the DataSender instance includes creating logins and users and applying permissions (see the next listing).

> **Listing 2   Enabling Service Broker and setting up transport security: DataSender**

```
USE master
-- SET UP TRANSPORT SECURITY

-- create the login that will be used to send the data through the Endpoint
CREATE LOGIN LoginDataTransferSender
WITH PASSWORD = 'Login__DataTransferSender_Password'
GO

-- Create a user for our login
CREATE USER UserDataTransferSender FOR LOGIN LoginDataTransferSender
GO

-- DO NOT FORGET THIS PASSWORD AND STORE IT SOMEWHERE SAFE
CREATE MASTER KEY ENCRYPTION
BY PASSWORD = 'Put_Your_Custom_Password_For_Senders_Master_DB_Here'

GO
-- create certificate for the service broker TCP endpoint for secure
-- communication between servers
CREATE CERTIFICATE CertificateDataTransferSender
```

```
WITH
    SUBJECT = 'CertDataTransferSender',
    START_DATE = '20111001',
    EXPIRY_DATE = '20500101'
    ACTIVE FOR BEGIN_DIALOG = ON
GO
-- create a certificate from the file we've copied over from the
-- DataReceiver instance to our c: drive
-- and use it to authorize the UserDataTransferSender user
CREATE CERTIFICATE CertificateDataTransferReceiver
    AUTHORIZATION UserDataTransferSender
    FROM FILE = 'c:\CertificateDataTransferReceiver.cer'

GO
-- create endpoint which will be used to send data to the DataReceiver
CREATE ENDPOINT ServiceBrokerEndPoint
    STATE = STARTED
    AS TCP (LISTENER_PORT = 4022)
    FOR SERVICE_BROKER
    (
        AUTHENTICATION = CERTIFICATE CertificateDataTransferSender,
        ENCRYPTION = SUPPORTED
    )
-- grant the connect permissions to the endpoint to the login we've created
GRANT CONNECT ON ENDPOINT::ServiceBrokerEndPoint TO LoginDataTransferSender
```

Now you've taken care of the setup in master databases on both the DataReceiver and DataSender instances. If you look at the setup in the master database on Data-Sender, you can see that you can easily add new instances that send data to the DataReceiver instance without changing anything. You just have to run the Data-Sender script on every new instance that will send data.

Creating Service Broker objects

The next step is to create Service Broker objects in the DBSender and DBReceiver databases. For this you'll need the IP address of each instance. Again, note that if you have the instances on the same physical server, you need to use different ports for each instance. Let's assume the DataReceiver instance has the IP of 111.111.111.111 and the DataSender instance the IP of 222.222.222.222.

You can have the Service Broker support objects like error tables and various stored procedures inside their own schema to make manageability easier. That way, you can add permissions to the schema if needed and not to each object directly; you also know where all the objects are and maintenance is easier. Let's call the schema DataTransfer on both instances.

Each instance will also have an error table. On the DataReceiver instance you'll have a ReceiveErrors table, and on the DataSender instance you'll have a SendErrors table. Any error that happens will be stored in those two tables.

Let's take a look at the DBReceiver database on the DataReceiver side and the DBSender database on the DataSender side. First you'll create the Service Broker sup-port objects like the error table to store any errors that occur when receiving messages, a table to store your received messages that you can use to process them further, and an activation stored procedure that will run and receive messages when they arrive in the Service Broker queue (see the following listing).

Listing 3 Creating support objects in DBReceiver on the `DataReceiver` instance

```
USE DBReceiver
GO
-- enable service broker for our database
ALTER DATABASE DBReceiver SET ENABLE_BROKER
-- get the Service broker ID to use later
SELECT service_broker_guid FROM sys.databases WHERE name = 'DBReceiver'
-- returns 962FF4B4-428B-482D-A0A7-748F62D3C41C on my machine
GO
-- create the schema that holds service broker support objects
CREATE SCHEMA DataTransfer
-- create table to hold errors when receiving messages
CREATE TABLE DataTransfer.ReceiveErrors
(
    ID BIGINT IDENTITY(1, 1) PRIMARY KEY,
    ErrorProcedure NVARCHAR(126) NOT NULL,
    ErrorLine INT NOT NULL,
    ErrorNumber INT NOT NULL,
    ErrorMessage NVARCHAR(MAX) NOT NULL,
    ErrorSeverity INT NOT NULL,
    ErrorState INT NOT NULL,
    TransferData XML NOT NULL,
    ErrorDate DATETIME NOT NULL DEFAULT GETDATE()
)
-- create table to hold received messages
CREATE TABLE DataTransfer.ReceivedMessages
(
    ID INT IDENTITY(1, 1) PRIMARY KEY,
    TableSchema NVARCHAR(128) not null,
    TableName NVARCHAR(128) NOT NULL,
    TransferedRows XML NOT NULL,
    DialogID UNIQUEIDENTIFIER NOT NULL,
    MsgSeqNum  BIGINT NOT NULL,
    CreatedOn DATETIME NOT NULL DEFAULT GETDATE()
)
-- stored procedure that writes the transferred data
-- from the queue to the DataTransfer.ReceivedMessages table
-- when the conversation ends those messages can be processed
-- with another stored procedure
GO

CREATE PROCEDURE DataTransfer.spReceiveTransferredData
AS
BEGIN
    DECLARE @msgBody XML, @dlgId uniqueidentifier, @msgSeqNum bigint,
@msgTypeName SYSNAME
    WHILE(1=1)
    BEGIN
        BEGIN TRANSACTION
        BEGIN TRY
```

```
               -- receive one message at a time
               ;RECEIVE top(1)
                          @msgBody = message_body,
                          @dlgId = conversation_handle,
                          @msgSeqNum = message_sequence_number,
                          @msgTypeName = message_type_name
               FROM   DataTransfer.QueueDataTransferReceive
               -- exit when the whole queue has been processed
               IF @@ROWCOUNT = 0
               BEGIN
                       IF @@TRANCOUNT > 0
                               ROLLBACK;
                       BREAK;
               END
               -- if we get the EndOfTransfer message we're closing
               -- the conversation
               IF @msgTypeName = N'//DataTransfer/EndOfTransfer'
               BEGIN
                       END CONVERSATION @dlgId;
/*
Here a stored procedure can be ran that processes messages
stored in the DataTransfer.ReceivedMessages table
*/
               END
               ELSE
               BEGIN
                       -- insert the message into the
                       -- DataTransfer.ReceivedMessages table
                       -- with a little XML querying magic
                       INSERT INTO DataTransfer.ReceivedMessages
   (TableSchema, TableName, TransferedRows,DialogID, MsgSeqNum)
                       SELECT  T.c.value('@TableSchema',
                                       'nvarchar(128)') as TableSchema,
                               T.c.value('@TableName',
                                       'nvarchar(128)') as TableName,
                               T.c.query('./rows') as rowsXml,
                                       @dlgId, @msgSeqNum
                       FROM    @msgBody.nodes('/*') T(c)
               END
               IF @@TRANCOUNT > 0
                       COMMIT;
       END TRY
       BEGIN CATCH
               IF @@TRANCOUNT > 0
                       ROLLBACK;
               -- insert error into the ReceiveErrors table
               INSERT INTO DataTransfer.ReceiveErrors(
                       ErrorProcedure, ErrorLine, ErrorNumber,
                       ErrorMessage, ErrorSeverity, ErrorState,
                       TransferData)
               SELECT ERROR_PROCEDURE(), ERROR_LINE(), ERROR_NUMBER(),
                       ERROR_MESSAGE(), ERROR_SEVERITY(),
                       ERROR_STATE(),
                       @msgBody
               -- here you can add extra logging to the error log
```

```
                              -- or email notifications, etc...
                END CATCH;
        END
END
```

You've ended the conversation in the spReceiveTransferredData stored procedure by using the //DataTransfer/EndOfTransfer message type. This is to avoid a very common and very wrong pattern developers like to use called "fire and forget." Here's how this pattern works: you send a message from DataSender to DataReceiver and then end the conversation from the DataSender side. The problem with this is that any returned messages are lost to the DataSender because the conversation is already over as far as it's concerned. That's the reason you always have to end the conversation from the DataReceiver side. This way, the DataReceiver sends the end conversation message to the DataSender, the DataSender responds with an "Okay, let's end this" message, and both close their ends of the conversation properly. Because the received messages are stored in a separate table, you can do whatever you want with them either when the conversation is over (look at the comment in the code in the spReceiveTransferredData stored procedure) or in some other scheduled job. Note that if you want to send the messages in order, they need to be sent on the same conversation. In any case, the way to end a conversation stays the same as just described.

Now that you have support objects, let's create the Service Broker objects (listing 4).

Listing 4   Creating Service Broker objects in the database on DataReceiver instance

```
USE DBReceiver
GO
-- create a message that must be well formed XML
CREATE MESSAGE TYPE [//DataTransfer/Message]
     VALIDATION = WELL_FORMED_XML
-- create a message to signal it's the end of the conversation
CREATE MESSAGE TYPE [//DataTransfer/EndOfTransfer]
     VALIDATION = NONE
-- create a contract for the message
CREATE CONTRACT [//DataTransfer/Contract]
      ([//DataTransfer/Message] SENT BY ANY,
      [//DataTransfer/EndOfTransfer] SENT BY ANY)
-- create a route on which the messages will be sent back to DataSender
-- instance
-- in our case these messages are acknowledgment messages
CREATE ROUTE RouteDataReceiver
     AUTHORIZATION dbo
WITH
     -- target server's service to which the data will be sent
     SERVICE_NAME = '//DataTransfer/DataSender',
     -- this is the Service Broker guid from the DBSender database on
     -- DataSender instance
     BROKER_INSTANCE = '030F00E8-386F-46AF-8622-655E320D2A1C',
     -- IP and PORT of the DataSender instance
     ADDRESS = 'TCP://111.111.111.111:4022'
-- create the queue to run the spReceiveTransferredData automaticaly when
```

```
-- new messages arrive
-- execute it as dbo
CREATE QUEUE DataTransfer.QueueDataTransferReceive
     WITH STATUS = ON,
     ACTIVATION (
             -- sproc to run when the queue receives a message
             PROCEDURE_NAME = DataTransfer.spReceiveTransferredData,
             -- max concurrently executing instances of sproc
             MAX_QUEUE_READERS = 1,
             EXECUTE AS 'dbo' );
-- create a target service that will accept inbound DataTransfer messages
CREATE SERVICE [//DataTransfer/DataReceiver]
     AUTHORIZATION dbo -- set the owner to dbo
     ON QUEUE DataTransfer.QueueDataTransferReceive
             ([//DataTransfer/Contract])
-- grant send on this service to everyone
GRANT SEND ON SERVICE::[//DataTransfer/DataReceiver] TO PUBLIC
```

Again notice that the [//DataTransfer/EndOfTransfer] message has no validation because it won't have any payload, as you'll see on the DataSender side. Another thing to look at is the creation of the route RouteDataReceiver, which has to be tied back to the sender. This works well with only two instances, but a problem arises when you have multiple data senders. You can solve this with a special route called TRANSPORT. This route can accept and properly route data on the DataReceiver instance from various services on multiple DataSender instances. It has to be created on the Data-Receiver instance in the DBReceiver database like this:

```
CREATE ROUTE [RouteDataReceiver] WITH ADDRESS = N'TRANSPORT'
```

Having a TRANSPORT route means you have to follow a few rules when naming your DataSender services. Each DataSender service must be named like this:

```
[tcp://xxx.xxx.xxx.xxx:PORT/UniqueServiceName]
```

xxx.xxx.xxx.xxx:PORT is the IP or name of the computer where the DataSender instance is and the port (between 1024 and 32767) it's sending data on. Unique-ServiceName is a service name that's unique per instance. That's why I put the database name where the service resides as the first part of the unique name. Here's an example of the service name:

```
[tcp://222.222.222.222:4022/DBSender/DataSender]
```

The following listing shows the code for creating the support objects on the DataReceiver instance.

Listing 5   Creating support objects in the database on the DataReceiver instance

```
USE DBSender
GO
-- enable service broker for our database
ALTER DATABASE DBSender SET ENABLE_BROKER
-- get the Service broker ID to use later
SELECT service_broker_guid FROM sys.databases WHERE name = 'DBSender'
```

```sql
-- returns 030F00E8-386F-46AF-8622-655E320D2A1C on my machine
GO
-- create the schema that holds service broker support objects
CREATE SCHEMA DataTransfer
-- create table to hold errors when sending messages
CREATE TABLE DataTransfer.SendErrors
(
      ID BIGINT IDENTITY(1, 1) PRIMARY KEY,
      ErrorProcedure NVARCHAR(128) NOT NULL,
      ErrorLine INT NOT NULL,
      ErrorNumber INT NOT NULL,
      ErrorMessage NVARCHAR(MAX) NOT NULL,
      ErrorSeverity INT NOT NULL,
      ErrorState INT NOT NULL,
      TransferData XML NOT NULL,
      ErrorUTCDate DATETIME NOT NULL DEFAULT GETUTCDATE()
)
GO
-- stored procedure that sends data in the form of XML payload
CREATE PROCEDURE DataTransfer.spSendTransferData
      @xmlData XML,
      @dlgId UNIQUEIDENTIFIER OUTPUT
AS
BEGIN
    BEGIN TRY
            -- begin the dialog.
            -- if @dlgId is NULL a new conversation is started
            -- if it's not null the conversation is reused
            BEGIN DIALOG CONVERSATION @dlgId
                  FROM SERVICE    [//DataTransfer/DataSender]
                  TO SERVICE      '//DataTransfer/DataReceiver',
                  -- tells us to which SB instance we're sending to
                  -- change to DataSenderDB service broker guid
                  '962FF4B4-428B-482D-A0A7-748F62D3C41C'
                  ON CONTRACT     [//DataTransfer/Contract]
                  WITH ENCRYPTION = OFF;

            -- Send our data to be DataTransfered
            ;SEND ON CONVERSATION @dlgId
                  MESSAGE TYPE [//DataTransfer/Message] (@xmlData)
    END TRY
    BEGIN CATCH
            INSERT INTO DataTransfer.SendErrors (
            ErrorProcedure, ErrorLine, ErrorNumber, ErrorMessage,
                          ErrorSeverity, ErrorState, TransferData)
            SELECT   ERROR_PROCEDURE(), ERROR_LINE(), ERROR_NUMBER(),
                  ERROR_MESSAGE(), ERROR_SEVERITY(), ERROR_STATE(),
                  @xmlData
            -- here you can add extra logging to the error log
            -- or email notifications, etc…
    END CATCH
END
GO
-- sproc that does some work and sends data.
-- it's an entry point and we call this sproc
```

```
-- from an application or a job
CREATE PROCEDURE DataTransfer.spDoWork
AS
    /*
    In the project I worked on we looped over the tables,
    got the needed data and sent it.
    So this is just META CODE!
    */
    WHILE Looping over the tables
    BEGIN
            -- create the xml message we'll send
            SELECT @msg = CONVERT(XML, '<M TableSchema="' + @TableSchema +
'" TableName="' + @TableName + '"><rows>Rows in XML go here</rows></M>')

            -- if our message is not null let's send it using our stored
            -- procedure for it.
            IF (@msg IS NOT NULL)
                    EXEC DataTransfer.spSendTransferData @msg, @dlgId OUT
    END
    -- after we've transferred all the data
    -- send the conversation is over message so the DataReceiver instance
    --  can end it
    ;SEND ON CONVERSATION @dlgId MESSAGE TYPE [//DataTransfer/EndOfTransfer]
```

The stored procedure spDoWork is the entry point to the Service Broker infrastructure. Everything else is transparent to the application. On a project I was working on, we used it to 1) check for changed rows in each table that we had to transfer over to the DataReceiver instance, 2) get those rows, 3) send per table changes in one message, and 4) send the [//DataTransfer/EndOfTransfer] message when we processed all the tables.

Having to do this in the application would require huge numbers of changes. This way we could abstract it all inside the database. That's one of the benefits of having an asynchronous messaging system inside the database. The code in the next listing creates the Service Broker objects on the DataSender instance.

> **Listing 6   Creating Service Broker objects in the database on the DataSender instance**

```
USE DBSender
GO
-- create a route on which the messages will be sent to receiver
CREATE ROUTE RouteDataSender
    AUTHORIZATION dbo
WITH
    -- DataReceiver service to which the data will be sent
    SERVICE_NAME = '//DataTransfer/DataReceiver',
    -- Service Broker id from DBReceiver database on DataReceiver instance
    -- BROKER_INSTANCE = '962FF4B4-428B-482D-A0A7-748F62D3C41C',
    -- IP and PORT of the DataReceiver instance
    ADDRESS = 'TCP://222.222.222.222:4022'
-- create a message that must be well formed
CREATE MESSAGE TYPE [//DataTransfer/Message]
    VALIDATION = WELL_FORMED_XML
```

```
-- create a message to signal it's end of conversation
CREATE MESSAGE TYPE [//DataTransfer/EndOfTransfer]
    VALIDATION = NONE
-- create a contract for the message
CREATE CONTRACT [//DataTransfer/Contract]
    ([//DataTransfer/Message] SENT BY ANY,
     [//DataTransfer/EndOfTransfer] SENT BY ANY)
-- create the initiator queue
CREATE QUEUE DataTransfer.QueueDataTransferSend
-- create an initiator service that will send messages to the target service
CREATE SERVICE [//DataTransfer/DataSender]
    AUTHORIZATION dbo
    -- no contract means service can only be the initiator
    ON QUEUE DataTransfer.QueueDataTransferSend
-- create service with IP and PORT of the initiator (this) server
GRANT SEND ON SERVICE::[//DataTransfer/DataSender] TO PUBLIC
```

The only thing to note in listing 6 is the lack of a contract on the [//DataTransfer/DataSender] service. This means that the service can only be the initiator and can't receive any messages except the system ones.

Summary

This chapter discussed a basic template used for Service Broker architecture. If the need arises, there are a few optimizations you can try, such as reusing conversation handles, receiving messages in batches instead of one by one, or having more than one instance of the activation stored procedure run at one time. These are advanced uses and optimizations that require an even deeper knowledge of your system and Service Broker itself.

About the author

Mladen Prajdić is a SQL Server MVP from Slovenia. He started programming in 1999 in Visual C++. Since 2002 he's been actively developing different types of applications in .NET (C#) and SQL Server. He's a regular speaker at various conferences and user group meetings. Mladen blogs at http://weblogs.sqlteam.com/mladenp and has authored various articles about SQL Server. He likes to optimize slow SQL statements, analyze performance, and find unconventional solutions to difficult SQL Server problems. He's developed a popular free add-in for SQL Server Management Studio called SSMS Tools Pack.

29 Effective use of HierarchyId

Denis Reznik

We find hierarchies in many places in our lives, such as organizational structures, sporting events, product categories in an e-market, social relationships, algorithms, classifications, and elsewhere. Modeling such systems means creating and storing information about the objects in a system. Tons of code was written using object-oriented programming principles, and many variants of storing information about objects in a database were invented. Hierarchy is a type of relationship between objects, and that's why modeling hierarchies is a common operation in writing code and databases.

Hierarchies in a database

There are many types of hierarchy implementations in a database. Parent-child relationships are one of the most common and at the same time the most native type of hierarchy modeling. Each row must have one parent row (parentId field related to the parent key) and several children rows (parentId field related to the current row key) in this implementation. It looks simple, but usually the query is recursive on this hierarchy, and data selection can have complex logic. This can cause a huge performance overhead and performance problems.

XML is another common implementation of hierarchy in a database. Using XML for hierarchy design is also native, but querying XML data in SQL has a poor track record.

The third popular implementation is Materialized Path. Each node stores as a `varchar` value in this implementation. This value consists of parent node identifiers separated by some kind of delimiter (for example, in `1 - 1.1 - 1.1.1 - 1.1.2 - 1.1.3` the dot is the delimiter). Each node contains all information about the parents and natively represents the path from the node to the top of the tree. Searching down this column (after indexing) can be quick and simple, but searching up and other such operations may not be. Other implementations are more specific and sometimes interesting, but they're complex and highly specialized.

Introduction to the HierarchyId data type

`HierarchyId` is a new way of introducing hierarchy to database. `HierarchyId` stores a hierarchy in an interesting way. Its logical representation is similar to that of Materialized Path. Type structure is organized like a tree of elements, where each element contains all information about its position in the hierarchy tree. In this scheme the root element is /, its children are /1/ and /2/, their children are /1/1/, /1/1/, /2/1/, and so on. Get it? It's interesting, for sure! This is the main principle of modeling hierarchies in databases using `HierarchyId`: each node knows its position in the hierarchy, and each node is self-describable. So, having one node, you can get a lot of information at once just by looking at a `HierarchyId` value. SQL Server optimizer will obtain information about the level of this node, its parent, and its children. This information is more than enough to produce an optimal query plan and to get data in the quickest way. `HierarchyId` doesn't use XML or strings. It's a Common Language Runtime (CLR) binary data type that exists in `SqlServer.Types` assembly.

`HierarchyId` was introduced in SQL Server 2008. Many developers and architects have used it in their projects since that time. Many of them said, "Wow! What a great thing Microsoft has made!" But there were also lots of complaints such as, "Ohhh! It takes too long to execute!" Why? Because of its performance, which you'd think would be great, but actually isn't. To avoid poor performance of the queries, you should understand internals and working principles and learn some best practices.

Using the HierarchyId data type

`HierarchyId` helps you design, manipulate, and query hierarchical data in simple hierarchies (one parent, many children). It was designed to perform many operations you use with hierarchical data, such as finding all children of some nodes, finding the parent of a node at a known level, and many other typical operations. The most common `HierarchyId` methods are as follows:

- `GetAncestor(@level int)`—Returns the parent for your node on the demanded level (@level). For example, you can get the parent of your node on the fifth level using this method.

- `GetDescendant(@child1, @child2)`—Returns the child of your node that lies between @child1 and @child2. If @child2 is NULL, it returns the child of your node that's higher than @child1. If @child1 is NULL, it returns the child of your node that's lower than @child2.

- `IsDescendantOf(@node hierarchyId)`—Returns True if @node is a parent for your node on some level. This is one of the most common methods. Searching all children in a hierarchy can be a complex operation, but not with this method. It's easy to use it in your queries.

- `GetLevel()`—Returns the level of the current node in the hierarchy. It can be useful in some indexing techniques and in some other cases.

- ToString()—Each HierarchyId value has a string representation. The string representation shows the logical organization of a node. It can be called explicitly or implicitly (when casting to a string).
- GetRoot()—Static method (which means that it must be called directly at type HierarchyId using this syntax: HierarchyId::GetRoot()) of HierarchyId data type. It returns the root node of the hierarchy (the root node is always "/").

NOTE   Because HierarchyId is a SQL CLR type, all its methods are case sensitive.

In comparison with other hierarchy implementations in a database, it's very simple. Say good-bye to complex logic. You can do all these operations using one data type. Does it look exciting? Yeah! Let's look into it more deeply; it will be interesting.

Physical HierarchyId data organization

The next important part of understanding the power of HierarchyId is its internal organization. Let's look at HierarchyId storage, which is in binary format. The size of a node varies from 3 to 856 bytes depending on the hierarchy level. Creating an index on a HierarchyId field sometimes can cause the following warning message: "Index key size is more than 892. Some data cannot be inserted into this index." Don't worry. You'll never face this problem, because storage of HierarchyId data is extremely optimized and, in most cases, the key size won't be too big. But you must know what size your field is and how big it can be in your database. The following information will help you to deal with it.

The best way to understand this idea is to create a table with HierarchyId data and examine this data. The script for creating the table and inserting the test data is shown in the following listing.

> **Listing 1   Creating and populating a table with a HierarchyId field**

```
CREATE TABLE Categories
(
  Id int IDENTITY(1,1) NOT NULL,
  Node hierarchyid NOT NULL,
  Name nvarchar(100) NULL,
  IsShowOnSite bit NOT NULL,
  CONSTRAINT PK_CATEGORIES_ID PRIMARY KEY(Id)
)
GO

INSERT INTO Categories VALUES
  ('/1/', N'Automobiles', 1),
  ('/2/', N'Animals and Pets', 1),
  ('/1/1/', N'Autos for Sale', 1),
  ('/1/2/', N'Autos Wanted', 1),
  ('/1/1.5/', N'Auto Service', 1),
  ('/1/1/1/', N'Classic Cars', 1),
  ('/1/1/2/', N'Sedans', 1),
  ('/1/1/3/', N'Trucks', 1),
```

```
    ('/1/1/1.2/', N'Motorcycles', 1),
    ('/2/1/', N'Birds', 1),
    ('/2/2/', N'Dogs and Puppies', 1),
    ('/2/3/', N'Cats and Kittens', 1)
GO
```

After creating the table, you can query its data and look at it:

```
SELECT Node, Node.ToString()
FROM Categories
ORDER BY Node
GO
```

In the output you can see the straight tree structure: children of every parent are sorted based on their position in the hierarchy. The query output is shown in figure 1.

Looking at the hex values in the first column of this output, you can see that HierarchyId can be very small. It's 2 bytes for node /1/, 3 bytes for node /1/1/3/, and so on. The second column shows the node string (logical) representation. The HierarchyId node contains all information about its position in a tree. It looks natural in its string representation: /1/2/ or /1/1.1/1.2/1/. This organization also helps you find the parent of an item by parsing the node from the end, and it's very effective. Physically, this structure encodes in binary format. Each node is encoded with the help of this formula:

	Node	(No column name)
1	0x58	/1/
2	0x5AC0	/1/1/
3	0x5AD6	/1/1/1/
4	0x5AD8D0	/1/1/1.2/
5	0x5ADA	/1/1/2/
6	0x5ADE	/1/1/3/
7	0x5B23	/1/1.5/
8	0x5B40	/1/2/
9	0x68	/2/
10	0x6AC0	/2/1/
11	0x6B40	/2/2/
12	0x6BC0	/2/3/

Figure 1   Selecting hierarchy data

```
<NodeNumber><BitFlagOfNextLevel>
...
<NodeNumber><BitFlagOfNextLevel>
```

NodeNumber is a binary representation of a digit. BitFlagOfNextLevel is a bit that shows the level of the next digit. It can be the same or the next level. We use a slash (/) to represent the next level and a dot (.) for the same level. We use a dot for inserting a node between existing nodes in an existing hierarchy. This structure organizes nodes in a natural order. They're sorted in a hierarchy sequence by default. Comparing two objects requires a single quick operation in this schema. This is the first part of encoding a logical structure in binary format. The second part is more interesting.

Each NodeNumber is encoded by using a special diapason code. The encoded value is calculated by subtracting the NodeNumber from the diapason value and storing the results in binary format. This is a compact storage schema, because the most frequent combination in a hierarchy is encoded by smaller bit sequences. If SQL Server developers had used integers or strings for this schema, the number of bits would be larger. Diapason codes are shown in table 1.

Table 1 `HierarchyId` encoding standards

Diapason code	Bit size	Max bit size	Range
000100	48/53	60	-281479271682120 to -4294971465
000101	32/36	43	-4294971464 to -4169
000110	12/15	22	-4168 to -73
0010	6/8	13	-72 to -9
00111	3/3	9	-8 to -1
01	2/2	5	0 to 3
100	2/2	6	4 to 7
101	3/3	7	8 to 15
110	6/8	12	16 to 79
1110	10/13	18	80 to 1103
11110	12/15	21	1104 to 5199
111110	32/36	43	5200 to 4294972495
111111	48/53	60	4294972496 to 281479271683151

The Bit Size column has two values (without/with anti-ambiguity bits). Anti-ambiguity bits have a fixed size and a fixed position. They're used to prevent ambiguous backward parsing of a representation. You can also see that a maximum bit size of a node value plus the size of the diapason code doesn't equal the maximum bit size of the whole value. For example, the maximum bit size of a node value is 53 for the last row in the table, the diapason code size is 6, but the maximum node value size is 60; that is, 60 = 53 + 6 + 1. What is that 1 bit? Let me explain. `HierarchyId` must support sorting; for example, for such values as /1/ and /1.1/, the second value must be higher. A dot is represented by 0 and a slash is represented by 1 in binary representation, so /1/ will be higher than /1.1/. But that's not right! To fix this situation, an additional bit is added for each node with a dot, which explains that 1 bit. The value of the node is padded with 0 to the nearest byte.

Effective indexing

Finally, we've come to the most important part of using this type, and that's an indexing strategy. All of the examples you've seen in this chapter are nothing without the right index on the `HierarchyId` field. It's very important! Many developers don't understand the main idea of using this type. They think that it's a great tool for designing and using hierarchies in a database. And all you need to do is to write a query, and you'll get your data quickly and effectively. That's totally wrong! It's not the full picture. You need to understand `HierarchyId` queries and build correct indexes to achieve great performance. You can index a `HierarchyId` field in two ways: in depth or in breadth. Your choice of index type depends on your queries. We'll consider them further in a small example.

NOTE All of the following queries were executed on the table having the same structure as the table mentioned previously. But this table has real-world content and contains nearly 1,500 records.

Depth-first indexes

A depth-first index is used when your query drills down to the tree. Getting all children of the node is a good example of a situation where a depth-first index must be created on the table. The following code demonstrates such a query:

```
DECLARE @node hierarchyId = '/1/';
SELECT * FROM Categories
WHERE Node.IsDescendantOf(@node) = 1
GO
```

The query execution plan before index creation is shown in figure 2.

Actually, this isn't what we want from `HierarchyId`. For effective use of `HierarchyId` in such types of queries, we need an index on a `HierarchyId` field. It's a depth-first index this time:

```
CREATE INDEX IDX_CATEGORIES_NODE
    ON Categories(Node)
GO
```

Then we call our query again. You'll notice that nothing changes! Why? Because we've created a nonclustered index, and for each row in the result set, there would be a key lookup to a clustered key. So, it's more effective to scan a clustered index in this case. If we change our query to get fields, which are included in a nonclustered index (or we include needed fields in the leaf level of a nonclustered index with the `INCLUDE` clause), our depth-first index will be used:

```
DECLARE @node hierarchyId = '/1/';
SELECT Id, Node FROM Categories
WHERE Node.IsDescendantOf(@node) = 1
GO
```

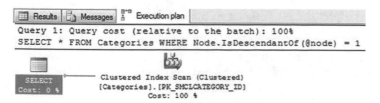

Figure 2 Execution plan before index creation

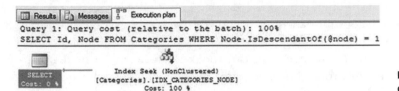

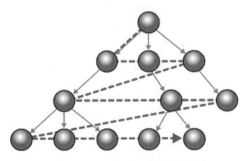

Figure 3   Selective query execution plan

In this code we can obtain all needed information from the IDX_CATEGORIES_NODE index without a lookup to the clustered index. Node is an index key, and Id is a clustered index key (which must be included in each record of a nonclustered index leaf level). The query plan will contain an index seek of IDX_CATEGORIES_NODE as expected this time, as shown in figure 3.

The main idea of a depth-first index is to store items in a certain order, where all subnodes of a node and subnodes of each subnode are located next to each other. So this type of index is efficient for selecting at all subtrees of the node. A graphic schema of this type of index is shown in figure 4.

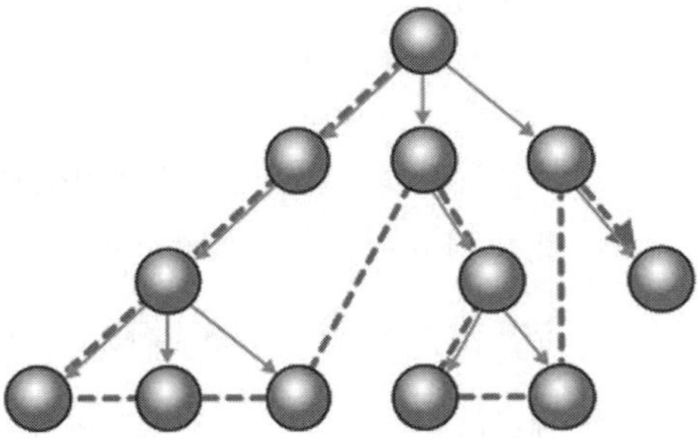

Figure 4   **Structure of a depth-first index**

Breadth-first indexes

The next type of index on HierarchyId is the breadth-first index. Breadth-first indexes are used for queries that process data of a specific level: getting all children of a node that lie at the same level of a hierarchy. A breadth-first index stores items of the same level of hierarchy together. You can see a schema of this type of index in figure 5.

Figure 5   **Structure of a breadth-first index**

To see how it works, we must add one more field to the Categories table (it can be a calculated column). It must return the level of a specific hierarchy node:

```
ALTER TABLE Categories
    ADD Level AS Node.GetLevel()
GO
```

Then we create a breadth-first index for this query using a level column created previously:

```
CREATE INDEX IDX_CATEGORIES_LEVEL_NODE
    ON Categories(Level, Node)
GO
```

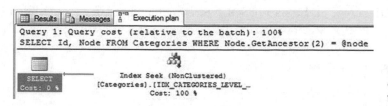

Figure 6   **Execution plan of a query on a breadth-first index**

Finally, we get all nodes that are the second-level children of node /1/ with the following query:

```
DECLARE @node hierarchyId = '/1/';
SELECT Id, Node FROM Categories
WHERE Node.GetAncestor(2) = @node
GO
```

Figure 6 shows its query execution plan.

Analyze your data and workload, and, if possible, use a unique nonclustered index. In many situations a node is unique, and it's a good candidate for a primary key. Don't miss this. Make `HierarchyId` a primary key, if possible, too. Choose a clustered index of your table (depth-first or breadth-first) depending on the top queries that use your table.

More information about HierarchyId

Sometimes using `HierarchyId` will result in suboptimal performance. For example, you may find that joins between the main table (Products) and the hierarchical table (Categories) are too expensive. In this case you can denormalize (at your own risk) your database schema and copy the `HierarchyId` field from the Categories table to the Product table and index it. When you do that, you won't need to have a join with the Categories table.

You know that `HierarchyId` is a SQL CLR type. But how does `HierarchyId` depend on SQL CLR? Will it work after disabling SQL CLR in SQL Server? Yes, it will. Like other internal CRL types (`geography` and `geometry`), `HierarchyId` doesn't depend on SQL CLR. Another side of this is that all methods of the `HierarchyId` data type are case sensitive, so `.ToString()` will work, but `.toString()` won't.

Unfortunately, there's no support for `HierarchyId` in Entity Framework and LINQ to SQL. There's a `SqlHierarchyId` type in .NET, but it's not really useful in the modern world, where ORM systems are everywhere. There are a couple of workarounds in using `HierarchyId` in EF or LINQ to SQL. You can choose any of the variants. My choice is to use stored procedures and wrap all hierarchy queries in procedures.

If you want to import `HierarchyId` data into your database using the SSIS package, use OLEDB Destination. ADO.NET and SQL Server Destination can't work with `HierarchyId` data.

SQL Azure is a cloud relational database from Microsoft based on the SQL Server database engine. Its features are different from on-premises SQL Server. There was no

HierarchyId data type at the start of SQL Azure in 2009, but later it was added (in the second half of 2010). So now there's no problem with using HierarchyId in SQL Azure or porting solutions, which use the HierarchyId data type, from on-premises SQL Server to SQL Azure.

Summary

HierarchyId is a great choice for storing and querying a hierarchy in a database. It gives us a clean query model, helping developers avoid difficult operations and complex T-SQL code, and it supports a brilliant performance of queries. This type is implemented as a CLR type, but it isn't dependent on SQL CLR. Every time you use HierarchyId, you should remember that the key to effective usage is an effective indexing strategy. Use HierarchyId effectively in your projects! Good luck!

About the author

Denis Reznik is the head of Web Development at Digital Cloud Technologies, a Ukrainian software company. Denis is excited about designing and developing high-load web applications. Most of those applications are based on SQL Server. Denis is also a trainer at the Microsoft Innovation Center of the Kharkov National University of Radioelectronics (KNURE). He teaches SQL Server courses and provides training for students, developers, and other IT specialists. He's an active member of the Ukrainian professional developer community UNETA and often speaks at user groups and conferences. A fan of an active lifestyle, Denis loves playing football (soccer) and basketball, snowboarding, and traveling around the world with his wife.

30 Let Service Broker help you scale your application

Allen White

Service Broker is an asynchronous messaging service, but that term does it a serious disservice. It limits the imagination and stifles creativity. In practice it becomes The Scalability Architecture of the Future! Okay, maybe that's a little over the top, but in this chapter you'll see some interesting ways to use asynchronous messaging to build applications that aren't limited to single-database/single-server environments and that can easily grow from small- to large-scale implementations.

Scalable solutions

Let's look at a couple of common application scenarios.

Many companies have decided to build a web-based interface to their services—not just traditional retail sales companies, but just about any company that provides products or services will create a website where customers can purchase their product. The last application where I implemented this solution was for a company that provides pet insurance, and the customers were able to purchase policies and track claims using the web interface. The database structures on the internal transaction application were well normalized, whereas the databases on the web-facing application were flattened for fast response. Instead of implementing a solution like replication, updates from each side to the other were initiated using Service Broker messages. The messages were automatically forwarded through the dual firewalls in a secure, encrypted package, and the database on the other end automatically updated when the messages were received.

Another implementation was an extract, transform, and load (ETL) source solution for a data warehouse. Small companies using the Standard Edition of SQL Server don't get the benefit of features like Change Data Capture. So the ETL implementation uses triggers added to the source tables that send Service Broker messages into a queue when changes occur in the transaction processing database; at the scheduled ETL times, the messages are received, the updated data is sent into the ETL process, and the data warehouse is updated. This solution provides the additional benefit of not holding transaction log pages open waiting for the ETL process to run, allowing the log pages to be reused after backups are complete.

Distributed applications can also work more efficiently if designed with asynchronous updates in mind. There are many cases where data doesn't need to be updated immediately but can be updated at "the earliest convenience" of the receiving application. Service Broker is the perfect solution for these kinds of applications.

Service Broker objects

When using Service Broker, you'll need to configure a number of objects, which I refer to as the "plumbing." It's important that all the pieces are configured properly, but once you understand what they are, it's fairly straightforward to get your solution up and running. Service Broker objects are generally defined using Uniform Resource Locator (URL) syntax, which you can shorten to meet your needs as long as you're certain you won't inadvertently create duplicate object names. (I typically leave the scheme and domain components off the names I use.)

Security

Because communication needs to be secure, you can create a certificate in the database where you're using Service Broker and create a certificate-based user (without login), which then sends and receives all messages. This approach allows you to filter triggers to distinguish updates coming from messages from those coming from the local application. See the following listing.

Listing 1   Creating a certificate-based user

```
USE AdventureWorks
GO

CREATE MASTER KEY
    ENCRYPTION BY PASSWORD = N'<enter REALLY secure password string here>';
GO

CREATE USER IntUser WITHOUT LOGIN;
GO
CREATE CERTIFICATE IntCert
    AUTHORIZATION IntUser
    WITH SUBJECT = 'Int Certificate',
        EXPIRY_DATE = N'12/31/2012';

BACKUP CERTIFICATE IntCert
  TO FILE = N'E:\Certs\IntCert.cer';
GO
```

Message types

The basic object you need to define is the message type. This describes what you can send and allows the receiving end to know what it's received. In the message type definition, you also define the owner (authorization) of the message type and the validation for the message. Here's an example:

```
CREATE MESSAGE TYPE [//AWSync/Sync/HumanResourcesEmployee]
AUTHORIZATION dbo
VALIDATION = WELL_FORMED_XML
GO
```

This message will be owned by dbo and any message sent with this type must follow the rules of well-formed XML format.

Contracts

Messages are grouped together using contracts, and you define the direction in which messages can be sent. An important thing to remember as your application evolves is that there's no ALTER command for contracts, so new message types will have to be added with additional contracts. You create a contract like this:

```
CREATE CONTRACT [//AWSync/Sync/IntContract]
    AUTHORIZATION dbo
    ( [//AWSync/Sync/HumanResourcesEmployee] SENT BY ANY,
      [//AWSync/Sync/PersonContact] SENT BY ANY,
     [//AWSync/Sync/PurchasingVendor] SENT BY ANY )
GO
```

Queues

Queues define how messages are sent and received, and (if you want) an automated process that will handle the messages it receives. In Transact-SQL you retrieve messages from the queue in the same way you read data from a table—in fact, the queue behaves just like a table in your database:

```
CREATE QUEUE IntQueue
   WITH
   STATUS = ON,
   RETENTION = OFF
GO
```

Services

The service assigns the contract to the queue and does the work of sending the messages on the queue to their destination and receiving the messages coming from other senders:

```
CREATE SERVICE [//IntSite/Sync/IntService]
AUTHORIZATION IntUser
ON QUEUE IntQueue
([//AWSync/Sync/IntContract])
GO
```

Conversations

In Service Broker, all messages are sent via a conversation. At this point, the only valid conversation type is a DIALOG, so the terms are functionally interchangeable. But to send messages you need to BEGIN a DIALOG; then, once it's been established, you SEND the message ON CONVERSATION. Here's the syntax of both components together:

```
BEGIN DIALOG @InitDlgHandle
    FROM SERVICE [//IntSite/Sync/IntService]
    TO SERVICE N'//ExtSite/Sync/IntService'
    ON CONTRACT [//AWSync/Sync/IntContract]
    WITH
        ENCRYPTION = ON;

SEND ON CONVERSATION @InitDlgHandle
    MESSAGE TYPE [//AWSync/Sync/HumanResourcesEmployee]
    (@ChangeMsg);
```

Notice in the BEGIN DIALOG statement that the FROM SERVICE name isn't quoted but the TO SERVICE name is. This is because the FROM SERVICE must be defined, and SQL Server will check the syntax to ensure it's a valid service. But the destination service may not even exist on this server, so it's quoted. Another important fact is that Service Broker messages are guaranteed to be delivered in order to the receiving side, but only as long as they've been sent on the same conversation.

Now, in the ETL example I mentioned earlier, these are all the components I needed, because both sides of the conversation are within the same database. You can leverage this technology to dramatically reduce contention in your application for updates that don't need to occur immediately, which can help your applications perform faster. The remaining components are needed when messages are sent to other databases or other servers.

Endpoints

Endpoints define the channel for the message communication. They're usually defined using TCP ports, and those ports are used exclusively for Service Broker communications:

```
CREATE ENDPOINT IntEndpoint
STATE = STARTED
AS TCP ( LISTENER_PORT = 4022 )
FOR SERVICE_BROKER (AUTHENTICATION = WINDOWS );
GO
```

If both servers involved in the communication are in the same domain, then Windows authentication will work just fine. But if not, you'll need to use certificate-based authentication for the endpoints.

Routes

There needs to be a roadmap for the messages to get from one point to the other, and you do that by defining routes. In your application database, you define the destination route for your outgoing messages, but you need to define a route for your incoming messages in msdb. See the next listing.

Listing 2   Defining message routes

```
USE AdventureWorks
GO

CREATE ROUTE DMZRoute
AUTHORIZATION dbo
WITH
     SERVICE_NAME = N'//DMZSite/Sync/IntService',
     ADDRESS = N'TCP://SQLTBWS:4023'
GO

USE msdb;
GO

CREATE ROUTE IntRoute
AUTHORIZATION dbo
WITH
     SERVICE_NAME = N'//IntSite/Sync/IntService',
     ADDRESS = N'LOCAL'
GO
```

Remote service binding

This code binds a local Service Broker service to a remote one and identifies the owner of the remote service:

```
CREATE REMOTE SERVICE BINDING [DMZBinding]
  AUTHORIZATION dbo
  TO SERVICE N'//DMZSite/Sync/IntService'
  WITH USER = [DMZUser]
GO
```

And finally you'll need to grant the SEND privilege to the remote user like this:

```
GRANT SEND
     ON SERVICE::[//IntSite/Sync/IntService]
     TO DMZUser;
GO
```

Sometimes a graphic helps you put the components together more effectively, so figure 1 shows how the plumbing fits together.

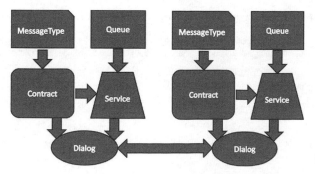

Figure 1   Service Broker objects

ETL trigger demonstration

The ETL example I mentioned at the beginning of this chapter uses triggers to identify which rows in which tables have been updated, and the triggers then send a message containing the key of the row changed. In this example you'll use the AdventureWorks (2005) database. Because the best format for messages is XML, you'll use the FOR XML clause in Transact-SQL, and you'll add the ELEMENTS keyword to the clause. (I prefer elements to attributes in my XML data.) Execute the following query:

```
SELECT TOP 1 c.[AccountNumber]
FROM [Sales].[Customer] c
FOR XML RAW, ELEMENTS, ROOT ('Customer')
```

It produces this result:

```
<Customer><row><AccountNumber>AW00000001</AccountNumber></row></Customer>
```

So, to enable Service Broker in AdventureWorks and set up the security objects you need, execute the commands in the following listing.

Listing 3

```
USE [MASTER]
ALTER DATABASE [AdventureWorks] SET NEW_BROKER
GO

USE AdventureWorks
GO

CREATE MASTER KEY
      ENCRYPTION BY PASSWORD = N'D8CT93u8XAr4ctcBopX7V7dm';
GO

CREATE USER ETLUser WITHOUT LOGIN;
GO
CREATE CERTIFICATE ETLCert
    AUTHORIZATION ETLUser
    WITH SUBJECT = 'ETL Certificate',
        EXPIRY_DATE = N'12/31/2012';

BACKUP CERTIFICATE ETLCert
  TO FILE = N'E:\Certs\ETLCert.cer';
GO
```

Next, create the message types you need and the contract shown in the next listing.

Listing 4   Creating message types and contract

```
CREATE MESSAGE TYPE [//WhseETL/Customer]
AUTHORIZATION dbo
VALIDATION = WELL_FORMED_XML
GO
```

```
CREATE MESSAGE TYPE [//WhseETL/Product]
AUTHORIZATION dbo
VALIDATION = WELL_FORMED_XML
GO

CREATE MESSAGE TYPE [//WhseETL/SalesOrderHeader]
AUTHORIZATION dbo
VALIDATION = WELL_FORMED_XML
GO

CREATE MESSAGE TYPE [//WhseETL/SalesOrderDetail]
AUTHORIZATION dbo
VALIDATION = WELL_FORMED_XML
GO

CREATE CONTRACT [//WhseETL/ETLContract]
    AUTHORIZATION dbo
    ( [//WhseETL/Customer] SENT BY ANY,
      [//WhseETL/Product] SENT BY ANY,
      [//WhseETL/SalesOrderHeader] SENT BY ANY,
      [//WhseETL/SalesOrderDetail] SENT BY ANY
    )
GO
```

Then, create the queues and services for both sides of the conversation (because the ETL process stays within this database). See the following listing.

Listing 5   Creating queues and services

```
CREATE QUEUE ETLQueue
    WITH
    STATUS = ON,
    RETENTION = OFF
GO

CREATE SERVICE [//WhseETL/ETLService]
AUTHORIZATION ETLUser
ON QUEUE ETLQueue
([//WhseETL/ETLContract])
GO

CREATE QUEUE ETLProcessQueue
    WITH
    STATUS = ON,
    RETENTION = OFF
GO

CREATE SERVICE [//WhseETL/ETLProcessSvc]
AUTHORIZATION ETLUser
ON QUEUE ETLProcessQueue
([//WhseETL/ETLContract])
GO
```

Now you need to begin the dialog. In my application I have a stored procedure to start a conversation, and then the triggers all use that same conversation "handle" to send messages, ensuring they're all delivered in order. See the following listing.

Listing 6   Starting a conversation

```
CREATE PROC [dbo].[StartETLConversation]
AS
SET NOCOUNT ON;

        DECLARE @ch UNIQUEIDENTIFIER;
        DECLARE @service_name nvarchar(512) = N'//WhseETL/ETLProcessSvc';

        SELECT @ch=[ch]
        FROM [dbo].[BrokerConversation]
        WHERE [service_name] = @service_name;

        IF @ch IS NOT NULL
                BEGIN
                DELETE FROM [dbo].[BrokerConversation]
                WHERE [service_name] = @service_name;

                END CONVERSATION @ch;
                END

        BEGIN DIALOG @ch
            FROM SERVICE [//WhseETL/ETLService]
            TO SERVICE N'//WhseETL/ETLProcessSvc'
            ON CONTRACT [//WhseETL/ETLContract]
            WITH
                ENCRYPTION = ON;

        INSERT INTO [dbo].[BrokerConversation]
                (ch, service_name)
        VALUES (@ch, @service_name);

GO
```

You can finally send a message as shown in the following listing. (This is the trigger logic.)

Listing 7   Sending a message

```
DECLARE @InitDlgHandle UNIQUEIDENTIFIER;
DECLARE @ChangeMsg XML;
DECLARE @ChangeCnt int;
DECLARE @service_name nvarchar(512) = N'//WhseETL/ETLProcessSvc';

SELECT @InitDlgHandle=[ch]
FROM [dbo].[BrokerConversation]
WHERE [service_name] = @service_name;

BEGIN TRY
```

```
set @ChangeMsg = (
SELECT TOP 1 c.[AccountNumber]
FROM [Sales].[Customer] c
INNER JOIN inserted i on c.[AccountNumber] = i.[AccountNumber]
FOR XML RAW, ELEMENTS, ROOT ('Customer')
);

IF @ChangeMsg IS NOT NULL  -- Make sure there's a message to send
BEGIN
  BEGIN TRANSACTION;
  -- Send the message, indicating the tblAddress as the message type
  ;SEND ON CONVERSATION @InitDlgHandle
    MESSAGE TYPE [//WhseETL/Customer]
     (@ChangeMsg);
  COMMIT TRANSACTION;
END
```

You can check the sys.transmission_queue catalog view to see that the message was
successfully sent. If the message is there, check the is_conversation_error and
transmission_status columns to determine what the problem might be. If the message was sent, no rows will be returned. You can then query the destination queue (//
WhseETL/ETLProcessQueue) to see the message. Retrieve the message with the code
shown in the next listing.

Listing 8   Retrieving a message

```
DECLARE @ch UNIQUEIDENTIFIER
DECLARE @messagetypename NVARCHAR(256),
    @service_name nvarchar(512),
    @service_contract_name NVARCHAR(256)
DECLARE @messagebody XML

WAITFOR (
    RECEIVE TOP(1)
        @ch = conversation_handle,
        @service_name = service_name,
        @service_contract_name = service_contract_name,
        @messagetypename = message_type_name,
        @messagebody = CAST(message_body AS XML)
    FROM ETLProcessQueue
), TIMEOUT 60000

SELECT @messagebody
```

I've built this into a stored procedure, which I run during the nightly ETL process. I
don't have to do anything special to store the data during the day; it's just there when
I run these queries.

Summary

Service Broker provides a versatile platform for scaling your application, using asynchronous messaging to eliminate a lot of the locking that can occur with live updates

of a very active database. You can use it to distribute your application; for ETL triggering, as I've shown here; for sharding your database to spread the load across multiple servers; and for many more solutions.

About the author

Allen White is a practice manager for UpSearch Technology Services in Northeast Ohio. He's spent more than 35 years in IT and has been using SQL Server since 1992. He's certified MCITP in SQL Server and MCT. Allen has been awarded Microsoft's MVP Award for the last five years. He's president of the Ohio North SQL Server User's Group and maintains a blog at http://sqlblog.com/blogs/allen_white/default.aspx.

## PART 4

Performance tuning and optimization

Edited by Brad M. McGehee

For most of my DBA career, I've focused on how to get the optimum performance out of SQL Server. I started a website in 2000 that focused exclusively on SQL Server performance. I don't think I'm alone in this regard. No matter where you look—blogs, forums, websites, conferences—the topic of SQL Server performance and optimization seems to be at the forefront. It's no wonder, because the biggest complaints DBAs hear from users are related to slow performance.

The sad part is that SQL Server can be lightning fast. With few exceptions, SQL Server–related performance problems aren't directly related to SQL Server itself but are related to other factors, such as inadequate hardware, poor configuration settings, poor database design, poor application design, poor indexing, poor database maintenance…the list goes on and on. SQL Server, the product, is seldom responsible for poor performance. Instead, it's the factors outside SQL Server that are often to blame for less-than-optimal performance.

Unfortunately, the DBA is seldom responsible for all aspects of a SQL Server–based application. For example, one team might be responsible for spec'ing out the hardware, configuring it, and maintaining it. Another team might be responsible for the database design. And another team might be responsible for writing the code that accesses SQL Server. Many people play a part in how an application gets designed and up and running.

Even if a DBA does his or her job perfectly, an application's performance can still suffer because of the areas outside of the DBA's control. I'd be willing to bet that, if a properly trained DBA could be totally responsible for all aspects of a SQL Server–based application, the application would rarely suffer poor performance. This is a bold claim, but I believe it to be true. The key to my claim is a "properly trained DBA"—and that's where this book comes into play.

To be a successful DBA, you must be constantly learning, expanding your knowledge and keeping up with the latest technology. DBAs can learn from many different sources, but my personal favorite is reading something like this book, where SQL Server experts share their practical knowledge and experience about SQL Server.

Although this part is called "Performance Tuning and Optimization," in reality almost every chapter in this book touches on this subject in one way or another. What's different about this part is that it's devoted specifically to SQL Server performance tuning and optimization, and what you learn from reading these chapters offers you insights into how you can get the best performance out of your SQL Servers, in spite of not being in total control.

This part includes nine chapters, all written by SQL Server MVPs, on a wide variety of performance-related topics. I want to thank each of the authors for donating their time in helping out not only the SQL Server community by sharing their knowledge, but also for helping out the children of the world, because all of the royalties for this book are being given to Operation Smile.

About the editor

 Brad M. McGehee, MCITP, MCSE+I, MCSD, and MCT (former), is the Director of DBA Education for Red Gate Software. Brad is an accomplished Microsoft SQL Server MVP with more than 16 years of SQL Server experience and over 7 years of training experience. He's a frequent speaker at SQL PASS, European PASS, SQL Server Connections, SQLTeach, devLINK, SQLBits, SQL Saturdays, TechFests, Code Camps, SQL Server user groups, and other industry seminars. A well-respected and trusted name in SQL Server literature, Brad is the author or co-author of more than 15 technical books and over 275 published articles. He blogs at www.bradmcgehee.com.

31 Hardware 201: selecting and sizing database server hardware

Glenn Berry

The absolute foundation of database performance is the underlying server hardware and storage subsystem. Even the best designed and optimized database application can be crippled by an inadequate hardware and storage infrastructure. Recent advances in new processors and chipsets, along with improvements in magnetic and SSD storage, have dramatically changed the hardware evaluation and selection process as compared to the past. Many database professionals struggle to keep up with new technology and often simply let someone else make their hardware selection and sizing decisions. Unfortunately, the DBA usually gets the blame for any performance or scalability issues that crop up later. This chapter covers current and upcoming hardware from both Intel and AMD, and gives you the tools and techniques to make better hardware selection decisions to support SQL Server OLTP workloads.

Why does database server hardware matter? After all, isn't it someone else's job to worry about all the gory details of your database hardware and storage subsystem? I'd argue that as a database professional, you have an ethical responsibility to have a decent level of knowledge about your hardware and storage environment. Your server hardware, and the underlying storage subsystem, form the foundation of your database environment, which will affect the success of your applications and of your organization's business.

Even if your organization is highly bureaucratic, with strict areas of responsibility and decision making for different business functions, you should still make a sustained effort to be aware of the details of your current environment. You should also do your best to influence what hardware is selected for future environments. Don't just be a passive observer in these decisions!

In many smaller organizations, all the hardware decisions may be left up to you, which may make you happy or may worry you. I think that it's an ideal situation, because I feel pretty confident about my ability to evaluate and select the best hardware possible for a given budget. After reading this chapter, you'll feel much more comfortable about performing this important task.

Why database server hardware is important

In most organizations, multiple applications probably depend on your database servers. If your database server is performing poorly, your users and management tend to notice quickly, putting you on the spot to do something to correct the problem as soon as possible.

Quite often, the immediate cause of poor application performance is poor application design, bad database design, an improper indexing strategy, stale statistics, or other common pain points. Always look at these higher-level issues before you suggest improving or replacing your hardware, lest you be accused of "throwing hardware at the problem."

Depending on the situation, and your performance-tuning skill and experience level, you may be able to make a dramatic improvement to your database performance by doing something as simple as adding an index or updating statistics on a table. In other cases, you may have already implemented nearly every tuning improvement possible (and you still have performance problems), or you may not have any option to make application or database changes (for example, with third-party applications and databases). In any case, having modern, high-performance server hardware that has been properly sized and configured will be extremely helpful to your efforts. It'll give you an extra margin of safety against a poorly designed application, and it'll make a well-designed application run even better. Good server hardware is affordable, especially compared to the cost of SQL Server processor licenses. It can be hard to compensate for poor hardware choices that you may have to live with for several years, which is why it's so important to make the right initial choices.

Scaling up or scaling out

Scaling up the data tier can be quite expensive, as you go from a two-socket machine to a four-socket machine to an eight-socket machine, and so on. As you do, your hardware cost (for the server itself) goes up much more quickly than the simple doubling at each step that you might expect. You'll also discover that your performance capacity doesn't scale in a completely linear fashion—for example, a four-socket server won't have twice the capacity of a two-socket server.

Scaling out the data tier can be difficult, because SQL Server currently doesn't offer a built-in solution for scaling out. Instead, you'll need to do architectural and engineering work to use techniques such as vertical partitioning, horizontal partitioning (database sharding), and data-dependent routing in order to scale out your data tier. These techniques are good long-term solutions if you have the time and engineering resources to perform this type of work. Again, having good database server hardware will give you more breathing room to survive until you can do the engineering work needed to scale out the data tier.

SQL Server and hardware selection

In my experience, nobody has complained that a database server is too fast! I think it's a big mistake to be frugal when it comes to selecting database server hardware, because so many applications and users probably depend on your database server. It's also important to avoid the temptation to reuse "old" database server hardware for a new version of SQL Server. For example, if you're upgrading from SQL Server 2005 to SQL Server 2008 R2, it's likely that your existing hardware is at least three to four years old, so it's probably out of warranty and woefully underpowered by today's standards.

Wise hardware selection can save a huge amount of money on SQL Server processor license costs. A modern two-socket server (with Intel processors) will have better single-threaded performance and more load capacity than a two-to-three-year-old, four-socket server. With increases in memory density over the past several years, it's possible to purchase a two-socket server with up to 288 GB of RAM. The increased CPU performance and capacity, along with the increased memory density available in two-socket servers, means that they're excellent platforms for most SQL Server workloads. One limitation of most two-socket servers is that they have fewer PCI Express (PCIe) expansion slots available; they are usually limited to three or four expansion slots. This restricts your ability to add additional RAID controllers (for direct attached storage) or host bus adapters (HBAs) for SAN storage.

If you need more expansion slots than that, you may be forced to move up to a four-socket server, which typically will support 8 to 10 PCIe expansion slots. Additional RAM capacity is another reason that you may need to move up to a four-socket server. By mid-2011, it was possible to buy a four-socket server that supports up to 2 TB of RAM, assuming you could afford it. With recent Intel processors, there's a substantial single-threaded performance difference between a processor meant for a two-socket server (such as an Intel Xeon X5690) and a processor meant for a four-socket server (such as an Intel Xeon X7560). The Intel two-socket server processors are typically about 9–12 months ahead of the four-socket processors in terms of technology and clock speed. This means that for the vast majority of OLTP applications, you'll get significantly better processor performance from a brand-new two-socket system than you will from a brand-new four-socket processor.

As you're looking at hardware specifications, don't forget to keep the new SQL Server 2008 R2 licensing limits in the back of your mind—they may take you by surprise. For example, SQL Server 2008 R2 Standard Edition is limited to four processor sockets and 64 GB of RAM, whereas SQL Server 2008 R2 Enterprise Edition is limited to eight processor sockets and 2 TB of RAM. These license limits are more restrictive than they were in SQL Server 2008. The most onerous issue for many people will be the 64 GB RAM limit for SQL Server 2008 Standard Edition, because a new two-socket server will support more than four times that amount of memory.

Database server–specific hardware factors

Database servers have much different workload characteristics than file servers or web servers. The exact type of workload your database server will see depends on the type of application workload that you have, whether it's an OLTP workload or a DW/DSS workload, but nearly all database workloads share some common characteristics. They're typically I/O intensive and memory intensive, but are often not particularly CPU intensive. Because of this, I often see people make the mistake of economizing by selecting lower-cost processors for database servers, which is a big mistake!

SQL Server is most commonly licensed by the physical processor socket, meaning that you don't pay any more for a multicore processor in that socket. Because of that, you should always select a processor that has the most cores possible for the server model you're considering. For example, you'd want to select an Intel Xeon X5690 processor (with six cores, plus hyperthreading) instead of an Intel Xeon E5620 processor (with four cores, plus hyperthreading); the SQL Server license cost would be the same for either choice, but the six-core processor would give you significantly better scalability and performance. The added hardware cost of an Intel Xeon X5690 over an Intel Xeon E5620 is currently about $1,200 per processor, which is pretty insignificant compared to your overall hardware costs and SQL Server license costs for a two-socket server. This is true if you're using SQL Server Standard Edition, and even more so with SQL Server Enterprise Edition.

As you're considering which processor to choose for your database server, you should also pay close attention to the processor L2 and L3 cache sizes. SQL Server is sensitive to the processor cache size; larger cache sizes are important for better performance. Having a larger L2 or L3 cache increases the likelihood that an application (like SQL Server) will find the instructions or data it needs in that cache, instead of having to retrieve it from main memory or even the disk subsystem. You'll notice that the more expensive processors in a given processor generation and family will have larger cache sizes, along with higher clock speeds. Because you're paying for a quite expensive processor license for each physical processor socket, you should just get the best processor available for that socket. The added incremental cost for the top-of-the-line processor is small compared to the overall cost of the server, especially if you factor in the SQL Server license cost.

You're likely to be stuck with whatever processors you initially buy for the life of the server, so you should get the best one available at that point in time. You may remember that I said most database servers have I/O- and memory-intensive workloads, so why am I pushing so hard for the best processor? The reason for this is that you can use that "excess" processor capacity that you purchased for a low incremental cost to help alleviate your bigger and more expensive I/O and memory scalability and performance bottlenecks. If you have SQL Server 2008 Enterprise Edition or later, you can use data compression to potentially reduce your I/O and memory requirements dramatically, by trading extra CPU utilization for reduced memory and I/O utilization. With SQL Server 2008 Enterprise Edition or SQL Server 2008 R2 Standard Edition, you can use backup compression to reduce your I/O requirements for database backups at the cost of some extra CPU utilization. You can do the same thing with any of the many available third-party database backup products.

Another advantage of having a top-of-the-line processor is that you'll enjoy better single-threaded OLTP performance (from the faster clock speeds and larger cache sizes) and better DW/DSS performance (from the additional cores and larger cache sizes). You'll also get additional scalability from having more cores in each processor. Having more processor cores will benefit parallel query plans as well. If you're budget constrained when you first buy the server, I'd choose processor over memory, because although you're likely to be stuck with your original processors for the life of the server, you'll probably be able to get approval to add more RAM later (if you need to).

Two interesting processor features that are currently Intel specific are hyperthreading and Turbo Boost technology. Intel hyperthreading was initially introduced in 2002 as a way to try to keep a single processor busy instead of having it idle, waiting to retrieve data from main memory. By creating two logical cores that are visible to the operating system (and SQL Server), you could allow multiple threads of execution to run nearly in parallel, resulting in up to a 20–30 percent performance boost for many workloads. Although this worked quite well on the desktop, many server workloads, such as those typically experienced by SQL Server, didn't always work as well. This was mainly due to a phenomenon known as *cache thrashing*, where the data in the L1 and L2 caches was shared between the two logical cores and was frequently forced to be reloaded from main memory as the application context switched between logical cores. Because of this, hyperthreading eventually got a bad reputation in database circles, with many people making a blanket recommendation to disable hyperthreading for all SQL Server workloads.

This blanket recommendation is a mistake. The performance effect of hyperthreading will vary based on your workload characteristics. It's much more effective with an OLTP workload that has many short duration queries that are unlikely to be parallelized by the query optimizer. This is particularly true if you've set the maximum degree of parallelism to 1 at the instance level. Hyperthreading is much less effective with long-running, complex queries that are more typical of a DW/DSS workload. You should also be aware that the second-generation hyperthreading, available in the Intel Xeon 5500 and 7500 series and later, is much more effective than the initial version that you may have dealt with in the past. Rather than taking my word for it, test with your environment and workload before you decide whether to enable hyperthreading.

Intel Turbo Boost is a much newer technology that's far less controversial. Available in the Intel Xeon 5500 and 7500 series and later processors, it's essentially "intelligent overclocking" that simply increases the clock speed of individual processor cores, in steps, based on how hard the rest of the cores in the processor are working. This gives you a nice single-threaded performance boost that's very beneficial for OLTP workloads. I don't see any possible performance downside to having Turbo Boost enabled. The latest Intel Sandy Bridge processors—available in the server space in late 2011—have Turbo Boost 2.0, which is more aggressive about overclocking more cores, by a greater percentage, for a longer period of time, subject to the operating temperature of the system. Turbo Boost 2.0 should be quite effective as a performance boost for database server workloads.

Intel vs. AMD processors

One basic choice that you have to make when you choose a database server model is whether you want a system with Intel processors or one with AMD processors. The fact of the matter is that Intel has been completely dominant in terms of pure performance in the two-socket space since December 2008 (with the Xeon 5500 series) and in the four-socket space since April 2010 (with the Xeon 7500 series). AMD processors are somewhat less expensive than Intel processors, but the processor cost is a small component of the total cost of your server, as previously discussed.

Intel has an advantage in market share, which gives them more money to spend on research and development, and more money to improve their fabrication technology; they're 18–24 months ahead of AMD. Intel has pretty much completed their transition from 45nm to 32nm lithography, which helps their processors perform better and use less power. The best AMD processors tend to perform somewhat better on DW/DSS workloads compared to OLTP workloads, whereas the best Intel processors are quite dominant with OLTP workloads.

AMD was able to become somewhat more competitive in 2010 (especially for DW/DSS workloads) with the introduction of the 12-core, Opteron 6100 series Magny-Cours processor. There's some hope that AMD may be able to close the gap even more with the release of the 16-core Bulldozer processor family in 2011. The Bulldozer is supposed to have 50 percent better throughput than the Magny-Cours, along with many other improvements that may make it successful.

In the meantime, I'll describe my current recommendations. The Intel processors I recommend are:

- *Two-socket server*—Xeon X5690 (32nm Westmere-EP); 3.46 GHz, 12 MB L3 cache, 6.40 GT/s Intel QPI; six cores, Turbo Boost (3.73 GHz), hyperthreading; three memory channels
- *Four-socket server*—Xeon E7-4870 (32nm Westmere-EX); 2.40 GHz, 30 MB L3 cache, 6.40 GT/s Intel QPI; ten-cores, Turbo Boost (2.80 GHz), hyperthreading; four memory channels

The AMD processors I recommend are:

- *Two- or four-socket servers*—Opteron 6180SE (45nm Magny-Cours), 12 cores; 2.5 GHz, 12 MB L3 cache, 6.4 GT/s

Memory recommendations

SQL Server can never have too much RAM. I'm a strong proponent of having as much RAM as you can afford, or as much RAM as will fit in your particular model server.

Server RAM is relatively inexpensive, as long as you avoid buying the highest-capacity sticks of RAM, which always have a significant price premium. Having a large amount of RAM is beneficial in several ways. Having lots of RAM will directly reduce your I/O requirements. Your read I/O requirements are reduced by having a larger buffer pool where SQL Server is more likely to find the data it needs in memory rather than having to go to your disk subsystem to get it. Having more RAM will also reduce the frequency of your checkpoint operations, which will help even out your write I/O workload. SQL Server will issue a checkpoint operation to write changed pages to the data file(s) when a certain percentage of data pages in memory are "dirty" (meaning they've been changed). Having more RAM in your server allows SQL Server to go longer before it has to issue a checkpoint.

It's ridiculous for a new two- or four-socket server to only have 16 or 32 GB of RAM in 2011. My personal laptop has 16 GB of RAM, and my workstation has 24 GB of RAM. If you're running SQL Server 2008 R2 Standard Edition, you're limited to 64 GB of RAM, which is about the minimum amount you should have for a production database server. With SQL Server 2008 R2 Enterprise Edition, I consider 128–144 GB to be a useful minimum figure to consider for a two-socket server. For a four-socket server, you should have at least 256 GB of RAM, and more if you can afford it. Even if you have a relatively small database right now (that comfortably fits in memory, with only 16 or 32 GB of RAM), you should plan on that database growing over time, often much faster than you expect.

Compared to SQL Server licenses and additional I/O capacity, server RAM is quite affordable. One trick to help minimize your RAM cost is to buy modules that are in the price/capacity "sweet spot," rather than going for the highest-capacity modules, as you can see in the following memory price sample:

Table 1 DDR3 ECC memory prices in late 2011

32 GB module	$2799	$87/GB
16 GB module	$559	$35/GB
8 GB module	$266	$33/GB
4 GB module	$115	$29/GB

Memory prices change over time but generally follow a downward trend, especially as larger-capacity modules are introduced. When a larger-capacity module becomes available, the existing smaller-capacity modules usually become much more affordable. Usually, the price/capacity sweet spot is the module size one down from the largest size available.

Traditional storage subsystems

The two most popular types of storage subsystems for SQL Server are a *storage area network* (SAN) and *direct attached storage* (DAS). A traditional SAN is quite complex and expensive, but also feature-rich and flexible. It allows you to support a number of host servers from a single SAN, with the ability to easily change RAID levels (with most SAN implementations) and expand logical drive sizes on the fly. You can also use features like SAN snapshots to recover from accidental data changes in many cases. SANs are usually optimized for I/Os per second (IOPS) rather than raw throughput, which makes them well suited for OLTP workloads. When evaluating a SAN, be sure to consider your complete data path, including the HBAs, switches, and so forth.

Unfortunately, SANs are usually accompanied by a cranky SAN administrator who probably has far different priorities than you, the database administrator. You should cultivate your relationship with your SAN administrator and communicate your I/O requirements in a specific and clear manner. Don't make the common mistake of just giving the SAN administrator a space requirement! If you do that, you'll most likely get a single logical drive, with poor performance characteristics. Your I/O requirements should include your required IOPS and required throughput, along with an estimate of the relative volatility of the data that will be on the volume, as well as your redundancy requirements.

Direct attached storage is much more affordable than a SAN but is also much less flexible. Current DAS devices typically use 6 Gbps 2.5-inch 15K SAS drives in an external enclosure directly attached with an SAS cable to a RAID controller in a single database server. It's much more difficult to do things like change your RAID level or expand the size of a logical drive. DAS storage is usually optimized for throughput, especially if you have dedicated RAID controllers that each control a single DAS enclosure.

New developments in storage subsystems

One recent development that's starting to become more popular in database servers is solid state disks (SSD). SSDs use flash memory instead of a spinning magnetic platter and a drive arm that has to move back and forth to access data on different parts of the disk. Because of this, SSDs have excellent random I/O performance and excellent sequential read performance. Some early SSDs had relatively bad sequential write performance, but newer models have improved upon this weakness. Generally speaking, SSD performance depends on the specific drive controller that the SSD uses and whether the SSD uses single-level cell (SLC) memory or multilevel cell (MLC) memory—SLC drives have better performance.

Enterprise-class SSDs (which are more expensive and more reliable) typically use SLC memory, whereas consumer-class SSDs usually use less expensive MLC memory. Initially, there were some questions about the long-term durability of SSDs, because at some point you won't be able to write to the SSD (flash memory has a finite write limit that you'll eventually run into, typically after many years of writes). SLC SSDs are more durable in this respect, and newer SSDs have better wear-leveling algorithms that extend their life. SSD storage is still expensive compared to traditional magnetic storage, but the price continues to come down. One advantage of SSDs is reduced power usage, especially as you may be able to replace multiple traditional magnetic drives with fewer SSDs.

Another new storage development is the increasing popularity of a series of products from a company called Fusion-io. Fusion-io makes several PCIe-based expansion card products that use flash memory (similar to SSDs). Rather than being restricted to the bandwidth of a SATA or SAS interface, a Fusion-io card can use the full bandwidth of a PCIe slot. Their main products are the ioDrive Duo—with 320 GB, 640 GB, and 1.28 TB capacities—and the new ioDrive Octal, with a 5.12 TB capacity and a 6 GB/sec read bandwidth. Fusion-io products have high performance at a relatively high cost. It's pretty common to use software RAID with multiple Fusion-io cards to get a better level of redundancy.

Benchmarking and sizing tools

When it comes time to do server selection and sizing, it makes good sense to use some of the freely available tools and techniques to do a better job than just guessing about the relative performance of different servers. One of my favorite free tools is CPU-Z, which is available from www.cpuid.com. CPU-Z lets you identify exactly what processor(s) and memory you have running in an existing system. Another handy tool is Geekbench, a cross-platform processor and memory benchmark from Primate Labs; Geekbench gives you a good idea of your processor and memory performance in just a couple of minutes and is available at www.primatelabs.ca/geekbench/. There's an online database of Geekbench results that makes it easier to compare the performance of an existing system to a system that you're considering but don't have access to.

Another useful set of evaluation and sizing tools are the TPC benchmarks from the Transaction Processing Performance Council. For OLTP workloads, I like to use the newer TPC-E benchmark (which is much more realistic that the old TPC-C benchmark). The TPC-E benchmark has been around since 2007, so there are enough published results that you should be able to find a published result that uses a system similar to your current system and to a proposed new system. By using those results, along with the Geekbench results of similar systems (and your own good judgment) you can make accurate sizing and capacity estimates from a processor and memory perspective. For DW/DSS workloads, look at published TPC-H results for database sizes that are closest to what you'll be dealing with.

As you evaluate these various benchmark results, you may have to make some adjustments for slight differences in the configured systems. For example, you might find a published TPC-E benchmark for a system similar to an existing system that you own but the TPC-E system is using a slightly better processor from the same generation and family compared to your system. Because the TPC-E benchmark is processor dependent, you could adjust the score in your estimation process to take that sort of difference into account. For example, if you want to informally adjust a TPC-E benchmark score to account for the difference between those two fairly similar processors, compare their Geekbench scores and use the percentage difference to change the TPC-E score.

Summary

Don't make the mistake of reusing old hardware for a new SQL Server installation or upgrade. Even hardware from a couple of years ago is completely outclassed by new database server hardware. Processors have gotten so much better over the past several years that you may be able to move from a traditional four-socket database server to a two-socket database server and save a lot of money in SQL Server license costs. Modern two-socket database servers can handle a high percentage of SQL Server workloads.

When you select your processor(s), you want to spend the extra money to get the absolute best processor possible for the model of server you're going to be using. This will give you more performance and scalability potential for each one of those expensive SQL Server processor licenses, as well as extra processor headroom to take advantage of data compression and backup compression to reduce your I/O requirements.

You should get as much RAM as possible, given your budget constraints. Having lots of RAM will reduce the pressure on your I/O subsystem, and RAM is much less expensive than additional I/O capacity.

You also don't want to make the common mistake of neglecting the I/O subsystem. I've seen many powerful servers crippled by an inadequate I/O subsystem. You want to base your sizing requirements not on just size but on your required IOPS and throughput figures. For performance, having a higher number of smaller capacity disks is always better than a smaller number of larger disks.

Finally, use the available component- and application-level benchmarks to compare and evaluate different systems rather than just guessing. This approach will help you make much more accurate estimates about the performance and capacity of different systems. Above all, don't be afraid to learn more about hardware, and stay current with new developments. You can do this by reading enthusiast websites, such as AnandTech, because such sites do a great job of reporting on new hardware developments that are relevant to database servers.

About the author

Glenn Berry works as a database architect at Avalara in Denver, CO. He's a SQL Server MVP and has a whole collection of Microsoft certifications, including MCITP, MCDBA, MCSE, MCSD, MCAD, and MCTS—which he says proves he likes to take tests. His expertise includes DMVs, high availability, hardware selection, full-text search, and SQL Azure. He's also an Adjunct Faculty member at University College – University of Denver, where he's been teaching since 2000. Glenn is the author of *SQL Server Hardware* (Red Gate Books, 2011) and blogs regularly at http://sqlserverperformance.wordpress.com.

32 Parameter sniffing: your best friend... except when it isn't

Grant Fritchey

Lots of people have heard the phrase *parameter sniffing*. Usually it's heard in conjunction with some horrific performance problem that has occurred within their system. But what most people don't know is that parameter sniffing is a process that's occurring all the time within your servers, and most of the time it's helping you. Only sometimes does parameter sniffing lead to problems, but when it does create a problem, it's a big one. My goal is to show you what parameter sniffing is and how it's constantly helping your database applications run better. You'll also learn how parameter sniffing can go wrong and why it happens. I'll be able to show you several ways to fix parameter sniffing when it goes wrong and which are the better choices depending on your situation. But, hopefully, the most important thing you'll take away from this chapter is that parameter sniffing is a desirable behavior that's useful to you and your systems...except when it isn't.

Understanding parameter sniffing

To understand parameter sniffing, you need to know a bit about how the query optimizer works. The optimizer relies heavily on statistics as a major part of its decision-making process. Statistics are used by the optimizer to help decide whether it should perform a seek or a scan on an index, among several other decisions related to creating an execution plan. The degree of accuracy of the plans created by the optimizer depends on the accuracy of the statistics and the distribution of the data used to create the statistics.

Often, in your stored procedures and parameterized queries, you use local variables and parameters. A local variable is a variable declared in the code with the DECLARE keyword, whereas a parameter is declared in the header of the procedure or as part of the parameterized query definition. When you use a local variable in SQL Server, the optimizer can't know what value that variable is going to be. This means that when the optimizer sees a local variable, it looks at all the statistics of any potentially applicable indexes and uses an average value from those statistics in determining the execution plan.

Parameters are different. When a parameter for a stored procedure is defined, SQL Server doesn't know the value for the parameter until the procedure is called for the first time. After you supply the values for the parameter, the value is passed to the optimizer. This allows the optimizer to use that value to search the statistics. Because the search within the statistics is more accurate, it makes the execution plans generated from those searches much more accurate most of the time. This process of using the value from the parameter is known as parameter sniffing. Parameter sniffing occurs for every procedure or parameterized query you call.

Let's create a small stored procedure for use with the AdventureWorks2008R2 database:

```
CREATE PROC dbo.spAddressByCity @City NVARCHAR(30)
AS
    SELECT   a.AddressID,
             a.AddressLine1,
             a.AddressLine2,
             a.City,
             sp.[Name] AS StateProvinceName,
             a.PostalCode
    FROM     Person.Address AS a
             JOIN Person.StateProvince AS sp
             ON a.StateProvinceID = sp.StateProvinceID
    WHERE    a.City = @City ;
```

To see parameter sniffing in action, you'll execute this new procedure. There are a number of ways to tell if a parameter value was used to help create the execution plan, but the simplest way to tell is to look at the execution plan itself.

NOTE   For the rest of the chapter, if you're following along on your own database, enable the Actual Execution plan in your T-SQL window by pressing Ctrl-M. Also, if you turn on IO and Time Statistics in the query window, you can see how long the execution takes and how many reads and scans are involved with the query.

We'll execute the stored procedure with this code:

```
EXEC dbo.spAddressByCity 'London'
```

SQL Server will use the value from the parameter @City to create the execution plan. The query ran in about 200ms on my system with 2 scans and 219 reads. The execution plan on my system looks like figure 1.

If you look at the properties page for the SELECT operator, the first operation at the left of the execution plan, you can find the parameter values that were used to create the plan. To do this, hover your mouse over the SELECT operator and right-

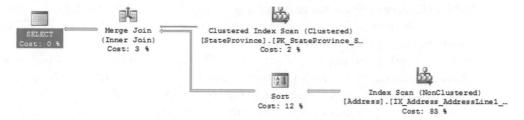

Figure 1   The execution plan created by running the stored procedure `dbo.spAddressBycity`

click. In the resulting context menu, select Properties to open the Properties page for that operator. It'll look something like figure 2.

Near the bottom of the full Properties page, the highlighted section in figure 2, you can see the values that were used to call the procedure and to compile the procedure. In the example, the city value of London was used to compile the procedure and create the execution plan. This process of the query optimizer looking at, or "sniffing," the value of a parameter during the first execution is called parameter sniffing.

To better understand how parameter sniffing helps your queries, try running this code instead:

Estimated Operator Cost	0 (0%)
Estimated Subtree Cost	0.218273
Logical Operation	
Memory Grant	6656
⊞ MissingIndexes	
Optimization Level	FULL
⊞ Parameter List	@City
Column	@City
Parameter Compiled Value	N'London'
Parameter Runtime Value	N'London'
Physical Operation	
QueryHash	0x6D09B759A0382ABB
QueryPlanHash	0x83B6639C4E926FC8
Reason For Early Termination Of	Good Enough Plan Found
⊞ Set Options	ANSI_NULLS: True, ANSI_PADDING
Statement	SELECT a.AddressID, a.Addr

Figure 2   Part of the Properties page from the `SELECT`
operator, with the parameter values highlighted

```
DECLARE @city VARCHAR(75) = 'London' ;

SELECT   a.AddressID,
         a.AddressLine1,
         a.AddressLine2,
         a.City,
         sp.[Name] AS StateProvinceName,
         a.PostalCode
FROM     Person.Address AS a
         JOIN Person.StateProvince AS sp
         ON a.StateProvinceID = sp.StateProvinceID
WHERE    a.City = @City ;
```

This query is essentially identical to the stored procedure you created earlier, but it runs in about 400 ms and with 1 scan and 1,084 reads, which is considerably slower and more resource intensive than the original stored procedure. This is because the local variable in the script prevented parameter sniffing from occurring. SQL Server was unable to "sniff" the parameter because none was used. Local variables are never sampled because SQL Server can't know their values at compile time. This means that the optimizer samples the data within the statistics rather than using an actual value. This estimate, based on a sampling of the statistics, leads to a different execution plan with different performance metrics.

The ability for the optimizer to use the exact values passed to the procedure through the parameters is a great advantage to the accuracy of your execution plans. The advantage occurs because knowing the exact value of the parameter that was passed in greatly increases the chance the query optimizer can find an exact match in the statistics as opposed to guessing by coming up with an average value. Remember, parameter sniffing is going on in all your parameterized stored procedures, each time they're called, making sure that you get the best plan for the parameters passed. But sometimes, things go wrong.

Parameter sniffing gone wrong

Using the same processes that created accurate execution plans, parameter sniffing can sometimes create wildly inaccurate plans. Let's go back to the stored procedure that you called earlier. To see the change in the execution plan that can result from a difference in the parameter values passed to it, you first need to remove that plan from the procedure cache. In a development environment, the easy way to do this is to run DBCC FREEPROCCACHE(). Once you've run it on your development machine, run the stored procedure again, but this time use the following code:

```
EXEC dbo.spAddressByCity 'Mentor'
```

NOTE Don't run DBCC FREEPROCCACHE() on a production server or you'll cause all queries to have to be recompiled.

This parameter returns considerably fewer rows than the original parameter of 'London'. This time the query ran in 65 ms and had a single scan with 218 reads. This is quite quick and can simply be explained by the fact that there's less data being returned. But take a look at the execution plan shown in figure 3.

This time a much simpler plan has been created. If you look at the Properties page of the SELECT operator again and check the parameters, you can see that 'Mentor' was used to create the plan instead of 'London'. That created an execution plan optimized to return a single row. Now, to see bad parameter sniffing in action, you'll run the query again with the original parameter value, 'London', which returns a lot more than one row.

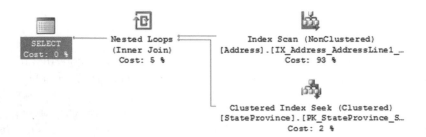

Figure 3 A new execution plan resulting from a change in the parameter used by the optimizer

On my machine, running the stored procedure again using `'London'` as the parameter but with the execution plan optimized for `'Mentor'` results in a query that runs in about 300 ms and with a single scan, but this time with 1,084 logical reads. The execution plan in figure 3 is optimal for retrieving a small dataset, but it's killing the performance of the large dataset. This is an example of parameter sniffing gone wrong. The question is: which of the two plans is right?

There isn't a single correct answer to that question. As I stated at the beginning of this chapter, statistics drive execution plans and data drives statistics. In this case, there's a wide divergence in the data stored in the Address table. The index in question on the City column mostly has only a few entries for each city. `'Mentor'` is typical of the average value in the index. `'London'` is an outlier. Each set of returned data is best retrieved by a different execution plan. This wide divergence is what's causing two different plans to be created. The right plan is the one that's best for the majority of your data. But getting that plan all the time can be hard, as you've seen. It's important that you get the right plan because once it's created, it'll be cached so each subsequent query run against the system will use that plan. So how do you deal with bad parameter sniffing?

Dealing with bad parameter sniffing

There are a number of techniques you can use to help assist parameter sniffing so it produces an optimal execution plan. Which one you use depends on the situation. You have to ask yourself whether your data is distributed in such a way that a fairly consistent number of rows are returned for most key values, with maybe only a few key values that return more or less than the average number of rows. In the earlier example, most cities returned around 25–40 rows with a couple of cities returning 60 and a couple returning 20. If your data is distributed in this way, you have some specific options. If you have extremely volatile or widely distributed data, you may need to use other methods that result in a generic plan that works well in most cases, or that create a new plan each time the stored procedure is called. Let's review some of the options you have available to deal with parameter sniffing gone wrong.

OPTIMIZE FOR

One of the most common methods for dealing with bad parameter sniffing is to use a query hint called `OPTIMIZE FOR`. You can use this hint to have the query optimizer develop a plan for a particular value or for an unknown value. It just depends on how you define the hint. Taking our sample stored procedure, you could modify it as follows in order to force the optimizer to create a plan that favors the value `'Mentor'` instead of the actual value passed:

```
ALTER PROC dbo.spAddressByCity @City NVARCHAR(30)
AS
    SELECT  a.AddressID,
            a.AddressLine1,
            a.AddressLine2,
            a.City,
```

```
            sp.[Name] AS StateProvinceName,
            a.PostalCode
    FROM    Person.Address AS a
            JOIN Person.StateProvince AS sp
            ON a.StateProvinceID = sp.StateProvinceID
    WHERE   a.City = @City
    OPTION  (OPTIMIZE FOR (@City = 'Mentor')) ;
```

Re-creating the procedure clears it automatically from cache. If you execute the query after modifying the procedure using the parameter 'London', you'll see that the execution plan is the one that favors 'Mentor', shown in figure 3, instead of the actual value passed. If you look at the parameter list in the SELECT operator, you'll see that the Compile Value is 'Mentor'.

Setting key values through OPTIMIZE FOR works best when your data is well known and its distribution is stable. Although this approach can work to address some parameter sniffing issues, it does require you to be confident of your data and its distribution. It's also subject to changes in data over time, so you may have to go back and reassess the values you selected and possibly change them at some point in the future. Because you may have to readdress this fix, or if your data distribution isn't well known or stable, sometimes a more generic approach is better.

Instead of going for a particular key value, you could address the issue by ensuring that you always get a sampled value. Modify the procedure again, this time substituting the key word UNKNOWN for the value:

```
ALTER PROC dbo.spAddressByCity @City NVARCHAR(30)
AS
    SELECT  a.AddressID,
            a.AddressLine1,
            a.AddressLine2,
            a.City,
            sp.[Name] AS StateProvinceName,
            a.PostalCode
    FROM    Person.Address AS a
            JOIN Person.StateProvince AS sp
            ON a.StateProvinceID = sp.StateProvinceID
    WHERE   a.City = @City
    OPTION  (OPTIMIZE FOR (@City UNKNOWN)) ;
```

If you run this stored procedure again passing it the value 'London', you'll see that the execution plan is the same as it was for the value 'Mentor'. There's one difference, though: because of the use of UNKNOWN as the value, the optimizer has treated this as if it were a local variable. There's no longer a Compile Value in the parameter list because none was used to create the execution plan.

This method would work well if you're unsure of the distribution of your data and the effects that picking a particular value might have. In some cases, using the sampled data can result in plans that are less than optimal for part of the data. This is the case for the earlier query when calling the larger 'London' dataset. You'll need to assess the distribution of your data in order to determine which approach will provide you with the most consistently best-performing procedure.

WITH RECOMPILE

Another popular method for addressing the issue of bad parameter sniffing is to recompile the statement every time it runs. This makes sure that, regardless of the values of the parameters passed you get a new execution plan each and every time the stored procedure is called. If you modify the original procedure as follows, the statement will be recompiled every time it executes:

```
ALTER PROC dbo.spAddressByCity @City NVARCHAR(30)
AS
    SELECT  a.AddressID,
            a.AddressLine1,
            a.AddressLine2,
            a.City,
            sp.[Name] AS StateProvinceName,
            a.PostalCode
    FROM    Person.Address AS a
            JOIN Person.StateProvince AS sp
            ON a.StateProvinceID = sp.StateProvinceID
    WHERE   a.City = @City
    OPTION  (RECOMPILE) ;
```

Now if you execute the stored procedure with the parameters you've been using, the execution plan will be different for each parameter. The `Compile Value` in the parameter list will be different each time as well. This approach won't work if there are multiple statements within the procedure that are all suffering from bad parameter sniffing. In this case you'd want to modify the code so that the entire procedure recompiles instead of just the statement:

```
ALTER PROC dbo.spAddressByCity @City NVARCHAR(30)
WITH RECOMPILE
AS
    SELECT  a.AddressID,
            a.AddressLine1,
            a.AddressLine2,
            a.City,
            sp.[Name] AS StateProvinceName,
            a.PostalCode
    FROM    Person.Address AS a
            JOIN Person.StateProvince AS sp
            ON a.StateProvinceID = sp.StateProvinceID
    WHERE   a.City = @City;
```

The `RECOMPILE` hint, either at the statement or the procedure level, works best when:

- Your data isn't that well known.
- Your data is extremely volatile and thus unlikely to benefit from a single plan, which means custom plans for each parameter set are needed.

Although this approach does address the parameter sniffing issue, it can introduce a new issue that could be as painful as parameter sniffing. Depending on the complexity of the procedure or the statement, compiling the execution plan each time the stored procedure is run can be expensive. One of the main reasons SQL Server stores plans in cache is to avoid the cost of query optimization. Further, while the procedure recompiles, it's locked to other users until the recompile completes. If this is a frequently called procedure, this method for fixing parameter sniffing could be worse than the original problem.

Local variables

As you've already seen, using a local variable affects the way the optimizer creates execution plans. The optimizer is forced to scan the statistics and use a sampled value instead of the specific "sniffed" value. In some situations, this will help. It's similar to using OPTIMIZE FOR UNKNOWN. In general, if you're in a situation where you can modify the code, I'd be more inclined to use the OPTIMIZE FOR method, but there's nothing wrong with this approach. If you want to modify the procedure we've been working with, do something like this:

```
ALTER PROC dbo.spAddressByCity @City NVARCHAR(30)
AS
DECLARE @LocalCity VARCHAR(30);
SET @LocalCity = @City;

    SELECT  a.AddressID,
            a.AddressLine1,
            a.AddressLine2,
            a.City,
            sp.[Name] AS StateProvinceName,
            a.PostalCode
    FROM    Person.Address AS a
            JOIN Person.StateProvince AS sp
            ON a.StateProvinceID = sp.StateProvinceID
    WHERE   a.City = @LocalCity;
```

Custom variables is an older approach and not one I'd normally recommend; it's best used in situations where your data distribution is consistent but a specific value can't readily be determined. If you do use this approach, just make sure that you use the same data types and lengths for the local variables so that you don't run into any implicit conversion issues. By using local variables, you'll get generic plans, which can be good in some situations. If your dataset is demanding that you get plans for specific values, this approach won't work. Further, you introduce a confusing bit of code, passing in a parameter and then switching it to a local variable—and someone editing the code in the future might not understand why you chose this particular option.

Plan guides

All of the examples of addressing bad parameter sniffing that you've seen so far require access to the T-SQL code. What happens in the situation where you're dealing with a vendor application and you can't modify the code? That's where a plan guide comes in handy. A plan guide is a mechanism for applying hints to a query without modifying the query. There are three types of guides: OBJECT, SQL, and TEMPLATE. The OBJECT type is for stored procedures, triggers, and functions. A SQL guide is for ad hoc queries and batches. TEMPLATE is applied to automatically parameterized queries, such as those that are created by forced parameterization (a topic outside the scope of this chapter).

Because we're working with a stored procedure in our example, we'll create an OBJECT plan guide for demonstration purposes, but you can use similar methods for a SQL or a TEMPLATE plan guide. You must supply three basic things to create an OBJECT plan guide: the code, exactly as it exists in the query; the object you're interested in; and the query hint itself. Here's an example of how you'd supply the OPTIMIZE FOR hint in an OBJECT plan guide for our sample stored procedure:

```
EXEC sys.sp_create_plan_guide @name = 'SniffFix', -- sysname
    @stmt = N'SELECT  a.AddressID,
            a.AddressLine1,
            a.AddressLine2,
            a.City,
            sp.[Name] AS StateProvinceName,
            a.PostalCode
    FROM    Person.Address AS a
            JOIN Person.StateProvince AS sp
            ON a.StateProvinceID = sp.StateProvinceID
    WHERE   a.City = @City ;', -- nvarchar(max)
    @type = N'Object', -- nvarchar(60)
    @module_or_batch = N'dbo.spAddressByCity', -- nvarchar(max)
    @params = NULL, -- nvarchar(max)
    @hints = N'OPTION(OPTIMIZE FOR(@City = ''Mentor''))' -- nvarchar(max)
```

This code will operate much the same way as the OPTIMIZE FOR code modification worked but doesn't require the code modifications you originally performed on the procedure. The plan guide will be recognized and accepted by the optimizer and the hint applied in the appropriate place, all without touching the code.

If you again look at the properties sheet for the SELECT operator, not only will you see the Parameter Compiled Value set to 'Mentor', which means that the query hint OPTIMIZE FOR has been applied, but you'll also see that the plan guide is identified, as shown in figure 4.

Estimated Subtree Cost	0.193818
Logical Operation	
⊞ MissingIndexes	
Optimization Level	FULL
⊟ Parameter List	@City
Column	@City
Parameter Compiled Value	N'Mentor'
Parameter Runtime Value	N'London'
Physical Operation	
PlanGuideDB	AdventureWorks2008R2
PlanGuideName	SniffFix
QueryHash	0x2A6897E5300E2EE7
QueryPlanHash	0x3293F572143F569B
Reason For Early Termination Of Statement Optimization	Good Enough Plan Found
⊞ Set Options	ANSI_NULLS: True, ANSI_PADDING: True, ANSI_WARNINGS:
Statement	SELECT a.AddressID, a.AddressLine1, a.Addressl

Figure 4 The SELECT operator Properties page with the plan guide information highlighted

Plan guides are best used in situations where you can't edit the code. You could also replace the OPTIMIZE FOR with a RECOMPILE hint if you were in a situation where that query hint was more applicable. You can apply any valid query hint through a plan guide. Plan guides, as you can see, are somewhat cumbersome to create and maintain. They're difficult to create because you have to get the code just right. They're difficult to maintain largely because they're not immediately visible. If you're editing a stored procedure, there's no indication that a plan guide exists until you attempt to save the query and you get an error. Be sure you need them before you get very far into creating a lot of plan guides.

Turn off parameter sniffing

What if you're in a situation where, after lots of investigation and time spent working on your statistics and tuning queries, you determine that the vast majority of your queries and stored procedures are still suffering from bad parameter sniffing? This is a rare situation. You'd need to establish the fact that a majority of your data is distributed across all of its indexes so poorly that a strong majority of your stored procedures or parameterized queries are in fact suffering from bad parameter sniffing. You'd also have to prove that those queries that are benefiting from parameter sniffing won't be seriously negatively impacted by the loss. In short, you need to be sure that your parameter sniffing problem is out of control and there are no more options to address it. Once you're sure, it's possible to turn off parameter sniffing. Doing so turns off good parameter sniffing as well as bad parameter sniffing, so I repeat, be sure this is what you need before taking this drastic step.

Here's how to turn off parameter sniffing. First, be sure you're running an up-to-date cumulative update. The update to completely turn off parameter sniffing was released for SQL Server 2005, 2008, and 2008 R2 and is available here: http://support.microsoft.com/kb/980653. Once you have the update in place, it's just a matter of setting a traceflag, 4163, to on. Turning this traceflag on results in *all* queries being treated as if they all had the OPTIMIZE FOR UNKNOWN query hint. If you were to execute our test procedure, you wouldn't see the Parameter Compiled Value.

Remember, this technique turns off all parameter sniffing, including the good parameter sniffing. But you might have a third-party system that's poorly designed, and creating hundreds of plan guides may not be an option. Or you might have a situation where all the code is generated through an object relational mapping engine and you can't edit it or affect how it's put together. In situations where there are no other options, you may want to consider turning off parameter sniffing.

Summary

The most important thing to remember is that parameter sniffing is, on the whole, a good thing. It absolutely improves the ability of the optimizer to find the right plans for your queries. The best thing you can do to ensure that parameter sniffing works as it's designed is to provide the best possible statistics to the optimizer at all times by keeping your statistics up to date through regular maintenance. But if you do run into a situation where parameter sniffing has gone bad, evaluate which solution is most suitable for your situation. Then test that solution to be sure your evaluation was accurate. Although you can completely disable parameter sniffing, I strongly advocate against it. You'll have a better system in the long run if you help the optimizer to do what it was designed for without trying to interfere.

About the author

 Grant Fritchey is a SQL Server MVP with more than 20 years' experience in IT, including time spent in support and development. He's worked with SQL Server since 6.0, back in 1995. He's developed in VB, VB.NET, C#, and Java. Grant volunteers at the Professional Association for SQL Server (PASS) and is president of the Southern New England SQL Server Users Group (SNESSUG). He's authored books for Apress and Simple-Talk and joined Red Gate as a Product Evangelist in January 2011.

33 Investigating the plan cache

Jason Strate

There lies within SQL Server a treasure trove of information that has the ability to provide insight into many different ways to tune your SQL Server databases. You can use this information to discover opportunities to reduce scans on indexes, identify potentially useful indexes, and find where specific operations are being performed. This information, and more, is contained within the plan cache (formerly known as the procedure cache).

The plan cache is where SQL Server stores compiled query plans. When a request is first made to execute a SQL statement, trigger, or stored procedure, SQL Server compiles a plan for executing that request. This plan is stored in memory in the plan cache. SQL Server can then reuse the plan when an identical or similar request is made in the future.

With the release of SQL Server 2005, a number of things changed with the plan cache, the most significant of which is your ability to access plans in the plan cache in the SHOWPLAN XML format through dynamic management objects (DMOs). By looking into the plan cache, you can examine its contents and make judgments based on frequency of use in order to determine what queries SQL Server is most often executing. By focusing your attention on these areas, you can identify opportunities for performance tuning with minimal effort.

Plan cache dynamic management objects

Before diving into the specifics of investigating the plan cache, let's examine the DMOs that provide insight into the plan cache. You can choose from a number of DMOs to view items in the plan cache. These DMOs begin with sys.dm_exec_*.

For the purpose of our discussion, we'll focus on only two: sys.dm_exec_cached _plans and sys.dm_exec_query_plan. Several others provide additional insight into the resources used by queries, but we won't discuss them in this chapter.

sys.dm_exec_cached_plans

The DMO `sys.dm_exec_cached_plans` provides insight into all the compiled plans in the SQL Server instance. For each plan that you compiled and placed in the plan cache, there will be one entry in this DMO.

This DMO includes many columns. For our purposes we'll focus on the columns in table 1.

Table 1 Columns of interest in `sys.dm_exec_cached_plans`

Name	Definition
plan_handle	`VARBINARY` value that provides an identifier for a query plan. This value is unique for each compiled plan and is valid only while the plan is in the plan cache.
usecounts	The number of times the compiled plan has been used since being added to the plan cache.
cacheobjtype	The type of object in the plan cache. In most cases, when you're investigating the plan cache the items returned will be compiled plans.
objtype	The object type for the plan cache item. It identifies whether the compiled plan is for a stored procedure, trigger, ad hoc statement, and so forth. This information is useful in determining the source of a compiled plan.

sys.dm_exec_query_plan

The DMO `sys.dm_exec_query plan` is a table-valued function that returns the query plan for each plan_handle passed into it. The query plan returned is represented as an XML document that can be opened as a graphical execution plan. The columns we're interested in are defined in table 2.

Table 2 Columns of interest in `sys.dm_exec_cached_plans`

Name	Definition
dbid	Database ID that corresponds to the database context when the plan was compiled. This value can be NULL for ad hoc or prepared statements.
objectid	Object ID for the object for which the plan was compiled, such as the stored procedure or trigger. This value can be NULL for ad hoc or prepared statements.
query_plan	XML value representing the compiled plan in SHOWPLAN XML format. This value can be NULL if the query plan contains more than 128 nest levels.

When investigating cached plans, remember that the plan may not always contain all the activity from the execution. For instance, the execution plan for a user-defined function will be represented by a single operator within the compiled plan. In actual-ity, there's another plan in the plan cache for the user-defined function that should also be considered in conjunction with the plan that calls the user-defined function.

WARNING   Queries against the plan cache can be expensive. Only run them on nonproduction servers until you understand their costs. Never leave the plan cache queries to run unattended.

Investigating missing indexes

Missing indexes are the best place to start investigating the plan cache. Finding the right indexes to add to a table can often be a challenge. When you discover the right ones, they often lead to noticeable performance improvements.

An often recommended process for adding missing indexes is to use the sys.dm_db_missing_index_* DMOs. These DMOs provide information on indexes that could be added to improve the performance on some queries in the database. Unfortunately, with the missing index DMOs, no clear relationship exists between the indexes and the queries that are being executed on the SQL Server. When adding indexes to a database, you must be able to identify which queries are improved; these DMOs don't help with that. The plan cache provides a solution to this issue. When missing index information is collected for the DMOs, the same process includes the information in the plan that's compiled and placed in the plan cache. Through queries run against the plan cache, you can discover missing index information and quantify the value of the improvement based on the number of times the plan was used.

The SHOWPLAN XML for a compiled plan contains an element named MissingIndex. This element contains information about an index that, if created, would improve the performance of the compiled plan.

In the query shown in listing 1, all query plans with the MissingIndex element are being returned. The MissingIndex element is then shredded to provide information on missing indexes.

Listing 1   Querying the plan cache for missing indexes

```
WITH XMLNAMESPACES (DEFAULT
'http://schemas.microsoft.com/sqlserver/2004/07/showplan')
,PlanMissingIndexes
AS (
  SELECT query_plan, cp.usecounts
  FROM sys.dm_exec_cached_plans cp
    OUTER APPLY sys.dm_exec_query_plan(cp.plan_handle) tp
  WHERE tp.query_plan.exist('//MissingIndex')=1
)
SELECT
  stmt.value('(//MissingIndex/@Database)[1]', 'sysname') AS database_name
  ,stmt.value('(//MissingIndex/@Schema)[1]', 'sysname') AS [schema_name]
  ,stmt.value('(//MissingIndex/@Table)[1]', 'sysname') AS [table_name]
  ,stmt.value('(@StatementText)[1]', 'VARCHAR(4000)') AS sql_text
```

```
        ,pmi.usecounts
        ,stmt.value('(//MissingIndexGroup/@Impact)[1]', 'FLOAT') AS impact
        ,stmt.query('for $group in //ColumnGroup
          for $column in $group/Column
          where $group/@Usage="EQUALITY"
          return string($column/@Name)
          ').value('.', 'varchar(max)') AS equality_columns
        ,stmt.query('for $group in //ColumnGroup
          for $column in $group/Column
          where $group/@Usage="INEQUALITY"
          return string($column/@Name)
          ').value('.', 'varchar(max)') AS inequality_columns
        ,stmt.query('for $group in //ColumnGroup
          for $column in $group/Column
          where $group/@Usage="INCLUDE"
          return string($column/@Name)
          ').value('.', 'varchar(max)') AS include_columns
        ,pmi.query_plan
FROM PlanMissingIndexes pmi
  CROSS APPLY pmi.query_plan.nodes('//StmtSimple') AS p(stmt)
ORDER BY stmt.value('(//MissingIndexGroup/@Impact)[1]', 'FLOAT') DESC
```

Executing this query provides information about the database and table that the missing index would benefit. It also includes the impact, equality columns, inequality columns, and the included columns with sys.dm_db_missing_index_* DMOs. The impact value is an estimation of the percentage improvement that the query should expect in the query cost. The equality columns are those that the query would use for exact matches to values in the index. The inequality columns would be nonexact matches, such as greater-than or less-than comparisons. Figure 1 shows sample output from the missing indexes query.

The value in adding an index can only truly be measured with additional information to support the index, such as the SQL text, query plan, and use counts. Although this information isn't available in the sys.dm_db_missing_index_* DMOs, you can get this data by querying the plan cache. Bringing this all together helps you know what indexes you need to create and enables you to measure and justify the performance improvements.

In a similar vein, reviewing missing index information along with the associated plans provides an opportunity to review more than just the missing index recommendation. You can also review the text of the query and identify areas where a reworking of the SQL statements will both improve the performance of the query and remove the recommendation for the missing index.

	database_name	schema_name	table_name	sql_text	usecounts	impact	equality_columns	inequality_columns	include_columns	query_plan
1	[AdventureWorks]	[Sales]	[SalesOrderHeader]	SELECT DueDate FR...	1	99.3245	[DueDate]			<ShowPlanXML xmlns...
2	[AdventureWorks]	[Sales]	[SalesOrderHeader]	SELECT DueDate FR...	1	96.4259		[DueDate]		<ShowPlanXML xmlns...
3	[AdventureWorks]	[Sales]	[SalesOrderHeader]	SELECT OrderDate FR...	1	94.906		[DueDate]	[OrderDate]	<ShowPlanXML xmlns...
4	[AdventureWorks]	[Sales]	[SalesOrderHeader]	SELECT DueDate, Ord...	1	94.906		[DueDate]	[OrderDate]	<ShowPlanXML xmlns...

Figure 1   Sample output from missing indexes query

Investigating index usage

Occasionally, you'll need to remove indexes from a table. Although it'd be great to be able to add indexes without any considerations for their cost, this isn't the case. As indexes are added to a table, they're done so with a cost. Every index needs to be maintained and the more indexes there are on a table, the more I/O that needs to be expended when changes are made to the data. Therefore, you should remove from tables any indexes that are never or slightly used in order to strike a balance between the benefits of the indexes on a table and their value. Before an index is removed from a table, though, its value must be known, and this is where trouble can arise.

In most cases, indexes are built to assist with queries that are run frequently in a database. In these cases, the use count for the indexes will be high, which makes their value apparent. But the number of times an index is used isn't the only measure of the value of an index.

An index can exist to improve the performance of infrequent transactions. For example, an index may assist in processing that only occurs once per month. This infrequent transaction may execute in a few minutes with the indexes in place. But without the indexes, it may take hours to execute. In these situations, the value of the index isn't a count of the times the index has been executed; instead, its value lies in the time savings and possible prevention of blocking.

Consequently, you should know the effect that dropping an index will have on a database. By investigating the plan cache, you can determine whether an index is being used in a cached plan and what the plan is doing.

For every table used within a compiled plan, the SHOWPLAN XML stores information about the table in an `Object` element. In these cases, the `Object` element also contains the database, schema, and index names. By searching for this element in the plan cache, you can find all the plans that would use (and have already used) the index.

To demonstrate, the query in listing 2 searches the plan cache for plans that contain `Object` elements with the index specified in the `@IndexName` variable.

Listing 2   Querying the plan cache for index usage

```
SET TRANSACTION ISOLATION LEVEL READ UNCOMMITTED
GO

DECLARE @IndexName sysname = 'PK_SalesOrderHeader_SalesOrderID';
SET @IndexName = QUOTENAME(@IndexName,'[');

WITH XMLNAMESPACES (DEFAULT
'http://schemas.microsoft.com/sqlserver/2004/07/showplan')
,IndexSearch
AS (
  SELECT qp.query_plan
    ,cp.usecounts
    ,ix.query('.')AS StmtSimple
  FROM sys.dm_exec_cached_plans cp
    OUTER APPLY sys.dm_exec_query_plan(cp.plan_handle) qp
```

```
        CROSS APPLY qp.query_plan.nodes('//StmtSimple') AS p(ix)
    WHERE query_plan.exist('//Object[@Index = sql:variable("@IndexName")]') =1)
    SELECT StmtSimple.value('StmtSimple[1]/@StatementText', 'VARCHAR(4000)') AS
        sql_text
      ,obj.value('@Database','sysname') AS database_name
      ,obj.value('@Schema','sysname') AS schema_name
      ,obj.value('@Table','sysname') AS table_name
      ,obj.value('@Index','sysname') AS index_name
      ,ixs.query_plan
    FROM IndexSearch ixs
      CROSS APPLY StmtSimple.nodes('//Object') AS o(obj)
    WHERE obj.exist('//Object[@Index = sql:variable("@IndexName")]') = 1
```

Through the use of the `exist()` method, the query plan associated with the index and the SQL text are returned in the output. As a result, a good understanding of the impact of removing an index can be identified. For instance, figure 2 shows that there are seven plans in the plan cache that utilize `PK_SalesOrderHeader_SalesOrderID`.

This technique applies to more than just indexes that are candidates for being dropped. You can also use it to identify plans that may be affected by a modification to an index, such as adding to or removing columns from the index.

	sql_text	database_name	schema_name	table_name	index_name	query_plan
1	CREATE PROCEDURE x...	[Adventure Works]	[Sales]	[SalesOrderHeader]	[PK_SalesOrderHeader_SalesOrderID]	<ShowPlanXML xmlns="htt...
2	CREATE PROCEDUR...	[Adventure Works]	[Sales]	[SalesOrderHeader]	[PK_SalesOrderHeader_SalesOrderID]	<ShowPlanXML xmlns="htt...
3	SELECT DueDate FROM ...	[Adventure Works]	[Sales]	[SalesOrderHeader]	[PK_SalesOrderHeader_SalesOrderID]	<ShowPlanXML xmlns="htt...
4	SELECT DueDate FROM ...	[Adventure Works]	[Sales]	[SalesOrderHeader]	[PK_SalesOrderHeader_SalesOrderID]	<ShowPlanXML xmlns="htt...
5	SELECT OrderDate FRO...	[Adventure Works]	[Sales]	[SalesOrderHeader]	[PK_SalesOrderHeader_SalesOrderID]	<ShowPlanXML xmlns="htt...
6	SELECT DueDate, Order...	[Adventure Works]	[Sales]	[SalesOrderHeader]	[PK_SalesOrderHeader_SalesOrderID]	<ShowPlanXML xmlns="htt...
7	SELECT DueDate FROM...	[Adventure Works]	[Sales]	[SalesOrderHeader]	[PK_SalesOrderHeader_SalesOrderID]	<ShowPlanXML xmlns="htt...

Figure 2   Results from the index usage query

Investigating operations

Some of the most useful queries that you can execute against the plan cache are those where you want to investigate properties of the `RelOp` element. The `RelOp` element represents all of the operations that occur when a query is executing. For instance, when a value is calculated, the Scalar operator is used. Or when an index seek is required, the Index Seek operator is used. Both of these, and many others, are represented in the compiled plan through the `RelOp` elements. From the perspective of the graphical execution plan, there's a `RelOp` element in the SHOWPLAN XML for every icon in the graphical plan.

One easy yet powerful way to demonstrate the value in querying the `RelOp` element is by executing a query to identify all the plans in the plan cache that use parallelism. Parallelism, which is represented by the CXPACKET wait type, occurs when queries execute across multiple CPUs. Oftentimes, especially in online transaction processing (OLTP) environments, queries that use parallelism can be associated with performance issues. This is often the case if the CXPACKET wait type has a large number of waits.

If you've determined that parallelism is an issue, one of the next steps is to identify the queries that use parallelism to reduce or mitigate their use of parallelism. To find the plans in the plan cache that utilize parallelism, use the query in listing 3.

Listing 3   Querying the plan cache for plan that utilizes parallelism

```
SET TRANSACTION ISOLATION LEVEL READ UNCOMMITTED;

WITH XMLNAMESPACES
(DEFAULT 'http://schemas.microsoft.com/sqlserver/2004/07/showplan')
SELECT
COALESCE(DB_NAME(p.dbid), p.query_plan.value('(//RelOp/OutputList/
     ColumnReference/@Database)[1]',
'nvarchar(128)')) AS DatabaseName
,DB_NAME(p.dbid) + '.' + OBJECT_SCHEMA_NAME(p.objectid, p.dbid) + '.' +
OBJECT_NAME(p.objectid, p.dbid) AS ObjectName
,cp.objtype
,p.query_plan
,cp.UseCounts
,cp.plan_handle
,CAST('<?query --' + CHAR(13) + q.text + CHAR(13) + '--?>' AS xml)
AS SQLText
FROM sys.dm_exec_cached_plans cp
CROSS APPLY sys.dm_exec_query_plan(cp.plan_handle) p
CROSS APPLY sys.dm_exec_sql_text(cp.plan_handle) as q
WHERE cp.cacheobjtype = 'Compiled Plan'
AND p.query_plan.exist('//RelOp[@Parallel = "1"]') = 1
ORDER BY DatabaseName, UseCounts DESC
```

The output from this query, shown in figure 3, can identify the database and the number of times the plan has been executed. By reviewing this output, you can hone in on the specific plans that use parallelism and take steps to mitigate the use of parallelism, possibly through the addition of indexes to the database or by improving selectivity within the query. Because you're focused on the most used cached plans, you can affect a larger number of improvements across the entire environment, compared to picking a single plan that happens to be currently running and using parallelism.

Through the RelOp element, you can uncover various attributes of each operation within a cached plan. The element allows you to determine the physical or logical operation being used for all operations within a compiled plan. That way, you can identify where Key Lookup operations are occurring. Reviewing these operations can provide opportunities to add included columns to indexes that cause the Key Lookup to occur. Also, you can look for hash aggregate operations. In these cases, an index that covers the columns in the operation can often be created to allow the operation

	DatabaseName	ObjectName	objtype	query_plan	UseCounts	plan_handle	SQLText
1	NULL	NULL	Adhoc	<ShowPlanXML xmlns=...	1	0x06000F005C518F3740...	<?query – WITH I0 AS (s...
2	[AdventureWorks]	NULL	Adhoc	<ShowPlanXML xmlns=...	5	0x06000F002D32080F40...	<?query – SELECT TOP 10 ...

Figure 3   Results from the parallelism query

to change to a stream aggregate, which can result in improved performance. Another good example of the type of information available in the `RelOp` element is the estimated CPU, I/O, and rows for an operation. By querying for this information, you can look for potential resource bottlenecks.

Investigating index scans

The previous two examples demonstrated how to query the plan cache to find the usage of an index and locate specific properties, such as parallelism of an operation in a compiled plan. These two activities can be combined into a single activity to provide fine tuning and investigation of the plan cache. Doing so can help leverage the information in the plan cache even further.

Consider a situation where an index begins to have a number of scans run against it. These scans require that the entire index be read into memory. This leads to a shift in the contents of the data cache and can result in memory pressure if competing data is attempting to be loaded into memory. The cause of these scans could be a poorly constructed query that a few minutes of tuning can easily resolve.

The plan cache contains the information necessary to discover the plans using the index as well as those plans that are accessing it with an index scan physical operation. The query to do this is provided in listing 4.

Listing 4 Querying a plan cache for index scans

```
SET TRANSACTION ISOLATION LEVEL READ UNCOMMITTED;
GO

DECLARE @IndexName sysname;
DECLARE @op sysname;

SET @IndexName = 'IX_SalesOrderHeader_SalesPersonID';
SET @op = 'Index Scan';

WITH XMLNAMESPACES(DEFAULT
N'http://schemas.microsoft.com/sqlserver/2004/07/showplan')
SELECT
     cp.plan_handle
    ,DB_NAME(dbid) + '.' + OBJECT_SCHEMA_NAME(objectid, dbid) + '.'
+ OBJECT_NAME(objectid, dbid) AS database_object
  ,qp.query_plan
  ,c1.value('@PhysicalOp','nvarchar(50)') as physical_operator
  ,c2.value('@Index','nvarchar(max)') AS index_name
FROM sys.dm_exec_cached_plans cp
  CROSS APPLY sys.dm_exec_query_plan(cp.plan_handle) qp
  CROSS APPLY query_plan.nodes('//RelOp') r(c1)
  OUTER APPLY c1.nodes('IndexScan/Object') as o(c2)
WHERE c2.value('@Index','nvarchar(max)') = QUOTENAME(@IndexName,'[')
AND c1.exist('@PhysicalOp[. = sql:variable("@op")]') = 1;
```

From the query results (see figure 4), you can begin to tune the specific plan that's causing the scans to occur. With some luck, the scan can be avoided and data that was

	plan_handle	database_object	query_plan	(No column name)	(No column name)
1	0x06000F00C2882D1...	NULL	<ShowPlanXML xmlns=...	Index Scan	[IX_SalesOrderHeader_SalesPersonID]

Figure 4   Results from the index scan query

previously in the data cache will no longer need to be there, leaving room for other data from other tables.

Investigating parameters

At times, queries may begin executing poorly without any warning. This can sometimes happen when the plan for a stored procedure is compiled, or recompiled, and the parameters used for the plan aren't representative of the rest of the data that the stored procedure returns. This situation is known as *parameter sniffing*.

When it appears that this has happened, it's useful to know what values the stored procedure used to create the plan. By determining these values, you can assist your investigation into why performance has changed.

The parameters used to compile a plan are stored in the plan cache along with the information on how to execute the query. They're stored in the `ParameterList` element. The query in listing 5 can be used to shred the execution plan for the stored procedure `dbo.uspGetWhereUsedProductID`. The results from this query would look similar to those in figure 5.

Listing 5   Querying a plan cache for parameterization

```
SET TRANSACTION ISOLATION LEVEL READ UNCOMMITTED
GO

WITH XMLNAMESPACES (DEFAULT
'http://schemas.microsoft.com/sqlserver/2004/07/showplan')
,PlanParameters
AS (
  SELECT ph.plan_handle, qp.query_plan, qp.dbid, qp.objectid
  FROM sys.dm_exec_cached_plans ph
    OUTER APPLY sys.dm_exec_query_plan(ph.plan_handle) qp
  WHERE qp.query_plan.exist('//ParameterList')=1
  and OBJECT_NAME(qp.objectid, qp.dbid) = 'uspGetWhereUsedProductID'
)
SELECT
  DB_NAME(pp.dbid) AS DatabaseName
  ,OBJECT_NAME(pp.objectid, pp.dbid) AS ObjectName
  ,n2.value('(@Column)[1]','sysname') AS ParameterName
  ,n2.value('(@ParameterCompiledValue)[1]','varchar(max)')
AS ParameterValue
From PlanParameters pp
  CROSS APPLY query_plan.nodes('//ParameterList') AS q1(n1)
  CROSS APPLY n1.nodes('ColumnReference') as q2(n2)
```

In these results, you can see that the value 15 was used for the `@StartProductID` and 2011-04-01 was provided for the `@CheckDate` parameters. If the values for these two

	DatabaseName	ObjectName	ParameterName	ParameterValue
1	AdventureWorks	uspGetWhereUsedProductID	@CheckDate	'2011-04-01 00:00:00.000'
2	AdventureWorks	uspGetWhereUsedProductID	@StartProductID	(15)

Figure 5 Results from the parameterization query

parameters don't represent the typical values that are supplied to the stored procedure, the performance of the stored procedure may not match expectations. See
chapter 32, "Parameter Sniffing: Your Best Friend…Except When It Isn't," for some
workarounds and more information on how this impacts performance.

Plan cache considerations

There are a number of things you should keep in mind when querying the plan cache
to avoid misinterpreting the results of your queries:

- The plan cache resides in memory. As such, when the SQL Server instance is
  restarted or the server is rebooted, all the information in the plan cache is lost.
- The contents of the plan cache change over time. Plans that are used less frequently can age out of the plan cache. If it's been a few days or weeks since a
  plan has been used, it will likely no longer be available to query. If database
  objects used by a cached plan are changed, the plans associated with them will
  be removed from the plan cache.
- Some plans won't be stored in the plan cache. For instance, plans that include
  OPTION RECOMPILE can miss the cache. Also, most zero-cost plans aren't stored
  in the plan cache.

There are a few other things to remember when writing and executing queries against
the plan cache:

- Because the compiled plans are returned in the SHOWPLAN XML format, you
  should learn XQuery to aid in writing queries against the plan cache.
- Use TRANSACTION ISOLATION LEVEL READ UNCOMMITTED when querying the
  plan cache. Doing so minimizes blocking related to queries investigating the
  plan cache.
- Test your queries against nonproduction environments before executing them
  against a production plan cache. Depending on how busy your production environment is, it may be advisable to only run plan cache queries in the test environment or during nonpeak times in production. If you use your test
  environment, be certain that a workload representative of a production workload has been run against it before starting your investigations.

These are a few of the key lessons learned and things that I've encountered while
investigating the plan cache. By keeping these items in mind, you'll find more success
and less frustration in your own investigations.

Summary

In this chapter, we looked at how you can investigate the plan cache through the use of DMOs. The examples provided in this chapter only scratch the surface of the wealth of information that DMOs can provide. The opportunities to investigate the plan cache are far and wide.

Besides the examples found in this chapter, here are some additional ways the DMOs can be used:

- Identify plans with Key Lookups to determine if columns could be included in a different index
- Search the plan cache for the use of specific functions or T-SQL
- List T-SQL statements with the highest I/O, CPU, or row estimates
- Determine plans that have implicit conversions occurring within them

When you tune queries in your environment, you often address issues one at a time. By leveraging the ways to explore the plan cache, you can address issues that may be affecting other queries similar to the ones you're already looking at. With this information, instead of tuning one query at a time, you can begin to tune one plan cache at a time.

About the author

Jason Strate, a database architect with Digineer Inc., is a DBA with more than 15 years of experience. He's a recipient of the Microsoft Most Valuable Professional (MVP) for SQL Server. His experience includes design and implementation of both OLTP and OLAP solutions, as well as assessment and implementation of SQL Server environments for best practices, performance, and high-availability solutions. Jason is a SQL Server MCITP and participated in the development of certification exams for SQL Server 2008.

34 What are you waiting for? An introduction to waits and queues

Robert Pearl

The purpose of this chapter is to help fellow DBAs, developers, and other database professionals by spreading the word about *waits and queues*. This performance-tuning methodology became significant with the release of SQL Server 2005, with all its dynamic management views and functions, collectively known as dynamic management objects (DMOs). With waits and queues, you can quickly identify the cause of a performance bottleneck on your SQL Server systems. Although this methodology was introduced without much fanfare, there wasn't a substantial amount of early adoption by those who would benefit from it the most: database administrators.

This topic is detailed and broad, so I'll focus only on the fundamental concepts as they apply to online transaction processing (OLTP) systems. My goal is to help you understand the topic so you can pursue your own independent investigation into more advanced aspects.

Introduction to total response time

In SQL Server 2000 and earlier, you had to use multiple methods to cast a wide net and set up various counters and tools to capture the underlying cause of a performance bottleneck. Traditional tools such as profiler traces, Performance Monitor (PerfMon), network sniffers, and other third-party software were also used to assist in this effort. Using these tools, you'd eventually get to the root cause of the issue, but the process was time consuming.

The biggest question then, and now, is "What are you waiting for?" What's the SQL Server engine waiting on that's causing performance to be slow? The greatest concern to end users is total response time (TRT), or total query response time.

TRT is the delay between a request and an answer. For example, when a user executes a query, essentially a request to retrieve data, TRT is the time it takes from when the user executes the query to the time the user receives the output; TRT measures the total time of an individual transaction or query.

Therefore, to accurately measure TRT, you must know what the SQL Server engine is waiting on and whether it experiences resource waits or signal waits. I'll discuss these a little later in the chapter. Essentially, if you add the resource wait time, signal wait time, and CPU time together, you get the TRT.

To optimize the TRT, you need to know about waits and queues.

What are wait stats?

Before I dive into a discussion of the waits and queues performance methodology, here's Microsoft's definition of wait statistics: "Whenever a request is made within SQL Server that—for one of many reasons—can't be immediately satisfied, the system puts it into a wait state. The SQL Server engine internally tracks the time spent waiting, aggregates it at the instance level, and retains it in memory."

So, in the simplest terms, when you run a query and SQL Server can't complete the request right away because either the CPU or some other resource is being used, your query must wait for the resource to become available. In the meantime, your query gets placed in the suspended, or resource, queue, or on the waiter list, and is assigned a wait type reflective of the resource for which the query is waiting. The question that can be answered by using wait stats is, "What's my query waiting for?" SQL Server exposes this data to DBAs, giving them the ability to track and query this data through the use of various DMOs.

Why use wait stats?

Let's look at reasons why you should use wait stats. For example, when a user calls to complain about slow performance, or your boss asks you to fix an urgent performance issue, they don't necessarily understand the time it might take to identify the cause of the problem, let alone to resolve it. Another example is when your developer colleagues are about to release code into production and suddenly find in their final testing that the application is running slowly. Whatever the scenario, perhaps the quickest way of identifying the issue is to look at wait stats first. Once you've found what a query or session is waiting on, you've successfully identified the likely bottleneck. You'll then want to set up relevant performance counters related to the resource wait in order to dig deeper.

Wait type categories

As SQL Server tracks more than four hundred wait types, I'll only discuss a handful of them in this chapter and focus on potential resource contention or bottlenecks, such as CPU pressure, I/O pressure, memory pressure, parallelism, and blocking. These few cover the most typical waits. Before I dig into the different wait types, let's discuss the four major categories of wait types:

- *Resource waits*—Occur when a worker thread requests access to a resource that's not available because it's being used by another worker. These are the most common types of waits and typically surface as locks, latches, and network and I/O wait states.

- *Signal waits*—Represents the time worker threads spend waiting for the CPU to become available to run. The worker threads are said to be in the runnable queue, where they wait until it's their turn. Because there's no specific wait type that indicates CPU pressure, you must measure the signal wait time. Signal wait time is the difference between the time the waiting thread was signaled and when it started running.

- *Queue waits*—Occur when a worker is idle, waiting for work to be assigned. This wait type is most typically seen with system background tasks, such as the deadlock monitor and ghost record cleanup tasks.

- *External waits*—Occur when a SQL Server worker is waiting for an external event, such as an extended stored procedure call or a linked server query, to finish.

The execution model

Before you jump into learning about wait states, there's one other important concept to cover: how SQL Server manages the execution of user requests using the SQL Server SQLOS execution model. To manage these requests, SQL Server uses schedulers, and each of these schedulers map to a CPU. Therefore, if the number of CPUs on the system is eight, there would be eight OS schedulers, one for each CPU. This mapping is to *logical CPU* and not to physical CPU cores or sockets. The reason why only one scheduler is created for each logical processor is to minimize context switching. Context switching occurs when the OS or the application is forced to change the executing thread on one processor to be switched out of the CPU so that another process can run. Excessive context switching can cause high CPU and I/O contention and is expensive. Once the SQLOS creates the schedulers, the total number of workers is divided among the schedulers. This keeps context switching to a minimum because the scheduler is doing the work and schedulers are bound one for one with CPUs.

The SQLOS implements what's called *thread scheduling*. In a multithreaded world, SQL Server can execute more than one thread simultaneously across multiple processors. It also implements cooperative scheduling (or nonpreemptive scheduling), where a thread yields the processor, voluntarily, to another thread when it's waiting for a system resource or non-CPU event. These voluntary yields will often show up as SOS _SCHEDULER_YIELD waits, which require further investigation to prove CPU pressure. If the current thread doesn't yield the processor within a certain amount of time, it expires, or is said to have reached its execution *quantum*. You can think of quantum as the amount of time a thread is scheduled to run. You can see the number of existing OS schedulers on your SQL Server by querying the sys.dm_os_schedulers DMV, like this:

```
SELECT COUNT(*) AS NO_OF_OS_SCHEDULERS FROM sys.dm_os_schedulers
WHERE status='VISIBLE ONLINE'
```

To best demonstrate the SQL Server execution model, I'll use an analogy by comparing it to a supermarket checkout line. For simplicity and easy visualization, let's focus

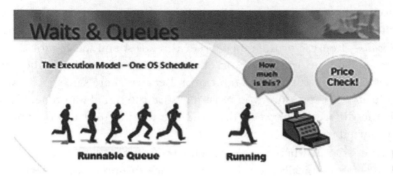

Figure 1   The execution model: running

on one OS scheduler. In figure 1, you can see what happens to a query that starts out executing on the CPU. The cashier represents the CPU, and all the folks standing in line are sessions or threads that represent the runnable queue. Each session or thread has a session ID, or SPID. The folks on this line who are waiting to be checked out are like the threads waiting for the CPU to become available. The person (or thread) that's at the front of the line about to be checked out is said to be running, or currently using the CPU. A thread using the CPU is running until it has to wait for a resource that's not available.

In our supermarket analogy, the customer is trying to purchase an item that doesn't have a price and therefore must step aside to let the next customer in line check out. The next thread moves to the front of the line of what's called the FIFO (first-in, first-out) queue; its state becomes *RUNNING* on the CPU; and if the resource is available, it continues until it needs to wait or the query execution is completed.

Meanwhile, the previous customer is now waiting for a price check, as shown in figure 2. The customer (or thread) now moves into the suspended, or resource, queue, is assigned a wait type, and is said to be on the waiter list. This is an unordered list of

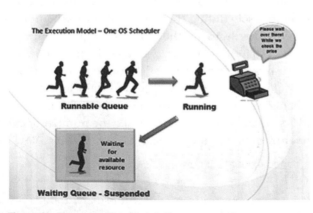

Figure 2   The execution model: the suspended queue

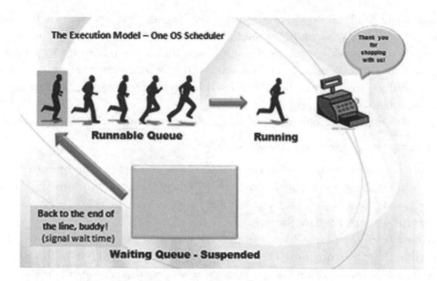

Figure 3
The execution model: the runnable queue

threads that are suspended and stay here until the needed resource becomes available. The time spent here is known as the resource wait time.

Once the resource becomes available, it's notified or signaled and moves out of the suspended queue, back to the bottom or end of the line in the runnable queue.

Higher-priority tasks will run before lower-priority tasks, as illustrated in figure 3. The time spent waiting in the runnable queue, or for the CPU to become available, is known as the signal wait time.

So, the execution model can be visualized as threads moving in a clockwise circular motion alternating between the various states from RUNNING to SUSPENDED, to RUNNABLE, to RUNNING again. This continues until the task or query is completed, as shown in figure 4. You can see the current status of a thread by querying the `sys.dm_exec_requests` DMV.

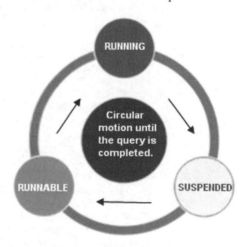

Figure 4   The query cycle

Viewing and reporting on wait statistics

To know what's happening on your server, SQL Server tracks the wait statistics, the wait types, and the wait times, and exposes this useful data to the user in the following DMOs:

- `sys.dm_os_wait_stats`
- `sys.dm_os_waiting_tasks`
- `sys.dm_exec_requests`

The main DMO you'll use to view wait stats is sys.dm_os_wait_stats, which shows the time for waits that have already completed. Within this DMO, you'll see the wait type, the number of waits for each type, the total wait time, the maximum wait time, and the signal wait time. Wait stats are presented at the instance level and aggregated across all session IDs since the SQL Server was last restarted or since the last time that the wait statistics were cleared.

The way to manually clear the wait stat data is by running the following command:

```
DBCC SQLPerf("sys.dm_os_wait_stats",CLEAR).
```

You should run this command only once in your test and development environments, or when you're trying to establish a baseline for performance monitoring. Although sys.dm_os_wait_stats provides you with the aggregated historical data, it doesn't show current sessions that are waiting.

To view current suspended sessions that are waiting to see what SQL Server is waiting on "right now," you must use the sys.dm_os_waiting_tasks DMO. This one shows you the actual waiter list of all waiting sessions as well as the reasons for the waits, and it filters out all other nonwaiting sessions. You can also see blocking and all the sessions involved. This DMO returns a lot of information, but the query in listing 1 shows the most important columns.

Listing 1   What's happening now: querying the sys.dm_os_waiting_tasks DMO

```
SELECT dm_ws.session_ID,
dm_ws.wait_type,
UPPER(dm_es.status) As status,
dm_ws.wait_duration_ms,
dm_t.TEXT,
dm_es.cpu_time,
dm_es.memory_usage,
dm_es.logical_reads,
dm_es.total_elapsed_time,
dm_ws.blocking_session_id,
dm_es.program_name,
DB_NAME(dm_r.database_id) DatabaseName
FROM sys.dm_os_waiting_tasks dm_ws
INNER JOIN sys.dm_exec_requests dm_r ON dm_ws.session_id = dm_r.session_id
INNER JOIN sys.dm_exec_sessions dm_es ON dm_es.session_id = dm_r.session_id
CROSS APPLY sys.dm_exec_sql_text (dm_r.sql_handle) dm_t
WHERE dm_es.is_user_process = 1
```

Finally, you can view all the current activity (e.g., active sessions) on the server by using sys.dm_exec_requests. Each SQL Server session has a unique session_id, and you can filter out user queries by specifying session_id > 50 in the WHERE clause.

Calculating wait time: signal waits vs. resource waits

Because there's no specific wait type to indicate CPU pressure, you measure this by looking at the signal wait time, which is stored in the signal_wait_time_ms column of the primary wait stat DMO, sys.dm_os_wait_stats.

The overall wait time reflects the time that elapses when a thread leaves the RUNNING state, goes to the SUSPENDED state, and returns to the RUNNING state again. Therefore, you can capture and derive the resource wait time by subtracting the signal wait time from the overall wait time. You can use the simple query shown in listing 2 to get the resource, signal, and total wait time. You also want to order by total wait time descending, to force the highest wait times to the top of the results.

Listing 2 Querying the `sys.dm_os_wait_stats` DMV to calculate wait times

```
Select wait_type, waiting_tasks_count, wait_time_ms as total_wait_time_ms,
signal_wait_time_ms,
(wait_time_ms-signal_wait_time_ms) as resource_wait_time_ms
FROM sys.dm_os_wait_stats
ORDER BY total_wait_time_ms DESC
```

Before we continue our discussion, you must understand that the nature of a healthy OLTP system is such that there will always be a runnable queue and a waiting queue for resources. This is how the SQL Server scheduling system is intended to work. A real issue might surface when the individual wait times are high, indicating a bottleneck; whether it's I/O, memory, disk, network, or CPU. Although the length of a queue may indicate a busy system, it's not the queue length that will cause a performance issue, but how fast the queue gets processed.

So there will always be waits on an OLTP system, but that doesn't necessarily indicate a problem. Just because you see that 85 percent of your waits are PAGEIOLATCH_X waits, for example, doesn't immediately imply a performance issue. What users want to be concerned with are recurring waits where the total wait time is greater than some number— for example, >30 seconds. In addition, as shown in the script in listing 3, there are certain system and background process wait types that can be excluded from your analysis.

Listing 3 is a query (written by Glenn Berry) that utilizes the sys.dm_os_wait_stats DMO . The query gets the top waits on the server by percentage and converts wait time to seconds. You can set the percentage threshold and thus eliminate nonimportant wait types.

Listing 3 Isolating top waits for server instance by percentage

```
WITH Waits AS
(SELECT wait_type, wait_time_ms / 1000. AS wait_time_s,
100. * wait_time_ms / SUM(wait_time_ms) OVER() AS pct,
ROW_NUMBER() OVER(ORDER BY wait_time_ms DESC) AS rn
```

```
FROM sys.dm_os_wait_stats
WHERE wait_type NOT IN
('CLR_SEMAPHORE','LAZYWRITER_SLEEP','RESOURCE_QUEUE',
'SLEEP_TASK','SLEEP_SYSTEMTASK','SQLTRACE_BUFFER_FLUSH',
'WAITFOR','LOGMGR_QUEUE','CHECKPOINT_QUEUE',
'REQUEST_FOR_DEADLOCK_SEARCH','XE_TIMER_EVENT',
'BROKER_TO_FLUSH','BROKER_TASK_STOP','CLR_MANUAL_EVENT',
'CLR_AUTO_EVENT','DISPATCHER_QUEUE_SEMAPHORE',
'FT_IFTS_SCHEDULER_IDLE_WAIT','XE_DISPATCHER_WAIT',
'XE_DISPATCHER_JOIN', 'SQLTRACE_INCREMENTAL_FLUSH_SLEEP'))
SELECT W1.wait_type,
CAST(W1.wait_time_s AS DECIMAL(12, 2)) AS wait_time_s,
CAST(W1.pct AS DECIMAL(12, 2)) AS pct,
CAST(SUM(W2.pct) AS DECIMAL(12, 2)) AS running_pct
FROM Waits AS W1 INNER JOIN Waits AS W2 ON W2.rn <= W1.rn
GROUP BY W1.rn, W1.wait_type, W1.wait_time_s, W1.pct
HAVING SUM(W2.pct) - W1.pct < 99 OPTION (RECOMPILE) -- percentage threshold
```

You can also compare the signal waits vs. resource waits on the SQL Server system with the following script:

```
Select signalWaitTimeMs=sum(signal_wait_time_ms),
'%signal waits' =
cast(100.0 * sum(signal_wait_time_ms)
     / sum (wait_time_ms) as numeric(20,2))
  ,resourceWaitTimeMs=sum(wait_time_ms - signal_wait_time_ms),
'%resource waits'=
cast(100.0 * sum(wait_time_ms - signal_wait_time_ms)
     / sum (wait_time_ms) as numeric(20,2))
from sys.dm_os_wait_stats
```

Figure 5 shows the output for this query. You can see the highlighted percentages for signal waits as compared to resource waits. You also see the cumulative wait times, respectively. Remember, these are the cumulative wait times since SQL Server was last restarted or statistics cleared. The useful information you must interpret are the percentages.

So what does the output in figure 5 tell you? Here you're measuring the resource waits—all the threads that are put into a suspended queue—and the signal waits—the time waiting for the threads to run on the CPU. Although the percentage of resource waits is significantly higher than the percentage of signal waits, this shouldn't be misinterpreted as a problem. In fact, that's exactly what you want to see. But if the

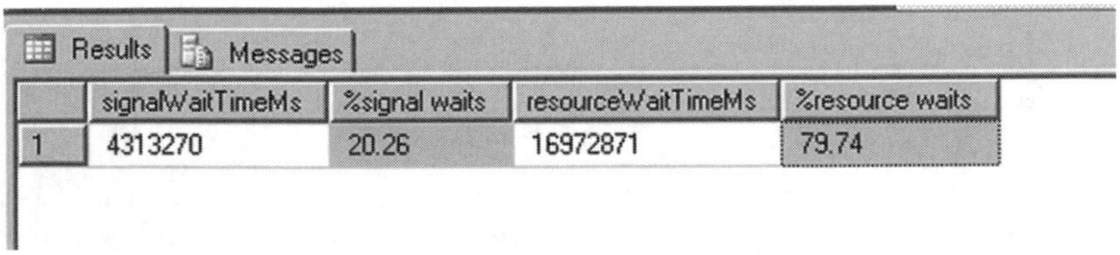

	signalWaitTimeMs	%signal waits	resourceWaitTimeMs	%resource waits
1	4313270	20.26	16972871	79.74

Figure 5   Query results of signal vs. resource waits

percentage is much higher on the signal waits, then you know the CPU itself is the bottleneck. It could indicate that there are too few or not fast enough cores to keep up with a given workload.

At this point, you can consider more or faster CPUs to keep up with the requests. You also can take a look at your indexing strategy to avoid unneeded sorts, order by, and group by options in your queries. You also want to reduce the number of excessive joins and compilations that force the query to utilize more CPU.

So, in sum, to understand the output of this simple query you want to see more resource waits than signal waits. Thus the output shows you all the resource waits versus signal waits as a percentage of the overall wait time.

Correlating performance data: putting it together

Thus far, we've discussed the waits side of the equation, and now it's time to demonstrate how you can interpret the data and determine which performance counters and other DMOs you can use to further investigate and isolate the cause of performance bottlenecks.

Let's focus on the following areas of possible contention, their associated wait types, what they mean, as well as the next steps in performance troubleshooting. After this final section, you'll have a basic picture of this methodology called waits and queues.

General I/O issues

Let's take two common wait types called `ASYNC_IO_COMPLETION` and `IO_COMPLETION`. These tasks are both waiting for I/O to finish. These generally represent non–data page I/O. Frequent and consistent occurrence of these wait types likely indicate a bottleneck with the I/O subsystem, and you can set up specific PerfMon physical disk counters for further analysis, such as Disk sec/read and Disk sec/write.

Possible actions to take include adding additional I/O bandwidth and balancing I/O across other drives. You can also reduce I/O with proper indexing, thus reducing the number of joins and fixing bad queries.

Buffer I/O latch issues

Requests that are currently blocked pending the completion of a physical disk I/O can surface as `PAGEIOLATCH_X` waits. Latches are lightweight internal structures used to synchronize access to buffer pages. Page I/O latches such as these are used for disk-to-memory transfers. After a data page is modified in memory, it must be written to disk. Before writing the data page to disk, SQL Server latches it to prevent further modifications. Once the page is successfully written to disk, the latch is released. When the percentage of these waits is high, it can indicate disk subsystem issues but possibly memory issues as well. PerfMon counters to look at are Page Life Expectancy, Page Lookups/sec, Page Reads/sec, and Full Scans/sec.

Another handy DMO to look at is `sys.dm_io_virtual_file_stats`, which returns I/O statistics for data and log files. You can look for I/O stalls, as well as view the I/O usage by database, file, or drive. This will give you the opportunity to move files on one physical array to other physical arrays by determining which files have the highest I/O.

Blocking and locking

With respect to blocking and locking, you'd typically see various LCK_M_* wait types that indicate blocking issues, or sessions waiting for a lock to be granted. Blocking occurs when one SQL Server session puts a lock on one or more records, whereas the second session requires a conflicting lock type on the record(s) locked by the first session. The second session will wait indefinitely until the first releases, causing a blocking chain that can significantly affect performance. It could also be a lock escalation issue, or increased memory pressure that causes increased I/O. The greater I/O can cause locks to be held longer and transaction time to go up, as well. Transaction duration should be as short as possible. You can see more information about currently active lock manager resources in the sys.dm_tran_locks DMO, and whether a lock has been granted or is waiting to be granted. You can set up the Lock wait time (ms) PerfMon counter, and check the isolation level for shared locks.

CPU pressure

You already know that you can see a pretty good indication of CPU pressure on the system when the percentage of signal waits is above 30 percent. Another sign of a stressed CPU is a large recurring number of SOS_SCHEDULER_YIELD waits. This means that a thread voluntarily yields CPU to another thread. This behavior is normal, but excessive yields increase pressure on the CPU. Furthermore, you can see if the SQL Server schedulers are waiting on CPU, wherein if the runnable_task_counts is >0, by querying sys.dm_os_schedulers:

```
SELECT scheduler_id, current_tasks_count, runnable_tasks_count
    FROM sys.dm_os_schedulers
    WHERE scheduler_id < 255 AND runnable_tasks_count >0
```

The traditional PerfMon counters to view are Processor: % Processor Time, System: Processor Queue Length, and System: Context Switches/sec.

Parallelism

Another common wait type is CXPACKET, and I often see DBAs jump to the wrong conclusion about this one. Although it indicates parallelism, it doesn't mean you should automatically change your instance-level configuration MAXDOP setting to 1, effectively turning off parallelism. As multiple threads are created for a single query, not all threads are given the same amount of work to do, thus causing one or more to lag behind and producing CXPACKET waits affecting the overall throughput. Missing indexes must be identified, because they could cause the query optimizer to use a parallel plan to compensate for the missing index. So, first try correcting any index problems to avoid large table scans, and ensure statistics are up-to-date to prevent a bad query plan. At that point, you might want to play with the MAXDOP setting, perhaps first experimenting with hints with the offending queries before you change it at the instance level. Another trick you can use is changing the Cost Threshold for Parallelism option to a higher value, reducing the number of queries running under parallelism but still allowing more expensive queries to utilize parallelism.

Memory pressure

A memory grant is memory used to store temporary rows for sort and hash join operations. The life of a memory grant is equal to that of the query. Because it's desirable that a query run in memory, the lack of available memory will force a query to use disk. This is due to pressure on memory resources and affects query performance. The Resource Semaphore is responsible for satisfying memory grant requests while keeping overall memory grant usages within the server limit. Only if there's enough free memory available does the Resource Semaphore allow a query to reserve memory. If query memory can't be granted immediately, the requesting query is forced to wait in a queue and is assigned the Resource Semaphore wait type. You can confirm this by setting up these PerfMon counters: Memory Grants Pending and Memory Grants Outstanding.

If you want to find all queries waiting in the memory queue or know which queries are using the most memory grants, you can run DMO queries. This query will display those waiting in the memory queue for memory grants:

```
SELECT * FROM sys.dm_exec_query_memory_grants where grant_time is null
```

Next, you can find which queries are using the most memory grants:

```
SELECT mg.granted_memory_kb, mg.session_id, t.text, qp.query_plan
FROM sys.dm_exec_query_memory_grants AS mg
CROSS APPLY sys.dm_exec_sql_text(mg.sql_handle) AS t
CROSS APPLY sys.dm_exec_query_plan(mg.plan_handle) AS qp
ORDER BY 1 DESC OPTION (MAXDOP 1)
```

Summary

This chapter has provided a brief introduction to waits and queues. We focused on the analysis of wait statistics as a streamlined way to quickly identify the root cause of a performance bottleneck by highlighting why queries are waiting and performing suboptimally. You also learned how to correlate the data with other traditional performance measures and counters. I described some of the common wait types indicative of I/O, memory, CPU, parallelism, and locking. We explored only a small portion of the wait types that exist in SQL Server. As always, performance tuning is more art than science. The next time your queries are performing slowly and your users are hovering by your desk, remember to look at wait stats first.

About the author

Robert Pearl is president of Pearl Knowledge Solutions, Inc., and a SQL MVP. He's a senior DBA with more than 12 years of experience in Microsoft SQL technology. Robert has developed SQLCentric, a web-based database monitoring and alert system, with the DBA in mind. This system won Best Performance and Database Monitoring in *SQL Server Magazine*'s Reader's Choice in 2004, and the Silver Award in the Community Choice Awards in 2010. Robert also participates in online forums, contributes articles to SQLServerCentral.com as well as other sites and publications, and covers local events in the New York City area. He blogs at www.sqlservercentral.com/blogs/pearlknows/default.aspx. For more information, visit www.pearlknows.com.

35 You see sets, and I see loops

Linchi Shea

Within the SQL Server community, the predominant view on writing T-SQL for performance is that you should think in sets instead of procedures. In addition, it follows that you should focus on what result you want in terms of the set operations, and let SQL Server figure out how to get the result under the hood. This view has served the community well, especially when developers versed in indexed sequential access method (ISAM)-style databases, such as Microsoft Access, migrate to SQL Server and carry with them the habit of interacting with databases on a row-by-row basis. The set-oriented approach is an effective counter measure to minimize the potential damage to SQL Server performance by the ISAM-style interaction.

That was then, and this is now. The SQL Server community has been thoroughly educated in the set-oriented approach. In fact, having become comfortable in expressing complex logic in the set-based SQL constructs, some SQL developers may have carried the set orientation, as wise and sound as it is, to the extreme and gone overboard. For the past few years, I've seen increasing evidence, in real-world applications, of the performance damage done by overzealous application of the set-oriented approach, the symptom of which is often overly complicated SQL queries.

In this chapter, I highlight a different perspective on T-SQL performance tuning that pays explicit attention to loops around your T-SQL code, in your T-SQL code, and under the hood, below your T-SQL code. Looking at T-SQL performance from a loop perspective complements the set-oriented approach and may help prevent its abuse.

What loops?

In the broadest sense, loops are one of the most fundamental constructs in computing. All computer programs, including SQL Server and the T-SQL queries you write, are made up of layers upon layers of loops, and performance tuning of any computer program fundamentally boils down to optimizing these loops.

At the lowest level, a program is no more than a loop of a small set of simple operations, such as fetching data or instructions from memory, doing arithmetic operations, and putting data back in to memory. At many layers higher, you can view an OS application as loops of API calls into the operating system. Loops at these layers are, of course, too remote from a T-SQL developer to be of little practical concern.

So what loops are practically relevant to writing or tuning T-SQL queries for optimal performance?

The most obvious loops in T-SQL code are those written by a developer or a DBA. Who hasn't written a WHILE loop through a collection of servers, databases, tables, or more generically, a result set of rows? Who hasn't written code to iterate through an explicitly declared T-SQL cursor? Your set-oriented instinct may urge you to stay away from these procedural constructs, but these explicit loops may be the right solutions for problem scenarios that are procedural in nature. For instance, there's no strictly set-oriented solution for changing the owners to SA for all the user databases on all your production SQL Server instances. You must explicitly loop through the SQL Server instances and all the databases on each instance.

More interesting loops are those implicit in perfectly set-oriented queries. Processing any nontrivial T-SQL query eventually translates into loops around the lower-level SQL Server constructs, such as disk I/Os, database pages, and cached rows. The more complex your query is, the more prominent the loops are in processing the query. If you look at the execution plan of a query, it consists of various query processing operators, many of which are essentially loops around one or more input streams of rows, and they only differ in what they do in the loops.

For instance, the Compute Scalar operator may look harmlessly simple. It's nonetheless a loop on the input rows, repeatedly calling the same scalar function. If that scalar function is heavy in computing resource consumption and the input rows are numerous, the loop can hurt your database performance. T-SQL joins are always executed in loops over the participating streams of rows regardless of whether they're processed with a hash match, a merge join, or a plain old nested loop.

A recursive common table expression (CTE) is inherently an iteration of—or a loop of—joins whether or not you may consider it a set-oriented construct. It's difficult, if not impossible, to understand the behavior of a recursive CTE query strictly from a declarative perspective without seeing the iterations or the loops in how it works.

You can also find loops inside an application or in a job, and from within these loops calls are made to T-SQL constructs such as stored procedures, ad hoc queries, and functions. It becomes deceiving as you concentrate on a piece of simple T-SQL code and consider the code to be sufficiently optimized, not knowing that the T-SQL code is called by a tight loop in an application.

The loop perspective

Now that you see that there are explicit loops and implicit loops in T-SQL, that there are loops in processing set-oriented T-SQL queries, and that there may be loops wrapping around T-SQL in applications or scheduled jobs, where does it lead you, and does it add any value to tuning T-SQL performance?

Yes, indeed. It leads you to a performance-tuning perspective that can yield significant targets for your troubleshooting efforts. From a loop perspective, all T-SQL performance problems are loop problems, and potentially problematic loops generally fall into one of these four categories:

- *Superfluous loops*—Your code contains loops that do no useful work but consume significant computing resources. Superfluous loops can creep into your code in numerous ways. Perhaps they're originally introduced to meet a specification that's no longer required. Perhaps they're included to retrieve a piece of data that's no longer needed. Superfluous loops can also be introduced by the SQL Server query processor through a bad query plan.
- *Superfluous iterations*—The loops in your code are necessary, but some of their iterations may not perform any useful work. A frequent example is to loop through all the rows in a table only to find the majority of them not meeting any of the conditions further checked inside the loop.
- *Expensive iterations*—The loops in your code are necessary for the requirement, but each iteration does more work than necessary. One of the most common examples is to place a significant piece of work inside a loop when the work can be done outside the loop. The adverse impact can be dramatic when there are multiple layers of loops and the work is placed in an inner loop.
- *Loop parallelism*—Your code includes serial loops that should be performed in parallel, or your code includes parallel loops that should be performed in sequence.

The next time you embark on a T-SQL performance-tuning task, try to look for loops that may fall into these four categories. Although not a full-blown performance-tuning methodology, some general guidelines have proven to be useful in seeking out problematic loops:

- Explicitly identify the loops in your code, the loops that implement/execute your code under the hood, and the loops that call your code.
- Focus on the expensive loops. These are the loops with a significant number of iterations or that do significant work, in terms of resource consumption and in each iteration of the loop.
- Identify and eliminate superfluous loops or superfluous iterations in a loop. You may be surprised with how often you can find useless loops that drag down your database performance.
- Squeeze the fat out of the loops. Keep the loops lean by moving as much work out of loops or moving work from inner loops to an outer loop, and looking for opportunities to eliminate unnecessary work from inside a loop altogether, if possible.
- Merge multiple loops into a single loop. When looping itself is significantly expensive as compared to the work done inside the loop, try to find if the work done in one loop can get a free ride in another loop, thus eliminating one loop.

- Parallelize independent loops if the goal is to finish the work as fast as possible and if there's additional processing capacity. Serialize loops if the goal is to reduce the load on the system so that there's processing capacity for other processes.

The most important first step is to consciously seek out loops that are adversely impacting your T-SQL performance. Once they're in sight, the steps to systematically analyze and optimize them follow naturally.

Let's now turn to specific examples to help flesh out this perspective and demonstrate its application. These examples come from real-world database applications and firsthand experience in tuning their performance through analyzing potentially problematic loops.

Loops in a query execution plan

A SQL Server query plan is a tree of logical and physical operators. To examine the loops in executing a query, you may want to focus more on the physical operators that implement their corresponding logical operations, such as joins and unions. Most of the more expensive physical operators involve looping through input rows in some fashion to execute their algorithms. Nothing evil here! But what you may want to look for in an execution plan is excessively large loops around a physical operator (as opposed to merely the number of rows an operator touches).

Let's look at a concrete example. To set it up, run the script in listing 1 to populate a test table with one million rows.

> **Listing 1   Creating a test table and populating it with a million rows**

```
CREATE TABLE test (i INT, j INT, filler CHAR(2000))
go
WITH tmp(i, j, filler) AS (
    SELECT CAST(1 AS INT), CAST(1 AS INT), 'abc'
    UNION ALL
    SELECT i + 1, j+1, filler
      FROM tmp
     WHERE i < 1000000
)
INSERT test
SELECT * FROM tmp
OPTION (maxrecursion 0)
go
CREATE CLUSTERED INDEX cix_test ON test(i)
CREATE INDEX ix_test ON test(j)
go
```

Then, run the script in listing 2 to get the average length of the filler column. This is to force a table scan (i.e., clustered index scan) through the test table because the filler column isn't indexed.

Listing 2 Scanning the test table with the clustered index

```
DBCC DROPCLEANBUFFERS
go
SET STATISTICS PROFILE ON
SET STATISTICS IO ON
go
SELECT AVG(LEN(filler)) FROM test
OPTION(MAXDOP 1)
go
SET STATISTICS PROFILE OFF
SET STATISTICS IO OFF
go
```

For comparison, run the script in listing 3. This time, use an index hint to force SQL Server to use the nonclustered index.

Listing 3 Scanning the test table with the nonclustered index

```
DBCC DROPCLEANBUFFERS
go
SET STATISTICS PROFILE ON
SET STATISTICS IO ON
go
SELECT AVG(LEN(filler)) FROM test WITH (INDEX=ix_test)
OPTION(MAXDOP 1)
go
SET STATISTICS PROFILE OFF
SET STATISTICS IO OFF
go
```

Table 1 shows the partial query execution plan produced by SET STATISTICS PROFILE ON in listing 2.

Table 1 Partial query plan from SET STATISTICS PROFILE ON in listing 2

Rows	Executes	StmtText
1	1	|--Stream Aggregate(DEFINE:([Expr1011]=COUNT_BIG(
0	0	|--Compute Scalar(DEFINE:([Expr1005]=len([db].[
1000000	1	|--Clustered Index Scan(OBJECT:([db].[dbo].[test

Table 2 shows the partial query execution plan produced by SET STATISTICS PROFILE ON in listing 3.

Table 2   Partial query plan from SET STATISTICS PROFILE ON in listing 3

Rows	Executes	StmtText
1000000	1	`|--Nested Loops(Inner Join, OUTER REFERENCES:([Uniq1002]`
1000000	1	`     |--Compute Scalar(DEFINE:([Expr1005]=len([db].[`
1000000	1000000	`          |--Clustered Index Seek(OBJECT:([db].[dbo].[test`

Pay attention to the values under the column Executes in the last row of both table 1 and table 2. The value in the Executes column is the number of times the corresponding operator, shown in the StmtText column, is called in a loop.

With the script in listing 2, the clustered index scan operator is called once to scan all one million rows in the test table. With the script in listing 3, the clustered index seek operator is called repeatedly one million times to scan the same one million rows. Generally speaking, calling a clustered index scan operator is significantly more expensive than calling a clustered index seek operator on the same table if the number of rows you're looking for is small. But when the clustered index seek operator is called a million times in a loop, it becomes much more expensive than scanning through the table once.

In fact, on the test server that produced the results in table 1 and table 2, the script in listing 2 returned in 8 seconds with 250,498 logical reads and 13 physical reads, whereas the script in listing 3 returned in 53 seconds with 3,214,040 logical reads and 28,876 physical reads. In terms of the response time, listing 3 was almost seven times as expensive as listing 2. Keep in mind that many factors can influence the result of a database performance test. If you run the scripts in listing 2 and listing 3, you can expect to see wide variations in their performance difference. But in most environments the script in listing 2 should consistently and significantly outperform the script in listing 3.

Loops in complex queries

The SQL Server optimizer isn't infallible and will never be. In fact, it's not rare that the optimizer gets the query plan wrong. And when that happens, you often see a loop problem in one of the four categories identified previously. An interesting case is when a query references complex and heavily layered views.

Many database developers find views a convenient abstraction and freely write queries with views layered on top of other views. The top-level query may appear to be deceivingly simple, and that's the main attraction because the complexity is hidden. But these queries are dangerous and can easily end up with wildly inefficient query plans.

When it comes to views, it's absolutely critical to remember that SQL Server doesn't automatically materialize any of the nested views during the query optimization process or the query execution process. In fact, the optimizer doesn't see the views in a query, and by the time it starts optimizing the query, the optimizer sees only the underlying tables from the view definitions. Because the complexity isn't hidden to the optimizer, and the complexity makes it difficult to estimate the cardinalities of intermediate results reliably, the chance for the optimizer to arrive at an incorrect plan becomes significant.

Fortunately, in real-world applications, the result of such a complex query often remains valid if you yank out an inner view, force it to materialize once into a temporary table (or even a table variable), and use the temporary table in place of the view in the query. This strategy is one stone killing two birds—first, it simplifies the query and therefore significantly improves the probability of the optimizer getting a correct plan, and second it can cut down the number of loops that may otherwise be present when the view is referenced in multiple places in the query.

The next time you run into performance problems with nested views, give this strategy a try. It may not always produce further optimization. But if past success is any indication, odds are good that your query performance and, more importantly, the stability of its query plan will both improve. To the user of an application, the stability of application performance is far more important than whether the queries are set oriented or to what extent they're set oriented.

User-defined scalar functions in implicit loops

Look at the following query fragment:

```
SELECT fsFuture(t1.PositionID), fsSwap(t2.PositionID), …
  FROM Positions t1 JOIN SecurityInfo t2 ON …
 WHERE …
```

Note that two user-defined functions, fsFuture() and fsSwap(), are applied to the two columns in the result set. The query may run fine, but there's a potentially expensive loop around the two user-defined functions, and the number of iterations is the number of rows in the returned result set because each user-defined function will be called once for every row in the result set. Clearly, that's a loop, albeit implicit.

Assume that the query returns 20,000 rows in 2 seconds and each call to either function takes 5 microseconds. The total amount of time to finish the loop on these two functions would be 200 milliseconds. In this case, the cost of looping through the functions is about 10 percent of the total query processing time.

Now if each call to the functions takes 100 microseconds instead of 5 microseconds, the loop with 40,000 iterations (20,000 for each function) would multiply the relatively small individual increment and return the query in about 6 seconds instead of 2 seconds, which may become unacceptable to the application.

Why should you be concerned that the function calls may go from 5 microseconds to 100 microseconds? This can easily happen when you make a change to the function or the tables used in the function are modified or grow larger. In addition, the function call can suddenly become more expensive when you start a trace to track the Statement Started or Statement Completed events in SQL Profiler.

Be aware of the multiplier effect of loops!

Merging multiple loops into one

In batch processes, such as when you archive or purge data weekly or monthly, you may not be able to avoid looping through large tables. It can be explicit loops using the T-SQL WHILE statement block, or it can be implicit in the form of multiple SQL queries, each of which scans through the tables.

I worked on a T-SQL script whose purpose was to prepare transaction data for purging and archiving. The script had multiple loops. The first one was to scan a large transaction table and apply logic to identify transactions eligible for archiving. Another loop went through the result from the first loop and applied more business logic and join operations to further filter out transactions that shouldn't be purged. And finally, a third loop was applied to group the identified transactions into batches, each of which was purged/archived as a transaction unit. The script would run for more than four hours from beginning to end.

The question was, "Can we apply all the logic once by scanning through the large transaction in one pass instead of three times?" It turned out that this was easily doable. For instance, grouping the transaction data into smaller batches was modified to use a simple math operation with the help of the T-SQL RANK() function during the first loop. The marginal cost of applying additional logic to data already cached was infinitesimally small compared to the cost of doing another scan through a large table. In the end, the work previously done in the second and the third loops got a free ride in the first loop. With three loops collapsed into one and some additional optimization, the script now completes in less than 15 minutes.

Parallelizing loops

Opportunities for parallelizing T-SQL loops abound in real-world applications. I worked on an application that required counting the number of rows in 140 tables scattered on four servers. The T-SQL stored procedure that did the row counting took more than seven hours to finish. The stored procedure was straightforward. It had a loop through the four servers, accessing them via linked servers, and on each server it looped through all the tables, counting each in turn. The total time for counting all the tables was the sum of counting each table. The problem was that the application couldn't wait that long for the row count to finish.

Because all the tables must be counted to ensure the integrity of the business process, there was no opportunity to slim down any of the loops. But note that it was completely independent work to count these tables. In other words, counting table B didn't have to wait until counting table A had finished. There was no dependency whatsoever.

That observation resulted in converting the T-SQL stored procedure into a C# program that counts each table in a separate thread. The C# program spawns 140 threads to count the 140 tables concurrently, and finishes in about 10 minutes, which is the time it takes to count the largest table.

Currently, although SQL Server supports intra-query parallelism, it doesn't have any feature for the user to mark a piece of T-SQL code as a unit for parallel execution. You must resort to an external language, such as C#, that supports multiple threading to parallelize a T-SQL script.

Linked server calls in a loop

The following query performs a distributed join between a local table TableA and table TableB on another SQL Server instance NYSQL02 via a linked server:

```
-- the local instance is named NYSQL01
SELECT a.C1, b.C2, b.C3
  FROM TableA a
       JOIN NYSQL02.myDB.dbo.TableB b ON a.C1 = b.C1
 WHERE a.C3 = 'XYZ'
   AND b.C2 like 'abc%'
```

In evaluating this query, note that it's much more expensive to access data on a remote server than it is on the same instance locally. In addition, depending on how SQL Server decides to process the query, you may or may not see a loop doing round-trips to retrieve data from TableB on NYSQL02. Furthermore, doing round-trips to NYSQL02 isn't necessarily inefficient. If the columns are highly selective, doing round-trips to NYSQL02 can be an efficient execution plan.

The danger with distributed queries is that the optimizer on NYSQL01 may not have the correct statistics from NYSQL02 and can end up choosing to process the linked server call in an expensive loop. If you know the data distribution, you can build that knowledge into the query to prevent the optimizer from making a costly mistake. For instance, if you know that column C2 on TableB is by itself highly selective, you could try to rewrite the query as follows:

```
-- the local instance is named NYSQL01
SELECT a.C1, b.C2, b.C3
  FROM TableA a JOIN OPENQUERY(NYSQL02,
          'SELECT C1,C2,C3 FROM TableB
             WHERE C2 like ''abc%''') b
       ON a.C1 = b.C1
 WHERE a.C3 = 'XYZ'
```

This retrieves all the qualifying rows from NYSQL02 in one fell swoop. It may not lead to the most efficient plan (for instance, when the additional condition on column C1 results in even more selective data), but it completely eliminates any chance of an expensive loop around the linked server calls, thus giving you stability in performance.

Being conscious of the potential loops around the linked server calls and their cost factors can help you in deciding whether to rewrite or how to rewrite the original query for better and/or more stable performance.

Squeezing the fat out of loops with a slim table

One effective way to speed up a loop is to look for ways to reduce the amount of data you carry through the loop. Some of the data may be excess fat that can be trimmed.

I once reviewed a T-SQL script with an explicit loop that executes multiple SQL statements in each iteration. What caught my attention was this large and wide table that was scanned multiple times inside the loop. The table was more than 90 GB in size and couldn't be all cached in memory, resulting in significant disk I/O activities. Even if all 90 GB could be cached, looking through this much data multiple times would still be expensive.

Upon further examination, it was clear that only a small subset of the integer columns of this table were used by the script. A temporary and much slimmer table was created and populated before the loop with data from the selected integer columns. Inside the loop, all references to the large fat table were replaced with references to this slim table, which was about 1.5 GB in size and was all cached by the time the loop started. Although there was an initial onetime cost of scanning the large table to populate the slim table, the end result was that the script ran twice as fast.

So be on the lookout for excess in loops, and try to cut it down as much as you can!

Summary

Looking at T-SQL performance from a loop perspective and thinking in sets aren't mutually exclusive. Continue to think in sets, but also go beyond thinking in sets and look at performance from multiple perspectives. Seeking out loops that are a significant time and resource contributor in your T-SQL code gives you an alternative perspective in practical T-SQL performance tuning. Seeing loops may uncover problems that aren't obviously exposed in the set operations and may reveal targets to help effectively focus your performance-tuning efforts.

About the author

Linchi Shea has been working with SQL Server since it was distributed on floppy disks. He enjoys database performance tuning and is interested in building robust SQL Server infrastructure in an enterprise environment. Linchi lives in New Jersey and currently works in the financial services industry in the New York City area. You can find him speaking at various user group meetings and conferences, and blogging at sqlblog.com.

36 Performance-tuning the transaction log for OLTP workloads

Brad M. McGehee

SQL Server can experience various types of bottlenecks that can negatively affect its performance. In this chapter, I'll focus on a specific and often overlooked bottleneck: the transaction log. I'll briefly describe how the transaction log works, the factors that can contribute to it being a bottleneck, how to determine if you have a transaction log bottleneck, and best practices you can employ to help prevent future bottlenecks or to correct existing bottlenecks.

How can the transaction log be a bottleneck?

To understand how the transaction log can become a bottleneck for SQL Server, let's first take a brief look at how the transaction log works. The following example has been simplified to make it easy for you to understand. In the real world, what happens is a lot messier, but the principles remain the same.

1 Let's assume that a) an application wants to insert a single row into a table and calls a stored procedure wrapped within an explicit transaction to perform the task, b) the stored procedure is the only code in the batch that's being submitted to SQL Server from the application, and c) there are no other transactions going on at the same time.

2 As the transaction begins, the first thing that happens is that a BeginTran log record is written to the log cache. The log cache is a place in memory where SQL Server temporarily stores log records before they're written to the transaction log file. Transaction log data is cached instead of being immediately written to disk, in order to bunch disk writes together so they can be written to disk more efficiently.

3   Let's also assume that the page where the row needs to be inserted isn't in the data cache but is stored on disk. Consequently, SQL Server will have to read in the appropriate page from disk into the data cache.

4   Once the page is in the data cache, the required locks are acquired and the page is latched. Locking is required to maintain the transactional integrity of the data, whereas the latch is used to maintain the physical integrity of the data.

5   SQL Server then creates an Insert log record, which is then added to the log cache.

6   The new row is then added to the data page stored in the data cache and the page is marked as being dirty.

7   The latch that was acquired for the INSERT is now released.

8   Now that the row has been inserted, a Commit log record is created, and all of the log records associated with the transaction are now flushed (written) to the transaction log file from the log cache. It's only at this point the transaction is complete. This process is known as *write-ahead logging*. In other words, all data modifications must first be made to the transaction log before they're written to the data file. Because of write-ahead logging, should the SQL Server fail before the dirty data page is written back to the data file, the transaction can be rolled forward during the recovery process when SQL Server is restarted.

9   Now that the transaction is complete, transactional locks are released and the batch is now considered complete, and the client is notified that the batch completed successfully.

So how does this example explain how a transaction log can become a bottleneck? Instead of just one row being inserted, let's assume that tens of thousands of rows per second are being modified in a database from hundreds of simultaneous transactions. This means that all the log records for every data modification have to be written to the log file. If the I/O subsystem isn't up to the task, transactions will have to wait before their log records can be written to the transaction log file, keeping them open longer than necessary and starting a potential chain of events (extra wait states, blocking, and so forth) that result in a bottleneck that can further hurt the performance of the server.

Factors that contribute to transaction log bottlenecks

Although the previous example was simple and illustrates the potential for the transaction log becoming a SQL Server bottleneck, a production server is much more complex. Although I think most DBAs understand that all data modifications in a database are logged, many DBAs don't fully appreciate what this means. For example, for every data modification the following activity can occur, which also needs to be logged, further straining transaction log resources.

- If your tables have indexes (including indexed views), every time a row is modified, then all the related indexes have to be modified, and each of these modifications are logged. The more indexes you have, the more logging overhead there will be. And even if your table is a heap and doesn't have indexes, logging has to take place to track location of the rows.

- Page splitting is a fact of life in tables, and each time a page is split, this modification has to be logged. So if your indexes experience a lot of page splitting, logging overhead increases.
- Whenever auto-create or auto-update statistics kicks in, all statistics creation and updates are logged.
- If your tables have off-row LOB storage, additional logging has to occur just to keep track of the off-row storage.

Besides the data modification–related transaction log activity, there are many activities that you can manually perform that can also cause transaction log activity, such as the following:

- Creating or altering database objects
- Rebuilding or reorganizing indexes
- Updating statistics

Most DBAs understand that the transaction log is written to sequentially, which is good for performance because sequential I/O activity is more efficient than random I/O activity on conventional disk arrays. But DBAs often don't realize that the transaction log is also often read, which can result in random reads and writes, further contributing to transaction log I/O overhead. Here are some examples:

- Every time a transaction has to be rolled back, log records have to be read so the rollback can occur.
- Creating a database snapshot requires crash recovery to be run, which reads the transaction log.
- Running DBCC CHECKDB creates a database snapshot as part of its internal process, and as you just saw, creating a database snapshot requires crash recovery to be run and the transaction log read.
- Any kind of backup—full, differential, or log—requires the transaction log to be read.
- If a database is in the simple recovery mode, every time a checkpoint occurs, the transaction log has to be read.
- Transactional replication reads the transaction log in order to move changes from the publisher to the subscriber.
- Using Change Data Capture uses the transactional replication log reader to track changes, which in turn reads the transaction log.
- Database mirroring reads the transaction log in order to move changes from the primary database to the secondary database.

And if these examples don't convince you that the transaction log's I/O can be strained, think about this: if you store more than one transaction log on the same array, which is a common practice, the disk head has to hop among the various transaction log files to read and write out the log records, introducing even more random I/O activity.

Although it's true that transactions logs have mostly sequential read and write activity, they experience much more random read and write activity than many DBAs realize.

Determining whether the transaction log is a bottleneck

The transaction log can become a bottleneck in one of two ways. The most common is I/O related. As you've seen so far, the transaction log is subject to substantial write (and potentially read) activity, and this will be the focus for the rest of this chapter. The second reason why the transaction log might become a bottleneck is that the Log Manager within SQL Server has some of its own built-in limitations. Other than in large online transaction processing (OLTP) systems, you shouldn't run into this limitation, and this topic is beyond the scope of this chapter. For more information on Log Manager–related bottlenecks, see the SQLCat Team article *Diagnosing Transaction Log Performance Issues and Limits of the Log Manager* at http://sqlcat.com/technicalnotes/archive/2008/12/09/diagnosing-transaction-log-performance-issues-and-limits-of-the-log-manager.aspx.

You can determine if a transaction log has an I/O bottleneck using the same tools that you'd use to identify any I/O performance bottlenecks. These can include using:

- fn_virtualfilestats
- sys.dm_io_virtual_file_stats
- sys.dm_io_pending_io_requests

as well as Windows Performance Monitor counters (logical or physical disk objects):

- Current Disk Queue Length
- Avg. Disk/sec Read
- Avg. Disk/sec Write
- Disk Reads/sec
- Disk Writes/sec

Although all of these can be used to help identify I/O bottlenecks, I always start with these two Performance Monitor counters:

- Average Disk sec/Read (the average time, in milliseconds, of a read of data from disk)
- Average Disk sec/Write (the average time, in milliseconds, of a write of data to disk)

The two counters provide you with the disk latency for the array where your transaction log(s) are located. Here's a list I use to help me determine whether I/O is becoming a problem:

- Less than 5 ms = excellent
- Between 5 and 10 ms = very good
- Between 10 and 20 ms = okay

- Between 20 and 50 ms = slow
- Greater than 50 but less than 100 ms = potentially serious I/O bottleneck
- Greater than 100 ms = definite I/O bottleneck

As with most recommendations, these numbers are generic and may not fit your particular environment. Ideally, in a busy OLTP system, I like to see five ms latency or less for both reads and writes for my transaction log. On less busy systems, a higher latency may not be a problem. But the higher the latency, the higher the potential for transaction log I/O performance issues. When I check out a server, and if the read and write latency is very good to excellent, I'm generally satisfied. If they're higher than 10 ms, I start checking my options for boosting transaction log I/O throughput.

Strategies for dealing with transaction log I/O bottlenecks

There are two ways to approach dealing with transaction log I/O bottlenecks. The first is taking proactive steps to help ensure you won't have a transaction log I/O bottleneck in the first place by implementing best practices before your SQL Server goes into production. The second is to identify a transaction log I/O bottleneck after you're in production and then try to implement best practices after the fact.

In this section, I'll introduce a set of best practices that you can implement before your server is put into production, which is usually the easiest time to implement them. Or these same best practices can be implemented after your server has gone into production, but in most cases, they're much more difficult and time-consuming to implement. For example, many of the recommendations require that SQL Server be brought down in order to implement them after the fact.

The best practices listed here are generic and, because of this, may or may not always be the best recommendations for your particular server environment. As the DBA, you need to evaluate each option and decide whether it will work for you. If you're not sure whether a particular recommendation is best for your servers, perform your own tests in a test environment and see for yourself.

Start with standard performance-tuning techniques

As with many cases when dealing with SQL Server performance issues, one of the best places to begin is with the application and database and ensure that they're properly tuned. In other words, employ as many of the standard performance-tuning best practices as you can, because they can help reduce transaction log activity, along with overall I/O. I don't have the space to cover all the techniques (books have been written about just this topic), but here are some of the most common recommendations that can significantly affect transaction log activity:

- Keep transactions short.
- Minimize the possibility that a transaction has to be rolled back.
- Eliminate redundant or unused indexes (including indexed views), because they all need to maintained, and maintenance requires log activity.

- Take steps to minimize page splitting. For example, use a monotonically increasing clustered index for each of your tables, and select a fill factor that will minimize page splitting.
- Considering the number of records modified in a batch. For example, tests by Paul Randal indicate that a batch size of multiple rows may be more efficient, from a transaction log perspective, than a batch size of a single row. For more information, check out "Optimizing Log Block I/O Size and How Log I/O Works" at www.sqlskills.com/BLOGS/PAUL/post/Benchmarking-1-TB-table -population-(part-2-optimizing-log-block-IO-size-and-how-log-IO-works).aspx.

Take advantage of minimally logged operations if appropriate

Although all database modifications are logged in SQL Server, some database modifications can be minimally logged, which incur less overhead than fully logged operations. These include BCP, BULK INSERT, INSERT INTO, and SELECT INTO, among several others. For these operations to be minimally logged, the database has to be using the bulk-logged recovery model. In addition, some of the operations have specific requirements in order to be minimally logged, and they can introduce other complexities that have to be handled. See the "Operations That Can Be Minimally Logged" section of Books Online for additional information.

Select a fast I/O subsystem

Because you know the potential negative effect of transaction logs on the overall performance of SQL Server, you want to ensure that they run on the fastest I/O subsystem possible, given your budget restrictions. Ideally, the transaction log should be located on a RAID 10 array (RAID 1 if you can't afford RAID 10). In some very high-end OLTP systems, some companies have been using RAID 1 SSDs (solid state drives) or Fusion-I/O devices for maximum performance.

Align disk partitions

For optimum performance, the partitions on your disk need to be properly aligned, or you risk losing a lot of your I/O subsystem's performance. If you aren't familiar with this topic, read the Microsoft white paper "Disk Partition Alignment Best Practices for SQL Server" by Jimmy May and Denny Lee, available at http://msdn.microsoft.com/en-us/library/dd758814(v=sql.100).aspx.

Remove physical file fragmentation

Use the Windows defrag.exe command to see if the array with your transaction logs has physical file fragmentation. If it does, use the same tool to remove it. Unfortunately, you have to take SQL Server down to defrag the log files. The best way to deal with physical file fragmentation is to prevent it from happening in the first place, which can be done by following the next best practice.

Preallocate transaction log file size

When a database and its transaction log are first created, ideally both should be pre-sized so that autogrowth doesn't have to be used to grow your files. This approach offers three benefits to transaction logs. First, it helps to prevent physical file fragmentation because the transaction log is created at one time, and autogrowth won't need to kick in and grow the file. Autogrowth is one of the leading causes of physical file fragmentation. Second, when autogrowth kicks in and grows the transaction log, the space has to be zeroed out (unlike database files with instant file initialization turned on). This process can take time, and during the autogrowth, SQL Server has to pause all activity in the log, which might make your users upset if the transaction log has to grow a lot. Third, autogrowth can lead to a situation where your transaction logs have too many virtual log files, which can impact performance. More on this topic shortly.

So what size should your transaction log file be? Unfortunately, there's no easy answer other than to test before you put your database into production. This is because so many factors can determine the size of a transaction log, factors such as the level of activity, the recovery model selected for the database, how often you back up your transaction logs, your database maintenance, and whether you use transactional replication or mirroring. If you're dealing with an existing production system, you can observe how much actual transaction log space is needed, and then use that figure to resize your transaction log size, if necessary.

You only need to create a single transaction log file, because SQL Server can use only one at a time. Only add additional transaction log files if you should run out of space on the existing array and you need to allocate more transaction log space on another array.

As you preallocate your transaction log files, be sure to change the default autogrowth setting of 10% to a fixed amount that makes sense in relation to the size of the preallocated transaction log file and won't take too long to grow. Remember, should autogrowth kick in, the newly allocated space has to be zero initialized, which can take some time. Because of this, pick a fixed amount no larger than 1 GB, and only pick a number this large if your transaction log is large in the first place. Ideally, autogrowth won't ever have to kick in if you preallocate the transaction log correctly in the first place, but autogrowth needs to be left on in case of some unexpected event that will cause the log to grow.

Separating data and log files

You've probably heard this advice a hundred times, but it's important to put your data (MDF, NDF) and log (LDF) files on separate arrays in order to reduce contention. This is one of the easiest things you can do, and it's effective in reducing I/O contention between data and log files.

Although many DBAs have heard this advice before, one question that usually doesn't come up is should this separation be done on a database-by-database basis, or is it okay to group all the log files from multiple databases on the same array? In other words, if you have a server with five databases, should each of the five log files be on five different arrays, or can all five log files reside on the same array?

In a perfect world with an unlimited budget, each log file should be on its own array, because mixing multiple log files on the same array will introduce a lot of random reads and writes, as discussed earlier in this chapter. The more log files there are on the same shared array, the bigger this problem becomes. Storing multiple log files on the same array is not ideal, but it's still better than storing them on the same array as your data files.

In many cases, storing multiple log files on the same array will be fine, but if your workload is so busy that the I/O system is overwhelmed, you'll need to consider putting each log file on its own array, assuming that you've done everything else you can to reduce the I/O bottleneck and this is one of your last options.

Managing virtual log files

Transactions logs are divided internally into what are called virtual log files (VLFs). If you aren't familiar with them, check out the article "Understanding Logging and Recovery in SQL Server" by Paul Randal, available at http://technet.microsoft.com/en-us/magazine/2009.02.logging.aspx. What you need to know is that having too few, or too many, VLFs, can hurt transaction log performance. According to Kimberly Tripp, in her article "Transaction Log VLFs: Too Many or Too Few," available at http://www.sqlskills.com/BLOGS/KIMBERLY/post/Transaction-Log-VLFs-too-many-or-too-few.aspx, VLFs have to be approximately 500 MB in size for optimum transaction log performance. The problem is that SQL Server won't do this for you automatically. To accomplish this, you'll need to preallocate transaction log space in 8,000 MB chunks. For example, if you plan to allocate 16,000 MB to your transaction log, first create an initial log file at 8,000 MB, and then immediately use the ALTER DATABASE command to extend it another 8,000 MB manually, for a total of 16,000 MB. Read Kimberly's article for all the details on why this is the case and the best way to implement it.

But what if you're currently in production? How do you find out how many VLFs you currently have? To find out, run DBCC LOGINFO (this is an undocumented command not directly supported by Microsoft) against each database, and the number of rows returned will equal the number of VLFs you currently have in your transaction log. If you have more than the recommended one VLF for each 500 MB of transaction log file size, consider shrinking the transaction log (after a transaction log backup) and then using ALTER DATABASE to grow the transaction log back to the preallocated size based on the earlier recommendations.

Perform transaction log backups often

When a database uses the bulk-logged or the full recovery model, every time a transaction log backup is made, unused portions of it are cleared out and can be used for new logging. The more often you perform transaction log backups, the quicker they take, helping to reduce overhead on the transaction log. If you don't back up the transaction logs often and they grow large, there will be a larger I/O hit during the operation. So, smaller and more frequent transaction log backups are preferred over larger and less frequent transaction log backups.

Schedule database maintenance during slow times

As I mentioned earlier in the chapter, full and differential database backups, index rebuilds, index reorganization, statistics updates, and DBCC CHECKDB all can contribute to transaction log activity. These are all important tasks that need to be done and can't be skipped. Because of this, consider performing these operations at times of the day when your server isn't so busy, and be sure you don't overlap running them at the same time. This approach will help spread out transaction log I/O throughout the day, minimizing any potential bottlenecks.

Summary

Your SQL Servers may or may not be experiencing a transaction log bottleneck, but you won't know until you check for yourself. If you don't have a transaction log I/O bottleneck, count yourself lucky, but don't be complacent. Be a proactive DBA and implement as many of these strategies as possible to mitigate future transaction log bottlenecks. If you do discover you have a transaction log bottleneck, use the strategies in this chapter, as appropriate to your environment, until the bottleneck has been minimized or completely eliminated.

About this author

Brad M. McGehee is the Director of DBA Education for Red Gate Software. He's an accomplished Microsoft SQL Server MVP with over 16 years of SQL Server experience and more than 7 years of training experience. Brad is a frequent speaker at SQL PASS, European PASS, SQL Server Connections, SQLTeach, dev-LINK, SQLBits, SQL Saturdays, TechFests, Code Camps, SQL Server user groups, and other industry seminars. A well-respected and trusted name in SQL Server literature, Brad is the author or co-author of more than 15 technical books and more than 275 published articles. He blogs at www.bradmcgehee.com.

37 Strategies for unraveling tangled code

Jennifer McCown

When you inherit an application or a database, you often become the proud owner of overly complex, poorly performing T-SQL code. These queries rarely come equipped with meaningful documentation or with system architects who are willing and able to explain the code.

This chapter covers several methods to make sense of the mess. The overall approach is to organize, break down, and then streamline the code to identify and remove some of the nastier coding mistakes and inefficiencies.

The sample database is a small model of a vending machine business, called *VendCo*. Tables in the VendUnit schema store data about each vending machine (including model and location information) and product inventory. Maintenance and Product schema hold technician and sales product data, respectively. You can download the scripts to create and populate the database from my blog: http://www.MidnightDBA.com/Jen/Articles/.

Organize: make it readable

Imagine that you've just received (or discovered) an undocumented mystery query. The first thing you notice is that the query is a solid chunk of code, without spacing or line breaks. Before you can do anything with the query, get it into a readable format and begin adding comments. The following two sections show you how.

Formatting

People are capable of reading large, solid blocks of text, but it's far easier to understand the written word when it's broken down into meaningful chunks. This book, for example, uses page breaks between chapters, and whitespace between sections, paragraphs, and words. Chapters are divided into fairly short paragraphs, each of which covers a complete, discrete thought.

In the same way, it's far easier to comprehend code when it's broken into discrete sections, with whitespace between queries and clauses. SQL Server ignores line breaks and whitespace, so arrange your code on multiple lines and add indentation. Here's a checklist for formatting a query:

1 Begin each major clause—for example, SELECT, FROM, JOIN, or WHERE—on a new line.

2 Indent each subquery, CASE statement, and comma-delimited list.

3 Reorder JOIN clauses into logical groupings. For example, if the statement selects from TableA, which joins to TableB, and then to TableC, arrange the JOIN clauses in that order. Keep each ON clause with its associated JOIN.

4 Add sensible table aliases as needed to make the column memberships easier to understand.

Auto-formatting software, like Red Gate's SQL Prompt, can significantly shorten the time it takes to insert line breaks and add indentation in your code, but you'll also need to touch up the code by hand.

Follow these formatting guidelines to transform your query into something much easier on the eyes (see listing 1).

Listing 1   An inherited mystery query, formatted

```
USE VendCo;
GO
WITH CurrentInventory
AS (
    SELECT   *
           , ROW_NUMBER() OVER( PARTITION BY MachineID, SlotID ORDER BY
DateReported DESC) AS ReportGroup
    FROM VendUnit.MachineInventory
    )
SELECT Mach.MachineID,
    INV.SlotID,
    PROD.ProductID,
    PROD.ProductName,
    INV.UnitsInStock,
    INV.DateReported
FROM VendUnit.Machine AS Mach
CROSS JOIN VendUnit.MachineModel AS MModel
INNER JOIN VendUnit.Location AS LOC
    ON LOC.LocationID = Mach.LocationID
INNER JOIN VendUnit.Territory AS TERR
    ON TERR.TerritoryID = LOC.TerritoryID
LEFT OUTER JOIN Maintenance.Technician AS TECH
    ON TECH.TerritoryID = TERR.TerritoryID
INNER JOIN CurrentInventory AS INV
    ON INV.MachineID = Mach.MachineID
INNER JOIN Product.Product AS PROD
    ON PROD.ProductID = INV.ProductID
WHERE ReportGroup = 1
    AND (
        PROD.ProductName LIKE '%soda%' OR
```

```
        PROD.ProductName LIKE '%cola%' OR
        PROD.ProductName LIKE '%pop%' )
AND Mach.MachineModelID = MModel.MachineModelID
AND ProductTypeID = 2;
```

Comments

There's nothing in SQL Server so universally useful, yet neglected, as comments. You, and the entire SQL-writing world, should make copious use of comments in every stored procedure and query that you detangle or create. The advantages are numerous:

- Comments are a reminder you write to yourself about particular code choices, purpose, context, and more.
- Comments instruct and guide the next person that touches the code.
- Comments serve as documentation that can never get lost. It's also easy to keep this "documentation" up to date; it's there every time you open the stored procedure!

Comment your code as you break it down and begin to understand what it does. Include the date, your name, and contact information. If you're concerned about being *too* verbose, follow the axiom, "Explain it like you're talking to the new guy." If you add the comments into existing stored procedures, the DBA who opens up this mystery query in three months will thank you…especially if you're that DBA.

Break down: what does it do?

Now that your code is prettified, determine what *kind* of query it is. Does it pull new membership data from the last quarter? Is it an aggregation of sales figures per salesperson per year? You have a few strategies for determining the query's purpose.

SELECT columns

Read over the column list to get an idea of what this query does:

```
SELECT Mach.MachineID,
    INV.SlotID,
    PROD.ProductID,
    PROD.ProductName,
    INV.UnitsInStock,
    INV.DateReported
```

This mystery query selects machine and product IDs, product name, units in stock, and date reported. So this query is related to vending machine inventory on a given date. With any luck, the data and remaining clauses hold more answers.

Data

Look at the data returned. If possible, run the query in a test environment. Alternately, run it in production if it's safe and you have sign-off from all the business owners.

First, if the query contains any common table expressions (CTEs) or noncorrelated subqueries, highlight and execute just the code from each CTE and subquery in turn. The CTE from your mystery query returns inventory data: ID, product ID, price, and date reported units in stock and units sold. This data comes with columns MachineID and SlotID, as shown in table 1.

Table 1 Output of CTE

MachineID	SlotID	ProductID	UnitsInStock	UnitsSold	DateReported	ReportGroup
1	1	2	13	2	2011-03-04	1
1	1	2	14	1	2011-03-03	2
1	1	2	15	0	2011-03-02	3
1	2	3	13	2	2011-03-04	1
1	2	3	14	1	2011-03-03	2

At this point, the CTE data supports the theory that this query relates to vending machine sales on a given date. (Note that the ProductSalesPrice column isn't displayed in the output, for readability.)

Next, run the query as a whole. A partial view of the data returned also supports your theory (table 2); this data is a listing of vending machines (by machine ID and name), and the number and type of product in each slot in a machine, on a given date.

Table 2 Output of the complete query

MachineID	MachineName	SlotID	ProductID	ProductName	UnitsInStock	DateReported
1	Soda Std 8	3	4	Soda Wow	13	2011-03-04
1	Soda Std 8	4	5	Cola Boo	7	2011-03-04
1	Soda Std 8	5	6	Yum Yum Pop	0	2011-03-04
1	Soda Std 8	6	7	Soda Wow	4	2011-03-04
1	Soda Std 8	7	8	Cola Boo	9	2011-03-04
1	Soda Std 8	8	9	Yum Yum Pop	8	2011-03-04
5	Master 4x10	95	8	Cola Boo	11	2011-03-04
5	Master 4x10	96	9	Yum Yum Pop	15	2011-03-04

Sketch

Sketch the tables and joins on paper to get the general shape of the query. The main body of the query joins six tables and a CTE. When you make a quick drawing, you can immediately see the hierarchy between tables and you can see that Machine is a very central data source; it's the table with the most joins to other tables (see figure 1).

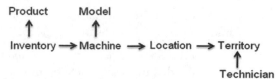

Figure 1 Sketch of tables and joins

Pseudocode

Translate the query into pseudocode. The pseudocode for your query might look like that shown in listing 2.

Listing 2   Pseudocode for the mystery query

Declare a CTE – This gets data from the machine inventory table, numbers rows within Machine-SlotID groups, and orders by most recent first. (So, Machine 1 Slot 2A is a group that has several records, and the most recent record will be row number 1.)

Get machine and slot, product, inventory, and date reported. Pull this data from Machine, cross joined to Machine Model and inner joined to the CTE, Product, Location, and Territory. Query left outer joins to Technician.

Only return rows with the CTE row number 1 (remember, the most recent inventory report per machine/slot); where the product name is like soda, cola, or pop; Machine and Model ModelID match; AND the product type is 2.

One thing that becomes clear after you perform these exercises is that the query joins to Location, Territory, and Technician but doesn't seem to *use* these joins. The query certainly doesn't pull any columns from these tables. Location and Territory are INNER JOINs, so perhaps they're used to restrict the result set to only Machine rows that have parent Location rows (which, in turn, have parent Territory rows). In other words, maybe these INNER JOINs are the equivalent of this WHERE clause:

```
… WHERE Mach.LocationID IN
( SELECT LocationID
  FROM VendUnit.Location
  WHERE TerritoryID IN
    (SELECT TerritoryID
    FROM VendUnit.Territory)
 )
```

A quick check of the underlying data model shows foreign key constraints between all of these tables. This means that the parent rows *must* be there, because the foreign keys enforce that relationship.

These Location and Territory joins aren't being used to enforce referential integrity; they're simply extra joins! Test and verify that removing the joins to Location, Territory, and Technician doesn't otherwise violate business logic and remove them to streamline the query.

Streamline: resolve obvious issues

In many inherited queries, there's one conspicuous thing wrong, something blindingly obvious. What this one thing is differs from one query to another. For example:

- *Pulls far more columns or rows than it needs*—A query that pulls more data than needed makes the SQL engine do more work and puts a heavier strain on disks, memory, and network bandwidth.

- *Performs unnecessary calculations, aggregations, ordering, or functions*—All of these take up CPU cycles and memory and extend the query runtime.
- *Contains non-SARGable* WHERE *clauses*—These prevent the use of useful indexes.

If there's something obviously wrong with the query, take care of that first.

NOTE These kinds of major problems are typically systemic. Application and database developers, and *teams* of developers, form conventions and habits. So, if a query or data model displays a major problem, you'll likely find that problem throughout the system.

Too much data

In the previous example, there are several red flags. The first one is the SELECT * in the CTE. SQL Server coders and administrators dislike SELECT *, because if the underlying table changes, the query may break.

A query rarely needs every column from a table. This query certainly doesn't need all six columns from MachineInventory in the CTE. Change the query to only get the columns you need—in this case, MachineID, SlotID, UnitsInStock, DateReported, and ProductID.

Another issue is that the CTE pulls every record from the MachineInventory table. The main query only uses rows with row number = 1 from the CTE—that is, the most recent row.

Confirm with the business owners that (a) inventory reports come in no less than once a week, and (b) this query is only concerned with current machine inventories. Add a WHERE clause to the CTE that limits the result set to the last month or weeks' worth of data, at most (see listing 3).

Listing 3   CTE code with updated SELECT list and WHERE clause

```
USE VendCo;
GO
WITH CurrentInventory
AS (
SELECT MachineID, SlotID, UnitsInStock, DateReported, ProductID
        , ROW_NUMBER() OVER( PARTITION BY MachineID, SlotID ORDER BY
DateReported DESC) AS ReportGroup
    FROM VendUnit.MachineInventory
    WHERE DateReported > DateAdd(dd, -7, GetDate())
    )
...
```

This WHERE clause is an improvement to the CTE—it limits the amount of data the query pulls back—but it's not the ideal solution. See the following section to learn how to further improve this clause.

Functions

Avoid using functions in WHERE and ON clauses, especially user functions, and especially for queries against large tables. User functions, system functions, and data type conversions (explicit and implicit) in the WHERE clauses and JOIN criteria normally cause table scans.

There are several strategies for removing functions from the WHERE clause, ranging from schema changes down to simple alterations to your query:

- *Computed columns*—Add computed columns to the underlying tables for common computations. This solution requires that you be able to make changes to tables, which may not always be possible.
- *Indexed views*—Create indexed views with the involved computations and conversions. This moves the bulk of the work to INSERT and UPDATE statements. An indexed view is materialized, so user queries just pull the precalculated values instead of running the same functions on the same values again and again.
- *CTEs and table variables*—When the function is table valued, you can replace it with a CTE or a table variable. This prevents you from having to force the query to run the function for every row considered.
- *Variables*—Depending on the needs of your query, you might simply use a variable to remove a function.

In the last section, I added a WHERE clause to the CTE to reduce the returned number of rows. In doing so, I introduced a function (DateAdd()) to the WHERE clause:

```
WHERE DateReported > DateAdd(dd, -7, GetDate())
```

This particular formula returns a single, discrete value at each runtime: the date seven days ago. Offload the function work and streamline the query with a variable, as shown in listing 4.

Listing 4   CTE code with refined WHERE clause

```
USE VendCo;
GO
DECLARE @LimitDate SMALLDATETIME;
SELECT @LimitDate = DATEADD(dd, -7, GETDATE());
WITH CurrentInventory
AS (
SELECT MachineID, SlotID, UnitsInStock, DateReported, ProductID
        , ROW_NUMBER() OVER( PARTITION BY MachineID, SlotID ORDER BY
DateReported DESC) AS ReportGroup
    FROM VendUnit.MachineInventory
    WHERE DateReported > @LimitDate
    )
```

Non-SARGable WHERE Clauses

A non-SARGable search item is anything that prevents the SQL optimizer from using a useful index. For example, a query with WHERE *colName* NOT IN followed by 200 hard-coded values can't make good use of an index on *colName*. The query would benefit if you rewrote it to use an INNER JOIN to a lookup table, or a range scan (such as WHERE value1 BETWEEN 200 AND 400).

This query has two problems in the WHERE clause: there are a lot of non-SARGable search items, and a lot of ORs:

```
WHERE ReportGroup = 1
    AND (
        PROD.ProductName LIKE '%soda%' OR
        PROD.ProductName LIKE '%cola%' OR
        PROD.ProductName LIKE '%pop%' )
    AND Mach.MachineModelID = MModel.MachineModelID
    AND ProductTypeID = 2;
```

In this query, the leading wildcard (%) sign in PROD.ProductName LIKE '%soda%' prevents the use of an index. This is exactly like opening a book and scanning the index for anything with "soda" in the term (soda-pop, baking soda, and so on). You'd have to read the entire index instead of going right to the correct leading character.

So far, there's no obvious solution to the leading wildcard issue in this query. But ProductTypeID 2 in the ProductType lookup table is Drink (shelvable). With more investigation, you determine that this query is meant to include all items of type 2, not just those with ProductName LIKE soda, cola, or pop. In other words, the business rule for this query is "all products of type 2," not "all products with the words 'soda,' 'cola,' or 'pop.'" Therefore, you can get rid of the ProductName LIKE '%...%' clauses:

```
WHERE ReportGroup = 1
    AND Mach.MachineModelID = MModel.MachineModelID
    AND ProductTypeID = 2;
```

It's good luck that the business rules support getting rid of the ORs and the non-SARGable % searches at once. You won't always be able to eliminate poorly coded WHERE clauses. Sometimes you're forced to rewrite the query or (gasp!) leave inefficient code as it is.

Streamline: optimize joins

Joins are essential in a relational database; they link together data held in separate tables. The work done under the covers for the simple word "JOIN" can be immense. A healthy JOIN does the least amount of work possible, but no more. It has a useful index, and it has clearly delineated join criteria.

The most common misuse of joins stems from developers who copy and paste code from other queries without performing appropriate reviews and performance tests. These thrown-together queries often contain extraneous joins and duplicate joins. Your mystery query (listing 5) has an example of a duplicate join, as you discovered in the "Pseudocode" section earlier.

Listing 5   Mystery query excerpt: unused joins

```
FROM VendUnit.Machine AS Mach
CROSS JOIN VendUnit.MachineModel AS MModel
INNER JOIN VendUnit.Location AS LOC           -- UNUSED JOIN!!
    ON LOC.LocationID = Mach.LocationID
```

```
INNER JOIN VendUnit.Territory AS TERR          -- UNUSED JOIN!!
    ON TERR.TerritoryID = LOC.TerritoryID
LEFT OUTER JOIN Maintenance.Technician AS TECH -- UNUSED JOIN!!
    ON TECH.TerritoryID = TERR.TerritoryID
INNER JOIN CurrentInventory AS INV
    ON INV.MachineID = Mach.MachineID
INNER JOIN Product.Product AS PROD
    ON PROD.ProductID = INV.ProductID
```

Another common problem is the overuse of CROSS JOINs, which can pull far more data than needed. A CROSS JOIN joins every row from one side of the join (x number of rows) to every row on the other side (y rows), and so it results in $x \times y$ rows. If you use CROSS JOIN on tables with large numbers of rows, or do more than one cross join (resulting in $x \times y \times z$ rows), you could tie up memory and CPU and fill up TempdDB. You'll occasionally need a CROSS JOIN for a query, but using them is a rarity. The defining difference is whether the result set of the query matches up with expectations. Try checking with a user who pulls this kind of data to see if the data makes sense.

CROSS JOINs are also misused as INNER JOINs, with a join definition in the WHERE clause. For example, the mystery query CROSS JOINs the Machine table with the MachineModel table:

```
FROM VendUnit.Machine Mach
CROSS JOIN VendUnit.MachineModel MModel
```

The WHERE clause contains join criteria:

```
AND Mach.MachineModelID = MModel.MachineModelID
```

A CROSS JOIN with a join condition in the WHERE clause is functionally identical to an INNER JOIN that uses the same join condition. Rewrite these "hidden inner joins" to improve the query's readability. Just move the join condition from the WHERE clause to the join and make it an inner join:

```
INNER JOIN VendUnit.MachineModel Mmodel
ON Mach.MachineModelID = MModel.MachineModelID
```

Streamline: similar subqueries and queries

The most common problem with subqueries is overuse. Often, if there are too many subqueries in a single query, they're identical or nearly so. This causes the SQL engine to hit the tables in the subquery multiple times, leading to double logical reads (for two nearly identical subqueries), triple (for three), or more. It's far better to remove multiple subqueries and consolidate them into a CTE, table variable, or indexed temporary table.

Additionally, systems are frequently architected with multiple queries stored in (or generated by) the calling application, instead of encapsulated in stored procedures. An application that sends T-SQL queries instead of stored procedure calls will, by necessity, have some or many nearly identical queries to provide for similar functionality. This practice complicates system support; any change to the database must be propagated through multiple application-side queries, instead of one or a few stored procedures.

On the other hand, sometimes a database has multiple stored procedures that all do nearly the exact same work—joining the same two large tables or pulling most of a table into a temporary table. In these cases, you can schedule a job to pull a superset of the data used by these stored procedures into a rollup table, and have the stored procedures query off that rollup table. Alternately, implement an indexed view to improve performance and simplify code across the board.

Streamline: dynamic SQL

Dynamic SQL queries are by definition very flexible, but they have several disadvantages over nondynamic queries, such as the following:

- Dynamic SQL queries are complex and difficult to read, making them hard to support and modify.
- They tend to be overinflated, as coders try to cram in as many variations as possible into one statement.
- SQL developers frequently use dynamic SQL queries to compensate for poor database architecture.

Simply refactoring dynamic SQL into traditional SQL queries (where feasible) will take you a long way toward a manageable, supportable database.

Let's take a simple example in the vending machine database. There are two types of vending machines, food and drink, and the attribute refrigerated is either on or off. The database contains four views based on these classifications: vwFoodNotRefrigerated, vwFoodRefrigerated, vwDrinkNotRefrigerated, and vwDrinkRefrigerated.

One stored procedure builds a dynamic SQL statement that varies depending on which view is called for (in this case, using the INT parameter @param), as shown in listing 6.

Listing 6   Stored procedure with dynamic T-SQL

```
USE VendCo;
GO
CREATE PROCEDURE getFoodData
  @param tinyint
AS
DECLARE @sql varchar(4000);

SET @sql = 'SELECT * FROM '

IF @param = 1
    SET @sql = @sql + 'vwFoodNotRefrigerated '
    ELSE IF @param = 2
        SET @sql = @sql + 'vwFoodRefrigerated '
        ELSE IF @param = 3
            SET @sql = @sql + 'vwDrinkNotRefrigerated '
            ELSE
                SET @sql = @sql + 'vwDrinkRefrigerated '
```

```
SET @sql = @sql
    + 'WHERE ExpirationDate < DATEADD(dd, -4, getdate());';

EXEC (@sql);
```

Even the simple code in listing 6 is overly complicated and will make syntax errors difficult to track down in the dynamic query.

You could break this code into a separate stored procedure for each type of call, each with a nondynamic SELECT, and alter the calling application. This approach would be marginally better for database supportability, but it doesn't completely address the underlying problem. By using these four separate views, the query has an additional layer of complexity.

A better option is to look at the (probably nearly identical) queries that define these views, and use variations of those queries within the stored procedure (listing 7).

Listing 7   Stored procedure without dynamic T-SQL

```
USE VendCo;
GO
CREATE PROCEDURE getVendData
  @IsFood BIT,
  @IsRefrigerated BIT
AS

IF @IsFood = 0
    SELECT MACH.PurchaseDate
          , MODEL.MachineModelName
          , MODEL.ProductsPerSlot
    FROM VendUnit.Machine AS MACH
    INNER JOIN VendUnit.MachineModel AS MODEL
        ON MACH.MachineModelID = MODEL.MachineModelID
    WHERE VendType = 'Drink'
        AND Refrigerated = @IsRefrigerated

ELSE IF @IsFood = 1
    SELECT MACH.PurchaseDate
          , MODEL.MachineModelName
          , MODEL.ProductsPerSlot
    FROM VendUnit.Machine AS MACH
    INNER JOIN VendUnit.MachineModel AS MODEL
        ON MACH.MachineModelID = MODEL.MachineModelID
    WHERE VendType = 'Food'
        AND Refrigerated = @IsRefrigerated
```

The rewrite in listing 7 is far easier to read; the query isn't buried in a lot of quotes and plus signs, and the actual code isn't hidden behind redundant views.

It won't always be so easy to rewrite dynamic SQL, especially if it's embedded in the application. In that case, if you aren't able to remove the offending code from the client side, the best you can do is just index for the queries appropriately.

Summary

We've all had to deal with mystery queries, and sometimes entire mystery databases, that are difficult to manage and support. In these cases, standards are often inconsistently enforced, bad coding practices abound, and there's no one left who really understands the relevant business rules.

The culprit is lack of good development practices and most especially the scarcity of good documentation for a given system. It's up to you to break the cycle as you explore the uncharted territory. To do so:

- Make your code readable with formatting and extensive comments.
- Figure out what it does. Look at the columns and data, sketch out the tables, and break it down with pseudocode.
- Resolve obvious issues, like returning too much data and other unnecessary work.
- Optimize your joins to what's essential.
- Eliminate duplicate queries and subqueries (if possible) by refactoring.
- Eliminate unnecessary dynamic SQL.

Make changes only when they won't have a detrimental effect on the outcome of the query. When possible, be sure to get confirmation and sign-off from business and project owners. Always test, test, and test your code changes before moving them into production, and be sure to have a rollback plan in place.

The keys to detangling unmanageable queries are to organize, comment, break down, and streamline the code. Armed with that and some performance know-how, you can divide and conquer!

About the author

 Jennifer McCown is a SQL Server MVP and long-time SQL developer and DBA. She is Senior Editor of MidnightDBA.com, where she creates technology tutorials, articles, and the DBAs@Midnight webshow. Jen is a member, volunteer, and speaker for the Professional Association for SQL Server, the North Texas SQL Server User Group, and the PASS Women in Technology virtual chapter. She's presented at multiple SQL Saturdays, conferences, and online training events.

Rick!
Happy, happy days!) #SQL Karaoke
(And funeral nights.) — *Jen McCown*

38 Using PAL to analyze SQL Server performance

Tim Chapman

Here's a common scenario for a database administrator. Someone stops by your cubicle and complains that the system is running "slow." Regardless of whether it's the database or the application, you're tasked with determining what's causing the slowdown, and you must diagnose the problem as quickly as possible. The problem worsens when the performance issue begins to impede normal business functions, ultimately costing the company revenue. Once management becomes involved, stress levels rise, and it becomes even more critical to resolve the issue quickly and accurately. Sometimes the issue is diagnosed easily, such as when a runaway process has locked a table. In other cases, the problems aren't so obvious.

Even great applications can experience performance problems. The ability to troubleshoot and resolve these issues when they occur is critical. Monitoring Windows Performance Monitor counters is one of the first things you should do when performance problems arise. But which ones should you look at? There are hundreds of counters to potentially capture, and making sense of the information once captured is often difficult and time consuming.

Performance Analysis of Logs (PAL)

Enter the Performance Analysis of Logs (PAL) tool. PAL is a labor of love developed by Microsoft Premier Field Engineer Clint Huffman. Constantly battling Windows performance issues, Huffman created PAL in an effort to easily diagnose performance problems through the analysis of Windows performance counters.

PAL is an open source application, freely downloadable from pal.codeplex.com. Not only is PAL a great addition to your toolset, but you have full access to the PowerShell and GUI source code, giving you the ability to customize it to fit your needs.

PAL analysis is driven by the type of workload to be consumed. Application-specific threshold files are used by PAL to identify performance trends. These threshold files are maintained by Microsoft Subject Matter Experts for a given application space. Applications that PAL can help analyze include SQL Server, Active Directory, SharePoint, and Exchange. David Pless, a Microsoft Senior Premier Field Engineer, is the content owner for the PAL SQL Server thresholds.

Using PAL with SQL Server

Performance Monitor counters captured for a SQL Server instance are an ideal use for PAL to identify database performance problems. PAL can quickly and easily analyze one or more performance log files, using a SQL Server threshold file to identify issues and find correlations between the counters gathered. Upon completion, PAL produces intuitive reports, highlighting any potential performance problems.

You can start PAL from the shortcut placed in the Start menu upon installation, or you can navigate to the executable in the Program Files\PAL folder. Note that PAL doesn't need to be installed on a production machine in order to perform the analysis, nor is network connectivity required.

Capturing performance counter data

To use PAL to diagnose SQL Server performance issues, specific counters must be gathered. If you plan to gather SQL Server counter data for named instances, you'll need to modify any templates to include the instance name, because SQL Server counters for instance names are always unique. In the following sections, I'll outline three methods for capturing performance counters needed by PAL for SQL Server analysis.

Data collector sets using PAL template files

PAL includes the ability to take an existing threshold file and export it to a Performance Monitor template file. This approach has the advantages of using the application-specific counters that the PAL content owner has deemed important and eliminating the need for you to have to remember the specific counters to capture.

To export the PerfMon template file definition, navigate to the Threshold File section within the PAL tool. In the Threshold File Title drop-down box, choose Microsoft SQL Server 2005/2008. A dialog box opens where you can specify a location to save the template file.

Once the threshold file has been exported, it can then be used to create a data collector set (DCS) that will capture the counters. You can create a DCS using the following steps:

1 Start perfmon.exe from the Run menu.
2 Expand Data Collector Sets.
3 Right-click User Defined and select New > Data Collector Set.
4 Give the set a name, and choose Create from a Template (recommended).

5 Click Browse, and navigate to the PerfMon template file you exported from the PAL tool.

6 Choose a directory to store the DCS data.

7 Once created, you can adjust the properties of the DCS, such as the schedule and stop conditions.

Logman

Logman is a Windows command-line tool that allows you to create Event Trace sessions or Performance Log sessions for local or remote machines to capture logs at regular intervals. The great thing about Logman is that you're able to save the SQL Server template file from PAL to a Logman template file, enabling it to be used to capture the specific metrics needed for PAL analysis. The following is an example of how to create a Logman counter trace using a counter template file named logman.txt, which was exported from PAL:

```
logman create counter sqlperf -cf "c:\logmansql.txt" -o
➥ "C:\perflogs\sqlperf"
logman start sqlperf
```

Note that the output from creating a Logman counter trace is a DCS.

SQLDiag

SQLDiag is one of my favorite tools to use when it comes to capturing performance-tuning data. SQLDiag is a command-line utility created by the Microsoft Product Support Services (PSS) team to gather performance metrics (such as SQL trace events, performance counters, and MSInfo) related to the Windows operating system and SQL Server. SQLDiag ships with SQL Server and is located in the \Tools\Binn directory of your SQL installation.

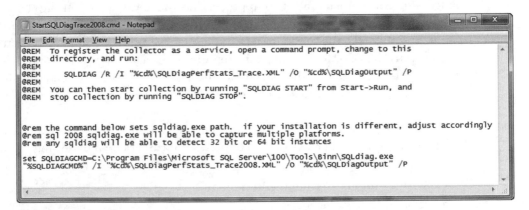

Figure 1   An example command file that invokes the SQLDiag utility

SQLDiag data collection is driven by enabling events to be captured via an XML configuration file. By default, SQLDiag generates three different XML configuration files each time it's run; each file specifies a different level of granularity for data capture. Don't modify these files, because your changes will be overwritten when SQLDiag executes. You should modify a copy of these files to enable or disable events as necessary.

The native SQLDiag XML configuration files don't have all necessary Windows counter events gathered in order to satisfy the PAL tool, but you can download the PerfStats scripts from sqlnexus.codeplex.com. The PerfStats scripts are maintained by Microsoft and capture all necessary events to feed SQL Server open source tools like PAL and SQL Nexus. Figure 1 shows an example command file for passing a PerfStats configuration file to SQLDiag.

Performing PAL analysis

Once you've collected a performance counter log from one or more machines, you can feed the files into PAL for analysis. In the following sections I'll review the screens in the PAL tool where you'll need to make decisions for how PAL processing will occur.

Counter Log

The Counter Log screen (see figure 2) is where you specify the performance counter file (.csv or .blg). This file can contain counter data from multiple computers, and you may also restrict the processing to certain data points from a particular date range.

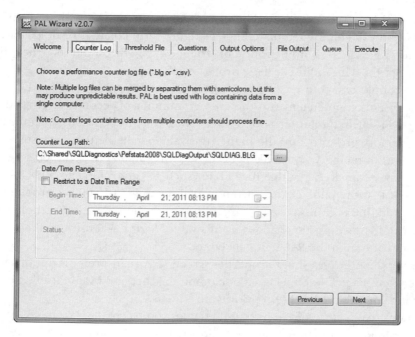

Figure 2 Specify the path to the Performance Counter log file on the Counter Log screen.

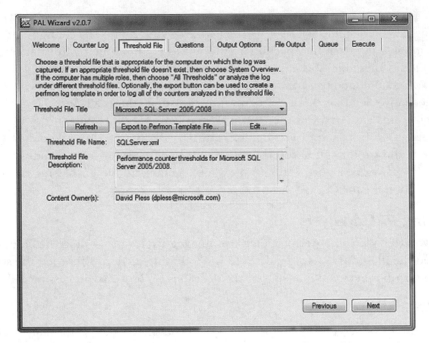

Figure 3   Use the Threshold File screen to edit or export PAL templates.

Threshold File

The Threshold file is the command center of the PAL tool. The real power of PAL is exposed when you edit the template file (see figure 3) to create thresholds and counters that are relevant to your environment. To modify the threshold file, click the Edit button under the Threshold File Title drop-down box.

One example of a counter you may want to consider editing is Page Life Expectancy (PLE). This counter tells you the average number of seconds an unreferenced data page will stay in the buffer pool. Lower values for this counter may indicate buffer pool memory pressure, and the higher this value is, the better. For systems with a large amount of memory, you'll likely never see this value approach 300 seconds. In fact, you may see an average value for PLE for such a system closer to 50,000 seconds. In the event that the value changes from 50,000 seconds to 10,000, a problem might have occurred that warrants research. PAL allows you to modify this threshold value so that you can identify drastic changes in this value. Figure 4 illustrates the Page Life Expectancy counter in the PAL template editor.

Opening the Edit Threshold Properties screen (figure 5) presents options for variables related to Page Life Expectancy, including the threshold value itself, along with the warning and critical condition priority thresholds.

Another great feature of PAL is that it enables you to create custom counters and define thresholds for them. A majority of the analysis in PAL is performed on custom counters, such as ratios between two or more counters. For example, PAL contains a

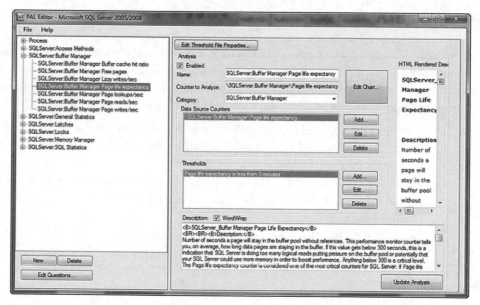

Figure 4   **Use the Edit button beside the Thresholds box to modify a threshold value.**

custom counter that calculates when the Target Server Memory counter is 500 MB greater than the Total Server Memory counter, which indicates that your instance may need more memory. You can use this feature to build rich, custom counters specific to your environment.

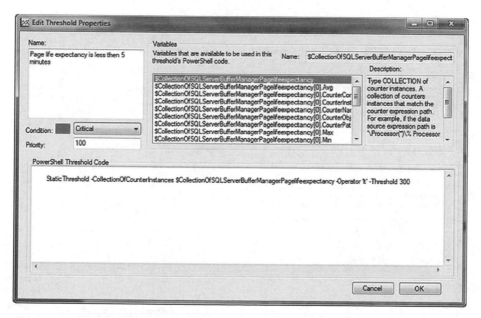

Figure 5   **Edit Threshold properties as necessary in PAL to suit your environment.**

Questions

The goal of the Questions screen of the PAL wizard is to gain insight into the server environment from which the performance counters were gathered. These questions may change depending on the threshold file chosen, and you can modify PAL to include your own questions, if you wish. For a SQL Server analysis, answer these questions accurately, as the answers you give greatly influence the PAL analysis.

- *NumberOfProcessors*—How many logical processors does the server have? Include each virtual core and take hyperthreading into account. You can look up this information using Task Manager or MSInfo.
- *ThreeGBSwitch*—Was the /3GB switch being used on the server? This question is only relevant for 32-bit systems, and you indicate if the /3GB switch is enabled in the boot.ini file.
- *SixtyFourBit*—Was the computer a 64-bit machine?
- *TotalMemory*—How many gigabytes of memory did the server contain?

Output Options

On the Output Options screen (see figure 6), you specify the analysis interval along with the option to process all counters in the collection. The analysis interval identifies trends in the counter analysis by specifying time slices. The default value for the Analysis Interval option is AUTO, which breaks the analysis into 30 intervals of equal size. Adjust this interval based on how long you plan to capture data. For extended counter capture sessions, it may make sense to break the analysis into one-hour segments.

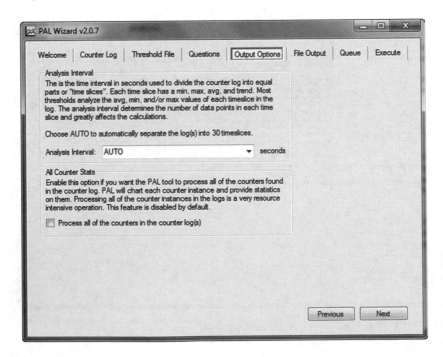

Figure 6 The Analysis Interval value of AUTO is recommended for most environments.

Choosing the option to process all counter stats will include in the report the counters that would normally be skipped due to not matching in the threshold file. This feature is great if you have third-party counters or need to include counters in the report that aren't already defined in the threshold file. You can modify the threshold files as necessary to include the counters you need. Additionally, some internet browsers can have difficulty rendering a large amount of counter log output.

File Output

The File Output screen lets you specify the physical location and the format in which you want the PAL output saved. Output can be saved as an HTML report or as an XML document. The most common option is HTML because it produces a handy graphical report that outlines time slices and counters and identifies potential problems using different colors that represent different warnings.

Queue

The Queue screen represents the work items that are in the queue to be processed by PAL. Queue items are the actual PowerShell batch statements that must be executed to invoke PAL analysis. You can remove items from the queue on this screen. If you have several work items to process, you can queue them here and step away while processing occurs.

Execute

Use the Execute screen (figure 7) to specify how PAL should execute the items currently in the queue. The options allow you to execute what's currently in the queue,

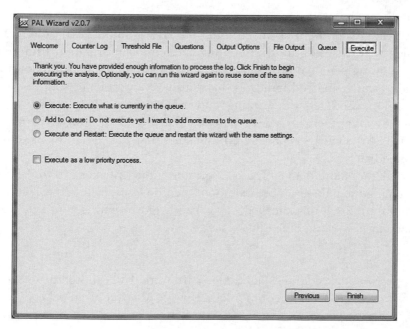

Figure 7 Use the Execute screen to indicate how you want the analysis performed.

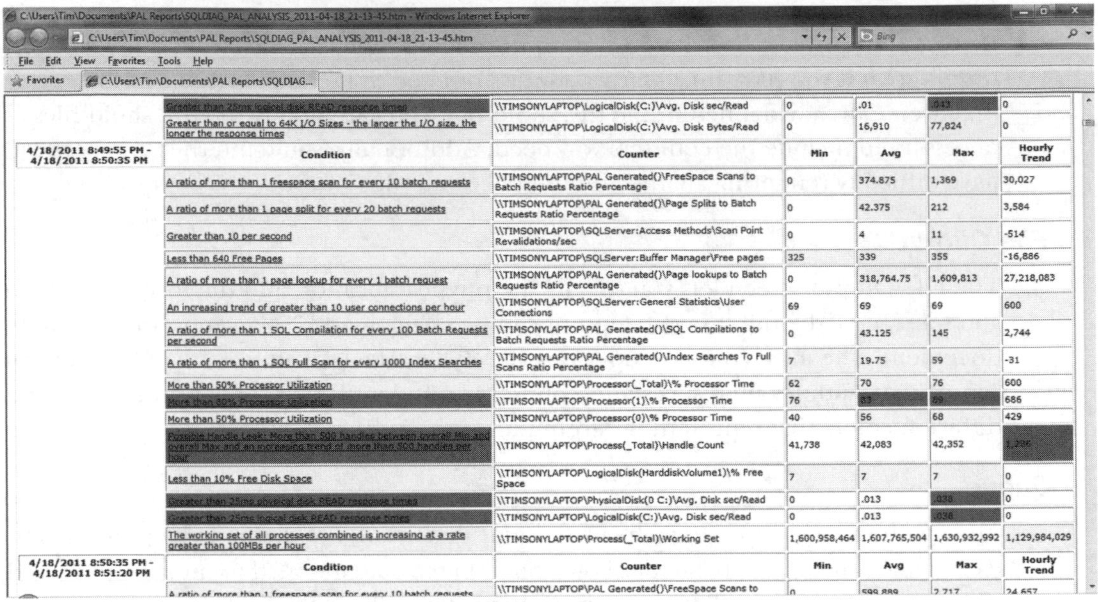

Figure 8   The PAL report will highlight potential performance problems encountered during the analysis.

add items to the queue, or execute what's in the queue and restart the PAL wizard using the same settings. The output of the Execute screen is the report.

The PAL report

Once you've captured the counter data and have processed it using PAL, you're ready to reap the rewards of the tool. When using the HTML output, PAL produces a rich and detailed report (see figure 8), outlining all counter information gathered, with highlights showing potential problem areas. The areas highlighted in yellow indicate a potential warning, and red indicates that you have a problem. Note that you can adjust the colors associated with warnings and critical issues in PAL.

In figure 8, notice there are several potential warnings, indicating areas you should investigate. The red entries represent critical issues that you should focus your attention on immediately.

If you click the "More than 80% processor utilization" critical alert, you're taken to a chart detailing the time-series breakdown of the Processor: % Processor Time counter (see figure 9). From this knowledge, you can begin reviewing your SQL workload to see what may have caused the CPU spikes.

Summary

Analyzing performance counter data can be hard work. PAL can significantly ease the pain of analyzing performance counter logs. Download it free from pal.codeplex.com and start using it right away, and you'll find it helps you make sense of the many

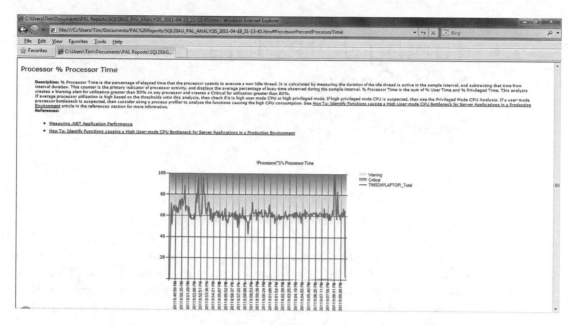

Figure 9   The charts included in the PAL report make it easy to see performance trends.

performance counters available to you. A major benefit of PAL is that it lets customize thresholds for existing counters and develop your own derived counters that are meaningful to your environment. Once the counters are captured, PAL analyzes the log and produces wonderful graphical reports, which provide a significant amount of insight into any hardware or SQL Server problems you may have.

About the author

Tim Chapman resides in Chapel Hill, NC, with his wife, Brittany, and Bernese mountain dog, Sam. For the past decade, Tim has worked with SQL Server in a variety of roles, ranging from administration to architecture, and recently accepted a position at Microsoft as a SQL Server Dedicated Premier Field Engineer. Tim has been awarded the SQL Server MVP each year since 2008.

39 Tuning JDBC for SQL Server

Jungsun Kim

When I look at the queries sent to SQL Server via JDBC, the query methods are often not optimized for SQL Server, resulting in performance issues. This problem has occurred in all of my customers' systems that use JDBC to access SQL Server. JDBC-based applications will have performance issues if appropriate steps aren't taken to correct the problems caused by JDBC.

For the last few years, I've diagnosed many performance problems for Java-based applications using the JDBC driver to access SQL Server. Doing so has required a lot of trial-and-error testing, but eventually I was able to come up with techniques to help resolve the performance issues.

In this chapter, I'll share what I've learned, so if you face similar problems, you'll know how to approach solving them.

JDBC performance tuning can be effective

The best way to start out is to review a recent case. The system consisted of Apache Tomcat, SQL Server, and Microsoft JDBC. As part of diagnosis and performance tuning, I decided to change a single attribute in Tomcat to modify the behavior of JDBC. I'll tell you about this change in the next section.

Figures 1 and 2 display the resource usage by duration, CPU, and logical I/Os for a given time period while running a common workload. Figure 1 shows the resource usage values before the change, and figure 2 shows the values after the change.

Each box represents one of the resources being monitored. We kept track of the number and total cost of "expensive" queries, and we defined "expensive" as being queries with a duration or CPU time of more than 1,000 ms, or queries that read more than 1,000 pages. For each resource, there are two columns, with the first indicating the counts and the second indicating the total cost. The two colors in each column represent the expensive queries (top) and the nonexpensive queries

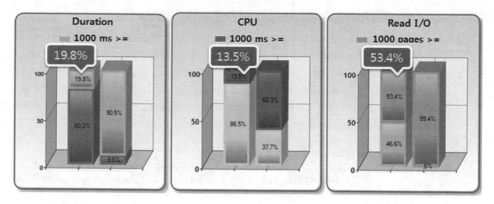

Figure 1   Resource usage before tuning

(bottom). So look at the first box in figure 1, duration. The first column indicates that 19.8 percent of all queries were ones with a duration of more than 1,000 ms, and the second column indicates that the sum of all the durations for those expensive queries was 90.5 percent of the total duration of the workload. The second box indicates that 13.5 percent of the queries were expensive in terms of CPU time and took 62.3 percent of the total CPU time. The third box indicates that 53.4 percent of the queries read more than 1,000 pages, and these queries comprised 99.4 percent of the total reads for the workload.

Figure 2 shows the same measurements after tuning, and you should note that duration, CPU, and I/O all show significant improvements with just a single change. For example, the number of expensive queries in the workload dropped from 19.8 percent to 1.4 percent and total time for the expensive queries dropped from 90.5 percent of the workload to 38.5 percent.

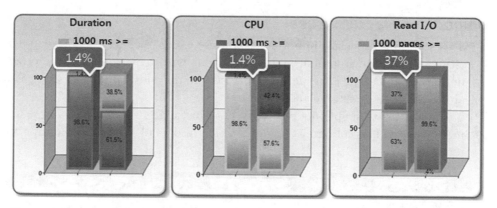

Figure 2   Resource usage after tuning

Recommendations for tuning jTDS configuration

Now that you can see how a single configuration change can boost performance, let's take a look at this change, along with other changes that can be made to help boost performance. As I explain these configuration settings, I'll focus on the jTDS JDBC driver (which is a commonly used open source JDBC driver) and compare the settings to Microsoft's own JDBC driver. I'll address the differences related to performance in each case. Table 1 shows the results from a system I tested.

Table 1   Summary of jTDS standard tuning items

Item	Recommendation	Attribute and code	Note (exceptions)
Unicode character	Non-Unicode	`sendStringParametersAs Unicode = false;`	Column type in UNICODE not applicable
API cursor	Default (Firehose)	`(default) useCursors = false;`	Affects ResultSet Type
ResultSet Type	Default (TYPE_FORWARD_ONLY)	`createStatement();`	Unimportant; API cursor not recommended
Prepared statement mechanism	sp_executesql	`prepareSQL = 2;`	

Let's review each of these items in detail.

NOTE   The test environment was JDK 6 Update 21 (x64), jTDS 1.2.5, and Microsoft JDBC 3.0 Driver. I've listed Java snippets as examples throughout.

Unicode character issues

This section is especially important if you use `varchar` or `char` as the data type. Java (JDBC) or .NET environments default the string type to `nvarchar` unless you explicitly define the data type. The performance suffers the most when the string is used in either the JOIN or WHERE clause.

Let's review a simple query (listing 1). It has a WHERE clause with the search argument `pub_id`. This column is a `char(4)` and is also a PRIMARY KEY column with a clustered index.

Listing 1   Example query

```
SELECT pub_id, pub_name
FROM Pubs.dbo.Publishers
WHERE pub_id = N'0736'
```

The value for pub_id is N'07236', which is a UNICODE literal, not a character literal. What will happen in this case? I'll first show you the query plan from an instance of SQL Server 2000 (see figure 3).

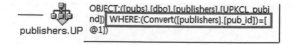

Figure 3   Execution plan from SQL Server 2000

As you can see in figure 3, the query can't use the available clustered index. The value of pub_id is converted implicitly, so the plan shows convert() to pub_id, and it changed the logical operator to WHERE, not SEEK. As a result, the query scans the entire table and then filters the results.

Now, what will happen in SQL Server 2005, 2008, and 2008R2? You might see the same Clustered Index Scan or Clustered Index Seek in the query plans. If you see the Clustered Index Seek, it means that the query used the improved implicit conversion feature of SQL Server 2005 (or later).

Next, let's check if the query really submitted an nvarchar in JDBC. I used the PreparedStatement class for sending parameterized SQL statements (also known as a parameterized query) to the database, as shown in listing 2.

Listing 2   Call parameterized query

```
Try
{
Class.forName("net.sourceforge.jtds.jdbc.Driver");

Connection cn          = null;
PreparedStatement stmt = null;
String strURL = "jdbc:jtds:sqlserver://localhost;";
String strID  = "sqluser1";
String strPWD = "sqluser1";

cn = DriverManager.getConnection(strURL, strID, strPWD);
stmt = cn.prepareStatement("SELECT pub_id, pub_name" +
                    " FROM Pubs.dbo.Publishers " +
                    " WHERE pub_id = ? ");
stmt.setString(1, "0736");
ResultSet rs = stmt.executeQuery();
```

Let's view the output from a Profiler trace. It shows the @P0 parameter in sp_prepare is declared nvarchar(4000), and the following sp_execute uses N'0736' as its value (see figure 4).

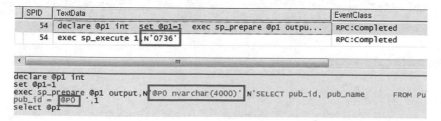

**Figure 4
Trace results
from Profiler**

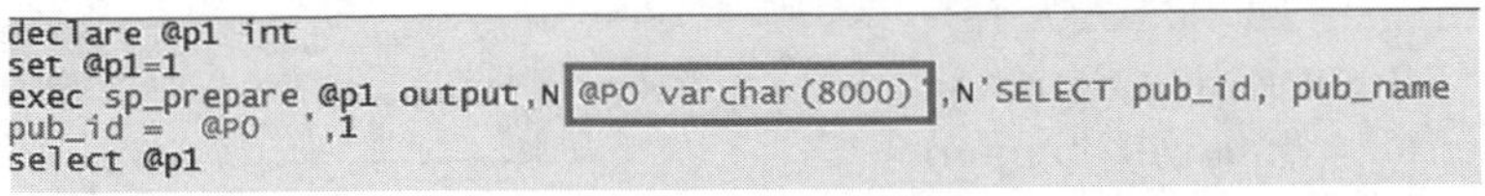

```
declare @p1 int
set @p1=1
exec sp_prepare @p1 output,N'@P0 varchar(8000)',N'SELECT pub_id, pub_name
pub_id =  @P0 ',1
select @p1
```

Figure 5   Profiler trace results when not passing a Unicode parameter

Now that you've uncovered the root cause of the problem, you must find a solution. The data type in the table is VARCHAR, not NVARCHAR, but the parameters are passed as nvarchar by the JDBC driver itself. That's the problem. So, you must find how to change the JDBC drivers. The first way is to change the connection property in the jTDS URL to this:

```
sendStringParametersAsUnicode = false;
```

Listing 3 shows the code and figure 5 the result.

Listing 3   Adding `sendStringParametersAsUnicode`

```
String strURL =
"jdbc:jtds:sqlserver://localhost;sendStringParametersAsUnicode=false;";
String strID  = "sqluser1";
String strPWD = "sqluser1";
```

Yes, this is exactly what you wanted. This simple step is one of the key points I begin with whenever I review systems with JDBC and SQL Server. It's the single change I referred to earlier, where I made one change and performance increased dramatically.

API cursor issues

There are also issues with cursors when using JDBC. The ResultSet Type is related to this issue, specifically to API server cursor usage. The jTDS and the JDBC drivers don't use an API server cursor by default. They use what is called a *firehose cursor*, which is also known as "direct select." In other words, it's a forward-only, read-only result set. It sends all the requested result rows from the database as a stream to the client, and it's the fastest type of cursor to use. SQL Server's documentation sometimes uses the term "default result set" instead of firehose cursor.

When you set useCursors = true; jTDS uses an API server cursor if you don't change the ResultSet Type. But if you set the ResultSet Type to FORWARD_ONLY, then a fast forward–only cursor is used. I'll discuss the server cursor type later in this chapter.

Now let's review the real action. Listing 4 shows code that sets useCursors = true; in the URL format, and figure 6 shows the Profiler trace of using an API server cursor.

Listing 4   `useCursors` property

```
Try
{
Class.forName("net.sourceforge.jtds.jdbc.Driver");

Connection cn = null;
Statement stmt= null;
String strURL = "jdbc:jtds:sqlserver://localhost;useCursors=true;";
```

```
String strID  = "sqluser1";
String strPWD = "sqluser1";

cn    = DriverManager.getConnection(strURL, strID, strPWD);
stmt = cn.createStatement();
ResultSet rs = stmt.executeQuery("SELECT * " +
                        " FROM AdventureWorks.Sales.SalesOrderHeader " +
                        " WHERE SalesOrderID <= (43659 + 200)");

while(rs.next())
{
System.out.println(rs.getString("CustomerID"));
}
```

The Profiler trace output (see figure 6) shows the system procedures sp_cursoropen, sp_cursorfetch, and sp_cursorclose sequentially, which demonstrates that an API server cursor is being used. The 16 in sp_cursoropen, set @p3 = 16 means Cursor Type = 16, a fast forward–only cursor.

In OLTP and web-based systems, the requirement is often just HMTL code that produces the entire record set from beginning to end. Therefore, you don't need to create a cursor on SQL Server. Such a cursor would cause many round-trips with small-sized row blocks. You also don't need to use scrollable movement instead of forward only. These actions as described would only cause performance overhead.

For example, I did some performance tuning as a consultant for an online store. Their application used server cursors from within their ASP code. I advised the development team to switch from an API cursor to a client-side cursor, and they executed the ADO code changes. After the change, the CPU usage dropped by 15 percent. This change in performance occurred within a matter of minutes, and my clients who were monitoring the system expressed astonishment.

ResultSet Type issue

The jTDS and the JDBC drivers both use the FORWARD_ONLY READ_ONLY ResultSet Type by default, and these are direct selects, which I mentioned earlier. But when you use a

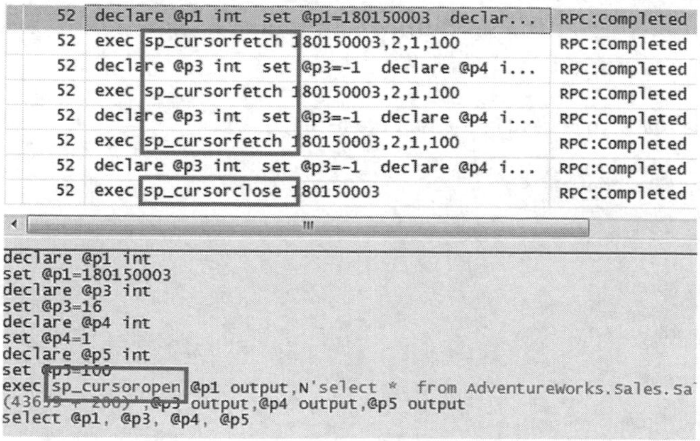

Figure 6   The Profiler trace shows the API server cursor.

scroll cursor—which allows forward or backward movement—the cursor automatically changes to an API server cursor. It doesn't follow the useCursors property.

Table 2 shows the cursor types supported by SQL Server according to JDBC's Result-Set Type. These types are mentioned in jTDS documents.

Table 2   ResultSet Types supported by jTDS on SQL Server

JDBC type	SQL Server cursor type	Server load	Description
TYPE_FORWARD_ONLY	Firehose cursor (direct select) where read-only	Light	Fast
	Fast forward–only (static) cursor when read-only and useCursors = true	Heavy	Slower than firehose cursors
	Forward-only dynamic cursor when updatable	Heavy	
TYPE_SCROLL_INSENSITIVE	Static cursor	Heavy	SQL Server generates a temporary table, so changes made by others aren't visible.
TYPE_SCROLL_SENSITIVE	Keyset Cursor	Medium	Others' updates or deletes visible, but not others' inserts.
TYPE_SCROLL_SENSITIVE+1	Dynamic cursor	Heavy	Others' updates, deletes, and inserts visible.

As you can see in table 2, all the other options, except the firehose cursor, place a burden on SQL Server that can cause performance problems. In addition, they sometimes make heavy use of temporary tables, further hindering performance.

Let's check the code example and the trace to find out what kind of cursor type is used. I'll skip the fast forward–only cursor, because it's been already discussed. The cursor type is set in the @scrollopt option in the sp_cursoropen system procedure, which you can see by looking at the @p output parameter in figure 7. Table 3 shows some of the cursor type parameter values.

Table 3   Cursor scroll type (only types used in the test are listed)

Value	Description
0x0001	Keyset-driven cursor
0x0002	Dynamic cursor
0x0004	Forward-only cursor
0x0008	Static cursor
0x0010	Fast forward–only cursor

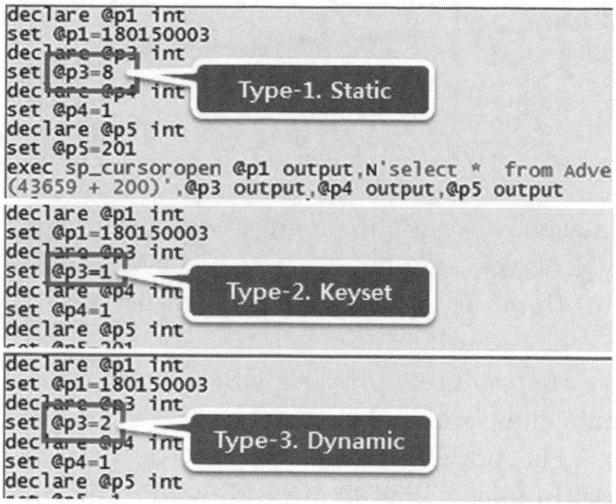

Figure 7   Trace results for each type

Listing 5 is almost the same as listing 4, except I modified TYPE in createStatement().

Listing 5   Three example codes for ResultSet Type

```
// Type-1)
stmt = cn.createStatement(ResultSet.TYPE_SCROLL_INSENSITIVE,
                          ResultSet.CONCUR_READ_ONLY);
// Type-2)
stmt = cn.createStatement(ResultSet.TYPE_SCROLL_SENSITIVE,
                          ResultSet.CONCUR_READ_ONLY);
// Type-3)
stmt = cn.createStatement(ResultSet.TYPE_SCROLL_SENSITIVE+1,
                          ResultSet.CONCUR_READ_ONLY);
```

Prepared statement mechanism issue

Temporary procedures have been used by some people or some database APIs such as JDBC in place of running the same queries in the same connection in an effort to improve performance and reduce expensive compiles. Another way to get better performance is by using the Prepare/Execute methods, which separates the processing into two steps: a preparing step that compiles the query and an execute step that uses the actual parameters and executes the compiled query. This two-step processing is useful only when a query is executed repeatedly in an application—for example, when it's contained within a WHILE loop. But it has the overhead of the round-trip to the server as an RPC event for each Prepare/Execute. It's reasonable to use this method only when you repeatedly use the same query in a connection.

When SQL Server 2000 was released, Microsoft recommended using the sp_executesql procedure instead of temporary procedures or Prepare/Execute. Prepare/Execute makes it difficult to analyze the query performance with Profiler, because it isn't straightforward to determine which Prepare operation corresponds to which Execute operation. (Yes, there are some workarounds for this, but I've never been comfortable using them.)

```
declare @p1 int
set @p1=1
exec sp_prepare @p1 output,N'@PO int',N'SELECT * FROM AdventureWorks.Sales.
WHERE SalesOrderID <=  @PO ',1
select @p1
go
exec sp_execute 1,43959
go
```

**Figure 8   Profiler
trace results using
the Prepare/
Execute method**

Using `sp_executesql` is advantageous because it generates execution plans that are more likely to be reused by SQL Server. Another advantage of using `sp_executesql` compared to dynamic SQL sent from the client is that fewer bytes travel across the network, thus reducing traffic and overhead.

So how do the jTDS and the Microsoft JDBC driver handle parameters? First, jTDS uses the Prepare/Execute combination with a default value of 3 for the `prepareSQL` property in the URL format. The possible values that can be provided for the `prepareSQL` property are shown in table 4, and figure 8 shows Profiler trace results using the Prepare/Execute method.

Table 4   Table 4 Values for the `prepareSQL` property

Value	Description	
0	SQL is sent to the server each time without any preparation; literals are inserted in the SQL (slower).	
1	Temporary stored procedures are created for each unique SQL statement and parameter combination (faster).	
2	`sp_executesql` is used (fast).	
3	`sp_prepare` and `sp_cursorprepare` are used in conjunction with `sp_execute` and `sp_cursorexecute` (faster; SQL Server only).	

jTDS supports changing the method of calling queries by setting the `prepareSQL` property in the URL format when you call `prepareStatement()`. For example, when you set `prepareSQL = 0;` as shown in table 4, the query runs as ad hoc by changing the whole query to a literal, not as a parameterized query. Let's confirm whether `sp_executesql` functions as expected when we change the value of `prepareSQL` property to 2. We'll validate the findings through trace results (figure 9) and the sample code shown in listing 6.

Listing 6   The `sp_executesql` mechanism

```
Try
{
Class.forName("net.sourceforge.jtds.jdbc.Driver");

Connection cn          = null;
PreparedStatement stmt = null;
String strURL          = "jdbc:jtds:sqlserver://localhost;prepareSQL=2;";
```

```
String strID          = "sqluser1";
String strPWD         = "sqluser1";

cn = DriverManager.getConnection(strURL, strID, strPWD);
stmt = cn.prepareStatement("SELECT * " +
                    " FROM AdventureWorks.Sales.SalesOrderHeader " +
                    " WHERE SalesOrderID <= ?");
stmt.setInt(1, 43959);
ResultSet rs = stmt.executeQuery();
```

```
exec sp_executesql N'SELECT *
 FROM AdventureWorks.Sales.SalesOrderHeader
 WHERE SalesOrderID <=  @P0 ',N'@P0 int',43959|
```

Figure 9　Trace results for `prepareSQL=2`

So how does the Microsoft JDBC Driver work by default? Figure 10 shows that it's handled as `sp_prepexec` and `sp_unprepare`.

```
declare @p1 int
set @p1=1
exec sp_prepexec @p1 output,N'@P0 int',N'SELECT *
FROM AdventureWorks.Sales.SalesOrderHeader
WHERE SalesOrderID <= @P0            ',43959
select @p1
go
exec sp_unprepare 1
go
```

Figure 10　Trace of the JDBC driver queries

So how does JDBC handle stored procedures? In jTDS, they're handled correctly by using `prepareCall()` in the `Connection` object. The Microsoft JDBC Driver calls `sp_prepexec/sp_unprepare`, like a parameterized query.

Controlling global configuration

Finally, I'd like to discuss how to control the URL format options, such as `useCursors`, `sendStringParametersAsUnicode`, or `prepareSQL`, with just one click. Are there any global configurations to change for all these options? After some research, I found the answer. Because I was working with Tomcat, I'll use Tomcat for an example. Figure 11 shows how you can set the `sendStringParametersAsUnicode` attribute in the URL of the `Context/Resource` element in C:\Tomcat5.5\conf\Catalina\localhost\ROOT.xml.

Another way to control the URL format option is to modify mssql.url in the server.properties file.

```
- <Context docBase="         " privileged="true" antiResourceLocking="false" antiJARLocking="false" reloadable="true">
    <Resource auth="Container" driverClassName="com.microsoft.sqlserver.jdbc.SQLServerDriver"
      factory="orq.apache.tomcat.dbcp.dbcp.BasicDataSourceFactory" maxActive="20" maxIdle="10" maxWait="-1"
      name="         " password="         " type="javax.sql.DataSource"
      url="jdbc:sqlserver://         ,databaseName=    ;sendStringParametersAsUnicode=false"
      username='    " />
    <!-- Link to the user database we will get roles from
```

Figure 11　Setting the URL attribute in ROOT.xml

Summary

When you use jTDS or the JDBC driver with SQL Server, you should review the following items in order to optimize performance: UNICODE parameters, API server cursor, a method to handle parameterize queries, and the ability to choose the proper ResultSet Type. Using the right options for your environment can greatly boost a JDBC-based application's performance.

About the author

 Jungsun Kim works as a senior consultant in SQLRoad, a consulting company in Korea. He became the first MVP in Asia (2002), and has been awarded the MVP title every year through 2011. He shares his knowledge in online communities, TechNet forums, his blog, Twitter, and many SQL Server seminars. He's written books on SQL Server, as well. For the last two years, he developed BigEyes, a utility tool for self-monitoring and tuning SQL Server performance. Jungsun enjoys introducing BigEyes to his clients and regularly releases enhancements with passion. You'll find his blog at http://blog.naver.com/visualdb. He'd like to thank William Wonhyuk Chung, an expert in SQL Server and his CEO, who helped translate this article into English.

## PART 5

Business intelligence

Edited by Greg Low

Thank you for purchasing this book. We appreciate your support and hope that you find it provides a different experience to other books that you may have purchased in the past.

In the Business Intelligence section for volume 1, I wrote about why BI was so important for businesses and discussed how far the Microsoft BI platform has come since it first appeared. This time, for volume 2, I want to discuss why it's important for you to be involved in BI for your career development.

Many SQL Server professionals have worked predominantly with the database engine and are now beginning to take tentative steps toward broadening their skill sets to include BI. There are several good reasons for doing this, but I feel that the most important reason is to increase your value to your organization and your own marketability.

Most organizations seem to see database engines as a commodity. Although the applications that run against those database engines are often critical to the business operation, the database engine and the staff who support it are often considered a cost of doing business. Whenever you work in an area that's considered a cost of doing business, you'll often experience constant cost reduction pressures from the business. Further, the slow but steady move into cloud-based systems will inevitably erode the career prospects for personnel wishing to use low-level database engine skills. Skills that are important today will be less important in the future.

By contrast, BI applications appeal directly to the people in the business who pay the bills. They're seen as a direct enhancement to the profitability of the business, and companies are often keen to invest in such applications. This means that BI is a good area to invest your time in developing skills. Some BI applications, particularly those involving data mining technologies, often contribute directly to the profitability of the organization. Although it can still be challenging to implement effective projects using these technologies today, working in an area that's seen by managers as being highly critical to the profitability of the business is a great way to build a career for the future. I encourage you to become involved if you aren't involved as yet.

I particularly want to thank the SQL Server MVPs who have written chapters for this section. Many are friends whom I've known for years. I'm constantly amazed by the contributions they make to the community.

About the editor

 Greg Low is an internationally recognized consultant and trainer. He's a SQL Server MVP and Microsoft RD and is the CEO for SolidQ in Australia. Greg is best known for his www.sqldownunder.com podcast and is a former board member of PASS. He regularly speaks at SQL Server–related events around the world.

40 Creating a formal Reporting Services report part library

Jessica M. Moss

Before entering the design process, an organization must incorporate every application into its existing processes and structures. The organization must decide how the new application replaces existing functionality or provides new features. A reporting solution is just another application that must go through these same steps. This chapter walks through the process of determining whether a formal Reporting Services report part library works for your organization, explains how to set up the server, and describes the process for using the report parts.

Report parts defined

Over the last eight years, SQL Server Reporting Services has come out with multiple versions to allow report writers to design and develop reports for their organizations. Whether the reports are analytical or operational, the design principles are typically the same: gather requirements, create a mock-up, pull data, and make the report. This process is repeated over and over again to produce an output shareable with executives and managers. But how do we make this process easier?

Reporting Services introduced an addition to their suite in 2010 (version 2008 R2) to allow report writers to create abstractions of particular report pieces and share them with other report writers. By reusing a report part in multiple reports, report writers can decrease their initial development time, increase their ease of maintenance, and create a cleaner, more aesthetic look across all their reports.

NOTE A *report part* is a component in Reporting Services that can be shared, reused, and modified by utilizing the report part gallery.

When designing reports, certain report items are used over and over again, including data and design elements. Report items that can act as a report part are shown in table 1, broken down into logical report item categories.

Table 1   Report items that can act as a report part

Report item category	Report items
Data	Data source
	Dataset
Design	Charts
	Gauges
	Images
	Maps
	Rectangles
	Tables
	Matrices
	Lists

You should keep in mind a few caveats when using report parts. Both report items that reference a Reporting Services custom code method and children report items can't be published to the report part gallery. You'll need to publish the top level of the nested report items to include the children items. In addition, report variables won't be included—and report parameters only sometimes—in the report part gallery.

Although using report parts can be a blessing for some organizations, it can be a curse for others. Depending on the structure of reporting in different environments, using a report part library may not make sense for your organization. Let's discuss some of the factors that may persuade your organization one way or the other.

Deciding to create a report part library

Although every organization can find some benefit from using report parts, creating and maintaining a formal report part library may not be required. You may think that a formal process is always better, but it's not necessarily so in this case. Let's start by defining a formal report library instead of just the report part gallery that Reporting Services comes with. Dedicating the time, work, and energy to creating and maintaining a formal report part library may not provide enough benefit to your organization to outweigh the drawbacks.

NOTE   A *report part library* is a gallery of data sources, datasets, and report parts in Reporting Services that are created, maintained, and supported by members of your organization.

Keep in mind that a report part library can be created in either Reporting Services native or SharePoint integrated mode. Figure 1 shows the process for setting up a report part library.

To create your report part library, begin by deciding which report parts to share with the report writers. Once this decision has been made, you create each report part and upload it to the report part gallery. Then, your report writers can start using the report parts. But once they start looking at the report parts, they usually want to make changes. Some examples of typical changes are listed here:

Figure 1   The process for setting up a report part library

- Add an additional column to a dataset
- Change the color on a bar chart
- Modify the target value on a gauge

The report writer has the ability to make a change directly on the report part and save it to the report gallery. The next time another report writer opens a report that uses that report part, they decide if they want to keep their old version or use the new version. Determining whether the change is specific to the report or a global change is something to be decided. Now you start to see where the maintenance piece comes in. The original report writer submits a request to change the report part, and an administrator decides if it's a one-off change or if propagation to the rest of the reports is required.

Now if your organization can't support this type of structure or doesn't have the staff to help manage this process, you may not benefit from a formal report part library. Additionally, if every report needs to go through an in-depth evaluation and review process, you don't want to throw small changes into the mix. Then you may not want this kind of library. Finally, if your reports don't share a lot of similar attributes, you may not see the speedy development and maintenance advantages of setting up the process.

If your organization doesn't fall into any of these categories and you think a formal report part library may be the way to go, you'll then decide how to initially set up your library. Let's begin by picking which report parts to create.

Selecting report parts

Before anyone starts using report parts, you'll want to create a set of base report parts to start the report library process. It's important to determine where you want your report parts to go before you start developing reports. Moving report parts to new folders after the fact can cause unhappy consequences with existing reports. Deciding which report parts to use is a feat all in itself!

Let's use the publicly available AdventureWorks samples to walk through the addition, usage, and modification of a report part. You can download the SQL Server 2008 R2 product sample databases from http://msftdbprodsamples.codeplex.com/ and the AdventureWorks Sample Reports SS2008R2 from http://msftrsprodsamples.codeplex.com/.

In the Reporting Services project named AdventureWorks 2008R2, take a look at the reports that the bicycle reseller store uses on a regular basis. You're not interested in the base or lesson reports, so you can exclude those from your project. What remains can be seen in figure 2.

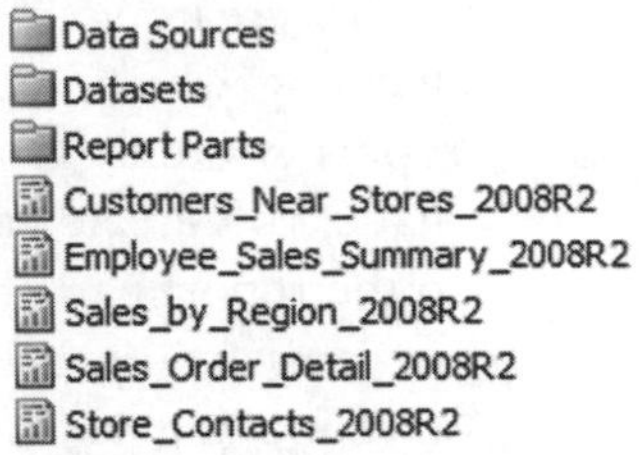

Before uploading your reports to the report server, you need to determine their correct location. The folder structure in the report server divides your report part library for report writers' convenience and security. The sample folder hierarchy in figure 3 is based on the reports from AdventureWorks. Following the figure, I'll walk you through the process of determining the items in each level of the hierarchy.

📁 Data Sources
📁 Datasets
📁 Report Parts
📊 Customers_Near_Stores_2008R2
📊 Employee_Sales_Summary_2008R2
📊 Sales_by_Region_2008R2
📊 Sales_Order_Detail_2008R2
📊 Store_Contacts_2008R2

Figure 2   AdventureWorks 2008R2 Sample Reports with base and lesson reports excluded from project

Level 1

The highest level, Level 1, contains two item types: a Data Sources folder and a folder for each department. This is a typical corporate folder structure for a Reporting Services environment even without report parts. The structure specific to the report part library starts under each department folder.

Level 2

The next level down, Level 2, contains all data sources in the Data Sources folder, all the reports per department, and an additional set of department Subject Area folders. Each

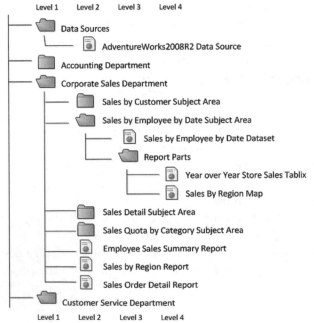

Figure 3   Sample folder hierarchy

	Departments					
	Customer Service	Retail Locations	Corporate Sales			
	Subject Areas	Subject Areas	Subject Areas			
	Customer Detail	Store Detail	Sales by Employee by Date	Sales Detail	Sales Quota by Category	Sales by Customer
R e p o r t s Customers_Near_Stores	☑	☑				
Employee_Sales_Summary			☑	☑	☑	
Sales_by_Region			☑			☑
Sales_Order_Detail				☑		
Store_Contacts		☑				

Figure 4 Sample reports linked to subject areas

Subject Area folder contains the report items that can be logically grouped together and typically has a one-to-one relationship with a shared dataset, included in Level 3. To decide what subject areas your organization has, take a look at your existing reports and data to see how you can sort the data and grouping elements.

For the AdventureWorks example, I've split the data from the provided reports into six subject areas. Figure 4 shows the list of reports and the linked subject areas.

Level 3

The Level 3 items include one dataset that directly relates to the Subject Area folder in which it resides and one folder named Report Parts.

Level 4

The final level, Level 4, includes all the report parts for that subject area, recognizable because each report part uses the dataset also in its parent Subject Area folder. Multiple reasons make a report part special enough to be included in the formal report part library, including reusability, commonality, and discoverability. Reusability means that multiple reports use the same report part, such as a standard header for external reporting. For a report part to show commonality, report writers use the report part's base data elements but make slight modifications for their needs without having to re-create the entire report part. A matrix with prepopulated sales and territory data is a great candidate for providing a common report part. Finally, if new data or a new way of viewing data is introduced into your organization, exposing a new report part using that data or data view can provide discoverability into your data.

Using a report part library

At this point, you've decided that a report part library fits your organization like a glove, and you've decided what base report parts your reports need. Using the AdventureWorks sample you already downloaded, let's work through the rest of the report part library process. Although you can create and publish a report part from both Business Intelligence Development Studio and Report Builder 3.0 (Report Builder), only Report Builder allows for searching and importing of report parts. Because of this, you'll use Report Builder for these examples.

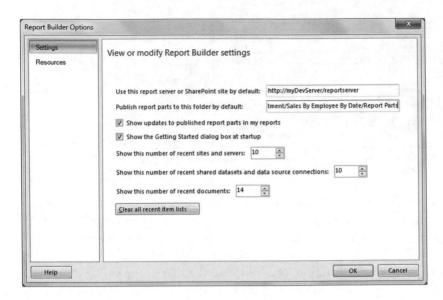

Figure 5   Configuration of publishing folder for report parts in the Options window

Creating the initial report part

To start setting up your report part, open the existing completed report, Sales_by_Region_2008R2. In Report Builder, begin by setting the publishing folder property for the report part to go to the report part folder in the Sales by Employee by Date Subject Area folder in the Options window, as shown in figure 5.

Next, you can publish the Map1 report item by clicking the Report Builder button in the top-left corner of the application and choosing Publish Report Parts. In the

Figure 6   Selection of a report part to publish to the report server

Select Report Parts To Publish dialog box, give the report part a name, such as Sales-ByRegionMap, and a description to ensure easy searching later on, as shown in figure 6.

Follow a similar pattern for the other report parts you picked in our earlier exercise.

Using report parts and change requests

Once the report part is available, you can reuse the report part in your report. In Report Builder, open the Insert menu and choose Report Parts. You can search for "map," "SalesBy-Region," or something similar to find the existing report part. The completed search screen appears in figure 7. Once you find the desired object, you can double-click or drag the item to the report. All dependent objects, such as data sources and datasets, are included in the report at this time.

If you decide you like the report part as is, you can save your report. But if you decide to change something, you have two options:

- Make the modification only in your report
- Change the global report part

Figure 7   Report part search in the Report Part Gallery

If you make the modification to your own report, your changes are not populated to other reports and you can ignore notifications when the original report part changes. This could be a valid option if you need to make a slight color change, or if you use a report part as a base report part.

If you decide to make a global change, you request a report part change from the administrator. Examples of global changes include new business logic that affects all reports, a change in the organization's color scheme that affects reports, or the inclusion of a column that report writers add over and over again.

Keep in mind that no matter which option you choose, changes to shared data sources and shared datasets are automatically pushed to the report, regardless of whether that's what you want.

Existing report part changes and publication

If you decide to change the report part globally, you make the change in Report Builder. After importing the report part onto a report, you make the desired change, republish the report part, and inform the report writers. Change the map report part and republish it to the report server to see the effects.

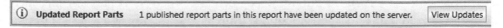

Figure 8   Notification of updated report part

Open the original report, Sales_by_Region_2008R2, in Report Builder to see that the report part has changed. Figure 8 shows the message you receive.

Each report writer can make the decision to accept the newest version or keep the old one the next time they work on that report. In this way, appropriate changes are populated across the organization, whereas inappropriate changes aren't.

Summary

If your organization is ready for it, a report part library can greatly increase your development speed. It's important to weigh all the options in making this important decision. Although it isn't the only way of working with the Reporting Services report part gallery, a formal report library can be a useful tool in the right environment. This chapter helped you decide if a formal report library is best for your company and taught you how to create one.

About the author

Jessica M. Moss is a well-known architect, speaker, author, and Microsoft MVP of SQL Server business intelligence. Jessica has created numerous data warehousing solutions for companies in many industries and has authored technical content for multiple magazines and websites. She coauthored the book *Microsoft SQL Server 2008 Integration Services: Problem, Design, Solution* (Wrox, 2009). Jessica enjoys working with the central Virginia community and speaks regularly at user groups, code camps, and conferences. You can read more on her website, www.jessicammoss.com.

41 Improving report layout and visualization

Greg Low

One of the things I love to do is to send suggestions to the SQL Server product team about how I'd hope to see the product improved. I usually joke that I know when a new version is about to be shipped because I start receiving all the emails saying "closed" and "won't fix." But with SQL Server 2008 R2, I was impressed by the number of emails I received from the Reporting Services team that said "closed" and "fixed."

I often get the feeling that there's a level of fixation within the product group about features that will appear in the next marketing brochure for the product. What also impressed me about the Reporting Services team was the number of small issues that they fixed in SQL Server 2008 R2. None of these are the things that you'll ever see in a marketing brochure, yet they're the sorts of things that can make developers happy. In this chapter, I focus both on issues from my suggestions that I was excited to see implemented and on issues that just make development easier.

Target-based rendering

Reporting Services has the ability to render reports for different targets such as HTML, Microsoft Word, Microsoft Excel, PDF, and others. The format that I've had the most difficulty with in the past has been the Excel format. The product team must have gone to extreme lengths to make the Excel rendering of the reports look similar to the HTML versions. They've adjusted fonts, line heights, cell layouts, and so forth. Yet when I supply one of these reports to an end user, they invariably look at it, smile, say "thanks," and then add "But what I really want is just the data."

This means that I often found myself needing to generate two versions of each report. One version was used for rendering as Excel; the other version was for all other formats. Because of this, I sent a suggestion asking for the ability to determine layout based on where the report was being rendered to. In essence, I wanted to be able to use a target like "EXCEL" or "PDF" within the expression language in Reporting Services.

The product team has supplied this and more. The expression language now includes an object called `RenderFormat` in the `Globals` collection. This means I can build expressions such as the following:

```
=Iif(Globals!RenderFormat.Name = "EXCEL",12, 100)
```

That did satisfy my requests, but what the team supplied was even better than that. The `RenderFormat` object also includes an `IsInteractive` property. This means I can format my output based on whether the report is in an interactive format without having to know the name of all the rendering formats in advance. For example, I could format hyperlinks differently only when the report is being used interactively.

Control over pagination

Another big issue for me was the control over pagination. The first time the need for this struck me was when I had to create a report that printed a number of client invoices. My report was a table that included invoices as subreports. Although I could include the page number in the footer of each invoice, I'd see a series of page numbers throughout the entire set of invoices. I wanted to restart the page number at the start of each invoice. Achieving that goal wasn't easy, so I also sent a request to be able to restart page numbers at the group level.

Again, the product group exceeded my needs. At the group level, a new set of properties was added, as shown in figure 1.

The first of these properties determines if a page break occurs at all, and if it does occur, where the page break occurs in relation to the group that the property is defined on. It's possible to specify the `Break-Location` as one of the following values:

⊟ PageBreak	
BreakLocation	**None**
Disabled	**False**
ResetPageNumber	**False**
PageName	

Figure 1   Pagination properties for a group

- None
- Start
- End
- StartAndEnd
- Between

Each of these properties can be set by an expression. This allows you to create scenarios such as Excel-based output that breaks groups into separate worksheets yet have HTML-based output that has no page breaks at all.

The property that surprised me in this list was `PageName`. It wasn't immediately obvious to me where I'd use a name for a page. But it turns out that this property is very useful. The `PageName` property is used to name worksheets when rendering to Excel, as shown in figure 2.

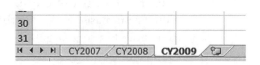

Figure 2   Use the `PageName` property to name Excel worksheets

Joining across datasets

Reports can be based on more than one dataset. Where a difficulty arises is when a report control such as a table needs to use data from more than one dataset. For example, while iterating through a list of products you might have a need to add a column for the most popular model of each product.

If one dataset has product details and another dataset has product model details, the solution to this problem has been to create a dataset based on a join of the underlying data. This approach works well if both datasets were based on the same data source. But if the datasets were based on different data sources, there might be no easy way to join the data before it arrives in Reporting Services.

Reporting Services now provides the ability to perform lookups from one dataset into the rows of another dataset. For example, consider the following code:

```
=Lookup(Fields!ProductID.Value,Fields!ProductID.Value,
        Fields!Name.Value,"ProductModel")
```

Note that the code has been split across two lines just for readability.

In this example, the table is bound to the Product dataset and is iterating through the products. The ProductModel dataset contains details of the most popular product model for each product. The `Lookup` function indicates that the ProductID field in the Product dataset should be used to find the matching ProductID field in the Product-Model dataset and to return the Name field from the ProductModel dataset.

This example used a one-to-one lookup, but Reporting Services provides other options as well that process sets of data: `MultiLookup` and `LookupSet`.

Aggregates of aggregates

You might not have tried to create an aggregate over an existing aggregate, but had you tried, you'd have found that it wasn't supported. For example, if I'd aggregated the sum of sales for a customer over each month and then wanted to calculate the average of these monthly totals, there was no easy way to do so.

In SQL Server 2008 R2, it's now possible to create an aggregate over an existing aggregate. Based on the example that I just mentioned, I could build the following expression:

```
=Avg(Sum(Fields!SalesTotalIncludingTax.Value,"MonthNumber"))
```

Writing mode

Previous versions of Reporting Services included the property `WritingMode` for controls such as text boxes. What changed in Reporting Services for SQL Server 2008 R2 was the addition of a new value for this property: `Rotate270`. The `Rotate270` property allows text to be rotated, as shown in figure 3.

	Sales Amount
Accessories 2001	20,235
2002	92,735
2003	296,533
2004	161,794
2001	7,395,349
2002	19,956,015

Figure 3   Rotating text in a textbox by using the `WritingMode` property

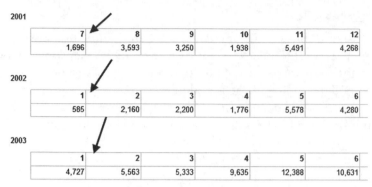

Figure 4 Ragged output in a matrix with missing data

Domain scope

Domain scope is one of my favorite new additions to Reporting Services. It only applies in limited situations, but when it's needed, it's so useful. When you use a tablix control that's configured as a matrix, the number of columns that appear is dependent on the data contained in the dataset. For example, I might use separate columns for the sales for each month. A particular month would only appear in the output if any data exists for that month. Where the problem arises, though, is when you create a list of these controls. The output then appears to be very ragged, as shown in figure 4.

Although there were ways of "fixing" this in earlier versions, doing so was messy. In SQL Server 2008 R2, you can set the DomainScope subproperty of the Group property of the inner tablix to the name of the outer tablix. Reporting Services then magically aligns the data for you, as can be seen in figure 5.

2001

1	2	3	4	5	6	7
						1,696

2002

1	2	3	4	5	6	7
585	2,160	2,200	1,776	5,578	4,280	10,478

2003

1	2	3	4	5	6	7
4,727	5,563	5,333	9,635	12,388	10,631	31,152

Figure 5 Aligned output in a matrix by using the DomainScope subproperty of the Group property

Databars

When you're viewing a column of data values, it's always good to have a visual indication of the magnitude of the values. This fact became apparent to me a short while back when I was doing some performance-tuning work. I'd stared at a column of numbers for about half an hour and all looked very similar. Eventually, though, I noticed that one of the values had one less digit. This wasn't obvious to me when viewing the numbers in a proportional font.

In previous versions of Reporting Services, it was possible to add a Databar, but the typical method for adding one involved these steps:

1 Create a subreport that contains a chart control.

2 Configure the chart control to look like a single bar.

3 Remove anything else from the subreport that doesn't look like the bar.

4 Add a parameter to the subreport for the value and another for the scale.

5 Add the subreport as a column in the main report.

6 Work out how to scale the charts across all current values.

7 Pass the value for the row plus the overall scale as parameters to the subreport.

	Sales Amount	
2001	20,235	
2002	92,735	
2003	296,533	
2004	161,794	
2001	7,395,349	
2002	19,956,015	
2003	25,551,775	
2004	13,399,243	
2001	34,376	
2002	485,587	
2003	871,864	
2004	386,013	
2001	615,475	
2002	3,610,092	
2003	5,482,497	
2004	2,091,012	

Figure 6   Databar representing sales for the row

You can imagine that this process wasn't all that easy. With SQL Server 2008 R2, this task is now trivial. You drag a Databar from the toolbox into a cell on your report and configure it by selecting the chart type and the value to be displayed. And that's it. It then appears similar to the report shown in figure 6.

Sparklines

Sparklines are also used to show the magnitude of numeric values, but instead of showing a single value, they show a set of values. Mostly, the set of values is being shown across a period of time. Sparklines are configured similarly to the way you configure Databars. But in addition to selecting the field to display, you need to select the grouping for the field. In figure 7, you can see a report that shows a sales value by year. What

	Sales Amount	
2001	20,235	
2002	92,735	
2003	296,533	
2004	161,794	
2001	7,395,349	
2002	19,956,015	
2003	25,551,775	
2004	13,399,243	
2001	34,376	
2002	485,587	
2003	871,864	
2004	386,013	
2001	615,475	
2002	3,610,092	
2003	5,482,497	
2004	2,091,012	

Figure 7   Sparkline representing sales by month for the row

the Sparkline adds to the report is that you can also see the month-by-month break-down of the sales value. This provides a large amount of information in a compact yet easy-to-understand format.

Summary

In this chapter I shared details of a number of the less obvious enhancements that the SQL Server Reporting Services team made in SQL Server 2008 R2. I hope you find them as useful in your own Reporting Services projects as I've found them in mine.

About the author

Greg Low is an internationally recognized consultant and trainer. He's a SQL Server MVP and Microsoft RD and is the CEO for SolidQ in Australia. Greg, best known for his www.sqldownunder.com pod-cast, is a past board member of the Professional Association for SQL Server (PASS). He regularly speaks at SQL Server–related events around the world.

42 Developing sharable managed code expressions in SSRS

William (Bill) Vaughn

Anyone who's been tasked with creating a customized report knows that it's all about the expressions. Once the parameters are defined, the datasets built, the groups configured, and the columns laid out, it's the expressions that give the report the readability and functionality customers demand. As the number of reports grows, the need to reuse common expression code grows with it. This chapter is about *sharing* expression code. As I walk you through how you can apply bits of logic to report expressions, I'll point out ways to build strategies that make it easier to update several reports when the expression code has to change.

Although the report processor (the engine that interprets the Report Definition Language [RDL]) only understands how to compile and execute Visual Basic, I'll discuss how to execute report expression code written in other .NET managed languages—even C#. I'll show you how to create a managed code dynamic link library (DLL), move it to a secret location, and tell the report processor how to identify it at runtime.

> **NOTE** This material can be reinforced by attending my 9-hour lecture/lab webinar on the same subject. Consult my website (http://betav.com) for more details.

Coding report expressions

Consider that most report and report element properties can be set with an expression. All expressions are embedded in the RDL as Visual Basic code, invocations of Visual Basic code functions, or invocations of external DLL class libraries written in any CLR language. What the code functions are permitted to do and what they can access is determined by a number of factors, such as Code Access Security (CAS) and the access permitted by the compiled code. So don't be surprised when your report fails to render due to code-rights restrictions.

There are three types of report expressions:

- *Report element property expressions*—These expressions are embedded as Visual Basic source in the RDL where they're used to set element properties at render time. For example, you probably use expressions to set the BackgroundColor, Visibility, and Value properties. Due to limitations in the report processor, only a subset of the full Visual Basic language is supported for this type of expression. In this approach, changes to report expressions require visiting each place the expression is used, making changes, and retesting the report.

- *Report Code property expressions*—In this case, a set of expression functions is saved in the report's Code property. Individual property expressions are coded to call into functions or leverage variables in the Code property. This means the property expressions are simpler and less change-dependent. The report Code property can contain functions that use virtually all of the Visual Basic language—but no other.

- *External DLL code classes*—If expression code needs to be shared between several reports or it's confidential, proprietary, or overly complex, it can be (and probably should be) compiled into a custom DLL. In this case, the code can be written in any .NET managed code language. The code is invoked by the report processor via references to the registered DLL's functions. Changes to the coded functions need not require any changes to the report at all. In many cases, you can simply update the DLL and move it to the appropriate location, where it's invoked by the report processor.

This chapter isn't about creating reports, so I'm not going to waste a lot of paper showing you how to create the report that I'll use to illustrate the expressions. The report itself is simple. It executes the following query against the AdventureWorks-2008 database:

```
SELECT
   Production.Product.ProductID
   ,Production.Product.Name
   ,Production.Product.Color
   ,Production.Product.StandardCost
   ,Production.Product.ListPrice
   ,Production.Product.ProductLine
   ,Production.Product.[Class]
   ,Production.Product.Style
FROM
   Production.Product
WHERE
   Production.Product.ProductLine IN (@ProductLine)
```

Adding a report element property expression

Our first challenge is to create a report property expression. In this case, the expression code replaces the property Value assignment in the RDL. One of the more common ways to customize any report that contains a Tablix control is to alternate the row

BackgroundColor so it's easier to read. In the mainframe days you'd use "greenbar" striped paper, but to get the same effect on the screen you'll have to add some logic to the RDL. The expression needed to alternate colors is fairly simple. The code divides the current row number by two and, if there's no remainder, sets BackgroundColor to Tan—otherwise BackgroundColor is set to White.

Follow along to apply this expression to the Tablix control's details rows:

1 Open your Business Intelligence Development Studio (BIDS) tools (or Report Builder), and install the sample report MA 1.0 Products By Line (Base). Rename it to `MA 2.0 Products By Line (Greenbar)`.

2 Select the entire details row of the Tablix and view the properties pane, as shown in figure 1. Note that the current BackgroundColor property is set to No Color.

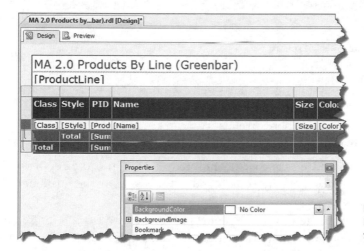

Figure 1 Inspecting the BackgroundColor property of the Details row in the Tablix

3 Select the BackgroundColor property, and click the drop-down list that shows a matrix of colors. Choose Expression to open the Expression editor.

4 Replace No Color with this expression

```
=IIF(RowNumber(Nothing) Mod 2,"Tan","White")
```

as shown in figure 2.

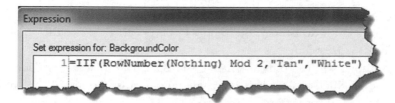

Figure 2 Setting the BackgroundColor expression to simulate greenbar

Class	Style	PID	Name	Size	Color	Standard Cost	List Price
		845	Mountain Pump			$10.31	$24.99
		871	Mountain Bottle Cage			$3.74	$9.99
		878	Fender Set - Mountain			$8.22	$21.98
		879	All-Purpose Bike Stand			$59.47	$159.00
		921	Mountain Tire Tube			$1.87	$4.99
	Total	4394				$83.60	$220.95
	U	709	Mountain Bike Socks, M	M	White	$3.40	$9.50
		710	Mountain Bike Socks, L	L	White	$3.40	$9.50
		861	Full-Finger Gloves, S	S	Black	$15.67	$37.99

Figure 3   The modified greenbar report

Preview the report and voilà, greenbar—well, "tanbar," but you get the idea. Your report should look like figure 3.

So what have you learned here? Well, as you can see, it's easy to change an existing element property to display a computed value. There are a couple of other points:

- When you choose this approach, you'll have to dig into the report properties one at a time to correct the code if you get it wrong or the customer changes their mind.
- The Visual Basic code you use in report property expressions is limited to those Visual Basic operators that are exposed in the Expression editor—a subset of the full Visual Basic language.

Coding a report Code property expression

If the expression logic is subject to change (you haven't ironed out the details) or it has to be applied in many places or in many reports, you need to consider the next alternative—report Code property expressions. In this case, the report property value does *not* contain the expression logic, only code that calls into a common block of functions that are visible throughout the report. With this approach, you can create far more sophisticated expressions and maintain them more easily. If the logic changes, all you need to do is open the report Code property, make the change, and hope that it fixes the problem.

For this example, you're going to change the BackgroundColor of a specific cell that displays the product's color. This is a challenge because not all of the colors are valid colors as far as the report processor is concerned. For example, some items have a color of Silver/Gray or Mixed. In addition, once the BackgroundColor is set, the

Using a Visual Basic application to create the functions

As with report property expressions, building, testing, and deploying Code property expressions can be difficult—especially given the lack of functionality (beyond a simple editor) in the Expression editor or the Code property window (which doesn't even support right-click Paste). This means you're going to want to create a Visual Basic application to help code, debug, and manage the functions used in these expressions—even the more complex property expressions. As I demonstrate in my *Sharing Managed Code in Report Expressions* webinar, it's not that difficult to build a Windows Forms application to collect input parameters and display the results of the functions that are destined to be used as your report Code (or property) expressions.

text color might become obscured by the background (black text on a black background). To deal with these issues, you'll also change the Color property to a contrasting color.

The first of these functions (SetBGColor as shown in listing 1) accepts a Color value (which is extracted from the report dataset) and returns either the same color or an alternative color in a few special cases. Notice that this code also deals with those products that have no known color (where Color is set to NULL).

Listing 1   The `SetBGColor` function

```
' Set Background color based on color except for non-standard colors
Public Function SetBGColor(ByVal strColor As String) As String
    ' Test for NULL color
    If String.IsNullOrEmpty(strColor) Then
        Return "Kakhi"
    Else
        Select Case LCase(strColor)
            Case "silver/black" : Return "Gray"
            Case "multi" : Return "Gold"
            Case Else : Return strColor
        End Select
    End If
End Function
```

The second function (SetTextColor as shown in listing 2) determines the Text Box's text Color property based on the Dataset Color property (being used for the BackgroundColor).

Listing 2   The `SetTextColor` function

```
' Return a contrasting color for the color provided
Public Shared Function SetTextColor(ByVal strColor As String) As String
    Dim strRet As String = "Black"    ' Default to black
    If (String.IsNullOrEmpty(strColor)) = True Then
        strRet = "Black"
    Else
        Select Case lcase(strColor)
```

```
                    Case "black", "blue" : strRet = "white"
                    Case "red" : strRet = "green"
                    Case "silver", "white", "yellow" : strRet = "black"
                    Case Else : strRet = "white"
            End Select
        End If
        Return strRet
End Function
```

Now that you have the functions coded, let's step through the process of setting the simple report's Code property to contain these functions so they can be called by report property expressions:

1 Right-click in the whitespace below the Tablix control, and choose Report Properties.

2 Click the Code tab on the left to select the report Code property.

3 Paste in the code shown in listings 1 and 2 (the functions `SetBGColor` and `Set-TextColor`) to manage the Color and Text properties into the report Code property editor, as shown in figure 4.

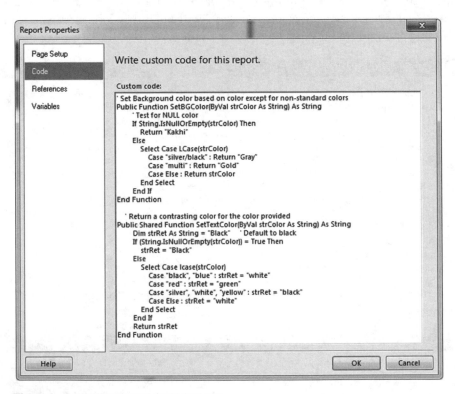

Figure 4   Setting the report Code property

You're now ready to hook up the functions you've added to the report Code property. To do so, you need to visit each report element that invokes the function.

4 Navigate to the [Color] cell in the details row of the Tablix control.

5 Right-click the cell, and choose Expression. Notice that the cell's Value property is set to =Fields!Color.Value, which means it takes its value from the Color column (field) in the dataset. You don't want to change that. You *do* want to change the properties of the Text Box that contains this value.

6 With the [Color] Text Box (not the selected text) highlighted, find the cell's Color property. It's currently hardcoded to Black. Change the Color property to call the SetTextColor function, as shown in figure 5. Note that the report Code property functions are invoked by prefixing the function name with =Code.<function>. Don't be concerned that the function name has a red underscore. Because of issues with the RDL development tools, function names can't be resolved until the report is rendered.

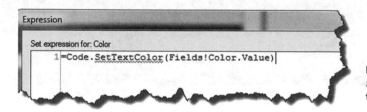

Figure 5   Referencing the SetTextColor function in the Code property

7 Next, reselect the [Color] cell in the Tablix, and locate the BackgroundColor property. Notice that it's already set to the greenbar expression. At this point, you're going to override that expression with your own cell-specific expression. Choose Expression from the drop-down list on the BackgroundColor property.

8 Enter the appropriate reference to the SetBGColor Code property function, as shown in figure 6.

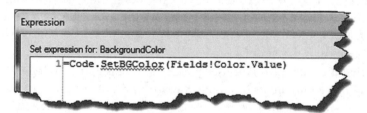

Figure 6   Referencing the SetBGColor function in the Code property

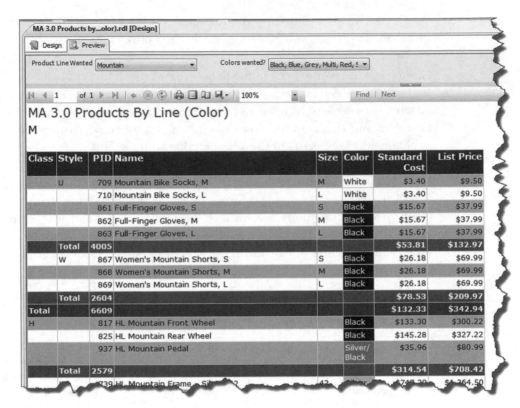

Figure 7　The rendered report with Code property expressions in place

9　You're now ready to test the report again with your new report Code property functions being referenced by the report element expressions. Your report should look something like figure 7.

As a wrap-up for this section, consider the following points:

- In a typical customer situation, the client doesn't know what they want until they *don't* get it. This means you'll be back tweaking the color assignment settings or other property expressions to make them happy. This is now easy—for this report. But if this Code property is assigned to a dozen reports, you have other problems to worry about.

- Consider that if each report that uses this technique is edited independently to meet changing requirements or an odd variation, you'll end up with lots of different versions of this same Code property list of functions—not good.

- Multiply these problems times the number of reports you have to manage and square that by the number of developers, report DBAs, and "users who just want to help," and you understand the gravity of the overall problem.

You need a more manageable and efficient alternative—and that's what I'll talk about next.

Creating sharable managed code expressions

This rather long trip has led you to the main point of this chapter—you need to create a mechanism to implement tunable expressions that can be referenced by as many expressions as necessary in the report while still being able to share this block of functions called by the expressions from multiple reports. Before we venture off into unknown territory, let's take a look at the roadmap:

- First, in this approach you can use any managed language, including Visual Basic.NET, C#, or F#, to create a class containing the functions, variables, constants, and supporting objects; subroutines; and other code used to glue it all together.
- Next, you configure the class to be accessible by the Report Manager—this is a CAS issue I'll discuss later.
- You also sign the class so you can keep it secure and (optionally) stick it in the global assembly cache.
- You compile the class into a DLL and mechanically copy the compiled class DLL to a hitherto secret location so the BIDS report processor can find it at runtime. Again, I'll discuss this location later.
- In BIDS, open the report and add a reference to the class DLL in the report properties.
- Change the function-invoking expressions in the report to call into the DLL instead of into the Code property functions.
- Test the result in BIDS, and if it's working, recopy the DLL to another hitherto secret location so the Reporting Services report processor can see it at runtime.
- Deploy the report to Reporting Services, and test it again from Report Manager.

Simple? Well, perhaps it doesn't seem so. But once you get the mechanism set up, it's easy to create a custom class DLL—especially from a tested set of functions. On that count, you're way ahead of the game because you have a set of functions you want to persist to a DLL. Let's get started:

1 Open Visual Studio, and create a new Visual Basic.NET Class project. If you don't know how to code Visual Basic, you can open a C# class or any .NET CLR language class project. Just keep in mind that all the examples from this point forward are in Visual Basic.NET. I'm using Visual Studio 2010, but any version (2005–2008) will do. In this case I named the class `MAFunctionClass`.

2 Open the project's property page. Select the Application tab, and open the Assembly Information dialog box. Make sure the copyright information is set correctly. Note the Assembly version and File version. They should both be set to 1.0.0.0.

3 On the Compile tab, ensure that Option Strict is set to On.

4 Click the Advanced Compile Options button, and ensure that Target Framework (All Configurations) is set to .NET Framework 3.5 (not 4.0) if you're targeting a

2008 or 2008 R2 report processor. If you don't, you'll throw a "…this is not an assembly" exception when you try to reference the assembly in a report.

5 On the Signing tab, check Sign the Assembly.

6 Create a new strong key file, and enter a password.

7 Insert the function code extracted from your previous Visual Basic project or the Code property of the report into the Public Class.

8 Make sure each function is declared as Public Shared. Any variables, constants, subroutines, or other classes that you don't want to be visible should be declared as Private.

9 Click the Solution Explorer, and click Show All Files to expose the project support files.

10 Open AssemblyInfo.vb. There's an equivalent CS file for C# classes. This file contains compiler directives to specify the version and other DLL class properties.

11 Add the following element to the AssemblyInfo file to permit the report processor to access these functions:

```
<Assembly: Security.AllowPartiallyTrustedCallers()>
```

12 Save the project.

13 Build the solution (using either Debug or Production configuration).

14 Note the location of the DLL in the Build dialog box at the bottom of the screen.

15 Return to the project properties and the Compile tab. If your version of Visual Studio supports it, click the Build Events button at lower right.

16 Code two Copy commands to move the newly built DLL to the Private Assemblies folder, as described in table 1.

Table 1   Path for expression DLL

Report processor	Path
BIDS (2008, 2008 R2)	Microsoft Visual Studio 9.0\Common7\IDE\PrivateAssemblies
Reporting Services (2008)	Microsoft SQL Server\MSRS10.SS2K8\ReportServer\Bin
Reporting Services (2008 R2)	Microsoft SQL Server\MSRS10_50.SS2K8R2\ReportServer\Bin
ReportViewer (Visual Studio 2010)	Microsoft Visual Studio 10.0\Common7\IDE\PrivateAssemblies\DataCollectors
Report Builder 3.0 (2008 R2)	Microsoft SQL Server\Report Builder 3.0
Report Builder 2.0 (2008)	Microsoft Visual Studio 9.0\Common7\IDE\PrivateAssemblies

Note that these paths vary based on the version of Reporting Services or report development tool installed and the name of the Reporting Services instance. The locations are not well documented (as far as I can tell).

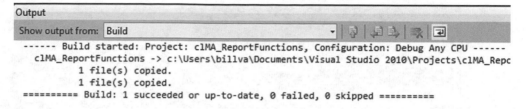

Figure 8   The Output Build messages

The Build Events command processor supports a number of Post Build macros that make it easy to address the newly created DLL. The following code shows the commands you use to copy your new DLL to the local BIDS folder (so you can preview the report) and to the target Reporting Services engine so it can be viewed postdeployment to the Reporting Services catalog. This copy operation assumes you have sufficient rights to copy into the report server's bin folder:

```
Copy /Y /B /V "$(TargetPath)" "C:\Program Files (x86)\Microsoft Visual
  Studio 9.0\Common7\IDE\PrivateAssemblies"
Copy /Y /B /V "$(TargetPath)" \\BETAV9\Croot\Program Files\Microsoft SQL
  Server\MSRS10_50.SS2K8R2\Reporting Services\ReportServer\bin
```

When you've filled in the postbuild commands, build the project and examine the Output Build messages to ensure that the DLL was built and the copy operations succeeded, as shown in figure 8.

Referencing DLLs from your report

Now that the DLL is in place, you can return to the report and reference the shared code:

1   Open the report properties, and select the Code tab. Clear out all of the code that's in the Code property editor that's implemented in the DLL. Sure, you can use both the Code property as well as DLL-sourced functions for your expressions, but for this example you're only going to be invoking code in the new DLL.

2   Click the References tab, and click Add to add a reference to your new DLL.

3   Click the ellipsis (…) button on the right, and use the Add Reference dialog box to browse for your new DLL. You know where the DLL is saved; you saw the path when you examined the build target location in your project (shown in figure 8). Your Report Properties References dialog box should look something like figure 9. Notice that I altered the version to permit minor changes to the assembly version to be acceptable by using the * notation.

4   Now comes the hard (tedious) part—you have to revisit each report expression you created that references the report Code property functions and replace the =Code. reference with =clMA_ReportFunctions.MAFunctionClass., as shown in

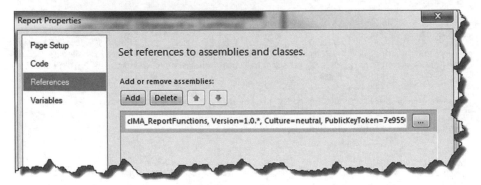

Figure 9   Setting a reference to the custom DLL

figure 10. Yes, this is a lot easier to do with a Find and Replace against the RDL (and won't miss any expressions buried deep within your report properties).

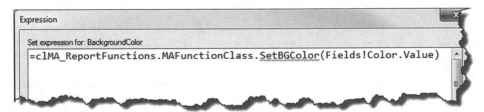

Figure 10   Replacing the report Code property references with DLL references

5 You're ready to test the modified report. Try the Preview pane in BIDS. Your report should run exactly as it did when it invoked functions in the report Code property.

At this point you can make alterations to the functionality in the DLL, but I suggest that you don't change the "signature" of the functions (the input parameters or returned values) without bumping the version. When you rebuild the project, the postevent build commands will automatically move the finished DLL to the target locations where the development tools will find them.

Summary

That about wraps up this chapter. Along the way I discussed a number of methods for embedding logic in your reports. This code can be tucked into (almost) every conceivable corner of the report as you hardcode property behavior. But as you can imagine, doing so can make your report difficult to maintain—and guess what? It might be *you* who has to go back and fix it a year from now. At that point you'll look back and wish you had at least used report Code property functions or, better yet, created a common set of functions that can be seen by all of your reports—persisted in a DLL that's easy to maintain and keep up to date.

About the author

William (Bill) Vaughn is an industry-recognized author, mentor, Microsoft MVP, and subject-matter expert on Visual Studio, SQL Server, Reporting Services, and data access technologies and has worked in the computer industry for nearly 40 years. He's written over a dozen books; his latest include the five-star *Hitchhiker's Guide to Visual Studio and SQL Server,* 7th edition (Addison-Wesley Professional, 2006) and the critically acclaimed *Hitchhiker's Guide to SQL Server 2000 Reporting Services* (Addison-Wesley Professional, 2004).

43 Designing reports with custom MDX queries

Paul Turley

On the Reporting Services forums, I see many report developers trying to build analytical reports with relational data sources, using complex and convoluted coding techniques. They might populate temporary tables, using inefficient and complicated subqueries to derive calculated values. OLAP cubes, queried with the Multidimensional Expression (MDX) query language, make this kind of reporting work easier to manage and the data much easier to query. For many, at first MDX seems strange and foreign, until arriving at a moment of clarity when the mechanics of the language begin to make practical sense.

This chapter will show you many of the essential report and MDX query design techniques, beyond the fundamentals, related to OLAP reporting. I'll show some examples that may help newcomers get started if you're willing to venture out of your comfort zone. You'll see how to use techniques in Reporting Services that will let you take advantage of the power of MDX and Analysis Services cubes. I'll provide enough direction to build a report if you already know the basics. You should know what to do when I provide directions like "create a new dataset with the provided query script" or "create a new parameter and use the dataset for the available values." If you don't have prior report design experience, there are several good books available on Reporting Services that teach essential report design. I encourage you to pick up one and learn report design basics before you read this chapter.

The report shown in figure 1 has been completed and deployed to SharePoint. It includes a trend analysis for a selected measure value over a 30-day period beginning on a specified date. The light shaded line shows a 30-day trend for the same selected measure, for a period of time that's a specified number of months behind the chosen date. By using parameters to drive these variables, the user's reporting experience can be adjusted to meet a variety of reporting needs.

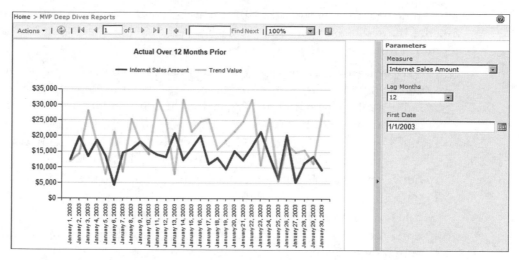

Figure 1   Trend analysis chart

Using the Adventure Works sample data

You can find the Adventure Works Analysis Services database at www.codeplex.com. Search for "Adventure Works SQL Server Sample Databases," and then download and install the correct version: http://msftdbprodsamples.codeplex.com/releases/view/55926.

I've tested these examples with SQL Server 2008 and SQL Server 2008 R2. After installing the relational data warehouse database and the Analysis Services project, open the Enterprise Analysis services project in Business Intelligence Development Studio, and then deploy and process the database on your server.

MDX query builder

The MDX graphical query builder is a useful tool for designing basic queries by dragging and dropping objects into the grid and various landing zones. Beyond this, it may not provide the flexibility to make manual modifications to the query script. Because it's so convenient, I often use the graphical query builder to prototype an MDX query. For highly parameterized queries, I usually start over and write the query from scratch, as you'll see in the following examples. To write the query manually, use the leftmost toolbar button named Edit as Text and switch to generic text mode.

Building a report

For the remainder of this chapter, I'll demonstrate query and report design techniques by progressively building a report, adding steps and features. The examples will focus on the capabilities of the query and results rather than the visual design of the report. This report could easily be enhanced with groups, Sparklines, gauges, a geographic map, or other visuals. I trust that you can find the most effective way to visualize the results on your own. We'll start with a simple query and then layer on additional features:

1 Start by creating a new report in either a Business Intelligence Development Studio (BIDS) report project or the newest version of Report Builder. Report Builder 2.0 can be used for SSRS 2008, and Report Builder 3.0 or newer can be used for newer product versions.

2 Add a data source that uses SQL Server Analysis Services, and connect to a database server containing the Adventure Works sample SSAS database.

3 Add a new embedded dataset to the report, and open Query Builder.

4 Click the leftmost toolbar button, labeled Edit as Text. This will allow you to type the query rather than using the graphical query builder.

5 Enter the following query script, and then execute the query by clicking the "!" button on the toolbar:

```
select {[Measures].[Internet Sales Amount]} on columns
, NON EMPTY [Date].[Date].members on rows
from [Adventure Works]
;
```

The execution results should include two columns for the Date and Internet Sales Amount measure. To get more business value from the query, we'll design it to show a specified range of dates. This is done by adding the LASTPERIODS function to return 30 days of results, up to and including a specified date.

1 Replace the expression [Date].[Date].members with the function name and a set of parentheses. The LASTPERIODS function takes two arguments separated by a comma: the number of periods and a member reference. The easiest way to add this date member reference is to use the Metadata pane on the left.

2 Expand the Date dimension and then the Date attribute hierarchy.

3 Expand Members, and then find January 31, 2003.

4 Drag and drop this member to the right of the comma so it looks like this query script:

```
select {[Measures].[Internet Sales Amount]} on columns
, NON EMPTY LASTPERIODS( 30, [Date].[Date].&[20030131] ) on rows
from [Adventure Works]
;
```

Execute the query to check the results. You should see 30 dates ending with January 31.

Adding a calculated member

Next, we'll add a calculated member that will return the Internet Sales Amount for a period 12 months prior to the current date period. This value will be returned as a member named TrendValue. In the following example, the with clause defines this member. The earlier date is returned by the ParallelPeriod function, which takes as arguments a hierarchy level, the number of prior periods (12 months), and a reference to the current member of the Calendar hierarchy. This expression will be processed for every Date member on the rows axis, to return a corresponding trend value. See listing 1.

1 Add the `with member` expression shown in the following example to apply the `ParallelPeriod` function as described.

2 Modify the `on columns` expression to return the TrendValue measure as shown.

3 Compare your query script to the following example, and click the Execute (!) button on the toolbar to test the results.

Listing 1   Example query script

```
with
    member Measures.TrendValue as ([Measures].[Internet Sales Amount]
                        , ParallelPeriod([Date].[Calendar].[Month], 12
                        , [Date].[Calendar].CurrentMember))

select
    {[Measures].[Internet Sales Amount], Measures.TrendValue} on columns
    , NON EMPTY LASTPERIODS(-30, [Date].[Calendar].[Date].&[20030131])
        on rows
from
    [Adventure Works]
;
```

Take a look at the results returned in Query Designer, as shown in figure 2. The first row shows that the Internet Sales Amount for the January 31, 2003, was approximately

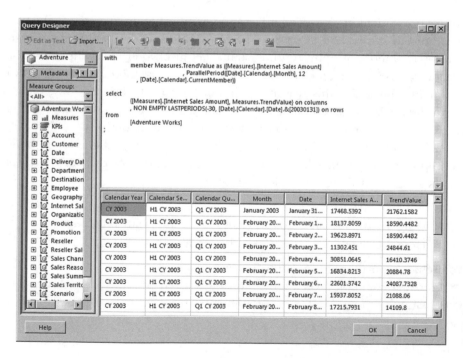

Figure 2 Query Designer results

$17,468.54. The TrendValue is the Internet Sales Amount for January 31, 2003; which was approximately $21,762.16.

In the previous examples, the Internet Sales Amount was hardcoded as the first measure. In this enhancement, we'll pass the measure name as a string and return the value as a member called Selected Measure. Later, we'll pass the measure name using a parameter so the report will analyze any measure the user chooses.

1 Modify the query script, adding another `member` clause for the Selected Measure, as shown in the example in listing 2.

2 Execute the query and check the results.

Listing 2 Modified query script

```
with
    member Measures.[Selected Measure]
        as [Measures].[Internet Sales Amount]
    member Measures.TrendValue as ([Measures].[Internet Sales Amount]
        , ParallelPeriod([Date].[Calendar].[Month], 12
        , [Date].[Calendar].CurrentMember))

Select
    {[Measures].[Selected Measure], Measures.TrendValue} on columns
    , NON EMPTY LASTPERIODS(-30, [Date].[Calendar].[Date].&[20030131])
        on rows
from
    [Adventure Works]
;
```

At this point, the Report Designer has enough information to generate the field metadata, and in subsequent query modifications, this metadata will remain unchanged. This is an important point to understand, because when the complexity of a query reaches a certain point, it can be more difficult to go back and make changes to things like field names. For this reason, it's important to establish this baseline and lock down the fields returned by a dataset. It's also a good idea to save a copy of this query in a separate script file for reasons that will soon be more obvious.

Before moving on to the next step in the query design, I'd like you to build a simple report interface. In a line chart the category represents the horizontal axis, and values are plotted along the vertical axis scale.

1 Add a line chart to your report.

2 Drag the two measures to the Values list in the Chart Data pane.

3 Drag the Date field to the Category Groups list.

Your chart report should resemble figure 3.

Here's a common MDX report flaw that's often overlooked in design and often gets past unit testing. Most dimension members return string values. This isn't always

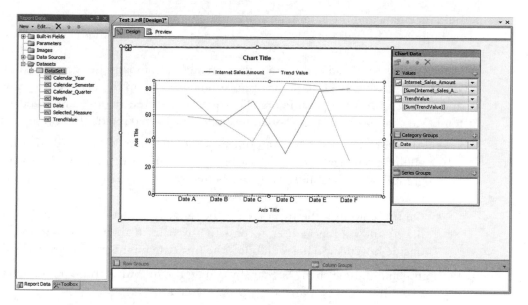

Figure 3   Line chart

the case, but it's more common than in relational solutions. In our case, the Date attribute returns string values and not actual date values, such as January 31, 2003 and February 1, 2003. These members are already sorted in the right order in the query result set, but if the category group were sorted on these field values, February 1… would appear before January 31…. By default, the Report Designer adds a sort expression when a group is created. As a rule, you should always check the groups for any data region and remove the sort expressions when designing reports with MDX datasets.

1   Preview the report and take note of the date order on the horizontal axis. Expect the dates to be in the wrong order.
2   Correct the automatic sorting issue by modifying the category Date Group.
3   Delete the sort expression for the group.
4   Preview the report again and verify that the dates are sorted correctly.

You can adjust the design to your liking.

Handling parameters

When an MDX query is created using the graphical Query Designer, parameters can be added automatically along with the datasets needed to drive the parameter list values. In our case, when writing the query manually, it's necessary to do this work ourselves. One convenient option is to use the graphical Query Designer to build the field metadata and the parameter lists and then modify the query script using manual techniques. This will work as long as the field order, names, and hierarchies aren't changed.

In our case, we'll add and set up the parameters manually. Let's go back to the last version of the query and look for opportunities to extend the capability of the query and report with some parameters. The query has three values hardcoded into the logic. We can make this query much more flexible by making the following changes:

- Alias the Internet Sales Amount as a member-named Selected Measure. The ability to change out the measure at will by using this placeholder provides a great deal of flexibility. This means that one query could be used to measure practically anything in the database.
- On the Rows axis, the first date for the range is hardcoded. It would be preferable to allow a report user to pass in any date of their choosing and then to decide how many dates will follow the first date member in the specified range.

Let's implement these changes. Start by adding the following three parameters to the report. Use the default for any other property values.

1 Add the parameters shown in table 1 to the report. In the Report Data pane, right-click the Parameters node and choose the menu option to add a parameter.
2 Enter the appropriate name and properties for each new parameter, and then close and save each parameter with the properties shown in the table.

Table 1 You'll open, edit, and close the Parameter Properties dialog box for each of these parameters.

Parameter Name	Prompt	Data Type	Default Value
MeasureName	Measure Name	Text	Internet Sales Amount
LagMonths	Lag Months	Integer	12
FirstDate	First Date	Date/Time	1/31/2003

My example for the FirstDate parameter default value uses a U.S.-formatted date. If your machine is configured for a different locale, use a date format appropriate for your region.

Passing parameters

Because we're building the dataset query manually, the parameters will be referenced right in the query script, and there's no need to map report parameters to query parameters as you normally would if you were using a common T-SQL or MDX query. A few different approaches are used to customize a query using parameters. Under some conditions you can embed a query parameter reference, prefixed with the @ symbol, into the query script, but the query parser is a bit restrictive about the components of a query that can be parameterized. If your mission is to use parameters more creatively than these restrictions will allow, you can use an expression to convert the entire query into a string value. For this effort, you'll have a query that can be used to control aspects of the report that would otherwise require starting over with a different report design. The trick with the technique is to write a query first to return all of the members and measures. Executing this query builds the report's field metadata. After that, you can use code and expressions to customize the query, as long as it continues to return results consistent with the metadata schema (all of the fields are returned using the same field structure).

BUILDING A DYNAMIC QUERY

To serve our purposes, the entire query will be converted to a string using a Visual Basic .NET expression.

1 In the Report Data pane, double-click the name of the dataset.
2 In the Dataset Properties dialog box, click the Expression Builder button next to the Query box.

The Expression Builder button has an *fx* on it, which stands for "Expression Builder." No, really, I think it actually stands for "Functions and Expressions," or something like that. Anyway, click that button.

3 Modify the query expression so it becomes a series of concatenated strings. You can use the ampersand (&) to combine each literal string or expression.

Every element of the query is a literal string except for the parameter references. In the following listing I've broken some of the strings into separate lines so they fit on the printed page. You're welcome to simplify this if you choose to, but you can copy it verbatim as a working starting point.

Listing 3 Query expression as concatenated strings

```
="with member Measures.[Selected Measure] as "
& "[Measures].[Internet Sales Amount] "
& "member Measures.TrendValue as ([Measures].["
& Parameters!MeasureName.Value
& "] , ParallelPeriod([Date].[Calendar].[Month], "
&     Parameters!LagMonths.Value & ", [Date].[Calendar].CurrentMember)) "
& "select "
& " {[Measures].[Selected Measure], Measures.TrendValue} on columns "
& " , NON EMPTY LASTPERIODS(-30, [Date].[Calendar].[Date].&["
& Format(Parameters!FirstDate.Value, "yyyyMMdd") & "] ) on rows "
& "from "
& " [Adventure Works];"
```

HANDLING DATE PARAMETERS

Working with date parameters and dimensions can be a bit tricky. To be successful, it's important to understand some of the common unique differences between working with date values in SQL and the way that date values are represented in an OLAP dimension. The fact is that there's no hard-and-fast standard for all date attributes, but there are some common approaches used by most experienced SSAS practitioners. In the Adventure Works sample cube, the Date attribute's key value is an integer converted to a string using the format yyyymmdd. For example, January 9, 2011 would be 20110109. Because the FirstDate parameter is a true `Date/Time` data type, it would be converted to the intended format using the `Format` function using the appropriate format mask.

Parameterizing measures

We have one more enhancement to make, and then we'll be finished. Because we're already focusing on the query design, let's make this change and wrap it up.

1 Replace the literal measure name in the Selected Measure calculated member expression with a reference to the MeasureName parameter, as shown in the following example. (See listing 4.)

Listing 4   Final query enhancement

```
="with member Measures.[Selected Measure] as [Measures].["
& Parameters!MeasureName.Value & "] "
& "member Measures.TrendValue as ([Measures].["
& Parameters!MeasureName.Value
& "] , ParallelPeriod([Date].[Calendar].[Month], "
&     Parameters!LagMonths.Value & ", [Date].[Calendar].CurrentMember)) "
& "select "
& "    {[Measures].[Selected Measure], Measures.TrendValue} on columns "
& "    , NON EMPTY LASTPERIODS(-30, [Date].[Calendar].[Date].&["
& Format(Parameters!FirstDate.Value, "yyyyMMdd") & "] ) on rows "
& "from "
& "    [Adventure Works];"
```

2 Close and save the expression and the Dataset Properties dialog box.

RETURNING METADATA WITH A DYNAMIC MANAGEMENT VIEW

This is one of those little-known secrets that, with some creativity, you can use to take your solutions to a completely new level. Data Management Views return metadata about database objects such as object names, attribute values, and member sets. Dynamic Management View (DMV) queries can return information for just about any system object. This example will touch only the tip of the iceberg. Data Management View queries are parsed by the Analysis Services data provider, but the query execution is handled by a different set of objects than the OLAP storage engine. As such, the syntax isn't standard MDX. It's a blend of SQL, but it's not really pure MDX, and the rules are a little different.

1 Create a new dataset using the same data source. Let's name it `MeasureList`. Because the DMV query isn't MDX, you must use the Expression Builder, rather than the Query Builder, to enter the query script.

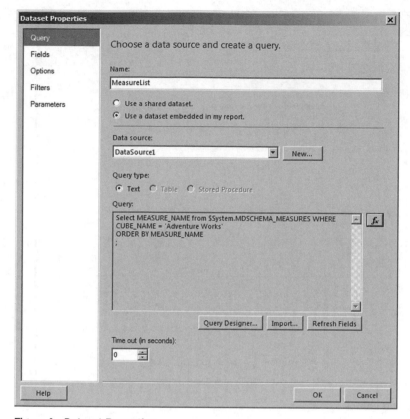

Figure 4   **Dataset Properties**

2   In the Dataset dialog box, click the Expression Builder (*fx*) button and enter the following text:

```
Select MEASURE_NAME from $System.MDSCHEMA_MEASURES WHERE CUBE_NAME =
    'Adventure Works'
ORDER BY MEASURE_NAME
;
```

3   Close and save the Expression Builder, and then click the Refresh Fields button, shown in figure 4.

4   Click the OK button to close the Dataset Properties dialog box.

5   Edit the MeasureName parameter, set it to use the new dataset for the Available Values, and then set the Default Value to Internet Sales Amount.

6   Close and save the parameter properties.

You should be ready to rock and roll, so let's make sure everything works. Preview the report, and it should look similar to my example in figure 5.

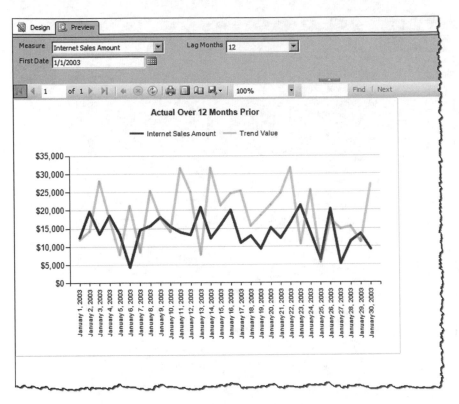

Figure 5   Report preview

I've dressed up this report just a little by applying formatting to the vertical axis label, and I've changed the series line colors and borders. This is a good time to go through the design and make adjustments to be consistent with company report standards.

Summary

I've shown you several techniques that should get you started building more dynamic and flexible report designs that use MDX to consume data from Analysis Services databases and cubes. By parameterizing things like the measure and field names, function arguments, and key property values, you can add a tremendous amount of flexibility to your reports. With just a little guidance, your business users can have a dynamic report to gain valuable insights and get answers to many important business questions without having to design additional reports. You'll find similar examples and other related tutorials on my blog at www.sqlserverbiblog.com. Also, check out www.reportsurfer.com to see live examples of several unique report designs. As I said, this is just a starting point, but you now have the tools to apply these techniques to your own unique problems and build flexible reports to meet your own business needs. Happy reporting!

About the author

 Paul Turley is a Microsoft Most Valuable Professional (MVP) for SQL Server, specializing in business intelligence, and is a multidisciplined consultant. He has been architecting, managing, and developing applications and business solutions for large and small businesses since 1992, and he has developed custom databases, BI, and reporting solutions for diverse industries. His expertise includes project lifecycle management, database modeling and design using SQL Server versions 6.0 through current, application development and user interface design, and enterprise BI solutions using SQL Server Reporting Services, Integration Services, and Analysis Services, actively working with product teams at Microsoft to advance the next-generation BI platform. He teaches, develops training courseware, speaks at industry conferences, and has authored and coauthored several technical books.

Paul works with hundreds of organizations to build business intelligence and analytical reporting solutions and has traveled throughout the United States, in Latin America, and in Asia to conduct on-site training and mentoring. He's an active contributor to several community forums and a moderator for the MSDN Reporting Services forum.

44 Building a scale-out Reporting Services farm

Edwin Sarmiento

In a SQL Server 2008 R2 Reporting Services scale-out deployment, two or more report server instances share a single report server database. This type of deployment enables you to increase the number of users who concurrently access reports and improve the availability of the report server.

What is network load balancing?

Network load balancing (NLB) is a clustering technology offered by Microsoft as part of the Windows Server operating systems. The good thing about Windows NLB is that it's available on nearly all the editions of Windows Server 2008 R2, unlike the failover clustering feature where you need at least the Enterprise Edition to have it configured. NLB uses a distributed algorithm to provide network load-balanced traffic for IP-based services such as web, virtual private networking, streaming media, terminal services, proxy, and so forth. This makes Windows NLB an ideal choice for SQL Server 2008 R2 Reporting Services because it's hosted as a web service.

Similar to the failover clustering technology, NLB assigns a virtual IP address to the cluster. When a client request is made using this virtual IP address, the NLB maps it to the physical IP address of one of the cluster nodes based on the configurations made as well as availability of the nodes. As far as the end user is concerned, only a single server is serving the request. The NLB nodes run separate copies of the server application—in this case, SQL Server Reporting Services. Because Reporting Services requires a backend SQL Server database for the report metadata, the NLB nodes should be able to access a shared database in order for the data access and updates to be synchronized. A supported scenario is to have the report server database on its own server where it can be accessed by all nodes of the NLB cluster.

Preparing your network

Although the task of preparing your network isn't typically a DBA's responsibility, it's important to understand what needs to be prepared prior to deploying your

Windows NLB cluster. This is one of the reasons why you need to be on good terms with your systems administrator.

Create a DNS entry for the NLB cluster application

Your DNS administrator will have to create a DNS entry for the NLB cluster application unless you're granted permissions to administer your DNS servers. Users will access the NLB cluster using a friendly name, so you must create a DNS entry mapping to the virtual IP address that will be used by the NLB cluster for SQL Server 2008 R2 Reporting Services. Make sure that you already have an address allocated for the virtual IP. For this example, use the name `SSRS2008R2NLB` with an IP address of `172.16.0.80`. This means that requests made to the application name will be directed to the specified IP address. You can have multiple applications hosted in the NLB cluster, so it's important to have different application names with their corresponding virtual IP address. For this example, you'll host only one application: the SQL Server 2008 R2 Reporting Services instance.

Configure the server network cards

Depending on how your network infrastructure is configured, you may have different network card configurations. Your servers may have only a single network card configured with a single IP address or multiple network cards each with its own IP address. Configuration of the NLB cluster will depend on how your network cards are configured. It's important to consider the IP address that you'll use to listen to requests—this will be the IP address that you need to use for the NLB cluster. Unlike in failover clustering technology, where you'd need an additional network card to act as the heartbeat, NLB can create a unique cluster adapter based on how your network adapter is configured. I recommend that you have an additional network adapter on a different subnet from the production network specifically for heartbeat use to improve communication between cluster nodes. For this example, you have only a single network card with a single IP address.

Adding the network load balancing feature

Similar to enabling the failover clustering feature in Windows Server 2008 R2, you'll use the Server Manager console to add the Network Load Balancing feature. Follow these steps:

1 Open the Server Manager console and select Features.
2 Click the Add Features link to launch the Add Features Wizard.
3 On the Select Features page, select the Network Load Balancing check box and click Next. (And while you're at it, you can include the .NET Framework 3.5.1 Features as well because they'll be used by the SQL Server 2008 R2 installation.)

4   On the Confirm Installation Selections page, click Install to confirm the selection and proceed with the installation of the Network Load Balancing feature.

5   On the Installation Results page, click Close. This completes the installation of the Network Load Balancing feature on the first node.

You must repeat these steps on all the other nodes of the NLB cluster before proceeding with creation of the new NLB cluster.

Creating the NLB cluster

Now that the Network Load Balancing feature has been installed on both of the servers, you can create network load-balanced clusters using the Network Load Balancing Manager console. You can run this administrative console on any of the servers that will become nodes of the NLB cluster. For this environment, you'll be configuring a two-node NLB cluster with the servers SSRS2008R2A and SSRS2008R2B. To create the NLB cluster, follow these steps:

1   Open the Network Load Balancing Manager console either by navigating to the Start > All Programs > Administrative Tools menu or running nlbmgr in the command line. For you to create a new NLB cluster, your account must be a member of the local Administrators group of the servers that will be a part of the cluster. Under the Cluster menu, select New to create a new NLB cluster using the New Cluster wizard.

2   On the New Cluster : Connect page, enter the hostname or IP address of the first server that will be a part of the NLB cluster. Click Connect. Network Load Balancing Manager detects the available network cards on the server and uses a specific IP address that will be used by the NLB cluster traffic. The network card configuration will play an important role in how your NLB cluster works.

   NLB clustering can be configured using various types of modes, depending on the number of network cards available on the server. Although using more than one network card is recommended for optimum performance and high availability, a single network card configuration works just fine. A thorough discussion of the various NLB clustering mode types is beyond the scope of this topic. For more information, check out "Specifying Cluster Network Connectivity" at http://technet.microsoft.com/en-us/library/cc787374(WS.10).aspx. The Microsoft TechNet article mentions Windows Server 2003 in the Applies To section, but the concepts still apply to Windows Server 2008 and later. Understanding how you want your NLB cluster to function will help guide you in configuring your network cards prior to creating the cluster. For this example, you'll use a single network card configured in multicast mode.

3   On the New Cluster : Host Parameters page, select a value for Priority (Unique Host Identifier). This parameter specifies a unique ID for each host that you'll add in your NLB cluster. The host with the lowest numerical priority among the current members of the cluster handles all of the cluster's network traffic that's

not covered by a port rule. Think of it as the active node in a failover cluster. Click Next to continue.

4   On the New Cluster : Cluster IP Addresses page, click Add to enter the cluster IP address that's shared by every host in the cluster. Enter the virtual IP address of the NLB cluster and click OK. This IP address will be used by the clients to communicate with the application—in our case, the SQL Server 2008 R2 Reporting Services instance. This IP address is the same as the one you added in your DNS server: 172.16.0.80.

NLB adds this IP address to the TCP/IP stack on the selected network card of all servers chosen to be part of the cluster. NLB supports IPv6 but doesn't support Dynamic Host Configuration Protocol (DHCP). Because I don't have IPv6 configured on my network cards, the option is disabled. NLB also disables DHCP on each network card it configures, so the IP addresses must be static.

Note that the first IP address listed is considered the primary cluster IP address and also used for cluster heartbeats. This information will be useful later on when you want to capture network traffic as part of troubleshooting. Click Next to continue.

5   On the New Cluster : Cluster Parameters page, under the Cluster IP configuration section enter the fully qualified domain name of the application that will be running on the NLB cluster. In this example, use the DNS entry that you created earlier: SSRS2008R2NLB.TESTDOMAIN.local.

In Cluster operation mode section, select Multicast and click Next.

6   On the New Cluster : Port Rules page, click the Edit button to modify the default port rules.

Clicking the Edit button opens the Add/Edit Port Rule page. Because SQL Server 2008 R2 Reporting Services is a web service, you'll use the default port number for HTTP traffic, port 80. In cases where you'd use a nondefault port number for the web service, assign that port number in this page. You'll use the Port Range section for this task and, for security reasons, limit the port number to only allow traffic for that specific port number. In the Protocols section, select TCP. In the Filtering mode section, select Multiple Host, which specifies that multiple hosts in the NLB cluster will handle network traffic for this port rule. In the Affinity section, select Single. This configuration is commonly used for web servers, especially when the application isn't capable of maintaining state across servers. Single affinity forces clients to use the same server as the previous connection, thus maintaining session state. Although traffic from multiple clients will be distributed over multiple cluster nodes, the load may not be spread evenly, because depending on the application requirement, one client could generate more traffic and sessions than another client. Click OK to close the Add/Edit Port Rule page.

7   On the New Cluster : Port Rules page, click Finish to create the NLB cluster.

The installer creates a new NLB cluster with just a single server.

Adding hosts to the NLB cluster

To add hosts to the cluster, right-click the new cluster SSRS2008R2NLB.TESTDO-MAIN.LOCAL and then click Add Host to Cluster. Configure the host parameters (including host priority and dedicated IP addresses) for the additional hosts by following the same instructions that you used to configure the initial host. You're adding hosts to an already configured cluster, which means all the cluster-wide parameters remain the same; therefore, these options, such as the Add/Edit Port Rule page, will be disabled.

Similar to how you'd test a Windows failover cluster, you can run a continuous ping test on the virtual IP address or the fully qualified domain name while rebooting one node at a time to see how the NLB cluster responds. Because this NLB cluster will host SQL Server 2008 R2 Reporting Services, a Telnet test on port 80 would be helpful to see if the cluster is indeed listening.

Installing Reporting Services on the NLB cluster

You're installing SQL Server 2008 R2 Reporting Services R2 on the NLB cluster, so you'll have to perform these steps on both of the nodes. Because the .NET Framework 3.5.1 is already installed as part of the steps outlined earlier, you can immediately proceed with running the setup.exe file:

1   In the SQL Server Installation Center, click the Installation link on the left side and then click the New Installation or Add Features to an Existing Installation link. The SQL Server 2008 Setup wizard launches.

2   On the next screens, choose the defaults until you see the second Setup Support Rules page, where you should click Install. Validate that the checks return successful results. If the checks returned a few warnings, make sure you fix them before proceeding with the installation. Click Next.

3   On the Setup Role page, select the SQL Server Feature Installation to install SQL Server 2008 R2 Reporting Services and then click Next.

4   On the Feature Selection page, select the Reporting Services check box to install SQL Server 2008 R2 Reporting Services and then click Next. You can install the client tools and other components as well, but as a best practice, only install those that you need to minimize surface area as well as the components that you need to patch later on.

5   On the Installation Rules page, validate that the next round of checks returns successful results and click Next.

6   On the Instance Configuration page, select either Default Instance or Named Instance, depending on your custom configuration, and click Next. For this example, use the default instance.

7   On the Disk Requirements page, click Next.

8   On the Server Configuration page, enter the service account that you'll use for the Reporting Services instance. Click Next.

9 On the Reporting Services Configuration page, select the Install, But Do Not Configure the Report Server option. This is what Microsoft refers to as the "files-only" mode installation for SQL Server 2008 R2 Reporting Services. You'll configure the report server after installation using the Reporting Services Configuration Manager. Click Next.

10 On the Error Reporting page, click Next.

11 On the Installation Configuration Rules page, review all the validation checks, making sure that they all return successful results. Click Next.

12 On the Ready to Install page, review all the configuration settings and click Install to proceed with the installation.

13 When you see the Complete page, click Close to complete the installation.

Before proceeding to the next part of the installation, make sure that you've successfully installed the SQL Server 2008 R2 Reporting Services binaries on all the nodes of the NLB cluster and that the SQL Server instance that will host the report server database has been configured for remote connections.

Configuring the first Reporting Services instance

You'll use the Reporting Services Configuration tool to connect the first report server to the shared database. You'll have to do this for all the Reporting Services instances that you've installed as part of the NLB cluster. For this example, begin with the first SQL Server 2008 R2 Reporting Services instance running on the server SSRS2008R2A:

1 In the Reporting Services Configuration Connection dialog box, enter the server name and report server instance name and click Connect.

2 Click the Web Service URL link. Verify the following values and click Apply:

- *Virtual Directory: ReportServer*—The virtual directory name identifies which web application receives the request. Because an IP address and port can be shared by multiple applications, the virtual directory name specifies which application receives the request. This is the default value.

- *IP Address: All Assigned (Recommended)*—This option specifies that any of the IP addresses that are assigned to the computer can be used in a URL that points to a report server application. This value also considers friendly hostnames (such as computer names) that can be resolved by a DNS server to an IP address that's assigned to the server. This Reporting Services instance will be a part of the NLB cluster, so you'll use this value and allow the NLB cluster to manage the URL-to-IP address resolution for the incoming traffic.

- *URLs: http://SSRS2008R2A:80/ReportServer*—This will be the URL to access the Reporting Services instance on this server. Because this server is a part of the NLB cluster, the NLB will be responsible to map the URL http://SSRS2008R2NLB:80/ReportServer to this URL.

3 Click the Database link and click the Change Database button. Doing so opens the Report Server Database Configuration Wizard.

- On the Actions page, select the Create a New Report Server Database option and click Next.
- On the Database Server page, enter the SQL Server database server instance name in the Server Name field. In this example, the SQL Server database instance name is SQL2008R2DB. Click Next.
- On the Database page, accept the default database name ReportServer and select Native Mode (you can also choose SharePoint Integrated if you want this report server instance to work with SharePoint) under the Report Server Mode option. Click Next.
- On the Credentials page, select the authentication type that you want to use to allow the report server instance to connect to the report server database. In this example, use the service account that you used for the Reporting Services instance. Click Next.
- On the Summary page, review all the report server database configuration settings. Click Next to create the report server database using the credentials that you provided earlier.
- On the Progress and Finish page, verify that all the processes completed successfully. If you encounter issues in any of the steps, make sure you resolve them before continuing. The two most common issues in creating the report server database are credential permissions and remote connectivity. Click Finish to go back to the Database page of SQL Server Reporting Services Configuration Manager.

4 Click the Report Manager URL link. Accept all the default values and click Apply.

5 Verify that the Reporting Services instance is configured and working properly. You can do so by opening a web browser and accessing the URL defined in the Web Service URL page.

Once you have a SQL Server 2008 R2 Reporting Services installation working for the first node, repeat steps 1-4 to add the second node to the NLB cluster.

Configuring the second Reporting Services instance

Before we proceed with configuring the SQL Server 2008 R2 Reporting Services instance on the second node, make sure that you already have it installed in files-only mode as defined in the first server. You'll use the Reporting Services Configuration tool to connect the second report server instance named SSRS2008R2B to the shared database. Follow steps 1 to 4 in the earlier section "Configuring the first SQL Server 2008 R2 Reporting Services instance," and accept the default values for the Web Service URL and Report Manager URL pages. The only difference here is step 3 because you already have an existing report server database. All you have to do is connect the second instance to it.

1 Click the Database link and click the Change Database button to launch the Report Server Database Configuration Wizard.

2 On the Actions page, select the Choose an Existing Report Server Database option and click Next.

3 On the Database Server page, enter the SQL Server database server instance name in the Server Name field. This should be the same as what you used for the first Reporting Services instance. For this example, the SQL Server database instance name is SQL2008R2DB. Click Next.

4 On the Database page, select the name of the database you used to configure the first report server instance. From the first Reporting Services instance, choose the database name ReportServer from the drop-down list. The Report Server Mode option value will automatically be filled in based on the report server database selected. Click Next.

5 On the Credentials page, use the same values from the first Reporting Services instance. Choose Service Credentials as the Authentication Type as per the previous configuration. Click Next.

6 On the Summary page, review all of the Reporting Server Database configuration settings. Note that this should be the same as the first Reporting Services instance that you configured. Click Next.

7 On the Progress and Finish page, verify that all the processes completed successfully. Click Finish to go back to the Database page of SQL Server Reporting Services Configuration Manager.

Although step 5 from "Configuring the first SQL Server 2008 R2 Reporting Services instance" talks about verifying that the reporting services instance is working properly, you won't do it this time around. The report server will be unavailable until the report server instance is joined to the scale-out deployment.

Joining the second Reporting Services instance

Up to this point, you may not have paid attention to the last link in the Reporting Services Configuration Manager: the Scale-Out Deployment link. When you click that link, you'll see a message stating that you should connect to the report server that has already been joined to this scale-out deployment.

This means that you need to connect to the first Reporting Services instance that you configured and accept the second Reporting Services instance to join the scale-out deployment. As shown in figure 1, run the Reporting Services Configuration Manager and connect to SSRS2008R2A.

You should see the second Reporting Services instance with a Waiting to Join status. Select the report server instance that's waiting to join the scale-out deployment and click the Add Server button. You can now verify that both Reporting Services instances are working properly by using the Web Service URL field values to test the Reporting Services individually as if they were still standalone instances.

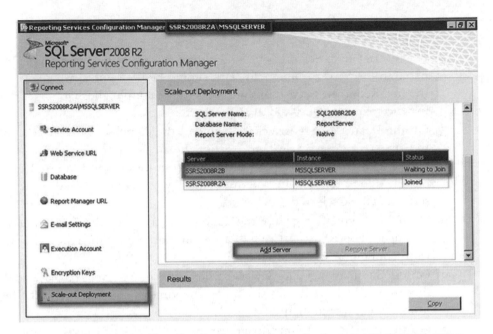

Figure 1   Adding the other Reporting Services instance on the Scale-Out Deployment page

Configuring view state validation

The web service URLs work fine after testing access, but you still need to take care of a few things. Note that SQL Server 2008 R2 Reporting Services still uses ASP.NET in its core platform but without IIS. You also need to remember that, because Reporting Services is a web application, the web is stateless. This means that once a web page is processed on the server and rendered on the browser, the server no longer remembers the page anymore. In order for end users to be able to view web pages (or, in this case, HTML reports) interactively, some form of state management must occur. This can be done by ASP.NET's view state validation. A full discussion of ASP.NET View State is beyond the scope of this chapter, but I'll discuss a few things to move forward.

By default, view state validation in ASP.NET is enabled and uses automatically generated keys for both validation and encryption. For Reporting Services, view state validation uses the identity of the Report Server web service to perform the validation. But because you're dealing with multiple machines in a NLB cluster, there will be multiple Reporting Services instances and therefore multiple Report Server web service identities to deal with. This would mean that you can't simply rely on a single process identity to perform the view state validation.

To work around this situation, you can manually generate both the validation and encryption keys instead of relying on the autogenerated values provided by ASP.NET. You'll use these key values across all of the nodes in the NLB cluster. You can do so by modifying the web.config files for both the report server as well as for the Report Manager. Microsoft KB article 312906 describes how you can create a .NET application that will generate these key values, but I'm not about to open up Visual Studio just to write my own utility. Luckily, there are a lot of utilities out there that will do this for you. I've used a machineKey generator utility from http://aspnetresources.com to generate the key values for me.

To update the validation and encryption keys, follow these steps:

1 Using any text editor, open the web.config file for the Report Manager. By default, this can be found in \Program Files\Microsoft SQL Server\MSRS10_50 .MSSQLSERVER\Reporting Services\ReportManager\Web.config.

2 Look for the `<system.web>` section and paste the `<machineKey>` element that you generated either from the machineKey generator utility from http:// aspnetresources.com or your own utility. The values I generated from the machineKey generator utility is shown here and I pasted it immediately after the `<system.web>` section just so I can easily find it later in case I need to do some troubleshooting:

```
<machineKey
validationKey="00A2CEAEF8A91B29F63399CBEE18F272159F114991EA7CF2FD78BC5D9BB0
821825C7332C4A4C1698FA58E39634365A97DA8F720377B84F471A3A166CFCDD31DF"
decryptionKey="009CA6A1D48DC4DB59E54865C470DFB75FBC1B73AA4833523C9795B1FA88
CBE3"
validation="SHA1" decryption="AES" />
```

3 Save the web.config file

4 Repeat the previous steps for the report server's web.config file. By default, this can be found in \Program Files\Microsoft SQL Server\MSRS10_50.MSSQLSERVER\ Reporting Services\ReportServer\web.config.

5 Repeat steps 1 to 4 on all the nodes in the NLB cluster.

6 Verify that the `<machineKey>` element in the `<system.web>` section of the web.config files for both the Report Manager and report server are identical across all of the nodes in the NLB cluster.

Configuring the hostname and UrlRoot

These configuration items can be found in the RSReportServer.config file. The Url-Root property is used by the report server delivery extensions to compose URLs that are used by reports delivered in email and/or file share subscriptions. This property has to be set correctly to avoid having incorrect links generated by the reports. Because you're dealing with multiple nodes in the NLB cluster, you wouldn't want end users to see the physical computer name where the subscriptions were generated. You also wouldn't want end users to be directed to the physical server and bypass the NLB cluster because this would affect their session state information.

You need to configure the UrlRoot property so that the subscribed reports will display the virtual server name of the NLB cluster instead of the physical server names of the NLB cluster nodes. The Hostname property defines how the network traffic to the reporting environment is directed. By default, this property isn't defined and will use the physical server name. Remember, you want the network traffic to be directed to the virtual server name so that the NLB cluster will be the one to handle and distribute the requests among the cluster nodes.

To configure the Hostname and UrlRoot properties, follow these steps:

1   Using any text editor, open the RSReportServer.config file. By default, this can be found in \Program Files\Microsoft SQL Server\MSRS10_50.MSSQLSERVER \Reporting Services\ReportServer\RSReportServer.config.

2   Look for the `<Service>` section and add the following information to the configuration file. Use the Hostname value of the virtual server name of your NLB server. For this example, use SSRS2008R2NLB.TESTDOMAIN.local. Similar to what I've done in the `<machineKey>` element in the web.config file, I pasted it immediately after the `<Service>` section just so I can easily find it later in case I need to do some troubleshooting.

    `<Hostname>SSRS2008R2NLB.TESTDOMAIN.local</Hostname>`

3   Look for the `<UrlRoot>` element. By default, it has no value but the default value used is in the format http:// or https://<physicalServerName>/<reportserver>, where <reportserver> is the virtual directory name of the Report Server Web service.

4   Type a value for UrlRoot that includes the virtual server name in this format: http:// or https://<virtualServerName>/<reportserver>. For this example, use http://SSRS2008R2NLB.TESTDOMAIN.local/ReportServer:

    `<UrlRoot>http://SSRS2008R2NLB.TESTDOMAIN.local/ReportServer</UrlRoot>`

5   Save the RSReportServer.config file.

6   Repeat steps 1–6 on all of the nodes in the NLB cluster.

7   Verify that the `<Hostname>` and `<UrlRoot>` elements in the `<Service>` section of the RSReportServer.config files are identical across all the nodes in the NLB cluster.

Workarounds for the HTTP 401 error message

At this point, you may be tempted to test access to the Reporting Services instance via the virtual server name. But if you do so, you may get an HTTP 401 error message. If you look at the web page, you'll notice the user interface associated with SQL Server Reporting Services, which tells you that the Reporting Services instance is working except that it encounters an HTTP 401 error. According to Microsoft KB article 896861, this behavior is by design if the fully qualified domain name or the custom host header doesn't match the local computer name, which is the case in a Reporting Services scale-out implementation. And although the Microsoft KB article describes the behavior for a web application running on IIS, it does apply to our scenario. You can implement any of the methods described in the KB article, but Method 1 is the approach Microsoft recommends. You'd need to reboot your server in order for the changes to take effect immediately because you don't have IIS on the NLB cluster nodes. Your BackConnectionHostNames key would look something like this for one of the nodes, considering including both the hostnames and the fully qualified domain names for the physical computer name as well as the virtual server name:

```
SSRS2008R2A
SSRS2008R2NLB
SSRS2008R2A.TESTDOMAIN.local
SSRS2008R2NLB.TESTDOMAIN.local
```

Make sure you make this Registry change across all the nodes in your NLB cluster, making the necessary changes to the Value Data box to reflect the corresponding physical server name for each node. Once all the nodes in the NLB cluster have been rebooted, you should be able to access the approach instance using the virtual server name.

Summary

Congratulations! You now have a highly available, scalc-out SQL Server 2008 R2 Reporting Services farm running on a two-node Windows network load-balanced cluster. Now you can add your reports and data sources.

About the author

 Edwin Sarmiento is a Microsoft SQL Server MVP from Ottawa, Canada, specializing in high availability, disaster recovery, and system infrastructures running on the Microsoft server technology stack. He's passionate about technology but has interests in business, music, professional and organizational development, leadership, and management when not working with databases. He lives up to his primary mission statement—"To help people and organizations grow and develop their full potential as God has planned for them."

45 Creating SSRS reports from SSAS

Robert Cain

Many developers, be they .NET developers, database developers, or business intelligence developers, have become accustomed to using SQL Server Reporting Services (SSRS) to create professional-looking reports, using relational databases of all kinds as their data source.

The real power of Reporting Services is unleashed when SQL Server Analysis Services (SSAS) is used as a data source. Reports that show aggregations at the highest level, yet still allow users to drill down to the detail level, can be quickly and easily generated. Many developers have shied away from Analysis Services, assuming they had to learn MDX (Multi-Dimensional Expressions, the SQL-like language used to query an SSAS database). Fortunately, using the tools built into SSRS requires no MDX knowledge.

For those unfamiliar with the concepts behind SSAS, let's review a few quick definitions before we get started. A database in Analysis Services is often referred to as a *cube*, due to the way data is stored and referenced. The term *measure* refers to the values stored in a cube; items such as sales amounts or inventory quantities are examples of measures. *Dimensions* are typically things like country, product name, date, or anything that measures are analyzed by.

For example, let's say the book *SQL Server MVP Deep Dives* sold 40,000 copies for a total of $23,000 in sales in the United States. The product *SQL Server MVP Deep Dives* and the geography of United States would be our dimensions; the quantity of 40,000 and the sales value of 23,000 are the measures.

For this chapter, you'll be creating a report that displays sales data by product for each year. Further, you'll allow the user to filter the data by country. All of the data comes from the Contoso Analysis Services example database, which you can download from www.microsoft.com/downloads/en/details.aspx?FamilyID =868662DC-187A-4A85-B611-B7DF7DC909FC&displaylang=en, where you'll find complete instructions on downloading and installing the database.

Creating the report project

Most readers are likely familiar with creating a report project, so I'll just quickly cover the basics here. Open Business Intelligence Developer Studio (BIDS). Create a new project, and in the Business Intelligence Projects section click Report Server Project. Assign your project a good name, such as `SSRS SSAS Sample` (see figure 1).

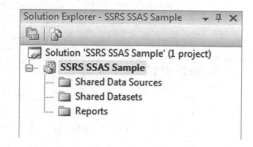

If you're using a version of SQL Server prior to 2008R2, you won't see the Shared Datasets branch. This is a new feature introduced with the R2 release. You'll still be able to accomplish all the objectives in this chapter, but you'll have to create the datasets for each report rather than being able to create the datasets once and reuse them.

Figure 1   Solution Explorer for a report server project

Adding a shared data source

Next you'll create the shared data source. If you've used tools like SSRS or SSIS (SQL Server Integration Services) in the past, you know how useful setting up a shared data source can be. They'll allow you to easily change your database as you move your project from development to testing to production.

Right-click on the Shared Data Sources branch, and select Add New Data Source from the menu. Give the new data source a descriptive name, such as `Contoso`. Next, change the type to Microsoft SQL Server Analysis Services.

Finally, you'll set up the connection string. The easiest way is to click the Edit button. If you're using the same computer that you have SQL Server installed on, you can enter `localhost` for the server name; otherwise, enter the name of the server where you've restored the Contoso sample database. In the database drop-down you should then be able to select `Contoso_Retail`. Click Test Connection to test, and if all is well you can click OK to close this dialog box. Click OK again to save the new shared data source.

Creating shared datasets

Because shared datasets are new in 2008R2, I'm including a brief instruction for those of you still on a previous version of SQL Server. You should create a new, blank report as described at the beginning of the next section. Once it's created, you can add each dataset following the instructions in this section. The dialog boxes you'll see for creating a dataset within a report are identical to those you'll see when creating a shared dataset.

So what is a dataset? Simply put, a dataset defines the tables you want to extract data from, along with the columns and any calculated columns. In previous versions of SQL Server, you were forced to re-create the dataset for every report.

Needless to say, this created many issues when using the same data in multiple reports. This was especially true in situations where calculations were included, because you were forced to open each report to make any changes. For this chapter you'll be taking advantage of shared datasets, but if you're running SQL Server 2008 (non-R2) or SQL Server 2005 you can still accomplish everything in this chapter. Instead of using a shared dataset you'll need to create the dataset when the report is created.

Creating the main dataset

Start by right-clicking on the Shared Datasets branch and selecting Add New Dataset. If you recall, our objective for this report is to display sales amounts by product for each year and to filter the data by country. Our first dataset will bring back the main data for the report.

Give the shared dataset a good name, such as `Sales Data`. In the data source select the Contoso shared data source you set up in the previous section. Next, you'll enter the query text that will bring back the report data.

SQL is the language used to query the relational databases many developers are accustomed to, and T-SQL is the specific version used with SQL Server. With SQL Server Analysis Services, the language used to query the SSAS database is called MDX. It looks somewhat like SQL (but looks can be deceiving). It has a unique format and syntax, one that many developers find quite daunting.

Fortunately the folks at Microsoft knew that having to learn MDX could be a barrier to getting reports created from an SSAS cube. So they added a query designer to the dataset creation window. Look under the Query part of the dialog box and you'll see a button labeled Query Designer (see figure 2). Click the Query Designer button to reveal the query designer.

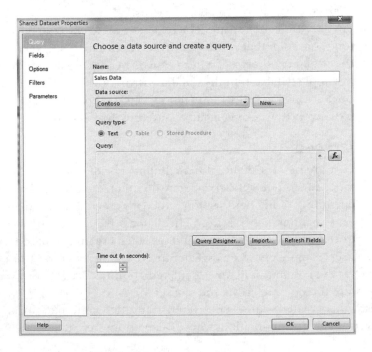

Figure 2
Shared Dataset Properties

In the upper left you'll find the cube selection area under Inventory. By clicking the ellipsis button (…), you'll be able to select the particular cube you wish to work with. In the Measure Group area, you can select the measures and dimensions you want on your report. Simply click on the one you want and drag it into the main area, the one that reads "This area will hold the values to be returned." At the top of the dialog box is an area for filters and parameters. Here you can drag any dimensions you wish to be able to filter your report on.

Begin by changing the cube you're working with. Click the ellipsis and select the Sales cube. You'll see the Measure Group area refresh; expand the Measures branch, then the Sales branch. Click the Sales Amount and drag and drop it into the main query area.

Next, scroll down to the Products folder and expand it. At the bottom of the list you'll see a Product group. This has a different icon than the other items. Although the other items appear as a series of six blocks, this appears as a stack of blocks, indicating it's actually a hierarchy. Click on it and drag into the query area. Note how it expands into its three levels: Product Category, Product Subcategory, and Product Name.

Recall that you also wanted to view your data by time. Scroll back up to the Date branch and expand it. At the bottom you'll see three hierarchies; for this report use the Calendar YQMD. Drag and drop it just to the left of the Product Category column.

Finally you wanted to be able to filter your report by the country (or region) where a sale was made. To do this, first expand the Geography branch. In this case you don't want to filter by a hierarchy but rather by a specific item. Grab the Region Country Name and drag and drop it into the Filters area at the top of the query designer, just above the list of fields you picked out.

You should set a default item, so click in the Filter Expression box and a drop-down icon should appear. Pick one of the countries to use; for this example, use United States. You'll notice a column to the right of the Filter Expression labeled Parameters, with a check box. Select this check box to allow you to connect this filter to a parameter in the report. Also note the text in the Dimension and Hierarchy columns. This will become the name of the parameter in the report (with any spaces removed). In this example it would be GeographyRegionCountryName. Now that you're all done your completed dialog box should look like the one in figure 3.

Clicking OK to close the query designer will return you to the Dataset Properties dialog box. Here you can see the query text has now been populated with the MDX you need to retrieve your data. Click OK to close and save the dataset, and you're now ready to create your next shared dataset.

WARNING In addition to the default visual designer mode, the query designer also supports a mode for entering MDX directly. If you switch from the MDX direct mode back to the visual designer, you will lose your custom MDX and have to re-create your query from scratch

Creating the parameter list shared dataset

In the previous example you created a filter from the Region Country Name column in the Geography dimension. You then set this up as a parameter. When you create

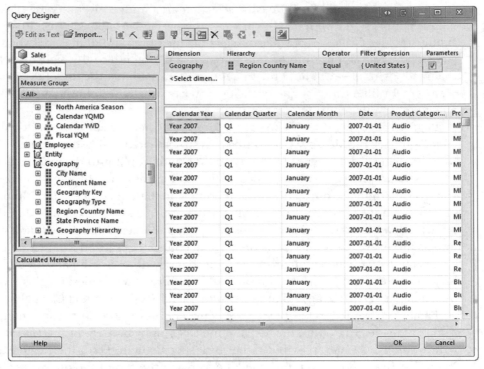

Figure 3   Completed query designer dialog box

the report, you'll need to supply a list of values to populate the drop-down of the parameter. To get those values you'll create a second dataset.

As before, right-click on the Shared Datasets branch in Solution Explorer and add a new shared dataset named `Countries`. Change the cube to Sales. Navigate to the Geography branch then drag the Region Country Name into the center area. At first glance, you might expect the list of countries to appear and thus be surprised when nothing happens. In order for the dataset to be valid, it can't display just a dimension; it has to be accompanied by a measure. Use the same one as before; expand the measures branch, then Sales, and finally drag and drop the Sales Amount onto the query area. You'll now see a list of countries along with their sales amounts. Click OK to close the query designer, and then click OK again to close and save the dataset.

The report

Now that you have your datasets ready, you can create your report. If you've used SSRS before, you're probably accustomed to right-clicking on the reports branch, selecting Add New Report, and following the report wizard. Unfortunately you won't be able to do that here because the report wizard doesn't recognize shared datasets.

Instead, right-click on Reports, click Add, and then click New Item. Next click Report (not Report Wizard), assign it a good name such as `Sales Report`, and click OK. You now have a blank report to work with.

Datasets

Begin by adding your datasets. In the Report Data area, right-click on the Datasets branch and click Add Dataset. Give the dataset a name, such as `SalesData`, and from the list choose the shared dataset for the main report, Sales Data. If you click the Parameters branch you'll see the Parameter you set up earlier. I'll revisit this later, but for now just click OK.

Repeat these steps to add the Countries shared dataset to the report.

The matrix

Start by giving yourself a bit more room and expand the size of the report body. Click the Toolbar tab, and drag and drop a Matrix tool onto the report body. Return to the report data so you can begin dropping fields onto your matrix.

First drag and drop the Product_Category_Name onto the Rows area. Then drag and drop the Product_Subcategory_Name and place it on the thin line between the Rows and Data area. Repeat with the Product_Name.

You now need to place your columns. Grab the Calendar_Year column and drop it into the Columns area. Next grab Calendar_Quarter and drop it on the thin line under Calendar_Year and above Data. Repeat with Calendar_Month. Note for this report you won't use the individual date, so ignore that field.

Finally, drag the Sales_Amount column into the Data area. If you preview the report, you'll see a nice matrix of the sales amount, divided by products and dates. Wouldn't it be nice, though, if the report was a bit more interactive, allowing the users to drill down on dates and products?

Adding hierarchy drill-down capabilities

Fortunately, adding interactivity is straightforward, although it does require you to do it for each item to be drilled down upon. Start by right-clicking on the Product_Name in the matrix control. In the menu select Row Group > Group Properties. In the properties dialog box, click in the Visibility area. Change the visibility from Show to Hide. Then check the box that reads "Display can be toggled by this report item" and select Product_Subcategory_Name from the drop-down. Click OK to save the setting.

Repeat these steps for Product_Subcategory_Name, instead using Product_Category_Name as the toggle.

You can do the same with your columns. Right-click on Calendar_Month, and select Column Group > Group Properties. Set the visibility as you did with the rows, using Calendar_Quarter for the toggle. Repeat for the quarter, using the year for the toggle.

Now preview the report, and you should see the data appear in a collapsed format, by year and product category, with + buttons that allow you to drill down.

Parameters

Let's tackle that parameter that's sitting up there doing nothing. In the Report Data section, expand the parameters branch. Note there's a parameter already in place. Right-click and delete it, because you'll be creating your own.

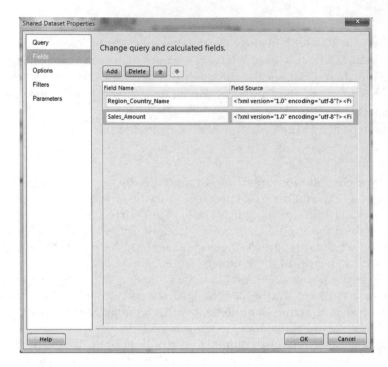

Figure 4
The fields section of the dataset editor

The value that you need to pass into your Sales dataset is of the form `[Geography].[Region Country Name].&[United States]`. How do you know? Well, the syntax is in the form `[Dimension].[Column].&[Key Value]`. If you recall from the query designer where you set up the shared dataset, you'd selected the Geography dimension, then the Region Country Name column, all enclosed in square brackets. After that you'd enter the value. Note the `&` in front of the final set of brackets; this indicates that the value is a Key column value rather than a Name column value. In this example they happen to be the same. Luckily, Reporting Services provides an easy way to get this value so that you don't have to construct it yourself.

Double-click on your `Countries` Shared Dataset, and choose the Fields section. You should see the fields `Region_Country_Name` and `Sales_Amount`, as in figure 4.

Now click the Add button and choose to add a Calculated Field. Give this new field the Field Name `Region_Country_Name_Unique`, and click the fX button beside the Field Source field. Type in `=Fields!Region_Country_Name.UniqueName`, ignoring the fact that it will be underlined as if it doesn't understand what you mean. This UniqueName property of the field is the form that your parameter expects.

Before you can use this field in your report, you should double-click on your `Countries` dataset in the Report Data pane and click the Refresh Fields button.
Now you can create your parameter. Right-click on the parameters folder and add a new one. For the name, use `pCountry`, and for the prompt use `Country/Region`.

Now click the Available Values tab and click Get Values from a Query. Select the `Countries` dataset. Select `Region_Country_Name_Unique` for the Value field and

Product Category Name	Product Subcategory Name	Product Name	⊞ Year 2007	⊞ Year 2008	⊞ Year 2009
⊞ Audio			17977874.2084999	30046682.4435	35567468.2935002
⊞ Cameras and camcorders			674849703.167011	460936577.551001	329720849.417502
⊞ Cell phones			222693504.919505	144060664.532	140282155.176498
⊞ Computers			682587335.801006	561783628.352003	591639242.919525
⊞ Games and Toys			25815311.4926001	24341961.8811004	25417791.1607003
⊞ Home Appliances			834288875.553527	796715200.163375	573726054.437117
⊞ Music, Movies and Audio Books			46111254.4674991	30196704.5380001	19568633.4895006
⊞ TV and Video			263099192.232001	269648019.234003	235581772.052002

Figure 5   The report using data from Analysis Services, before any formatting is applied

Region_Country_Name for the Label. Next, click the Default Values page and click the Specify Values option. Click Add; then for your default choose the fX button and enter ="[Geography].[Region Country Name].&[United States]". Click OK to close the dialog box.

Now you must connect this parameter to the dataset. Right-click on the SalesData dataset and click Properties. There should already be a parameter called Geography-RegionCountryName; if not, add it. For Parameter Value, select the [@pCountry] parameter you just created. Save your report and preview it. The parameter at the top of the report should now have its drop-down populated correctly. In addition, changing the value and clicking View Report should update the data with the new values. Figure 5 shows what your report should look like.

At this point you can begin applying formatting to clean up the report. Rename the column headers, apply currency formatting to the sales amounts, and perhaps apply a particular color scheme. Because these techniques are fairly basic to report creation, and due to the wealth of information available on report formatting, I'll leave this as an exercise for the reader.

Charts

Text-based reports aren't the only type of report you can create from an Analysis Services database. Adding a chart to a report using data from SSAS is every bit as easy as creating a matrix. Back on the toolbox, grab a chart control and drop it on the report; I put mine above the matrix. For the chart type, I went with the default column chart. Click inside the chart to make the Chart Data dialog box appear to the right of the chart. Click the green + button beside Values; in the menu pick Datasets > Sales Data > Sales_Amount. Now click the + next to Category Groups, and select Product _Category_Name. Finally, click the + beside Series Groups and select Calendar Year.

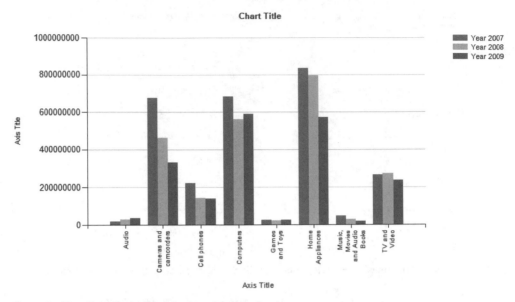

Figure 6   **The chart displaying data from Analysis Services**

Save your work and preview the report to see your chart (figure 6).

Summary

By now you can see how easy it is to tap the power of SSAS to create an interactive SSRS report, without having to know a great deal about SSAS and MDX.

About the author

Robert C. Cain is a Microsoft MVP in SQL Development, MCTS certified in BI, and works as a consultant for Pragmatic Works. He's a technical contributor to Pluralsight Training, and co-author of the first volume of this book, *SQL Server MVP Deep Dives*. Robert has more than 20 years' experience in the IT field, working in a variety of fields ranging from manufacturing to telecommunications to nuclear power. He maintains the popular blog http://arcanecode.com. Robert enjoys spending time with his wife and two daughters. His hobbies include digital photography and amateur radio; he holds the highest amateur license available and operates under the call sign N4IXT.

46 Optimizing SSIS for dimensional data loads

Michael Coles

SQL Server Integration Services (SSIS) is Microsoft's enterprise solution for extract, transform, and load (ETL) operations from a wide variety of sources to any number of destinations. In this chapter, I'll talk about practical methods for optimizing SSIS ETL data flows. The examples I'll use are dimensional data loads, because they provide some of the most interesting data loading scenarios, but the optimization opportunities I'll discuss here are useful in many different SSIS ETL scenarios.

Before we dive into performance tuning, I'll define the term *dimensional data* for those readers who haven't built ETL for dimensional data marts yet and may not be familiar with the terminology. Dimensional data marts are stored in relational database management systems (RDMBSs), like SQL Server, using either a *star schema* or *snowflake schema* with a *fact table* and its related *dimension tables*.

The fact table contains the measures and metrics related to business processes, sometimes in aggregated form, with keys (usually integer keys) referencing the dimension tables. A fact table might contain an entry for a sales order including item price, quantity, and tax information, for instance. The dimension tables hold attributes that add context to your fact table entries. Dimension tables may include geographic, time, and customer attributes. Dimension tables might hold descriptive information to answer questions like when and where a sale occurred and who was the customer involved in the transaction.

Dimensional data structures are often queried directly for reporting purposes or used to populate online analytical processing (OLAP) cubes, like those created by SQL Server Analysis Services (SSAS).

Optimization quick wins

Now that we have the definitions of dimensional data structures, let's look at some general-purpose quick win optimizations for SSIS. The first quick win is to touch rows as few times as possible. This has to do with the way SSIS processes data. Unlike

SQL Server, which is set-based in its processing, SSIS uses row-by-row processing. SSIS is essentially a powerful, flexible, optimized client-side cursor that loads and manipulates input rows one at a time. The key is to perform all transformations required in as few passes over the same data as possible.

Another quick win is to eliminate "dead-end" data flow components. Consider the data flow in figure 1, which has two Lookup components that redirect unmatched rows to Row Count components. In this example, the Row Count components are updating SSIS variables that aren't used anywhere else in the package. Despite the fact that these are true dead-end, or "bit-bucket," data flow components, SSIS still has to move data along the data flow path to the components. That means it still has to allocate buffers and copy data along the way. Because the row counts that are generated aren't used elsewhere in the package, SSIS is doing a lot of extra work for no additional benefit in this example.

Another related optimization comes from the RunInOptimizedMode setting, which can be set on a Data Flow task or at the Project level. (The Project level setting overrides the Data Flow task-level settings, but only in BIDS debugging mode.) When you set this property to True, SSIS eliminates unused outputs, columns, and components from the data flow. I recommend setting this property to True on all Data Flow tasks, except in debugging scenarios where the extra information may be useful in troubleshooting.

Logging is another place where you can optimize your packages. A policy of minimal logging in production packages ensures SSIS won't waste resources tracking a bunch of useless information. Although it's important to log errors, warnings, and other events, some SSIS events like OnProgress and OnInformation generate a lot of logging activity with little or no added value outside of a debugging scenario. For example, the OnProgress event fires whenever "measurable progress is made" by a task. In a data flow this can mean an OnProgress event fired for every 1 percent

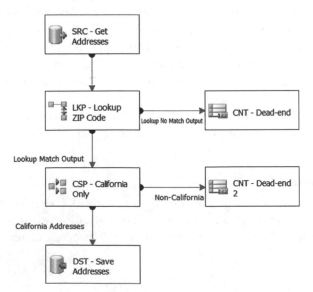

Figure 1   Eliminate dead-end data flow components.

completion, or 100 times per task. That's a lot of extra resources spent on logging with no real benefit in a production scenario.

Now that I've covered a handful of quick wins you can implement immediately, I'll consider some of the data flow optimizations you can apply to various dimensional data load scenarios.

Type 0 dimensions

Slowly changing dimensions (SCDs) are sets of attributes stored in the dimension tables we covered earlier in the chapter. What differentiates the types of SCDs is how they track historical changes. A Type 0 SCD (also known as a "nonchanging dimension" or a "very slowly changing dimension") is a type of dimension that very rarely (if ever) changes. Examples of Type 0 dimensions include Date/Time and Gender dimensions. Often Type 0 dimensions are loaded using onetime static scripts, with possibly rare one-off updates also performed with scripts. Because updates are rare events and are usually just additions to the existing data (e.g., adding another 10 years' worth of dates to your Date/Time dimension), Type 0 dimensions, by definition, don't concern themselves with tracking historical changes.

For demonstration purposes, I created a simple SSIS package to load a Type 0 dimension. This package loads a Date dimension with about 13,000 rows of data, representing about 35 years' worth of dates. The data flow is extremely simple, reflecting the fact that a Type 0 dimension doesn't need to handle changes or track history.

The OLE DB Destination Editor uses Table or View data access mode. The sample package loads about 13,000 rows of data in 9 seconds on my laptop, for a rate of about 1,445 rows per second. The reason for the poor performance is the Table or View mode setting on the OLE DB Destination adapter. This setting generates a separate INSERT for each row of data pushed into it, resulting in a separate round-trip to the server for every single row. You can use SQL Server Profiler, as shown in figure 2, to verify this fact.

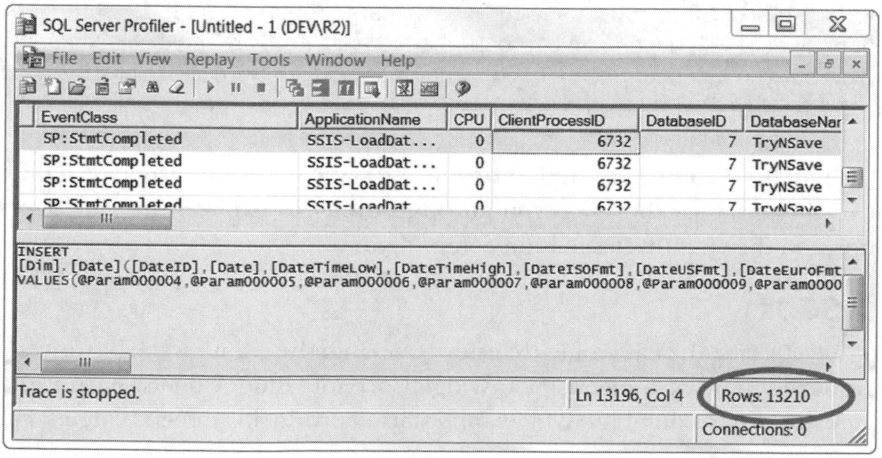

Figure 2   Verifying individual inserts generated by Table or View mode in SQL Server Profiler

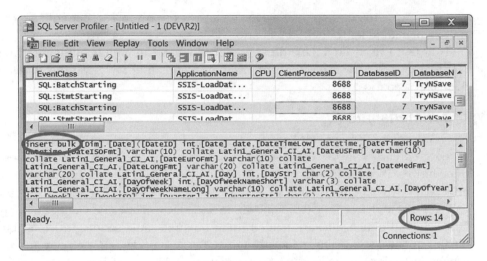

Figure 3   Profiling the Table or View - Fast Load data access mode in SQL Server Profiler

You can overcome this slow insert mechanism by changing the OLE DB Destination data access mode to Table or View - Fast Load. This mode of operation uses the OLE DB `IRowsetFastLoad` interface, which queues up rows of data in memory and commits them in batches. The same 13,000-row load on my test machine in Table or View - Fast Load mode completed in 1.5 seconds, or about 8,667 rows per second. As you can see in figure 3, the OLE DB driver generates a handful of INSERT BULK statements that commit the data to the server in batches.

INSERT BULK or BULK INSERT?

You may have heard of the T-SQL `BULK INSERT` statement before, but there's also a Tabular Data Stream (TDS) protocol statement called `INSERT BULK`. TDS is the low-level protocol SQL Server uses to transfer data. The `INSERT BULK` statement isn't directly accessible (you can't type `INSERT BULK` into SQL Server Management Studio), but you can see it being used by database drivers with SQL Server Profiler.

As I mentioned earlier, you'll probably use static scripts to load Type 0 dimensions, but in this instance they gave you an opportunity to explore the data access mode options on the OLE DB Destination component.

Type 1 SCDs

Type 1 SCDs take the easy route to history tracking; they don't track historical changes. Consider a simple example: last year WidgetCorp sold Blue Widgets. Starting on January 1, they stopped making Blue Widgets and started producing Green Widgets. When they updated their Type 1 Product dimension, they replaced the Blue Widgets with Green Widgets. They overwrote the history of Blue Widget products in the Product dimension. It's as if they always sold Green Widgets, and Blue Widgets never even existed.

With a Type 1 SCD, you need a true "upsert" design pattern: incoming rows of data are either inserted into the target dimension table or they update/overwrite an existing row in that table. When you're loading Type 1 SCDs, your job is to compare the inbound rows of data to the existing rows in the dimension table. The main question surrounding Type 1 SCDs is where do you want to do this comparison: in the SSIS data flow or on the server?

Type 1 SCDs and lost information

As you can see from the example, WidgetCorp lost some information when they replaced Blue Widgets with Green Widgets in their Product dimension. For instance, they won't be able to track sales of Blue Widgets versus Green Widgets over time, to see if color had any noticeable effect on sales performance or other metrics. In some cases this is acceptable, but the factors that weigh into that decision are beyond the scope of this chapter; you have to determine this on a case-by-case basis when planning your data mart.

The first choice of some is the SSIS SCD component. Setting up the SCD component takes a bit of effort, but it does all the work of comparing your dimension attributes in the data flow. For comparison purposes, I set up a simple package to update a Type 1 SCD called the Product Dimension using the SCD component, as you can see in figure 4.

NOTE   Unfortunately I don't have space to cover the setup and configuration of the SCD component in this chapter, but don't worry. If you're interested in pursuing the SCD component option, it is well described in several books and blogs and on the MSDN website at http://msdn.microsoft .com/en-us/library/ms141715.aspx.

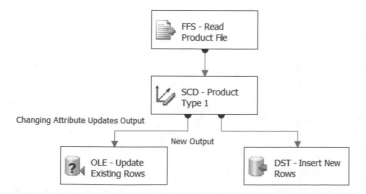

Figure 4   Updating a Type 1 SCD with the SCD component

To test the stock SCD component, I loaded two Product dimension files on my laptop. The first had 1,500 products in it. The second file had about 25,500 products, including updates to the 1,500 original products. The results of the loads are shown in table 1.

Table 1   Comparison of SCD component Type 1 dimension loads

Load description	Time	Rows per second
First load: 2,500 rows, empty target table	1.1 sec.	2,272 row/sec.
Second load: 25,300 rows, updates to 2,500 initial rows	88.6 sec.	286 rows/sec.
Third load: 25,300 rows, no updates	118.9 sec.	212 rows/sec.

The bottlenecks in this data flow were the SCD component, which runs extremely slowly and compares every column of every inbound row to the matching columns of existing rows in the target dimension table, and the OLE DB Command component, which issues a single UPDATE statement for every changed row. What you need is an optimized method of detecting changes and a more efficient way to update the target table than you get with the SCD component.

To optimize change detection, you'll use SHA1 hash codes. SHA1 is a collision-free hash function, which is like a 160-bit fingerprint for your data. The advantage of the SHA1 hash function is that you can compare the business key (in this case the 12-digit Universal Product Code [UPC] number) to a single hash code column to detect changes. That way, you avoid comparing every column in the target table to every inbound column value. The main tradeoff is the cost in performance to produce the hash code, which is generally minimal (or at least less than a column-by-column comparison of several columns), and the additional 20 bytes per row required to save the hash codes.

The SHA1 hash function accepts a binary array/binary string as input and outputs a 160-bit (20-byte) hash code. You can access SHA1 via SQL Server's built-in HASHBYTES function or you can generate the SHA1 hash code in .NET using a script component. In keeping with the concept of touching rows as few times as possible, I chose to use .NET to generate SHA1 hash codes in the SSIS data flow in this example. Figure 5 shows the control flow and data flow of the Product Type 1 SCD package.

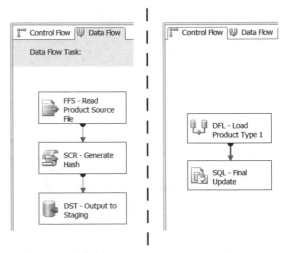

Figure 5   Data flow and control flow for updating Product Type 1 SCD

NOTE More information on the SQL Server HASHBYTES function can be found in
SQL Server Books Online at http://msdn.microsoft.com/en-us/library/
ms174415.aspx.

The data flow of the Type 1 Product SCD package reads in the source file, generates a
hash code for each row, and outputs to a staging table. I'm using a Script component
and the .NET SHA1Managed class to generate an SHA1 hash code for the non–business
key columns of every inbound row. The contents of the ScriptMain class in the script
component look like the code in listing 1.

Listing 1 ScriptMain class

```
[Microsoft.SqlServer.Dts.Pipeline.SSISScriptComponentEntryPointAttribute]
public class ScriptMain : UserComponent
{
    SHA1Managed sha1;
    MemoryStream ms;
    BinaryWriter bw;

    public override void PreExecute()
    {
        base.PreExecute();
        sha1 = new SHA1Managed();
    }

    public override void PostExecute()
    {
        base.PostExecute();
    }

    public override void Input0_ProcessInputRow(Input0Buffer Row)
    {
        ms = new MemoryStream(2000);
        bw = new BinaryWriter(ms);
        bw.Write(Row.Category);
        bw.Write('|');
        bw.Write(Row.Manufacturer);
        bw.Write('|');
        bw.Write(Row.Color);
        bw.Write('|');
        bw.Write(Row.Price);
        bw.Write('|');
        bw.Write(Row.ProductName);
        bw.Write('|');
        bw.Write(Row.Size);
        bw.Write('|');
        Row.Hash = sha1.ComputeHash(ms.ToArray());
        bw.Close();
        ms.Dispose();
    }
}
```

Observant .NET developers will notice that I use the `BinaryWriter` to write the data in each inbound row to a `MemoryStream` for efficiency. The output of this data flow is pushed into a staging table called Staging.Product. The final step in the control flow is an Execute SQL task that performs a `MERGE` to update the Dim.Product table, as shown in listing 2. On SQL Server 2005 you can use separate `UPDATE` and `INSERT` statements in place of `MERGE`.

Listing 2   Final `MERGE` statement to update the Product Type 1 SCD table

```
MERGE INTO Dim.Product_Type1 AS Target
USING Staging.Product AS Source
ON Source.UPC = Target.UPC
WHEN MATCHED AND Source.Hash <> Target.Hash
THEN UPDATE SET Target.Category = Source.Category,
     Target.Manufacturer = Source.Manufacturer,
     Target.ProductName = Source.ProductName,
     Target.Size = Source.Size,
     Target.Color = Source.Color,
     Target.Price = Source.Price,
     Target.Hash = Source.Hash
WHEN NOT MATCHED
THEN INSERT
(
     UPC, Category,Manufacturer,
     ProductName, Size, Color,
     Price, Hash
)
VALUES
(
     Source.UPC, Source.Category, Source.Manufacturer,
     Source.ProductName, Source.Size, Source.Color,
     Source.Price, Source.Hash
);
```

The performance of this optimized solution is shown in table 2.

Table 2   Comparison of optimized Type 1 dimension loads

Load description	Time	Rows per second
First load: 2,500 rows, empty target table	0.5 sec.	5,000 row/sec.
Second load: 25,300 rows, updates to 2,500 initial rows	1.5 sec.	16,866 rows/sec.
Third load: 25,300 rows, no updates	1.5 sec.	16,866 rows/sec.

As you can see, the performance of this optimized design is an order of magnitude faster than the stock SCD component. Using this method requires you to generate hash codes for comparison and to stage the data in a database table, but for enterprise ETL solutions, the performance increase can be well worth the additional design and development work.

Type 2 SCDs

Type 2 SCDs track all historical changes for a dimension. Let's revisit WidgetCorp with a Type 2 Geography dimension. Widget-Corp decides to implement a Type 2 Product dimension so they can keep track of historical changes to their product line. Now when they swap out Blue Widgets for Green Widgets, they maintain a history of the change. By keeping Type 2 historical data, they'll be able to track and compare their historical sales of Blue Widgets to their future sales of Green Widgets.

The SCD component data flow for updating the Type 2 Product dimension is shown in figure 6. Even more than with the Type 1 SCD component data flow, the Type 2 SCD component data flow adds a considerable number of component steps

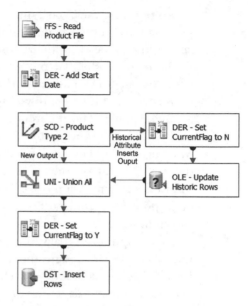

Figure 6 SCD component Type 2 dimension data flow

to the data flow and additional complexity to the process.

The general idea is that new rows are output from the New Output of the SCD component and existing changed rows are output to the Historical Attribute Inserts Output. Along with the Historical Attribute Inserts Output, the historic matching rows are updated so that their CurrentFlag is set to N using an OLE DB Command component. This means a single UPDATE statement is issued for every row that passes through this branch of the data flow. Afterward, both branches of the data flow are brought back together with a Union All component, the CurrentFlag is set to Y, and the rows are inserted into the target table. Table 3 shows the performance of this particular data flow.

Table 3 Comparison of SCD component Type 2 dimension loads

Load description	Time	Rows per second
First load: 2,500 rows, empty target table	2.1 sec.	1,190 row/sec.
Second load: 25,300 rows, updates to 2,500 initial rows	53.4 sec.	474 rows/sec.
Third load: 25,300 rows, no updates	130.2 sec.	194 rows/sec.

As you can see, the performance is pretty miserable. You must find a way to improve performance similar to what you did with the Type 1 dimension. You need to improve on the performance of the comparisons you get from the SCD component and a more efficient method of updating the target table.

To optimize the Type 2 dimension load, you'll use a pattern similar to the Type 1 optimization. You'll read in the flat file data, generate an SHA1 hash code for each row, and insert the rows into a staging table. The difference is in the last step of the control flow, where you'll update the effective dates (`StartDate`) and `CurrentFlag` for the dimension rows. The data flow and control flow are shown in figure 7.

The optimized data flow is much simpler in design and utilizes far fewer components. The

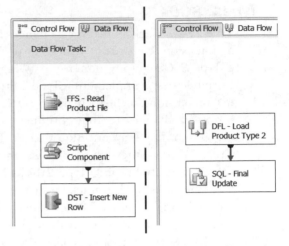

Figure 7   Optimized Type 2 dimension data flow and control flow

Script component uses the same code as the Type 1 dimension Script component to generate the SHA1 hash code.

The final Execute SQL task in the Type 1 control flow had a basic `MERGE` statement to update existing rows or insert new rows in the target table. In the case of the Type 2 dimension, it's a little more complex because all new rows or changes to existing rows are inserts. At the same time, if a row is an update to an existing product you need to update the old rows (set their `CurrentFlag` to N). You can accomplish both tasks in a single statement by using a `MERGE` statement with an `OUTPUT` clause to feed an outer `INSERT` statement, as shown in listing 3.

Listing 3   Using `MERGE` to feed `INSERT` for Type 2 Product dimension update

```
INSERT INTO Dim.Product_Type2
(
    UPC, Category, Manufacturer,
    ProductName, Size, Color,
    Price, Hash, StartDate, CurrentFlag
)
SELECT UPC, Category, Manufacturer,
    ProductName, Size, Color,
    Price, Hash, GETDATE(), 'Y'
FROM
(
    MERGE INTO Dim.Product_Type2 AS Target
    USING Staging.Product AS Source
    ON Source.UPC = Target.UPC
    WHEN MATCHED AND Source.Hash <> Target.Hash
    THEN UPDATE SET Target.Category = Source.Category,
            Target.Manufacturer = Source.Manufacturer,
            Target.ProductName = Source.ProductName,
            Target.Size = Source.Size,
```

```
                Target.Color = Source.Color,
                Target.Price = Source.Price,
                Target.Hash = Source.Hash,
                Target.CurrentFlag = 'N'
        WHEN NOT MATCHED
        THEN INSERT
          (
                UPC, Category, Manufacturer,
                ProductName, Size, Color,
                Price, Hash, StartDate, CurrentFlag
          )
        VALUES
          (
                Source.UPC, Source.Category, Source.Manufacturer,
                Source.ProductName, Source.Size, Source.Color,
                Source.Price, Source.Hash, GETDATE(), 'Y'
          )
        OUTPUT $action, inserted.UPC, inserted.Category,
inserted.Manufacturer,
                inserted.ProductName, inserted.Size, inserted.Color,
                inserted.Price, inserted.Hash
)
AS T
(
    action, UPC, Category, Manufacturer,
    ProductName, Size, Color,
    Price, Hash
)
WHERE action = 'UPDATE';
```

The inner MERGE statement inserts new products that don't yet exist and sets the CurrentFlag to N for existing product rows that have changed. The OUTPUT clause feeds the rows back to the outer INSERT statement, where new rows are inserted for product updates. This is an interesting feature of SQL Server 2008, although you can accomplish the same results with INSERT and UPDATE statements in SQL Server 2005. The performance of this optimized solution is shown in table 4.

Table 4   Performance of the optimized solution

Load description	Time	Rows per second
First load: 2,500 rows, empty target table	0.5 sec.	5,000 row/sec.
Second load: 25,300 rows, updates to 2,500 initial rows	1.4 sec.	18,071 rows/sec.
Third load: 25,300 rows, no updates	1.4 sec.	18,071 rows/sec.

The performance of the optimized Type 2 Product dimension solution is considerably better than the SCD component data flow.

Summary

There are several ways to optimize your SSIS ETL data flows. In this chapter you learned about quick wins that you can start implementing in your data flows immediately to increase their performance. This chapter also looked at the performance of the slowly changing dimension (SCD) component and discussed how to optimize dimension updates with hash codes and staging tables.

About the author

Michael Coles is a SQL Server MVP and consultant based in New York City. He's written several articles and books on a wide variety of SQL Server topics, including *Pro SQL Server 2008 XML* (Apress, 2008) and *Pro T-SQL 2008 Programmer's Guide* (Apress, 2008). He can be reached at www.sqlforge.com.

47 SSIS configurations management

Andy Leonard

SQL Server Integrations Services (SSIS) is a wonderful platform for migrating data around and between enterprises. SSIS ships with many powerful features and functionalities. One of the most powerful is package configurations.

Package configurations allow data integration developers to externalize SSIS package values. When software facilitates a separation between modules, or between code and configurable options, the application is described as decoupled. *Decoupling* is an important principle and best practice for developing object-oriented software.

Externalizing SSIS package values adds flexibility to a data integration solution and promotes code reuse. For example, an SSIS package can load data from one of several flat file sources if the location of the flat file is externalized. Instead of writing a separate SSIS package to load data from each source location, an externalized source serves as a parameter, allowing a single SSIS package to load data from many source locations.

But making data integration packages dynamic involves more than flexibility and best practices; it clears the way for SSIS developers to participate in an enterprise software development life cycle (or SDLC). SDLCs aren't just a good idea; they're the subject of compliance audits and, in some cases, the law.

In this chapter I'll share a design pattern for managing SSIS configurations for SSIS 2005, 2008, and 2008R2. Specifically, I'll focus on connections management. There are several variations of SSIS design patterns in the wild; most share significant overlap. This is due to neither malevolence nor coincidence: SSIS simply lends itself to certain patterns for execution, logging, and configurations management. If you can accept that two people discovered or invented calculus independently, separate individuals developing similar SSIS frameworks and design patterns should be relatively easy to accept.

Building the demo database

Let's create a demo database to use with our SSIS solution. Execute the script in listing 1 in SQL Server Management Studio (on a development server please!).

| Listing 1   Creating the demo database |

```
use master
Go

Create Database MVPDeepDivesDev
go

use MVPDeepDivesDev
go

Create Table MySource
(Id int identity(1,1) constraint PK_MySource primary key
   ,SourceName varchar(255) ,SourceValue int)

Insert Into MySource  (SourceName ,SourceValue)
Values ('Andy',0),('Christy',1),('Stevie Ray',2)
     ,('Emma Grace',3) ,('Riley',4)

Create Database MVPDeepDivesTest
go

use MVPDeepDivesTest
go

Create Table MySource
(Id int identity(1,1) constraint PK_MySource primary key
 ,SourceName varchar(255)  ,SourceValue int)

Insert Into MySource (SourceName,SourceValue)
 Values ('Andy',0),('Christy',1)

Create Database MVPDeepDivesProd
go

use MVPDeepDivesProd
go

Create Table MySource
  (Id int identity(1,1) constraint PK_MySource primary key
    ,SourceName varchar(255) ,SourceValue int)
```

Starting in the middle

Let's build an SSIS solution to demonstrate. The example is in SQL Server 2008R2. Open Business Intelligence Development Studio (BIDS). Create a new Integration Services project and name it MVPDeepDivesSSISConfigurations. When the new project opens, rename Package.dtsx to Configurations.dtsx in Solution Explorer.

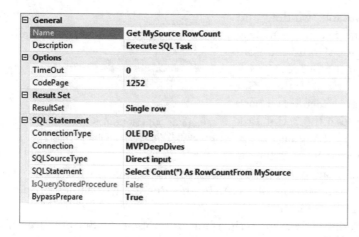

Figure 1 Enter these values for properties on the General page.

Right-click in the Connection Managers area at the bottom of the Control Flow. Click New OLE DB Connection. When the Configure OLE DB Connection Manager window displays, click the New button. This brings up the Connection Manager editor. In the Server Name drop-down, enter or select the SQL Server instance you used earlier to create the demo databases in SQL Server Management Studio. Click the "Select or Enter a Database Name" drop-down and select the MVPDeepDivesDev database. Click the OK button to close the Connection Manager editor, and again to close the Configure OLE DB Connection Manager window. Rename the connection manager MVPDeep-Dives. Drag an Execute SQL task onto the Control Flow canvas and open its editor. Set the properties shown in figure 1 on the General page.

On the Result Set page, click the Add button. Type RowCount into the Result Name column and click the Variable Name drop-down. Click <New variable…> and configure the variable properties as shown in figure 2.

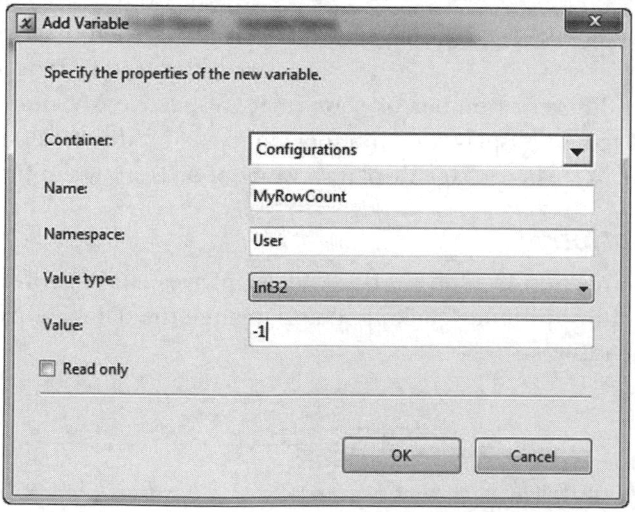

Figure 2 Set these variable properties.

Close the New Variable window and click OK to close the Execute SQL Task Editor. Drag a Script task onto the Control Flow and connect a Success Precedence Constraint from the Get MySource RowCount Execute SQL task to the Script task. Open the Script Task editor and set the ScriptLanguage property to Microsoft Visual Basic 2008 (or

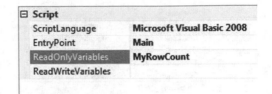

Figure 3   Add MyRowCount in the ReadOnlyVariables property.

the version of Visual Basic that appears in the ScriptLanguage property drop-down on the Script page of your version of SSIS). In the ReadOnlyVariables property, add MyRowCount, as shown in figure 3.

Click the Edit Script (or Design Script) button to open the Script editor and edit the `Sub Main()` subroutine to read as follows:

```
Public Sub Main()
    Dim iMyRowCount As Integer
    iMyRowCount = Convert.ToInt32(Dts.Variables("MyRowCount").Value)
    MsgBox("MyRowCount: " & iMyRowCount.ToString)
    Dts.TaskResult = ScriptResults.Success
End Sub
```

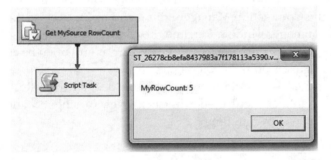

Figure 4   Execution results with a message box

This code creates an integer variable in the Script named iMyRowCount and reads the value of the SSIS variable MyRowCount into this variable. It then pops up a message box displaying a message containing the value of the MyRowCount SSIS variable. From the demo script, you'll recall the different environments; each contains a different number of rows in its respective MySource tables. Execute the SSIS package to display the number of rows in the MVPDeepDivesDev.dbo.MySource table. My SSIS package displays a value of 5, as shown in figure 4.

Changing the connection

You can change the connection by altering the MVPDeepDives connection manager properties. Open the editor by double-clicking it, and change the database from MVPDeepDivesDev to MVPDeepDivesTest, as shown in figure 5.

Figure 5   Changing the database name

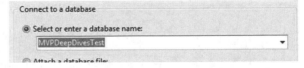

Close the connection manager and re-execute the Configurations SSIS package. Note the value of MyRowCount is 2 because there are two rows in MVPDeepDives-Test.dbo.MySourcee.

Externalizing the connection

Let's externalize the MVPDeepDives connection manager's connection string property. Click the SSIS drop-down menu and choose Package Configurations. Select the Enable Package Configurations check box to enable the controls in the Package Configurations Organizer window. Click the Add button to add a new package configuration, and click past the Welcome screen in the wizard (if it displays). On the Select Configuration Type page, leave Configuration Type set to XML Configuration File and click the Browse button to select a location for the configuration file.

After selecting a file location, click the Next button to display the Select Properties to Export page. On this page of the wizard you'll find all the properties you can externalize. Some of them aren't useful (like the Package Description property); others can expand package functionality, flexibility, and usefulness (like the Package CheckpointFilename and CheckpointUsage

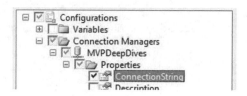

Figure 6   Selecting the properties to expose in the configuration

properties). Expand the MVPDeepDives node under Connection Managers, and then expand Properties. Select the ConnectionString property, as shown in figure 6.

Click the Next button and supply a name for this package configuration, such as cm_MVPDeepDives. Click the Finish button and then the Close button in the Package Configurations Organizer window.

You've just changed the package to use a file to manage the connection for your SSIS package. This may seem small, but it's huge! Don't believe me? Let's make a small change to that file. Open it in Notepad and find the string "Initial Catalog=MVPDeepDivesTest". Change it to read "Initial Catalog=MVPDeepDivesProd" and save the file.

Return to BIDS and re-execute your SSIS package. When I do this, I get a row count of 0. That's because I'm now executing a Count() statement against the empty MySource table in the MVPDeepDivesProd database... *and I didn't change the SSIS package to make this happen!* I told you—this is huge.

Taking a step back

I have a confession to make: I don't like storing connection manager connection strings. I can hear you asking, "Why not, Andy?" I'm glad you asked! I have this dream. I want to store and manage all my connection strings in a central location. It would be cool to store them in a SQL Server table somewhere, because that would allow me to use Transact-SQL to manage them. I like T-SQL.

Now SSIS facilitates storing configurations metadata in SQL Server by way of the SQL Server package configuration. But let's say you want to manage connection strings differently for these reasons:

- You want to encrypt connection strings using SQL Server's built-in encryption.
- You want to treat connection strings as ETL metadata.
- You want to manage connection strings as part of the enterprise Application Lifecycle Management protocol.

Abstracting a bit

To begin, create a database called SSISConfig to hold SSIS metadata:

```
Use master
go
Create Database SSISConfig
```

Inside this database, create a schema named cfg:

```
Use SSISConfig
go
create schema cfg
```

Inside this schema, create a table named Connections:

```
Create Table cfg.Connections
  (ConnectionName varchar(255) constraint PK_Connections primary key
    ,ConnectionString varchar(255) Not Null)
```

I'm not going to cover encryption in this chapter, but in real life I encrypt the ConnectionString column in this table—even at the development database level.

Now insert some data:

```
Insert Into cfg.Connections
Values
 ('DEV_MVPDeepDives','Data Source=(local);Initial
  ➥ Catalog=MVPDeepDivesDev;Provider=SQLNCLI10.1;Integrated
 Security=SSPI;Auto
  ➥ Translate=False;')
,('TEST_MVPDeepDives','Data Source=(local);Initial
 ➥ Catalog=MVPDeepDivesTest;Provider=SQLNCLI10.1;Integrated Security=SSPI;Auto
 ➥ Translate=False;')
,('PROD_MVPDeepDives','Data Source=(local);Initial
 ➥ Catalog=MVPDeepDivesProd;Provider=SQLNCLI10.1;Integrated Security=SSPI;Auto
 ➥ Translate=False;')
```

Next, you need a way to reach the SSISConfig database. In your SSIS package, create a new OLE connection manager named SSISConfig aimed at the SSISConfig database you just created.

Access the Package Configurations Organizer, delete the existing package configuration, and create a new package configuration. Repeat the earlier steps for creating an XML Configuration File package configuration with the following exceptions (see figure 7):

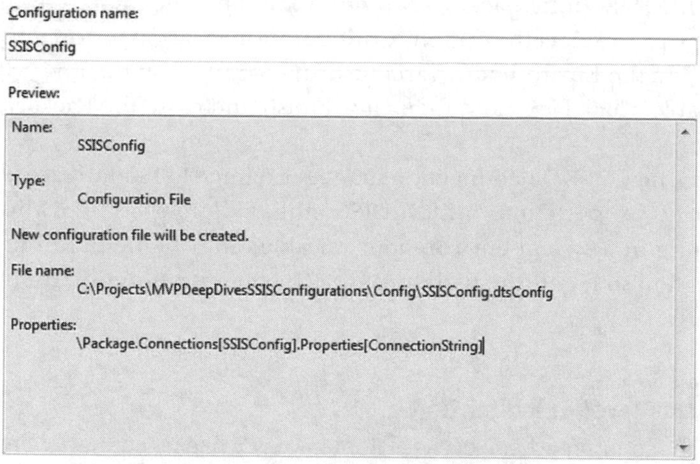

Configuration name:

SSISConfig

Preview:

Name:

     SSISConfig

Type:

     Configuration File

New configuration file will be created.

File name:

     C:\Projects\MVPDeepDivesSSISConfigurations\Config\SSISConfig.dtsConfig

Properties:

     \Package.Connections[SSISConfig].Properties[ConnectionString]

**Figure 7
Naming the configuration**

- Name the file `SSISConfig.dtsConfig`.
- Select Package > Connections > Properties and choose the ConnectionString property to export (I know I said I don't want to export connection strings…be patient!).
- Name the package configuration `SSISConfig`.

Now, access the system environment variables of the server or workstation you're using to develop this sample. For example, if you're using Windows 7 Ultimate 64, you can access the system environment variables by the following process: Click Start, right-click Computer, and click Properties. In the Control Panel Home window, click Advanced System Settings, and then click the Environment Variables button.

To create a new system environment variable, click the New button beneath the System Environment Variables pane in the lower half of the Environment Variables window. Name the environment variable `Env_SSISConfig` and set the value to the path of the SSISConfig .dtsConfig file you just created for the XML Configuration File package configuration, as shown in figure 8.

Click OK several times to exit (and save) the new system environment variable. Visual Studio enumerates environment variables when it starts, so you have to save your SSIS project, close, and reopen BIDS before proceeding. Then return to the Package Configurations

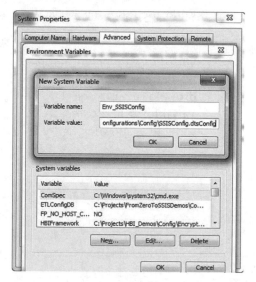

Figure 8 The New System Variable dialog box

Organizer, select the SSISConfig package configuration, and click Edit. On the Select Configuration Type page, select the option "Configuration location is stored in an environment variable." In the Environment Variable drop-down, select the Env_SSISConfig environment variable. Click Next, and then click Finish and close the Package Configurations Organizer.

You've created a new OLE DB connection manager named SSISConfig, externalized its connection string property into a file (SSISConfig.dtsConfig), stored the path to SSISConfig.dtsConfig in a system environment variable, and then edited the existing package configuration so it gets the path to this XML configuration file from the environment variable.

> ## Rationale for this level of indirection
>
> Imagine a time in the future when you've built many SSIS packages that are running in Production but a new security mandate requires you to *move* your XML configuration file. (It happens, trust me.) Without the use of a system environment variable to store the path to this file, you have to open each package, change the location, resave, and then redeploy the packages. But wait, there's more! What if you miss one of the SSIS packages and move your XML configuration file? Well, SSIS will dutifully attempt to execute using your default package values. Your worst-case scenario here is reading data from a development or test environment into Production. Don't think it can happen? It happened to me.

Now your SSIS package can locate the SSISConfig database. Let's use it! Drag an Execute SQL task onto the Control Flow, name the Execute SQL task `Get MVPDeepDives Connection`, and set the Connection property to the SSISConfig connection manager. Enter the following SQL statement:

```
Select ConnectionString From cfg.Connections Where ConnectionName = ?
```

On the Parameter Mapping page, from the Variable Name drop-down list, select <New Variable…> and configure the variable as shown in figure 9.

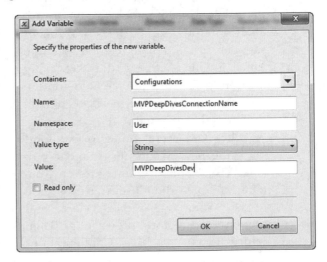

Figure 9   Adding a variable

Change Value type to Varchar and Parameter Name to 0. On the General page, change the ResultSet property to Single Row. On the Result Set tab, click the Add button. Set Result Name to 0 and create another new variable, as shown in figure 10.

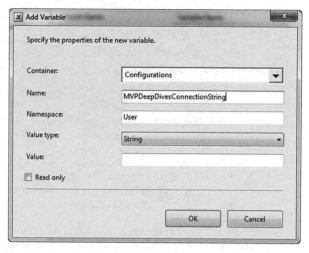

The Execute SQL task is now configured to execute a Transact-SQL statement that will return the Connection-String value associated with a ConnectionName in the SSIS-Config.cfg.Connections table

Figure 10   Adding a second variable

for the ConnectionName MVPDeepDivesDev. It will push the connection string into the SSIS variable named MVPDeepDivesConnectionString. How cool is that?

Once you have the connection string in the variable, now what? You need to map that value into the ConnectionString property of the MVPDeepDives connection manager. To map the variable value into the MVPDeepDives connection manager's Con-

nectionString property, right-click the MVPDeepDives connection manager and click Properties. Click the Expressions property, and then click the ellipsis in the Value text box of the Expressions property. This displays the Property Expressions Editor. Click the Property drop-down and select Connection-String, and then click the ellipsis in the Expression text box to display the Expression Builder window. Expand the Variables virtual folder in the upper left of the Expression Builder. Click and drag the User::MVPDeepDivesConnectionString variable into the Expression text box, as shown in figure 11.

Click OK twice to close the Expression Builder and the Property Expressions Editor windows.

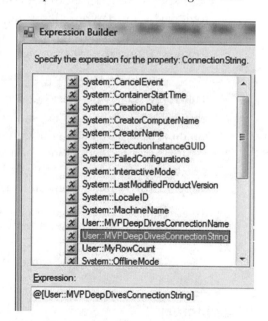

Figure 11   Choosing the user variable

Let's take a peek

Double-click the Script task to open the editor and add MVP-DeepDivesConnectionString to the ReadOnlyVariables property, as shown in figure 12.

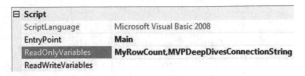

Figure 12   ReadOnlyVariables selection

Click the Edit Script button (Design Script if you're using SSIS 2005) and add the following code:

```
Dim sMVPDeepDivesConnectionString As String =
➥ Dts.Variables("MVPDeepDivesConnectionString").Value.ToString
        MsgBox("MVPDeepDivesConnectionString: " &
            ➥ sMVPDeepDivesConnectionString)
```

Close the Code Editor window and click OK to close the Script Task editor. Execute the SSIS package by pressing F5 and examine the messages shown in the message boxes. They should indicate you're connected—dynamically—to the MVPDeepDives-Dev database.

Runtime overrides

To utilize this functionality, open a command prompt to execute this package using DtExec, the SSIS command-line execution utility. Navigate to the folder containing your MVPDeepDivesSSISConfigurations solution, and then navigate to the project sub-folder. On my laptop, this brings me to C:\Projects\MVPDeepDivesSSISConfigurations\MVPDeepDivesSSISConfigurations. Enter the following command to execute the Configurations.dtsx SSIS package:

```
dtexec.exe /FILE Configurations.dtsx /REPORTING E
```

The /FILE switch tells DtExec you're executing SSIS from a file and accepts a path parameter. The /REPORTING switch controls the information displayed from the execution. The E parameter configures the execution to only display errors.

It's possible to override variable values from the command line using the SET switch. Add the following SET switch and package path; value parameters override the MVPDeepDivesConnectionName variable, setting it to TEST_MVPDeepDives:

```
dtexec.exe /FILE Configurations.dtsx /REPORTING E /SET
➥ "\Package.Variables[MVPDeepDivesConnectionName].Properties[Value]";
➥ TEST_MVPDeepDives
```

Executing this command causes the package to run against the MVPDeepDivesTest database.

Summary

This chapter discussed a design pattern for SSIS connections management. You leveraged the built-in SSIS Package Configurations functionality to build a dynamic connection to a central metadata repository (the SSISConfig database). Next you used a combination of a table, Execute SQL task, and variables to retrieve connections meta-data. Finally, you explored one method for changing the connection from the command line at runtime.

I hope you've enjoyed this chapter and the demo project!

About the author

Andy Leonard is Chief Servant Officer for SQLPeople and Linch-pin People LLC, an SSIS Trainer and Consultant, SQL Server database and Integration Services developer, SQL Server data warehouse developer, community mentor, SQLBlog.com blogger, and engineer. He is a coauthor of *Professional SQL Server 2005 Integration Services* (Wrox, 2006) and volume 1 of this book, *SQL Server MVP Deep Dives* (Manning, 2009). His background includes web application architecture and development, VB, and ASP; SQL Server Integration Services (SSIS); and data warehouse development using SQL Server.

48 Exploring different types of enumerators in the SSIS Foreach Loop container

Abolfazl Radgoudarzi and Shahriar Nikkhah

There are two types of loop structures in SQL Server Integration Services (SSIS): the For Loop container and the Foreach Loop container. The Foreach Loop container will loop through items in the specified collection, where the collection is divided into seven different enumerators. You may need to loop through files, items in a directory, records in a data table, nodes in XML data, and SMO objects.

Make it dynamic

Expressions provide a dynamic way of working in SSIS, particularly when combined with a Foreach loop. For example, you can change data sources in data flow tasks at runtime or change the path of an FTP address without changing the package and recompiling it. There are times when you encounter situations that require the processing of several similarly structured .csv files in one table. This is achieved with a single dataflow task inside a Foreach Loop enumerator. This ability to use combinations of expressions and the Foreach loop is illustrated in some of the examples of this chapter to familiarize you with dynamic SSIS development.

Foreach Loop enumerators

The following sections offer brief descriptions with examples for all seven enumerators in the Foreach Loop container.

FILE ENUMERATOR

The File enumerator loops through files in a directory. For example, you may need to loop through Excel/.csv files with the same structure in a directory and import them all with a single data flow task. The File enumerator achieves this.

Suppose that addresses in each city are in a .csv file in a specified directory, and each .csv file contains two columns of data: AddressLine and City. Sample data in the .csv file for the city of Seattle is displayed in figure 1. The whole scenario is to loop through the .csv files in the speci-

```
AddressLine,City
7126 Ending Ct.,Seattle
4598 Manila Avenue,Seattle
5666 Hazelnut Lane,Seattle
1220 Bradford Way,Seattle
```

Figure 1   Seattle_AddressLines.csv

fied directory and import each data file into a destination SQL Server table. The destination table named Address contains two columns: AddressLine of `varchar(60)` and City of `varchar(50)`.

Solution

Create a package variable of the `string` data type in the package `scope` and name it `FilePath`. Set one of the .csv source file paths as the default value.

Add a Foreach Loop container in the control flow. Double-click the Foreach Loop container, and in the Foreach Loop Editor in the Collection tab, set Enumerator to `Foreach File Enumerator`. In the Enumerator Configuration section, set Folder to the specified folder that contains the .csv files. In the Files box, enter *.csv to loop through only .csv files. Set the Retrieve File Name field to Fully Qualified. (You can choose among Fully Qualified, Name and Extension, and Name Only. This is based on your scenario for each of these options.) In this example you don't need to check Traverse Subfolders, because this is required only when looking for files in root and subfolders. The configuration is displayed in figure 2.

Your next step is to fetch each fully qualified file path into the `FilePath` string variable. On the Variable Mappings tab, set the Variable column to `User::FilePath` and the Index column to 0. See figure 3.

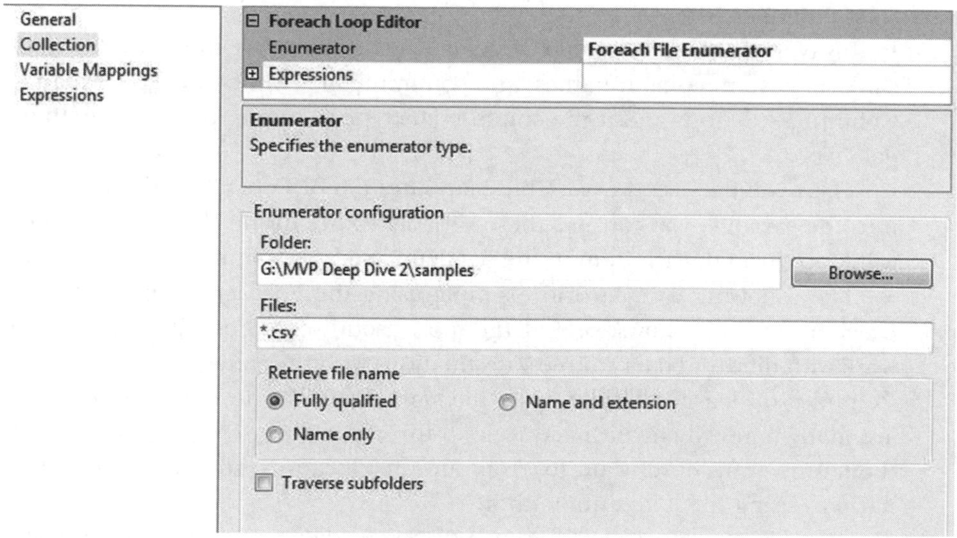

Figure 2   File Enumerator Collection configuration

General
Collection
Variable Mappings
Expressions

Select variables to map to the collection value.

Variable	Index
User::FilePath	0

**Figure 3
File Enumerator
variable
mappings**

Next, create the data flow structure in the Loop container. Add a data flow task inside the Foreach Loop container, and set a flat file source pointing to one of the .csv files. Then set OLEDB Destination to the destination table, and set all mappings and configurations.

This is a simple data flow task that reads data rows from .csv source files and transfers them into a destination SQL Server table. In this scenario you need to make this data flow task dynamic. To implement this, right-click the flat file connection manager in

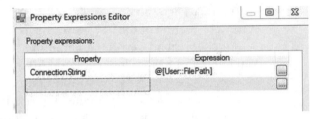

Figure 4   Property Expressions Editor settings for the File enumerator example

the Connection Manager pane, and select Properties. In the Properties window, find the Expressions property and click the Browse (...) button in front of it; the Property Expressions Editor window will open. In the Property column, select Connection-String, and in the Expression field enter this expression: @[User::FilePath]. This configuration will make a flat-file connection manager dynamically based on the User::FilePath variable value. See figure 4.

ITEM ENUMERATOR

In this type of enumerator you can create a custom data table as the enumerator; you can't set custom column names, and column names will be in this format: Column 0, Column 1, …. You can set the column data type as required from a predefined list of data types.

Then you can use the Variable Mappings tab of Foreach and read column values into the variable; you can use these variable values inside the Foreach loop. Foreach will loop through each item in the data table and fill column values into the variables.

The following is real-world example using the Foreach Item enumerator. As the previous example shows, one of the most useful scenarios with a Foreach loop is to work with different data sources/destinations with the same structure. In the previous example you learned how to loop through files with the File enumerator, but there are many times when you need to loop through database servers, connect to each of them, and transfer all data to/from another location. You can accomplish this scenario by using the Item enumerator.

Suppose you have two different SQL Server database servers. Each of them has a database with the name MVPDeepDive2, and each of them has an Address table that contains a few lines of data (this example is similar to the previous example in that one of the tables has data rows for Seattle and the other has data rows for Bellevue). You want to integrate this data into a third database server table. The structure of the source and destination table(s) is the same as in the previous example.

Solution

Create a package variable of type `String`, name it `ServerName`, and set a default valid value for it. (Note that you should set a default valid value because SSIS will check this value when you assign it to the data source as an expression at compile time.)

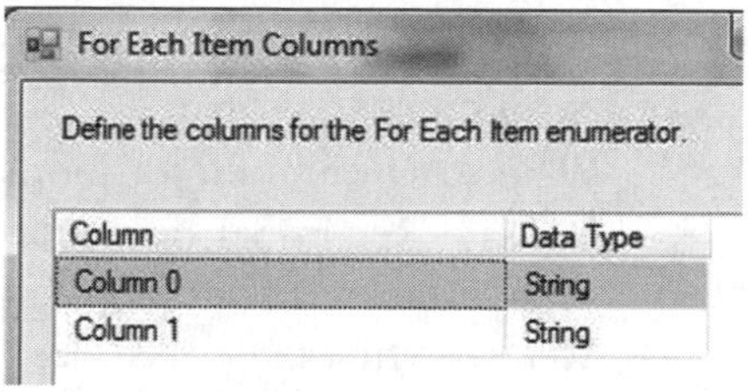

Add a Foreach Loop container in the control flow. In the Foreach Loop Editor,

Figure 5　Defining Foreach Item columns

click the Collection tab. Set Enumerator to `Foreach Item Enumerator`. Then in the Enumerator Configuration section, click the Columns tab, and add two columns of type `String` (note that you can't change the column names). See figure 5.

Then click OK, and go back to the Foreach Loop Editor, click the Collection tab, and add two data rows for two different database servers. The configurations in the Collection tab are displayed in figure 6.

Map each column of this data table to a package variable. Click the Variable Mappings tab, set the variable to `User::ServerName`, and set Index to `1`. (Note that Index is zero based, and you can set it based on enumerator columns; in this example, the enumerator has two columns, so if you want to fetch ServerName, you should retrieve it from the second column, which has its index set to `1`.)

The loop configuration is complete. Now you should create a simple data flow task that reads data from an OLEDB source and writes it to an OLEDB destination, where the structure of both source and destination is the same, so you don't need any extra transformations.

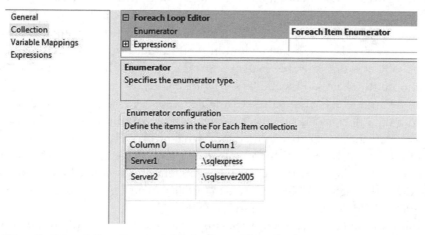

Figure 6　Foreach Item Enumerator Collection configurations

Make a dynamic source that will change its connection to a different server each time. Right-click the Source Connection Manager, and select Properties. In the Property Expression Editor window, set Property to ServerName. (Note that in this example, the database name, table names, and authentication are the same, and you just need to change ServerName. You can use the ConnectionString property if you need to change all of these items.) Set Expression to @[User::ServerName].

ADO ENUMERATOR

The ADO enumerator loops through an ADO object. The ADO object can be filled from a RecordSet destination, from a Script task, or from an Execute SQL task. You can choose the Loop option to loop through all tables in a DataSet or loop through only the first table records.

Let's dive in deep with an example. In the previous example you created a data table that contains server names in the Foreach Item Enumerator configuration, but in this example you want to read it from a database table. The source/destination and data structure are the same as for the previous example. Use a data flow task and the Connection Managers of the previous example. The only changes are in the Foreach loop.

Solution

First, create two package variables with these definitions: ServerName variable of type String with a default valid servername value and ServersData variable of type Object.

Add a data flow task in control flow, and set an OLEDB Source to the Server table that contains the server's information. Then add a RecordSet Destination (RecordSet Destination will save the result of an input data stream into an Object type variable in ADO format). In the RecordSet Destination, set VariableName to ServersData, and in the Input columns, select all columns.

This step will load the server's information from the database table into an Object type variable named ServersData. Configure the Foreach loop to loop through this data.

Add a Foreach Loop container in control flow right after the first data flow task, and connect a precedence constraint from the data flow task to this Foreach Loop container. In the Foreach Loop Editor, choose the Collection tab and set the enumerator to Foreach ADO Enumerator; and in the Enumerator Configuration section, set the ADO object source variable to User::ServersData. In the Enumeration Mode section, choose Rows in the First Table; see figure 7.

In the Variable Mappings tab, set Variable to ServerName, and set Index to 1.

Add a data flow task inside the Foreach loop as you did in the previous example. Note that you should set the Connection Manager property of the expression ServerName to the User::ServerName variable. Run the package and review the results.

You can also loop through an object variable in an Execute SQL task in full result-set mode or through an object variable that holds an ado.net dataset and is populated from a Script task with the ADO enumerator.

A question that may arise is why SSIS implemented two types of enumerators (Item enumerator and ADO enumerator) based on the data table. To answer this question,

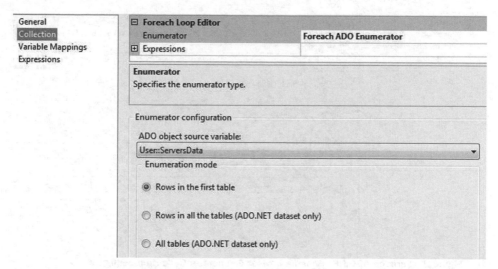

Figure 7 Foreach ADO Enumerator Collection configuration

note that in the Item enumerator you can have only a static data table applicable at the package level, but in the ADO enumerator you can dynamically fill an object type variable from any source in the ADO type.

ADO.NET SCHEMA ROWSET ENUMERATOR

In this enumerator, you can use information schema views in SQL Server and iterate in each of them as you want. Information schema views are views that contain metadata of a SQL Server database. To use this type of enumerator, you need to set an OLEDB connection to a SQL Server database and select the schema desired (for example, Table Info). Lists of all information schema views are available here: http://msdn.microsoft.com/en-us/library/ms186778.aspx.

You should create a connection of type OLEDB. If you don't, you'll get this error:

```
The new connection, <connection name>, is not an OLE DB connection so it
cannot be used by the schema rowset enumerator and, therefore, will not be
added to the connections list.
```

The following is a real-world scenario for this type of enumerator. The sample database is AdventureWorks; you can download this database from http://msftdbprod-samples.codeplex.com/. Your mission is to export all tables in the HumanResource schema to .csv files. Note that the structure of the data isn't the same, so you can't use a data flow task.

Solution

Add four package variables of type `String`; name them `Database`, `Schema`, `TableName`, and `SQLCommand`.

Add a Foreach loop in control flow, set the Enumerator field to `Foreach ADO.NET Schema Rowset Enumerator`, and then in the Enumerator Configuration section, under Connection, create an OLEDB connection. If your default connection type isn't

General
Collection
Variable Mappings
Expressions

⊟ **Foreach Loop Editor**	
Enumerator	Foreach ADO.NET Schema Rowset Enumerator
⊞ Expressions	

Enumerator
Specifies the enumerator type.

Enumerator configuration

Connection:
LocalHost.AdventureWorks1

Schema:
Tables

Set Restrictions...

Figure 8   Foreach ADO.NET Schema Rowset Enumerator Collection configuration

OLEDB, you can change it in this way: click the Provider drop-down list and under .NET Providers for OLEDB, select Microsoft OLEDB Provider for SQL Server.

After creating a connection to the AdventureWorks database, in Enumerator Configuration click the Schema drop-down. Here you'll find a list of all information schema views, and you can use them as you want. In this example you should choose Tables because you'll want to loop through tables of the AdventureWorks database. See figure 8.

The Tables schema will return all tables and views from all schemas in the database, but you need to fetch only HumanResource schema tables, so you should set a filter. You can do this with the Set Restrictions option. Click the Set Restrictions button to open the Tables Schema Restrictions window. There are four restrictions: TABLE_CATALOG means the database name. You should check every restriction for which you want to filter its data. In this example you should check TABLE_CATALOG first and then enter AdventureWorks in the Text box. TABLE_SCHEMA, as its name implies, is the schema of the table. Check this restriction too, and enter Human-Resources in the Text box. TABLE_NAME is the name of the table; you don't need to set any filter here because you have no filter on table names. TABLE_TYPE is the type of table, which can be TABLE or VIEW in this case. Check this restriction and enter TABLE in the Text box. Note that when you check the TABLE_TYPE restriction, TABLE_NAME

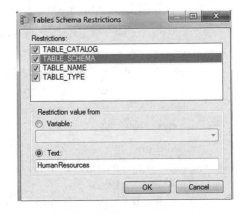

Figure 9   The Tables Schema Restrictions window

will also be checked. Don't worry about this, because you didn't set any text as a filter there, so all tables will be listed. This is the logic of restrictions: as you check the downward restriction, upward restrictions will be included in the filter. See figure 9.

After configuring the enumerator, fetch the enumerator items into package variables. As you see in the Restrictions window, there are four columns in the enumerator, and you can fetch data from these columns. In this case you need the databasename, schema, and tablename. In the Variable Mappings tab, set these rows: User::Database variable with Index 0, User::Schema variable with Index 1, and User::TableName variable with Index 2.

The order of columns in the enumerator is exactly the same as the order of the restrictions in the Tables Schema Restrictions window.

Now that you have each table name, schema, and database name, implement the export to .csv for tables. As you may know, the SSIS data flow task doesn't support dynamic metadata, so you can't use the data flow task when the structure of data is different. But there are other options that can help you overcome this issue; you can use the BCP command to export data from SQL Server to .csv files. The only restriction for using BCP is to enable xp_cmdshell on the database server. The script in the following listing enables xp_cmdshell.

Listing 1 Enabling xp_cmdshell

```
---- To allow advanced options to be changed.

EXEC sp_configure 'show advanced options', 1
GO
-- To update the currently configured value for advanced options.
RECONFIGURE
GO
-- To enable the feature.
EXEC sp_configure 'xp_cmdshell', 1
GO
-- To update the currently configured value for this feature.
RECONFIGURE

GO
```

Use the following script to export each table to the destination .csv file:

```
"declare @sql varchar(8000)
select @sql = 'bcp "+ @[User::Database] +"."+ @[User::Schema] +"."+
    @[User::TableName] +" out c:\\BCP\\"+ @[User::Database] +"."+
    @[User::Schema] +"."+ @[User::TableName] +" -c -C850 -t, -T -S'+
    @@servername
exec master..xp_cmdshell @sql"
```

You should use this script as sqlstatement in an Execute SQL task, which is why you create the SQLCommand variable. Right-click the SQLCommand variable, select Properties, and in the Properties window set the Expression property with this script. Also set EvaluateAsExpression to True.

Now add an Execute SQL task inside the Foreach loop and set an OLEDB connection. Set SQLSourceType as a variable, and set SourceVariable as User::SQLCommand.

Another hint to using the BCP command is that the destination file should exist, so you can use a script task to create each file with the lines of code in the following listing.

> **Listing 2   Code in Script task of ADO.NET schema rowset enumerator example**

```
public void Main()

    {
        string filename = string.Format("{0}.{1}.{2}"
            , Dts.Variables["User::Database"].Value
            , Dts.Variables["User::Schema"].Value
            , Dts.Variables["User::TableName"].Value);
        if (!System.IO.File.Exists(@"c:\BCP\" + filename))
            System.IO.File.Create(@"c:\BCP\" + filename);
        GC.Collect();
        Dts.TaskResult = (int)ScriptResults.Success;

    }
```

You should put the script task inside the Foreach Loop container, right before the Execute SQL task, and connect the Precedence constraint from the Script task to the Execute SQL task.

Note that you should set the language in the Script Task Editor to Visual C# and also set User::Database, User::Schema, and User::TableName as ReadOnlyVariables in the Script Task Editor.

After running the package, some files will be created in C:\BCP containing data rows.

FROM VARIABLE ENUMERATOR

Suppose you have a .NET ArrayList that contains the names of persons, and you need to perform logic in another task on each of these people.

Solution

First, create two package variables of Object data type; name them Collection and Item. Then add a Script task to initialize the Collection variable with an ArrayList, as shown in the following listing.

> **Listing 3   Code in Script task initializes the Collection variable with an ArrayList**

```
public void Main()

    {
        System.Collections.ArrayList arr = new
    System.Collections.ArrayList();
        arr.Add("Reza Rad");
        arr.Add("Shahriar Nikkhah");
        Dts.Variables["User::Collection"].Value = arr;

        Dts.TaskResult = (int)ScriptResults.Success;

    }
```

Loop through Collection variable items, add a Foreach Loop container right after the first Script task, connect the Precedence constraint from the Script task to this

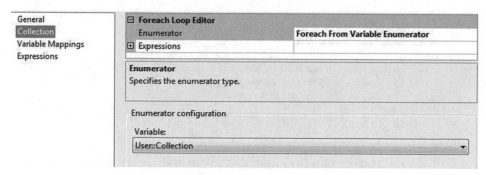

Figure 10   Foreach From Variable Enumerator Collection configuration

Foreach Loop container, and set Enumerator to `Foreach From Variable`. Then under Enumerator Configuration, set Variable to `User::Collection`. See figure 10.

Choose the Variable Mappings tab, and set the `User::Item` variable to Index 0. The reason for defining the `User::Item` variable as an object is that you can have any data type in the collection array.

Then you can add any other task inside the Foreach Loop container as required.

NODELIST ENUMERATOR

In addition to the XML task that has the ability to apply XPath, XSLT, and other changes in to an XML source, a built-in enumerator feature loops through the XML source structure based on the applied XPath; this is the NodeList enumerator.

In this type of enumerator, you can set XML Source to DirectInput under Variable, or you can set a FileConnection to an XML file. Also you can set EnumerationType as Navigator, Node, NodeText, or ElementCollection.

If you aren't familiar with XML structures, use this link, which is an introduction to XML: www.w3schools.com/xml/default.asp. As you may know, you can apply XPath to XML data to fetch data. We don't cover XPath queries in this chapter, but you can find helpful information about XPath here: www.w3schools.com/xpath/default.asp.

In all types of enumerations, you need to define OuterXPathStringSourceType and OuterXPathString. If you choose ElementCollection as EnumerationType, you should also define an InnerElementType, InnerXPathStringSourceType, and InnerXPath-String for access to subelements of nodes retrieved by OuterXPathString.

Here's a real-world example for the NodeList enumerator. Suppose you have a students.xml file with the data shown in the following listing. In this case you want to loop through the students, fetch each email, and perform actions on that email.

Listing 4   students.xml

```
?<?xml version="1.0" encoding="utf-8"?>

<Students>
    <Student>
        <FirstName>Reza</FirstName>
```

```
        <LastName>Rad</LastName>
        <Email>a.raad.g@gmail.com</Email>
    </Student>
    <Student>
        <FirstName>Shahriar</FirstName>
        <LastName>Nikkhah</LastName>
        <Email>snikkhah@live.ca</Email>
    </Student>
</Students>
```

Solution

First, create a variable for the enumerator item as the `string` data type; name it `Email`.

Add a Foreach Loop container, and set Enumerator to `Foreach NodeList Enumerator`. Then under Enumerator Configuration, set DocumentSourceType to `FileConnection`, and configure DocumentSource with a connection to an XML data file.

In figure 11, you can see all configurations under XPath. Note that OuterXPathString will fetch all student nodes, and InnerXPathString will fetch the Email element. Choose the Variable Mappings tab, and set the `User::Email` variable to Index 0.

Select the `User::Email` variable in the tasks that you use inside the Foreach Loop container. Because using an enumerator item variable inside the container is the same as for the other examples, we omitted this step; you can implement this step per the previous examples.

This was an example of ElementCollection as EnumerationType, but you can use the same method if you want to use the Navigator, Node, and NodeText options. The only difference is that you should set only OuterXPathString with these enumeration types.

SMO ENUMERATOR

Last, we have the SMO enumerator. SMO stands for SQL Server Management Objects, and as its names implies, it contains a collection of SQL Server management objects

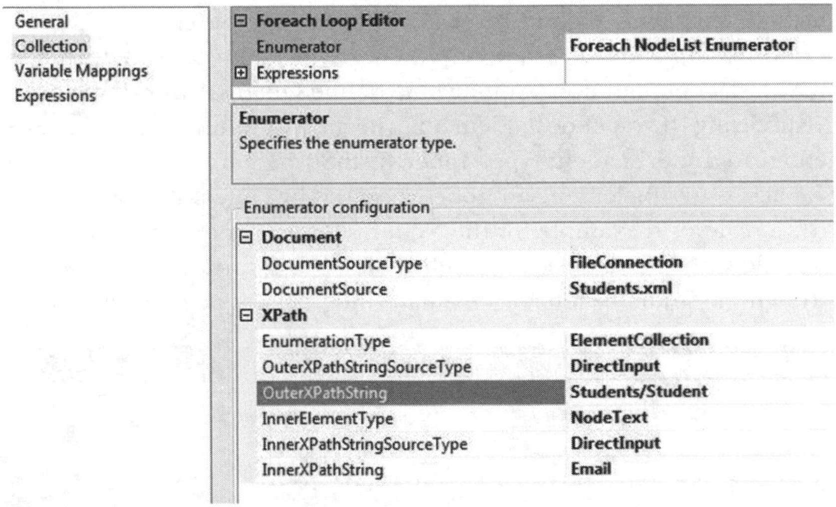

Figure 11   Foreach NodeList Enumerator Collection configuration

that can be accessed through programming. More information about SMO is available at this URL: http://msdn.microsoft.com/en-us/library/ms162169.aspx.

You may need to loop through logins on SQL Server or loop through jobs or data files of a database and perform an action. You can easily use the SMO enumerator in all of these situations.

All you need to do is to set a Connection Manager to an instance of SQL Server, and then enter an Enumerate string. There's a built-in SMO Enumerate string generator you can use if you like. If you click the Browse button and explore all objects in the SMO list, you can choose every object collection you want, and you can set Enumeration Type to fetch the whole object or part of it.

Here's a real-world example of the SMO enumerator. Suppose that you need to grant execute permission on a special stored procedure to all logins in a database server.

Solution

Create two package variables of `String` data type; name them `LoginName` and `SQLCommand`.

Add a Foreach Loop container, set the Enumerator field to the SMO enumerator, and then in Enumerator Configuration, set a connection to a database server. Click the Browse button. When you see the Select SMO Enumeration window,

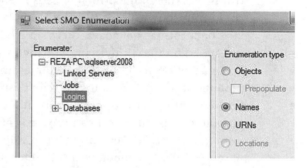

Figure 12   The Select SMO Enumeration window

select Logins from the Enumerate tree, and then select Names under Enumeration Type. See figure 12.

You'll see the autogenerated string under Enumerate, as shown in figure 13.

Choose the Variable Mappings tab, and set the `User::LoginName` variable to Index 0.

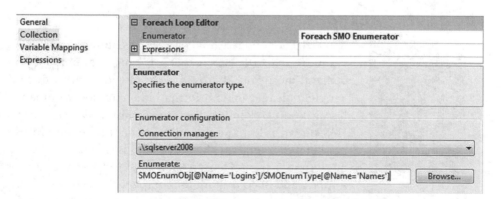

Figure 13   Foreach SMO Enumerator Collection configuration

Generate a grant SQL statement in the SQLCommand variable. Click the SQLCommand variable, and choose the Properties window. Set the expression to this value:

```
"Grant exec on sample_storedprocedure to "+ @[User::LoginName]
```

Also set the EvaluateAsExpression property to True. Then add an Execute SQL task inside the Foreach Loop container, create a connection to the database server, and set sqlstatement to the User::SQLCommand variable.

Summary

The Foreach Loop container provides a powerful looping structure with a variety of enumerators that cover many kinds of collections. There are two enumerators especially for SQL Server database servers that can loop through SMO or Information Schema Views: SMO enumerator and ADO.NET Schema Rowset enumerator. Working with files is one of the primary needs in SSIS, so there's a special File enumerator that can loop through files in a directory with a mask. Because XML is considered a standard data format nowadays, there's a NodeList enumerator that loops through XML data based on the XPath string provided.

In addition to all of these enumerators, there may be times when you need to implement your own collection that isn't a built-in type. SSIS has three custom Foreach enumerator types for this: Item enumerator, ADO enumerator, and From Variable enumerator. You can use each of these in appropriate situations. For example, you can use the Item enumerator where you need to use a static collection as enumerator. The ADO enumerator will fetch some data rows from a data source (Oracle, Excel, Sybase, and MySQL, to name a few) and loop through these data rows. Use the From Variable enumerator when you have an array of data filled from a .NET script and you want to loop through this array. These seven types of enumerators will help you to improve the design of the SSIS package.

About the authors

Abolfazl Radgoudarzi holds a BSC in computer engineering; he has more than 10 years' experience in programming and development, mostly on Microsoft technologies. Currently he's a software team leader in an information technology company. He got his Microsoft MVP in SQL Server in 2011 for his dedication to SSIS. He's known as Reza Rad in online communities and forums. Reza has been working on the Microsoft Business Intelligence suite more than 5 years. He's an SSIS/MSBI/.NET trainer and is also a software and BI consultant for companies and private institutions. His articles on various aspects of technologies, and especially on SSIS, can be found on his blog: www.rad.pasfu.com.

Shahriar Nikkhah's database development career started in 1990; he's been working with Microsoft Business Intelligence tools for more than 10 years in a variety of roles and industries. His biggest challenge was dealing with an SSIS farm environment for the leading telecommunication companies at Toronto. He specializes in SQL-SSIS, BI, ETL, and database design, implementation, and administration, using SQL Server technology. He focuses primarily on SQL Server SSIS and ETL, and the Microsoft SQL Server BI range of tools completes the list. His last word is, "Thank you, Microsoft."

49 Late-arriving dimensions in SSIS

John Welch

SQL Server Integration Services (SSIS) is a great tool for populating data warehouses. Straightforward, common approaches in data warehousing are easy to implement. But certain scenarios can be more complex to implement using SSIS, particularly if you're moving a lot of data and have aggressive performance requirements. Late-arriving dimensions are one of those scenarios.

Late-arriving dimensions (sometimes called early-arriving facts) occur when you have dimension data arriving in the data warehouse later than the fact data that references that dimension. This chapter discusses several options for handling late-arriving dimensions in SSIS.

A late-arriving dimension scenario

In the typical case for a data warehouse, extract, transform, and load (ETL) processes are written so that dimensions are fully processed first. Once the dimension processing has been completed, the facts are loaded, with the assumption that all required dimension data is already in place. Late-arriving dimensions break this pattern, because the fact data is processed first, before the associated dimension information. The ETL processes can encounter fact records that are related to new dimension members—members that have yet to be processed.

One real-world example of this can occur at online retailers. To make it convenient for customers, online retailers allow several options when placing an order. Customers can log into an existing account, create a new account, or place the order as a guest. Although this makes it easy for a customer to place an order, it also allows the customer to create multiple new accounts and means the company may end up with multiple accounts for the same customer.

This isn't really a problem for the operational system, but for reporting and analytics, the company wants to combine the multiple accounts into a single view of the customer. Doing so requires some additional processing, and in some cases, manual intervention. So, customer data has to go through a separate business process and may not be available right away. The sales record should show up in the warehouse immediately so that reports on sales are up to date.

Natural keys and surrogate keys

When discussing late-arriving dimensions, it's helpful to have a clear understanding of natural keys and surrogate keys. In the context of dimensional models, natural keys (sometimes referred to as business keys) are a column or set of columns that uniquely identify an entity from a business perspective. For a person, this could be a Social Security number, national ID, or a combination of first name, last name, and the person's email address. Sometimes, the natural key is combined with effective dates, when the dimension needs to store multiple versions of the entity.

Surrogate keys, on the other hand, are system-generated keys that uniquely identify a record. This is typically a uniquely assigned integer or GUID value. Surrogate keys are often generated by using an identity column or sequence object. They are often used in data warehouses to simplify data relationships between the facts and dimensions. They also minimize the space used in fact tables to store the dimension keys, in cases where the natural key is large or has multiple columns.

When processing late-arriving dimension rows, the natural key helps in identifying whether the dimension record is new or whether it already exists in the dimension table. The surrogate key allows you to link the fact table to the dimension. The remainder of this chapter assumes that the natural key for the dimension is included with the incoming fact data. Scenarios where it's not included are beyond the scope of this chapter.

The example data structure

So, you're processing your fact data, and you encounter a row that doesn't have a matching dimension record. What do you do with it? For the following examples, you'll use a data warehouse structure like that in figure 1. In this model, SalesSource represents the source of sales transactions. FactSales is the fact table where the sales transactions are recorded. DimCustomer is the late-arriving dimension and is where customer records are stored. CustomerName is the natural key for a customer, and CustomerID is the surrogate key assigned to a customer record.

This model has been simplified so you can focus on the core workings of the late-arriving dimension processing.

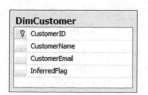

Figure 1   The data model

Working around late-arriving dimensions

Before adding complexity to your ETL processes, it's worth investigating whether you have to handle the late-arriving dimension directly. There are several approaches that may not fully address the needs of a late-arriving dimension but may be adequate in some scenarios and allow you to incorporate it into the ETL process in a relatively simple manner. You should validate these approaches carefully against your business requirements to ensure they fully meet the requirements.

File it

One approach is to place the fact row in a suspense table. The fact row will be held in the suspense table until the associated dimension record has been processed.

In SSIS, this would be implemented by adding a Lookup transformation to the data flow that matches records in the customer dimension and redirecting nonmatching rows to the suspense table. This approach is shown in figure 2.

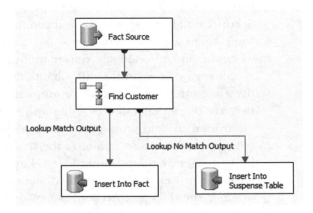

Figure 2   Redirecting to a suspense table

This solution is relatively easy to implement, but the primary drawback is that the fact row isn't available for reporting until the associated dimension record has been handled. Depending on business requirements, that may not be acceptable.

Ignore it

Another approach is to simply assign the "Unknown" dimension member to the sales fact record. On the positive side, this approach does allow the fact record to be recorded during the ETL process. But it won't be associated with the correct customer. Eventually, when the customer data is processed, the business is probably going to want the sale record associated with a real, valid customer record.

In SSIS, this solution can be implemented by configuring the Lookup transformation to ignore failures to match the customer record, as shown in figure 3. Following the Lookup, you can add a Derived Column transformation to

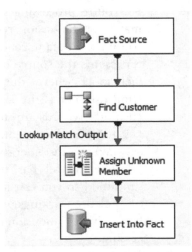

Figure 3   Ignoring missing customers

assign the customer ID to the Unknown dimension member, using the following expression (note that this assumes the Unknown member's ID is −1):

```
ISNULL(CustomerID) ? -1 : CustomerID
```

Update the fact later

To update the fact row at a later time to point to the correct customer record, you'd initially assign the Unknown dimension record to the fact, or a dimension record specially designated to represent customers that haven't been processed yet. In addition, you'd need to record the natural key of the late-arriving dimension (CustomerName in this example) either directly on the fact record itself or associated with the fact record. This is necessary so that you can look up the correct Customer record later.

On future runs of the ETL process, you look for fact records associated with the Unknown or Unprocessed customers, and using the associated natural key, attempt to match them to a customer. If it were found, the fact record could be updated with the appropriate surrogate key from the Customer dimension.

This approach has a few downsides. First, it requires you to store the natural keys for the late-arriving dimensions along with the facts. As mentioned in the earlier section "Natural Keys and Surrogate Keys," generally storing natural keys with facts is avoided because of the overhead in storing larger values. Second, updating fact records can be problematic in large data warehouses, due to performance constraints. Third, if the data warehouse has an OLAP cube built from it, updating fact information can have a significant impact, forcing data to be reprocessed for the OLAP cube.

The second pass update can be implemented through a SQL command, similar to the one in listing 1. Note the use of the natural key (CustomerName) in the join condition.

Listing 1   Updating the fact

```
UPDATE FactSales
    SET CustomerID = customer.CustomerID
FROM FactSales sales
        INNER JOIN DimCustomer customer
            ON sales.CustomerName = customer.CustomerName
```

Handling late-arriving dimension members in fact processing

Although the approaches I've discussed may accommodate simple requirements for late-arriving dimensions, in most cases they'll require more robust handling. One approach is to insert a placeholder (or inferred) dimension member for the new customer as the information is encountered in the fact table. The placeholder row will have the natural key information filled in, but the rest of the record will be filled in later, when the dimension data arrives. The placeholder row should also have a flag set on it that indicates it was created automatically. In this example, the InferredFlag column is used for this, and it will be used later, when updating the dimension data.

A key part of inserting the placeholder row is to determine when and how the new surrogate key for the customer record will be created. One approach is to generate the surrogate key as an identity column. When you use identity columns or sequences, the row has to be inserted into the dimension table before the surrogate key can be determined.

A second challenge is that, during the fact table load, the same natural key may be encountered multiple times, associated with a different fact record each time. This could occur if a new customer placed multiple orders in a short time period. In this case, only one dimension placeholder record should be created.

Both of these needs can be met by using a stored procedure to handle the insert of the placeholder. For example, see the stored procedure in listing 2; it first checks to see whether the natural key already exists. If it does, the associated surrogate key is returned. If it doesn't, the placeholder record is inserted, and the newly created identity value is returned.

Listing 2   Inserting a dimension record

```
CREATE PROCEDURE pInsertCustomer
    (@CustomerName NVARCHAR(50)
    , @CustomerID INT OUTPUT) AS

SELECT @CustomerID = CustomerID
    FROM DimCustomer
    WHERE CustomerName = @CustomerName
IF @CustomerID IS NULL
    BEGIN
            INSERT INTO DimCustomer (CustomerName, InferredFlag)
                VALUES(@CustomerName, 1)
                SELECT @CustomerID = SCOPE_IDENTITY()
    END
```

In SSIS, handling late-arriving dimension members can be accomplished by redirecting any non-matched dimension rows to an OLE DB Command transformation. The pattern shown in figure 4 illustrates this. The OLE DB Command transformation calls the stored procedure, and then the results are joined back and inserted into the fact table.

This approach does have some performance implications in SSIS. The OLE DB Command requires a round-trip to the database for each row that passes through it to determine whether the row already exists.

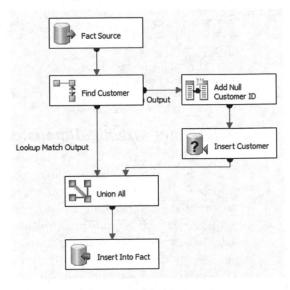

Figure 4   Adding a placeholder row

If it doesn't, a second round-trip is made to insert the record and return the key. These round-trips can slow down the performance of the data flow significantly.

For a better-performing approach in SSIS, you want to reduce round-trips as much as possible and insert the placeholder dimension rows in batches. You can accomplish this goal in SSIS, but doing so requires a few changes to the patterns used until now. For one, instead of using identity columns, the pattern will generate its own surrogate keys for the customer dimension. Please see www.ssistalk.com/2007/02/ 20/generating-surrogate-keys/ for an explanation of how to generate surrogate keys in SSIS. Second, foreign keys can't be enforced between the fact and the dimen-

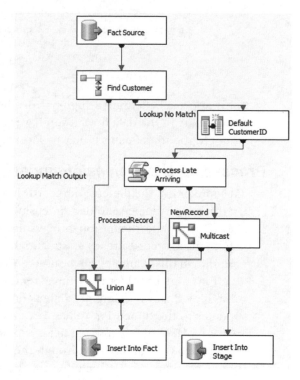

Figure 5   High performance pattern

sion during the ETL process, because fact rows could be inserted before the dimension placeholder rows.

In figure 5, a Script component is used to both assign the surrogate key and to determine whether the record has already been seen. A portion of the script can be seen in listing 3. In short, the code checks to see if the natural key for the dimension has already been cached by the component. If it has, the assigned surrogate key is returned. If it hasn't, a new surrogate key is assigned and the record is cached. The unique set of natural keys is directed to a staging table. These will be inserted later into the Customer dimension through a batch operation.

Listing 3   Caching late-arriving rows

```
public override void Input0_ProcessInputRow(Input0Buffer Row)
{
    int key;
    if (LateArrivingRows.TryGetValue(Row.CustomerName, out key))
    {
        Row.CustomerID = key;
        Row.DirectRowToProcessedRecord();
    }
    else
    {
```

```
        LastKeyUsed++;
        LateArrivingRows.Add(Row.CustomerName, LastKeyUsed);
        Row.CustomerID = LastKeyUsed;
        Row.DirectRowToNewRecord();
    }
}
```

This approach delivers a high-performing data flow at the cost of some additional complexity in the data flow. If you have a relatively small number of late-arriving rows, though, the initial pattern may be more appropriate.

Processing the dimension update

At some point, the dimension record should be updated with the correct information. At this point, the placeholder dimension record needs to be updated with the latest values. During the dimension processing, the natural key can be used to determine whether the record already exists, and the flag value discussed earlier (the InferredFlag column, in this example) can be used to determine whether it was a placeholder record.

If it's a placeholder row, it may require special handling. For example, in the case of a Type 2 slowly changing dimension, the default approach might be to write any updates to the dimension values as a new version of the record. But if this dimension row is a placeholder, updated fields should overwrite the current dimension values.

In SSIS, you can do this through the slowly changing dimension (SCD) transformation (see figure 6). It includes an option for inferred member support. The SCD

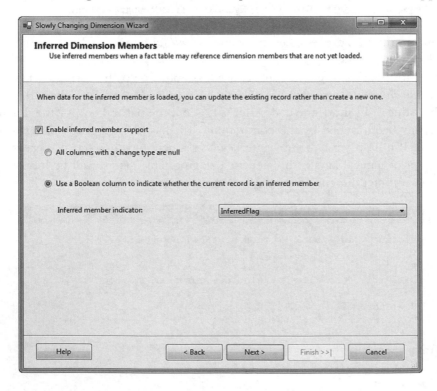

Figure 6
Slowly changing dimension transformation

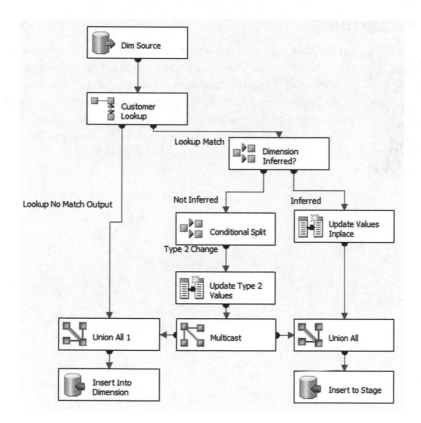

**Figure 7
Redirecting
inferred rows**

transformation has a few drawbacks, though, including potentially slow performance and configuration challenges.

Another approach is to use a Lookup transformation to determine whether the dimension record exists, based on the natural key. The InferredFlag can be returned and used to direct processing down a different path, as shown in figure 7.

In this package, the Conditional Split transformation is used to determine whether the InferredFlag was set on the dimension row. If it was, the dimension values are updated on the existing row, and the record is sent to a staging destination to be used for a batch update of the dimension table after the data flow completes. If it wasn't an inferred member, the row goes through standard Type 2 dimension handling, with a new version of the record being created.

Summary

Late-arriving dimensions can pose some challenges to process efficiency, but SSIS provides all the tools needed to handle them. By leveraging the range of approaches shown in this chapter, you can implement the right approach for meeting your specific business requirements for late-arriving dimension members.

About the author

John Welch is a BI architect with Varigence, which builds tools and frameworks that enable the creation and management of end-to-end business intelligence solutions with unprecedented ease and speed. John has been working with business intelligence and data warehousing technologies since 2001, with a focus on Microsoft products in heterogeneous environments. He's an MVP and a frequent presenter on SQL Server BI topics.

50 Why automate tasks with SSIS?

Ted Krueger

SQL Server Integration Services (SSIS) is a platform that offers many benefits when Windows Server and SQL Server are the primary technologies used. For cost reasons, SSIS is a good choice when SQL Server is already implemented. This is because a license is required only if SSIS is installed on a server other than one that has a fully licensed SQL Server Engine installed. SSIS integrates directly with SQL Server, and the integrated development environment (IDE) of Visual Studio .NET is used to develop SSIS packages. This can be valuable when Visual Studio .NET is already being used in house for other Microsoft-based development by limiting learning curves of the IDEs. By default, SQL Server installs a version of Visual Studio .NET called Business Intelligence Development Studio, or BIDS. This version has specific projects that are related to BI development. If a full version of Visual Studio .NET is already installed, it can be used as well. SSIS works with many other database server technologies, including Oracle and DB2. This makes SSIS a sound solution when the database server technologies used in-house are a mix of technologies.

With these strengths in mind and an existing or future implementation of SQL Server, SSIS is a sound choice for use, not only for BI tasks but also for automation initiatives. Automating tasks has one key result: efficiency. The more efficient administrators and developers are with repetitive tasks, the more time they have to work on other priorities. This can virtually add members to a team, by doing more with the same number of people.

Both of the packages that are used in the following examples to show how you can develop SSIS packages are available on http://blogs.lessthandot.com as downloads. This chapter won't cover their complete setup and design because of the volume required to do so. It will focus on key steps and configuration methods from them that can be used in other SSIS packages to automate similar tasks.

Automation by example

To show the added value in using SSIS to automate certain tasks, this chapter will review and discuss aspects of two common tasks that have been automated with SSIS:

- Refresh development by means of restoring databases
- Back up files by storing system-level files in SQL Server

The Refresh Development package is designed to remove the manual process of restoring production databases to a development or staging SQL Server. As shown in figure 1, the workflow for this task includes requirements for making decisions on how to perform the restore. Those decisions would be based on how the package is executed by use of runtime settings. This task is often a manual and tedious one that's been part of a database administrator's daily routine for years. The time required for determining the backup files to move, moving them, changing RESTORE scripts, and then performing the restore can be hours if not an entire day. By automating this task, the entire time is freed for other more critical tasks. All that remains is to review and monitor the task.

The Backup Files package shows that SSIS can be utilized for tasks that involve objects that are outside the control of SQL Server, as shown in figure 2. These objects

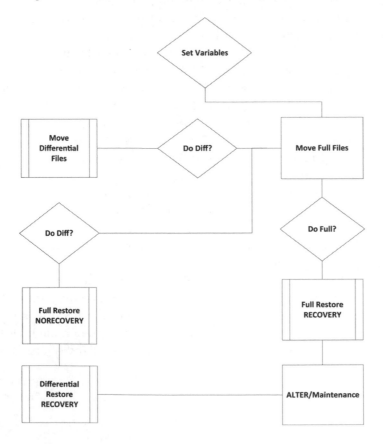

Figure 1   Workflow of the Refresh Development SSIS package

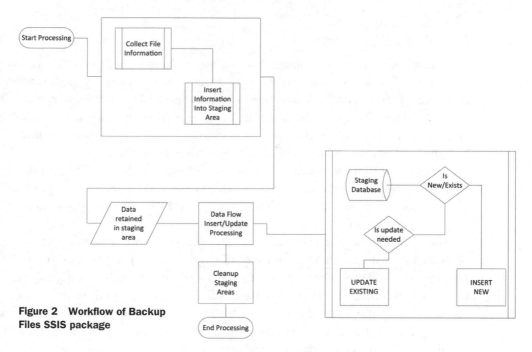

Figure 2   Workflow of Backup Files SSIS package

are still a critical part of the overall functionality and stability of a system's up time, and there's a need for recovering them in the event of a disaster.

Although backing up files may seem trivial, and other vendor-supplied software may seem more suited for this task, the concept of pulling files such as configuration files that run out of systems into SQL Server requires that those files be included in SQL Server's Disaster and Recovery strategies. Doing so provides a secondary recovery or the first point of recovery for these files. At times, files like these are backed up to tape and sent offsite for retention. Retrieving those tapes can take quite some time while systems are down. Retrieving the contents from SQL Server can greatly decrease this recovery time.

SSIS key tasks and components

SSIS has a set of key tasks, containers, and components that can be exploited in automating otherwise manual and lengthy tasks. This section will cover some of those tasks, containers, and components by exploring the Refresh Development and Backup Files packages discussed previously.

Many objects are available in SSIS that can be used to successfully automate different tasks that an administrator or developer must perform repetitively. Out of the many objects, a few tasks, containers, and components stand out above the others that allow the flexibility needed when involving other obstacles that are outside the control of SQL Server:

- Script task
- File System task

- Execute SQL task
- Foreach Loop container

In this list, the Script task is listed first because of the vast abilities it brings to a package. The Script task provides the ability to execute functions or methods written in C# or VB.NET that extend the capabilities of a package beyond the built-in tasks already available. With this ability, almost any task can be performed from within an SSIS package. But with any platform that allows you to write custom code, there are many things that should be done within it and many things that should not.

An example of a task that SSIS may not be best utilized for would be a user application with a task to upload an Excel file. This task could be accomplished by calling a package to import the Excel file either using DTEXEC or a stored procedure call that starts a SQL Agent job.

File operations and manipulating variables based on other events are a perfect use of the Script task and take advantage of the high-level coding abilities. In the Refresh Development package, the files that need to be copied from the primary source directory to the destination location are based on a pattern supplied to the package. This pattern is used to search for parts of the filenames in the source directory. SSIS has the File System task, but this task is limited in the ability to search based on a pattern. To get around this limitation, you can use the Script task.

In order to search files based on their names, you use the DirectoryInfo and FileInfo classes. The DirectoryInfo class is used to create an object instance of the directory where backup files are stored. Once this instance of the object is created, the FileInfo class is used to inspect each filename. If the file matches the criteria, a variable value is set to that filename. The variables are then used in other variables that are evaluated as expressions (discussed later in this chapter) so they can be supplied to a File System task. This is shown in the following code segment from the Script task in the Refresh Development package:

```
DirectoryInfo dir = new DirectoryInfo(backup_folder);

foreach (FileInfo file in dir.GetFiles())
{
 if (file.Name.IndexOf(GetFileDate) !=
     -1 && file.Name.IndexOf("FULL") != -1)
 {
  Dts.Variables["FullBackup"].Value = file.Name;
 }
}
```

The Script task could be used to copy the files that are found to the destination directory, but the built-in File System task can perform this task without further coding required. This both simplifies the code in the Script task and takes full advantage of the tasks available in SSIS.

The File System task has four main file operations available: copy file, move file, rename file, and delete file. There are also directory operations available for these

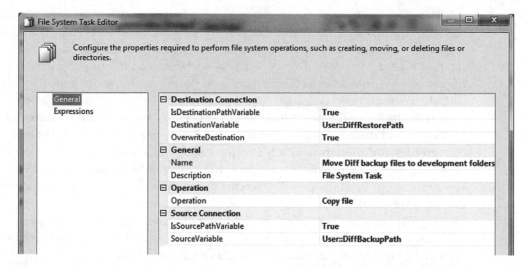

Figure 3   File System Task Editor and use of variables for Source and Destination connections

four methods, along with the ability to delete all the contents of a directory and set attributes. The copy file operation is required in the Refresh Development package to move the backup files to the destination directory. This allows the restore and file activity to not affect the disk I/O on the source to which other backup files may be actively writing.

In the File System task, the properties IsDestinationPathVariable and IsSource-PathVariable change the way the task's connections are interpreted. If either of these tasks is set to True, the connection will be altered to be evaluated at runtime based on a variable value or as a preset value from a file connection.

In figure 3, both destination and source have been changed to be evaluated from variables. These variables are set based on what the Script task found in the previous steps.

With these two changes to the File System task, the task itself is now capable of accepting dynamic values, making it flexible for the needs at hand. If higher-level file operations are required, you'd use the Script task along with the System.IO class.

So far, the tasks that we've covered have been used to manipulate properties and variables and to move files between directories. Up to this point, we've sent no commands to SQL Server. The needs of either a database administrator or database developer often require one or more commands to be sent to SQL Server to complete the process. Although SSIS is a great tool for manipulating files and other tasks that don't involve communicating with SQL Server, SSIS may not be the most optimal tool at this point if it isn't being used to communicate with SQL Server in some way.

To send T-SQL statements to SQL Server, SSIS has the Execute SQL task. The Execute SQL task can send either one SQL statement or a batch to SQL Server. One important note in using a batch in an Execute SQL task is that it can return only one result set from that batch. This is important to remember when you're relying on the results of the task to base your precedence constraints or the results of the entire package.

The Refresh Development package utilizes the Execute SQL task to send the RESTORE command to SQL Server. Because the Execute SQL task is easily configured by requiring only the main properties of a connection and statement, it's the perfect method for this step. If more complexity is introduced in the requirements for multiple statements or batches to be executed, you should combine the Execute Script task with the Foreach Loop container.

For example, in the case where there's a need to restore multiple transaction log backups, the Foreach Loop container could be used to enumerate through all the backup files and then dynamically execute each restore statement based on each file matching the criteria. This can also be extremely valuable in processing file repositories or locations in which the file contents themselves dictate the type of statement or mapping required.

The File Backup package utilizes both the Execute SQL task and property expression (explained in detail later in this chapter) in a Foreach Loop container. For each filename found in the enumeration of a directory, the Execute SQL task dynamically builds the following statement in order to INSERT each file's contents and metadata required to further process the package:

```
INSERT DBA.dbo.XMLConfigRepository_Temp
    (ModifiedDate,ConfigPath,XMLContents,ImportBy,Filename)
  SELECT '1/21/2011 8:35:00 PM','',BulkColumn,SUSER_NAME(),'' FROM
    OPENROWSET(Bulk '', SINGLE_BLOB) [rowsetresults]
```

The Foreach Loop container is invaluable when multiple files have to be processed. With each file found, a full subset of tasks can be executed. This container of tasks can then be run in parallel to other tasks outside the container.

In SQL Server 2008, the execution pipe was redesigned to take full advantage of parallel processing and the use of multicore processor-based systems. This was a major change and increase in performance for SSIS 2008 over 2005. As shown in figure 4, for

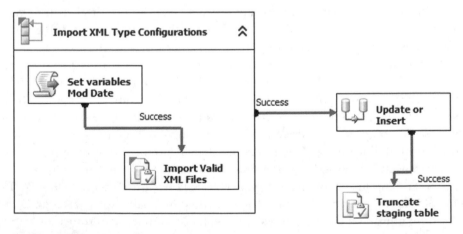

Figure 4   Backup Files package outlining the use of the Foreach Loop container with inner tasks and control flow to ending Data Flow task and cleanup tasks

the example of backing up files on a server, the Foreach Loop container is utilized as the method to enumerate files in a given directory.

For each new file that's found in the collection, the filename is set to a variable named `IndexFile`. The variable is then passed to the internal tasks and is available to all those internal tasks as needed. This is shown here from the coding used in a Script task to check for the file's existence as a secondary validation and then set the critical variables that will base the Data Flow task's job of determining if the file is to be inserted, updated, or unchanged:

```
if (File.Exists(Dts.Variables["IndexFile"].Value.ToString()))
{
  FileInfo file = new FileInfo(Dts.Variables["IndexFile"].Value.ToString());
  Dts.Variables["FileModDate"].Value = Convert.ToDateTime
  ➥(File.GetLastWriteTime(Dts.Variables["IndexFile"].Value.ToString()));
  Dts.Variables["FileNameOnly"].Value = file.Name.ToString();
  Dts.TaskResult = (int)ScriptResults.Success;
}
```

Without this ability built in, Script tasks or other much more complicated methods would be required. This would add to development time and completely lose the value in using SSIS for this type of task.

Creating reusable and mobile SSIS packages

Automating tasks is beneficial only if that automation can be used for any or all SQL Server instances in an environment. All of the design methods and tasks that we've discussed will function for one instance of SQL Server. In reality, teams oversee many instances, and many databases exist on those instances. With this volume, there's a need to have SSIS freely move from SQL Server to SQL Server and database to database. If an SSIS package can't be easily reused on multiple SQL Servers, the task of updating them per instance is tedious. This negates the reasoning for automation altogether.

Variables, expressions, and configurations all allow SSIS packages to become reusable and mobile. Transportability of an SSIS package means that an SSIS package can be provided a value that's of a specific data type, and either the workflow of that package will be altered or the instance and database the package uses as a source and destination will be changed. This allows the package to not be restricted in use to a specific SQL Server, database, or even directory.

Take the example of the Refresh Development package. In the Connection Managers area, an ADO.NET connection is created that will provide the connectivity to the SQL Server instance the database will be restored to. This connection object could be set to look at the default instance of the server it's executed on. This would be fine if the environment consists of only default instances and characters as the period or localhost were used in the connection object. But if the default instance wasn't used and a named instance was used, the package would require a change to the connection object for each server it's executed on.

NOTE   In order to prevent the need to change these properties, you can use variables and expressions to change them at runtime.

The Refresh Development package has the variables `ServerName` and `DatabaseName`. These two variables are used to set the ADO.NET connection at runtime. The scope of these variables is set to the root of the package so the connection and variables can be used freely throughout the entire package.

Scope in SSIS packages is a term used to identify where a variable or object is visible. Each object in SSIS has a scope. For example, if a package has a Foreach Loop container in the workflow and a Bulk Insert task is within the Foreach Loop container, all variables that have a scope of the Bulk Insert task won't be usable by the Foreach Loop container itself.

In figure 5, the Bulk Insert task is selected, and the Variables viewer shows the variable `BulkInsert`. If the Bulk Insert task focus is changed to the Foreach Loop container, the Variables viewer won't show `BulkInsert` as an available variable.

Changing the scope of variables can be difficult but is done by manipulating the XML that makes up SSIS packages. Tools like BIDSHelper exist to make these changes in scope easier. BIDSHelper is a free add-in to BIDS that assists in tasks while developing SSIS packages; you can find it on CodePlex at http://bidshelper.codeplex.com/.

To make full use of the variables and pass new values into the package upon execution, you set property expressions to use the variables. Property expressions are expressions that can change certain properties dynamically when a package is executed. These expressions can be used to change some properties on packages, tasks, Foreach loops, For loops, sequences, Foreach enumerators, event handlers, connection managers, or log providers.

With the ADO.NET connection in the Refresh Development package, the expression property ConnectionString is set to take advantage of both the `ServerName` and `DatabaseName` variables. This is done by going into the property expressions from the Properties window of the ADO.NET connection. Once you're in the Property Expression

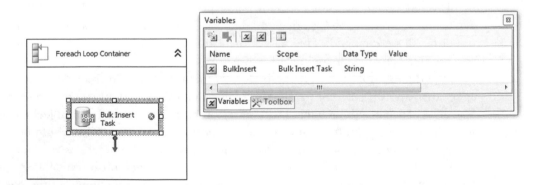

Figure 5   Variable scope shown on task

Editor, you select properties and then build expressions on them. For the Connection-String property, the following expression is used to dynamically build the connection string from the `ServerName` and `DatabaseName` variables:

```
"Data Source=" + @[User::ServerName]  + ";Initial Catalog=" +
    @[User::DatabaseName]  + ";Integrated Security=True;"
```

If the `ServerName` value is set to `localhost` and the `DatabaseName` is set to `MASTER`, this expression will evaluate to the following string:

```
Data Source=localhost;Initial Catalog=MASTER;Integrated Security=True;
```

The value in the ability to manipulate properties in this manner is that you can execute SSIS packages in several different ways and on multiple different SQL Server instances with few changes required.

Precedence and manipulating control flow

SSIS packages are controlled by precedence constraints. *Precedence constraints* are links that dictate whether a step is executed or not based on the previous steps results. The most common precedence constraints utilized in SSIS packages are Success, Completion, and Failure. These types of constraints are execution result constraints. In order to fully take advantage of a multitude of steps and control these steps, you may find that execution result constraints aren't intelligent enough for the needs in the control flow. Fortunately, you can utilize other types of precedence constraints. These are listed here in full detail as referenced from Books Online:

- An expression that's evaluated to determine whether the constrained executable runs. If the expression evaluates to True, the constrained executable runs.
- An expression and a constraint that combine the requirements of execution results of the precedence executable and the return results of evaluating the expression.
- An expression or a constraint that uses either the execution results of the precedence executable or the return results of evaluating the expression.

The Refresh Development package has two distinct needs that the precedence constraints must dictate. These needs are for a Full Restore or Full and Differential restore to be performed. In order to restore a differential backup, the database should be initially restored with `NORECOVERY`. To do this in the SSIS package, use a variable as a flag indicating that a Differential restore is needed. You can also use this to copy that Differential backup file so it's available while the Full restore is being performed.

To accomplish this type of precedence, use an expression evaluation operation. This requires the expression to evaluate to True or False, and based on that result, the precedence will allow the next step to be executed. For the Refresh Development package and the variable flag of `ApplyDiff`, the expression used is as follows:

```
@[ApplyDiff] == 1 ? True : False
```

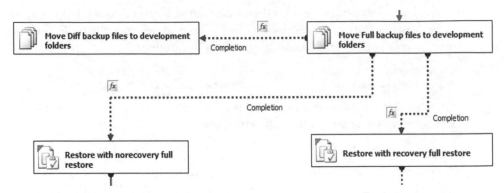

Figure 6   Expression-based precedence constraints

In this expression, the `ApplyDiff` variable is checked for the value of 1. If the value is found to be 1, the expression result is True, and if not, it's False. This allows two different Execute SQL tasks to be run based on whether only a Full restore or a Full and Differential restore is needed. In figure 6, the three precedence constraints are used to control whether a Differential restore is applied and the Differential backup file is moved by use of a File System task.

By changing the results of the expression from True to False as a result of the value being found, the precedence will allow the Full restore to be the next step executed.

Based on the ability to use these types of variables and expressions as properties and control workflow, the ability to create reusable and mobile SSIS packages is much more applicable. With this, you can change the Refresh Development package to be run exclusively from variables and expressions. This value is shown explicitly in the Refresh Development package in the restore statement itself.

The Execute SQL statement for the restore requires several values that are required to restore the database successfully. These values are the logical database and transaction log names, the paths that are used in the MOVE option, and the path of the backup to use:

```
"RESTORE DATABASE [" + @[User::DatabaseNameRestore] + "] " +
"FROM  DISK = N'" + @[User::FullRestorePath]  + "' " +
"WITH  FILE = 1,  " +
"NORECOVERY,  NOUNLOAD, " +
"MOVE N'" + @[User::DataFile] + "' TO N'" + @[User::RestoreLocMDF] + "'," +
"MOVE N'" + @[User::LogFile] + "' TO N'" + @[User::RestoreLocLDF] + "'," +
"NOUNLOAD, " +
"REPLACE,  STATS = 10 "
```

This expression with the values all set correctly in the variables evaluates to the following well-formed SQL statement:

```
RESTORE DATABASE [DBA_DEV]
FROM DISK = N'c:\restores\DBA.BAK'
WITH  FILE = 1,  NORECOVERY,  NOUNLOAD,
MOVE N'DBA' TO N'C:\SQL2008R2\MSSQL10_50.TK2008R2\MSSQL\DATA\DBA_DEV.mdf',
```

```
MOVE N'DBA_LOG' TO
N'C:\SQL2008R2\MSSQL10_50.TK2008R2\MSSQL\DATA\DBA_DEV_1.ldf',
NOUNLOAD, REPLACE,  STATS = 10
```

Monitoring the results

Monitoring what's automated can be as important as successfully automating the tasks. Logging is used within SSIS packages to provide high-level monitoring of how a package is executing. Event handlers in SSIS are also used to make decisions to execute secondary tasks based on an event the primary tasks have triggered. The use of event handlers in packages that automate tasks such as we've discussed can be used to notify administrators or developers when the tasks fail or environment objects have changed. This handling of events is useful because events can be handled and notifications sent or logged, and the package execution can proceed without completely stopping.

Logging in SSIS has a set base of events that will be logged. OnError, OnInformation, and OnTaskFailed are common events used for the built-in logging mechanisms in SSIS.

NOTE   When adding events like OnInformation or Diagnostic to troubleshoot and debug packages, performance may be affected by the amount of information being logged. Use these types of events for logging only when there's a distinct need for them.

In order to log internal events in a Script task, the Refresh Development package uses the ScriptTaskLogEntry event, as shown in figure 7. This event is set on Script task containers and is triggered when the Dts.Log method is called within the Script task

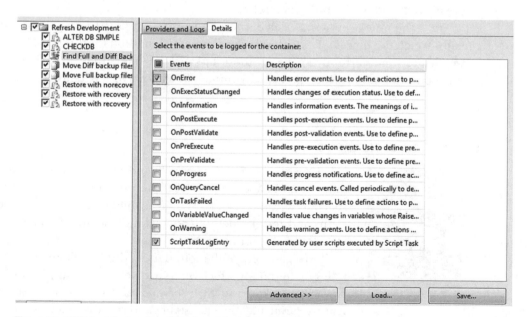

Figure 7   SSIS Logging and custom Script task event logging

code. The Script task can also force a failure based on error handling internally by calling the `Dts.Events.FireError` method.

These two methods are used in the package to log the variable results and any errors from the script's findings. The `Dts.Log` method is called as shown here:

```
Dts.Log("Successfully set variables for Full or Differential distinction:
Backup folder=" + backup_folder + " Pattern search=" + GetFileDate +
" Full Backup File=" + Dts.Variables["FullBackup"].Value.ToString() +
" Differential backup File=" +
Dts.Variables["DiffBackup"].Value.ToString(), 0, emptyBytes);
```

Wrapping the code in the Script task in a `Try Catch` block is a method to control and handle errors that occur within the script. If an error is found and the `Catch` block called, the `Dts.Events.FireError` is then issued as follows:

```
Dts.Events.FireError(0, "Error setting Full or Differential variables",
ex.Message + "\r" + ex.StackTrace, String.Empty, 0);
```

This will then log to the SSIS logging destination selected without further logging configurations needed. With this logging mechanism built into SSIS, you can easily develop and implement proactive monitoring and alerts.

Summary

Many tasks throughout the day cause you to lose time that can be better utilized. With SSIS and other features that are available in SQL Server, many tools assist you in automating them. When they're automated and developed in a manner so that they're reusable across systems, reviewing and monitoring are all that's needed, and time is greatly reduced on the tasks themselves.

Take the time to review a week or month's worth of tasks that are performed manually. Weigh the time it takes to develop an automated method for those tasks, and then weigh the time currently spent on those tasks. More often than not, time is saved through automation, which in turn saves money and allows you to focus on other areas.

About the author

Ted Krueger is a SQL Server MVP and has been working in development and database administration for more than 13 years. His specialties range from high availability and disaster recovery setup and testing methods to custom assembly development for SQL Server Reporting Services.

Ted is also one of the founders of the LessThanDot.com technology community, which offers articles on backup, recovery, security, SSIS, working with SQL Server, and using all of the SQL Server features available to create stable and scalable database services.

Ted lives in the Greater Chicago area.

51 Extending SSIS using the Script component

Tim Mitchell

The data flow workspace in SQL Server Integration Services (SSIS) is packed full of useful source, transformation, and destination components that can be used to address the most common extract, transform, and load (ETL) data challenges. But anyone who works in this space for long will quickly discover that some ETL problems don't fit neatly inside those little boxes. Fortunately, SSIS includes a flexible and powerful tool for handling custom data flow needs: the SSIS Script component.

The Swiss Army knife of SSIS

The SSIS Script component is, as the name suggests, a scripting interface within Integration Services that allows the direct inclusion of custom code within a data flow. Unlike the preconfigured components that are a part of SSIS, the Script component is very much a blank slate. This allows the ETL developer an immense amount of flexibility to fill the void between the built-in functionality of the SSIS data flow objects and the off-the-beaten-path ETL requirements that can't easily be addressed using those native components. In various presentations that I've done on this topic, I refer to the Script component as the Swiss Army knife: it's lightweight, easy to keep around, and great to have within reach when you're in a tight spot. Versatile enough to serve multiple roles, the Script component can be used as a data source, transformation, or destination, and with the full power of the .NET runtime under its hood, it's capable enough to handle almost any imaginable ETL requirement. To help streamline repetitive operations and avoid duplicate code, you can also reference existing assemblies, allowing the reuse of external code within the script task. Further, this tool uses the familiar Visual Studio interface, eliminating the need to learn to play in a new sandbox, and any prior coding experience (especially in C# or VB.NET) is easily leveraged in the Script component.

The Script component lives with its counterparts in the toolbox within the data flow components, residing by default with the transformations. Not to be confused with the *script task* (which is a function of the control flow workspace and can perform a variety of tasks unrelated to the data flow), the Script component is used almost exclusively for direct data interaction.

Before we get started...a word of caution

Obviously, I'm a big fan of the Script component in SSIS. Yet I must offer my standard disclaimer that just because you *can* use this tool doesn't mean you *should*. The Script component differs greatly from the other data flow elements in that the most significant parts of the logic will exist outside the GUI, purely in code. Any time you step outside the constraints of the preconfigured components, you have to consider the additional time and effort required for testing, debugging, and maintenance, not to mention the possible performance implications. So, if you find yourself in need of the flexibility offered by the Script component, use it! But for tasks that can be easily accomplished by using native components, I don't recommend reinventing the wheel.

Sources, destinations, and transformations...oh my!

As mentioned earlier, the SSIS Script component can function as a source, a destination, or a transformation. Immediately upon introducing the Script component to a data flow surface, you'll be prompted to set the behavior for the current instance (see figure 1). It's important to select the correct behavior for this component, because there are some type-specific settings that are built into the component upon creation, and changing type from one to another after initial configuration can be difficult.

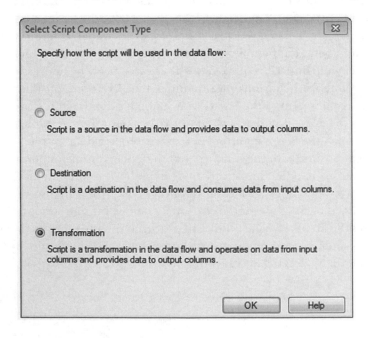

Figure 1
Choose your configuration.

We'll take a brief walk through each of these Script component types. I'll focus mainly on the use of the Script component as a transformation, because this is the most typical use of this component, and it allows me to demonstrate the use of inputs and outputs as well as the synchronicity between the two.

SCRIPT COMPONENT AS A SOURCE

Configured as a source, the Script component can be used to shred difficult data structures such as inconsistently formatted input files, or to process data from other atypical stores such as web services or serialized objects.

When you create a new instance of a Script component configured as a source, you'll get a shell with no inputs and a single output. Because there are, by design, no inputs to the Script component source, you'll only be configuring the column metadata for the output, as well as defining when and how data is sent to the output. Rows are added to the output by calling the `<Output Name>Buffer.AddRow()` method, which we'll explore momentarily.

A useful feature of the Script component is the support of multiple outputs. This behavior is valuable when you find yourself connecting to a specific data object that contains multiple domains of data—for example, an Excel document that stores in a single sheet your customer demographic data as well as financial transactions for those customers. By configuring multiple outputs in your script source, you can selectively pass data to the appropriate output, potentially avoiding multiple round-trips to that source to extract all the information required.

SCRIPT COMPONENT AS A DESTINATION

The Script component used as a destination is the inverse of a Script component source, and is preconfigured with a single input and no outputs. Using this setting, you'll have full control over the output of data to whatever destination is selected—because there are no direct output paths, you'll be responsible for passing values from your input into whatever "buckets" you define in your destination structure. Although using the Script component as a destination can be complex, the upside is that you can send data down unconventional and otherwise inaccessible output paths, including custom-formatted emails or nonrelational message queues (if you're familiar with healthcare data, think HL7 messages). Incoming rows are handled a row at a time, using the `<Input Name>_ProcessInputRow` method.

In my experience, the use of the Script component as a destination isn't as common as its role as a source or transformation. But there are enough legitimate use cases that call for a scripted destination that it's worthwhile to keep it in your tool belt.

SCRIPT COMPONENT AS A TRANSFORMATION

When you choose to configure your Script component as a transformation, it will be built with exactly one input and one output, which will be joined together synchronously (more on synchronous and asynchronous operations in a bit).

The power and flexibility of this tool are best demonstrated when it's utilized as a transformation—the list of possibilities available here is almost limitless. The Script component transformation can apply complex business rules to in-flight or stored data, consolidate many rows into few (or vice versa), perform vast amounts of data cleansing, and create complex rules to split a single stream of data into multiple output paths.

Synchronous and asynchronous behavior

When using the Script component as a transformation, you have the choice to configure the synchronicity of the data between the input and output. Synchronizing the inputs and outputs represent a pass-through transformation approach and establishes a mandatory relationship between the input and output. In contrast, using the script transformation asynchronously breaks that hard link between input and output, allowing for greater control of the transformation of data.

SYNCHRONOUS SCRIPT TRANSFORMATION

The synchronous transformation is relatively easy to set up and configure, though it's also the more restrictive of the two options. Figure 2 shows the default behavior when creating a Script component transformation: you can see that the indicated setting shows Output 0 synchronously joined with Input 0. In this scenario, any changes to

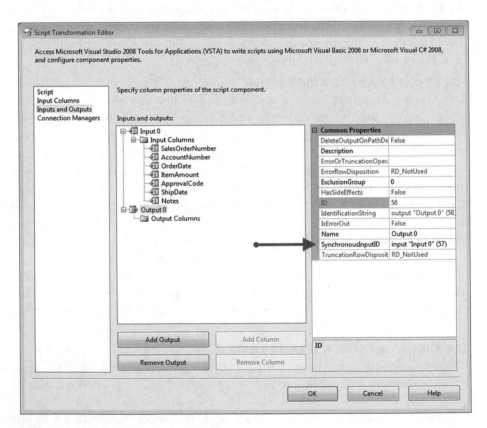

Figure 2   Synchronous transformation

the data are performed inline; you can't change the number of rows sent to the output, nor can you modify the data types of the existing columns. All modifications to the data must be coded within the method `<Input Name>_ProcessInputRow`.

A synchronous transformation is most useful when you need to do some manner of data manipulation on the in-flight data without changing data types or length. To relate this behavior to an RDBMS concept, you can think of it as performing an UPDATE statement against existing data—no rows are added or deleted, and only existing values are modified.

It's interesting to note that you can synchronously attach more than one output to your input. But because this would send the same data to multiple outputs, the use of multiple synchronous outputs doesn't add much value.

ASYNCHRONOUS SCRIPT TRANSFORMATION

The script transformation used asynchronously requires more effort to configure but offers significant flexibility in return. Used in this manner, it gives the developer complete control over the intrascript data flow, including the manipulation of the number and types of columns, and the number of rows processed, and it even allows you to selectively send dissimilarly structured data to different outputs. Common uses for this type of script transformation include the following:

- Consolidating multiple rows from the source into a single row in the output
- Splitting each row of data from the source into multiple rows in the output
- Conditionally sending rows of data to different outputs (similar to the conditional split transformation, but this allows the outputs to have differing metadata)

Unlike the synchronous transformation, which handles the generation of output rows automatically, you'll be responsible for executing each output row manually using the `<Output Name>Buffer.AddRow()` method. There's no requirement to send *any* data to an output: as with a native SSIS component, you can send zero rows of data.

You can change a synchronous transform to behave asynchronously by adjusting the SynchronousInputID setting on the output (see the callout in figure 2) to None. You'll also need to create and configure your output columns, because the asynchronous output is unwired from the input and won't receive its metadata from that input.

Script component inputs and outputs

Although they're not as exciting to discuss as the complex transformations you'll perform within the script, the inputs and outputs comprise the foundation of a successful Script component instance. By design, there's little to do to configure a script input because the metadata is defined by the data pipeline leading into the script. On the output side, though, you have the flexibility to add and configure additional outputs to the Script component, and you can modify some of the properties of the existing outputs. Again referring back to figure 2, you'll notice some of the output-level settings exposed in the output designer; the two most notable (and user-configurable) settings for the script output are the output name and the previously discussed SynchronousInputID selection.

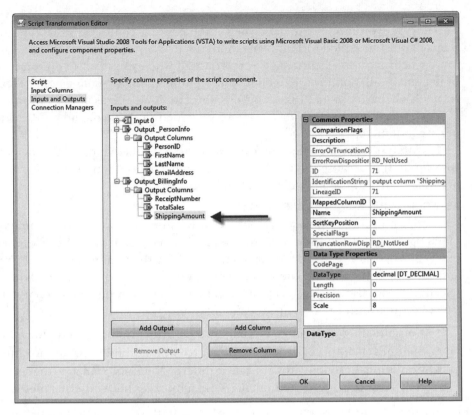

Figure 3   Output column configuration

Within each of the outputs in your script, you have control over the column definitions as well. You can add additional columns, rename existing columns and change data types, and even delete columns from the output. Figure 3 highlights some of the settings that are configurable at the column level. I must point out that you have *some* control of this columnar metadata; if you're working with a Script component instance used as a synchronous transformation, you won't be able to edit or delete any existing columns that are synchronously bound to the input, although you can still add new columns in this case. When using the script as a source or an asynchronous transformation, you're free to add, edit, or delete any of the columns as necessary.

Into the code

Having reviewed the GUI elements of the Script component, let's jump in and investigate some code!

THE SCRIPT DESIGNER

Before you open the Script designer, your first key decision point is the selection of the language to use in the script. Currently, the only languages directly supported are C# and VB.NET (which is an upgrade from SSIS in SQL Server 2005, where only VB.NET was available). In addition, you can include assemblies written and compiled externally—in any .NET-compliant language—by referencing these assemblies in your Script components. This is a great way to leverage existing code without having to embed the same logic repeatedly into multiple packages.

Just as the configuration of the Script component will differ greatly when used in its various roles (source, transformation, and destination), so will the way you must construct your code for these three uses.

WHERE DID ALL THIS CODE COME FROM?

One of the first things you'll notice when you dive into the code of the Script component is that there's a significant amount of code already present. When you introduce a Script component into your data flow—more specifically, when you choose which type of script to use—the component is preconfigured with some essential functionality. I'll review some of these role-specific code inclusions in a bit.

As shown in figure 4, the Script designer in SSIS is a slightly trimmed-down version of the Visual Studio development environment. As such, you'll have access to the full power of the .NET runtime along with design features such as IntelliSense, Object Explorer, code snippets, and many other attributes of the Visual Studio environment. For BI professionals who have spent time working in Business Intelligence Development

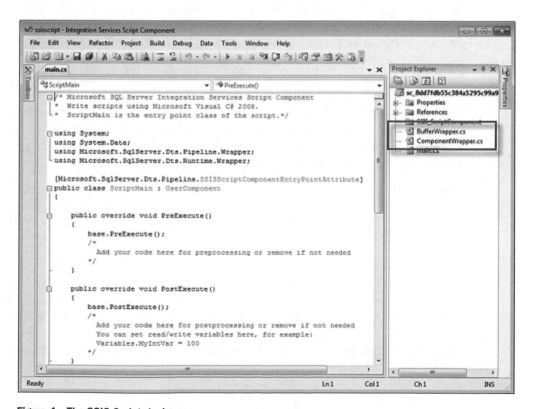

Figure 4   The SSIS Script designer

Studio (BIDS), and for those who have developed applications in Visual Studio, the scripting environment should feel comfortable.

You'll notice in figure 4 that there are several files shown in the Project Explorer window; I've highlighted a couple of files for review. The two highlighted code files, BufferWrapper.cs and ComponentWrapper.cs (or suffixed as .vb, for my VB.NET colleagues), are containers for the preconfigured code I mentioned earlier. A comprehensive examination of these file contents is beyond the scope of this chapter, but there are a couple of things worth pointing out. First, you're free to explore the code in these files, and I recommend doing so to familiarize yourself with the plumbing of the Script component. Much of the core functionality of the Script component is hidden in these files, and having at least a working knowledge of their contents can give you a better idea of the entire life cycle of the Script component. Second, you should resist the urge to modify these files in any way! A brief warning appears at the top of these ancillary resources, but it bears restating here: because these files are system generated, they're subject to being overwritten at any time, so don't spend valuable development time trying to modify them; any changes made to those code files are volatile.

One file that you *can*—in fact, *should*—modify is the Main.cs file (Main.vb if you're using VB.NET). This file is the business end of the Script component, and it's the code file that's opened by default when you start the Script designer. In this file, you'll embed your custom transformations, business logic, and other routines and algorithms specific to your ETL processes. This file compiles to become the main entry point for your script logic.

Note that Main.cs/Main.vb isn't the only file in which you can code within the Script component. As with a Visual Studio project, you're free to add resources to the Script component—specifically, you can add additional code files to your Script component project. If you expect to construct a significant amount of code in your Script component (particularly if you utilize multiple complex classes), I encourage you to consider using separate files for this logic.

NOTE   If you're writing complex code within your scripts and this logic is generic enough to be used in multiple packages, consider developing a custom component instead. It's a much better way to reuse complex code in SSIS!

SCRIPTING A SOURCE

When you build a Script component source, you're starting off with an empty shell, and as such, you'll be responsible for creating each row of output data and populating each column. As mentioned earlier, some of the baseline code will be prepopulated when you create the instance of the Script component. When using it as a source, you'll be working in the method named `CreateNewOutputRows()`, which starts out like this:

```
    ...
public override void CreateNewOutputRows()
{
    /*
```

```
        Add rows by calling the AddRow method on the member variable
        named "<Output Name>Buffer".  For example, call
        MyOutputBuffer.AddRow() if your output was named "MyOutput".
        */
}
...
```

Within this code block, you'll add the logic to connect to whatever mechanism is storing your data. Generating a new row of data to be sent to the output is done through the `<Output Name>Buffer.AddRow()` method; from there, individual columns may be populated using the convention `<Output Name>Buffer.<ColumnName> = "Value"`:

```
public override void CreateNewOutputRows()
{
        ... Your code to connect to and retrieve your data will go here. ...
        PersonnelOutputBuffer.AddRow();
        PersonnelOutputBuffer.FirstName = strFirstName;
        PersonnelOutputBuffer.LastName = strLastName;
        PersonnelOutputBuffer.SocialSecurityNo = strSocSecNo;
}
```

Keep in mind that the `CreateNewOutputRows()` function is fired exactly one time during the execution of the Script component. Therefore, if you're going to produce multiple rows of data, you'll have to include some sort of iterative or looping structure within this method to repeatedly fire the `AddRow()` function of the target output. You can call `AddRow()` as much and as often as required, but remember that this is a forward-only operation. Firing the `AddRow()` method will finalize the current row of data and start a new one, and there's no indexer to allow you to reference a previous row in the buffer within the Script component.

SCRIPTING A DESTINATION

Much like the Script component source, the Script component destination is a blank slate, only this time the canvas is on the output side.

When you open the Script designer for a script destination, you'll notice that the available methods have changed. Gone is the `CreateNewOutputRows()` function, and in its place you find the `<Input Name>_ProcessInputRow` method. Unlike `CreateNewOutputRows()` from the previous example, `<Input Name>_ProcessInputRow` will be called numerous times, once for each input row of data. From there, you can ferry the data to its next stop (or its final resting place, if that's the case). Each column of data can be referenced using the convention `Row.<ColumnName>`:

```
public override void Input0_ProcessInputRow(Input0Buffer Row)
{
        ...
        WebServices.UpdatePersonnel(Row.SSN, Row.OldSalary, Row.NewSalary);
        WebServices.NotifyPayroll(Row.SSN, Row.ControlID);
        WebServices.ConfirmChange(Row.ControlID);
        ...
}
```

SCRIPTING A TRANSFORMATION

Using the Script component as a transformation blends the behaviors of the script source and the script destination. You'll have an input and one or more outputs, and the code elements for both are included. When you open the Script designer for a transformation, you'll see that you have the <Input Name>_ProcessInputRow function, the same as occurs with scripting a destination:

```
   ...
   public override void Input0_ProcessInputRow(Input0Buffer Row)
{
}

   ...
```

The data should be dealt with in the <Input Name>_ProcessInputRow method; its natural iterative behavior helps to avoid reinventing the wheel while providing enough flexibility to handle even complex transformation requirements. This is true when using the Script component synchronously, because you're sending the rows directly from the input to the output and making any changes inline.

If you're working with an asynchronous Script component transformation, don't forget that you can utilize multiple outputs in the transformation (you can do this with a Script component configured as a source as well). This is particularly useful when attaching to a data source that has varying metadata within the same feed: for a practical example, think about a flat file that has a record type identifier in each row, with each distinct record type having its own metadata definition:

```
...
if (Row.RecordType == 1)        // Patient Data
{
    PatientsBuffer.Name = thisRow[0];
    PatientsBuffer.SocSecNo = thisRow[1];
    PatientsBuffer.AddressCode = thisRow[2];
}
else if (Row.RecordType == 2)   // Billing Data
{
    BillingBuffer.ProcedureCharges = thisRow[0];
    BillingBuffer.EquipmentCharges = thisRow[1];
    BillingBuffer.FinanceCharges = thisRow[2];
}
...
```

If using the script transformation synchronously, your options are obviously more limited. But it's also much simpler to use in this manner because you're modifying existing cells without having to tinker with adding rows and/or columns:

```
...
if (Row.LastName.EndsWith(" JR"))
{
    PatientsBuffer.LastName = PatientsBuffer.LastName.Replace(" JR", "");
    PatientsBuffer.Suffix = "JR";
}
...
```

Summary

SSIS is a great tool, and in many cases its native components are sufficient to handle complex ETL challenges. But for those exceptions where built-in tools won't do, it's good to have the Script component at the ready. Used as a source, destination, or transformation, this tool can get you out of almost any jam.

About the author

Tim Mitchell is a Microsoft SQL Server consultant, speaker, and trainer, and is a Microsoft SQL Server MVP. He's been working with SQL Server for more than seven years, primarily in business intelligence, ETL/SSIS, reporting, and database development. You can find his complete profile at http://TimMitchell.net.

52 ETL design checklist

Rafael Salas

Your company's data warehouse project has finally taken off, and you've been asked to build a reliable system to extract, clean, integrate, and deliver the data. A preliminary check indicates you have the required elements to accomplish your mission: data from source systems and a handy ETL tool. It looks easy!

The reality is that building a data integration system is an endeavor that requires meeting complex requirements coming from different perspectives. In this chapter, you'll explore key tasks and subcomponents that should be included in every ETL solution for increased reliability, scalability, manageability, and data quality.

To facilitate the discussion, I'll break the chapter into five sections: data realities, extract, transform, load, and instrumentation and management. Each section includes design rationale aspects and guidelines that will help you during the design process of an ETL system to attain increased consistency, completeness, and reliability.

Discovering data realities

Once your source systems have been identified, you should invest time profiling their data in order to assess its health and quality. As Jack E. Olson explains in his book *Data Quality, The Accuracy Dimension* (Morgan Kaufmann, 2003), data has quality if it satisfies the requirements of its intended use. That means accuracy and relevance of data depends on the context of its use. For example, although data may be of good quality from a transactional system standpoint, it may not have the completeness or accuracy necessary for specific analytical requirements the data warehouse system has to support.

There are compelling benefits for analyzing and profiling source data before including it as part of the ETL solution:

- It provides the opportunity to confirm or exclude source systems that are to be included in the pool of candidate systems.
- It provides insight into the level of cleansing and transformation complexity that the ETL system will need to have. This is a key estimating factor of the

ETL development effort because it allows breaking the "dirty data" problem into more manageable pieces.

- It builds awareness about potential data quality issues early in the process. This information can be used to communicate potential risks and set business stakeholders' expectations.
- It uncovers new business rules or data relationships within the data that weren't accounted for in the target data model.

Data profiling activities may become overwhelming and meaningless quickly when not scoped correctly, but you can minimize that risk by taking some basic steps:

- Have a good understanding of business requirements and how the data will be used.
- Gather and review available documentation for each source system: data models, metadata, and data repository. This material can be used as reference when profiling and analyzing the data.
- Meet with source system owners to gain a better understanding of the underlying source data structures. Source system owners may provide additional insight into known data quality issues and help interpret the outcome of the data profiling exercises.

The method for profiling data may go from writing custom SQL queries, to validating specific conditions, to using advanced data profiling tools to get a broader profiling baseline. With the 2008 version, SQL Server Integration Services introduced the data profiling task, which relatively quickly facilitates creation of a data profiling baseline. Yet it has some limitations you should be aware of:

- For non–SQL Server sources, you need to stage data in a SQL Server database before profiling it. Profiling results are stored in XML format in the file system. If you need the results in a different format to use for further analysis or create reports, you need to account for the extra effort required to reformat the XML files. Fortunately, it's relatively simple to use the SSIS XML task to reformat the XML output file in a tabular format that can easily be loaded into a table.
- The data profile viewer application, a basic graphical interface to display the SSIS data profiling task results, is only available after installing SQL Server client tools. This is a drawback when you need to share the results with users who don't have SQL Server client tools installed. Your best bet in this case is to reformat the XML output file and load the results into a table.

Extract phase

Selecting data from source systems is pretty easy, but extracting only the data you are likely to need is a key step in any ETL process and not always that easy.

Detecting changed data

One of the first tasks you have to face when designing the extract phase of the ETL system is finding a reliable and efficient way to detect data that has changed or that has been added since the last time the extraction process ran. Although identifying changed data is irrelevant in initial load scenarios—a fixed portion or the entire content of the data source has to be extracted—having this ability is important for incremental load scenarios:

- Keeping the number of rows to be extracted to a minimum reduces the connection time required to the source system.
- Reducing the amount of data the ETL system has to process each time it runs increases system performance.
- Extracting entire datasets from source systems on each incremental load increases the risk of posting duplicate inserts or updates to the target tables.

There are multiple techniques you could use to detect changed data in data sources depending on particular conditions and realities of the source system. Each technique comes with different degrees of complexity and efficiency:

- *Using insert/update date metadata columns*—Today, most systems include columns in their data structures that provide the insert or last modification dates for each record. If these fields are available, and proven to be reliable, they can be referenced in the queries used to extract the data. This is by far one of the most cost-effective techniques. But you have to validate that those columns are in fact reliable and are updated with each insert and update operation. As an aside, avoid using system date values such as getdate()-1 when using this technique, because doing so makes your logic vulnerable to causing duplicates when rerunning the process after a failure or skipping rows if the process doesn't run as scheduled. Instead, create and maintain a table to store the maximum date from the previous load. This table will have a row for each source table and the date value is updated after each extraction is completed.
- *Using change data capture (CDC) technology*—Some RDBMSs include CDC capabilities that flag inserted, deleted, and updated rows and makes them available to be consumed by other applications. This is something you could use only if it's available in the targeted source system. This is well worth asking the system admin about if you're not familiar with the system's capabilities.
- *Using entire extract and elimination*—If there are no other alternatives to identify changed rows, you could extract the full dataset from the source table and then do a comparison against data you retain from the previous extraction period. You could maintain two staging tables for the current and the previous extract and then use a query for the comparison. This technique is resource intensive and may not be viable if you're dealing with very large datasets.

Data staging

The staging area is a working area that ETL processes use to store data in transit in a temporary or permanent way. Many ETL developers question the need of staging the data as part of the extract phase, arguing the performance cost of persisting data to disk and the capabilities of ETL tools of doing in-memory data transformations. But there are other aspects that you should take into account when evaluating the needs of staging data and whether this will benefit the ETL system. Consider the following points:

- Staging data upon extraction gives you the ability to capture data in source systems at a given point in time. This approach simplifies the recovery processes when an error occurs during the transform or load phase because you don't to have to re-extract the data. This is especially important when dealing with source systems that override their own data; you minimize the chances of skipping or missing changes in the source data.
- Staged data could be used for auditing and troubleshooting of the ETL process.
- The connection time to source systems can be greatly reduced when no data transformations are involved in the process. This factor may be particularly important when you have to extract large amounts of data from systems that support heavy transactional workloads.
- When data is staged in a database, data transformation operations may benefit from having the ability to offload some of the logic to the database engine.
- ETL processes incur additional overhead every time data is written to disk, because the I/O subsystem is typically the slowest component of the system.
- You need to design and build processes to prune and/or archive data in the staging database. Depending on your needs, this can be as simple as truncating the tables on each execution or may require more complex data archiving processes.

If you choose to stage the data, you have an additional decision to make: where to stage it. Filesystem storage gives you better I/O speeds, but database tables are easier to deal with when you need to analyze or manipulate staged data.

Transform phase

This phase is where you'll spend the most time in the development cycle. Once the data has been extracted from the sources, it's time to filter, scrub, and transform it as dictated by business rules and requirements. If you came to this point in your project without a good degree of familiarity with source data, your project is at risk! You should go back and read the "Discovering data realities" section in this chapter.

Data transformation requirements are generally different for each source and target table. But there are some principles and guidelines that, if followed correctly, can improve performance, maintainability, and manageability of the system:

- *Using aggregation and sort operations*—Sorting and aggregating data using the database system is, in most cases, simpler and more efficient than doing it in the ETL tool. SSIS sort and aggregate transformations are notoriously slow—they have to load all data into memory before performing the intended operation.

- *Joining datasets*—Database systems are, in general, better at this than ETL tools. In most cases, the SQL join operator is far more efficient than using ETL tools such as SSIS Merge Join or Lookup Transformations. You could add indexes to staging tables when using SQL operations to boost query performance. Keep in mind that indexes slow down insert operations; therefore, you may want to create and drop them each time the ETL process runs.

- *Monitoring memory usage*—ETL tools use lots of memory. Make sure memory settings inside packages and routines are aligned to the size of the workload and the resources available to the system. Monitor memory usage during performance testing. For SSIS, make sure you understand how package properties such as DefaultBufferMaxSize, DefaultBufferMaxRows, BufferTempStoragePath, and BLOBTempStoragePath work.

- *Comparing performance and business value*—As a member of the technical team, you invest much time focusing on the efficiency and performance of the ETL system, and although that's certainly important, building faster processes that deliver poor data quality or low business value may not be your best bet.

- *Using data error handling and tracking*—Your ETL architecture should include a system-wide data error handling process that allows identifying, handling, and tracking rows that don't pass data quality screens and business rules. This can be accomplished by adding a set of tables to your system such as the Error Event Fact table (shown in figure 1) that Ralph Kimball describes in his book *The Data Warehouse Lifecycle Toolkit* (Wiley, 1998). The table allows capturing detailed information about data errors, including row identifiers, the name of the

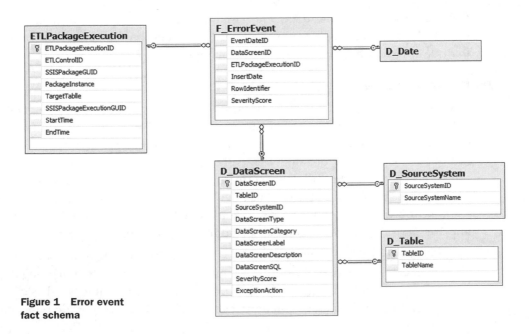

**Figure 1   Error event
fact schema**

source tables and columns, failed validation(s), and any other metadata you consider relevant for tracking and auditing purposes.

Once you have the desired set of tables in place, you need to define a standard method to collect relevant information inside each of the ETL packages and subroutines in a consistent way.

Load phase

At this stage, we are ready to deliver data for end user consumption and some important decisions are yet to be made.

Surrogate key generation

A surrogate key is a system generated value with no semantic meaning, typically numeric, that is used as a unique identifier in a table. You can use various approaches to generate surrogate key values during the ETL process, but all of them seem to follow one of two patterns. The first one is to use the relational database engine; the second is to do it inside the ETL tool as the data is loaded into the target tables.

SURROGATE KEYS MANAGED BY THE DATABASE ENGINE

This approach can be simple to implement and maintain. In SQL Server, identity columns seem to fit the requirement perfectly. This approach adds virtually no overhead to the ETL process because the values are automatically generated by the database and you can control the starting point of the key sequence and its increment. Moreover, the values are generated directly in the database upon inserting each row, so this approach allows concurrent process to load data into the same table without the risk of assigning duplicate key values. On the other hand, you need to be aware of some caveats:

- The key value is known only after the insert operation has been completed. This is a limitation in scenarios where you need to know the key value beforehand. For example, when loading parent-child tables simultaneously, you have to know the value to be assigned as a primary key of the parent row, because it's also a foreign key in the child table.
- In SQL Server, there are known issues with `@@IDENTITY` and `SCOPE_IDENTITY()` functions that can cause them to return invalid values. See Microsoft Knowledge Base article 2019779 for more details.
- You'd need to take additional steps when copying data from tables that use identity columns if you want to preserve referential integrity or avoid creating duplicate key values. Consider this example:

```
/* Create Table to move data from */
CREATE TABLE TestTable_A (ID INT IDENTITY(1,1), TestVal VARCHAR(50))

/* Insert some rows */
INSERT TestTable_A (TestVal) VALUES ('Value 1')
INSERT TestTable_A (TestVal) VALUES ('Value 2')
INSERT TestTable_A (TestVal) VALUES ('Value 3')
```

```
/* Delete a row in the middle of the key sequence */
DELETE FROM TestTable_A WHERE ID=2

/* Create table to move data to. Notice it has an identity column too*/
CREATE TABLE TestTable_B (ID INT IDENTITY(1,1), TestVal VARCHAR(50))

/* copying data */
INSERT INTO TestTable_B (TestVal)
SELECT TestVal FROM TestTable_A

/* Compare the keys for rows where TestVal='Value 3' - They are
different!*/
SELECT * FROM TestTable_A
SELECT * FROM TestTable_B

/* Clean up */
DROP TABLE TestTable_A
DROP TABLE TestTable_B
```

Although you won't typically move data in this way as part of the ETL process, you may need to do it for testing or troubleshooting purposes. You can avoid this issue by disabling the identity column in the destination table before moving the data, and then re-seed the sequence and re-enable it once the insert operation is completed.

SURROGATE KEYS GENERATED AS PART OF THE ETL DATA PIPELINE

This method involves two basic steps. The first step is to store the maximum key value in the target table inside a variable, typically using a query with a MAX function. In the second step, you use the value from the previous step to seed the current load key sequence and then increment the value for each row that passes through the data pipeline. In SSIS, this can be easily done with an Execute SQL task for step one and a Script component inside a data flow for the second. The benefits of this method are that you have fine control of key value generation, you can move data from table to table and not be concerned about breaking the referential integrity of the data, and the potential for creating gaps/overlaps in the key sequence is very low. But there are a couple of drawbacks that are worth noting:

- The key generation logic needs to be replicated in each package or routine loading data. The effort may be greatly reduced by the use of templates or reusable components available to ETL developers.
- There's no easy way to support concurrent processes loading data into the same target table.

Data update strategy

Changes to data warehouse tables require insert, update, and, in some cases, delete operations. These operations are resource intensive and must be done in an efficient way and without sacrificing other aspects of the ETL system, such as the ability to resume the ETL process after a failure or data integrity maintenance.

From the performance standpoint, it's desirable that insert, delete, and update transactions affect batches of rows as opposed to individual rows. Transactions affecting one row at a time create unnecessary overhead at the database level and seriously impact performance.

Insert operations are in most cases straightforward. Several options are available that offer optimal performance in most scenarios, such as SSIS OLE DB destination, the Bulk Insert task, or the BCP utility.

Yet update and delete operations require special attention in order to perform efficiently. For example, no built-in component in SSIS allows updating or deleting batches of rows in the data flow. A common approach to circumvent this limitation is to create a separate staging table to queue all rows to be updated or deleted, and then use a single SQL statement to update or delete all rows at once. Notice that in SQL Server 2008 or later, you can perform deletes, inserts and updates using a single MERGE SQL statement.

ETL system instrumentation and management

Building processes that clean, transform, integrate, and deliver data is just half the work. The other half is to make sure it does so in a reliable, consistent, and transparent way each time the ETL process is executed. For that, you need to include capabilities and components in your ETL architecture to facilitate management and monitoring activities.

Alerting

The system should have the ability to alert users when important events occur in the ETL process. It's common to configure the system to send email notifications upon successful completion or failure of each ETL batch. In some scenarios you may want to send additional messages containing information about data exceptions, such as the number of rows rejected or cleaned by the ETL process. In all cases, the notifications should include vital information about the event, such as job name, event date and time, last error message, phase/step of the event, and so forth.

Most scheduling tools provide alerting functionality, but you should validate that they provide the appropriate level of details about the event. In some cases, you may want to embed additional alerting logic inside of ETL routines in order to have more control over the notification logic.

Recovery and restart ability

ETL systems should have the ability to stop, start, and retry without producing inconsistent results or requiring complex data cleanup procedures. Designing the recovery strategy involves finding the smallest grain of the recovery points while keeping a workable level of complexity and performance. For example, having a row-level recovery strategy would require more complex logic than one that's at the table level—given it has to determine which rows have already been processed versus which ones haven't—and would typically yield suboptimal performance than the latter. Here are some guidelines to consider when designing the "restartability" strategy:

- Salvage as much of the data that was successfully loaded prior to the failure as possible. Doing so will save processing time when dealing with long-running processes.

- Any data cleanup should require no human intervention. This may include rolling back incomplete transactions or deleting data committed by the failed process.

- Break the ETL process into smaller chunks, giving you greater flexibility when establishing recovery points. A good rule of thumb is one process or package per target table.

- The built-in checkpoint functionality in most ETL tools, including SSIS, doesn't support complex control flow logic and has limited functionality. Make sure you test the checkpoint functionality within the tool and understand how it works before you implement it.

- The ETL processes should be re-entrant. This means they can be executed a second time, even after a failure, without posting duplicate transactions or skipping unprocessed rows.

You can create a simple but effective recovery strategy by storing ETL execution metadata in a set of tables like the ones shown in figure 2:

- *ETLControl*—A new row is inserted in this table each time the process is started. That row is updated at the end of the process to indicate the completion of the process. ETLControlID is used to identify each ETL batch. You can interrogate this table at the beginning of each process to confirm whether the current execution is a new batch or an attempt to complete a previously failed one.

- *ETLPackageExecution*—This table gets a new row each time a subprocess runs, and it's updated when the subprocess is successfully completed. A subprocess is a self-contained unit of work of the ETL process. In this case, an SSIS package loads data to a target table. You can interrogate this table at the beginning of each subprocess to determine whether the current execution is a new one or an attempt to complete it after a failure. New executions should load data normally. Incomplete executions after failures should perform required data cleanup and reload all data for that batch. Completed executions after a failure should be halted and control returned to the main ETL routine.

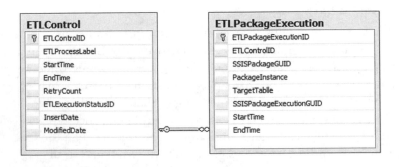

Figure 2   ETL execution metadata tables

Using this approach, the ETL process has the ability to identify and skip all the packages that were successfully executed and completed before the failure point and execute those remaining. Let's revisit these tables and extend them to support other key tasks, such as monitoring, logging, and troubleshooting.

Audit, balance, and control support

ETL systems must generate and capture metadata at each point where a major data transformation occurs to support audit enquiries and data reconciliation efforts. Having the ability to answer questions like "How many rows were rejected/loaded in the last process?," "Where is this row coming from?," and "How many duplicates were there in the last load?" will increase confidence in the transparency, accuracy, and reliability of the system. You can create or extend existing ETL metadata tables to accommodate audit information about the load process, such as the number of records inserted, deleted, updated, and rejected in each subroutine of the process. Figure 3 illustrates a basic set of tables you can design to store the data. Once the data structures are in place, you should take the time to design standard reusable routines to insert and update data into the tables. For example, in SSIS it's a common practice to include this type of logic in packages that are used later as templates.

Runtime event logging

Logging is to the ETL process what flight recorders are to planes. Logging metadata provides crucial information about the execution of the process to support auditing, monitoring, and diagnostic activities. One of the challenges of designing the logging subsystem is to decide the level of detail to be captured. Capturing too much detail could generate huge amounts of data and degrade system performance. But a more restricted level of logging could limit your ability to diagnose and troubleshoot execution errors. Here are a few pointers to guide you when you're designing the logging strategy:

- Evaluate logging output options available in the ETL tool and understand their performance implications and usability. Although text files may have reduced performance impact, tables may be easier to interact with.

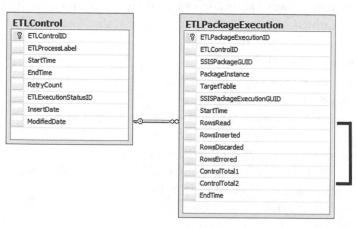

Figure 3   Extending ETL execution metadata tables for audit, balance, and control support

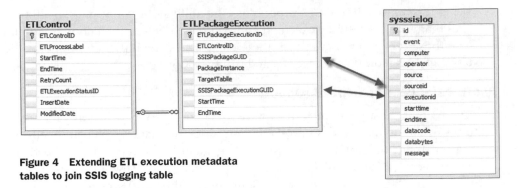

Figure 4   Extending ETL execution metadata tables to join SSIS logging table

- Find the optimal level of information detail to be captured. It should be enough for tracking and troubleshooting purposes without becoming overwhelming.
- Validate that logging information generated is meaningful. This is one of the first places where you'll look for clues when dealing with ETL execution–related errors.
- Consider enhancing and extending built-in logging capabilities to fill possible reporting gaps.
- Design a pruning process to remove aged logging records. Logging tables and files can grow to unmanageable sizes very quickly.

In SSIS, you have fine control over the type of events to be logged, but its output tends to be verbose to the extent that it becomes difficult to analyze when too many of them are selected. You can use `OnError`, `OnWarning`, and `Diagnostics` events as a starting point and then add events if required. For reporting purposes, you can configure SSIS packages to write log information to the SysSSISLog table and then join it to the custom ETL metadata tables presented in earlier sections to get more precise logging information (see figure 4).

ETL metadata and reporting

ETL processes have many moving parts and can generate large amounts of metadata that's valuable for various audiences and purposes. For that reason, you're often required to design reporting layers that allow the different ETL audiences to consume this data. Here are some examples:

- ETL operators are mainly interested in near real-time metadata that facilitates monitoring activities.
- ETL developers use execution logs extensively for testing and troubleshooting purposes.
- Business users require the time of the last data refresh.
- Project owners may require capture and analysis of more complex audit, balance, and control metrics, such as the duplication ratio across source systems providing overlapping data.

Summary

Data integration systems are complex in nature and crucial to the success of data warehouse implementations. As a responsible professional building the ETL solution, you need to ensure your system delivers high quality data while maintaining a high level of reliability, security, manageability, and scalability. You can't accomplish these goals without investing time in planning and architecting the solution.

About the author

Rafael Salas is an accomplished professional with more than a decade of experience helping Fortune 500 companies and public agencies to improve decision making, financial management, and customer engagement processes by using business intelligence and data warehousing technologies. Rafael has been a Microsoft SQL Server MVP since 2007 and is an active member of the SQL Server community. He's an author, a blogger, and a frequent speaker at technical conferences. Visit his blog at www.rafael-salas.com.

53 Autogenerating SSAS cubes

Johan Åhlén

This chapter describes how to autogenerate cubes in SQL Server Analysis Services (SSAS) and the underlying relational database. It comes with a step-by-step example of how to build a tool, InstantCube, that could drastically reduce the development time of simple SSAS cubes. With a few lines of code, you can significantly reduce the effort of analyzing your data manually. InstantCube isn't intended to be a full-featured tool but serves as an example of how to programmatically build cubes.

This chapter is divided into the following sections:

- Background—usage scenarios and technology overview
- Step-by-step example of how to implement a simple cube generator in C#
- Results and conclusions

NOTE   This material can be reinforced by downloading the InstantCube source code from CodePlex and reading my blog at http://www .joinsights.com for further details.

Background

When I started programming around 1983, writing even small programs was a time-consuming process. I used paper and pen together with a list of CPU instruction codes to manually compile my programs and then had to load them into memory using POKE statements in the built-in BASIC interpreter. If the program hung, which it often did, I had to restart the computer.

Today, developers are getting more productive with languages and tools that enable us to work at a higher level. We don't have to reinvent the wheel as we did earlier. Some of us never liked doing manual repetitive tasks, so we wrote programs that did the job for us. This is exactly what got me started automatically generating SSAS cubes (and ETL packages). The first tool that I wrote in 2006, read its metadata from Excel spreadsheets and created relational tables, SSIS packages, and SSAS cubes. It helped me create and manage a lot of cubes and ETL packages that were similar and to respond quickly to changing user needs. A few years later I read a white-paper called "Metadata-Driven ETL Management (MDDE)" and found that Microsoft IT had been thinking along the same lines.

Sample usage scenarios

Here are some examples of where programs can be used to automate repetitive tasks:

- Independent software vendors, adding analytical capabilities to their business systems
- Consultants, cutting BI project delivery time drastically
- In-house BI Competency Centers, delivering many similar projects

Technology overview

A number of related technologies exist:

- XMLA (XML for Analysis), a SOAP-based protocol used for communications with SSAS
- ADOMD.NET, a .NET Framework data provider used for XMLA communications
- ASSL (Analysis Services Scripting Language), a language for describing SSAS objects
- AMO (Analysis Management Objects), a .NET API on top of ASSL

The documentation of all these technologies is sparse, so expect some trial and error to succeed.

Developing InstantCube, a simple cube generator

There are no suitable general purpose-languages for expressing *simple* cubes. ASSL is a domain-specific language for cubes, but it isn't *simple*. Something else is needed. I've created a language I call DWML (Data Warehouse Markup Language) that's based on XML. In this language, I've included elements representing the most common objects in simple cubes such as `<dimension>`, `<hierarchy>`, and `<measure>`.

Creating the Visual Studio project

InstantCube was created as a Windows Forms application in C#, but it could be written in any other .NET language. You'll need to add a reference to the AMO assembly Microsoft .AnalysisServices.dll, which typically is located in C:\Program Files (x86)\Microsoft SQL Server\100\SDK\Assemblies. The project consists of a model, representing the DSL, a user interface, emitters for SQL and SSAS, and a sample file, as shown in figure 1.

Figure 1   The InstantCube project

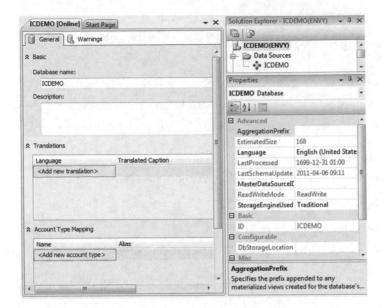

Figure 2   ICDEMO database settings

Creating the relational database emitter

Because the focus of this chapter is on SSAS, I'll briefly touch on how to generate the relational database. The cube needs to be supported by fact and dimension tables and some sample data. It relies on foreign key relationships between the fact tables and the dimension tables through surrogate keys. Columns need to be created for the key, name, and value of each dimension attribute.

You can accomplish all this with T-SQL code. InstantCube contains a number of methods that transform the user model (written in DSL) into T-SQL. They are then executed against the SQL Server through an OLE DB connection. For further details, see the source code of InstantCube.

Creating the Analysis Services emitter

The SSAS objects can be generated in different ways. I've chosen to use AMO because it's the most convenient way. AMO works only when connected to an SSAS server (online), but you can easily create an offline solution by choosing Import Analysis Services Database in Visual Studio.

Creating the SSAS database

The first thing you need in SSAS is a database. The database is the root object in SSAS and contains some global settings such as collation. A screenshot from Visual Studio is shown in figure 2.

To create the database you first need to connect to the server. You do this by instantiating the `Microsoft.AnalysisServices.Server` object and calling the `Connect` method. This could be implemented in the constructor of the `SSASEmitter` class as shown in the next listing.

Listing 1   Connecting to SSAS

```
public SSASEmitter(Project project)
{
  this.Project = project;
  server = new Server();
  server.Connect(Project.Connections.SSASConnection);
}
```

Before creating a database, you should check to see if a database already exists. Then you need to decide how to handle it; for example, drop and re-create it. If you drop a database, you must call the Update method on the server object before the database is dropped.

The InstantCube implementation that drops previous databases, is in the following listing.

Listing 2   Database initialization

```
public void EmitDatabase()
{
  if (server.Databases.ContainsName(dbName))
  {
    server.Databases[dbName].Drop();
    server.Databases.Remove(dbName);
    server.Update();
  }
  var database = server.Databases.Add(dbName);
  // Add additional code here to set database properties like Collation
  database.Update();
}
```

Creating the data sources

The next object you need to create is a data source. In most cases, as in InstantCube, you read from only one relational database, so you need only one data source. The settings for the data source include the connection string, which is always an OLEDB connection string, but you can also set the isolation level and maximum number of parallel connections. In the data source, you also set the impersonation information used for connecting to the relational database.

To add a data source, you create an object of type RelationalDataSource, initiate some properties, and add it to your SSAS database object. The following listing is an example from InstantCube.

Listing 3   Data source emitter

```
public void EmitDataSource()
{
    var database = server.Databases[dbName];
    var datasource = new RelationalDataSource(dbName, dbName);
    datasource.ConnectionString = Project.Connections.OLEDBConnection +
            "Initial Catalog=" + Project.Namings.SqlDbName;
    database.DataSources.Add(datasource);
    datasource.Update();
}
```

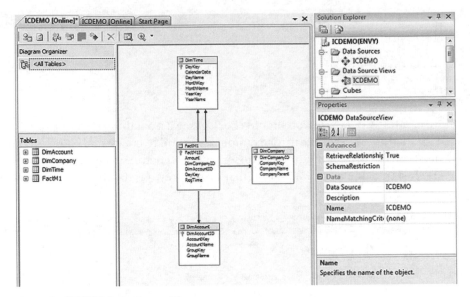

Figure 3   ICDEMO Data Source View

Creating the Data Source View

The Data Source View is an abstraction layer between the physical database and the relational model used by Analysis Services. It can be used to create custom columns and tables, but the best practice is to use views in the relational database instead. In InstantCube, the Data Source View is an exact mapping of the relational data source, including referential integrity, as shown in figure 3.

What causes some confusion in AMO is that the Data Source View is represented by an ADO.NET dataset. That means you'll have to map your relational database columns into .NET types. For instance, a SQL Server `varchar` needs to be converted to a .NET `string`. Another example is a SQL Server `smallint` that needs to be converted to a .NET `Int16`.

The complete code for creating the Data Source View is a bit too comprehensive to be included here, but the main method in InstantCube, provided in this next listing, provides a reasonable overview of the necessary steps:

Listing 4   DSV Emitter

```
public void EmitDSV()
{
    var database = server.Databases[dbName];
    var dsv = new DataSourceView(dbName);
    database.DataSourceViews.Add(dsv);
    dsv.Schema = new DataSet();

    foreach (var dimension in Project.Dimensions.Values)
    {
        EmitDSVTable(dsv, dimension.GetTableName(), dimension.GetFields(),
```

```
                    dimension.GetPrimaryKey());
    }

    foreach (var cube in Project.Cubes)
    {
        foreach (var mg in cube.MeasureGroups)
        {
            var tbl = EmitDSVTable(dsv, mg.GetTableName(), mg.GetFields(),
                mg.GetPrimaryKey());

            foreach (var fk in mg.GetForeignKeys())
            {
                var col1 =
                dsv.Schema.Tables[fk.RemoteTable].Columns[fk.RemoteField];
                var col2 = tbl.Columns[fk.LocalField];
                var relation = new DataRelation(fk.ID, col1, col2);
                dsv.Schema.Relations.Add(relation);
            }
        }
    }

    dsv.DataSourceID = dbName;
    dsv.Update();
}
```

Creating the dimensions

Dimensions can be simple or complex objects depending on your data warehouse design. The easiest are regular star schemas with a simple hierarchy consisting of a few attributes. More advanced dimensions can have many-to-many relations, snowflake schemas, and a few other more complex features. Supporting these features is certainly possible, but for the InstantCube example, we'll confine ourselves to simple dimensions, as shown in figure 4.

You should pay special attention to the Time dimension. For the Time dimension you need to set Dimension Type to Time and map the attributes to date parts (Days,

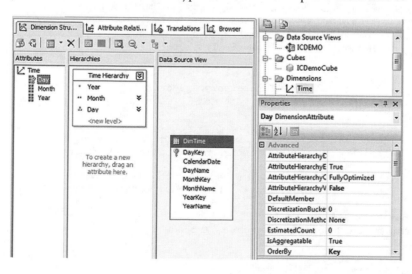

Figure 4 ICDEMO dimensions

Months, Years). Other dimensions can be mapped to type `Regular` and their attributes can be of type `Regular` as well.

To create a dimension, you first create an object of type `Microsoft.Analysis-Services.Dimension`. Then follow these steps:

1 Set the Source property to a `DataSourceViewBinding` that references your previously created Data Source View.

2 Set the Type property to either Time or Regular.

3 Create the attributes by calling `Attributes.Add` on your dimension, and set the attribute properties and column references for Key, Name, and Value.

4 Add the attribute relationships by adding them to the `AttributeRelationships` property of your attribute.

5 Finally, add your hierarchies by calling `Hierarchies.Add` on your dimension and then call `Levels.Add` on all your hierarchies.

Parent-child hierarchies are, as opposed to regular dimensions, created by adding an attribute with `Usage` set to `Parent` and `KeyColumns` set to the column that contains the parent reference.

The main method in InstantCube for creating dimensions is shown in the following listing.

Listing 5 Dimension Emitter

```
public void EmitDimensions()
{
    var database = server.Databases[dbName];

    foreach (var modelDimension in Project.Dimensions.Values)
    {
        var dimension = new
            Microsoft.AnalysisServices.Dimension(modelDimension.ID);
        dimension.Description = modelDimension.ID;
        dimension.Source = new DataSourceViewBinding(dbName);
        if (modelDimension is TimeDimension)
            dimension.Type = DimensionType.Time;
        else
        {
            dimension.Type = DimensionType.Regular;
            EmitSurrogateKeyAttribute(modelDimension, dimension);
        }

        foreach (var attribute in modelDimension.Attributes.Values)
            EmitAttribute(modelDimension, dimension, attribute);

        foreach (var hierarchy in modelDimension.Hierarchies)
            EmitHierarchy(dimension, hierarchy, modelDimension);

        database.Dimensions.Add(dimension);
        dimension.Update(UpdateOptions.ExpandFull);
    }
}
```

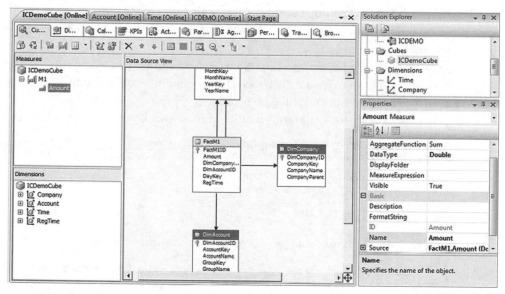

Figure 5   ICDEMO cube properties

Creating the cubes

The cubes are the most complex objects to generate because they can have a lot of different contents. A cube contains a number of measure groups, each of which contain measures, and references a number of dimensions, as shown in figure 5. For simple star schemas these references are made up of a reference between a column in the fact table and an attribute in the dimension. In other cases such as in many-to-many relations, the references are more complex. The cube also contains calculations, one or more MDX scripts that contain calculated members, calculated measures, named sets, and the like. In addition, KPIs and actions can be defined. Cubes can also be partitioned and have aggregations (which is important for performance). Finally, there can be perspectives and translations on the cube, which we won't cover here.

The main steps involved in creating a cube are as follows:

1 Call the `Cubes.Add` method on your SSAS database.
2 Set the `Source` using a `DataSourceViewBinding` object.
3 Set the `StorageMode`.
4 Create the Measure Groups by calling `MeasuresGroups.Add` on the cube.
5 Create at least one partition on each Measure Group by calling `Partitions.Add` on the Measure Group.
6 Add the Measures and Dimension references to your Measure Groups.
7 Add one or more MDX scripts to the `MdxScripts` collection of your cube, providing the script code in the `Command` property.
8 Add any actions as either `StandardAction`, `DrillThroughAction`, or `ReportAction` on the `Actions` collection of the cube.

9   Add KPIs as `Kpi` objects on the `Kpis` collection of the cube.

10 Finally, call `Update` on the cube with `UpdateOptions.ExpandFull` to create all
    dependent objects.

As you may remember, in the Data Source View you had to work with .NET types. In
the cubes you have to use OLE DB types for the measures. For instance, the SQL Server
type `numeric` becomes OLE DB type `Double`.

The main body for generating a cube in InstantCube is in the next listing.

Listing 6 Cube Emitter

```
var cube = database.Cubes.Add(modelCube.ID);
cube.Source = new DataSourceViewBinding(dbName);
cube.StorageMode = StorageMode.Molap;
cube.DefaultMeasure = "";

foreach (var modelMeasureGroup in modelCube.MeasureGroups)
{
    var measureGroup = cube.MeasureGroups.Add(modelMeasureGroup.ID);
    var partition = measureGroup.Partitions.Add(modelMeasureGroup.ID);
    partition.StorageMode = StorageMode.Molap;

    foreach (var measure in modelMeasureGroup.Measures)
        EmitMeasure(modelMeasureGroup, measureGroup, measure);

    foreach (var cubeDim in modelMeasureGroup.Dimensions)
        EmitCubeDimension(modelCube, modelMeasureGroup, cube, measureGroup,
            cubeDim);
}

var script = EmitMDX(modelCube);
var command = new Command(script.ToString());
cube.MdxScripts.Add("MDX").Commands.Add(command);

EmitActions(modelCube, cube);
EmitKPIs(modelCube, cube);

cube.Update(UpdateOptions.ExpandFull);
```

Summary

A resulting sample cube generated with InstantCube is shown in figure 6. With relatively little coding, InstantCube can generate simple cubes. An improved tool and
domain-specific language (DSL) can generate more complex data warehouses and
cubes, drastically reducing the delivery time, enforcing best practices, and tracking
the lineage of data between different domains (SSAS, SSIS, relational database). My
prediction is that in the future we'll move toward a dominant general-purpose DSL for
describing the whole ETL, relational, multidimensional, and BISM model with a toolset built into Visual Studio either from Microsoft or a partner. But already today
there's good potential for ISVs, in-house BI Competency Centers, and consultants to
invest in autogenerating cubes.

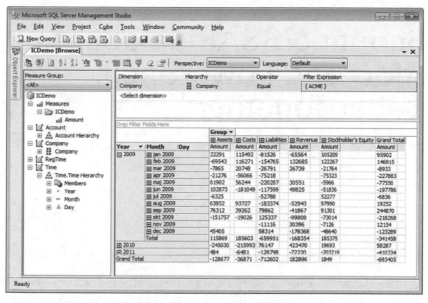

Figure 6 Sample cube generated with InstantCube

References

Check out these sources for further information:

- InstantCube
  http://instantcube.codeplex.com

- Microsoft SQL Server Metadata-Driven ETL Management Studio (MDDE)
  http://sqlservermddestudio.codeplex.com/

- AMO documentation
  http://msdn.microsoft.com/en-us/library/microsoft.analysisservices.aspx

- My blog
  http://www.joinsights.com

About the author

Johan Åhlén is the CEO of SolidQ Sweden and a business intelligence specialist, cloud enthusiast, entrepreneur, and SQL Server MVP living in South Sweden. He's a frequent speaker at conferences and a technical writer. Johan is co-founder of the PASS SQLRally Nordic conference and chairman of the Swedish SQL Server User Group. In his spare time, Johan enjoys playing his grand piano and spending quality time with his family. He keeps blogging at http://www.joinsights.com.

54 Scripting SSAS databases – AMO and PowerShell, Better Together

Darren Gosbell

Have you ever found yourself clicking repetitively through an action in Business Intelligence Development Studio (BIDS)? Or struggling to compose XML for Analysis (XMLA) `Create` or `Alter` statements? Then read on to find out how to make your life a whole lot easier.

For designing and building Analysis Services databases, Microsoft has given you a great tool in the form of BIDS. For administrative tasks, you have SQL Server Management Studio (SSMS). These are both great GUI tools, but like all GUI tools, they fall short when you need to perform repetitive actions or when you have to automate a series of actions. Fortunately, both of these GUI tools have been implemented over the top of the Analysis Management Objects (AMO) library. The fact that both SSMS and BIDS use AMO internally is significant; it means that every single piece of functionality that these two GUI tools expose can be replicated programmatically. There's no action that they perform that you can't replicate in your own program or script.

AMO is a .NET library, so when it comes to working with AMO you have two choices:

- Write a .NET program and compile it
- Write a PowerShell script

Advantages of PowerShell

Using PowerShell presents a number of advantages.

- There's no separation of source code and compiled code; there's only PowerShell code, and thus little danger of someone accidentally editing an old version of the code.

- PowerShell scripts are just text, so they can be modified quickly and easily.
- PowerShell scripts can be signed if you wish to prevent unauthorized alterations.
- PowerShell was designed as an administrative scripting language, so it was designed to "get out of your way" and let you get work done.

Advantages of compiled code

Using compiled code also has some advantages.

- Compiled code is potentially faster than a PowerShell script, which has to be parsed and interpreted on the fly. But if you look at most programs that use AMO, you'll find that the vast majority of the time is spent inside AMO function and method calls and little time is spent in your program.
- If you're worried about the potential for people stealing the intellectual property of your AMO code, a .NET program may be more suitable provided that you make sure to run an obfuscation tool. (Otherwise your .NET code can be easily decompiled.)

Rather than continuing to talk abstractly about the benefits of PowerShell and AMO, I'll provide a few practical examples to demonstrate the true power of this combination of technologies.

Automating processing

Suppose you have a situation where you want to automate the processing of all dimensions that have a name beginning with the letter P. To do this in C#, you'd have to start Visual Studio, create a new console application, add a reference to the Microsoft.AnalysisServices.dll, and enter the code shown in listing 1.

Listing 1   C#: processing dimensions beginning with P

```
using Microsoft.AnalysisServices;

namespace ProcessDims
{
    class Program
    {
        static void Main(string[] args)
        {
            Server svr = new Server();
            svr.Connect("localhost");
            Database db = svr.Databases.GetByName("Adventure Works DW 2008");
            foreach (Dimension dim in db.Dimensions)
            {
                if (dim.Name.StartsWith("P") )
                    dim.Process(ProcessType.ProcessUpdate);
            }
        }
    }
}
```

To do the same thing in PowerShell, you could type the code in listing 2 interactively in the PowerShell console. Or you could save these lines in a text file with a .ps1 extension or enter them directly in PowerShell job step in a SQL Agent job.

Listing 2　PowerShell: processing dimensions beginning with P

```
$amo = "Microsoft.AnalysisServices"
[System.Reflection.Assembly]::LoadWithPartialName($amo) > $null
$svr = New-Object Microsoft.AnalysisServices.Server
$svr.Connect("localhost")
$db = $svr.Databases.FindByName("Adventure Works DW 2008")
$procType = [Microsoft.AnalysisServices.ProcessType]::ProcessUpdate
$db.Dimensions | Where { $_.Name -like "P*" } | % { $_.Process($procType) }
```

As you can see, although there's still some ceremony in the PowerShell code, particularly when dealing with the `processType` enum, there's a lot less when compared to the C# version. Even if you don't count the lines with only opening and closing braces, there are still 10 lines in the C# version, which is 40 percent more than the PowerShell version. If you want to reduce the overall line count, it's possible to get the PowerShell version down to four lines, but the readability would suffer and there'd be no real benefit to doing this.

Reducing the amount of code isn't the main benefit—by far the biggest benefit is that the code you write is the code that executes. With compiled code, the code that executes is in an EXE file, which is separate from the source code, so there's always the potential for a disconnect. Also, a lot of overhead is involved in making changes or creating new scripts or utilities.

If you haven't worked with PowerShell, some of the code may look a bit cryptic, so let's walk through the previous example one line at a time and see what's going on:

```
$amo = "Microsoft.AnalysisServices"
```

This first line creates a string variable called `$amo` and sets its value to `"Microsoft .AnalysisServices"`. Notice that there's no need to declare the type of the variable; PowerShell is able to determine the variable type from the value used to set it.

```
[System.Reflection.Assembly]::LoadWithPartialName($amo) > $null
```

This is one of the more cryptic lines, but all it's doing is loading up the AMO assembly so that you can use its objects and methods from PowerShell. The end of this line, `"> $null"`, redirects the output from loading the assembly so that the output doesn't clutter the screen. It's completely a cosmetic thing. This step wasn't needed in the C# version because the same thing was done declaratively by adding a reference to the AMO assembly to the project.

```
$svr = New-Object Microsoft.AnalysisServices.Server
$svr.Connect("localhost")
```

The next two lines are where you create an `AMO Server` object, store it in the `$svr` variable, and then connect to the localhost server.

```
$db = $svr.Databases.FindByName("Adventure Works DW 2008")
```

On the fifth line, you call the `FindByName` method of the `Databases` collection to find the database called `Adventure Works DW 2008`.

```
$procType = [Microsoft.AnalysisServices.ProcessType]::ProcessUpdate
```

The next line creates the `$procType` variable and sets it equal to the value of the `ProcessUpdate` enumeration value. Referencing enumeration values is one area where PowerShell is more verbose than usual due to the need to use the fully qualified reference.

```
$db.Dimensions | Where {$_.Name -like "P*"} | % {$_.Process($procType)}
```

This next line is where all the magic happens. It's technically three statements in one line and uses an important PowerShell concept called *pipelining*. Here you use the vertical pipe character (|) to pass the output of one expression as the input to another.

So let's break out the three expressions and see what they're doing:

```
$db.Dimensions
```

The first part of our final line, `$db.Dimensions`, is an expression that returns a collection of all the dimensions in the database.

```
| Where {$_.Name -like "P*"}
```

This collection is then piped through to the `where-object` cmdlet (which is aliased as simply `Where`) and you filter for names starting with the letter P. You may be wondering where the strange underscore variable `$_` came from. This is a special intrinsic variable that's available in any cmdlet that can iterate over a collection of objects; it simply returns the current object for the iteration. It should be a familiar concept to Analysis Services developers because it's similar to the `CurrentMember` function in multidimensional expressions (MDX).

```
| % {$_.Process($procType)}
```

This last expression uses the `%` sign, which is the `foreach` operator. It will loop through each of the objects that are piped into it one at a time and call the `Process` method on each one.

This example is definitely a little contrived. It's probably not a common situation to want to process dimensions that have a name beginning with a certain letter. But you could easily take this simple example and extend it in a number of ways. If you have multiple cubes in your database, you could write a script to process only dimensions that are associated with a specified cube. Or you could check the last processed date of each dimension and only process those that haven't been processed within a given time frame.

Repetitive design changes

Another area where scripting is extremely beneficial is in making repetitive design changes. One issue that I commonly see are databases where the dimension names all start with "Dim" and the measure groups all start with "Fact." This usually happens

A PowerShell primer

You may be looking at the previous example and thinking, "That's all well and good, but if I don't have a lot of experience with AMO, how would I know that the `Server` object has a `Databases` collection that has a `FindByName` method? Or that the `Process` method needs to be passed a `ProcessType` parameter?" The answer to these questions is that PowerShell was specifically designed with consistency and discoverability in mind to make it easy for you to figure out these sorts of things. You need to remember only three core cmdlets to be able to work with PowerShell:

- `get-help`—This one should be fairly self-explanatory. You pass it the name of a keyword or cmdlet or concept and it outputs the relevant help topic.
- `get-command`—This cmdlet returns a list of all the commands available in the current session.
- `get-member`—When you pass an object to this cmdlet, it will return a list of all the properties and methods for that object. This is probably one of the most useful cmdlets when working with a .NET assembly like AMO. `get-member` is often invoked using its short alias of `gm`. To list all the properties and methods of the database object in our example, use the expression `$db | get-member`.

because it's a common naming practice in data warehouses to prefix the fact and dimension tables. So the customer dimension table is `dimCustomer` and the sales fact table is `factSales`. The names of your objects are effectively the user interface of your cube. I don't have an issue with using a naming standard like this in the data warehouse (but arguments that it's becoming redundant are valid now that tables can play the role of both a dimension and a measure group). Yet when it comes to the names of objects in your SSAS database, I strongly feel that these should be named in business-friendly terms.

So if you have one or more databases where all of the dimensions have a "Dim" prefix and all of the measure groups have a "Fact" prefix, how could you fix this? One option would be to open the database in BIDS and work through each dimension and measure group removing these prefixes. That would be rather tedious work—especially when you consider that it's not just the dimension name in the database, but also the cube dimension name, that need changing. When a dimension is used in a cube, it inherits the name of the database dimension by default, but you can change the name in the cube—this is what allows you to implement role-playing dimensions. If you have more than three or four dimensions in your database or if you have multiple cubes, it doesn't take long before it's much simpler to use a PowerShell script. The script in listing 3 will loop through the specified database and remove any "Fact" and "Dim" prefixes.

Listing 3   Removing name prefixes with PowerShell

```
$amo = "Microsoft.AnalysisServices"
[System.Reflection.Assembly]::LoadWithPartialName($amo) > $null
$svr = new-Object Microsoft.AnalysisServices.Server
$svr.Connect("localhost")
```

```
$DatabaseID = "Adventure Works DW 2008"
$db = $svr.Databases.FindByName($DatabaseID)

# Update the name of each database dimension
foreach ($dim in $db.Dimensions)
{
    if ($dim.Name.StartsWith("Dim "))
    {
        $dim.Name = $dim.Name.Substring(4)
        $dim.Update
    }

}

foreach ($cube in $db.Cubes)
{
    # Update the name of each cube dimension
    foreach ($dim in $cube.Dimensions)
    {
        if ($dim.Name.StartsWith("Dim "))
        {
            $dim.Name = $dim.Name.Substring(4)
            $dim.Update
        }
    }

    #update the name of all of the measure groups
    foreach ($mg in $cube.MeasureGroups)
    {
        if ($mg.Name.StartsWith("Fact "))
        {
            $mg.Name = $mg.Name.SubString(5)
            $mg.Update
        }
    }
}
```

Another closely related scenario to this was one that a friend of mine came across a few years ago. He'd been called in to fix a client's database where the source relational database had all of its table and column names in uppercase letters. And because the cube wizard had been run with the minimum of intervention, this meant that every object in the Analysis Services database also had uppercase names. The firm had started manually updating the dimension names, but there were more than a hundred attributes to work through. The script in listing 4 worked through that process in a minute or so.

Listing 4 Converting attribute names to title case

```
$amo = "Microsoft.AnalysisServices"
[System.Reflection.Assembly]::LoadWithPartialName($amo) > $null
$svr = new-Object [Microsoft.AnalysisServices.Server]
$svr.Connect("localhost")
$DatabaseID = "Adventure Works DW 2008"
$db = $svr.Databases.FindByName($DatabaseID)

# This small function is extracted to improve readability
function ToTitleCase([String]$in)
```

```
{
  (Get-Culture).TextInfo.ToTitleCase($in.ToLower())
}

# Foreach dimension loop through each attribute and call ToTitleCase()
foreach ($dim in $db.Dimensions)
{
    "Dimension: $($dim.Name)"
    foreach ($att in $dim.Attributes)
    {
        $oldName = $att.Name
        $newName = ToTitleCase($oldName)
        $att.Name = $newName
        "  Name Changed from: $oldName to: $newName"
    }
    $dim.Update()
}
$svr.Disconnect()
```

Scripting databases

Another area where the combination of AMO and PowerShell is effective is in the automation of maintenance tasks. This is due to the fact that you can work with resources like files and folders just as easily as you can work with .NET classes. It's easy to create a script to make a backup of all of your Analysis Services databases with a specified naming convention and then remove backups that are older than a specified date. You can find good examples of scripts like this with a quick internet search.

Another similar administration task that you might need to perform is that of scripting your Analysis Services databases to XMLA. There are a number of reasons why you may want to script your database's XMLA:

- You may have automated processes that create partitions in your cube and this is one way of recording the state of your database at a given point in time.
- Your production database may have different role memberships and this is a good way of recording the state of those role memberships.
- If you have people connecting directly to the server to make changes to the database (which isn't a recommended practice), this is one way of making regular backups of their work.
- If you have multiple developers deploying changes, this can provide an audit trail for the design that was deployed to the server.

The script in listing 5 will loop through all of the databases on the specified server and use the Scripter class in AMO to generate an XMLA script of each database.

> **Listing 5 Scripting all the Analysis Services databases on a server**

```
# load the AMO and XML assemblies into the current runspace
$assembly = [System.Reflection.Assembly]
$assembly::LoadWithPartialName("Microsoft.AnalysisServices") > $null
$assembly::LoadWithPartialName("System.Xml") > $null
```

```
$serverName = "localhost"
$outputFolder = "C:\data\"
$dateStamp = (get-Date).Tostring("yyyyMMdd")

# connect to the server
$svr = new-Object Microsoft.AnalysisServices.Server
$svr.Connect($serverName)
foreach ($db in $svr.Databases)
{
    Write-Host "Scripting: " $db.Name
    $utf8encoding = [System.Text.Encoding]::UTF8
    $scriptFile = "$($outputFolder)DBScript_$($db.Name)_$($dateStamp).xmla"
    $xw = new-object System.Xml.XmlTextWriter($scriptFile, $utf8encoding)
    $xw.Formatting = [System.Xml.Formatting]::Indented
    $scripter = [Microsoft.AnalysisServices.Scripter]
    $scripter::WriteCreate($xw,$svr,$db,$true,$true)
    $xw.Close()
}
$svr.Disconnect()
```

One of the interesting parts of this script is how the file path is constructed. It uses a feature of PowerShell that will expand variables within string expressions. In the following line I've highlighted the variables:

```
"$($outputFolder)DBScript_$($db.Name)_$($dateStamp).xmla"
```

Note that in this string the variables are also surrounded by a dollar sign and brackets to denote them as an expression. This is because no whitespace is used to delimit the variables so you need some way of telling PowerShell how to differentiate between the variable and the constant text in the expression. When run against the Adventure Works DW 2008 database on April 5, 2011, the script generated the following string:

```
"C:\data\DBScript_Adventure Works DW 2008_20110405.xmla"
```

NOTE Although it would be entirely possible to create an Analysis Services database from scratch using PowerShell, doing so would take a lot of effort. Probably a better approach is to design a baseline cube using BIDS and then deploy and modify it with PowerShell.

Modules and snap-ins

I've shown you scripts that you can run on a server with SQL Server 2008 or later without any additional software. But PowerShell has the concept of snap-ins and modules, which allow developers to extend PowerShell with additional functionality. Snap-ins are a PowerShell v1 concept, whereas modules were introduced in PowerShell v2. Projects like PowerShell Community Extensions (http://pscx.codeplex.com), an open source project that adds useful general functionality to PowerShell, are also available.

For working specifically with Analysis Services, you can use the PowerSSAS module (http://powerssas.codeplex.com). This module allows you to simplify your scripts by providing convenience cmdlets for working with Analysis Services. It includes cmdlets that let you access all the major Analysis Services objects. If you'd used PowerSSAS in the first PowerShell script in this chapter (listing 2), you could've reduced the code from seven lines to four, as shown in listing 6.

> **Listing 6   PowerSSAS: Processing dimensions beginning with P**

```
Import-Module PowerSSAS
$procType = [Microsoft.AnalysisServices.ProcessType]::ProcessUpdate
$dims = Get-ASDimension localhost "Adventure Works DW 2008"
$dims | Where { $_.Name -like "P*" } | % { $_.Process($procType) }
```

In addition, `PowerSSAS` contains a PowerShell provider. This feature allows you to map a drive to an Analysis Services server and then navigate it as you would a filesystem.

   `PowerSSAS` also has one fairly unique feature in that it has a pair of cmdlets that allow you to load an Analysis Services project file as an AMO database object and another that allows you to save an AMO database object as a project. That way, you can make changes to your database before it's deployed to a server, which isn't something you can easily do with AMO on its own.

Summary

I hope that by now you're convinced that the approach of using PowerShell and AMO is one that's definitely worth pursuing. This approach is more flexible and agile than compiling utilities using C# or VB.NET—and infinitely simpler than using raw XMLA commands.

   If you're interested in reading more about PowerShell, these sites provide a good starting point:

- PowerShell Code Repository: www.poshcode.org
- PowerShell.com: www.powershell.com
- "Scripting with Windows PowerShell": www.microsoft.com/powershell

About the author

Darren Gosbell is a Solution Architect with James & Monroe, a consulting firm whose specialties include the areas of business intelligence, data warehousing, and business performance management. He's been building and implementing data warehousing and business intelligence solutions on the Microsoft platform as a consultant since 1999. Darren also enjoys coding and is a founding member of the BIDS Helper, ASStoredProcedures, and PowerSSAS projects on Codeplex. He's been a Microsoft MVP in SQL Server since 2006, in recognition of his contribution to the community, specifically in the areas of Analysis Services and MDX. Darren lives in Melbourne, Australia with his wife and two children.

55 Managing context in MDX

Boyan Penev

When writing MDX queries, you usually start with a goal you need to achieve. Whether this goal is to return a simple data set or to perform calculations, you need to be aware of context. Context affects all sections of your queries and is an important background setting. Understanding and managing it correctly greatly simplifies and demystifies the query logic and outcomes.

To begin our exploration of context, we will start with its broader side, distinguishing and describing the three overarching context types: cube, session, and query context.

- *Cube context*—When you define calculations and named sets in the cube script, they can be used and shared by all sessions and queries against that cube. But as you'll see later in this chapter, they aren't affected by some MDX query statements.
- *Session context*—You can also define calculations and named sets in your MDX query sessions. If you do that, all queries in the same session can share the same calculations for the duration of the session. Session context overrides cube context.
- *Query context*—The smallest grain of context you can use is the query context. Calculations in the query context exist only for the duration of the query and are visible only within the query. Query context overrides both session and cube contexts.

One important implication of these three context types is caching. Calculations performed in each of the contexts are cached, and the cache is shared. This is an important facet of query optimization. Defining calculations in the correct context is an important usability consideration, but it's also an important performance optimization technique.

To better understand these three context types, review the sample script extracts in the following listing (all of these can be deployed or executed against Adventure Works DW 2008R2).

Listing 1   Comparing cube context, session context, and query context

```
// This set definition is placed in the cube script
CREATE STATIC SET CURRENTCUBE.[Europe Cube Set]
AS
    {[Geography].[Country].&[France],
     [Geography].[Country].&[Germany],
     [Geography].[Country].&[United Kingdom]};

// Creating a session set - e.g. in an SSMS query window
CREATE SESSION SET [Adventure Works].[Europe Session Set]
AS
    {[Geography].[Country].&[France],
      [Geography].[Country].&[Germany],
      [Geography].[Country].&[United Kingdom]};

// Creating a query set as a part of the query
WITH
SET [Europe Query Set]
AS
    {[Geography].[Country].&[France],
     [Geography].[Country].&[Germany],
     [Geography].[Country].&[United Kingdom]}
MEMBER [Measures].[Cube Set Count]
AS
    // This set has been defined in the cube script and the cube has been
    // deployed as showed above prior to executing the query
    [Europe Cube Set].Count
MEMBER [Measures].[Session Set Count]
AS
    [Europe Session Set].Count
MEMBER [Measures].[Query Set Count]
AS
    [Europe Query Set].Count
SELECT
{
    [Measures].[Cube Set Count],
    [Measures].[Session Set Count],
    [Measures].[Query Set Count]
} ON 0
FROM [Adventure Works]
```

The logic within the three measures and named sets is precisely the same, and the results from the query, as shown in table 1, which uses all of them, are identical in this case.

Table 1   Results of code from listing 1

Cube Set Count	Session Set Count	Query Set Count
3	3	3

But this doesn't hold true if you modify the query as shown in the following listing.

Listing 2   Applying a slicer

```
SELECT
{
    [Measures].[Cube Set Count],
    [Measures].[Session Set Count],
    [Measures].[Query Set Count]
} ON 0
FROM [Adventure Works]
WHERE [Geography].[Geography].[Country].&[Germany]
```

Now the `Query Set Count` result is different, as you can see in table 2.

Table 2   Results of code from listing 2

Cube Set Count	Session Set Count	Query Set Count
3	3	1

Here you can observe a peculiar situation: regardless of the logic being identical, we obtain different results. In the first and second cases, the measures are created in cube and session contexts, respectively. Therefore, the slicer statement doesn't affect them, but in the third case it does. This leads us to another very important consideration when working with MDX: when objects we define are evaluated.

Named sets

There are two types of named sets: DYNAMIC and STATIC. The difference between the two types is that STATIC ones get evaluated once—when they're created in the overall cube context—and DYNAMIC ones get evaluated with the context of each query. Therefore, DYNAMIC ones behave like query sets.

Both cube and session named sets are STATIC by default. It's wise to consider whether you need them to remain such or if you need to apply the DYNAMIC property when you create them.

Once you know what type your sets are, you need to understand how sets are evaluated—that is, what tuples they contain.

Simply put, named sets are evaluated in the context in which they're created. If you examine the previous query, which creates a query-scoped set, you'll notice that the slicer axis does indeed impact its contents. Change the query as shown here.

Listing 3   Named set

```
WITH
SET [Europe Query Set]
AS
    {[Geography].[Country].&[France],
     [Geography].[Country].&[Germany],
```

```
        [Geography].[Country].&[United Kingdom]}
MEMBER [Measures].[Query Set Count]
AS
    [Europe Query Set].Count
SELECT
{
    [Measures].[Query Set Count]
} ON 0,
{
    [Geography].[Geography].[Country].&[Germany]
} ON 1
FROM [Adventure Works]
```

The resulting value for `Query Set Count` is 3. This is because when they're created, named sets don't take into account the current coordinates defined on the axis in the query.

Calculated members

Explicit sets and set expressions in calculated members are independent of axis and slicer context. In the following query, the result is constant regardless of the fact that certain dimension members have been placed on both the column and the slicer axis.

Listing 4   Calculated member

```
WITH
MEMBER [Measures].[setExpression]
AS
    [Geography].[Geography].[City].COUNT
SELECT
{
    [Measures].[setExpression]
} ON 0,
{
    [Geography].[State-Province].&[WA]&[US]
} ON 1
FROM [Adventure Works]
WHERE [Geography].[Country].&[United States]
```

NOTE   Here and later in this chapter we're omitting .MEMBERS calls for retrieving the members of a level of a hierarchy, and we are using it for retrieving the whole hierarchy. In the previous example the [Geography].[Geography].[City].COUNT statement can be rewritten as [Geography].[Geography].[City].MEMBERS.COUNT, which explicitly shows the MEMBERS call. The two types of syntax are equivalent, and the former is used for brevity of the expressions.

Here, the members of the [Geography].[Geography].[City] level don't get restricted by either United States in the slicer axis or WA on the rows axis. If you changed the query and specified Australia in the WHERE clause and the state of Victoria on rows, the result would remain the same. This is different for query named sets, as described earlier; for them the slicer is taken into consideration when created.

You can enforce the context you want by using the EXISTING MDX function. Let's rewrite the query as shown in the following listing.

Listing 5 Calculated member with EXISTING

```
WITH
MEMBER [Measures].[setExpression]
AS
    (EXISTING [Geography].[Geography].[City]).COUNT
SELECT
{
    [Measures].[setExpression]
} ON 0,
{
    [Geography].[State-Province].&[WA]&[US]
} ON 1
FROM [Adventure Works]
WHERE [Geography].[Country].&[United States]
```

The result is very different. Our set expression now gets evaluated in the context of the current coordinate of each cell, and we do get the count of cities in Washington in the United States only. Changing the query to specify Victoria, Australia, yields different results, as expected.

You could expect that the EXISTING function would do the same for named sets. Let's try the following query in order to test this assumption.

Listing 6 Named set with EXISTING

```
CREATE SET [Adventure Works].[Cities]
AS
    [Geography].[Geography].[City];

WITH
MEMBER [Measures].[setExpression]
AS
    (EXISTING [Cities]).COUNT
SELECT
{
    [Measures].[setExpression]
} ON 0,
{
    [Geography].[State-Province].&[WA]&[US]
} ON 1
FROM [Adventure Works]
WHERE [Geography].[Country].&[United States]
```

Indeed, the result shows that the session set did get restricted to the current cell coordinates. This holds true for static and dynamic named sets defined in the cube script, as well.

Another detail we should examine is the subselect construct you can use to define cube context. SQL Server Reporting Services and Excel use subselect statements by default, and understanding the differences when dealing with them to set the query execution context is also necessary. Unlike the WHERE statement, the subselects in MDX don't change the current coordinate of the evaluated cells. To grasp this concept in full, we should first review the concept of *current coordinate.*

When you work with MDX, it's easy to omit the fact that tuples always include coordinates from all related dimensions and all of their hierarchies. For example, when you write [Measures].[Internet Sales Amount], this member definition statement gets implicitly translated to the lengthier but more complete:

```
([Measures].[Internet Sales Amount]
,[Dimension1].[Hierarchy1].DefaultMember
,[Dimension1].[Hierarchy2].DefaultMember
,...
,[DimensionN].[HierarchyN].DefaultMember)
```

In other words, the default member for each dimension and each hierarchy replaces missing members in the tuple definition. Once you specify some hierarchy member, you explicitly overwrite the default member in the tuple. Please note that SSAS doesn't necessarily use the ALL member from each hierarchy but the default one. This is important when considering non-aggregatable attributes.

When you place a set of members on an axis, the member on each position of the axis overwrites the default member in the tuple returned from the query. Therefore, when you place the set of all members in the Country level of the Country attribute of the Geography dimension on the rows axis and the Internet Sales Amount measure on columns, you explicitly overwrite two members in each retrieved tuple—one from the Country attribute and another one from the Measures dimension. Moreover, if you place a member from the City level of the City attribute of the Geography dimension in the WHERE clause, you explicitly overwrite a third member in each tuple in the result set. We refer to the coordinate of each cell as the current coordinate.

On the other hand, the subselect statement doesn't alter the current coordinate and doesn't overwrite any members in the query tuples. This is why you can place a hierarchy appearing on an axis in the subselect statement but not in the WHERE clause. For example, the first query in the following listing results in an error (shown below the first query), whereas the second one succeeds and returns an empty result set as expected.

Listing 7   Overwriting default members

```
SELECT
{
    [Measures].[Internet Sales Amount]
} ON 0,
{
    [Geography].[Country].&[United States]
} ON 1
FROM [Adventure Works]
WHERE [Geography].[Country].&[Australia]

The Country hierarchy already appears in the Axis1 axis.
```

```
SELECT
{
    [Measures].[Internet Sales Amount]
} ON 0,
{
    [Geography].[Country].&[United States]
} ON 1
FROM (
    SELECT {[Geography].[Country].&[Australia]} ON 0
    FROM [Adventure Works]
)
```

Because the subselect part of the query doesn't affect the current coordinate in which expressions are evaluated, let's see how it impacts named sets and set expressions. If you execute the following query, you'll see that just like with a WHERE clause, the result shows you the total count of cities in the Geography dimension.

Listing 8   Subselect to override default members

```
WITH
MEMBER [Measures].[cityCount]
AS
    [Geography].[Geography].[City].COUNT
SELECT
{

    [Measures].[cityCount]
} ON 0
FROM (
    SELECT {[Geography].[Country].&[United States]} ON 0
    FROM [Adventure Works]
)
```

In contrast to using EXISTING with a WHERE set, using EXISTING with a subselect as in the following listing seemingly doesn't work, and you get the same result.

Listing 9   EXISTING with a subselect

```
WITH
MEMBER [Measures].[cityCount]
AS
    (EXISTING [Geography].[Geography].[City]).COUNT
SELECT
{
    [Measures].[cityCount]
} ON 0
FROM (
    SELECT {[Geography].[Country].&[United States]} ON 0
    FROM [Adventure Works]
    )
```

In fact, the EXISTING function does work in exactly the same way: it enforces the current coordinate to the set expression. But the current coordinate isn't changed; it still includes the default (which in this case is the `ALL` member) from the Country attribute hierarchy. The subselect behaves in the same way as an overarching `EXISTS` clause (listing 10); listings 9 and 10 are equivalent.

Listing 10 EXISTS clause

```
WITH
MEMBER [Measures].[cityCount]
AS
    (EXISTING [Geography].[Geography].[City]).COUNT
SELECT
{
    EXISTS([Measures].[cityCount],[Geography].[Country].&[United States])
} ON 0
FROM [Adventure Works]
```

The automatic application of `EXISTS` to the sets and set expressions in the query is somewhat different when dealing with `WHERE` clauses and subselect statements. The distinction has been blurred in SQL Server 2008 and onwards, and currently you can assume that the `EXISTS` clause is always applied to the innermost expression. For example, you can assume that in the following expression the `EXISTS` clause will be applied around the set and not around the `COUNT` function.

Listing 11 Inner and outer EXISTS

```
// original expression
COUNT([Geography].[Geography].[City])

// inner EXISTS - this is how we can assume SSAS applies EXISTS for a
// WHERE clause or a subselect
COUNT(EXISTS([Geography].[Geography].[City], <slicer/subselect set>))

// outer EXISTS - this is how a WHERE clause used to be transformed before
// SQL Server 2008
EXISTS(COUNT([Geography].[Geography].[City]), <slicer/subselect set>)
```

In the case of using a `WHERE` clause, SSAS applies `EXISTS` logic to the set expressions within the query and also changes the current coordinate, whereas if you're using subselects it applies only the `EXISTS` logic. Therefore, you can reasonably expect that when it comes to set expressions in your queries, both `WHERE` and subselects will behave in exactly the same way, but the `EXISTING` keyword won't apply to subselects.

Indeed, the output from the two queries in the following listing is different for this reason.

Listing 12 EXISTING with subselects

```
// a definition of a session set
CREATE SESSION SET [Adventure Works].[sessionSet]
AS
    [Geography].[Geography].[City];
```

```
// WHERE clause
WITH
MEMBER [Measures].[cityCount]
AS
    (EXISTING sessionSet).COUNT
SELECT
{
    [Measures].[cityCount]
} ON 0
FROM [Adventure Works]
WHERE {[Geography].[Country].&[United States]}

// Subselect clause
WITH
MEMBER [Measures].[cityCount]
AS
    (EXISTING sessionSet).COUNT
SELECT
{
    [Measures].[cityCount]
} ON 0
FROM (
    SELECT {[Geography].[Country].&[United States]} ON 0
    FROM [Adventure Works]
)
```

Scope assignments

Scope assignments are a powerful way to affect context in MDX. The primary way of setting scope assignments is through the aptly named SCOPE function in the cube script. In brief, SCOPE sets the calculation logic for a specified subcube in SSAS. Its argument is a subcube definition, and the body defines a calculation. A simple example altering the way the Internet Sales Amount measure of the Adventure Works cube behaves is the following statement:

```
SCOPE([Measures].[Internet Sales Amount]);
    This = [Measures].[Internet Sales Amount]/2;
END SCOPE;
```

Here you tell Analysis Services to return the Internet Sales Amount measure divided by 2. The calculation affects a subcube including all hierarchies from all dimensions and only the Internet Sales Amount measure. This is a simple example, and you can greatly enhance its value by including more attribute members. For example, you could restrict this behavior to a smaller subcube by including the CY 2008 member of the Calendar Year attribute hierarchy in our Date dimension:

```
SCOPE([Date].[Calendar Year].[Calendar Year].&[2008],
        [Measures].[Internet Sales Amount]);
    This = 1;
END SCOPE;
```

After adding this statement to the cube script for the Adventure Works cube, SSAS will apply the calculation for Internet Sales Amount for 2008 and the ALL member, which is higher than it is in the hierarchy. Similarly, if you apply a scope assignment to the key attribute hierarchy Date, the calculation affects all levels higher than it:

```
SCOPE([Date].[Date].[Date], [Measures].[Internet Sales Amount]);
    This = [Measures].[Internet Sales Amount]/2;
END SCOPE;
```

Assignments to physical measures (as opposed to calculated measures, which are governed by logic implemented by the developer) aggregate up the hierarchy, and amounts for dates get aggregated to months, quarters, semesters, years, and the grand total. Similarly, if you change the scope assignment to affect a subcube including the Month attribute hierarchy, it will apply to the quarters, semesters, years, and the grand total but not to dates. You can change this by explicitly specifying the attributes that get affected. For example, if you want the scope assignment to take effect for all members under Calendar Year 2008, you can write the following:

```
SCOPE([Date].[Calendar].[Calendar Year].&[2008],
      [Date].[Date].[Date],
      [Measures].[Internet Sales Amount]);
    This = [Measures].[Internet Sales Amount]/2;
END SCOPE;
```

Note that we're not including the ALL member in the Date attribute hierarchy. The assignment didn't directly apply to the 2008 subtotal; it impacted only the 2008 subtotal because the assignment on dates aggregated up to 2008. If we were to include the ALL level, you could rewrite the statement like this:

```
SCOPE([Date].[Calendar].[Calendar Year].&[2008],
      [Date].[Date].Members,
      [Measures].[Internet Sales Amount]);
    This = [Measures].[Internet Sales Amount]/2;
END SCOPE;
```

There's a distinctive difference between the two, and they yield different results. In the second case the scope assignment works on the dates and the ALL member of the date attribute hierarchy, as well. Therefore, the Internet Sales Amount measure will be divided by 2 for each date and for all tuples, including the ALL Date member under 2008 (that is, the 2008 subtotal). Effectively, you tell SSAS to give you the overwritten value every time a tuple includes both the year 2008 and any member of the Date attribute hierarchy. This includes all tuples under and including the year 2008 in the user-defined hierarchy (for example, Q1 2008, Jan 2008, and so on). But instead of assigning a calculation (or a value) to Date and then aggregating up from Date, the logic will be applied directly to such tuples. An interesting illustration is the following scope assignment:

```
SCOPE([Date].[Calendar].[Calendar Year].&[2008],
      [Date].[Date].Members,
      [Measures].[Internet Sales Amount]);
    This = 1;
END SCOPE;
```

Notice that as a result, the Internet Sales Amount measure evaluates to 1 for all tuples that include the year 2008 and any Date member, including the default ALL member. Thus, the Internet Sales Amount measure gets overwritten with 1 for every hierarchy member between Year and Date (inclusive) for the CY 2008 branch of the calendar user-defined hierarchy. This isn't the case here:

```
SCOPE([Date].[Calendar].[Calendar Year].&[2008],
        [Date].[Date].[Date],
        [Measures].[Internet Sales Amount]);
    This = 1;
END SCOPE;
```

Here you actually get the aggregation over dates, and for different months you get the number of days in them instead of just a straightforward overwrite to 1. Because of this, the Month level members show the sum for all dates below them for the Internet Sales Amount measure, which is overwritten to 1. You see 31 for January, 29 for February (yes, 2008 was a leap year), and so on.

In addition to defining simple subcubes, you can further enhance the logic behind scope assignments by nested SCOPE statements. Doing this, you can refine the outer subcube definitions and apply different logic to its parts. The nested SCOPE statements can look like the following statement:

```
SCOPE([Measures].[Internet Sales Amount]);
    SCOPE([Date].[Calendar].[Calendar Year].&[2007]);
        This = [Measures].[Internet Sales Amount]*2;
    END SCOPE;
    SCOPE([Date].[Calendar].[Calendar Year].&[2008]);
        This = [Measures].[Internet Sales Amount]/2;
    END SCOPE;
END SCOPE;
```

In this case SSAS will multiply by 2 the Internet Sales Amount measure for 2007 and will divide it by 2 for 2008. Nested SCOPE statements give you a powerful way to implement conditional logic, which you'd normally do through CASE of IIF statements. Because they contain an explicit definition of subcubes, SSAS can efficiently calculate the expressions. The previous statement can be rewritten in a query to use an IIF call:

```
IIF([Date].[Calendar].CurrentMember IS
        [Date].[Calendar].[Calendar Year].&[2007],
    [Measures].[Internet Sales Amount]*2,
    IIF([Date].[Calendar].CurrentMember IS
            [Date].[Calendar].[Calendar Year].&[2008],
        [Measures].[Internet Sales Amount]/2,
        [Measures].[Internet Sales Amount]
    )
)
```

Such nested IIF statements can obstruct the efforts of the SSAS formula engine to derive the best possible execution path, especially when the logic runs deep and includes nontrivial calculations. In fact, the Formula Engine will still need to determine the subcubes in which the calculation applies and then apply the logic in the IIF branches. Even with the improvements to the IIF function in SQL Server 2008 and later, it's prone to estimating the complexity of the calculations incorrectly and resorting to inefficient algorithms for the calculations. Because of this possible pitfall, it's recommended to use scope assignments for this type of conditional logic.

Summary

Although the topic of context in MDX is wide and deep, understanding scope assignments and set expression context is an essential, core part of it. The demystification of these concepts and a deeper understanding of the reasons for their behavior help in determining the reasons for the outcome of calculation logic, and, from there, the results you obtain from your queries. Although designed to be intuitive, in some cases the complexity and power of MDX doesn't make sense to SSAS developers, and the behavior of similar statements can yield wildly different results. Working with MDX can be difficult but rewarding, and learning its concepts, as well as how SSAS functions, gives you the ability to manipulate vast amounts of data elegantly and efficiently.

About the author

Boyan Penev is a Microsoft MVP who specializes in the Business Intelligence stack of Microsoft SQL Server. He lives in Melbourne, Australia, and has delivered talks at Tech Ed Australia and various other events, including sessions on MDX in front of the Melbourne and Sydney SQL Server User Groups. He also publishes the *Boyan Penev on Microsoft BI* (http://www.bp-msbi.com) blog, which encompasses practical and technical topics from the world of SQL Server Business Intelligence.

56 Using time intelligence functions in PowerPivot

Thiago Zavaschi

PowerPivot is composed of two parts: an add-in that enhances the analytical capabilities of Microsoft Excel 2010 (PowerPivot for Excel) and a component for Share-Point 2010 that allows the deployment of workbooks with PowerPivot for SharePoint. The add-on also allows automated data refresh and control over managed workbooks. This chapter's focus is specifically on the expressions and functions that are used to manipulate data using Data Analysis Expressions (DAX) in Excel.

Introducing Data Analysis Expressions

DAX is an expansion of the native language of formulas from Excel specifically designed to deal with great amounts of relational data while providing ease of use. In the current version, DAX can be used to create new data columns or measures.

Several types of DAX functions are available:

- Date and time
- Filter and value
- Information
- Logical
- Math
- Statistical
- Text
- Time intelligence

The focus in this chapter is on the time intelligence functions and how they're used. Best practices associated with these functions are also discussed.

DAX data types

DAX assumes that the analyzed columns are one of six types:

- Whole number: Integer
- Decimal number: Double precision real number

- Currency: Four decimal places of precision
- TRUE/FALSE: Boolean
- Text: String
- Date: Datetime (starts at March 1, 1900)

Excel provides only two types (Number and String). The main data type discussed here is the Date type, which also stores the time information. Be aware that the Date type can only be used for dates from March 1900 on; prior dates can't be handled this way.

A number of other functions that return entire tables of data are also provided. These functions don't provide the final output of a DAX expression but an intermediate calculation that's used as part of the process of calculating final values.

Sample database

The examples in this chapter will use two datasets from the AdventureWorksDW2008R2 database: one for sales data from the FactInternetSales table and one from the time dimension (DimDate). This database contains data about the sale of bikes and accessories. The queries used to extract data are as follows:

```
SELECT
    dpc.EnglishProductCategoryName,
    dp.EnglishProductName,
    dd.FullDateAlternateKey AS OrderDate,
    fis.SalesAmount
FROM FactInternetSales fis
JOIN DimDate dd
    ON fis.OrderDateKey = dd.DateKey
JOIN DimProduct dp
    ON fis.ProductKey = dp.ProductKey
JOIN DimProductSubcategory dps
    ON dp.ProductSubcategoryKey = dps.ProductSubcategoryKey
JOIN DimProductCategory dpc
    ON dps.ProductCategoryKey = dpc.ProductCategoryKey

SELECT
    FullDateAlternateKey, CalendarYear, MonthNumberOfYear,
    EnglishMonthName, DayNumberOfMonth
    FROM DimDate
```

Time intelligence functions

Most of the analyses performed in PowerPivot are performed using simple aggregations such as SUM or AVERAGE (figure 1), but there are scenarios where more complex operations are needed, such as when analyzing time-specific information related to events.

Categories ▾	Sum of SalesAmount	Average of SalesAmount
Accessories	700759.96	19.42
Bikes	28318144.65	1862.42
Clothing	339772.61	37.33
Total	**29358677.22**	**486.09**

Figure 1   Common DAX use

A set of time intelligence functions are available. These 35 functions can be divided into three groups:

- Functions that return a single date
- Functions that return a table of dates
- Functions that evaluate expressions over a time period

Golden rules

One of the architects from the Analysis Services team, Marius Dumitru, defined a set of rules that are useful when working with time intelligence DAX functions:

1 Never use a datetime column from a fact table in time functions.

When working with PowerPivot, a common mistake is to take the easy path of using datetime columns from fact tables. Unfortunately these columns can contain gaps—which leads us to the second rule.

2 Always create a separate Time table with contiguous dates (without missing day gaps in the date values).

In this example, the database AdventureWorksDW2008R2 has been used as a data source. Fortunately, this database already contains a table for the time dimension (DimDate). When you're working with other data sources, there's usually a need to create a table to hold time dimension data. An example of a T-SQL script that could be used to create a time dimension can be found at http://www.sqlservercentral.com/scripts/Data+Warehousing/30087.

3 Create relationships between fact tables and the Time table.

It's important that the granularity of the fact table is in days (no time information is held); otherwise it's not possible to create the required association (e.g., because 01/07/2011 00:00:00 is different from 01/07/2011 00:00:01).

4 Make sure that relationships are based on a datetime column (and not on another artificial key column).

5 Ensure that at least a full year of data exists in the Time table. For instance, even though a transaction table may only contain sales data up to May 2010, the Time table should have dates up to December 2010. The same rule applies to fiscal year data.

6 The datetime column in the Time table should be stored at day granularity (without fractions of a day).

Now that a set of rules has been established, it's time to learn to work with the time intelligence functions. You'll find examples of how to use many of these functions in the "Samples" section of this chapter.

Functions that return a single date

The following functions operate on one column and return a single date:

- `FIRSTDATE (Date_Column)`
- `LASTDATE (Date_Column)`

OrderDate	STARTOFQUARTER	STARTOFYEAR	ENDOFMONTH
01/07/2005	01/07/2005	01/07/2005	31/07/2005
01/07/2005	01/07/2005	01/07/2005	31/07/2005
01/07/2005	01/07/2005	01/07/2005	31/07/2005
01/07/2005	01/07/2005	01/07/2005	31/07/2005
01/07/2005	01/07/2005	01/07/2005	31/07/2005
02/07/2005	01/07/2005	01/07/2005	31/07/2005
02/07/2005	01/07/2005	01/07/2005	31/07/2005

Figure 2
STARTOFQUARTER,
STARTOFYEAR, and
ENDOFMONTH functions

- FIRSTNONBLANK (Date_Column, Expression)
- LASTNONBLANK (Date_Column, Expression)
- STARTOFMONTH (Date_Column)
- STARTOFQUARTER (Date_Column)
- STARTOFYEAR (Date_Column [,YE_Date])
- ENDOFMONTH (Date_Column)
- ENDOFQUARTER (Date_Column)
- ENDOFYEAR (Date_Column [,YE_Date])

These functions are easy to understand. Figure 2 shows how the STARTOFQUARTER, STARTOFYEAR, and ENDOFMONTH functions can be used to compose new columns. These functions can also be used to compose DAX measures (using the current context of the calculation).

Functions that return a table of dates

Sixteen functions are available that return a table of dates. These are typically used for setting the SetFilter parameter of the CALCULATE function.

The first eight functions return a period relative to the current context (next year, previous month, and so on):

- PREVIOUSDAY (Date_Column)
- PREVIOUSMONTH (Date_Column)
- PREVIOUSQUARTER (Date_Column)
- PREVIOUSYEAR (Date_Column [,YE_Date])
- NEXTDAY (Date_Column)
- NEXTMONTH (Date_Column)
- NEXTQUARTER (Date_Column)
- NEXTYEAR (Date_Column [,YE_Date])

DATESMTD, DATESQTD, and DATESYTD are used to return a table of dates from the start of a month (or quarter, or year) up to the current date (based on the context of the expression, not the time the expression is run), and are commonly used with CALCULATE, as seen in some of the samples that are provided later in the chapter.

- DATESMTD (Date_Column)

- DATESQTD (Date_Column)
- DATESYTD (Date_Column [,YE_Date])

The following functions (which are slightly more complex) are used to change the current data context:

- SAMEPERIODLASTYEAR (Date_Column)
- DATEADD (Date_Column, Number_of_Intervals, Interval)
- DATESBETWEEN (Date_Column, Start_Date, End_Date)
- DATESINPERIOD (Date_Column, Start_Date, Number_of_Intervals, Interval)
- PARALLELPERIOD (Date_Column, Number_of_Intervals, Interval)
- Note that DATEADD is the most frequently used of these functions.

Functions that evaluate expressions over a time period

The final set of functions that are described here allow the evaluation of expressions across frequently used time contexts. For example, the expression CALCULATE (Expression, DATESQTD (Date_Column)[, SetFilter]) can be simplified to TotalQTD (Expression, Date_Column [, SetFilter]).

Here's a list of these functions:

- TOTALMTD (Expression, Date_Column [, SetFilter])
- TOTALQTD (Expression, Date_Column [, SetFilter])
- TOTALYTD (Expression, Date_Column [, SetFilter] [,YE_Date])
- OPENINGBALANCEMONTH (Expression, Date_Column [,SetFilter])
- OPENINGBALANCEQUARTER (Expression, Date_Column [,SetFilter])
- OPENINGBALANCEYEAR (Expression, Date_Column [,SetFilter] [,YE_Date])
- CLOSINGBALANCEMONTH (Expression, Date_Column [,SetFilter])
- CLOSINGBALANCEQUARTER (Expression, Date_Column [,SetFilter])
- CLOSINGBALANCEYEAR (Expression, Date_Column [,SetFilter] [,YE_Date])

Samples

Now that I've described the available time intelligence functions, the best way for you to understand their benefits is through some samples. These samples use data from the AdventureWorks database. To start with, imagine a pivot table such as the one shown (partially) in figure 3.

There might be a need to extract information from the source:

- Sum of sales amount
- The accumulated value of sales amount by quarter
- The accumulated value of sales amount by year

Figure 3 Initial pivot table

Year/Month
2005
7
8
9
10
11
12
2006
1
2
3
4
5
6
7
8
9

- The value from the previous year for comparison
- The percentage of the sales monthly growth amount (month-over-month growth)
- The accumulated value of sales amount by quarter (using `TotalQTD`)

The way that these requirements can be resolved follows:

1 Sum of sales amount

This problem is fairly simple to solve. No time intelligence functions need to be used.

> **NOTE** In DAX measures, it's a good practice to use the format `Table-Name[ColumnName]` when referencing a column from outside the table and to use the name of the column `[MeasureName]` when there's a need to reference the column from within the same table. Doing this also makes the DAX expressions easier to read.

```
= SUM(Sales['SalesAmount'])
```

2 The accumulated value of sales amount by quarter

This can be solved with `TOTALQTD` or by using `CALCULATE` plus `DATESQTD`. A later sample shows how to use `TOTALQTD`, so in this case, our example will use `CALCULATE`.

The `SUM` function needs to be applied to a specific context; to do that, use

```
= CALCULATE(SUM(Sales[SalesAmount]),
            DATESQTD('Date'[FullDateAlternateKey]))
```

3 The accumulated value of sales amount by year

Similar to the previous sample, but use the `DATESYTD` time intelligence function instead of `DATESQTD`:

```
= CALCULATE(SUM(Sales[SalesAmount]),
            DATESYTD('Date'[FullDateAlternateKey]))
```

4 The value from the previous year for comparison

To achieve this, use the `PARALLELPERIOD` function. This function returns a table of dates that are parallel to the given set of dates, offset by a specified interval.

The `CALCULATE` function is used with `SUM(SalesAmount)`, but the filter parameter uses the parallel period.

```
= CALCULATE(SUM(Sales[SalesAmount]),
            PARALLELPERIOD('Date'[FullDateAlternateKey],-12, MONTH))
```

The coolest thing in DAX is the ability to combine different functions. For example, if you need to calculate YTD from the last year, use the solutions from samples 3 and 4 together.

```
= CALCULATE(SUM(Sales[SalesAmount]),DATESYTD(
    PARALLELPERIOD('Date'[FullDateAlternateKey],-12,MONTH)))
```

5 The percentage of the sales monthly growth amount (month-over-month growth)

This task is a bit more complex to solve, because PowerPivot DAX works with columns whereas Excel works with reference to cells.

First, create two measures named [SumTotal] and [PrevMonthTotal]. If a filter is needed, use the CALCULATE and FILTER functions instead of a simple SUM.

```
[SumTotal] = SUM(Sales[SalesAmount])
```

```
[PrevMonthTotal] = CALCULATE([SumTotal],
    DATEADD('Date'[FullDateAlternateKey], -1, MONTH))
```

Now a simple arithmetic operation is needed:

```
[Growth] = ([SumTotal] - [PrevMonthTotal])/[PrevMonthTotal]
```

To avoid a division by 0, use an IF function:

```
[Growth] = IF ([PrevMonthTotal], ([SumTotal] -
    [PrevMonthTotal])/[PrevMonthTotal], BLANK())
```

6 The accumulated value of sales amount by quarter (using TotalQTD)

For convenience, instead of using CALCULATE and DATESQTD, TOTALQTD can be used to obtain the same result:

```
=TOTALQTD(SUM(Sales[SalesAmount]), 'Date'[FullDateAlternateKey])
```

The results of all these DAX functions are shown in figure 4.

Year/Month	Sum of SalesAmount	DATESQTD	DATESYTD	SalesAmount Last Year	YTDLastYear	Growth	TOTALQTD
⊟ 2005	3,266,373.66	1,812,850.77	3,266,373.66			30.09%	1,812,850.77
7	473,388.16	473,388.16	473,388.16				473,388.16
8	506,191.69	979,579.85	979,579.85			6.93%	979,579.85
9	473,943.03	1,453,522.89	1,453,522.89			-6.37%	1,453,522.89
10	513,329.47	513,329.47	1,966,852.36			8.31%	513,329.47
11	543,993.41	1,057,322.88	2,510,845.77			5.97%	1,057,322.88
12	755,527.89	1,812,850.77	3,266,373.66			38.89%	1,812,850.77
⊟ 2006	6,530,343.53	1,327,799.32	6,530,343.53	3,266,373.66	3,266,373.66	-2.66%	1,327,799.32
1	596,746.56	596,746.56	596,746.56			-21.02%	596,746.56
2	550,816.69	1,147,563.25	1,147,563.25			-7.70%	1,147,563.25
3	644,135.20	1,791,698.45	1,791,698.45			16.94%	1,791,698.45
4	663,692.29	663,692.29	2,455,390.74			3.04%	663,692.29
5	673,556.20	1,337,248.48	3,128,946.94			1.49%	1,337,248.48
6	676,763.65	2,014,012.13	3,805,710.59			0.48%	2,014,012.13
7	500,365.15	500,365.16	4,306,075.74	473,388.16	473,388.16	-26.07%	500,365.16
8	546,001.47	1,046,366.63	4,852,077.21	506,191.69	979,579.85	9.12%	1,046,366.63
9	350,466.99	1,396,833.62	5,202,544.20	473,943.03	1,453,522.89	-35.81%	1,396,833.62
10	415,390.23	415,390.23	5,617,934.44	513,329.47	1,966,852.36	18.52%	415,390.23
11	335,095.09	750,485.32	5,953,029.53	543,993.41	2,510,845.77	-19.33%	750,485.32
12	577,314.00	1,327,799.32	6,530,343.53	755,527.89	3,266,373.66	72.28%	1,327,799.32

Figure 4   Final pivot table

Summary

In this chapter, I described the time intelligence functions that are provided as part of the DAX language. These functions are powerful and can ease the task of analysis.

More information about each of the time intelligence functions is provided at http://social.technet.microsoft.com/wiki/contents/articles/powerpivot-dax-time-intelligence-functions.aspx.

About the author

 Thiago Zavaschi is a Microsoft SQL Server MVP, has several Microsoft certifications (MCT, MCTS, MCITP, MCPD), gives technical lectures, helps out in SQL Server and .NET communities, and is a moderator at PowerPivot FAQ. He currently works as a Microsoft SQL Server and business intelligence specialist helping customers and partners to adopt SQL Server solutions. He also writes articles about SQL Server in his blog (http://zavaschi.com, in Portuguese).

57 Easy BI with Silverlight PivotViewer

Gogula Aryalingam

Gone are the times when business intelligence (BI) was one of those things that only large enterprises could afford. More and more smaller organizations are now into BI. Microsoft has in many ways helped this cause. With the introduction of the Unified Dimensional Model (UDM) in SQL Server 2005 Analysis Services, business intelligence for the masses became a reality, or at least a step closer. But building the information base for BI is one thing; building BI information visualization is something else. BI users need to see data for business insight (for that's what BI is all about) that's presented in an intuitive way. Microsoft addresses this through several technologies, one of which is Silverlight PivotViewer.

Presenting Silverlight PivotViewer

Silverlight is Microsoft's implementation of a rich internet application (RIA) framework. It's similar to Adobe Flash and is used to create applications that require a rich web or multimedia user experience. Applications developed using Silverlight can be run on top of most browsers by means of a plug-in. Windows Phone 7 applications are also created using Silverlight.

Silverlight PivotViewer is a visualization tool in the form of a Silverlight control that runs on your browser via the Silverlight plug-in. PivotViewer uses a concept analogous to the nanoparticles (or micro-robots) idea in Michael Crichton's novel *Prey*. It makes use of a large collection of items (usually consisting of images that are related to underlying data) that can be visualized in ways that make sense by organizing them in different ways. The user starts with a high-level view of the entire collection and then zooms in by scrolling with the mouse.

Silverlight PivotViewer is an easy-to-use tool. You can derive business insight from the highest levels, right down to the grain level of business data, in an intuitive manner by clicking and scrolling with the mouse. It also allows for filtering information without effort. In a nutshell, Silverlight PivotViewer is a clever tool that you can give your boss to keep him or her occupied, amused, and happy. Well, at least mine was.

What makes up your pivot

Data for the PivotViewer comes in the form of a Collection XML (CXML) file and an associated collection called a `DeepZoom` collection. The content of the CXML along with that in the `DeepZoom` collection is parsed and rendered as a dynamic graphical pivot by the PivotViewer control.

Cards (or images)

The basic unit of a pivot is an image or more appropriately, a card. A pivot is composed of a large collection of these cards. When you analyze the pivot, you may arrive at an individual card, which is designed to display information from the grain level of your data. Your card may contain an individual image, an image (or multiple images) with

Figure 1   An example of a pivot card

additional textual information appropriately formatted, or textual information formatted in a certain way. Take, for instance, the data card from one of the samples dedicated to endangered animals from the PivotViewer site (figure 1). It displays not only the picture of an animal, but also its scientific name (main text), conservation status (top right), map of habitat (bottom left), and background color indicating its class. A pivot can also be created with plain pictures involving your subject area, as mentioned earlier.

Now when you click on the card you're presented with an Info panel with more information and (optionally) links so that you can navigate to another pivot (or another view of the same pivot) that has related information. Continuing with the same example, when you click on the name of the animal's class, as shown in figure 2, it will take you to a view of all animals in that class. Each piece of information is called a *facet*, and the groupings of these facets are called *facet categories*.

Figure 2   The Info panel

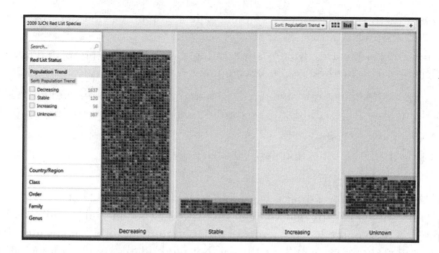

**Figure 3
PivotViewer**

Slicing and dicing options

The initial view of the pivot is one large rectangle made up of miniature cards, called the Grid view. When you zoom in by scrolling with your mouse, the images get bigger, providing a close-up view of the cards. But the grid view doesn't give you much. Clicking the Graph view icon provides a much better way of slicing and dicing the pivot. In the graph view, cards are grouped into a bar chart format where you can select the group you want and drill into it (see figure 3).

Filtering and sorting options

Toward the left of the PivotViewer you have the Filter panel, where the facet categories are listed. You can select the values in this section to see the pivot dynamically change to display the filtered results. You can also make use of the free-form text box to search for a particular piece of text. Sort the data cards on the various facet categories by selecting from the Sort drop-down.

The way to go

Let's start getting our hands dirty...

Which seat should I take?

To create the pivot, you need to generate a CXML and its associated `DeepZoom` collection. Choose among the following three ways, with their varying degrees of difficulty and flexibility:

- *Simple*—Involves one pivot, where you can have up to 3,000 cards.
- *Linked*—Involves multiple pivots, where you can link pivots with each other. For instance, you can have a pivot of cars for sale, and another with all the car marts. The cars pivot would hold cards of the different cars that are available, with each card holding a link saying "car marts." When clicked, the link will

open up the car marts pivot, automatically slicing into a view of cards of the car marts that sell that particular car.

- *Just-in-time*—Involves dynamically creating the CXML and the related image collections. This method results in complex development requirements.

To stay true to the title of this chapter, let's focus only on the simple and linked methods. Building your CXML (and DeepZoom collections) can be done in three ways:

- Using the Excel add-in
- Using the Pivot Collection Tool (also known as pauthor)
- Hardcore programming

Using the Excel add-in method is way too simple and not flexible at all. This option doesn't offer much except that you can use it to do your learning and preliminary research and development. The hardcore programming method goes against the gist of the chapter. Therefore, you'll use the pauthor method to generate your CXMLs and collections. Pauthor isn't a Microsoft-developed tool but one hosted on CodePlex and developed independently. Yet pauthor is talked about in the Microsoft PivotViewer learning site, which recommends its use for pivot generation.

The source

The source for your pivot can be anything as long as you can pull out the data onto a specially formatted Excel workbook. Because the emphasis here is on Microsoft technologies, the preferred source would be an Analysis Services (SSAS) cube or a SQL Server data mart/warehouse. This is so, because almost always, a BI platform would be one of these. The Excel workbook is critical for working with pauthor. Pauthor uses the data from the Excel workbook to generate the CXML file and the related DeepZoom collection. When generating, any images that are mentioned in the Excel workbook will be picked up from the computer. Therefore, the paths of these images also have to be included in the Excel workbook.

Preparation

There are a few things you need to prepare before implementation:

- HTML template of the card
- Excel workbook design
- PivotViewer hosting

HTML TEMPLATE

The HTML template is required to display static content on each card. Creating an HTML template with placeholders for the picture and additional data would look something like this:

```
<!DOCTYPE html PUBLIC "-//W3C//DTD XHTML 1.0 Transitional//EN"
     "http://www.w3.org/TR/xhtml1/DTD/xhtml1-transitional.dtd">
<html xmlns="http://www.w3.org/1999/xhtml">
```

```html
<head>
    <!-- size: 1200,720 -->
    <meta http-equiv="Content-Type" content="text/html;   charset=utf-8" />
    <title>Cars</title>
    <link href="styles.css" rel="stylesheet" type="text/css" />
</head>
<body>
    <div class="{redListStatus}">

        <div class="imageStyle" style="padding-left:5px">
            <img src="{image}" border="0"/>
        </div>

        <div class="body_wrapper">
            <div style="nameStyle">{name}</div>
            <div style="classStyle">{class}</div>
        </div>
    </div>
</body>
</html>
```

In this code snippet, notice the pieces of text within curly braces, such as {image}, {name}, {class}, and {red_list_status}. These are the placeholders for the business data coming in from the Excel file. They should share the same name as field names from the items sheet of the Excel workbook, mentioned later in this chapter. You could take advantage of CSS in order to impressively design your template.

Next you need to decide what needs to be in each section of your pivot control:

- Decide on the additional data that needs to be on the Info panel of each card.
- Decide on the facet categories that need to be displayed on the Filter panel.
- Decide on the facet categories that need to be in the Sort drop-down.
- Design the Excel workbook as per pauthor requirements

EXCEL WORKBOOK DESIGN

The Excel workbook should have three sheets:

- *collection*—Describes the entire collection as a set. This sheet (see figure 4) has a value only for the name field. The rest, because they're optional, are left blank.

	A	B	C	D	E	F
1	name	icon	brand_image	additional_search_text	copyright_title	copyright_url
2	Species					
3						

Figure 4 Excel workbook

- *facet_categories*—Describes the facet categories. The name field specifies the name of the category. The other fields are for data types, formatting, and sorting options. This sheet (see figure 5) also describes which facet category goes where in the various sections of the PivotViewer through the is...visible fields:

  - is_filter_visible—Indicates whether the facet category appears in the Filter panel.

	A	B	C	D	E	F	G	H
1	name	type	format	is_filter_visible	is_metadata_visible	is_wordwheel_visible	sort_name	sort_values
2	red_list_status	String		TRUE	TRUE	TRUE		
3	population_trend	String		FALSE	TRUE	FALSE		
4	class	Link		TRUE	TRUE	TRUE		
5	order	Link		TRUE	TRUE	TRUE		

Figure 5   Describes the facet categories

- is_metadata_visible—Indicates whether the facet category appears in the Info panel.
- is_wordwheel_visible—Indicates whether the values from the facet category appear in the text filter box as you type in filter values. The text filter box is part of the Filter panel.
- *items*—Contains the data for the pivot. Each facet category appears as a field and the values are populated here from the source as rows (see figure 6).

	A	B	C	D	E	
1	name	image	red_list_status	population_trend	class	order
2	Pygmy Raccoon	images\pygmy_raccoon.png	Critically Endangered	Decreasing	Mammals||Species?class=Mammals	Carnivorous||S
3	Grevy's Zebra	images\grevys_zebra	Endangered	Stable	Mammals||Species?class=Mammals	Grazing||Spec

Figure 6   Each facet category appears as a field.

If you look closely at the class field in figure 6, you'll notice the value Mammals|| Species?class=Mammals. This is a link to another sheet or another view of the same sheet. Let's take this line apart: the value Mammals before the double pipes indicates the value to display. The value Species indicates the name of the pivot that the value should link to. The ?class value indicates the field of the pivot that needs to be matched for the value succeeding the equals symbol, which is Mammals. In the Info panel, this will display a link stating Mammals. When clicked, the pivot will change to a view displaying all the mammals in the collection.

HOSTING THE PIVOT

The PivotViewer control needs to be hosted on an ASP.NET page. You can then include the page with the preferred application.

Implementation

Now that you've done the grunt work to define your collections, it's time for you to generate your pivot:

1 Extract data from the source to the Excel workbook.
2 Run pauthor to generate the CXMLs and collections.

You probably want these two tasks to happen one after the other and on a scheduled basis. Consider attaching the two processes at the end if you have a weekend or month-end data load process happening to your data mart/warehouse.

There may be scenarios where you have a need for real-time pivots. This will be an issue due to the time it takes for the collections to be generated. Depending on the number of cards, you could opt for a day's or week's latency. If in any case you (or the boss/client) insist on real-time data, then just-in-time is your solution, although it involves some complex coding.

Extracting data from the source to Excel can be done through SQL Server Integration Services (SSIS) to make things simpler. SSIS is a flexible tool that allows you to pull data from various types of sources, especially if you don't have a data mart/warehouse. You create separate packages for each Excel workbook that you have; this makes it easier for troubleshooting. Because pauthor is a command-line utility, you can use the Execute Process task in SSIS to construct the command to generate the CXML and collections from Excel and execute that command. Pauthor has the ability to generate collections from Excel, CSV, and pre-created CXMLs. An example of creating collections from an Excel workbook looks like this:

```
pauthor.exe /source excel "C:\Pivot\Excels\Cars.xlsx" /target deepzoom
 "C:\Pivot\DeepZoom\Cars.cxml" /html-template "C:\Pivot\Excels\Cars.html"
 log > "C:\Pivot\DeepZoom\Cars.log"
```

Here, the `source` and `target` switches indicate the source and destination where the generation will happen. Pauthor allows you to convert between any of these types: `excel`, `csv`, `deepzoom`, and `cxml`. CSVs are files with comma-separated values; the difference between the latter two types is that `cxml` refers to a CXML file that has images that are normal images in the local computer and `deepzoom` refers to a CXML file with a collection of associated `DeepZoom` pieces. The `html-template` switch indicates the HTML template that needs to be used to create the cards for the collection.

The locations of the files are important when executing pauthor. Because the images will be inserted into the cards, it's essential that images be located in the same folder as the HTML template if the Excel file has relative paths for the images.

Equally important is that once you've generated a `DeepZoom` collection the first time, always delete the entire collection before generating the collection again. Otherwise, you're bound to get undesirable results if data has changed in between. Deleting the folder is a time-consuming task, because thousands of `DeepZoom` files (or pieces) are created for a collection. You could use the `rmdir` command with the `/S /Q` switches to delete all content including subfolders. You could also rename the `DeepZoom` folder (which would happen almost instantaneously) and delete it at another time.

Figure 7 shows a high-level overview of the ETL for a simple BI solution using Silverlight PivotViewer.

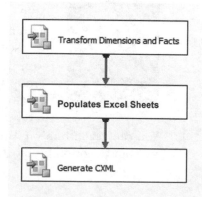

Figure 7   The ETL process

First, we have an ETL process transforming the business data to a dimensional model. Next, this data is pumped onto the Excel for pivoting. Finally, the CXMLs and DeepZooms are generated. Going further into the final step (see figure 8), you first have the old DeepZooms removed and then DeepZooms for each pivot generated separately.

At this point, you should be able to launch the pivot through your ASP.NET page and see new data.

Summary

This chapter explained how you can use PivotViewer to build a simple yet intuitive BI tool. The PivotViewer home page (http://www.microsoft.com/silverlight/pivotviewer/) and the learning site (http://www.silverlight.net/learn/pivotviewer/) give you a plethora of information and documentation.

PivotViewer Extension for Reporting Services is a tool from Microsoft for dynamically generating collections off business intelligence data and then publishing it on SharePoint 2010 via a webpart. As of this writing, the PivotViewer Extension is in CTP2 (community technology preview).

PivotViewer for SharePoint is a tool developed independently and available on CodePlex. This tool pulls out data from SharePoint lists and dynamically generates a pivot based on them.

Figure 8   DeepZooms generation

About the author

Hailing from Sri Lanka, Gogula Aryalingam has been a SQL Server MVP since 2008. Gogula is an MCITP in database development, administration, and business intelligence. He's the co-founder of the SQL Server Sri Lanka User Group (SS SLUG), which he runs with three other MVPs. Gogula co-founded and operates the user group's parent community website, SQLServerUniverse.com.

Gogula works as a SQL Server and BI trainer and has conducted several technical training sessions for a number of organizations. You can reach him on Twitter (@gogula), on LinkedIn (http://www.linkedin.com/in/gogula), or on his blog (http://dbantics.wordpress.com).

58 Excel as a BI frontend tool

Pedro Perfeito

The amount of business data is increasing exponentially, and computers and technology have made the world move faster. Uninformed decisions may be the result of a world moving faster than the minds of the decision makers, who increasingly need business intelligence (BI) systems.

The concept of BI is related to the ability to provide quality information at the right time to all layers of an organization (strategic, tactical, and operational), making it more competitive today than yesterday and more competitive tomorrow than today. The term was officially coined in 1989 by Howard Dresner, but the practices inherent in this concept have always been present in our daily lives. For Microsoft, BI is "getting the right information, to the right decision makers, at the right time." In the economic world crisis, a new phrase should be added to the original definition: "at lower cost." At lower cost and user-friendly, a tool like Excel could be a good option in the BI frontend spectrum.

This chapter explains the construction of an Excel dashboard from an IT and business perspective in a retail sector scenario. It isn't intended to show the best way to create a dashboard for the retail sector, but to describe some tips and tricks for a low-cost dashboard using a familiar tool commonly implemented across organizations: Excel.

Key points to consider when choosing a BI frontend tool

Frontend and *backend* are terms used to describe program interfaces. A frontend interface is one that users interact with directly, and a backend application or program serves indirectly to support the frontend services. An important point to remember is that the focus of a BI frontend tool should be the business processes and not the tool/software, which is just a commodity. Nevertheless, choosing a BI frontend tool should be based on several factors:

- Cost of ownership
- Corporate reporting needs

- Implementation costs
- Compliance with existing systems

Considering these factors, Excel 2010 seems to be the strongest candidate for a preferred tool. It's certainly true that Excel 2010 doesn't yet have the design features of some BI frontend competitors, but its low cost and acceptance from end users are big advantages. Naturally, there are huge commercial interests in favor of more robust solutions that generally stand by their promises, but the return on investment (ROI) is the issue.

Why Excel?

No matter how good and sophisticated a BI tool is, business users will invariably export data to Excel. They aren't concerned with the IT perspective and data integrity, because they want to get the data right now! Microsoft has acknowledged this trend and introduced an amazing and powerful Excel add-on named PowerPivot. This add-on provides the capability to process millions of rows using client resources. Could you imagine the chaos that could ensue?

This freedom goes against what companies have been fighting for in previous decades. But we all know that users like Excel, and if we can't change that, why don't we give them what they want with proper data management and enforcement of proper practices and standards? In defense of Excel, there are several factors in its favor:

- Organizations spend lots of money on BI frontend tools. They need low-cost and simple solutions that business users love and really use.
- Business users know Excel, so they can save the time and expense involved in learning a new tool.
- Office is one of Microsoft's main strategies; therefore, Excel discontinuation is not probable, even in the most pessimistic minds.

Assumptions

Naturally, there are some assumptions to meet the conditions necessary to implement this dashboard:

- All the data quality activities were performed during the ETL process responsible for extracting, transforming, and loading data from operational systems into a data warehouse.
- All the information provided in the dashboard is stored and integrated in OLAP cubes.
- All the data security rules were implemented in the OLAP cube.
- The dashboard was planned and validated by the business users.
- Dashboards don't need millions of rows. Their purpose is to display aggregated information to make decisions and not to display transactional data.

In essence, Excel should always be the destination of data and never the source.

Why use OLAP as a source?

The term *online analytical processing* (OLAP) was coined in 1993 by Ted Codd and is associated with decision support systems used for business analysis. With OLAP, business users can analyze and manipulate the information in various ways in the form of a cube. The most important advantages of OLAP tools are the intuitive multidimensional structure that brings an intuitive perspective of the business to end users, the fact that questions involving mountains of data can be answered within a few milliseconds, and finally the easy creation of complex calculations, particularly along the time dimension.

In addition to the previous advantages, and because we're using Excel, "the one version of the truth" also offers the following key benefits:

- IT can still control and ensure quality and security data rules.
- We avoid the duplication of data through several departments and teams.
- All the centralized work in the OLAP cube can be reused by other BI frontend tools, including those that may have more requirements in some specific or complex scenarios. All metrics and calculations are made centrally and are shared by individuals, teams, or departments. This effort will be made by those who have such knowledge and are aligned with the standards and objectives of the organization.
- Allowed new requirements are controlled by a BICC or IT department. Nevertheless, end users should have autonomy to explore information and even to make some XMLA updates into cubes through a controlled and automated channel (power users only).

Dashboard Implementation

Dashboard implementations tend to be divided into two areas: technology and business. BI consultants should be positioned between these two worlds in order to be successful with their BI implementations.

The business perspective

When designing a dashboard, it's important that you consider exactly what information is required and how it should be represented graphically. BI vendors provide several options for creating amazing dashboard layouts, which vary from business to business, even in the same process.

The dashboard design often assumes minor importance in a BI implementation and is usually planned by IT people. Decision makers are easily swayed by a beautiful design, often without concern as to how it was achieved. Complex functionality and design don't accommodate every problem. It's preferable to maintain a clean and useful dashboard instead of using it as decoration, which could be amazing but not useful for business.

Putting yourself in the mindset of a decision maker is an important step in creating a successful dashboard with end user acceptance. It's necessary that the metrics and key performance indicators (KPIs) be those desired by and useful for people who make decisions every day.

KEY BUSINESS METRICS

The retail company modeled in this example has several stores spread around Portugal, and monitoring and controlling the progress of each one are essential. It's therefore important that a BI system expose its sales process efficiently. Following is a list of the main metrics used to monitor the sales performance of each store. It's assumed that the budget process was already realized and the targets for the metrics were already settled. The metrics applied to this scenario are as follows:

- Sales amount, representing the total sales in a given period.
- Number of tickets or transactions realized in a given period.
- Number of visitors to each store for a given period.
- Conversion rate, representing the ratio between the number of visitors and tickets. It tracks how many visitors to the store are turned into customers.
- Average basket, representing the total sales amount for a given period divided by the number of baskets for the same period.
- Items per basket, representing the average number of items in each transaction for a given period. It measures the salesperson's ability to add to a sale.
- Gross margin, representing the total amount of sales minus the cost (brand dependency).

The technology perspective

Excel 2010 has strong new features that bring to end users the ability to create their own dashboards without a single line of code. Any user could connect to an OLAP cube and create a dashboard similar to the one described in this chapter. End users need freedom and the chance to get business answers through self-service systems like the one proposed here, where IT controls the data, has it all centralized and integrated, and assures quality. The BI team should resist the temptation to implement a dashboard without carefully describing it conceptually. The way information is presented in one screen and the way the data model is structured are important to ensure the success of the dashboard.

DIMENSIONAL MODEL

The data model usually applied to BI implementations is the dimensional model introduced by Ralph Kimball. This model is exclusively created for decision support systems, and in the design process the following three points should be considered:

- *Performance*—The model should be designed for faster answers to business queries. To achieve it, a denormalized model suggested by Ralph Kimball, known as star-schema, has proven effective. (Although beneficial, denormalization isn't mandatory.)
- *Flexibility*—The model should allow for structural changes to accommodate future needs, but it should also provide autonomy and freedom to business users to select the information they want when they want it.
- *Intuitive*—The model should provide a clean and simple layout to enable business users to easily navigate through the business model in search of information

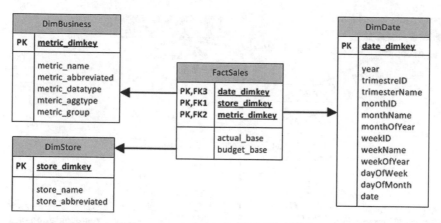

Figure 1   The physical dimensional model (Data Mart)

they need. Some examples would be the use of the smallest number of dimensions possible (creating dimension hierarchies), short and clean attribute names, and the display of only those items that need to be displayed.

Our retail company has sales data according to the model shown in figure 1. This model has been designed to reflect the three principles just described.

In the dimensional model, the DimBusiness dimension was created to enable a more flexible perspective for the business. Apart from exploring information from typical dimensions like DimDate, DimCustomer, DimStore, DimSupplier, DimProducts, and others, DimBusiness also lets you explore the metrics context in a hierarchical way as typically structured in a balanced scorecard. In figure 2, you can

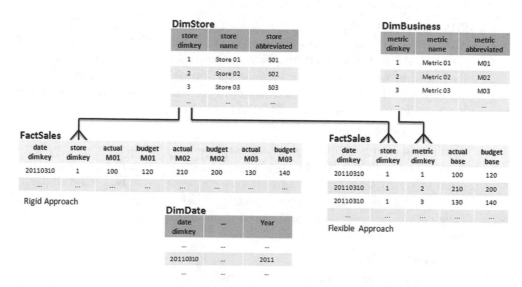

Figure 2   Dimensional model with some values entered to show the two different approaches

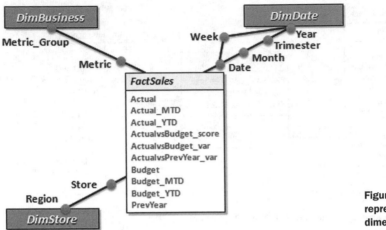

Figure 3   Semantic representation of the dimensional model

compare and evaluate two different approaches that could have been applied in the dimensional model.

This chapter follows the more flexible approach and requires just two metrics (actual_base and budget_base) in the physical model, as shown in figure 1. Furthermore, the calculations on the cube could be reused for all the metrics that exist in the DimBusiness dimension. These calculations provide end users with more answers to business questions, mainly through the date dimension, and can be seen in the semantic model shown in figure 3, which is exactly the information model end users will see.

The word *intuitive* should always be in the mind of those who will plan, design, and implement a dashboard. The intuitive way the dashboard is structured, the intuitive way information is displayed, and the intuitive way layout/navigation is made available to the business are critical success factors.

INTUITIVE STRUCTURE

The dashboard will fit the entire screen in just one worksheet. Each answer displayed in the dashboard is created in a different worksheet and uses a different pivot table. Each answer will be added to the main worksheet as a table, chart, or image. At the end, slicers will be linked to each answer in the dashboard, and the worksheets where the questions were answered will be hidden from view.

INTUITIVE INFORMATION

At the end of this chapter, the dashboard applied to this retail case scenario will be shown. The steps described next will help you create a similar one. The first step is to open Excel 2010 and create a connection to the OLAP cube placed under a multidimensional database located on a SQL Server Analysis Services (SSAS) server. This OLAP cube connection will be reused each time a business question is answered in a worksheet.

Add a pivot table

1 Rename the worksheet Sheet1 to DASHBOARD.
2 Create the OLAP cube connection through Menu > Data > From Other Sources.

3 Add a pivot table to the worksheet and add the following metrics: Actual, Pre-vYear (rename to N-1), ActualvsPrevYear_var (rename to %N-1), Budget, and ActualvsBudget_var (rename to % Budget).

4 Drag Store Name to the row labels, and drag Metric Name, CalendarMonth, Month of Year, and Day of Month to the Report Filter.

Add slicers

Slicers are an amazing new feature of Excel 2010 that are useful for filtering the information that comes from the OLAP cube. You can create a slicer for each dimension attribute of the dimensional model created previously. Place your cursor over the pivot table created in the previous step and choose Menu > PivotTable Tools > Options > Insert Slicer.

Then create slicers for the following dimension attributes: Year, Month of Year, Week Name, Day of Month, and Store Name.

Add a header

It's important to include a header in the dashboard to better convey the context of the business process that will be analyzed through it. This way, users will remain aware of the name of the business process and the granularity of the information being analyzed from the dimensions (date level, month level, country level).

The header example in figure 4 shows the business process name (Sales Dashboard), the granularity of DimStore (All level—Country Overview), and the granularity of DimDate (Date level—28-March-2011).

`="(" & IF(D8<>"All";D8 & " - ";"") & IF(D7<>"All";D7 & " - ";"") & D6 & ")"`

Sales Dashboard (Country Overview)   (28 - March - 2011)

**Figure 4
Dashboard header**

The date label in the header is an Excel formula that reads the selected data from the pivot table Report Filter when the user selects the existing slicers. The formula is simple:

`="(" & IF(D8<>"All";D8 & "-";"") & IF(D7<>"All";D7 & "-";"") & D6 & ")"`

Add in-cell data bars (for negative and positive values)

To rapidly highlight the strong and weak variations in the metrics, add an in-cell data bar. Apply this conditional formatting functionality to the metrics already added to the pivot table: %N-1 and %Budget. These two metrics show the variation in percentage of Actual compared to Budget and Previous Year (N-1) values; see figure 5.

	Actual	N-1	% N-1	Budget	% Budget	Month
Store 01	7.902 €	2.721 €	190,4%	8.400 €	-5,9%	
Store 02	7.129 €	9.176 €	-22,3%	10.600 €	32,7%	
Store 03	19.083 €	10.671 €	78,8%	19.800 €	-3,6%	
Store 04	11.242 €	5.909 €	90,3%	15.400 €	27,0%	
Store 05	10.477 €	6.011 €	74,3%	13.500 €	22,4%	
Store 06	2.276 €	1.998 €	13,9%	2.800 €	18,7%	
Store 07	9.374 €	6.254 €	49,9%	7.600 €	23,3%	
	67.483 €	42.740 €	57,9%	78.100 €	13,6%	

**Figure 5
The data bar for negative and positive variations of Actual compared to N-1 and Budget**

Select the cells to which you want to apply the data bar, and in the Main menu on the Home tab expand Conditional Formatting > Data Bars > Gradient Fill; then click Green Data Bar.

Add Sparklines

The term *Sparkline* was introduced by Professor Edward Tufte in his book *Beautiful Evidence.* He proposes Sparklines for "small, high resolution graphics embedded in a context of words, numbers, and images." Tufte describes Sparklines as "data-intense, design-simple, word-sized graphics." Microsoft implemented Tufte's idea in Excel 2010, which includes three types of small charts: line, column, and win/loss charts.

A Sparkline provides additional insight when applied to a long series of a specific metric combined with the same metric aggregated in time. In Excel you need to create a new pivot table to get the Sparkline at a low level of detail, and then copy it to the main pivot table created in the first step. In this case, a Sparkline is required to display the positive and negative actual under-budget value variations along a specific month selected in the Month of Year slicer.

1 Add a new worksheet to the Excel file, and rename it `AUX_Sparklines`.

2 Open the existing OLAP cube connection, and add a pivot table to this worksheet.

3 Drag ActualvsBudget_var to the metrics zone.

4 Drag Metric Name and Calendar Month to the Report Filter, Day of Month to the column labels, and Store Name to the row labels.

5 Select entire records for all stores, and in the rightmost cell of the pivot table, add a Sparkline of type Win/Loss. Figure 6 shows the result and the other two types of Sparklines that could be created and included in the Excel dashboard.

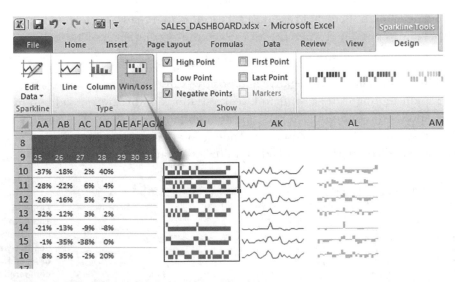

Figure 6   The three different types of Excel Sparklines

6 Because you need the Sparkline in the worksheet where the dashboard is created, repeat the previous step, and when prompted for the Location Range, set it to an appropriate value to have it displayed in the dashboard.

Add a bullet graph

The bullet graph was introduced by the visualization design expert Stephen Few, and his idea was to replace gauges and speedometer decorations that are often used in dashboards. Bullet graphs are easier to interpret, convey much more information, and have a simple structure comprising a text label, a quantitative scale along an axis, a base measure (for example, Actual), and a comparative measure (for example, Budget, N-1). The following steps demonstrate how to create a bullet graph in Excel 2010.

1 Add a new worksheet to the Excel file, and rename it `AUX_BulletGraph`.
2 Open the existing OLAP cube connection, and add a pivot table to this worksheet.
3 Drag the metric ActualvsBudget_score to the values area.
4 Drag the attribute Metric Name from the dimension DimBusiness to the pivot table row labels and delete Grand Totals.
5 Copy and paste the slicers you want to link to the bullet graph, and connect them to the pivot table through the Pivot Table Connections of each slicer.
6 Convert the pivot table to formulas and add three new columns, adding ranges to the chart.
7 Add a horizontal stacked bar chart, as shown in figure 7, and delete the legend.
8 Rename the chart title to `Sales Key Metrics` and change the font size to 14.
9 Set the chart height to 6.5 cm and the width to 10 cm.
10 Change the color of the series from dark gray to light gray or from red to green.

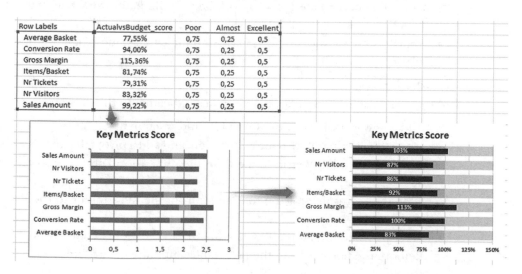

Row Labels	ActualvsBudget_score	Poor	Almost	Excellent
Average Basket	77,55%	0,75	0,25	0,5
Conversion Rate	94,00%	0,75	0,25	0,5
Gross Margin	115,36%	0,75	0,25	0,5
Items/Basket	81,74%	0,75	0,25	0,5
Nr Tickets	79,31%	0,75	0,25	0,5
Nr Visitors	83,32%	0,75	0,25	0,5
Sales Amount	99,22%	0,75	0,25	0,5

Figure 7 The bullet graph implementation in Excel 2010

11 Right-click under the series of actual values and select Format Data Series.

12 In Series Options tab, in the Plot Series On field, set this series to Secondary Axis, and in the Gap With field, set the value to 150%.

13 Delete the upper axis of the chart.

14 Set the font size of the axis (Percentages) to 8 and style it as bold.

15 Set the axis minimum to 0 and maximum to 1.5, set the major unit to 0.25, and format it as %.

16 Select one of the other series under the chart (not Actual) and set the GAP to 50%.

Add bar charts

A bar chart consists of rectangular bars with lengths proportional to the values that they represent. The bars can be plotted horizontally or vertically, and the color can be used to associate additional information with each bar. In this case, we'll create two bar charts, one for comparing sales amounts to those of the previous year and budget and another to rank sales by the sales amount achieved (other metrics should be used for a better ranking).

1 Add a new worksheet to the Excel file, and name it `AUX_SalesCompare`.

2 Open the existing OLAP cube connection, and add a pivot table to this worksheet.

3 Drag the attribute Metric Name from the dimension DimBusiness to the Report Filter.

4 Filter the pivot table by the Sales Amount value.

5 Select the metrics Actual, Budget, and PrevYear to compare the actual sales amount in a vertical bar chart.

6 Copy the chart created in this worksheet to the main worksheet named DASH-BOARD.

7 Repeat these steps (using the Sales Amount actual value in a new worksheet) to create a ranking bar chart for country stores.

Add KPIs

Add the two most important key performance indicators to the dashboard:

1 Add a new worksheet to the Excel file, and rename it `AUX_KPIs`.

2 Open the existing OLAP cube connection, and add a pivot table to this worksheet.

3 Drag the attribute Metric Name from the dimension DimBusiness to the Rows label.

4 Drag the Status field of the KPI_Metric from the KPI's folder to the Pivot Table values area.

5 Filter just Sales Amount and Gross Margin in the Metric Name drop-down list.

6 Remove the borders from the pivot table, and hide the gridlines from this worksheet.

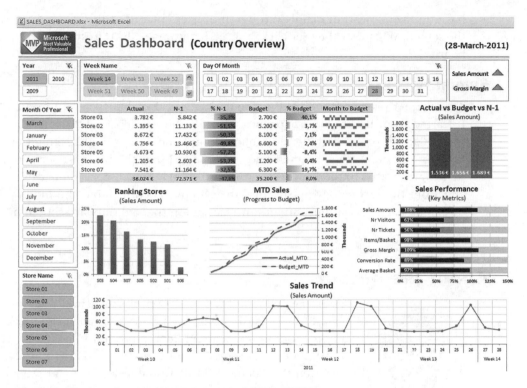

Figure 8   The completed dashboard created with Excel 2010

7 Use a new Excel feature called Camera Tool to take a snapshot of selected cells' Metric Names plus the icon that indicates performance.

8 Paste the snapshot into the DASHBOARD worksheet, as shown in figure 8, and update the dashboard slicers' connections to the pivot table created in this step.

Additional tips to make information more intuitive:

▪ Always include chart legends or titles to let your users quickly understand each series. Apply formats to the metrics, such as currency and percentages, and remove the decimal places from them.

▪ Display to the user just what they want to see. If there's any attribute in the dimensional model that the user doesn't want, just hide it (for example, dimension/surrogate keys, attributes that are already available from a hierarchy, and so on).

▪ Design the dashboard in grayscale, not only because there are end users with color blindness, but also because dashboards are frequently printed in grayscale.

INTUITIVE LAYOUT/NAVIGATION

Figure 8 is the result of all the tips and tricks described in the previous steps. The layout seems clean and actionable from the business user's perspective. Furthermore, it has intuitive navigation mainly through the slicers placed at the top and left side of the screen. Whenever the user clicks a slicer, it automatically refreshes the entire dashboard.

Summary

This chapter presented a set of tips and tricks to use Excel 2010 as a BI frontend tool. It started from the theory perspective to justify the use of Excel 2010 with an OLAP source, and it proceeded into a dashboard implementation, highlighting the importance of the two worlds: business and technology. From the business perspective, the person/team who implements the dashboard should have a decision-maker mindset, and from the technology perspective, they should keep in mind the intuitive structure, intuitive information, and intuitive navigation that a dashboard should have.

About the author

 Pedro Perfeito was born in 1977 in Portugal and currently works as a BI consultant at Novabase. He's also an invited teacher in master and postgraduate BI degree programs, by IUL-ISCTE (Lisbon) and UPT (Porto), respectively. In 2010 and 2011, he received the Microsoft Most Valuable Professional (MVP) award for his dedication and contribution to theoretical and practical issues in the various BI communities.

He has several Microsoft certifications including MCP, MCSD, MCTS-Web, MCTS-BI, and MCITP-BI and also worldwide certifications in the area of BI provided by TDWI/CBIP (The Data Warehouse Institute, www.tdwi.org). He's currently preparing for his PhD in BI. For further information you can visit his personal blog at www.pedrocgd.blogspot.com or even contact him directly at pperfeito@hotmail.com.

59 Real-time BI with StreamInsight

Allan Mitchell

In this chapter, we're going to look at a product that was new to the SQL Server suite in 2008 R2. That product is StreamInsight, Microsoft's first iteration of a complex event processing (CEP) engine. Don't worry if you've never heard this term; by the end of the chapter, everything will become clear, and you'll be thinking about ways to use it in your business. This chapter begins by introducing the architecture of StreamInsight and showing how it might be used. Following this introduction, the focus of the chapter is on the heavy lifting of the analytics: the querying of the streams. Being able to write your CEP applications in languages such as C# and leverage existing developer potential means that building an application and processing events can be achieved quickly. Later in this chapter, we'll further explore what a developer needs to know to build a successful and flexible StreamInsight application.

We'll start with some basics before moving on to some quite powerful design patterns and windowing of data.

What is StreamInsight?

StreamInsight is a complex event-processing engine from Microsoft that allows developers to write applications that can process potentially high-volume, low-latency streams of events within the business. StreamInsight is a .NET framework that allows you to write applications that can respond efficiently, in close to real time, to events occurring in your business. Businesses can obtain insight into the business events by being able to source, query, analyze, and react to potentially tens of thousands of events per second. They can then proactively drive decision making across the enterprise based on this insight. StreamInsight's query language is Language Integrated Query, or LINQ.

What are events and event streams?

Everyday events happen all the time in your business. Some of the types of events you can encounter are listed here, but this list is by no means exhaustive:

- Taking an order
- Sensor readings
- Reading RFID tags in your warehouse
- Placing trades
- Placing a bet
- ATM transactions

The power of StreamInsight is in its ability to easily consolidate varying events, stream inputs, and static data sources, providing a more comprehensive decision-making mechanism than viewing one source at a time.

To illustrate, these events could be considered as a cloud of events. CEP engines look into this cloud of events in order to determine relationships and derive analytics from what they find. Another important concept of event streams is that they're potentially unbounded: they have a beginning, but possibly no discernable end. This makes asking for the sum of an attribute in your event stream more challenging than querying an RDBMS. In the current version of StreamInsight, the payload of an event is somewhat limited. Although it supports most of the .NET scalar and elementary data types, nested types aren't permitted. This can, on occasion, lead to some interesting design choices.

Event shapes

Events in StreamInsight come in different shapes, and each one is designed around the shape of a real-world event. Choosing a shape depends on your needs, but the vast majority of examples you'll see are of the point shape. Later, I'll show you how to make this event shape look like the other two listed here, but first, I'll define these event shapes:

- *Point*—A point event is valid for a single point in time; its start time and end time are separated by one tick (formally referred to as one cronon). This shape is used when something is valid in the real world only for the time the event happened, an example being an RFID tag being read in your warehouse.
- *Interval*—The interval shape is used when you know the start and end times of an event. The developer must specify the start and end times of the event on the event header.
- *Edge*—The edge event shape is used when you know that an event has started but you have no idea when it will finish. The end time is open ended. This pattern is most often seen when looking at reference data.

Deployment

So, how do you take your CEP application and use it within your environment? Thankfully, the StreamInsight team has provided flexible methods for deploying your StreamInsight applications, enabling you to deploy the best solution for the best situation.

- *Hosted server*—This method allows for the publishing of a stream of data in real time in a centralized place. Think of it as a fire hose. A developer then can create a StreamInsight client, which connects to this hosted, publishing server and consumes the stream of events. The client can then apply filters and extra logic to the stream as required. Other clients can connect to the same stream and manipulate it in completely different ways. This is a flexible architecture that allows the client to drive the pattern in the events for which they're searching and also distributes the development of applications.
- *Embedded server*—This method could be deployed as an application or a Windows service. Everything the CEP application needs to do is encapsulated inside the application or service, which makes a tight, atomic unit for deployment. This is the model commonly found on the web when searching for examples of CEP code and applications using StreamInsight.

Architecture

StreamInsight is built around similar concepts to SQL Server Integration Services (SSIS). Figure 1 shows the StreamInsight architecture. Because SSIS is a familiar technology, it

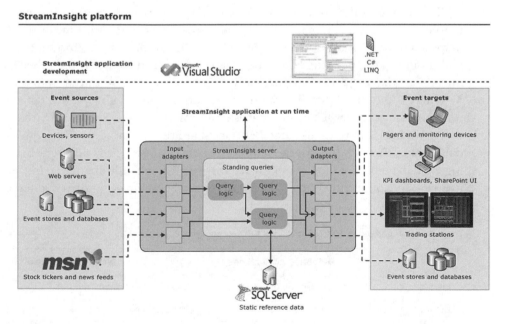

Figure 1 StreamInsight architecture

helps to relate the concepts in StreamInsight to SSIS for ease of understanding. Stream-Insight has two core concepts:

- *Adapters*—StreamInsight is built around the idea of adapters. Input adapters allow you to connect to data sources, consume event streams, and push those events into the StreamInsight engine. Output adapters take event streams from the StreamInsight engine and push them out to target data consumers.
- *Engine*—The engine is where the events arrive from source adapters and is where all the business intelligence is derived. By using standing queries (more on that later) written in LINQ, event streams can be correlated, aggregated, compared, and finally sent to the output adapters for consumption.

How does querying streams differ from querying an RDBMS?

Today, many businesses have some kind of data warehouse from which they derive their analytics of what has happened in the past. It's also possible that these enterprises use the same information to drive predictions of business activity or to streamline performance-management programs. Typically, these data warehouses are loaded by some batch process, such as SQL Server Integration Services, at regular intervals. These intervals could be every hour, day, week, or any other time unit that's in accordance with business requirements. It's practically impossible to do these batch processes in close to real time. There's one immediate downside to doing this: latency. By the time your users query your nice, information-rich, dimensionally modeled data, it's out of date. They're querying stale data. What they're seeing happened potentially a good distance in the past.

This is one of the areas where a CEP engine like StreamInsight wins. By hooking onto events—data streams within your business—in close to real time, StreamInsight helps to eliminate most of the staleness of data. Therefore, StreamInsight can provide real insight at the point at which the data is being produced. On the other hand, by introducing latency into querying, businesses become reactive rather than proactive.

There's another difference between the way StreamInsight queries data and, say, someone querying a SQL Server database using Management Studio. In StreamInsight you define the queries, and they become what are known as standing queries. The data washes through the queries and derives the results. This is different from querying a database in that the data in the database isn't constantly changing, but your queries can and often do change. The differences between event-driven querying and RDBMS are shown in table 1.

Table 1   Comparison of RDBMS and event-driven querying

	Database applications	Event-driven applications
Query paradigm	Ad hoc queries or requests	Continuous standing queries
Latency	Seconds, hours, days	Milliseconds or less

Table 1   Comparison of RDBMS and event-driven querying *(continued)*

	Database applications	Event-driven applications
Data rate	Hundreds of events/sec	Tens of thousands of events/sec or more
Query semantics	Declarative relational analytics	Declarative relational and temporal analytics

Let's examine a query that when using StreamInsight is relatively simple to answer but when using an RDBMS is more protracted and requires constant requerying:

- The data is meter readings (units used).
- Group the readings by post code.
- Divide the data in the groups into windows.
- Every minute, each window should look at the last five minutes' worth of dataAverage, the number of units used in each window.
- For each window, show the difference between this and the previous window.

Table 2 shows the average units used for every household in one post code in windows of five minutes and a new window being created every minute. The output is also shown in order to demonstrate the required output.

Table 2   Example query

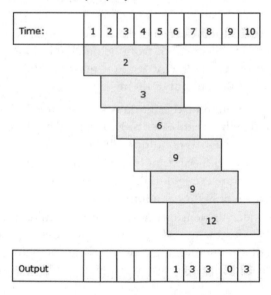

At the end of this chapter, the full solution to this conundrum will be presented, but you're free to mock up an example in your favorite RDBMS and try to solve it. This is one of the key tenets in StreamInsight: the ability to look at your data in flight and react to what you see.

Where is StreamInsight useful?

StreamInsight can be applied to a whole range of business questions and scenarios. It's fair to say though that it's most useful where your reason for using it is because of the ability to do something with that data in real time. StreamInsight can also be used as an aggregator for other applications but taking a potentially large and fast-flowing data stream and producing an aggregated view of that stream. This could be useful for RFID tag readings fed into BizTalk Server.

As mentioned previously, being able to react to data in real time provides unique opportunities where traditionally you may have relied on querying a stale data warehouse. For example, your credit card is being used by you and, unfortunately, by frauds who have cloned your card. Your credit card company receives each of the transactions on the card and loads them into its transactional database. Every hour, these transactions are loaded into the data warehouse. A job routinely queries the warehouse and does some predictive modeling of card transactions in order to highlight where there may have been suspicious activity. These queries, on finding dubious activity, initiate a workflow process that eventually ends up with the bank stopping the card and calling you to query the transactions. The question is, would you rather this happened in real time so the transactions are captured and analyzed and workflow initiated within seconds of the events occurring, or are you happy for the bank to phone you the following day when the offenders are currently relaxing somewhere with your money?

The answer is most definitely the first of these two options.

Many different industries can—and do!—benefit from being able to look at their businesses in real time in order to drive intelligent decision making. Following are some of those business areas and why CEP is useful to them:

- *Financial services*—Being able to monitor the markets in real time and look at trades being done by the traders has real benefits. Risk can be monitored and the necessary people informed as soon as conditions dictate.
- *Betting companies*—While receiving thousands of bets a second for an event, the CEP engine is able to look inside the event cloud and, based on previous knowledge, derive whether the pattern of betting is anomalous.
- *Oil companies*—Being able to watch the sensors transporting your fluids from wells to the surface and being able to see the mix of those fluids provides real business intelligence. Being able to tell when something is overheating and being able to shut down that potentially malfunctioning valve in real time could save lives.

Time

There are two aspects about time that I should mention here. The first is current time increments, or CTIs. One of the tasks of the CEP application developer is to inject these into the data stream. CTIs determine the liveliness of your stream. They determine when events from your source get pushed into the engine. Because StreamInsight provides aggregates over a stream, it needs to know when it's safe to output aggregated values. Without CTIs you can enqueue events all day long on your adapters, but your events will go nowhere. CTIs are like checkpoints in the stream. They tell the adapter that it shouldn't see an event coming through that has a header start time that's before the CTI start time. If it does, then StreamInsight has rules about what to do with those events, such as drop or adjust.

Time is also a fundamental StreamInsight thread/property/characteristic that, unfortunately, is one of the things that catch developers the most. When you join streams, or want to analyze streams of events, the first thing you need to know is that if these events don't exist in the same moment of space-time, then you're comparing two completely separate things. Remember what I mentioned earlier about event shapes?

- A point event is valid for one tick; its start time and end time are separated by one tick.
- The interval shape is used when you know the start time of an event and you know the end time of the event.
- The edge event shape is used when you know that an event has started but you have no idea when it will finish.

If you have two streams of point events that join on a particular payload attribute, coming from an RDBMS, this is an easy query to write:

```
SELECT <col list>
FROM Table 1 t1
JOIN Table 2 t2
ON t1.<col> = t2.<col>
```

In StreamInsight, if the events in Table 1 and Table 2 didn't occur within the lifetime of each other, then the result of this query would be empty.

Querying the streams

Once the events leave the input adapter, they enter the engine. The engine is where all the query logic is introduced and from where the intelligence is derived. The StreamInsight query definition language is Language Integrated Query. LINQ, as a language, has many incarnations, for example, LINQ to SQL, LINQ to Entities, and LINQ to XML. LINQ for StreamInsight is an evolving language. Hardcore LINQ developers are probably going to miss some things they can do outside of StreamInsight.

The aim of this final part of the chapter isn't only to give a sense of the language used when querying event streams but also to provide insight into how powerful the syntax can be. The examples will build quite rapidly from basics and then delve into some of the more colorful and powerful queries. Rather than being a list of examples with no real explanation, the following code demonstrates those areas of StreamInsight LINQ that are powerful and also relevant to developers on practically every application they'll write. The scenario focuses on a financial institution that's interested in exposing what's happening within the business in real time.

In order to keep the focus on StreamInsight, the scenario is simplified for the purposes of illustration. StreamInsight is capable of handling much more complex scenarios.

In this scenario, we have two streams of data. One of the streams is for the trades themselves, and the other stream provides the location of the traders. A trade event has the following shape:

```
public class TradeEvent
    {
            public DateTime EventDate;
            public int TraderID;
            public string InstrumentName;
            public string Exchange;
            public float Price;
    }
```

A trader event has the following shape:

```
public class Trader
    {

            public int TraderID;
            public string TraderLocation;
    }
```

This first query looks into the `tradeStream`, or stream of trades, and projects each of them into `simpleSelect`:

```
var simpleSelect = from e in tradeStream
                   select e;
```

Now what if we want to filter the stream and only look for trades where the price was greater than a certain value:

```
var simpleSelect = from e in tradeStream
                   where e.Price > 123.98
              select e;
```

We can further restrict that to trades where the price is above a certain value and the `InstrumentName` is a certain instrument:

```
    var simpleSelect = from e in tradeStream
                       where e.Price > 123.98 && e.InstrumentName == "BOND"
                       select e;
```

In the next query, we remove the filter on the `tradeStream` and join to the `traderStream`, a stream of traders matching on `TraderID`:

```
var simpleSelect = from e in tradeStream
                   join t in traderStream
                   on e.TraderID equals t.TraderID
                   select new {
                           TraderID = e.TraderID,
                           TraderLocation = t.TraderLocation,
                           Exchange = e.Exchange,
```

```
                InstrumentName =  e.InstrumentName,
                Price = e.Price
                  };
```

There's a problem with this statement. The join in the last query is an equijoin. This means the trader must exist in the trader stream as well as the trade stream. What if we're late adding new traders to the trader stream? The last thing we want to do is miss trades happening because of this. What we need is a left anti semi join to get those trades for which we don't know the trader. We then union the two streams together to get the full result set:

```
var missingTrades = from e in tradeStream
                    where (from t in traderStream
                            where e.TraderID == t.TraderID
                            select t).IsEmpty()
                    select new {
                        TraderID = e.TraderID,
                        TraderLocation = "unknown",
                        Exchange = e.Exchange,
                        InstrumentName =  e.InstrumentName,
                        Price = e.Price
                        };

var joinedStreams = simpleSelect.Union(missingTrades);
```

The final step in this example is to ask the average price of an instrument for each trader location against each exchange. The prices will be further calculated for each hour of the day:

```
var finalStream = from evt in joinedStreams
                  group evt by new {
                        evt.TraderLocation,
                        evt.Exchange,
                        evt.InstrumentName } into tradegroups
                  from win in tradegroups
                        TumblingWindow(TimeSpan.FromHours(1),
                        HoppingWindowOutputPolicy.ClipToWindowEnd)
                  select new
                      {
                      TraderLocation = tradegroups.Key.TraderLocation,
                      Exchange = tradegroups.Key.Exchange,
                      InstrumentName = tradegroups.Key.InstrumentName,
                      AveragePrice = win.Avg(e => e.Price)
                            };
```

Finally, we look at the solution, to the question posed earlier regarding meter readings, post codes, and grouping.

In the following solution, strm is a stream of meter readings from all households in all post codes. Our solution requires that we group by the post code and create sliding windows of five minutes, outputting the results every minute, over those groups. Within each of those windows we need to calculate the average meter reading for each post code:

```
var avg = from e in strm
            group e by e.PostCode into PostCodeGroups
            from win in PostCodeGroups.HoppingWindow(
                    TimeSpan.FromMinutes(5), TimeSpan.FromMinutes(1),
                    HoppingWindowOutputPolicy.ClipToWindowEnd)
            select new
            {
                    PostCode = PostCodeGroups.Key,
                    avgMeterReading = win.Avg(e => e.MeterReading)
            };
```

After calculating the average reading for a post code in a window, we convert those windows back to a stream of point events. Currently in StreamInsight, events in windows start when the window starts and end when the window ends. Converting to a point stream means we have one event per window per post code. The event start time is the start time of the window, and the end time is one tick later. The payload of the event is the `avgMeterReading` value for the window:

```
var ptstream =  from evt1 in avg
                    .ToPointEventStream()
                    select evt1;
```

After creating the point stream, we convert our point events to a signal. We do this by pushing each event end time out to infinity and then clipping on the next occurrence of the same post code in the stream.

```
var signal = from e in ptstream
            .AlterEventDuration(evt => TimeSpan.MaxValue)
            .ClipEventDuration(ptstream, (e1, e2) => e1.PostCode == e2.PostCode)
              select e;
```

Now we take our point stream after the window calculations and join it to our signal stream. We set the start time of our point stream to be one tick before the event happened. This means that the events are offset. This allows us to see the current event payload with the previous event payload. This in turn means we can do our calculation:

```
var joined = from e1 in signal
            join e2 in ptstream
            .ShiftEventTime(e => e.StartTime - TimeSpan.FromTicks(1))
            on e1.PostCode equals e2.PostCode
            select new
            {
                PostCode = e1.PostCode,
                PreviousValue = e1.avgMeterReading,
                CurrentValue = e2.avgMeterReading,
                Diff = e2.avgMeterReading - e1.avgMeterReading
            };
```

Summary

StreamInsight is a framework for building complex event-processing engine applications using .NET. Being able to correlate events around your business and do this in close to real time offers an incredible opportunity. No longer will managers have to wait until the following day to find out how their business is doing today. The ability to drive analytics and real business intelligence on the data while it's in flight opens a myriad of opportunities. Thinking in streams of data is a paradigm shift for a lot of people, but once you do, you'll find that a whole world of opportunity awaits.

About the author

Allan Mitchell is a data integration architect based in the UK. He has worked all over the world in a variety of industries on projects big and small. He specializes in StreamInsight, SSIS, and WF4. He has been a SQL Server MVP since 2004.

60 BI solution development design considerations

Siddharth Mehta

Every organization makes decisions necessary to keep its business functioning efficiently and profitably. These decisions can be categorized into one of three types: strategic (long term), tactical (short term), and operational (day to day). One of the factors that influences decision making is the analysis and measurement of business performance. Business intelligence (BI) solutions cater to business analysts and stakeholders with information related to performance measurement, predictive analysis, data discovery, and more. Developing a BI solution depends on the kind of decision support data that stakeholders require for their decision making. In this chapter, BI solution development using the Microsoft business intelligence technology stack is discussed, with special emphasis on architectural design considerations.

Architecture design

Consider any IT service or application that collects operational data and stores it in a relational data repository (generically referred to as OLTP, or online transaction processing). A typical business requirement is that clients have their OLTP systems in production, and they want analytics and reporting capability from them. A required solution would need to bridge the gap from OLTP to a dashboard, which is the end user interface, to present analytics and reporting capability to the decision makers of an organization. From an architecture design standpoint, the diagram in figure 1 depicts a typical OLTP-to-dashboard solution architecture.

Various artifacts of this solution can be categorized into different areas that can be seen as logical layers from an architecture design perspective, as follows:

- *Source systems*—Various OLTP source systems make up the source system layer. These source systems can be relational and nonrelational data sources that host data through some application interface or direct user inputs.

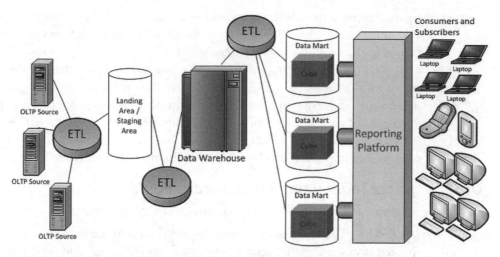

Figure 1   Typical BI design for an OLTP-to-dashboard solution

- *Landing area/staging area*—Data from different data sources needs to be gathered at a centralized area, commonly known as the landing or staging area. The landing area is used to extract as well as gather data, because there may be some data that is received in streaming format, such as in-flight data, which would need to be gathered into a common storage repository. The staging area is a common data warehousing practice, where incremental data extracted from source systems is gathered for temporary or permanent storage, depending on the design of master data management. This layer can be a mix of landing and staging areas. How to identify this area depends on the functional aspect of the layer. Landing and staging may be combined into one area.

- *Data warehouse*—This layer acts as the master repository of data collected from all the different source systems. Data mostly resides in a normalized form in this layer. From an industry standard, there are two major data warehouse design methodologies: Kimball and Inmon.

- *Data marts*—This layer acts as the business- or function-specific dimensional model, which sources data from the data warehouse. The benefit of having this layer is that it facilitates customization of the data model as well as temporary or permanent manipulation of data for different purposes, such as what-if analysis or storing data at a higher grain. Cubes are built on top of these data marts, based on the requirements they need to meet.

- *Reporting platform*—This layer acts as a uniform layer that hosts data from all the data marts and caters to reporting to its consumers or subscribers. Data regarding analytical reporting is sourced generally from data marts, and if the design is such that data isn't present in a data mart, it can always be sourced from the data warehouse. Data from operational reporting requirements is supplied from OLTP source systems, but considering the present scope, the diagram in figure 1 represents only the association with data related to analytical reporting. Consumers and subscribers can vary greatly and can include smart devices, as shown in the right-most side of the diagram.

- *Extract transform load (ETL) layer*—The ETL layer(s) manages the transfer of data across all the layers right from OLTP to the data marts or reporting platform, depending on the design. This ETL can be generic or source specific and primarily molds the data to the reporting requirements. There are different theories as to whether it should be an ETL or ELT layer, but you can view this as just a change of sequence in the way this layer acts; the functionality remains the same.

Other aspects influencing architecture design

There are a few additional considerations not already mentioned:

- *Decoupling*—The effect of this design aspect is seen in the long run, when either the requirements or the data model itself need scaling. Any business can be expected to grow over a period of time, or the business may be divided into different sub-businesses managed by the senior leadership of the organization. The solution would have been designed with the business at its original size, and when the organization grows or the business gets distributed or more business divisions step in to use this solution, only a balanced decoupling can keep the solution in shape. Considering the long-term vision, a BI solution should be developed using a generic product-development methodology instead of requirement-specific application-development methodologies.

- *Facades and contracts*—This factor comes as a direct requirement to support decoupling. If source systems that might want to plug in to take advantage of the BI solution are considered in advance, the scalability of the design is limited. There's a strong possibility that any source system might undergo a schema change because of evolving requirements. In this case, OLTP sources, the landing area, the data warehouse, and data marts can be seen as a source system in one form or another. For a robust design, each source system should expose a standard interface within itself or through an intermediate layer that can act as an interface to its subscribers, and whatever the change, data would be published in a standard format exposed by the interface. The facade layer should take care of the changes at the source system, so that impact is contained at this layer instead of cascading the impact to the final end point of the solution.

- *Lineage tracking*—Data gets exchanged and transformed at many layers, and if you intend to investigate the origin of a particular piece of data from the reporting platform back to the source system, lineage tracking is an important factor to consider while designing the solution. This kind of requirement arises frequently in finance-related businesses, where funds are exchanged from one system to another, and some investigation might need to track the origin of data from its primary source.

Solution development

After the architecture is designed, the next phase involves developing the logical and physical designs and implementing the solution using a suitable technology stack. For this chapter, we take for granted that Microsoft BI stack technologies would be used for the solution development.

The following sections of this chapter focus on the various categories of tasks from a solution planning and development perspective, related challenges, and technologies from the Microsoft BI stack and other freeware tools that can address the task requirements.

Conceptual design

This task requires involvement from a broad audience, including business analysts, senior leadership of the organization, and end users. The direct derivative of this task would be logical, physical, and dimensional design for the landing area, data warehouse, and data marts.

Design challenge

The main known challenge in this area is to get the stakeholders to agree on a common conceptual hierarchy of entity-relationship modeling.

Tools and technologies

Microsoft Visio is the diagramming and process modeling tool from the Microsoft tool stack. Apart from this, ERwin (not freeware) is one of the most popular tools for this task.

ETL layer

Designing and developing the ETL layer is an iterative activity, because it's needed to bridge data between different layers. Data profiling, data cleansing, and data quality control are some of the regular functionalities addressed in the ETL layer, which can also be perceived as a control point where data changes its lineage.

Design challenges

- Source systems might or might not support mechanisms to handle delta detection (differential data detection) at the source. If this isn't supported, a snapshot-based delta detection mechanism needs to be implemented, and this would be done at the staging area layer.
- Proper facades need to be implemented to shield the ETL from becoming tightly coupled with the source data model. Otherwise, the ETL design would be prone to errors. A common example is ETL packages reading data directly from source tables. When the table schema changes, the data is impacted. Instead, facades need to be implemented in the form of a stored procedure or view, so that changes at either end don't impact the design.
- Appropriate modular division should be maintained in implementing ETL logic. A single execution unit shouldn't be delegated functionality such that its failure can halt the execution of a number of tasks.

Tools and technologies

- SQL Server Integration Services (SSIS) is the technology for the ETL requirements of the solution. Business Intelligence Development Studio (BIDS) is the software used to develop SSIS packages. SSIS contains out-of-the-box functionality in the form of configurable tasks and transforms that can be used for simple to complex levels of ETL implementation, and it provides enterprise solution features such as modular development, debugging, auditing, security configuration, and deployment.

- In case out-of-the-box tasks and components aren't sufficient for development needs, the SSIS Tasks and Components Gallery is available on CodePlex, and it offers different ready-to-use SSIS tasks and transforms that have been shared by the SSIS community.

- The BIDS Helper add-in can add value to BIDS for certain SSIS package design-related functionalities not available out of the box. This added value is purely from a developer productivity–enhancement perspective. You can refer to the BIDS Helper home page on CodePlex to learn more details about these value additions.

Dimensional modeling and cube design

Dimensional modeling and cube design activity happens at the data mart layer and is dependent on whether a design is implementing Kimball or Inmon methodology and whether the data warehouse and data mart layers can exchange positions. Effectively, this would cause the dimensional modeling host to also change. Kimball methodology is usually preferred by practitioners for dimensional modeling using a bus architecture.

Multidimensional database objects commonly known as cubes are developed on top of a dimensional data store. Data can be stored in multidimensional OLAP, relational OLAP, or hybrid OLAP, and the differences among these are in the way data is aggregated and the repository where the data is stored. Also, a cube generally hosts the key performance indicators that are an essential element of performance monitoring using dashboards.

Design challenges

- Dimensional modeling in a typical bus architecture starts with a set of conformed dimensions. Identifying these conformed dimensions and modeling the relationships with other dimensions and facts require careful modeling. The design of the dimensional model paves the way for developing mapping details used by ETL logic, to bridge data between the source and the data warehouse or data mart layer.

- Cube design works on the philosophy of being able to identify each entity uniquely in the dimensional space. Cube design requires detailed study of the data to fine-tune each entity and its attributes to comply with this philosophy. Violation of this philosophy has the potential of rendering that entity completely useless in the dimensional space.

- Multidimensional Expressions (MDX) is an industry-standard query language for accessing data and defining multidimensional objects. Most professionals think of data in the form of a table or matrix. It can be quite a challenge to come to grips with this query language.

Tools and technologies

- SQL Server Analysis Services (SSAS) is the technology that caters to the OLAP requirements of the solution. BIDS is the software used to design and develop cubes. SSAS contains out-of-the-box functionality required to develop, configure, deploy, and maintain simple to complex cubes. SSAS also provides enterprise solution features like developing complex schemas, fine-tuning dimensions and facts or measures, support for MDX scripting, controlling cube processing, configuring security, associating relationships between dimensions and measure groups, and much more.

- The Dimensional Modeling workbook, available from the book *The Microsoft Data Warehouse Toolkit* (Mundy/Thornthwaite, 2011), is a useful template to start dimensional modeling. This is an Excel workbook, and it contains templates for documenting mapping details and other information for dimensions and facts. Also, once the documenting is complete, it can generate T-SQL using this information to create the relational data mart. This can save you a lot of work for your data mart development. It also provides documentation along with the implementation.

- The BIDS Helper add-in can add value to BIDS for certain cube design-related functionalities that aren't available out of the box. This value addition is purely from a developer productivity–enhancement perspective. The BIDS Helper home page on CodePlex can provide more details about these value additions.

Reporting platform

Developing the reporting platform includes developing operational reports from OLTP sources and analytical reports from OLAP sources. This layer needs to provide data reporting on a collaborative platform, where users can view their reports from a common medium as well as use the same medium to share their analysis from the reports. Analytical reports need specialized support for data representation and analysis, and this is provided through advanced analytical visualizations like heat maps, decomposition trees, and scatter plot graphs.

Design challenges

- Historically, reports were viewed and analyzed only over hard-wired or wireless computers with a standard screen resolution, using a web browser with HTTP as the communication protocol. Today, a broad variety of report consumers are available, including smart devices like smartphones, iPads, Netbooks, and more. Senior leadership of an organization has the highest probability of requesting report access on smart devices. Designing reports that are supported by a great variety of such devices remains a big design challenge.

▪ Any report is only as good as the user's ability to interpret and analyze the data. Analytical data tends to be complex, and depending on the purpose of analysis, such reports need specialized support to represent the data. This support is provided by advanced analytical visualizations. Data needs to be modeled in a form that such visualizations can use to represent it, and this can be tricky to do with some visualizations.

Tools and technologies

▪ SQL Server Reporting Services (SSRS) is the technology that supports reporting requirements of this solution. BIDS is the software used to design and develop reports. SSRS contains built-in functionality in the form of out-of-the-box controls that you can use for report development. Also, SSRS provides enterprise solution features such as modular report authoring, a ready portal to browse deployed reports, an integration interface with collaboration platforms like SharePoint and application development platforms like .NET, the option to export reports in standard document formats, a programmable API to manage and generate reports, and much more.

▪ SSRS can be operated in SharePoint integrated mode. SharePoint acts as the collaboration platform to make reports available to users from a common medium.

▪ Excel Services can be used to develop Excel-based reports from a variety of data sources, and it can be accessed using SharePoint as the collaboration platform.

▪ The BIDS Helper add-in can add value to BIDS for certain report design-related functionalities that aren't available out of the box. This value addition is purely from a developer productivity–enhancement perspective. See the BIDS Helper home page on CodePlex for details.

▪ RSScripter and Fiddler are two useful freeware tools for automated report deployment and debugging report performance over HTTP. These two utilities are useful for deploying reports and debugging traffic over HTTP, respectively, because the support for these is limited in BIDS.

▪ SCRUBS is a useful SSRS execution log analysis framework, available on CodePlex. Execution log analysis for reports requires manually analyzing details related to report performance. For automated reporting and analysis of execution log data, this ready-to-use framework can save a lot of development effort.

Dashboard development

This artifact is the face of the solution to end users. The main task that remains is to organize different reporting artifacts in a context-specific data representation methodology. Users generally start by analyzing higher-level data and then drill down into the details for problem decomposition and data analysis. This higher-level data is in the form of key performance indicators (KPI), analytical visualizations, strategy maps, and other reporting mechanisms. A detailed study of the dashboard leads to what-if analysis for defining the right business strategy, and this is one of the reasons why dashboards are also known as management information systems (MIS) or decision support systems (DSS).

Design challenges

- Dashboard designs often suffer from the issue popularly known as TMI—too much information. Designers often try to use too fancy gauges and indicators, colorful representations, and other techniques to represent lots of data on the screen space. Although this design might appear futuristic in nature, it often suffers from a usability perspective. Representing the right amount of data in the right context remains a key design challenge.

- Selecting the right visualization for the right kind of data to enable the right kind of analysis requires experienced analytical vision and skills. Today, independent vendors provide various kinds of visualizations, and using the right visualization can exponentially increase the usability index of a dashboard.

Tools and technologies

- PerformancePoint Services 2010 (PPS), which is available as a service in Share-Point 2010, is used for dashboard design and development. PPS contains features such as scorecard development, KPI development, analytical visualizations, and more. It also provides strong integration with a collaboration environment like SharePoint.

- Visio Services in SharePoint 2010 can be used to render strategy maps, which are data-driven diagrams authored using Microsoft Visio and hosted on Share-Point. These services can help you render visually appealing diagrams by exploiting the capability of Silverlight on a web browser. Reporting the health of the organization's business through a pictorial representation driven by data from predefined KPIs is an important feature of a dashboard.

Summary

An end-to-end business intelligence solution architecture and solution design commences from the OLTP sources or source system layer and concludes at the reporting or dashboard layer. Different layers in architecture design have different design challenges and effectively require factoring in the correct design considerations to meet those challenges. This chapter began with an introduction to a typical BI solution architecture design, followed by the functional details of each layer from a design perspective. A BI solution development lifecycle comprises some standard higher-level tasks. We discussed a few such tasks, commonly known design challenges of these tasks, and tools and technologies from the Microsoft SQL Server and SharePoint 2010 business intelligence stack that can help you tackle these tasks. After reading this chapter, you should be able to achieve a higher-level understanding of BI solution development from a design considerations perspective.

About the author

Siddharth Mehta is a business intelligence professional with more than nine years of experience. He presently works in the role of a technology architect for Accenture Services Pvt. Ltd. (Mumbai, India), in the capacity of associate manager. Prior to coming to Accenture, he worked at Capgemini, with clients including Walt Disney Pictures and Television, CitiBank, Transport for London, and ABN AMRO.

He started his career in 2002 with Visual Basic and SQL Server and since then has been mainly working with SQL Server, business intelligence, data warehousing, dimensional modeling, information visualization design, and related technologies. He's known for his writing in the field of Microsoft business intelligence. He authored a whitepaper for MSDN Library titled "Bulk Report Generation Using SSIS and SSRS 2008 R2." He continues authoring content on MS BI for community sites like MSSQLTips.com, SQLServerCentral.com, SQL-Server-Performance.com, and others.

He won the Microsoft Most Valuable Professional award in 2011, Capgemini India Envoy in 2010, and other awards through the course of his career. He shares his insights on business intelligence through his blog at http://siddhumehta.blogspot.com. You can reach him at siddhumehta_brain@yahoo.co.in.

index

Symbols

! button 426
(?:) construct 227
(?) construct 226
@ symbol 430
@[User::ServerName] 484
@@IDENTITY function 262, 531
@CheckDate parameter 328
@City parameter 310
@database_name parameter 142
@DateOfBirth parameter 264
@IndexName variable 324
@Name parameter 264
@restore_file parameter 142
@scrollopt option 390
@SSN parameter 263
@StartProductID parameter 328
@vDate parameter 206–207
@vPrice parameter 206–207
@WindowsUsersAnd-GroupsInSysadminRole field 134
#sqlhelp hash tag 177
%expression_column% 231
$amo variable 550
$instance variable 96
$procType variable 551
$Sheet variable 96

Numerics

64-bit server 141

A

ABA (abandonment rate) 171
absolute paths 246
abstracting, connections in SSIS 474–479
account names, and authentication 163–165
Activity Monitor. See AM
acts 208
actual_base metric 590
ActualvsBudget_score metric 593
adapters 600
Add Features link 437
Add Features Wizard 437
Add New Item dialog box 214
Add User-Defined Type option 214
Add-in method 580
add-ons, PowerPivot. See Power-Pivot add-on
Address table 313
AddRow() method 517, 519, 523
ADO enumerator 484–485, 492
ADO.NET Schema Rowset enumerator 485–488

Advanced button 144
Advanced Compile Options button 419
Advanced Micro Devices. See AMD
Advanced section 248
Adventure Works cube 565
Adventure Works DW 2008 549–551, 553, 555–556
AdventureWorks (2005) database 292
AdventureWorks 2008R2 project 400
AdventureWorks database 116, 186, 486, 573
AdventureWorks samples 399
AdventureWorks2008R2 database 177
aggregates, in Reporting Services 407
aggregation 529
alerting, in ETL system 533
ALL Date member 566
ALL member 562
allocation of expense model 125
ALTER DATABASE method 155
Alter statement 548
AM (Activity Monitor) 147
ambassadorship, by DBA 107
AMD (Advanced Micro Devices) processors 304

AMO (Analysis Management Objects) 539, 548, 550, 556
AMO library, and PowerShell framework 548–556
  advantages of 548–549
  automating processing 549–552
  repetitive design changes 551–556
Analysis Interval option 380
Analysis Management Objects. *See* AMO
Analysis Services databases 554
Analysis Services emitter 540
Analysis Services Scripting Language. *See* ASSL
Another database 108
ANSI standard 180
APIs (Application Programming Interfaces) 388–389
application functionality 68–69, 75
Application Programming Interfaces. *See* API
application quality, in unit tests 255
application sociability 122
Application tab 419
Applies To section 438
ApplyDiff 511–512
architecture design, for BI development 608–610
arithmetic overflow error 28
Array function 134
arrays, disk alignment on 56
artificial keys, arguments for 6–8
  are de facto standard 12
  can improve performance 7
  have meaning by virtue of being used 8
  issues with natural keys 6–8
  reduce fragmentation of clustered indexes 8
Aryalingam, Gogula 584
ASA (average speed to answer) 171
ASCII character 39
Assembly Information dialog box 419
AssemblyInfo file 420
ASSL (Analysis Services Scripting Language) 539
ASYNC_IO_COMPLETION 339
asynchronous output 232

asynchronous transformation, Script component 519
atomic data 41
attribute names 553
AttributeRelationships property 544
Attributes.Add function 544
audit support, in ETL system 535
authentication, and Microsoft Windows 163–165
AUTO option 380
AutoClose 101, 103
AutoComplete 179
auto-formatting software 363
autogenerating SSAS cubes 538–547
  background 538–539
  InstantCube simple cube generator 539–547
    Analysis Services emitter 540
    creating cubes 545–547
    Data Source View 542–543
    data sources 541
    dimensions 543–544
    relational database emitter 540
    SSAS database 540–541
    Visual Studio project for 539
autogrowth 359
automated testing, vs. manual testing 73
automatic execute 256
automating with SSIS 503–514
  common automation tasks 504–505
  key tasks and components 505–509
  monitoring results 513–514
  precedence and manipulating control flow 511–512
  reusable and mobile SSIS packages 509–511
automating, processing 549–552
automation, of unit testing 265
AutoRefresh property 118–119
AutoShrink 132
auto-update 355
AUX_BulletGraph 593
AUX_KPIs 594
AUX_SalesCompare 594
AUX_Sparklines 592

average speed to answer. *See* ASA
average total user cost 34
average user impact 34

B

BackConnectionHostNames key 447
BackgroundColor property 118, 413–415, 417
backing up, transaction log 360
Backup Files SSIS package 505
backup processes, snapshots as 58
backup sets 85
backups
  and restoration of tables 159–160
  log
    availability of 80
    misconceptions about 165
  restoring 73
balance support, in ETL system 535
bar charts, in Excel as BI frontend tool 594
baselines 76
BASIC interpreter 538
basic tests 260
BAT file 265
BEGIN DIALOG statement 290
BEGIN TRANSACTION statement 157
BeginTran log record 353
benchmarking, and sizing tools 307–308
Berry, Glenn 112, 308, 337
Bertrand, Aaron 184
best practice compliance 128–137
  Central Management Servers feature 130–131
  context for contemporary database administration 128–129
  importance of 129–130
  Policy-Based Management tool 131–135
    Surface Area Configuration policy 132–134
    Sysadmin membership 134–135
    with Central Management Servers feature 135–136

Best Practices Analyzer, Microsoft 129
best practices, for DBAs 155
BestPractice column 116
betas candidates 72
betting companies 602
BETWEEN operator 201
BETWEEN queries 182
BI (business intelligence)
  design considerations for 608–615
    architecture design 608–610
    conceptual design 611
    dashboard development 614–615
    dimensional modeling 612–613
    ETL layer 611–612
    reporting platform 613–614
  Excel as 585–596
    and navigation 595–596
    bar charts in 594
    bullet graphs in 593–594
    considerations for 585–586
    dimensional model for 588–590
    headers in 591
    in-cell data bars in 591–592
    key business metrics for 588
    KPIs in 594–595
    OLAP as source 587
    pivot tables in 590–591
    reasons to use 586
    slicers in 591
    Sparklines in 592–593
  with Silverlight PivotViewer 577–584
    cards in 578
    EXCEL workbook design 581–582
    filtering and sorting 579
    Graph view in 579
    hosting of 582
    HTML template for 580–581
    implementing 582–584
    overview 577–578
    simple vs. linked pivots 579–580
    source for 580
BIDS (Business Intelligence Development Studio) 118, 141, 413, 426, 470, 522, 548, 612

BIDS debugging mode 458
BIDS Helper add-in 613
BinaryWriter 464
Bit Size column 282
bit-bucket data flow components 458
BitFlagOfNextLevel 281
BizTalk Server 602
blank lines, removing 195
.blg file 377
blocking, locking and 340
blue key icons 18
Blue Widgets 465
Boles, Kevin 194
bottlenecking, of transaction log 353–357
breadth-first indexes 284–285
BreakLocation property 406
budget_base metric 590
buffer I/O latches 339–340
buffer pool 378
Buffer.AddRow() method 517, 519, 523
bugs 168
Build dialog box 420
Build Events command 421
BULK INSERT statement 460
BulkInsert variable 510
bulk-logged recovery 80
Bulldozer processor 304
bullet graphs, in Excel as BI frontend tool 593–594
Business Intelligence Development Studio. See BIDS
business intelligence. See BI
business keys 495
business meaning, of natural keys 8–9
business process-oriented structure 172
business value 530

C

C# class 419–420
C# code 113
cache sizes 303
cache thrashing 303
cacheobjtype column 321
caching, late-arriving rows 499–500
Cain, Robert C. 456
CALCULATE statement 572–575
calculated members, in MDX 560–565

Calendar Year attribute 565
candidate key 5
capacity planning 87–94
  description of 87–88
  gathering current database disk space usage 88–90
  performance metrics 90–94
capital expense 125
cards, in Silverlight PivotViewer 578
caret symbol 198
Cartesian product 235
CAS (Code Access Security) 411
CASE statement 363, 567
CATCH block 209, 263
Categories table 284–285
CDC (change data capture) 158, 528
Celko, Joe 6, 237
Central Management Servers feature 130–131, 135–136
Central Processing Units. See CPUs
CEP (complex event processing) 597
change control 75–76
Change Data Capture 355
Change Database button 441
changed data, detecting 527–528
changes, making with unit tests 255
Chapman, Tim 383
character masking 109
characters, Unicode standard 386–388
CHAR-based variable 180
chargeback model 124
chargebacks, implementing model for 125–127
Chart Data pane 428
charts, in SSRS reports from SSAS 455
Check Condition field 134
CHECK CONSTRAINT 181
Check Database Pages button 84
CheckpointFilename property 473
CheckpointUsage property 473
Cherry, Denny 59
Choose Objects page 143
City attribute 562
City column 313

Class Library template 113
classic DBA functions 128
client-oriented structure 172
clock cycles 162
clones 59
CLOSINGBALANCEMONTH (Expression, Date_Column [,SetFilter]) function 573
CLOSINGBALANCEQUARTER (Expression, Date_Column [,Set-Filter]) function 573
CLOSINGBALANCEYEAR (Expression, Date_Column [,SetFilter] [,YE_Date]) function 573
cloud computing 123
CLR (Common Language Runtime) 111, 211–214, 279
    deciding whether to use 212–213
    NULL value 214
    representations and conversions 213
    SQL 112–115, 229–230
CLR integration 214
CLR module 226
CLR object 112
CLR type 280, 285–286
Cluster IP Addresses page 439
cluster nodes 69
Cluster Parameters page 439
Clustered Index Scan 387
Clustered Index Seek 387
clustered indexes 8, 184, 347–348
clustered page locking 10
clustering, physical 10
clusters, for NLB
    adding hosts to 440
    creating 438–439
cmd.exe file 248
CMSs (content management systems) 245
cntr_type 92–93, 117
cntr_value 89, 92–93, 117
Codd, Edgar F. 3
code
    compiled, advantages of 549
    for SSRS 411–423
        adding 411–418
        creating sharable 419–421
        referencing DLLs from report 421–422

unraveling tangled 362–373
    determining kind of query 364–366
    organizing code to make readable 362–364
    streamlining 366–369
Code Access Security. See CAS
Code property 415–422
code reuse, and UDFs 192–193
CodePlex 177
coherent databases 38–40
    cohesive 40
    documentation of 40
    reasonable names and data types 39
    standards-based 38–39
cohesive databases 40
Coles, Michael 468
collapsing multiple lines, into single line 197–198
collation conflict error 159
collation selection, misconceptions about 158–159
Collecting database 100
collection sheet 581
Collection tab 481, 483–484
Collection variable 488
Collection XML file. See CXML
Colledge, Rod 137
Color column 24, 417
Color property 415, 417
column headers 97
Column type 386
TableName 574
Columns node 179
columns, identity 13
comma character 197
Command property 545
Command(s) completed successfully message 260
comments 364
Commit log record 354
COMMIT TRANSACTION statement 158
Common Language Runtime. See CLR
common table expressions. See CTEs
Community Technology Preview. See CTP1
Compile Value 314–315
compiled code, advantages of 549
Complex data type 219
complex numbers 211, 215
components, SSIS 505–509

ComponentWrapper.cs file 522
composite key 5
computational unit. See CU
Compute Scalar operator 191, 344
computed columns 368
computing resources 162
concatenated strings 431
conceptual design, for BI development 611
concurrency 46
Configuration Manager 247
configuration options, OS 247
configuration, global 393–394
Configurations.dtsx 470, 478
Configure OLE DB Connection Manager window 471
Confirm Installation Selections page 438
Connect method 540
Connection object 393
Connection property 476
connections, in SSIS
    abstracting 474–479
    changing 472–473
    externalizing 473
ConnectionString column 474
ConnectionString property 473, 475, 477, 511
conservation, of data 107
consistency concerns 10
constraints 16–19
    primary keys 17–18
    unique 18–19
    unique indexes 19
consumer-class SSDs 306
CONTAINS FILESTREAM attribute 249
content management systems. See CMSs
context types, in MDX 558
Contoso sample database 449
Contoso_Retail 449
CONTRACT, object for Service Broker 289
contracts 610
Control Flow canvas 471
control flow, SSIS 511–512
control support, in ETL system 535
CONVERSATION, object for Service Broker 290
conversions, representations and 213

CONVERT function 182, 194
convert() method 387
converting
    between .NET framework
        and serialized
        data 219–220
        custom serialization 220
        native serializa-
            tion 219–220
    between .NET framework
        and text 216–219
        PARSE() function 216–217
        TOSTRING() method
            218–219
Cook, John Paul 199
cooperative scheduling 333
copy on first write method 56
COPY_ONLY option 84
core, regular expres-
    sions 227–229
corrupted pages, identify-
    ing 81
cost of solution 125
cost recovery, SQL
    Server 121–127
COUNT function 564
Count property 98
Count() statement 473
Counter Log screen 377
counter_name 89, 92–93, 117
counters
    for PAL tool 375–376
        data collector sets using
            template files 375–376
        Logman tool 376
        SQLDiag tool 376
    performance, using SQL-
        CLR to get values 112–115
Countries dataset 452–454
Countries table 9–10
Country attribute 10, 562, 564
Country column 11
CountryID column 12
CountryID key 9
CPU bottlenecks 193
CPU comparison 238
CPU intensive 302
CPU spikes 382
CPU utilization 302
CPUs (Central Processing
    Units) 340
CPU-Z tool 307
CREATE ASSEMBLY DDL
    statement 229
Create column 97, 100

Create Database script 249
CREATE FUNCTION DDL
    statement 229
CREATE PARTITION PRI-
    MARY ALIGN=64 com-
    mand 56
Create Publication Wizard 161
CREATE SEQUENCE
    statement 203
Create statement 548
Create Utility Control Point
    screen 149
CreateNewOutputRows
    method 231, 522–523
createStatement()
    method 391
Credentials page 442
CROSS APPLY 190
CROSS JOIN 363, 369–370
CS file 420
.csv file 377
CTEs (common table
    expressions) 118, 201,
    344, 364
CTP1 (Community Technology
    Preview) 200
CU (computational
    unit) 125–126
cube context 557
cube design 612
cubes, autogenerating
    538–547
    background 538–539
    InstantCube simple cube
        generator 539–547
Cubes.Add method 545
CultureInfo.InvariantCulture
    217
current coordinate 562
CurrentFlag 465–466
CurrentMember 551
cursors, issues with 388–389
Custom Data Flow
    Component 232
custom serialization 220
Customer database 108
CustomerID 30, 495
CustomerName 495
Customers table 11
CXML (Collection XML)
    file 578, 580, 583
CXPACKET waits 325, 340

D

DAC (data-tier
    applications) 148
DAL (data access layer) 256
damaged pages, page types
    of 80–81
DAS (direct attached
    storage) 305
dashboard development, for BI
    development 614–615
DASHBOARD worksheet 595
data
    determining kind of query
        from returned 364–365
    streamlining 367
data access layer. See DAL
Data Analysis Expressions. See
    DAX
data cache 354
Data Collector 147
data collector set. See DCS
data conservation 107
data consistency, maintenance
    of by natural keys 9–10
data damage 173
Data Definition Language. See
    DDL
data driven 64
data error handling 530
data files, and log
    files 359–360
Data Flow task 482, 484, 487
data integrity 39
data manipulation language.
    See DML
data marts 457, 589, 609
Data Only option 145
data organization, in Hierar-
    chyId data type 280–282
data points 377
data quality, and ETL
    design 526–527
data recovery 172
data separation 108
Data Source View, InstantCube
    simple cube
    generator 542–543
Data Sources folder 400
data staging, in extract
    phase 528–529
data structures, example for
    late-arriving
    dimensions 495
data tiers, scaling 300

data types 211–222
  and scalability 28
  CLR user-defined 212–214
    deciding whether to
      use 212–213
    NULL value 214
    representations and
      conversions 213
  custom 214–222
    adding fields for native
      representation 215
    converting 216–220
    editing signature 215–216
    handling NULL
      values 220–221
    starting project 214
  DAX 569–570
  not choosing right 181–182
  of relational databases,
    reasonable 39
  VARCHAR, declaring with-
    out length 179–180
data warehouse 609
Data Warehouse Markup Language. See DWML
Data Warehouse tab 153
dataAverage 601
databars, in Reporting
  Services 408–409
database administration, con-
    text for
    contemporary 128–129
Database Administrators. See
  DBAs
database design flaws 4
database information,
    collecting 100–104
Database Mail 133
database mirroring 158, 355
database objects 355
database recovery 158
database server hardware
    299–308
  about author 308
  benchmarking and sizing
    tools 307–308
  factors concerning 302–304
  importance of 300
  Intel vs. AMD
    processors 304
  memory recommendations
    304–305
  scaling up or scaling
    out 300–301
  SQL Server and selection
    of 301

storage subsystems
  new developments
    in 306–307
  traditional 305–306
database sharding 300
Database_name
    parameter 142
Database.Schema.Table 34
DatabaseName variable
    510–511
databases 105–110
  configuring, for FILES-
    TREAM data
    type 249–250
  DBA 106–109
    assets of 106–107
    tools of 107–109
  gathering current disk space
    usage of 88–90
  hierarchies in 278
  InstantCube simple cube
    generator 540–541
  personally identifiable
    data 106
  restoring. See page restores
  sample for DAX 570
  scripting 554–555
  shrinking, misconceptions
    about 163
  tempdb 54
  unit test for 256–257
Databases collection 552
databases, relational. See rela-
    tional databases
DataCenter edition 80
data-dependent routing 300
DataReceiver instance
    268–273
DataSender instance 269,
    274–277
Dataset dialog box 433
Dataset Properties dialog
    box 431–433, 451
datasets 530
  in Reporting Services,
    joining 407
  in SSRS reports from SSAS
    453
DataSourceViewBinding
    object 545
data-tier applications. See DAC
DataTransfer/EndOfTransfer
    message 273
Date attribute 426, 429, 432,
    566
date metadata columns 528

date ranges, mishandling
    queries 182–183
Date type 570
Date/Time data type 432
DATE/TIME value 181
DATEADD 368, 372, 575
DATEADD (Date_Column,
    Number_of_Intervals,
    Interval) function 573
DateAdd() method 368
dates, time intelligence
    functions 571–573
DATESBETWEEN (Date
    _Column, Start_Date,
    End_Date) function 573
DATESMTD (Date_Column)
    function 572
DATESQTD (Date_Column)
    function 573
DATESYTD (Date_Column
    [,YE_Date]) function 573
datetime column 571
DATETIME type 181
Davidson, Louis 48
DAX (Data Analysis Expres-
    sions) functions 569–570
  data types 569–570
  sample database 570
DB type 546
DBA Common folder 142
DBA functions 128
DBAs (Database
    Administrators) 106–109
  assets of 106–107
  tools for 146–156
    best practices 155
    managing multiple instan-
      ces using UCP 148–152
    multiserver management
      and administra-
      tion 152–155
    SQL Server 2008
      R2 146–147
    SSMS 147–148
  tools of 107–109
    data separation 108
    education and
      evangelism 109
    obfuscation 108–109
    retention policies 107
    role-based permissions
      107–108
DBAToolbox 118
DBCC CHECKDB method 81,
    355, 361
DBCC command 90

DBCC FREEPROCCACHE()
method 312
DBCC LOGINFO
command 360
DBCC SHOWFILE-
STATS 89–90
dbid column 321
dbo.Events table 182
dbo.MySequence object 203
dbo.Orders table 204–205
dbo.SO_OrderID SEQUENCE
object 204
dbo.spAddressBycity 311
dbo.SpareParts table 205
dbo.ufn_clr_GetPerfCounter
Value 115, 117
dbo.usp_get_product_for_sell
procedure 206–207
dbo.uspGetWhereUsed
ProductID 328
DCS (data collector set) 375
DDL (Data Definition
Language) 132, 211
dead-end data flow
components 458
decision support systems. See
DSS
DECLARE keyword 89, 92,
309, 311, 316
decoupling 469, 610
DeepZoom collection
578–580, 583
default file specifications, misconceptions about 165–166
default signature 215
defrag.exe command 358
Denali, SQL Server. See SQL
Server Denali
depth-first indexes 283–284
Derived Column
transformation 496
design
considerations
for BI develop-
ment 608–615
architecture design
608–610
conceptual design 611
dashboard develop-
ment 614–615
dimensional model-
ing 612–613
ETL layer 611–612
reporting platform
613–614
of unit tests 256

repetitive changes in 551–556
modules and snap-
ins 555–556
scripting databases
554–555
destination
as Script component 523
Script component as 517
development environments 70
Development Servers group 130
DHCP (Dynamic Host Configuration Protocol) 439
Diagnostics event 513, 536
DIALOG type 290
DIFF page 81
differential backup 80, 83,
511–512
differential restore 511–512
Dim prefix 552
dimCustomer 495, 552
DimDate 570–571
<dimension>cube 539
dimension loads 462
dimension records, processing
updates in 500–501
dimension tables 457
dimensional data, optimizing
SSIS for 457–468
general optimizations
457–459
Type 0 SCDs 459–460
Type 1 SCDs 460–464
Type 2 SCDs 465–467
dimensional model
for BI development 612–613
for Excel as BI frontend
tool 588–590
Dimensional Modeling workbook 613
dimensions 448
beginning with P 549
InstantCube simple cube
generator 543–544
direct attached storage. See DAS
direct select 388
DirectoryInfo class 506
dirty data 354, 527
Disabled option 248
disaster recovery plans 74
disk alignment 54–56
correcting
after partition has been
created 56
on Microsoft Windows
55–56
on array 56

disk partitions, aligning 358
Disk Requirements page 440
disk space, gathering current
database usage of 88–90
diskpart.exe 55
DISTINCT keyword 20–21
Distinct Sort operator 22
dividend (Stockholder)
table 240
division, relational. See relational division
divisor (Portfolio) table 240
DLL (dynamic link
library) 411, 421–422
DLL classes 412, 420
DLL file 113–115
DML (data manipulation
language) 259
DMOs (dynamic management
objects) 320, 331
DMVs (dynamic management
views) 33, 111–112, 147,
432
document characteristics 172
documentation, of relational
databases 40, 42–43
dollar sign symbol 198
domain scope, in Reporting
Services 408
DomainScope property 408
domain-specific language. See
DSL
Double type 546
Double.Parse() method 217
downstream environments,
using snapshots to present
storage to 58
downtime 172
DROP command 19
DSL (domain-specific
language) 546
DSS (decision support
systems) 615
DTEXEC 506
Dts.Events.FireError
method 514
Dts.Log method 513–514
duration comparison 239
DW/DSS performance 303
DW/DSS workload 302
DWML (Data Warehouse
Markup Language) 539
dynamic functions 112
Dynamic Host Configuration
Protocol. See DHCP
dynamic link library. See DDL

dynamic management objects.
    See DMOs
DYNAMIC named set 559
DYNAMIC property 559
dynamic SQL 371–373
dynamic views 112

E

edge event 598, 603
Edit button 378
Edit Threshold Properties
    screen 378
education, and evangelism 109
ElementCollection 489–490
ELEMENTS keyword 292
elimination 528
ellipsis button 451
Email element 490
embedded server 599
enabling CLR integration 214
encapsulation, of relational
    databases 44–46
encoding 109
encryption 108
end user license agreement. *See*
    EULA
ENDOFMONTH (Date
    _Column) function 572
ENDOFQUARTER (Date
    _Column) function 572
ENDOFYEAR (Date_Column
    [,YE_Date]) function 572
ENDPOINT, object for Service
    Broker 290
enqueue events 603
Enter Backup File path in sin-
    gle quotes parameter 142
Enterprise edition 80
enterprise-class SSDs 306
entire extract 528
EnumerationType 489–490
enumerators in SQL SSIS
    Foreach Loop
    container 480–493
    ADO enumerator 484–485
    ADO.NET Schema Rowset
        enumerator 485–488
    File enumerator 480–482
    From Variable enumerator
        488–489
    Item enumerator 482–484
    NodeList enumerator
        489–490
    SMO enumerator 490–493
Env_SSISConfig variable 476

equality columns 34
error 824 81
Error Event Fact 530
Error Reporting page 441
errors, when GROUP BY clause
    is ignored 24–25
escape sequence 196
ETL (extract, transform and
    load) design
    and data quality 526–527
    extract phase 527–529
    for BI development 611–612
    load phase 531–533
        data update strategy
            532–533
        surrogate key generation
            531–532
    system
        management 533–536
        alerting 533
        audit support 535
        balance support 535
        control support 535
        metadata from 536
        recovery and restart
            ability 533–535
        runtime event logging
            535–536
    transform phase 529–531
ETL operators 536
ETL process 583–584
ETL type 42
ETLControl 534
ETLPackageExecution 534
EULA (end user license agree-
    ment) 168
Evaluate Policies option 136
evaluation mode 132
evangelism, education and 109
event streams, events and 598
Event Trace sessions 376
event-driven querying 600
events, and event streams 598
exact matches 323
Excel file 506, 581, 583,
    592–594
Excel object 96
EXCEL workbook design, for
    Silverlight
    PivotViewer 581–582
Excel worksheet 96
Excel, as BI frontend
    tool 585–596
    and navigation 595–596
    bar charts in 594
    bullet graphs in 593–594

considerations for 585–586
dimensional model
    for 588–590
headers in 591
in-cell data bars in 591–592
key business metrics for 588
KPIs in 594–595
OLAP as source 587
pivot tables in 590–591
reasons to use 586
slicers in 591
Sparklines in 592–593
EXE file 550
EXEC statement 263
EXECUTE command 205
Execute screen, for PAL
    tool 381–382
Execute SQL task 466,
    471–472, 476–477, 479
EXECUTE statement 205–208
Executes column 348
execution models 333–335
execution plan options 11
Execution Plan tab 33
execution plans, comparing
    results of 202
exist() method 325
EXISTING function 561,
    563–565
Existing Report Server Data-
    base option 443
EXISTS clause 179, 564
expansion slots 301
expensive iterations 345
expensive queries 384
Expression editor 413–415
Expression text box 477
Expressions property 477, 482
expressions, time intelligence
    functions 573
external DLL code classes 412
EXTERNAL NAME syntax 230
external waits 333
externalizing, connections in
    SSIS 473
extract phase, of ETL
    design 527–529
extract, transform and load. *See*
    ETL
extracted values 224

F

facades 610
facet_categories sheet 581
facets 132

Fact prefix 552
fact processing, handling late-
arriving dimensions
in 497–500
fact table 457
FactInternetSales table 570
FactSales 495
failures 69–71
Farley, Rob 25
FCR (first call resolution) 171
Feature Selection page 440
FETCH option 200–202
comparing execution plan
results 202
SQL Server solutions
2005 and 2008 201
Denali 201–202
Few, Stephen 593
Fibre Channel cards 168
Fiddler 614
field members 215
fields, adding for native
representation 215
FIFO (first-in, first-out)
queue 334
File enumerator 480–482
file fragmentation 359
File I/O Streaming Access 247
file id:page number
notation 81
File Output screen, for PAL
tool 381
file specifications,
default 165–166
File System task 505–507, 512
FileInfo class 506
FileInfo file 506, 509
FilePath variable 481–482
files, placement of 53–54
Filestream Access Level
option 248
FILESTREAM data
type 245–254
configuring for
database 249–250
operating system 247–248
SQL server 248–249
considerations for 251
creating table using 250–251
overview 245–246
retrieving files in 252–253
filesystems 246
filing, late-arriving
dimensions 496
fill factor, of indexes 36
Filter panel 579, 581–582

filtering, in Silverlight
PivotViewer 579
financial services 602
Find and Replace dialog
box 196
FindByName method 550–553
firehose cursor 388, 390
first call resolution. See FCR
FIRSTDATE (Date_Column)
function 571
FirstDate parameter 430, 432
first-in, first-out. See FIFO
FIRSTNONBLANK
(Date_Column, Expres-
sion) function 572
fixed rate model 125
fixes, testing each release to
see 71–72
flash memory 306
flexibility 588
fn_TotalPrice function 190
fn_virtualfilestats 356
FoodMart2008 database 152
FOR method 316
FOR XML clause 207, 292
Foreach File Enumerator 481
foreach flow control 99,
101–102
Foreach Item Enumerator
483–484
Foreach Loop container 506,
508–510
Foreach Loop Editor 481,
483–484
foreach operator 551
foreign keys 499
FORMAT function 181
Format.Native 219
formatting, code 362–364
FORWARD_ONLY 386,
388–389
four-socket server 301, 304
fragmentation 8, 359
FriendlyName column 116
Fritchey, Grant 319
FROM SERVICE name 290
From Variable
enumerator 488–489
fsFuture() method 349
fsSwap() method 349
Full Access Enabled option 248
full backup 80, 82
full database backup 82
full file backup 82
full filegroup backup 82

Full restore 511–512
FullName-style output 185
functions, stream-
lining 367–368
Fusion-io 307
future ORMs 45

G

GAM page 81
Gap With field 594
GB database 52
GDR (general distribution
release) 77
Geekbench tool 307
general distribution release. See
GDR
generalization 60–64
benefits of 63–64
definition of 62–63
lessons from UIX
discipline 61–62
proper place for
normalization 60–61
Generate Scripts 143, 145
Geography branch 451
Geography dimension 562
GeographyRegionCountry-
Name 451, 455
GET_FILESTREAM_TRANS
ACTION_CONTEXT()
method 252
GetAncestor(@level int)
method 279
get-command 552
GetCustomerInfo 29
getdate() function 528
GetDescendant(@child1,
@child2) method 279
get-help 552
GetLevel() method 279, 284
get-member 552
GetRoot () method 280
global configuration,
controlling 393–394
Globals collection 406
gold key icons 17
Gosbell, Darren 556
Govoni, Sergio 209
granular profiling 190
granularities, restoring data-
bases at 79–80
Graph view icon 579
Graph view, in Silverlight
PivotViewer 579

Graphical User Interfaces. *See* GUIs
Green Widgets 465
greenbar 413–414, 417
GROUP BY clause 16, 23–24
  DISTINCT keyword vs. 21–22
  error when ignored 24–25
Group class 226
Group property 408
grouping constructs 227
groupRestriction parameter 232
groups, introduction to 224–226
groupsToSkip 228
GUI tools 548
GUI wizard 84
GUID value 495
GUIDs, as primary keys 31–32

H

hands-off environment 70
hard disk drive. *See* HDD
hardware configurations 75
hardware failures 168
hardware, database server. *See* database server hardware
HASHBYTES method 109, 462–463
hashing 108
HAVING clause 24
HBAs (host bus adapters) 301
HDD (hard disk drive) 168
HDD damage 173
headers, in Excel as BI frontend tool 591
hierarchies, in database 278
Hierarchies.Add 544
<hierarchy> cube 539
hierarchy data 281
HierarchyId data type 278, 280, 285–286
  hierarchies in database 278
  indexing 282–285
    breadth-first 284–285
    depth-first 283–284
  introduction to 279–282
HierarchyId value 279
high availability 167–174
  and Service Level Agreements 171, 173–174
  and unavailability indicators 169–170
  types of 169
  defined 167–168

measurement indicators for 171–172
options in SQL Server 170–171
high performance pattern 499
hints, query
  OPTIMIZE FOR 313–314
  recompile 315–316
Hirt, Allan 78
horizontal partitioning 300
host bus adapters. *See* HBAs
Host Parameters page 438
hosted server 599
hosting, of Silverlight PivotViewer 582
Hostname property 445
hostname, configuring for NLB 445–446
hotfixes 71–72
HTML report 381
HTML template, for Silverlight PivotViewer 580–581
html-template switch 583
HTTP 401 error messages, workarounds for 446–447
human-caused errors 168
HumanResource table 486
hyperthreading 302–303

I

I/O bandwidth 339
I/O bottleneck 193
I/O intensive 302
I/O operations 162
I/O subsystem, and performance tuning transaction log 358
I/O utilization 302
I/Os per second. *See* IOPS
IAM pages 81
IBinarySerialize interface 213, 220
ICDEMO cube properties 545
ICDEMO database 540
IDE (integrated development environment) 503
IDENTITY column 202–203
identity columns 7, 13–14
Identity key 5, 7
IDENTITY property 204–205
IDX_CATEGORIES_NODE index 284
IEnumerable parameter 228
IF statements 115, 139, 260

implicit loops, user-defined scalar functions in 349–350
importers/outside sources 45
iMyRowCount variable 472
in-cell data bars, in Excel as BI frontend tool 591–592
INCLUDE 283
Include Actual Execution Plan option 33, 162, 190
include columns 34
independent loops 346
index advantage 33
index files 54
index scans 327
Index Seek operator 325
index sizes 7
index_keys 35
indexed sequential access method. *See* ISAM
indexed views 354, 357, 368
indexes 33–36, 354
  and plan cache
    missing 322–323
    scans of 327–328
    usage of 324–325
  clustered, fragmentation of 8
  fill factor of 36
  maintenance of 35
  overindexing 35
  underindexing 33–34
  unique, unique constraints vs. 19–20
IndexFile variable 509
indexing, HierarchyId data type 282–285
  breadth-first indexes 284–285
  depth-first indexes 283–284
indicators, of unavailability 169–170
inequality columns 34
inferred rows 501
InferredFlag column 497, 500
Info panel 578, 581–582
Information property 98
Initial database 46
inline table valued function. *See* iTVF
Inmon methodology 612
INNER JOIN 234, 240–241, 363, 368–370, 497
InnerElementType 489
InnerXPathString 489–490
input columns 230

<Input Name>_ProcessInput-
Row method 517, 519,
523–524
inputs, for Script
component 519–520
Insert log record 354
INSERT statement 89, 116, 143,
145, 203–205, 346, 467
insert trigger 261
INSERT/UPDATE/DELETE
command 158
Installation Results page 438
Installation Rules page 440
Instance Configuration
page 440
instance information, collecting 97–98
instances, multiple 148–152
Instant File Initialization 166
InstantCube 539–543, 546–547
Analysis Services emitter 540
creating cubes 545–547
Data Source View 542–543
data sources 541
dimensions 543–544
relational database
emitter 540
SSAS database 540–541
Visual Studio project for 539
INT data type 13
INT parameter 371
int type 39
integrated development environment. See IDE
Intel processors, vs. AMD
processors 304
intelligent overclocking 303
IntelliSense 140, 179
intent-based management
regime 137
interactivity, adding to SSRS
reports from SSAS 453
Internet Sales Amount
measure 565
interval shape 598, 603
intra-query parallelism 351
intuitive 588
invalid page checksum
error 81
InvokeIfReceiverIsNull
property 221
IO_COMPLETION 339
ioDrive Duo 307
ioDrive Octal 307
IOPS (I/Os per second) 306
IP address 441

is_conversation_error
column 295
is_filter_visible 581
is_metadata_visible 582
is_wordwheel_visible 582
IsActive column 116
ISAM (indexed sequential
access method) 343
IsByteOrdered property 215
IsDescendantOf(@node
hierarchyId) method 279
IsDestinationPathVariable
property 507
IsFixedLength property 215
IsInteractive property 406
IsMatch Regex method 232
IsNull method 220–221
IsRatioBased column 116
IsSourcePathVariable
property 507
IsSQLCounter flag 115–117
IT agreements 172
Item enumerator 482–484
items sheet 582
iTVF (inline table valued
function) 190–191

J

Java database connectivity. See
JDBC
Jayanty, Satya Shyam K 156
JDBC (Java database connectivity) driver,
tuning 384–394
API cursor issues 388–389
controlling global
configuration 393–394
effectiveness of 384–385
jTDS configuration 386
prepared statement mecha-
nism issue 391–393
ResultSet Type types
issue 389–391
Unicode standard character
issues 386–388
JDBC type 390
job information, SQL Agent
98–99
JobServer.Jobs property 98–99
JOIN 363, 368–370, 386, 570
joining datasets 407, 530
joins
on tables using natural
keys 9
optimizing 369–370

joint track data storage. See
jTDS
jTDS (joint track data storage)
configuration 386

K

Karaszi, Tibor 166
key business metrics, for Excel
as BI frontend tool 588
KEY column 386
Key Lookup operations 326
key performance indicators. See
KPIs
keys 3–15
arguments 6–10, 12
debate concerning 5–6
identity columns may result
in value gaps 13
in relational model 4–5
modularity, portability, and
future of 12–13
natural and surrogate 495
primary 17–18
recommendations for 13–14
simplicity and
aesthetics 14–15
Keys section 17
keyword expansion 179
Kharkov National University of
Radioelectronics. See
KNURE
Kim, Jungsun 394
Kimball methodology 612
Kimball, Ralph 588
Kline, Kevin 129
KNURE (Kharkov National
University of
Radioelectronics) 286
Koprowski, Tobiasz Janusz 174
KPIs (key performance
indicators) 587, 614
Kpis collection 546
KPIValue column 118
Krueger, Ted 514
Krug, Steve 38, 61

L

L1 cache 303
L2 cache 302–303
L3 cache 302
LagMonths parameter 430
Lah, Matija 233
Landrum, Rodney 145

Larsen, Greg 94
Larsson, Peter 244
last log backup 165
last user seek 34
LASTDATE (Date_Column)
    function 571
LASTNONBLANK
    (Date_Column, Expres-
    sion) function 572
LASTPERIODS function 426
LastRunOutcome property 99
latches, buffer I/O 339–340
late-arriving dimensions, in
    SSIS 494–501
  example data structure 495
  filing 496
  handling in fact processing
    497–500
  ignoring 496
  natural and surrogate
    keys 495
  processing dimension up-
    date 500–501
  scenario for 494–495
  updating later 497
late-arriving rows, caching
    499–500
LCK_M_* wait types 340
LDF file 158, 359
Lee, Denny 358
Leonard, Andy 479
Levels method 544
Levin, Ami 15
lightweight reports 119
lineage tracking 610
linked pivots, vs. simple
    pivots 579–580
linked server calls, in loops 351
LinkedServers 98
list disk statement 56
ListPrice column 206
live migration 171
load phase, of ETL
    design 531–533
  data update strategy 532–533
  surrogate key generation
    531–532
LoadWithPartialName 96
LOB data types 161
LOB storage 355
local variables 316
LocationID values 31
lock contentions, due to physi-
    cal clustering 10
locking 354
log backup chain 84

log backups, availability of 80
log cache 353
log files
  and data files, separating
    359–360
  transaction 54
Log Reader Agent job 158
log sequence number. See LSN
log shipping 84
logarithmic scale 239
logged operations 358
logging
  misconceptions about
    157–166
  output options 535
logical CPU 333
logical unit number. See LUN
Logman tool 376
logs, transaction 165
long-term strategies 77–78
Lookup function 407
Lookup transformation 496
LookupSet option 407
loop parallelism 345
loops
  description of 343–344
  in complex queries 348–349
  in query execution
    plan 346–348
  linked server calls in 351
  merging multiple into
    one 350
  parallelizing 350–351
  speeding up with slimmer
    table 352
  user-defined scalar func-
    tions in implicit 349–350
  viewing problems from per-
    spective of 344–346
lost information 461
Low, Greg 410
LowerLimit column 116
LSN (log sequence number) 83
LUN (logical unit number) 52

M

m_null placeholder 215
machine information, instance
    information and 97–98
Machine table 370
MachineInventory table 367
<machineKey> element
    445–446
machineKey generator 445
MachineModel table 370

MAFunctionClass 419, 421
Magnabosco, John 110
Magny-Cours processor 304
Main.cs file 522
Main.vb file 522
maintenance, of indexes 35
Manage Policy tab 153
Managed Instances 152
Management Data Warehouse.
    See MDW
management information sys-
    tems. See MIS
ManipulationLog table 262
manual testing, automated test-
    ing vs. 73
master boot record. See MBR
master.sys.sp_MSforeachdd 90
Match class 226
Match function 228, 230
matches, introduction
    to 224–226
Materialized Path 278
matrix, in SSRS reports from
    SSAS 453
MaxByteSize property 215
MAXDOP setting 341
May, Jimmy 358
MBR (master boot record) 54
McCown, Jennifer 373
McGehee, Brad 129, 361
MCT (Microsoft Certified
    Trainer) 120
MDDE (Metadata-Driven ETL
    Management) 539
MDF file 359
MDW (Management Data
    Warehouse) 147
MDX (multidimensional
    expression) 557–568
  calculated members
    in 560–565
  context types in 558
  in Reporting
    Services 424–435
    Adventure Works sample
      data for 425
    building report 425–429
    MDX query builder tool
      425
    passing parameters
      430–432
    returning metadata with
      DMV 432
  named sets in 559–560
  scope assignments in 565–568
MDX query builder tool 425

mean time between failures. *See* MTBF

mean time to recovery/repair. *See* MTTR

<measure> cube 539

Measure Group 451, 545

MeasureList 432

measurement indicators, for high availability 171–172

MeasureName parameter 430, 432–433

Measures dimension 562

Mehta, Siddharth 616

member clause 428

MEMBERS call 560

memory
  cost of 305
  intensive 302
  MLC 306
  pressure 341
  recommendations for 304–305
  SLC 306
  usage 530

Memory Grants Outstanding 341

Memory Grants Pending 341

MemoryStream 464

MERGE statement 464, 467

merging multiple loops 345

MESSAGE TYPE, object for Service Broker 289

message_id parameter 208

metadata
  from ETL system 536
  returning with DMV 432

Metadata-Driven ETL Management. *See* MDDE

meta-LUN 52

metrics, performance 90–94

Microsoft Certified Trainer. *See* MCT

Microsoft Excel, Microsoft PowerShell framework and 95–96

Microsoft Operations Framework. *See* MOF

Microsoft PowerShell framework
  and Microsoft Excel 95–96
  using SMO with 96

Microsoft Windows
  account names, and authentication 163–165
  correcting disk alignment on 55–56

Microsoft.AnalysisServices 550

Microsoft.AnalysisServices.Dimension 544

Microsoft.AnalysisServices.Server object 540

Microsoft.SqlServer.Server library 113

MiddleName value 186

Miller, Ben 254

minimally logged operations 358

MIS (management information systems) 615

missing indexes, and plan cache 322–323

MissingIndex element 322

Mitchell, Allan 607

Mitchell, Tim 525

ML page 81

MLC memory 306

mobile packages, SSIS 509–511

models 4
  chargeback, implementing 125–127
  execution 333–335
  recovery, and availability of log backups 80
  relational, keys in 4–5

ModifiedDate column 182

modularity, of keys 12–13

modules, and snap-ins 555–556

MOF (Microsoft Operations Framework) 76

monitoring SSIS automation 513–514

Month attribute 566

Moreira, Luciano 266

Moss, Jessica M 404

Most database 52

Most Valuable Professional. *See* MVP

MOVE option 512

msdb backup history 81

MSDB backup tables 83

msinfo32.exe 139

MTBF (mean time between failures) 170

MTTR (mean time to recovery/repair) 170

multicore processor 302

multidimensional database 612

multidimensional expressions. *See* MDX

multijoin queries 188

multilevel structure 172

MultiLookup option 407

multiple instances, managing using UCP 148–152

multiple loops 345

multiple spindles 52

multiserver management, and administration 152–155

multiserver query 131

MVP (Most Valuable Professional) 120, 596

MVPDeepDive2 database 482

MVPDeepDivesDev database 471

MVPDeepDivesDev.dbo.MySource table 472

MVPDeepDivesProd database 473

MVPDeepDivesSSISConfigurations project 470, 478

MVPDeepDivesTest database 478

MyRowCount variable 472–473

MySource table 472–473

N

Name column 22

Name field 134

name prefixes 552

Name property 216

named groups 226

named sets, in MDX 559–560

names, of relational databases 39

naming conventions 28–29

NAS matrixes 168

native representation, adding fields for 215

native serialization 219–220

natural disasters 168

natural keys
  and surrogate keys 495
  arguments for 8–10
    assist optimizer 11–12
    eliminate lock contentions due to physical clustering 10
    have business meaning 8–9
    maintain data consistency 9–10
    queries on tables using require fewer joins 9
  issues with
    can become long and complex 6–7
    cases where none exist 7–8
    values can change 6

NDF file 359

.NET data types 219
.NET framework
   and serialized data 219–220
   and text 216–219
   regular expressions
      and 226–227
.NET representation 213
NET SHARE 248
.NET string 542
Network Load Balancing check
   box 437
Network Load Balancing
   feature 438
Network Load Balancing Man-
   ager console 438
network load balancing. See NLB
New Cluster wizard 438
New Project dialog box 214
New Query option 131, 135
newline characters,
   removing 196–197
NEWSEQUENTIALID
   function 31
NEXT VALUE FOR
   function 203–204
NEXTDAY (Date_Column)
   function 572
NEXTMONTH (Date
   _Column) function 572
NEXTQUARTER (Date
   _Column) function 572
NextValue method 114
NEXTYEAR (Date_Column
   [,YE_Date]) function 572
Nielsen, Paul 64
NLB (network load balancing)
   adding feature 437–438
   clusters
      adding hosts to 440
      creating 438–439
   configuring first instance
      441–442
   configuring hostname
      445–446
   configuring second
      instance 442–443
   configuring UrlRoot 445–446
   configuring view state valida-
      tion for 444–445
   installing Reporting Services
      on 440–441
   overview 436
   preparing network
      for 436–437
   workarounds for HTTP 401

error message 446–447
NLB nodes 436
nlbmgr command 438
NO_TRUNCATE option 84
NodeList enumerator
   489–490, 492
NodeNumber 281
non VSS enabled storage
   arrays, snapshots
   with 57–58
nonaggregated fields 24
noncapturing groups 227
nonchanging dimension 459
nonclustered index 283–284,
   347
noncorrelated subqueries 364
nonexact matches 323
nonexpensive queries 384
nonmatched dimension
   rows 498
nonpreemptive scheduling 333
non-SARGable 182, 368–369
nonsensitive data 108
non-uniform memory access.
   See NUMA
nonwaiting sessions 336
NORECOVERY option 84,
   511–512
normal database restore 82
normalization 30–31
   of relational databases 40–41
   overnormalized 30
   proper place for 60–61
   undernormalized 30–31
NOT (negation) 235
NOT NULL constraint 214
NULL method 220–221
NULL values,
   handling 220–221
   InvokeIfReceiverIsNull and
      OnNullCall properties 221
   NULL and IsNull
      methods 220–221
NUMA (non-uniform memory
   access) 91
NumberOfProcessors 380
Numbers table 144
NVARCHAR 179, 388

O

obfuscation 108–109
Object element 324
Object Explorer 17, 248
Object table 63

OBJECT type 316
Object type variable 484
objectid column 321
object-relational mapping. See
   ORM
objects, for Service
   Broker 288–291
   CONTRACT 289
   CONVERSATION 290
   ENDPOINT 290
   MESSAGE TYPE 289
   QUEUE 289
   REMOTE SERVICE
      BINDING 291
   ROUTE 290–291
   security 288
   SERVICE 289
ObjectType table 63
objtype column 321
OFFSET option 200–202
   comparing execution plan
      results 202
   SQL Server solutions
      2005 and 2008 201
   Denali 201–202
OLAP (online analytical
   processing) 586–587
old hardware, reusing 301
OLE DB connection 485, 487,
   540
OLTP (online transaction pro-
   cessing) 60, 325, 331, 356
OLTP applications 301
OLTP database 45, 61
OLTP performance 303
OLTP workload 302
ON CONVERSATION
   type 290
On Demand mode 132
On Schedule mode 132, 134
one dimension placeholder 498
OnError event 536
ongoing expenses 125
OnInformation event 458, 513
online analytical processing.
   See OLAP
online transaction processing.
   See OLTP
OnNullCall attribute 221
OnNullCall property 221
OnProgress event 458
OnWarning event 536
OPENINGBALANCEMONTH
   (Expression, Date_Column
   [,SetFilter]) function 573

OPENINGBALANCEQUAR-
TER Quarter (Expression,
Date_Column [,SetFilter])
function 573
OPENINGBALANCEYEAR
(Expression, Date_Column
[,SetFilter] [,YE_Date])
function 573
operating systems,
configuring 247–248
operational costs 125
operations, and plan
cache 325–327
Opteron 6180SE 304
OPTIMIZE FOR
method 313–314, 316–318
optimizers, assistance to by natural keys 11–12
OPTION RECOMPILE 329
options argument 230
Options window 402
OR (disjunction) 235
ORDER BY clause 24, 183–184,
201
ORDER BY statement 177
OrderID column 204
ORM (object-relational
mapping) 12, 257
OS configuration options 247
OSVersion 98
out of space error 163
OuterXPathString 489–490
out-null cmdlet 96
output columns 230, 520
Output Options screen, for
PAL tool 380–381
outputs, for Script
component 519–520
overclocking 304
overhead model 125
overindexing 35
overly complicated database 63
overnormalized database 29, 63

P

package configurations 469
Package Description
property 473
Package.dtsx 470
Page Life Expectancy. *See* PLE
Page lookups/sec 92
Page reads/sec 92–93
page restores 79–85
granularities 79–80
GUI for, in SQL Server
Denali 84–85

performing 81–84
requirements and limita-
tions 80–81
page type of damaged
page 80–81
recovery model and avail-
ability of log backups 80
SQL Server Edition 80
page splitting 355, 358
page types, of damaged
page 80–81
PAGEIOLATCH_X waits 337,
339
PageName property 406
pagination, for Reporting
Services 406
PAL (Performance Analysis of
Logs) tool 374–383
Counter Log screen 377
counters for 375–376
data collector sets using
template files 375–376
Logman tool 376
SQLDiag tool 376
Execute screen 381
File Output screen 381
Output Options
screen 380–381
overview 374–375
Questions screen 380
Queue screen 381
report for 382
Threshold file
screen 378–379
PAL tool 382
pal.codeplex.com 374
parallelism 326, 340–341
parallelizing, loops 350–351
PARALLELPERIOD
(Date_Column,
Number_of_Intervals,
Interval) function 573
ParallelPeriod function
426–427
Parameter Compiled Value
317–318
Parameter Mapping page 476
parameter sniffing 309–319,
328
description of 309–312
faulty 312–318
local variables 316
OPTIMIZE FOR query
hint 313–314
plan guides 316–318

recompile query
hint 315–316
turning off parameter
sniffing 318
parameterization 328
parameterized query 387
ParameterList element 328
parameters
and plan cache 328–329
in SSRS reports from
SSAS 453–455
passing to MDX queries in
Reporting Services
430–432
parentId field 278
Parse() method 213, 217,
220–221
PARTIAL option 160
partitions, correcting disk
alignment after
creating 56
Partitions.Add method 545–546
PASS (Professional Association
for SQL Server) 137, 319,
410
PathName() method 252
pattern argument 230
pauthor utility 580–583
Pawar, Shashank 122
Payroll application 122
PBM (Policy Based Manage-
ment) 147
PCIe (PCI Express) expansion
slots 301
Pearl, Robert 342
peer-to-peer replication 171
Penev, Boyan 568
PerfCounters table 117, 119
Perfeito, Pedro 596
PerfMon counters 340–341
PerfMon template 375
performance 588
improvement of by artificial
keys 7
of relational databases 46–48
queries and misconceptions
about 162–163
Performance Analysis of Logs.
See PAL
performance bottlenecks 302
Performance Counter log
file 377
performance counters, using
SQLCLR to get values
112–115

performance dashboards
111–120
DMVs as source of
performance-related
information 111–112
performance monitoring
sample solution
for 115–118
SSRS for 118–119
tips for 119
using SQLCLR to get performance counter values
112–115
performance data, correlating
339–341
blocking and locking 340
CPU pressure 340
I/O issues 339
memory pressure 341
parallelism 340–341
performance issues, using
UDFs 185–188, 193
Performance Log sessions 376
performance metrics 90–94
Performance Monitor
counters 33, 356
performance monitoring
sample solution for 115–118
SSRS for 118–119
performance tuning, for transaction log 357–361
aligning disk partitions 358
and transaction log file
size 359
backing up often 360
fast I/O subsystem 358
managing virtual log files 360
removing physical file
fragmentation 358
separating data and log
files 359–360
standard techniques 357–358
using minimally logged
operations 358
PerformanceCounter class 114
PerformancePoint Services
2010. See PPS
PerfStats scripts 377
permissions, role-based 107–108
Person.Contact table 186, 201
personally identifiable data 106
PFS page 81
physical clustering, lock contentions due to 10
physical file fragmentation 359
pipelining 551
Pivot Table Connections 593

pivot tables, in Excel as BI frontend tool 590–591
PivotViewer control 578
PK (primary key) 161
PK_SalesOrderHeader_Sales
OrderID 325
PK_Vendor_VendorID 18
placeholder row 497–498
plan cache 320–330
and index scans 327–328
and index usage 324–325
and missing indexes 322–323
and operations 325–327
and parameters 328–329
considerations when
querying 329
dynamic management
objects for 320–322
plan guides 316–318
plan_handle column 321
planned system outage. See PSO
planning, capacity. See capacity
planning
PLE (Page Life Expectancy) 378
Plot Series On field 594
PLSSUG (Polish SQL Server
User Group) 120
point event 598, 603
Policy Based Management. See
PBM
Policy Details tab 153
Policy-Based Management
tool 131–135
Surface Area Configuration
policy 132–134
Sysadmin membership
134–135
with Central Management
Servers feature 135–136
Polish SQL Server User Group.
See PLSSUG
Port Rules page 439
portability, of keys 12–13
Portfolio table 240
Potasinski, Pawel 120
PowerPivot add-on 569–576
DAX functions 569–570
data types 569–570
sample database 570
time intelligence
functions 570–573
rules for 571
samples 573–576
that evaluate expressions
over time period 573
that return single date
571–572

that return table of dates
572–573
PowerShell batch state-
ments 381
PowerShell framework
advantages of 548
AMO library and 548–556
advantages of 548–549
automating processing
549–552
repetitive design
changes 551–556
PowerShell framework, Microsoft. See Microsoft Power-
Shell framework
PowerSSAS 555–556
PPS (PerformancePoint Services 2010) 615
Prajdi, Mladen 179, 277
precedence constraints, SSIS
511–512
Prepare/Execute method
391–392
prepareCall() method 393
prepared statements, mechanism issue 391–393
PreparedStatement class 387,
392
prepareSQL 386, 392–393
preproduction 70
PREVIOUSDAY (Date_Column)
function 572
PREVIOUSMONTH (Date
_Column) function 572
PREVIOUSQUARTER (Date
_Column) function 572
PREVIOUSYEAR
(Date_Column
[,YE_Date]) function 572
price/capacity sweet spot 305
PRIMARY filegroup 160
primary keys 17–18, 31–32
generating values for 32
GUIDs as 31–32
system-generated integers
as 32
Primate Labs 307
Private Assemblies folder 420
Private Cloud 123
Process method 551–552
processing, automating
549–552
processor cores 303
Processor: % Processor Time
counter 382

processors, Intel vs. AMD 304
processType parameter 550
ProcessUpdate 549–551, 556
Product Category level 451
Product Name level 451
Product Subcategory level 451
Product Support Services. *See* PSS
Product table 285
Product_Category_Name 453, 455
Product_Name 453
Product_Subcategory_Name 453
ProductID column 178
ProductID field 407
Production group 136
Production Servers group 130–131
production time 171
Production.Product table 22
ProductModel dataset 407
ProductName LIKE 363–364, 369
Products table 9
ProductSalesPrice column 365
ProductTypeID 2 369
Professional Association for SQL Server. *See* PASS
Profiler trace 190, 389
Program FilesPAL folder 375
Progress and Finish page 442
Properties option 248
Properties page 311, 317
Property Expression Editor 511
pseudocode 366
PSO (planned system outage) 169
PSS (Product Support Services) team 376
pub_id 386–387
Publish Report Parts option 402

Q

QA group 140
quantum 333
queries
  and performance, misconceptions about 162–163
  complex, loops in 348–349
  date range, mishandling 182–183
  determining kind of 364–366
    data 364–365

pseudocode 366
  SELECT columns 364
  sketching 365
loops in execution plan 346–348
on tables using natural keys, fewer joins required 9
working for all types of relational division 242
query context 557
Query Designer button 450
query hints
  OPTIMIZE FOR 313–314
  recompile 315–316
Query Plan 34
query_plan column 321
querying
  many servers at once 138–141
  streams 603–606
Questions screen, for PAL tool 380
Queue screen, for PAL tool 381
queue waits 333
QUEUE, object for Service Broker 289

R

R2 Management Studio Object Explorer screen 149
Radgoudarzi, Abolfazl 492
RAID (redundant array of independent disks) type 49–53
RAID 0 arrays 49–50
RAID 1 arrays 50
RAID 5 arrays 51–53
RAID 6 arrays 51–53
RAID 10 array 358
RAID 10 arrays 52
RAID 50 arrays 52
RAID controllers 301, 306
RAID levels 306
RAID type 49, 52
RAISERROR statement 263
RAISERROR() function 208
RAM capacity 301
RAM limit 301
Randall, Paul 129, 251, 360
RANK() method 350
RDBMS (relational database management systems) 235, 600–601
RDBMS concept 519
RDL (Report Definition Language) 411

RDP (remote desktop connect) 139
Read() method 213, 220
readable code 362–364
  comments 364
  formatting 362–364
ReadOnlyVariables property 472, 478
Ready to Install page 441
ReceiveErrors table 270
recompile query hint 315–316
recovery and restart ability, in ETL system 533–535
recovery mode 355
recovery models, and availability of log backups 80
recovery point objectives. *See* RPOs
recovery time objectives. *See* RTOs
recovery, replication and 160–162
redundant indexes 357
refactoring code, with unit tests 256
reference lists 224
referenced document 225
Refresh Development package 504, 506–513
Refresh Fields button 433
refrigerated attribute 371
Regex class 227, 232
RegexOptions enumeration 227
Region Country Name column 451, 454
Registered Servers 130, 141
regular expressions 223–233
  in SSMS 195–199
    collapsing multiple lines into single line 197–198
    eliminating blank lines 195
    removing extra newline characters 196–197
  solution 227–231
    core 227–229
    SQL CLR user-defined function 229–230
    SSIS script component 230–231
  understanding 223–227
    .NET framework 226–227
    background 224–226
    introduction to regular expressions, matches, and groups 224–226

Regular Expressions option 196
relational database emitter 540
relational database management systems. *See* RDBMS
relational databases 37, 41–48
  coherent 38–40
    cohesive databases 40
    documentation 40
    reasonable names and data types 39
    standards-based databases 38–39
  documented 42–43
  encapsulated 44–46
  fundamentally sound 41–42
  normal 40–41
  secure 43–44
  well performing 46–48
relational division 234–244
  background 235
  comparison charts 238–240
  defining 234–235
  query working for all types 242
  reasons to use 234
  sample data for two simple cases 236–238
  set-based solutions 240–241
relational models, keys in 4–5
RelationalDataSource object 541
releases, testing each to see fixes 71–72
relevant processes 74
RelOp element 325–326
remote desktop connect. *See* RDP
REMOTE SERVICE BINDING, object for Service Broker 291
RenderFormat object 406
repeating character masking 109
REPLACE option 165
REPLICATE method 109
replication, and recovery 160–162
Report Builder 401–402
Report Code property expressions 412
Report Definition Language. *See* RDL
report element property expressions 412
Report Manager URL link 442
Report Part Gallery 403

Report Server Mode option 443
Report Server Project template 118
reporting platform 609, 613–614
Reporting Services 405–410
  aggregates of aggregates 407
  databars in 408–409
  datasets in, joining 407
  deciding if needed 398
  domain scope in 408
  pagination for, controlling 406
  report parts
    changing 403
    creating 402
    defined 397
    level 1 400
    level 2 400
    level 3 401
    level 4 401
    using in reports 403
  scaling 436–447
    adding hosts to NLB cluster 440
    adding NLB feature 437–438
    configuring first instance 441–442
    configuring hostname 445–446
    configuring UrlRoot 445–446
    configuring view state validation 444–445
    installing Reporting Services on NLB cluster 440–441
    preparing network 436–437
    workarounds for HTTP 401 error message 446–447
  sparklines in 409–410
  target-based rendering 405–406
  with MDX queries 424–435
    Adventure Works sample data for 425
    building report 425–429
    MDX query builder tool 425
    passing parameters 430–432
    returning metadata with DMV 432
  WritingMode property 407

Reporting Services check box 440
Reporting Services Configuration Connection dialog box 441
Reporting Services Configuration page 441
REPORTING switch 478
ReportServer 441
representations
  and conversions 213
  native, adding fields for 215
requerying 601
requestedGroups 228
Rerun Validation button 150
Resource Governor. *See* RG
resource usage 385
resource waits 332, 337–339
response time, TRT 331–332
RESTART WITH option 204
restartability strategy 533
restore all log backups rule 160
RESTORE command 508
RESTORE DATABASE command 160, 165
RESTORE LOG commands 83
RESTORE scripts 504
RestorePending 83
restoring and backing up, tables 159–160
restoring backups 73
restoring data. *See* page restores
Result column 150
Result Set tab 477
RESULT SETS clause 205–208
results, uniqueness in 20–25
  DISTINCT keyword 20–21
  error when GROUP BY clause is ignored 24–25
  need for 22
  unnecessary grouping 23
ResultSet property 477
ResultSet Type types, issues with 389–391
retention policies 107
retrieval mechanism 246
retrieving files, in FILESTREAM data type 252–253
return on investment. *See* ROI
reusable packages, SSIS 509–511
Reznik, Denis 286
RFID tag 598, 602
RG (Resource Governor) 147
RIA (rich internet application) 577
rich internet application. *See* RIA

rmdir command 583
ROI (return on investment) 586
role-based permissions 107–108
ROLLBACK statement 204
Rotate270 property 407
ROUTE, object for Service Broker 290–291
RouteDataReceiver 274
row headers 100
ROW_NUMBER() function 201–202
row-by-row processing, using UDFs 188–190
RowCounts column 190
rows, late-arriving 499–500
RPOs (recovery point objectives) 68
RSReportServer.config file 445–446
RSScripter 614
RTOs (recovery time objectives) 68
Run all tests.bat file 265
Run command 89
RunInOptimizedMode setting 458
runnable queue 335
runnable_task_counts 340
RUNNING state 337
runtime event logging, in ETL system 535–536

S

SaaS (Software as a Service) model 122
Salas, Rafael 537
Sales Key Metrics chart 593
Sales_Amount column 453
Sales.SalesOrderDetail table 178
SalesOrderDetailID column 178
SalesOrderHeader table 187
SalesOrderID column 178
SalesPerson table 187
SalesSource table 495
SAMEPERIODLASTYEAR (Date_Column) function 573
SAN (storage area network) 305
SAN matrixes 168
Sarmiento, Edwin 447
Save Report button 150
scalability, and data types 28
scalar functions, user-defined 349–350

Scalar operator 325
scaling
    Reporting Services 436–447
        adding hosts to NLB cluster 440
        adding NLB feature 437–438
        and NLB 436
        configuring first instance 441–442
        configuring hostname 445–446
        configuring second instance 442–443
        configuring UrlRoot 445–446
        configuring view state validation 444–445
        creating NLB cluster 438–439
        installing Reporting Services on NLB cluster 440–441
        preparing network 436–437
        workarounds for HTTP 401 error message 446–447
    up or out 300–301
SCDs (slowly changing dimensions) 500
    Type 0 SCDs 459–460
    Type 1 SCDs 460–464
    Type 2 SCDs 465–467
Schema and Data option 145
Schema Only option 145
SCHEMABINDING condition 179
scope assignments, in MDX 565–568
SCOPE function 565
SCOPE statements 567
SCOPE_IDENTITY() method 262
Script button 84
Script component 515–525
    as destination 517, 523
    as source 517, 522–523
    as transformation 517–518, 524
    asynchronous transformation 519
    inputs and outputs for 519–520
    SSIS 230–231
    synchronous transformation 518–519

when to use 516
Script task 505–509, 513–514
Scripter class 554–555
scripting
    databases 554–555
    multiple objects and data 143–145
    solutions, with templates 141–143
    with AMO library and PowerShell framework 548–556
        advantages of 548–549
        automating processing 549–552
        repetitive design changes 551–556
Scripting Options page 144
ScriptLanguage property 472
ScriptMain class 463
ScriptTaskLogEntry event 513
SCRUBS execution log analysis framework 614
SDLC (software development life cycle) 469
second-generation hyperthreading 303
security
    object for Service Broker 288
    of relational databases 43–44
Security tab 153
SEEK operator 387
SELECT @@VERSION query 140
SELECT * statement 259
SELECT * stored procedure 177–179
SELECT clause 24, 189
SELECT columns 364
select disk N command 56
Select Features page 437
SELECT operator 310–312, 314, 317
Select Report Parts To Publish dialog box 403
SELECT SERVERPROPERTY query 139
SellEndDate column 206
SellStartDate column 206
SEND privilege 291
SendErrors table 270
sendStringParametersAs Unicode 386, 388, 393
separation, of data 108
SEQUENCE object 202–205
    restrictions 203–205
    tips for using 203
Sequence Project Task 202

serialization
  custom 220
  native 219–220
serialized data, .NET frame-
    work and 219–220
serialized representation 213
Series Options tab 594
server calls, linked 351
Server database 111–114,
    442–443
Server Manager console 437
Server object 96, 100, 552
server processors 301
Server table 473
Server type 546
Server.Information.Edition
    property 98
Server.Settings.LoginMode
    property 98
ServerName variable 510–511
SERVERPROPERTY object 73,
    139
servers
  discovering 95–104
    collecting information
      97–104
    Microsoft PowerShell
      framework 95–96
  querying many at
    once 138–141
  SQL
    and selection of database
      server hardware 301
    regular expressions
      and 226
ServersData veriable 484
<Service> section 446
Service Broker 267–277,
    287–296
  DataReceiver instance
    268–269, 273–274
  DataSender instance
    269–270, 276–277
  example using 287–288, 292
  objects for 288–291
    CONTRACT 289
    CONVERSATION 290
    ENDPOINT 290
    MESSAGE TYPE 289
    QUEUE 289
    REMOTE SERVICE
      BINDING 291
    ROUTE 290–291
    security 288
    SERVICE 289
Service Level Agreements 171,
    173–174

service packs. See SPs
service time 172
SERVICE, object for Service
    Broker 289
service-oriented structure 172
Services database 425, 434,
    455, 548, 553, 555
session context 557
SET CONTEXT_INFO
    command 164
SET STATISTICS IO ON
    command 162
SET STATISTICS PROFILE
    ON 347–348
SET STATISTICS PROFILE
    ON command 347–348
set-based refactoring 191–192
set-based solutions to relational
    division 240–241
SetBGColor function 415–417
SetFilter parameter 572–573
SetID function 242–243
SetTextColor function 415–417
Setup Role page 440
SGAM page 81
shapes, of events 598
sharable code expressions, for
    SSRS
  creating 419–421
  referencing DLLs from
    report 421–422
shared data sources, for SSRS
    reports from SSAS 449
Shared Datasets branch 452
shared datasets, for SSRS
    reports from SSAS 449–452
Shaw, Chris 36
Shaw, Gail 86
Shea, Linchi 352
SHOWPLAN XML
    format 320–321, 329
shrinking, databases 163
signal waits 333, 337–339
signatures, editing 215–216
Silverlight PivotViewer 577–584
  cards in 578
  EXCEL workbook
    design 581–582
  filtering and sorting 579
  Graph view in 579
  hosting of 582
  HTML template for 580–581
  implementing 582–584
  overview 577–578
  simple vs. linked
    pivots 579–580
  source for 580

simple cube generator 539–547
  Analysis Services emitter 540
  creating cubes 545–547
  Data Source View 542–543
  data sources 541
  dimensions 543–544
  relational database
    emitter 540
  SSAS database 540–541
  Visual Studio project for 539
simple key 5
simple pivots, vs. linked
    pivots 579–580
single-level cell. See SLC
SixtyFourBit 380
sizing tools, benchmarking
    and 307–308
sketching, shape of query 365
Skip method 228
SLA clauses 171
SLC (single-level cell)
    memory 306
slowly changing dimensions.
    See SCDs
SMALLDATETIME type 181,
    183
smallint 542
SMO (SQL Server Manage-
    ment Objects) 96
smokescreen tests 73
snap-ins, modules and 555–556
snap-sets 57
snapshots 56–58
  as backup process 58
  using to present storage to
    downstream environ-
    ments 58
  with non VSS enabled stor-
    age array 57–58
  with VSS enabled storage
    array 57
SniggleStr column 39
snowflake schema 457
Software as a Service. See SaaS
software development life
    cycle. See SDLC
software faults 168
solid state disks. See SSD
sort operations 529
sorting, in Silverlight
    PivotViewer 579
SOS_SCHEDULER_YIELD
    waits 333, 340
source
  as Script
    component 522–523
  Script component as 517

Source Connection
    Manager 484
Source property 544
source systems 608
sp_configure options 249
sp_configure procedure 249
sp_cursorclose procedure 389
sp_cursorfetch procedure 389
sp_cursoropen procedure
    389–390
sp_execute procedure
    386–387, 391–392
sp_executesql procedure 386,
    391–392
sp_help procedure 35
sp_prepare procedure 387, 392
sp_prepexec/sp_unprepare
    procedure 393
sp_setapprole procedure 164
sp_unprepare procedure 393
sp_who procedure 164
SP:StmtCompleted event 190
sparklines
    in Excel as BI frontend
        tool 592–593
    in Reporting Services
        409–410
Specify Values for Template
    Parameters icon 142
spindles 52
Split method 232
spReceiveTransferredData
    procedure 273
SPs (service packs) 68
SQL (Structured Query Lan-
    guage) Server
    and selection of database
        server hardware 301
    CLR user-defined function
        112–115, 164, 229–230
    configuring, for
        FILESTREAM data
        type 248–249
    cost recovery 121–127
        chargebacks 125
        SQL Server as a Service
            121–123
    dynamic 371–373
    misconceptions
        about 157–166
        authentication and Micro-
            soft Windows account
            names 163–165
        collation selection 158–159
        default file specifica-
            tions 165–166

difficulty of using SQL
    server 166
logging 157–166
queries and performance
    162–163
replication and recovery
    160–162
shrinking databases 163
table-level backup and
    restore 159–160
transaction log backups
    165
regular expressions and 226
SQL Agent job information,
    collecting 98–99
SQL Client Tools 142
SQL CLR module 226
SQL command 497
SQL Error Log 81
SQL guide 316
SQL Sentry Plan Explorer 178
SQL Server Agent job
    information 99
SQL Server Agent job
    schedules 149
SQL Server Agent service 148,
    154
SQL Server Analysis Services.
    See SSAS
SQL Server as a Service
    context for 121–122
    description of 122–123
SQL Server Best Practices
    Analyzer 129
SQL Server database 222
SQL Server Denali 200–210
    EXECUTE statement and
        WITH RESULT SETS
        clause 205–208
    GUI for page restores
        in 84–85
    OFFSET and FETCH
        options 200–202
        comparing execution plan
            results 202
        SQL Server solutions
            201–202
    SEQUENCE object 202–205
        restrictions 203–205
        tips for using 203
    THROW statement 208–210
SQL Server Edition, and page
    restores 80
SQL Server execution
    model 333
SQL Server Installation
    Center 440

SQL Server Integration Ser-
    vices. See SSIS
SQL Server Management
    Objects. See SMO
SQL Server Management Stu-
    dio. See SSMS
SQL Server OLTP
    workloads 299
SQL Server patches 71
SQL Server processor
    licenses 300
SQL Server Project
    template 112
SQL Server Reporting Services.
    See SSRS
SQL Server scheduling
    system 337
SQL Server sprawl 121
SQL Server Sri Lanka User
    Group. See SSSLUG
SQL Server table 481–482
SQL Server template 376
SQL2K8R2_SE instance 152
SQLCLR assembly 113
sqlcmd command 73
SQLCMD interface 148
SQLCommand variable 487,
    492
SQLDiag tool 376
SqlFileStream object 252–253
SqlFileStream.Write
    method 253
SqlFunction 113–114
SqlHierarchyId type 285
SqlMethod property 220–221
SqlServer.Types 279
SQLPrompt 179
SqlServer.Types 279
SQLSourceType variable 487
SSAS (SQL Server Analysis
    Services) 590, 613
    autogenerating
        cubes 538–547
        background 538–539
        InstantCube simple cube
            generator 539–547
    scripting with AMO library
        and PowerShell frame-
        work 548–556
        advantages of 548–549
        automating processing
            549–552
        repetitive design changes
            551–556
    SSRS reports from 448–456
        adding interactivity to 453
        adding shared data
            source 449

SSAS *(continued)*
　charts in 455
　creating report project 449
　creating shared
　　datasets 449–452
　datasets in 453
　matrix in 453
　parameters in 453–455
SSAS database 426, 448, 450,
　541, 545, 552
SSASEmitter class 540
SSD (solid state disks) 306
SSIS (SQL Server Integration
　Services) 226, 612
　building demo database 470
　building solution 470–472
　common automation
　　tasks 504–505
　connections in
　　abstracting 474–479
　　changing 472–473
　　externalizing 473
　extending with Script
　　component 515–525
　as destination 517
　as source 523
　asynchronous transforma-
　　tion 519
　inputs and outputs
　　for 519–520
　synchronous transforma-
　　tion 518–519
　when to use 516
　key tasks and components 5
　　05–509
　late-arriving dimensions
　　in 494–501
　example data structure 495
　filing 496
　handling in fact
　　processing 497–500
　ignoring 496
　natural and surrogate
　　keys 495
　processing dimension
　　update 500–501
　scenario for 494–495
　updating later 497
　monitoring results 513–514
　optimizing for dimensional
　　data load 457–468
　general optimizations
　　457–459
　Type 0 SCDs 459–460
　Type 1 SCDs 460–464
　Type 2 SCDs 465–467

precedence and manipulat-
　ing control flow 511–512
reusable and mobile
　packages 509–511
SSIS command 478
SSIS data flow component 232
SSIS variables 230
SSISConfig database 474–478
SSISConfig.cfg.Connections
　table 477
SSISConfig.dtsConfig
　file 475–476
SSMS (SQL Server Manage-
　ment Studio) 138–146,
　248, 258
　querying many servers at
　　once 138–141
　regular expressions
　　in 195–199
　collapsing multiple lines
　　into single line 197–198
　eliminating blank lines 195
　removing extra newline
　　characters 196–197
　scripting
　　multiple objects and
　　　data 143–145
　solution with templates
　　141–143
　tools for DBAs 147–148
SSMS Reports 147
SSMS Tools Pack 179
SSRS (SQL Server Reporting
　Services) 111, 614
　code expressions
　　for 411–423
　adding 411–418
　creating sharable 419–421
　referencing DLLs from
　　report 421–422
　for performance
　　monitoring 118–119
　reports, from SSAS 448–456
　adding interactivity to 453
　adding shared data
　　source 449
　charts in 455
　creating report project 449
　creating shared datasets
　　449–452
　datasets in 453
　matrix in 453
　parameters in 453–455
SSSLUG (SQL Server Sri
　Lanka User Group) 584
staged data 529
staging area 609

staging table 533
stakeholders 76
standard resource rates
　model 125
standards, relational databases
　based on 38–39
star schema 457
StartDate 466
STARTOFMONTH (Date
　_Column) function 572
STARTOFQUARTER (Date
　_Column) function 572
STARTOFYEAR (Date_Column
　[,YE_Date]) function 572
Statement Completed
　event 187
statements, mechanism
　issue 391–393
Static method 280
STATIC named set 559
STATISTICS IO output 185
StmtText column 347–348
Stockholder table 240
Stockname 237, 240
storage 49–59
　clones 59
　disk alignment 54–56
　correcting 55–56
　on array 56
　file placement 53–54
　selecting correct RAID
　　type 49–53
　snapshots 56–58
　as backup process 58
　using to present storage to
　　downstream
　　environments 58
　with non VSS enabled stor-
　　age array 57–58
　with VSS enabled storage
　　array 57
　subsystems
　　new developments
　　　in 306–307
　　traditional 305–306
storage area network. *See* SAN
storage arrays
　non VSS enabled, snapshots
　　with 57–58
　VSS enabled, snapshots
　　with 57
Storage Utilization tab 151
storage-based backups 75
StorageMode 545–546
Stored procedure 371–372
straight tree structure 281
Strate, Jason 330

strategies, long-term 77–78
StreamInsight CEP
 engine 597–607
 architecture of 599–600
 deployment of 599
 description of 597
 events and event
  streams 598
 querying streams 603–606
 uses for 602–603
streamlining, code 366–369
 dynamic SQL 371–373
 functions 367–368
 non-SARGable WHERE
  clauses 368–369
 optimizing joins 369–370
 similar subqueries and
  queries 370–371
 too much data 367
streams, querying 603–606
string data type 220, 481, 490
String() method 217
StringBuilder type 219
strm solution 605–606
Subject Area folder 400–401
subnodes 284
subqueries and queries,
 streamlining
  similar 370–371
substrings 225
Summary page 442
Summary tab 145
superfluous iterations 345
superfluous loops 345
support costs 125
support rollback 157
Surface Area Configuration
 policy 132–134
surrogate key generation, in
 load phase 531–532
surrogate keys, natural keys
 and 495
suspect_pages table 81
suspended queue 334
SUSPENDED state 337
suspense table 496
synchronous output 232
synchronous transformation
 519–520
SynchronousInputID 519
sys.dm_db_missing_index_*
 DMOs 322–323
sys.dm_exec_* 320
sys.dm_exec_cached_plans
 320–321
sys.dm_exec_query_plan
 320–322

sys.dm_exec_requests DMO 335
sys.dm_exec_sessions 164
sys.dm_io_pending_io_request
 s DMO 356
sys.dm_io_virtual_file_stats
 DMO 339, 356
sys.dm_os_performance
 DMV 92
sys.dm_os_performance
 _counters stored
 procedure 89–93, 112,
 116–117
sys.dm_os_ring_buffer stored
 procedure 91
sys.dm_os_schedulers DMV 333
sys.dm_os_wait_stats
 DMO 335, 337
sys.dm_os_waiting_tasks
 DMO 335
sys.dm_tran_locks DMO 340
sys.sequences view 203
sys.sp_refreshsqlmodule stored
 procedure 179
sys.transmission_queue catalog view 295
Sysadmin Check
 Condition 135
Sysadmin Check Policy 134
Sysadmin member-
 ship 134–135
sysadmin-privileged
 accounts 134
SysSSISLog table 536
System.Data.SqlDataTypes
 class 252
System.Diagnostics 113
System.Globalization 217
System.IO class 507
<system.web> section 445
system-generated integers, as
 primary keys 32
sysutility_MDW database 148,
 150

T

table column 246
table variables 368
tables
 backing up and
  restoring 159–160
 creating, with FILESTREAM
  data type 250–251
 of dates, time intelligence
  functions that
  return 572–573

speeding up loops with
 slimmer 352
using natural keys, fewer
 joins required on 9
Tables Schema Restrictions
 window 486–487
Tablix control 412–413,
 416–417
tail-log backup 165
Target Server Memory
 counter 379
target-based rendering in
 Reporting
 Services 405–406
targets 132
tasks, SSIS 505–509
TasksGenerate Scripts
 option 143
TAT (turnaround time) 171
TB database 53, 58
Team Foundation Server. *See*
 TFS
tempdb database 54
Template Explorer 141
template parameters 143
TEMPLATE type 317
templates, scripting solution
 with 141–143
Test Servers group 130
test/QA servers 140
testing 67–70, 72–78
 automated vs. manual 73
 change control 75–76
 each release to see
  fixes 71–72
 early and often 72–73
 failures 69–71
 list of situations for 73–75
 long-term strategies 77–78
 use beyond application
  functionality 68–69
testing, unit. *See* unit testing
Tests - usp_RegisterCustomer
 .sql project 259
Tests - usp_RegisterCustomer
 .sql script 265
text, .NET framework
 and 216–219
textual (string)
 representation 213
TFS (Team Foundation
 Server) 141
third-party vendors 129
thread scheduling 333
ThreeGBSwitch 380
Threshold File screen 378

Threshold File Title drop-down
box 375, 378
THROW statement 208–210
time intelligence functions
570–573
rules for 571
samples 573–576
that evaluate expressions
over time period 573
that return single
date 571–572
that return table of
dates 572–573
time service factor. *See* TSF
Time table 571
time, characteristic of Stream-
Insight CEP
engine 602–603
tiny int 28
title case 553
tools
for DBAs 146–156
best practices 155
managing multiple
instances using
UCP 148–152
multiserver management
and administration
152–155
SQL Server 2008
R2 146–147
SSMS 147–148
sizing, benchmarking
and 307–308
TOP expression 201
ToString() method 213, 217,
221, 280
Total Response Time. *See* TRT
Total Server Memory
counter 379
TotalMemory 380
TOTALMTD (Expression,
Date_Column [, SetFilter])
function 573
TOTALQTD (Expression, Date
_Column [, SetFilter])
function 573
TOTALYTD (Expression, Date
_Column [, SetFilter]
[,YE_Date]) function 573
TPC benchmarks 307
TPC-E benchmark 307
TPC-H results 307
TradeEvent class 604
Trader class 604
TraderID 604–605
tradeStream 604–605

transaction log 353–361
bottlenecking of 353–357
performance tuning
for 357–361
aligning disk partitions 358
and transaction log file
size 359
backing up often 360
fast I/O subsystem 358
managing virtual log
files 360
removing physical file
fragmentation 358
separating data and log
files 359–360
standard techniques
357–358
using minimally logged
operations 358
transaction log activity 357
transaction log data 353
transaction log files 54
transaction logs, backups 165
Transaction Processing Performance Council 307
transactional locks 354
transactional replication 158
transactions 357
Transact-SQL Access Enabled
option 248
Transact-SQL statement 477
Transact-SQL. *See* T-SQL
transform phase, of ETL
design 529–531
transformation
as Script component 524
Script component as 517–518
transformation component 230
transmission_status column 295
Tripp, Kimberly 166
TRT (Total Response
Time) 331–332
TRY block 209, 263
Try Catch block 514
TSF (time service factor) 171
T-SQL (Transact-SQL)
bad habits in 177–184
about author 184
declaring VARCHAR data
type without
length 179–180
making assumptions about
ORDER BY
clause 183–184
mishandling date range
queries 182–183

not choosing right data
type 181–182
SELECT * stored
procedure 177–179
unit test walkthrough
257–265
TSQLUnitTest database 258
Turbo Boost technology 303
Turley, Paul 435
turnaround time. *See* TAT
two-socket server 301, 304
Type 0 SCDs 459–460
Type 1 SCDs 460–464
Type 2 SCDs 465–467
type of references 225
Type property 544
Type value 241
TYPE_FORWARD_ONLY
JDBC type 390
TYPE_SCROLL_INSENSITIVE
JDBC type 390
TYPE_SCROLL_SENSITIVE
JDBC type 390
TYPE_SCROLL_SENSITIVE+1
JDBC type 390
types
data, DAX 569–570
of unavailability 169
page, of damaged
page 80–81
ResultSet Type, issues
with 389–391
wait, categories of 332–333
Types of Data to Script
option 144

U

UAT (user acceptance
training) 127
UCP (Utility Control
Point) 148–152
UCP Wizard 149
UDAs (user-defined
aggregates) 211
UDFs (user-defined
functions) 185–194
alternatives to 190–192
set-based refactor-
ing 191–192
using iTVF 190–191
and code reuse 192–193
performance issues when
using 185–188, 193
row-by-row processing
with 188–190

UDM (Unified Dimensional Model) 577
ufn_clr_GetPerfCounterValue 113–115
UI code-behind button 64
UIX (user interface design and user experience) 61–62
UMDW (Utility Management Data Warehouse) 148, 153
unavailability
    indicators 169–170
    types of 169
underindexing 33–34
undernormalized database 29–31
Unicode parameter 388
Unicode standard, character issues 386–388
Unified Dimensional Model. *See* UDM
Uniform Resource Locator. *See* URL
unique compiles 34
UNIQUE constraint 42
unique constraints 18–20
unique constraints, vs. unique index 20
unique indexes 19–20
uniqueidentifier column 161, 250
UniqueName property 454
uniqueness 16–25
    constraints 16–19
        primary keys 17–18
        unique 18–20
        unique indexes 19
    in results 20–25
        DISTINCT keyword 20–21
        error when GROUP BY clause is ignored 24–25
        need for 22
        unnecessary grouping 23
    introduction to 16
UniqueServiceName 274
unit testing 255–266
    automating execution of 265
    basics of 255–265
        T-SQL unit test walk-through 257–265
        unit test for databases 256–257
    objectives of chapter on 255
Universal Product Code. *See* UPC

Unknown dimension member 496
UNKNOWN statement 314
unplanned system outage. *See* USO
unpredictable events 168
UNSAFE statement 114–115
unused CU utilization 126
unused indexes 357
unused joins 369
UPC (Universal Product Code) 462
Update method 541
UPDATE statement 368, 500, 519
UpdateOptions.ExpandFull 544, 546
updating
    dimension records 500–501
    late-arriving dimensions 497
UpperLimit column 116
upsert 461
URL (Uniform Resource Locator) 288
<UrlRoot> element 446
UrlRoot, configuring for NLB 445–446
Use Counts 34
usecounts column 321
useCursors 386, 388, 390, 393
user acceptance training. *See* UAT
user seeks 34
User::Database variable 487
User::Email variable 490
User::Item variable 489
User::MVPDeepDivesConnectionString variable 477
User::ServerName variable 483–484
User::TableName variable 487
user-defined aggregates. *See* UDAs
user-defined data types, CLR 212–214
user-defined function 113
user-defined functions 349–350
user-defined functions. *See* UDFs
UserDefinedFunctions class 103, 113–115
UserTable 27
using substring statement 41
USO (unplanned system outage) 169
usp_RegisterCustomer procedure 258

usp_Restore_Database.sql script 142
Utility Administration node 153
Utility Control Point. *See* UCP
Utility Explorer Content tab 151
Utility Explorer screen 153
Utility Explorer tab 149
Utility Management Data Warehouse. *See* UMDW

V

ValidationMethodName property 215
value gaps, resulting from identity columns 13
Value property 417
Value type 477
var1 placeholder 215
VARBINARY value 321
varbinary(max) columns 247–248
varchar 278, 371, 386, 542
VARCHAR data type 179–180, 388
varchar(12) 39
Variable Mappings tab 481–484, 489–491
Variable Name drop-down 471
Variables viewer 510
Vaughn, William 423
verification path 256
vertical partitioning 300
vertical pipe character 551
View link 136
view state validation, for NLB 444–445
virtual log files, managing 360
Visual Basic SQL CLR Database Project 214
Visual C# SQL CLR Database Project 214
Visual Studio interface 515
Visual Studio project, for InstantCube simple cube generator 539
Volatile Resource Policy Evaluation tab 153
Volume Snapshot Service. *See* VSS
VSS (Volume Snapshot Service) enabled storage arrays 57

W

wait states, and queues 331–342
  calculating wait
      time 337–339
  correlating performance
      data 339–341
  execution model 333–335
  TRT 331–332
  wait stats 332–333, 335–336
wait stats 332–333
  reasons for using 332
  viewing and reporting
      on 335–336
  wait type categories 332–333
wait time, calculating 337–339
wait type categories 332–333
Ward, Peter 127
Web Service URL link 441
web.config file 445–446
Webb, Joe 104
Welch, John 502
WHERE clauses, non-
    SARGable 368–369
WHERE IsBusiness = 'Y'
    filter 20

WHERE statement 562
where-object 551
WHILE loop 344, 391
WHILE statement 350
White, Allen 296
WhseETL/ETLProcessQueue
    295
WidgetCorp 461
Win32 I/O streaming 248
Windows Authentication 131
Windows command-line
    tools 376
Windows domain account 154
Windows Management Inter-
    face. See WMI
Windows Performance Moni-
    tor counters 356
Winver.exe 139
with clause 426
with member expression 427
WITH NORECOVERY 83–84
WITH RESULT SETS
    clause 205, 207
WMI (Windows Management
    Interface) 95
workloads 302

Write() method 213, 220
write-ahead logging 354
WritingMode property 407

X

x column 179
x coordinates 213
Xeon X5690 304
Xeon X7560 304
XMLA (XML for
    Analysis) 539, 548
xp_cmdshell 487
xp_msver 139–140

Y

y coordinates 213
YEAR() function 182
YTD (year to date) 574

Z

Zavaschi, Thiago 576